HACKING JAVA®

The Java Professional's Resource Kit

HACKING JAVA®

The Java Professional's Resource Kit

Mark Wutka

David Baker
David Boswell
Ken Cartwright
David Edgar Liebke
Tom Lockwood
Stephen Matsuba
George Menyhert
Eric Ries
Krishna Sankar

Java Expert Solutions

Library of Congress Catalog No.: 96-70785

ISBN: 0-7897-0935-x

99 98 97 6 5 4 3 2 1

Interpretation of the printing code: the rightmost double-digit number is the year of the book's printing; the rightmost single-digit number, the number of the book's printing. For example, a printing code of 97-1 shows that the first printing of the book occurred in 1997.

Screen reproductions in this book were created using Collage Complete from Inner Media, Inc., Hollis, NH.

Credits

President
Roland Elgey

Publisher
Joseph B. Wikert

Publishing Manager
Jim Minatel

Title Manager
Steven M. Schafer

Editorial Services Director
Elizabeth Keaffaber

Managing Editor
Sandy Doell

Director of Marketing
Lynn E. Zingraf

Acquisitions Manager
Cheryl D. Willoughby

Acquisitions Editor
Stephanie Gould

Product Directors
Mark Cierzniak
Jon Steever

Production Editor
Sean Dixon

Editors
Kelly Brooks, Judith Goode,
Sidney Jones, Kelly Oliver

Product Marketing
Kim Margolius

Assistant Product Marketing Manager
Christy M. Miller

Strategic Marketing Manager
Barry Pruett

Technical Editors
Jim Hoffman, Russ Jacobs,
Ernie Sanders, Eugene W. Sotirescu,
Steve Tallon

Technical Support Specialist
Nadeem Muhammed

Acquisitions Coordinator
Jane K. Brownlow

Software Relations Coordinator
Patty Brooks

Editorial Assistant
Andrea Duvall

Interior Book Designer
Barbara Kordesh

Cover Designer
Barbara Kordesh

Production Team
Kevin Cliburn, Tammy Graham,
Jason Hand, Heather Howell,
Dan Julian, Bob LaRoche,
Casey Price, Erich Richter,
Laura Robbins, Marvin Van Tiem,
Paul Wilson

Indexer
Chris Barrick

Composed in *Helvetica Condensed* and *Stone Serif* by Que Corporation.

To my wife Ceal, who talked me into writing and then got me through it.

—Mark Wutka

Acknowledgments

Writing a book like this is quite an experience, and one of the most important parts of that experience has been the people I have worked with and the people who helped me get through it.

I would especially like to thank my wife Ceal, who somehow managed to keep me close to my normal level of sanity (which is minimal at best). Thanks also go to Chris, Amy, Samantha, and Kaitlynn, who had to endure endless hours of clicking keys and to my Mom, who taught me, by example, how to work hard and to strive constantly to improve myself.

Joe Weber, author of *Special Edition Using Java*, provided some excellent suggestions about the outline for this book, as well as some good advice about being an author. In addition, Cliff McCartney provided me with technical feedback on various aspects of the book, especially in the area of legacy system migration—a subject near and dear to both of our hearts.

This book was not written by a single person. I am extremely grateful for the work of the other authors. The technical expertise that each of them brought to this book has truly made it a book of expert solutions.

I would also like to thank the staff at Que, who have been great to work with—Stephanie Gould, Mark Cierzniak, Ben Milstead, Jon Steever, Sean Dixon, and the many people behind the scenes.

Finally, I would like to thank Geddy, Alex, and Neil for EXCELLENT music to code by. You guys have gotten me through hundreds of thousands of lines of code.

About the Authors

David W. Baker is a systems developer for BBN Planet, a business unit of BBN Corporation. He specializes in software development and system integration for Internet solutions. He also works as a freelance game writer, authoring materials for various roleplaying games. Until recently, he worked for Second Nature Interactive, a software development company, where he served as a Senior Game Writer. David's home page is available at **http://www.netspace.org/users/dwb/**.

David P. Boswell lives in Brigham City, Utah, with his wife Carma and four children. He works as a programmer/analyst for Thiokol Corporation and as an independent Internet consultant. David can be reached via **http://www.daves.net** or **dave@daves.net**.

Ken Cartwright is a software engineer with Science Applications International Corp. He has received a bachelor's degree from the University of Oklahoma and a master's degree in information systems and software engineering from George Mason University. He has been developing complex software systems for several years and has spent the last three years concentrating on object-oriented distributed system development using CORBA and object-oriented databases. Some of his most recent projects utilized the combination of Java and CORBA to support client/server systems. Ken can be reached at **KenCartwright@msn.com**.

David Edgar Liebke (**liebke@scripps.edu**) works at The Scripps Research Institute in La Jolla, CA. A member of the Research Computing group, he develops Java-based information systems and deals with issues of network security. David graduated from UC San Diego with a B.S. in cognitive science, where he studied artificial intelligence, neural networking, and emergent computation. He currently lives in Irvine, CA with his spousal-type unit, Rochelle, who is completing her doctorate in cognitive science. David hopes to one day rid the world of tyranny, or at least proprietary software "standards."

Tom Lockwood has 12 years' experience as a technical writer and marketing specialist with several computer graphic companies. He is currently employed at Cinebase Software where he championed the development of its Web site. Tom is also a freelance writer, a softball coach, and, most proudly, an Aries. He can be reached at **tom.lockwood@cinesoft.com** or via his personal Web site at **http://www.cris.com/~tlockwoo**.

Stephen N. Matsuba is cofounder of Alt.Reality Technologies Corporation, a company developing virtual reality and multimedia applications, and SHOC Interactive, a company developing multimedia games and educational applications. In his other life, he is completing his Ph.D. in computational linguistics and English literature at York

University, Canada. His research interests include Shakespeare, literary theory, computational linguistics, artificial intelligence and cognitive science, computer applications in humanities research and education, VR, and multimedia design. He also coauthored *Special Edition Using VRML* (Que, 1996) with Bernie Roehl.

George Menyhert is currently the Director of the Harmony Product and a member of the technical staff at Cinebase Software where he concentrates on multimedia application engineering. He is also a freelance Java developer. George has a degree in engineering from the University of Cincinnati. He can be reached via his Web page at **http://w3.one.net/~menyhert** or through one of his various e-mail accounts: **george.menyhert@cinesoft.com**, **menyhert@one.net**, or **menyhert@acm.org**.

Krishna Sankar has been a computer professional since 1980. He has worked on strategic business systems for companies like HP, AT&T, Pratt & Whitney, Testek, Ford, TRW, Caterpillar, Qantas Airlines, and Air Canada, as well as for the U.S. Air Force and U.S. Navy. He still believes in information re-engineering and development of competitive business systems and is excited about the possibilities of intranet applets and servlets in those areas. He has two master's degrees, one in production engineering and the other in computer science. He is now pursuing his MBA. He is a Microsoft Product Specialist as well as a Lotus Certified Professional. He is the founder of U.S. Systems & Services, a Silicon Valley intranet systems and Java technology company. Nowadays, you can meet him in the corridors of venture capitalists and banks promoting products "for those whose life is not Internet but want to leverage the net to enjoy it."

Mark Wutka is a senior systems architect who refuses to give up his programming hat. For the past two years he has worked as the chief architect on a large, object-oriented distributed system providing automation for the flight operations division of a major airline. Over the past eight years, he has designed and implemented numerous systems in C, C++, Smalltalk, and Java for that same airline.

He is currently the Vice President of Research and Development for Pioneer Technologies, a consulting firm specializing in distributed systems and legacy system migration. He can be reached via e-mail at **wutka@netcom.com**. He also claims responsibility for the random bits of humor found at **http://www.webcom.com/wutka.**

We'd Like to Hear from You!

As part of our continuing effort to produce books of the highest possible quality, Que would like to hear your comments. To stay competitive, we *really* want you, as a computer book reader and user, to let us know what you like or dislike most about this book or other Que products.

You can mail comments, ideas, or suggestions for improving future editions to the address below, or send us a fax at (317) 581-4663. Our staff and authors are available for questions and comments through our Internet site, at **http://www.mcp.com/que**, and Macmillan Computer Publishing also has a forum on CompuServe (type **GO QUEBOOKS** at any prompt).

In addition to exploring our forum, please feel free to contact me personally to discuss your opinions of this book: I'm **mcierzniak@que.mcp.com** on the Internet.

Thanks in advance—your comments will help us to continue publishing the best books available on new computer technologies in today's market.

Mark Cierzniak
Product Development Specialist
Que Corporation
201 W. 103rd Street
Indianapolis, Indiana 46290
USA

Contents at a Glance

Contents at a Glance

Contents

V Java Web Servers 459

23 Creating Web Services in Java 461

24 Writing Web Services for Jeeves 471

25 Writing Web Services for Jigsaw 505

Introduction

by Mark Wutka

Java is one of the most significant software products to hit the scene in a long time. Unlike Netscape, whose impact was big and immediate, Java's full impact won't be realized for a long time. Java is more than just a programming language. It requires a different mindset when developing applications.

Sure, you can use Java to spruce up your Web pages—it works quite well for that. This book will even give you some tips on ways to do it. But that's not the main purpose of Java. If you only use it for pretty Web pages, you are missing a lot.

Hacking Java: The Java Professional's Resource Kit not only gives you lots of useful Java classes and programming tips, it relates the "vision" of Java. You get an overview from the 30,000-foot level, as well as from down in the trenches, to borrow some management clichés. Both of these views are important. When you're digging a trench, you still need to look up to see where you're headed. Java will have a significant impact on the future of software development, and even the future of technology. If you don't already understand why this is so, you need this book.

One of the important things to realize about Java is that it is young and still evolving. There are many features yet to come, and many more uses of Java to be discovered. This book will help guide you in making design decisions that may be affected by some of these new applications of Java.

Who Should Read This Book

This book addresses Java on several different levels. Some people will be interested in hard-core programming techniques. There are plenty of those here. You may know the language, but you want to use it to solve different problems that aren't addressed in any of the Java programming books.

You may be a software designer, looking for new design techniques. This book has plenty of good object-oriented design strategies that apply not only to Java but to other O-O languages as well.

If you're a system architect creating your company's information infrastructure, there's plenty in here for you, too. This book discusses many architectural issues and shows you situations where you can use Java that you've probably never thought of. This is especially true when it comes to the overall philosophy of Java and its multitude of uses.

This book is not an introduction to programming in Java. There is no discussion of what classes and methods are. *Special Edition Using Java* by Que will give you a good introduction to Java. This book is meant to complement *Special Edition Using Java,* giving you the kind of advice that you don't get from a book on programming.

What This Book Is About

Hacking Java: The Java Professional's Resource Kit is more than just a how-to book. It's also a what-to book. A how-to book assumes that you already know exactly what you want to do, and it gives you step-by-step instructions showing you how to do it. This book gives you ideas about what to do with Java, and then tells you how to implement them.

How This Book Is Organized

This book starts out by addressing some of the burning issues of creating applets. It provides suggestions for improving the performance of your applets, as well as ways to get around some of the restrictions imposed on applets.

Section II discusses some of the aspects of Java applications, including a way to run an applet as an application. This section also discusses the JDBC database interface and the remote method invocation facility.

Section III discusses some of the CORBA products available for Java, how to use them, and what you can do with them. If you are unfamiliar with CORBA, you also get a brief introduction to CORBA.

Section IV shows you how you can speed up your applets, both in the download phase and once the applet is running.

Section V introduces some of the Java Web servers that are now available. You can use Java to implement new Web services that you previously could only do with CGI. In addition, since the servers are written in Java, you can run them anywhere you can run Java.

Section VI delves into some of the deeper aspects of security. It introduces digital signatures and data encryption, and discusses some of the issues involved in protecting your communications.

Section VII shows you how you can use Java to do business over the Web. It discusses some of the aspects of electronic commerce and shows you how to perform secure transactions.

Section VIII deals with "legacy" systems and how you can use Java to connect these older systems to the Internet. There is a large amount of system design philosophy in this section, much of which is applicable no matter what language you are using.

Section IX shows you how to expand capabilities of the HotJava browser, which is written entirely in Java. You will learn how you can add new networking protocols and how you can make HotJava understand new data formats.

Section X introduces some of the multimedia capabilities of Java. This is one field where Java will be expanding greatly. This section suggests possible uses of Java in the multimedia realm.

Section XI discusses some of the issues involved with running Java on small devices like cellular phones and personal digital assistants (PDA). As these devices become more readily available, your systems will have to cooperate with them. This section gives you guidelines that let you start planning for these devices now.

On the CD, three chapters will show you how Java integrates with the Virtual Reality Markup Language (VRML). You will see how you can add whole new dimensions to your Java programs, literally.

How to Use This Book

You can use this book either as a cookbook or as a learning tool. If you have a specific problem that you need to solve, you can consult the book for the solution, as you might use a reference book.

This book is also of immense use as a learning tool. It covers issues faced every day by professional programmers. These issues are rarely covered in a typical programming book.

While many of the example programs solve complex problems, you will find most of them to be relatively straightforward. If you are still fairly new to programming, you will learn a lot just by studying the example programs. They are fairly well-commented and are quite readable.

PART I

Applet Programming in Java

chapter 1

What Is Java?

by Mark Wutka

In this chapter

- **Writing applets in Java**
  The initial focus of Java has been in writing applets that belong in Web pages. There are some interesting advantages of applets beyond just making a Web page look pretty.
- **Writing applications in Java**
  Java is also a full-fledged programming language. Its simple design and various libraries make it an attractive general purpose language.
- **Future directions**
  Java is still young and is just hitting another growth spurt. There are many new and interesting features on the horizon.
- **Running Java in small devices**
  Java is suitable for running in small handheld devices. You need to take certain things into consideration when designing an application that supports these small devices.

Because this book assumes that you already know how to program in Java, you already have a good idea of what features are in the Java language. This book will not teach you how to program in Java; it takes the next step by showing you what you can do with Java and how to do it.

Java as a Web Programming Language

Much of the initial appeal of Java comes from the fact that it can be embedded in Web pages. It allows you to go beyond the static nature of Web pages by making your pages come alive. Using Java's Abstract Windowing Toolkit (AWT), you can create interactive forms that go beyond the simple act of filling in a bunch of fields and clicking the Submit button. You can perform error checking on forms, provide context-sensitive help, even give the user suggestions or examples. Some of these things you can do without Java, but not as quickly.

Java allows you to improve the interaction between the client and the server. The HTTP protocol, the native language of the World Wide Web, is very specific and somewhat restrictive as far as the interaction between the client and server. Whenever a client needs to send data to the server, it must open up a network connection, send a set of headers and the request data, and then sit and wait for a response. The server has very few options for sending data to a client. It must wait for the client to send it information, and the only option it has for sending back multiple responses is the "multi-part" message, in which the server sends part of a response, and then later sends more of the response. Given the static nature of Web pages, this has always been considered acceptable. Also, because the network connection is closed after a server has sent a response back to the client, there is no notion of a session within HTTP. Clients and servers have had to come up with their own interesting ways of maintaining session information between requests. The Netscape Cookie protocol is one such method.

The server puts Netscape cookies in a Web page when it sends information back to the browser. The pieces of information are tagged as being cookies, which the browser watches for and saves for later use. The next time the browser accesses that server, it sends the cookies back to the server. This allows the server to save information at the client-side and then receive the information at a later time. Cookies are discussed more fully in Chapter 6, "Communicating with a Web Server."

When you are writing serious applications, however, you need the interaction between client and server to be much more flexible. A client should be able to send information to a server at any time, and the server should be able to send data back to the client at any time. Java's networking support allows you to do this by creating a socket connection between the client and the server.

Look at an example of a real-world application and see how Java can improve your applications drastically.

Suppose you work for an airline and you are creating a program to display the current position of any of the company's aircraft. You would like this program to run on any Web browser within the company. Your server will be gathering aircraft position data and sending the information out to the browsers. You obviously want this to be a graphical program—you don't just want to list coordinates. You want the president of the company to be able to see immediately that flight 1313 is halfway between Cleveland and Detroit, without having to estimate its distance based on the latitude and longitude shown on some chart.

If you were to do this application using the traditional Web server and HTML forms, your server would have to generate entire images and send them to the client. Anytime a plane's position changed, you'd have to generate new images for each client that was watching that plane. Even if a plane's position changes once a minute, if you watch ten planes, you'll be receiving an average of one image every six seconds. That's an incredible burden to place on your server.

Now, suppose you were to create the same application in Java. The Java applet would download a blank map from the server and then open up a socket connection to the server. Anytime the Java applet wanted to watch a new plane, or stop watching a plane, it would send a message to the server. The server would track what clients were watching what planes. One of the keys here is that the connection between the client and the server stays up. This allows the server to keep track of clients based on their sockets. Now, suppose the server receives a position update for a plane. It looks through its tables and finds every client that was watching that plane and sends the new position down to that client. It does not have to perform any image generation. The amount of data sent to the client is probably 100–1,000 times smaller than the image that would be sent under the previous architecture.

The Java applet is responsible for creating the new image of the aircraft. Although this may take a little longer to generate on the client than on the server, the server is able to handle many times more clients than it otherwise would, because it doesn't have to do as much work for each client.

If you step back and take a look at this application, you'll see that the applet is really just implementing the user interface for the flight tracking system. The bulk of the work in gathering the flight data and analyzing it is done by the server. The interaction between the server and client is a clearly defined set of actions. The client starts watching a plane, the client stops watching a plane, the server sends a flight position to the client. That's a pretty simply protocol! The client does what it does best—it interacts with the user. The server does what it does best—it gathers and analyzes information.

Keep this in mind as you design and develop new applications. Don't heap all the work on the applet, just let it do what it does best—interact with the user.

Realizing that applets are going to need a reasonable way to communicate with the actual applications, Sun added two important subsystems to Java. Remote Method Invocation (RMI) allows a Java object to invoke methods in another Java applet somewhere else on the network. You don't have to come up with your own way of transmitting data between the applet and the application on the server. The applet can simply invoke methods on the server using RMI.

RMI is a nice feature, and is very easy to use since it blends into your applet and application almost seamlessly. There is another way to invoke methods remotely, however. It's called the Common Object Request Broker Architecture, or CORBA. There are many differences between RMI and CORBA. One of the biggest is that CORBA is a multi-language protocol. You can use CORBA in an applet to invoke methods in a C++ application running on your server.

You will be able to choose between RMI and CORBA for your applets. They will both be supported as part of the core of Java. You can expect both mechanisms to be present in a Java-compliant Web browser, or any Java-compliant environment.

Java as an Applications Programming Language

It's unfortunate that Java has gotten the reputation of being solely a Web programming language. It is a full-fledged application programming language. It contains all the features you need to write some pretty hefty programs—and they will all run on any system that runs Java!

Java is young and is still experiencing growing pains. One of these pains is the fact that although Java runs on multiple platforms, it doesn't quite run *exactly* the same on every platform. Most of the time, these differences are in the implementation of the AWT, causing the problems to appear more often in applets than applications (unless you're creating a graphical application, of course). Because most people see only the graphical programs, the platform-to-platform variations in Java look worse than they actually are. The Jigsaw WWW server, discussed in Chapter 25, "Writing Web Services for Jigsaw," is written entirely in Java—over 30,000 lines! It runs very well across all Java-enabled platforms.

The big difference between a Java application and a Java applet is the lack of security restrictions. Java applications are given free reign over the system (although they can't get around the operating system's security). A Java application is free to open a socket connection to any host it wants, open any file, and create its own custom class loaders. If you have been banging your head against a wall because you couldn't do these things in an applet, you might be tempted to turn your applets into applications (in other words, make them stand-alone) so you can have all these features. That is, of course, your choice. But you should seriously consider keeping the user interface and the application separate. For some quick hack program that isn't very significant, it probably won't matter. However, if you're writing a big commercial application, it does matter. There are many advantages to being able to run applets in a browser; one of the biggest advantages is that the browser performs automatic software distribution for you. You don't have to install the applet on a system ahead of time in order for someone to use it. If you start writing everything as a stand-alone application, you fall back into the old trap of trying to maintain a program on a large number of machines.

Java's database API, called JDBC, is a boon for application programming. You now have a standard interface for accessing a relational database. JDBC frees you from being tied to a specific database API, meaning you not only can create cross-platform applications, you can also create cross-database applications.

Java is a great language for handling little ten-minute hack programs, as well. You have immediate access to an excellent set of libraries that handle many tedious functions that you won't find in the standard library set of C or C++. You can buy these libraries for other languages, of course, but why bother if you get them free with Java? You may soon find that you are writing Java programs when you previously wrote C programs or Perl scripts.

New Features on the Horizon

While the Java language itself will remain fairly static for now, with only a few additions, the available APIs for the language will be growing at a rapid pace. The original APIs that came with Java were enough to generate great interest in Java. Now, as more and more companies use Java for serious work, they are discovering areas that Java hasn't addressed up to now.

Multimedia has become a hot topic on the World Wide Web. You can now use your Web browser to view animated news clips, listen to samples of new record albums, and even make video telephone calls halfway around the world. Java's support of multimedia has been minimal, so far, but that is being addressed. You will soon see a flurry of new multimedia APIs for Java. These APIs will provide improved audio service, full-motion video, 2-D and 3-D graphics, and even telephony. The APIs will really help level the playing field when it comes to selecting a platform for running your programs. You will be able to count on having these services available on whatever platform you choose, whether it be Windows, UNIX, or Mac.

In the area of audio, you will be able to synchronize your audio a little better, allowing you to create animation that is in sync with the audio. You should also be able to support varying sample rates. Most important of all, you will be able to find out when an audio clip finishes playing. This is one of the most glaring omissions in the current API. You can't even create a simple music jukebox under the current API, because you never know when to start the next piece of music.

The video API will allow you to display video clips in different formats, and even synchronize them with the audio. Rather than sticking to a single video format, the video API allows you to plug in different kinds of video handlers. You could support MPEG and QuickTime, for instance.

The 2-D API provides a rich set of drawing routines that is badly needed. The `Graphics` class in the AWT provides only the most basic drawing features. You will be able to perform complex pattern fills with the new API, for example. There will also be an API for doing sprite animation. Sprites are essentially graphical objects that move around the screen. You can do something similar right now, but you have to write all the animation and redrawing code yourself. The sprite API will take care of that for you, and will do it in a much more efficient manner. This should result in a lot of neat new games for Java, many approaching the capabilities of some home gaming systems.

You will be able to create interesting new effects with the 3-D API. There will be support for simple 3-D objects, as well as animated 3-D objects, and even some of the features you now find in VRML systems. Again, since these are part of the native Java environment, they should be very efficient.

The telephony API addresses the growing integration between the telephone and the computer. Essentially, the telephony API is a mechanism for placing and receiving phone calls. You may need special hardware to interface with the actual phone equipment, but eventually you'll be able to redirect phone calls over your home network to whatever device you happen to be near, whether it is your WebTV, your PDA, or your old desktop computer.

Network management is another important topic, especially at large companies. Right now, many operating systems and most network devices support the SNMP network management protocol. There are a number of tools available for configuring and monitoring SNMP-enabled devices. The JavaManagement API will allow you to create new programs for monitoring network devices. You will be able to monitor SNMP devices, or plug in your own protocols to manage devices using other network management protocols. The advantage here is that you will be able to take advantage of Java's ease of use, and create network management applications that will run on any Java-enabled platform.

One of the most exciting new Java APIs to come along is the Beans API. Beans is an API for creating and using software components. One of the dreams in software development has always been that software components could be used like electronic components. When you buy electronic components, they have a standard interface. Many times, the same kind of component is offered by a number of vendors, giving you freedom of choice. You can create an electronic board by looking at the specifications for the components and designing the board. Once you finally assemble the components, you have an excellent chance of things working as you had planned.

In the software arena, this is rarely the case. Beans doesn't necessarily solve this problem, but it brings you one step closer. The philosophy behind the Beans API is that you have a nice development tool for creating new applications. In a way, it's like your workbench.

You buy software components from different companies, and each component is a bean. You add the beans to your development tool, and the tool uses the Beans API to find out what interfaces each new bean supports. In addition, the Beans API defines mechanisms for customizing a bean.

For example, you might buy a nifty new pushbutton bean and add it to your graphical development environment. Your graphical environment presents you with a visual toolkit of all the beans you have. You could select the pushbutton and drag it onto your new application. Next, you could pop up a configuration menu that allowed you to customize the pushbutton. The Beans API uses a new Java feature called reflection to discover the parts of the bean that can be customized. As an alternative, you could supply your own customizer for a bean.

If you think you can do a lot with Java now, imagine what you'll be able to do when these new features become available.

Java as an Embedded Systems Language

The ability to run programs inside small devices like cellular phones and PDAs (Personal Digital Assistants) is one of Java's best kept secrets. Sun, and other hardware manufacturers, realized that Java's virtual machine could easily be implemented in silicon and placed in a wide variety of devices. Already, companies have created cellular phones and PDAs that run Java. In fact, Java itself came from a project that created a small handheld device.

One day, you may have a refrigerator that runs Java. What would that mean to you? Probably nothing, unless it makes you play Tetris in order to use the ice maker. The toaster has always been the appliance that everyone wants to connect to the Internet. Yes, someone has demonstrated a Java-enabled toaster. In fact, Sun has considered changing its trademark phrase "The Network Is The Computer" over to "The Toaster Is The Computer." Okay, not really. Still, if things continue in the direction they are going, you will have more and more pieces of equipment in your house that run Java. This can be upsetting to an application designer who is accustomed to thinking of the desktop as the sole realm of applications.

This is where the notion of separating the user interface from the application really becomes important. You can't cram some behemoth of an application into a cell phone. You shouldn't even try. Take the flight tracking system as an example.

Suppose the airline president handed you his Java-enabled organizer and said, "I want to see flights on this thing." Fortunately for you, you separated the application from the user interface, so all you have to do is create a special user interface for the organizer.

If you had written the flight tracking system as a big stand-alone application, you would have already torn your hair out in big clumps trying to figure out how you were going to fit all that code into an itty-bitty living space.

You may, in the future, have a completely different computing model at home than you do now. Right now, you probably have a single computer, a printer, a monitor, and a modem. Some of you even have your own ethernet networks now. In the future, you may have an application server on which all your favorite programs reside—your e-mail system, your word processor, and yes, your favorite games. This server may not even have a keyboard or a monitor, just a connection to your home network. On your desktop, you might have a Java-enabled monitor and keyboard that are also hooked to the network. In the living room, your Java-enabled television is also on the network. With the coming of digital TV and high-speed networking to the home, there may no longer be a difference between a computer monitor and a television. When you want to read your e-mail, you can access it from the computer monitor, your TV, or even your wireless digital assistant, all using your home network to access the e-mail application running on your home server. You may not even have a server at home—you might subscribe to an e-mail service over the network and access a server somewhere in Tuscaloosa. The point is that there are more and more ways for you to interact with computer systems, and in the future, one single way will no longer be sufficient.

As you design your applications, keep the image of a cell phone or a personal digital assistant hovering like a dark cloud over you, whispering menacingly, "Will your application run on me?"

chapter 2

Embedding Applets in Web Pages

2

by Mark Wutka

In this chapter

- **No Java? No problem**
  How to accommodate browsers that do not support Java.
- **Passing parameters to applets**
  Using the <PARAM> tag and reading parameters in an applet.
- **Faster applet response**
  How to make your applets come up faster.

While Java has been one of the hottest new technologies to hit the Web, it is still unfamiliar to many users. There are still only a handful of Web browsers that support Java. The rest simply ignore the <APPLET> tag that identifies an applet to the browser. For users whose browsers don't support Java, you want to provide at least some suggestion that there is something there that the browser cannot display. Otherwise, they might not realize that they are missing something. You also need to consider the fact that some applets may take a while to download. Most browsers just display a large blank area while downloading an applet, not giving the user an indication that there is anything more to display. You need to let the user know that there is something more to see and that they should be patient.

No Java? No Problem

Once you've written a Java applet and you want to display it in a Web page, you use the <APPLET> tag. This is probably one of the first things you learned when you started programming in Java. Making the jump from a simple "Hello World" applet to enhancing your company's Web page is a big step. You now have to consider the possibility that people cannot run Java. Many Web browsers still do not understand the <APPLET> tag. A browser that does not understand the <APPLET> tag simply skips over it. On the other hand, a browser that does understand the <APPLET> tag skips over any other tags and text up to the closing </APPLET> tag (except for the <PARAM> tags, of course). You can take advantage of this by providing alternative content, such as an image or text, to go in place of the applet.

Note

The most popular Java-enabled Web browsers are the Netscape Navigator (version 2 and later) and Microsoft Internet Explorer (version 3). Sun's HotJava browser not only runs Java, it is written entirely in Java.

Displaying an Image in Place of an Applet

You should consider displaying an image in place of an applet if your Web page expects something to occupy the applet's space. In other words, sometimes when you lay out your Web page, you place the applet somewhere and expect it to occupy a certain amount of space. The rest of the text is laid out accordingly. If you suddenly try to view the page on a browser that doesn't understand the <APPLET> tag, there will be nothing occupying that space and your page layout will be far from what you expected. You can still reserve that space, however, by using an image as the alternative content. The advantage of an image is that you can specify its exact size the same way you can with an applet. In fact, you may have noticed already that the <APPLET> tag contains a number of options that are identical to those of the <IMG> tag. If the image you want to display is smaller than the applet's display area, you can either expand the image or you can put padding around the image. Unfortunately, some older browsers, like Mosaic, won't even expand images, so if you are trying to accommodate really old browsers, you may want to avoid expanding the image.

Note
Some of the non-Java browsers you are likely to encounter are Netscape version 1, Microsoft Internet Explorer version 2 and earlier, Mosaic, and most custom browsers offered by Internet providers. In addition, Netscape version 3 does not support Java under Microsoft Windows version 3.

Listing 2.1 shows a Web page that displays an applet with an image as the alternative content. The image being displayed is only 100×100 pixels, but the applet is 200×200. The `<IMG>` tag specifies a width and height of 200, causing the browser to expand the image to fit the area.

Listing 2.1 Source Code for *PushButton.html*

```
<HTML>
<TITLE> Pushbutton Applet </TITLE>
<HEAD>
</HEAD>
<BODY>
Here is some text before the applet.
<APPLET codebase="." code="PushButton.class" width=200 height=200>
<IMG src="javacup.gif" width=200 height=200>
</APPLET>
Here is some text after the applet.
</BODY>
</HTML>
```

Figure 2.1 shows this page with the applet running.

Figure 2.2 shows how this page looks on a browser that doesn't understand the applet tag but is still able to expand images.

You can also match the image size to the applet size by adding padding to the image. This might be useful on browsers that cannot expand images to fit a particular size. Unfortunately, these browsers might not support the HSPACE and VSPACE attributes. Mosaic, for instance, doesn't expand images and it doesn't support HSPACE and VSPACE. Listing 2.2 shows a Web page that contains the same 200×200 applet and uses the same 100×100 image as the alternative content. Rather than expanding the image to fit a 200×200 space, it pads the image by 50 pixels on each side, making the effective image size 200×200.

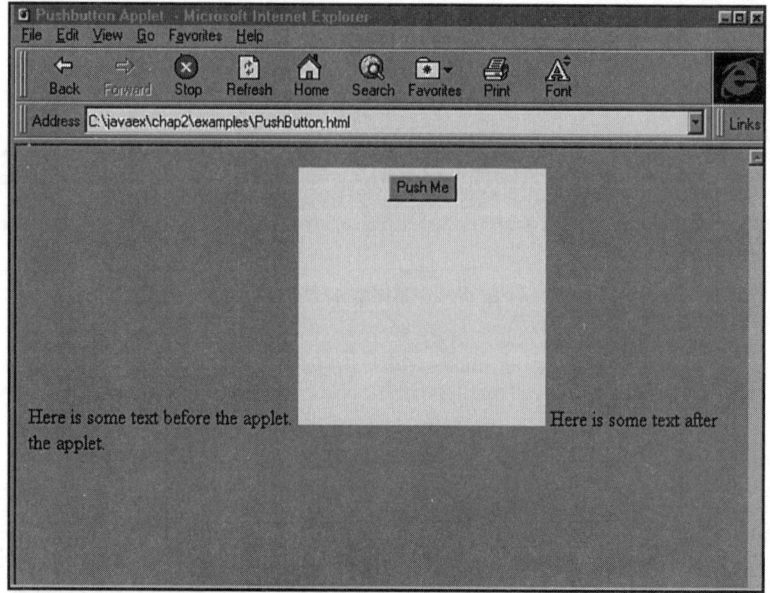

Fig. 2.1
A Java-enabled browser displays the applet defined by the `<APPLET>` *tag.*

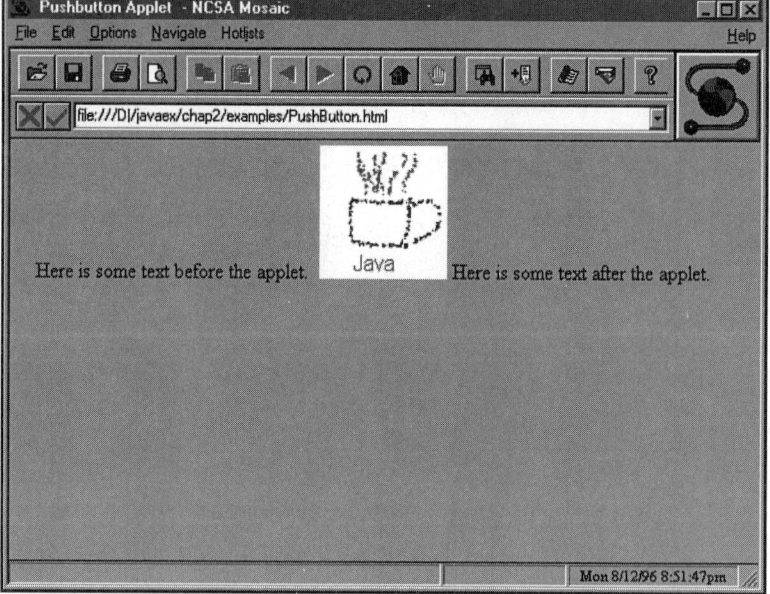

Fig. 2.2
A browser that does not support Java can display an image in place of the applet.

Listing 2.2 Source Code for *PushButton2.html*

```
<HTML>
<TITLE> Pushbutton Applet </TITLE>
<HEAD>
</HEAD>
<BODY>
Here is some text before the applet.
<APPLET codebase="." code="PushButton.class" width=200 height=200>
<IMG src="javacup.gif" width=100 height=100 hspace=50 vspace=50>
</APPLET>
Here is some text after the applet.
</BODY>
</HTML>
```

Figure 2.3 shows how the page appears on browsers that do not support applets.

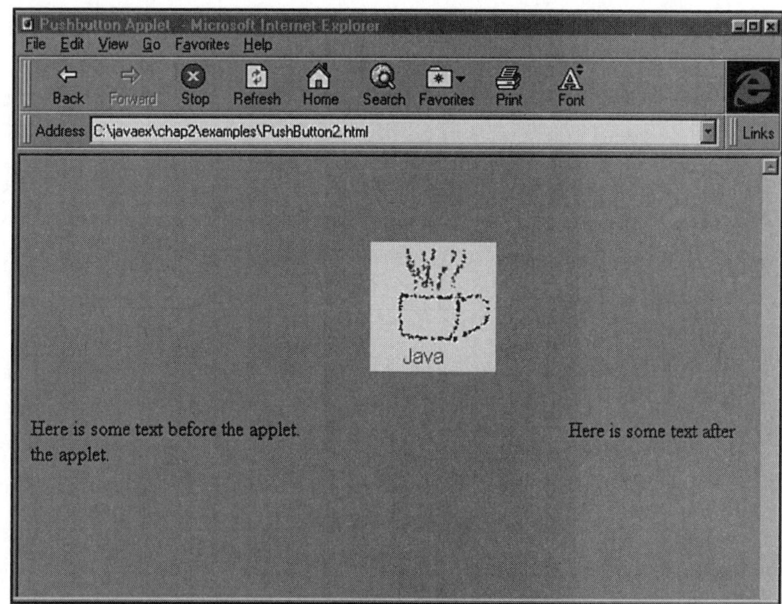

Fig. 2.3
The HSPACE *and* VSPACE *attributes add padding around an image.*

Note

Figures 2.1, 2.2, and 2.3 feature the Microsoft Internet Explorer browser. Figure 2.1 uses Internet Explorer version 3, while Figures 2.2 and 2.3 use IE version 2, which does not support Java. Since IE version 2 was shipped with Windows 95, there are many people still using it.

Passing Parameters to Applets

One of the many ways you can strive to make reusable applets is to make them very configurable. You want to be able to use the same applet in a number of Web pages without creating multiple versions of the applet. You can use the parameter mechanism to pass parameters from a Web page to the applet.

Tip

If you are able to reuse an applet on a Web page rather than use two separate applets, you save a lot of downloading time. The browser doesn't download the same applet twice.

One of the difficult aspects of the `getParameter` method in the `Applet` class is that it has only one option—it fetches a single named parameter. There is no support for having multiple values for a parameter or for having a default parameter value. You can solve this by creating a class that performs these functions for you.

The `Parameters` class presented here provides a more flexible interface to applet parameters. It allows you to specify a default value for a parameter and also retrieve an array of values for a parameter. You can provide multiple values one of two ways—either by grouping them into one string with one or more separators or by providing `<PARAM>` tags with parameter names that have numbers appended to them.

If you want to supply multiple parameter values from a single `<PARAM>` tag, you need to define the set of separator values that you will put in between the parameters. The following example of the `<PARAM>` tag provides multiple values separated by colons:

```
<PARAM name="foo" value="somevalue:anothervalue:thisvalue:lastvalue">
```

You can also provide multiple parameters by appending numbers to the parameter name, starting at 0:

```
<PARAM name="foo0" value="somevalue">
<PARAM name="foo1" value="anothervalue">
<PARAM name="foo2" value="thisvalue">
<PARAM name="foo3" value="lastvalue">
```

The numbered parameters are more useful when you want to have several sets of multiple parameters. You may have a scrolling marquee, for instance, in which you supply the marquee text and the speed. You would like to be able to group them like this:

```
<PARAM name="text0" value="This is my marquee">
<PARAM name="speed0" value="100">
```

```
<PARAM name="text1" value="I hope you like it">
<PARAM name="speed1" value="200">
```

Listing 2.3 shows the source code for the `Parameters` class.

Listing 2.3 Source Code for *Parameters.java*

```
import java.util.Vector;
import java.util.StringTokenizer;
import java.applet.Applet;

/**
 * Provides extra ways to access applet parameters. Allows multiple
 * values for a parameter either by separated values, or by adding an
 * index value to each parameter (i.e. param0=first param1=second, etc.)
 * You can either call static methods or create an instance and call
 * instance methods. The static methods require that you pass the
 * applet each time. Because you create instances by passing the Applet
 * to the constructor, the instance methods don't require you to pass
 * the applet.
 * @author Mark Wutka
 */

public class Parameters
{
     protected Applet applet;

/**
 * Creates a Parameters instance that will fetch parameters for a
 * particular applet.
 * @param applet The applet whose parameters will be retrieved.
 */

     public Parameters(Applet applet)
     {
          this.applet = applet;
     }

// All the instance methods just pass through to the static methods
// to avoid code redundancy.

/**
 * Returns the named parameter, or null if not set (this is identical
 * to the Applet.getParameter method).
 * @param paramName The name of the parameter to retrieve.
 */
     public String getParameter(String paramName)
     {
          return getParameter(paramName);
     }

/**
 * Returns the named parameter, or defaultValue if not set.
 * @param paramName The name of the parameter to retrieve.
```

continues

Listing 2.3 Continued

```
 * @param defaultValue The parameter value to use if there is no
 *          PARAM tag for this parameter.
 */
    public String getParameter(String paramName, String defaultValue)
    {
        return getParameter(applet, paramName, defaultValue);
    }

/**
 * Returns an array of parameters. The corresponding parameter names
 * in the PARAM tags should end with numbers starting with 0. For
 * example, for a parameter named "foo", the PARAM tags should use names
 * of foo0, foo1, foo2, etc:
 * <PRE>
 * <PARAM name="foo0" value="somevalue">
 * <PARAM name="foo1" value="anothervalue">
 * <PARAM name="foo2" value="thisvalue">
 * <PARAM name="foo3" value="lastvalue">
 * </PRE>
 * If you skip a number, the rest of the parameters will be ignored.
 *
 * @param paramName The base name for the parameters to be fetched.
 */

    public String[] getParameters(String paramName)
    {
        return getParameters(applet, paramName);
    }

/**
 * Returns an array of parameters. The parameters should be separated
 * by a specific separator character, or a set of separator characters.
 * For example, for the following call to getParameters:
 * <PRE>
 *    param.getParameters("foo", ";:,");
 * </PRE>
 * You could use :, ;, and , as separators:
 * <PRE>
 * <PARAM name="foo" value="somevalue:anothervalue;thisvalue,lastvalue">
 * </PRE>
 *
 * @param paramName The name of the parameter to fetch.
 * @param separators A string containing the separators for the parameters.
 */
    public String[] getParameters(String paramName, String separators)
    {
        return getParameters(applet, paramName, separators);
    }

/**
 * Returns the named parameter, or null if not set (this is identical
 * to the Applet.getParameter method).
 * @param applet The applet whose parameters will be fetched.
 * @param paramName The name of the parameter to retrieve.
 */
    public static String getParameter(Applet applet, String paramName)
```

```
    {
         return applet.getParameter(paramName);
    }

/**
 * Returns the named parameter, or defaultValue if not set.
 * @param applet The applet whose parameters will be fetched.
 * @param paramName The name of the parameter to retrieve.
 * @param defaultValue The parameter value to use if there is no
 *          PARAM tag for this parameter.
 */
    public static String getParameter(Applet applet, String paramName,
         String defaultValue)
    {
         String returnValue = applet.getParameter(paramName);
         if (returnValue == null) return defaultValue;
         return returnValue;
    }

/**
 * Returns an array of parameters. The corresponding parameter names
 * in the PARAM tags should end with numbers starting with 0. For
 * example, for a parameter named "foo", the PARAM tags should use names
 * of foo0, foo1, foo2, etc:
 * <PRE>
 * <PARAM name="foo0" value="somevalue">
 * <PARAM name="foo1" value="anothervalue">
 * <PARAM name="foo2" value="thisvalue">
 * <PARAM name="foo3" value="lastvalue">
 * </PRE>
 * If you skip a number, the rest of the parameters will be ignored.
 *
 * @param applet The applet whose parameters will be fetched.
 * @param paramName The base name for the parameters to be fetched.
 */
    public static String[] getParameters(Applet applet,
         String paramName)
    {
// Put the parameters into a vector first, because you don't
// know how many parameters you are getting.
         Vector vec = new Vector();

         for (int i=0; true; i++) {
// Try getting next numbered parameter
              String paramStr = applet.getParameter(paramName+i);
// If it isn't there, you're done
              if (paramStr == null) break;
// If you got the parameter, add the it to the vector
              vec.addElement(paramStr);
         }

// Create a string array to hold the values
         String[] returnValues = new String[vec.size()];

// Copy the vector values into the new string array
         vec.copyInto((Object[])returnValues);
```

continues

Listing 2.3 Continued

```
          return returnValues;
     }

/**
 * Returns an array of parameters. The parameters should be separated
 * by a specific separator character or a set of separator characters.
 * For example, for the following call to getParameters:
 * <PRE>
 *    param.getParameters("foo", ";:,");
 * </PRE>
 * You could use :, ;, and , as separators
 * <PRE>
 * <PARAM name="foo" value="somevalue:anothervalue;thisvalue,lastvalue">
 * </PRE>
 *
 * @param paramName The name of the parameter to fetch.
 * @param separators A string containing the separators for the parameters.
 */
     public static String[] getParameters(Applet applet,
          String paramName, String separators)
     {
          String paramStr = applet.getParameter(paramName);

// If the parameters weren't there, just return an empty array
          if (paramStr == null) {
               return new String[0];
          }

// Put the parameters into a vector first, because you don't
// know how many parameters you are getting.
          Vector vec = new Vector();

// The tokenizer will separate out the parameters from the string
          StringTokenizer tok = new StringTokenizer(paramStr,
               separators);

// Grab the parameters from the string
          while (tok.hasMoreTokens()) {
               vec.addElement(tok.nextToken());
          }

// Create a string array to hold the values
          String[] returnValues = new String[vec.size()];
// Copy the vector values into the new string array
          vec.copyInto((Object[]) returnValues);

          return returnValues;
     }
}
```

Tip

The `getParameters` method in the `Parameters` class deals with a common problem. It must create an array of strings without knowing ahead of time how many strings there are. To solve this problem, you store the strings in a vector. Once you have all the strings you need, you can create an array of strings, using the `size` method in the vector to determine how many strings there are. Once you create the array, you simply copy the strings from the vector to the array. The `copyInto` method in the Vector class will do the copying for you so you don't have to do it manually.

Improving Applet Startup Time

When you are creating a commercial Web page that is covered with Java applets, you want to get results to the user as quickly as possible. Web browsers tend to leave a big blank spot on the page where an applet is supposed to go. If your applet takes 30 seconds to load, someone may not be patient enough to wait for it. In fact, he may not even know there is an applet being loaded. It would be nice if you could at least print a message telling the user that an applet is being loaded that is going to blow his socks off, so he should sit in rapt anticipation for your wonderful-but-huge applet to be downloaded. As it turns out, this is a snap! You can create a very small applet that downloads the real applet in the background. The only trick to this is that when you create an applet manually, it doesn't know its code base or document base. It does, however, have a method called `setStub` that tells it where to go for this information. Almost every method in the `AppletStub` interface is implemented in the `Applet` class, which means that your loader applet can act as an applet stub for another applet. The only method in the AppletStub interface that isn't in the Applet class is `appletResize`. Your `appletResize` method can simply call the `resize` method in your loader applet, since that will perform the actual resize.

Tip

The `appletResize` method in this case is performing a technique called "delegation." The `appletResize` method delegates the responsibility of performing the resizing to the `resize` method. You often use this technique in object-oriented programming where one object has a set of methods that delegate their responsibility to methods in another object.

Listing 2.4 shows a quick applet loader that can be used to display information while you are loading a much larger applet. This applet is less than 2K in size, so it should take only a few seconds to load.

Listing 2.4 Source Code for *QuickLoader.java*

```
import java.applet.Applet;
import java.applet.AppletStub;
import java.awt.Graphics;
import java.awt.GridLayout;
import java.awt.Label;

// This applet is responsible for loading another applet in the
// background and displaying the applet when it finishes loading.
// The name of the applet to load is supplied by a <PARAM> tag.
// For example:
// <PARAM name="applet" value="RealApplet">
// which would load an applet class called RealApplet
//
public class QuickLoader extends Applet implements Runnable, AppletStub
{
      String appletToLoad;
      Label label;
      Thread appletThread;

      public void init()
      {
// Get the name of the applet to load
            appletToLoad = getParameter("applet");

// If there isn't one, print a message
            if (appletToLoad == null) {
                  label = new Label("No applet to load.");
            } else {
                  label = new Label("Please wait - loading applet "+
                        appletToLoad);
            }
            add(label);
      }

      public void run()
      {
// If there's no applet to load, don't bother loading it!
            if (appletToLoad == null) return;

            try {

// Get the class for the applet we want
                  Class appletClass = Class.forName(appletToLoad);

// Create an instance of the applet
                  Applet realApplet = (Applet)appletClass.newInstance();

// Set the applet's stub - this will allow the real applet to use
```

```
// this applet's document base, code base, and applet context.
                        realApplet.setStub(this);

// Remove the old message and put the applet up

                        remove(label);

// The grid layout maximizes the components to fill the screen area - you
// want the real applet to be maximized to our size.

                        setLayout(new GridLayout(1, 0));

// Add the real applet as a child component
                        add(realApplet);

// Crank up the real applet
                        realApplet.init();
                        realApplet.start();
                } catch (Exception e) {

// If we got an error anywhere, print it
                        label.setText("Error loading applet.");
                }

// Make sure the screen layout is redrawn
                validate();
        }

        public void start()
        {
                appletThread = new Thread(this);
                appletThread.start();
        }

        public void stop()
        {
                appletThread.stop();
                appletThread = null;
        }

// appletResize is the one method in the AppletStub interface that
// isn't in the Applet class. You can use the applet resize
// method and hope it works.

        public void appletResize(int width, int height)
        {
                resize(width, height);
        }
}
```

Once you are able to embed applets on a Web page, you can concentrate on the really fun part—creating interesting applets. Make your applets interesting, visually pleasing, and fast. And remember that not everyone will be able to run Java. Make sure you leave something for those poor souls.

chapter 3

Applet Security Restrictions

3

by Mark Wutka

In this chapter

- **Accessing Files**
  Most browsers place heavy restrictions on file access. In most cases, an applet can neither read nor write files on the local filesystem.
- **Using the Network**
  Applets can only perform a few network operations. This prevents applets from snooping around the local network, possibly breaking into other systems.
- **Other Restrictions**
  There are some other ways that a malicious applet could cause damage on the local system. Fortunately, the other applet security restrictions keep these kinds of violations from occurring.
- **Avoiding Security Restrictions**
  Sometimes you need to turn off the applet security, especially if you know that the applet you are loading is safe. There are several ways to turn off the security or to classify an applet as being trusted, giving it more access.

Applet Security

Applet security is generally regarded as a necessary pain by most Java programmers. The ability to download code on-the-fly is a major advantage, but it is also a wonderful tool for the same kind of people who like to write viruses that infect your PC. Fortunately, the designers of Java took that into account and developed a security model that protects your system from malicious attacks. You may consider some of the applet security restrictions draconian, but it is much better to have too much security than too little—especially when Java is still striving for acceptance. These restrictions do not apply to applications, because they are meant to access local files and the local network. The security restrictions are there to protect you from unknowingly loading a malicious program that can be hidden on a Web page. You have to manually run an application on your local system, however, so you are responsible if the application is malicious.

Security restrictions vary from browser to browser. Netscape, for instance, has a very tight security model, although HotJava allows you to switch off some of the security restrictions.

The Microsoft Internet Explorer version 3 (IE3) supports several security models from completely relaxed (no restrictions) to completely secure (won't download and run applets at all). In addition, IE3 allows digitally signed classes to have fewer restrictions.

Tip

Many browsers, including HotJava, IE3, and Netscape, relax the security policy for applets that are loaded from files on the local system—that is, files that are loaded with a type of "file:". If you load a file with "http:", even if the file is stored on your local drive, you will be under the full scrutiny of the security manager.

File Access Restrictions

File access is one of the most vulnerable places for malicious attacks. If someone were able to modify files on your system when you ran an applet, they could implant viruses on your system or just destroy data directly. For this reason, no applet is allowed to access the local filesystem in any way—not even in a read-only mode. After all, you wouldn't want someone implanting invisible applets on their Web page just so they could snoop your hard drive and copy files from it. You may be allowed to read and write files if your applet is loaded from the local filesystem using a URL of type "file:".

The inability to read and write files poses a major challenge for applet writers. For the moment, the only solution is to read and write files on applet's home Web server.

Network Restrictions

The network restrictions in Java may seem a little overboard, but they are there for good reason. The general philosophy of network security is that applets can only make network connections back to the Web server they were loaded from. An applet may not listen for incoming socket connections, nor can it listen for datagrams (connectionless network data) from anywhere but its home server. It also can only send datagrams back to its home server.

These security restrictions are intended to protect organizations that have Internet firewalls set up. In case you are unfamiliar with the intricacies of Internet security, many companies have large internal IP networks (the main networking protocol of the Internet). These networks are connected to the rest of the world through machines called "firewalls." A firewall's job in life is to protect the internal IP network from prying eyes in the outside world while allowing people on the inside to access data out on the Internet. These firewalls usually render the internal network invisible to the rest of the world. Given the clever ways people have found to attack systems, it is best to not give out any information about host names or addresses on the internal network.

The problem with Java is that applets run inside the firewall on your local machine. This means that without any network restrictions, your entire network is exposed to any malicious applets. You might be thinking that it would be nice if you could just tell your browser the names of hosts that you trust. It would not be difficult for the security system in Java to handle that, but it would keep your poor network administrator on a steady supply of indigestion medication, wondering when someone will trust an untrustworthy host. If you're an administrator at a site using HotJava, go ahead and get yourself a good spoonful of Maalox—you can completely turn off the networking restrictions in HotJava! Keep in mind, also, that Internet Explorer also lets you turn off all security restrictions. Netscape does not support such an option, however.

If your applet is loaded from the local filesystem, you can get around these security restrictions. You may have to set the `appletviewer.security.mode` system property to `unrestricted` to completely get around these restrictions. Because one of the other restrictions on applets is that they cannot change the system properties, you'll have to come up with unique ways of getting around this.

Other Security Restrictions

In addition to the file and network restrictions, most environments also place a few other interesting restrictions. They are discussed in this section.

Non-local applets may not access the system properties. A local applet may read and write the system properties. If an applet were able to change the system properties, any applet could change the `appletviewer.security.mode` property, for instance, and throw open a huge security hole. Other system properties contain information about the local machine, which could include the host name and IP address. If the machine is safe behind a firewall, you might not want this information getting out.

Non-local applets may not define their own class loaders. This is really an unfortunate restriction, because the ability to define new ways to add classes to the runtime system is one of Java's neatest features. The problem comes with the fact that when your class refers to another class, the system first goes to the class loader for your class to find the class you are referring to. If you wanted to create an applet that could read and write local files, you could create your own `InputStream` and `OutputStream` classes that did not consult the `SecurityManager` object for permission. When your applet is loaded via your custom class loader, the class loader will be asked if it can load the `InputStream` and `OutputStream` classes. A well-behaved loader would simply load the system versions of these classes, but an evil class loader will load the non-secure versions of these.

Applets may not call native methods. It would be terrible to have all these nice security measures built into Java, only to have an applet come along and bypass them completely by calling the native methods that are used by the system classes. For example, a malicious applet could call the native socket functions directly and snoop around the local network.

Applets cannot execute commands on the local system using the `Runtime.exec` method. Otherwise, a malicious applet could come along and execute commands to delete all your files.

Applets may not be able to define classes that belong to certain packages. Typically, they cannot define classes for the `java` and `sun` packages. Also, Netscape does not permit applets to define classes in the `netscape` package.

When a non-local applet opens a top-level frame (a window separate from the browser), the frame contains a warning message indicating that the applet is not trusted.

Getting Around Security Restrictions

This is a touchy subject because the Java security system is in place for good reason. Many companies would like to create Java applets that freely access other systems within the company's intranet, while denying such access to applets loaded from the Internet.

Companies can do this if they load their intranet applications from local files. This is not acceptable in many cases, however. One of the advantages of downloading code is that software distribution is a snap. You just put the new copy of the program on your Web server. If you have to copy your intranet applets to each client, you are back in the old system administration nightmare.

Using Digital Signatures for Increased Access

The Microsoft Internet Explorer version 3 is the first major browser to implement digital signatures for applets. This digital signature mechanism allows you to permit applets from certain trusted sites to have more access to your local system. Internet Explorer's approach to digital signatures is basically an all-or-nothing approach. If an applet is digitally signed, it is considered to be a trusted applet and is allowed much more access, including the ability to write local files.

In order to take advantage of digital signatures for Internet Explorer, you need to package your applets in Microsoft's cabinet format. Cabinets are discussed more fully in Chapter 14, "Creating Your Own Class Archive Files."

When you create your cabinet file, make sure you use the `-s` option to leave room for the digital signature. The following command packs all the .class files in the local directory into a cabinet called `MyCab.cab` and leaves 6,144 bytes at the beginning of the cabinet for the digital signature:

```
cabarc -s 6144 n MyCab.cab *.class
```

The tools for digitally signing your code are included with the Microsoft ActiveX SDK, available from **http://www.microsoft.com/activex**. The ActiveX development kit is free, and you can use the digital signature programs without any additional packages. If you want to develop ActiveX programs, however, you also need the Microsoft Windows SDK.

Note

To digitally sign your code for Internet Explorer you must have a Software Publishers Certificate, signed by a trusted certificate authority. You can find information on obtaining this certificate from Microsoft's Web server at **http://www.microsoft.com/intdev/signcode**.

Once you have created a cabinet file, use the SignCode program to digitally sign your code. If you simply type `signcode` on the command line, you will be presented with a handy step-by-step windowed interface for signing code. You can also use the command-line version of `signcode`. If your Software Publishers Certificate is in the file `MyCert.spc` and you want to use a private key called `MyKey` to sign `MyCab.cab`, you would use the following command:

```
signcode -name MyCab.cab -spc MyCert.spc -pvk MyKey
```

Once your cabinet is signed, any class loaded from that cabinet is trusted by Internet Explorer and is allowed free access to the local system.

Java 1.1 includes support for digitally signed Java classes. Under Sun's security policy, you are able to restrict access based on the signature. If a class is signed by Sun, you might permit it full access to your system. If the class is signed by a vendor that you do not completely trust, however, you might give it only limited abilities.

Because digital signatures are a part of Java 1.1, eventually all Java-enabled browsers will contain code to support digitally signed applets. These applets will be given much more freedom to access the local system. For now, however, if you really need to create applets that have little or no security restrictions, you have to create your own custom security manager.

Creating a Customized Security Manager

Creating a security manager is a difficult job, and any little error in programming can expose your system to attacks. Most security managers use the `inClassLoader` method to determine whether the current class was loaded by the `AppletClassLoader` class. If it was loaded by the applet class loader, it is subjected to the applet security restrictions. If you can legally get ahold of the source to an existing security manager, you should take a good look at it before attempting to create your own security manager.

Listing 3.1 shows a skeleton security manager. It performs no checks whatsoever, so you should use it only for your intranet applications—or better yet, just for testing.

Listing 3.1 Source code for *AppletSecurity.java*

```
// Uncomment one of these to create a security manager
// for the browser of your choice

// package Netscape.applet;      // for Netscape Navigator
// package sun.applet;           // for HotJava

import Java.io.FileDescriptor;
import Java.net.URL;
```

```
public class AppletSecurity extends SecurityManager
{
     public void checkAccept(String host, int port)
     {
     }

     public void checkAccess(Thread g)
     {
     }

     public void checkAccess(ThreadGroup g)
     {
     }

     public void checkConnect(String host, int port)
     {
     }

     public void checkConnect(String host, int port, Object context)
     {
     }

     public void checkCreateClassLoader()
     {
     }

     public void checkDelete(String file)
     {
     }

     public void checkExec(String cmd)
     {
     }

     public void checkExit(int status)
     {
     }

     public void checkLink(String lib)
     {
     }

     public void checkListen(int port)
     {
     }

     public void checkPackageAccess(String pkg)
     {
     }

     public void checkPackageDefinition(String pkg)
     {
     }

     public void checkPropertiesAccess()
     {
     }
```


continues

Listing 3.1 Continued

```
        public void checkPropertyAccess(String key)
        {
        }

        public void checkRead(FileDescriptor fd)
        {
        }

        public void checkRead(String file)
        {
        }

        public void checkRead(String file, Object context)
        {
        }

        public boolean checkTopLevelWindow(Object window)
        {
             return true;
        }

        public void checkURLConnect(URL url)
        {
        }

        public void checkWrite(FileDescriptor fd)
        {
        }

        public void checkWrite(String file)
        {
        }
   }
```

Once you have created your own custom security manager, you can install it over the existing security manager in the browser you are using. Netscape stores its classes either in moz2_x.zip (moz2_0.zip, moz2_01.zip, and so on) or moz3_x.zip, depending on whether it is Netscape 2.x or Netscape 3.x. HotJava stores its classes in classes.zip. Internet Explorer also stores its files in classes.zip, which is usually found in the C:\WINDOWS\JAVA\CLASSES directory.

You'll need a zip program to replace the old security manager. See the section "Creating Your Own Archive File with Info-ZIP" in Chapter 14, "Creating Your Own Class Archive Files," for more information on zip programs and creating Java class .zip files.

To install this security manager in a Netscape mozxxx.zip (moz2_0.zip, moz2_1.zip, and so on) file, perform the following steps:

1. Go to the directory in which the mozxxx.zip file is stored.

   Under Win 95/NT, this is probably Program Files\Netscape\Navigator\Program\Java\classes.
2. Create a subdirectory called Netscape, and then create a subdirectory under that called applet.
3. Copy the AppletSecurity.class file you compiled into the Netscape/applet (or Netscape\applet) subdirectory.
4. Make a backup copy of the mozxxx.zip file; you'll need it if you want to go back to the old security manager.
5. zip –0 –u mozxxx.zip Netscape/applet/AppletSecurity.class

The procedure for HotJava is almost identical:

1. Go to the directory in which the classes.zip file is stored.

   Under Win 95/NT, this is probably \hotJava\lib.
2. Create a subdirectory called sun, and then create a subdirectory under that called applet.
3. Copy the AppletSecurity.class file you compiled into the sun/applet (or sun\applet) subdirectory.
4. Make a backup copy of the classes.zip file; you'll need it if you want to go back to the old security manager.
5. zip –0 –u classes.zip sun/applet/AppletSecurity.class

The procedure for installing your own security manager for Internet Explorer is also very similar:

1. Go to the directory in which the classes.zip file is stored. It should be C:\WINDOWS\JAVA\CLASSES, but may be slightly different if your Windows directory is in a different place. For instance, it might be C:\WINNT\JAVA\CLASSES.
2. Create a subdirectory called com, and then create a subdirectory under that called ms. Under the com\ms directory, create another subdirectory called applet.
3. Copy the AppletSecurity.class file you compiled into the com\ms\applet subdirectory.
4. Make a backup copy of the classes.zip file; you'll need it if you want to go back to the old security manager.
5. zip –0 –u classes.zip com/ms/applet/AppletSecurity.class

The next time you start your browser, your applets should be completely unrestricted.

Caution

Warning! Turning off applet security like this is extremely dangerous. Don't do this unless you know what you are doing. Remember, there is a better solution coming in the form of digital signatures, so only do this if you need unrestricted applets immediately.

chapter 4

Displaying Images

by Mark Wutka

In this chapter

- **Displaying simple images**
  You can draw images, optionally scaling them to a new size.
- **Creating your own images**
  You can create an image by storing the pixel values in an array.
- **Displaying other image formats**
  Given a specific image format, you can create an array of pixel values from the image format and turn that into a drawable image.
- **Manipulating images**
  Using the image filtering mechanism, you can drastically change the appearance of an image.
- **Filtering image colors**
  Image filters allow you to change the color of each pixel, allowing you to create interesting color filters.
- **Downloading images**
  While downloading images, you can perform other tasks and be notified when an image has finished downloading.

Images in Java

Java applets frequently need to display images. Sometimes, these images are GIF and JPEG files downloaded from a Web server. Other times, they are images that are created internally by the applet. You can also create classes that load Java images in formats other than GIF and JPEG.

Once you create a Java image, you can either display it using the AWT Graphics class, or you can apply different filters to change the appearance of the image. When you display an image, you can either draw it as is, or resize it.

Java's image filtering mechanism is very powerful. It allows you to create classes that change the appearance of an image. Because the filters are implemented as classes, once you create a filter that performs a specific visual effect, you can use the filter in any number of applets and applications.

Since images tend to take a while to download, Java allows your applet to run while the images are still downloading. It provides ways to track images so you can tell when they finish downloading, or when there is an error in downloading. Although it isn't always a good idea, you can even wait for all the images to finish downloading before starting your applet.

Displaying Simple Images

The basic mechanism for displaying images within an applet is the `drawImage` method in the `Graphics` class. It displays instances of the `Image` class. The `getImage` method in the `Applet` class fetches a GIF or JPEG image from a URL and creates an instance of `Image`. Listing 4.1 shows an applet that loads an image and displays it.

Listing 4.1 Source Code for *DrawImage.java*

```
import java.applet.Applet;
import java.awt.Graphics;
import java.awt.Image;

// This is a simple example applet that loads an image and
// displays it.

public class DrawImage extends Applet
{
     Image image;

     public void init()
     {
          image = getImage(getDocumentBase(), "samantha.gif");
     }

     public void paint(Graphics g)
     {
          g.drawImage(image, 10, 10, this);
     }
}
```

Figure 4.1 shows the image displayed by this program.

Fig. 4.1
Java can display any GIF or JPEG file.

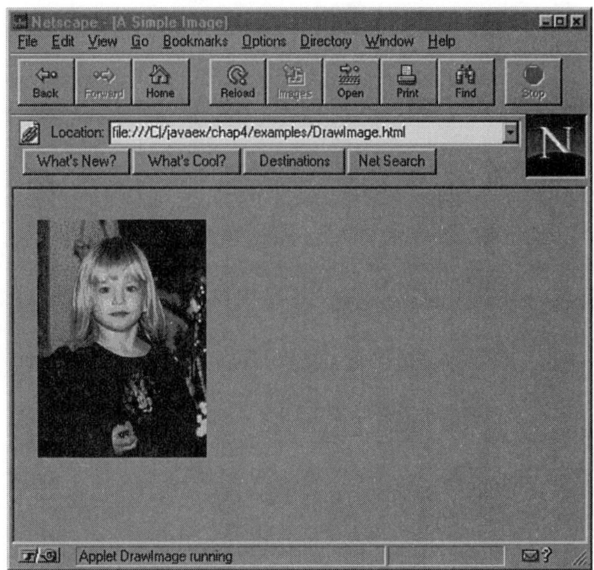

Shrinking and Stretching Images

Like the <IMG> tag in many Web browsers, the Java image display mechanism has the ability to shrink or stretch images to fit a particular size. Normally, when you display an image, you only specify the x- and-y coordinates for the upper left corner of the image. You can, however, specify an alternate width and height for the image. Java automatically scales the image to fit the new width and height. Listing 4.2 shows an applet that stretches and shrinks an image.

Listing 4.2 Source Code for *ShrinkStretch.java*

```
import java.applet.Applet;
import java.awt.Graphics;
import java.awt.Image;
import java.awt.MediaTracker;

// This applet takes an image and displays it stretched and shrunk.

public class ShrinkStretch extends Applet
{
      Image image;

      public void init()
      {
// Get the image
            image = getImage(getDocumentBase(), "samantha.gif");
```

continues

Listing 4.2 Continued

```
// Create a media tracker to wait for the image
            MediaTracker tracker = new MediaTracker(this);

// Tell the media tracker to watch the image
            tracker.addImage(image, 0);

// Wait for the image to be loaded
            try {
                    tracker.waitForAll();
            } catch (Exception ignore) {
            }
      }

      public void paint(Graphics g)
      {
// Get the width of the image
            int width = image.getWidth(this);

// Get the height of the image
            int height = image.getHeight(this);

// Draw the image in its normal size
            g.drawImage(image, 10, 10, width, height, this);

// Draw the image at half-size.
            g.drawImage(image, width+20, 10, width / 2,
                  height / 2, this);

// Draw the image at twice its size. Notice that the x coordinate
// for this image is width * 3 / 2 + 30. The 30 represents a 10-pixel
// padding between each image, for 3 images. The 3/2 represents the
// total image size of the previous two images. One full image, plus
// one half the original size.

            g.drawImage(image, width * 3 / 2 + 30, 10,
                  width * 2, height * 2, this);
      }
}
```

Figure 4.2 shows the output from this applet. The image on the left is the untouched image. The middle image is half the size of the original, and the image on the right is twice the size of the original.

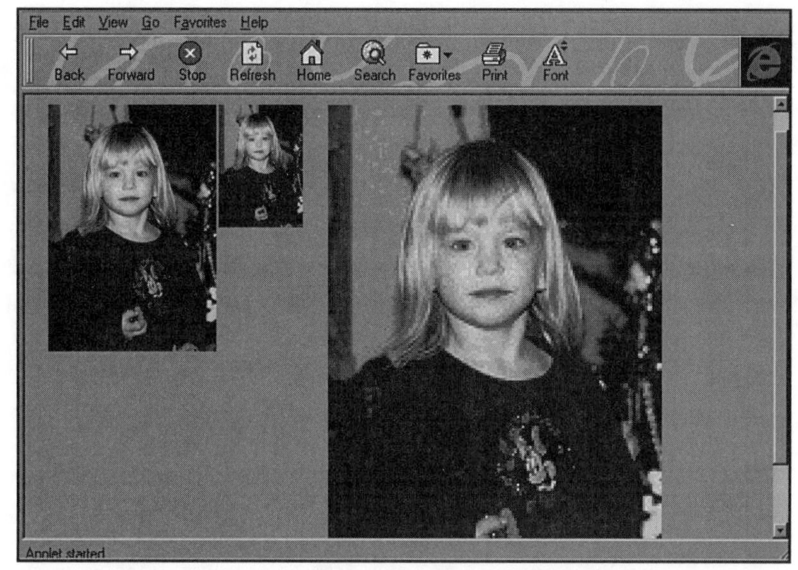

Fig. 4.2
Java automatically shrinks and stretches images.

Generally, images stretch better than they shrink. When you shrink an image, you are losing some part of the picture because there are fewer pixels. When you stretch an image, on the other hand, you don't lose any pixels. In addition, the stretching works best when the new size is a multiple of the original size. In other words, it is better to double or triple the size of an image rather than increasing it by only 50 percent. Figure 4.3 shows an image that has been stretched by 50 percent next to an image whose size has been doubled. Notice how the image on the left shows "stretch marks" where some areas are stretched a little more than others.

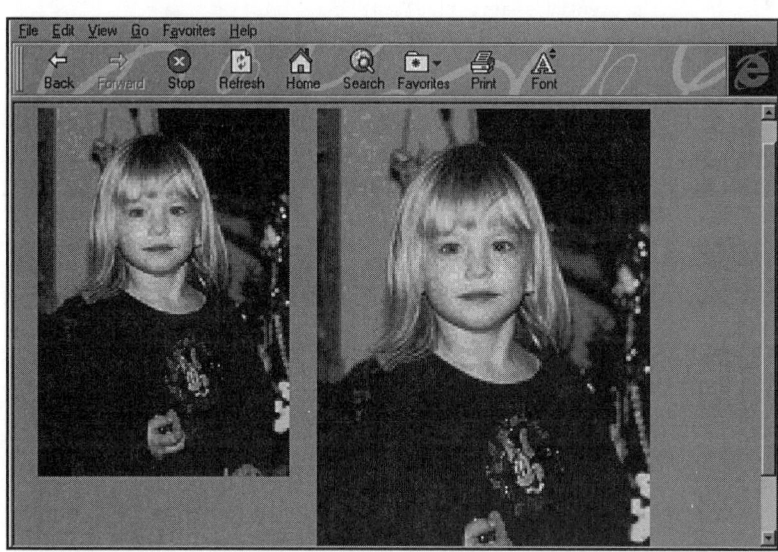

Fig. 4.3
Images scale better in whole multiples.

Creating Your Own Images

In addition to displaying GIF and JPEG images, you can also create images from an in-memory array. This enables you to create your own images on-the-fly. Usually a browser has native code to display GIF and JPEG files; however, the in-memory images go through some additional Java code before they are displayed. This means that the in-memory images usually take much longer to display than GIF or JPEG files. To create your own in-memory image, you first create a `MemoryImageSource` object, and then use the `createImage` method to create an `Image` instance. Listing 4.3 shows an applet that creates a memory image source and displays it.

Listing 4.3 Source Code for *MemoryImage.java*

```
import java.applet.*;
import java.awt.*;
import java.awt.image.*;

// This applet creates an image from an array of color values
// and displays it.

public class MemoryImage extends Applet
{
// Create some shortcut constants for yellow, black, and white

     protected static final int y = Color.yellow.getRGB();
     protected static final int b = Color.black.getRGB();
     protected static final int w = Color.white.getRGB();

// Define an array of pixel values. The pixels will be converted
// into a 16x16 image.

     protected static final int imageData[] = {
          w, w, w, w, y, y, y, y, y, y, y, y, w, w, w, w,
          w, w, w, y, y, y, y, y, y, y, y, y, y, w, w, w,
          w, w, y, y, y, y, y, y, y, y, y, y, y, y, w, w,
          w, y, y, y, b, b, y, y, y, y, b, b, y, y, y, w,
          y, y, y, y, b, b, y, y, y, y, b, b, y, y, y, y,
          y, y, y, y, y, y, y, y, y, y, y, y, y, y, y, y,
          y, y, y, y, y, y, y, y, y, y, y, y, y, y, y, y,
          y, y, y, y, y, y, y, y, y, y, y, y, y, y, y, y,
          y, y, y, y, y, y, y, y, y, y, y, y, y, y, y, y,
          y, y, y, b, y, y, y, y, y, y, y, y, b, y, y, y,
          y, y, y, y, b, y, y, y, y, y, y, b, y, y, y, y,
          y, y, y, y, y, b, b, y, y, b, b, y, y, y, y, y,
          w, y, y, y, y, y, y, b, b, y, y, y, y, y, y, w,
          w, w, y, y, y, y, y, y, y, y, y, y, y, y, w, w,
          w, w, w, y, y, y, y, y, y, y, y, y, y, w, w, w,
          w, w, w, w, y, y, y, y, y, y, y, y, w, w, w, w
     };
```

```
      Image smiley;

      public void init()
      {
// Create an image from the array of pixels
            smiley = createImage(
                  new MemoryImageSource(16, 16, imageData, 0, 16));
      }

      public void paint(Graphics g)
      {
// Display the image, stretched considerably from its original 16x16
// to a size of 128x128.
            g.drawImage(smiley, 10, 10, 128, 128, this);
      }
}
```


Figure 4.4 shows the output from this applet.

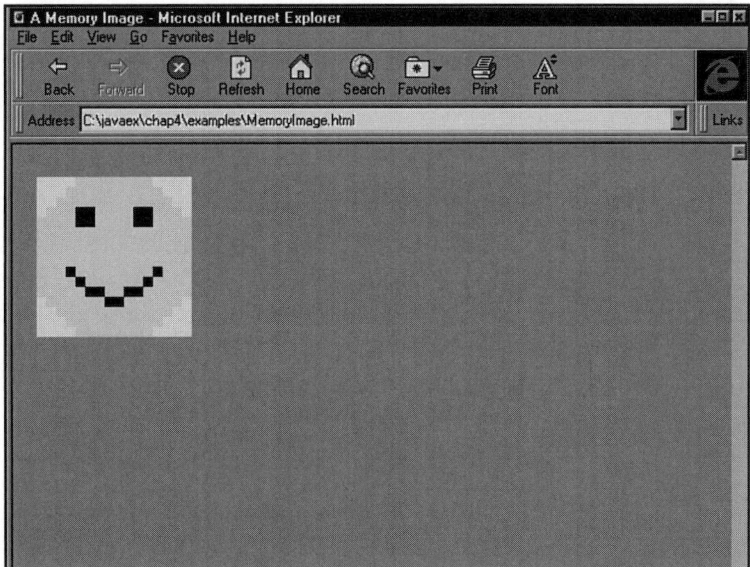

Fig. 4.4 *You can define your own image from an array of pixels.*

Displaying Other Image Formats

You may want to display images that aren't in either GIF or JPEG format. You can use the `MemoryImageSource`, along with a little programming finesse and knowledge of image formats, to display any image format you want. Most image formats contain similar information that is stored in different ways. You can usually find the dimensions of the image, the number of bits per pixel, an optional color map, and the pixel values. Your task is to take those pixel values and turn them into an array of RGB values that can be passed to the `MemoryImageSource` class. The hardest part of getting the pixel values is almost always the image decompression. Most popular image file formats have a compression algorithm to shrink the image before storing it. Some of these compression algorithms, like LZW, are not very easy to code. The Windows Bitmap (.BMP) format, on the other hand, uses a very simple compression method called run-length encoding (RLE) that is easy to write. Run-length encoding simply replaces a number of consecutive pixels of the same color with a count and the pixel color. In other words, if there were 97 blue pixels in a row, it would replace them with 97 blue. There's a little more to it, but that's the basic scheme.

Tip

Whenever you create a class that understands a particular image format, make sure that it can use an `InputStream` object. This allows you to read in images from either a file or an URL.

The Microsoft Windows Bitmap (BMP) File Format

Windows bitmaps are all over the place. Under the various Microsoft operating systems, you use bitmaps as icons, cursors, wallpaper, and other visual components. Windows bitmaps are not very popular on the Web, however. Since most windows bitmaps are not compressed, they tend to be larger than they would be if they were in GIF or JPEG format.

A Windows bitmap file consists of four parts: the bitmap file header, the bitmap info header, the color table, and the bits that make up the image.

Note

All numbers in a bitmap file are stored in Intel byte order, also known as little-endian. This means that the first byte in the file represents the little end of the number. For instance, if you wrote the hex number 0x1234 in little-endian format, you would write out 0x34, followed by 0x12. Java, on the other hand, uses big-endian format (sometimes known as network byte order, since it is employed by the TCP/IP suite). When you write out 0x1234 in big-endian format, you write out 0x12 followed by 0x34.

Table 4.1 shows the contents of the bitmap file header.

Table 4.1 Format of the Windows Bitmap File Header

# of Bytes	Type	Description
2	Character	File type (should be the characters 'B' and 'M')
4	32-bit Int	Total size of the file in bytes
2	16-bit Int	Reserved
2	16-bit Int	Reserved
4	32-bit Int	Byte-offset in file where the actual bitmap bits begin

The file type in the bitmap file header allows a program to make sure that this is a bitmap file before proceeding. If it doesn't start with "BM," it isn't a bitmap file. The byte offset for the bitmap bits is important, because there may be some padding between the headers and the actual bits. You need to know how much padding to skip over.

Note

The technique of putting a special value at the beginning of a file (like 'BM') is very common. This value is often referred to as a magic number. UNIX uses this same technique to identify the type of a file.

Table 4.2 shows the contents of the bitmap info header.

Table 4.2 Format of the Windows Bitmap Info Header

# of Bytes	Type	Description
4	32-bit Int	Size (in bytes) of the info header
4	32-bit Int	Width of bitmap (in pixels)
4	32-bit Int	Height of bitmap (in pixels)
2	16-bit Int	Number of bitplanes (should be 1)
2	16-bit Int	Number of bits per pixel (should be 1, 4, 8, or 24)
4	32-bit Int	Type of compression used
4	32-bit Int	Actual number of bytes in bitmap (only necessary if compression is used)

continues

Table 4.2 Continued

# of Bytes	Type	Description
4	32-bit Int	Number of horizontal pixels per meter (used for scaling)
4	32-bit Int	Number of vertical pixels per meter (used for scaling)
4	32-bit Int	Number of colors actually used
4	32-bit Int	Number of colors that are really important (helps when reducing the number of colors)

After the bitmap info header is a table of colors. The colors are stored in a format called RGBQUAD, which consists of 4 bytes. An RGBQUAD value contains an 8-bit blue intensity value, an 8-bit green intensity, an 8-bit red intensity, and 8-bits of 0. This may look backwards to you when you are used to thinking of colors in the order red-green-blue, but remember that this is actually just a 32-bit number stored in little-endian format. If you were to read in an RGBQUAD and perform the necessary byte-order adjustments, you end up with a normal RGB color value. For example, suppose an RGBQUAD contained the bytes 0x56, 0x34, 0x12, and 0. If you read this value in and converted it from a little-endian number to a Java big-endian number, you would have an RGB color value of 0x123456. The number of colors in the color table is given in the bitmap info header as the number of colors actually used.

Note

If a bitmap contains pixels using 24-bit color, there is no color table because the actual color values are stored in the pixel bits.

If the compression type in the bitmap info header is 0, then no compression is used. If the compression type is 1, the bitmap uses RLE8 compression. A compression type of 2 indicates that the bitmap uses RLE4 compression.

RLE4 and RLE8 compression are both simple run-length encoding schemes. The only difference is that RLE4 is used when you have 4-bit pixels, and RLE8 is used when you have 8-bit pixels. Basically, these two encoding schemes consist of a number of 2-byte codes and pixel values. A 2-byte code can contain a repeat count and a pixel value. The count indicates how many times in a row the pixel value is repeated. If the first byte of the code is 0, the second byte can indicate a number of things. It might indicate that you should skip to the next line, or you should skip to a certain x,y position, or that there are a certain number of unencoded bytes following this 2-byte code. You could completely ignore the run-length encoding and still support most of the Windows bitmaps you find. Very few of them actually use the run-length encoding.

The most peculiar thing about windows bitmaps is that they are stored upside-down. The last line in the bitmap is stored first, and the first line is stored last.

Listing 4.4 shows the `BMPReader` class that reads a Windows Bitmap from an input stream and creates an image.

Listing 4.4 Source Code for *BMPReader.java*

```
import java.awt.*;
import java.awt.image.*;
import java.io.*;

// This class provides a public static method that takes an InputStream
// to a Windows .BMP file and converts it into an ImageProducer via
// a MemoryImageSource.
// You can fetch a .BMP through a URL with the following code:
// URL url = new URL( <wherever your URL is> )
// Image img = createImage(BMPReader.getBMPImage(url.openStream()));

public class BMPReader extends Object
{
// Constants indicating how the data is stored
    public static final int BI_RGB = 0;
    public static final int BI_RLE8 = 1;
    public static final int BI_RLE4 = 2;

    public static ImageProducer getBMPImage(InputStream stream)
    throws IOException
    {
// The DataInputStream allows you to read in 16 and 32 bit numbers
        DataInputStream in = new DataInputStream(stream);

// Verify that the header starts with 'BM'

        if (in.read() != 'B') {
            throw new IOException("Not a .BMP file");
        }
        if (in.read() != 'M') {
            throw new IOException("Not a .BMP file");
        }

// Get the total file size
        int fileSize = intelInt(in.readInt());
```

continues

Listing 4.4 Continued

```
// Skip the 2 16-bit reserved words
        in.readUnsignedShort();
        in.readUnsignedShort();

        int bitmapOffset = intelInt(in.readInt());

        int bitmapInfoSize = intelInt(in.readInt());

        int width = intelInt(in.readInt());
        int height = intelInt(in.readInt());

// Skip the 16-bit bitplane size
        in.readUnsignedShort();

        int bitCount = intelShort(in.readUnsignedShort());

        int compressionType = intelInt(in.readInt());

        int imageSize = intelInt(in.readInt());

// Skip pixels per meter
        in.readInt();
        in.readInt();

        int colorsUsed = intelInt(in.readInt());
        int colorsImportant = intelInt(in.readInt());
        if (colorsUsed == 0) colorsUsed = 1 << bitCount;

        int colorTable[] = new int[colorsUsed];

// Read the bitmap's color table
        for (int i=0; i < colorsUsed; i++) {
            colorTable[i] = (intelInt(in.readInt()) & 0xffffff) + 0xff000000;
        }

// Create space for the pixels
        int pixels[] = new int[width * height];

// Read the pixels from the stream based on the compression type
        if (compressionType == BI_RGB) {
            if (bitCount == 24) {
                readRGB24(width, height, pixels, in);
            } else {
                readRGB(width, height, colorTable, bitCount,
                    pixels, in);
            }
        } else if (compressionType == BI_RLE8) {
            readRLE(width, height, colorTable, bitCount,
                pixels, in, imageSize, 8);
        } else if (compressionType == BI_RLE4) {
            readRLE(width, height, colorTable, bitCount,
                pixels, in, imageSize, 4);
        }
```

```
// Create a memory image source from the pixels
        return new MemoryImageSource(width, height, pixels, 0,
            width);
    }

// Reads in pixels in 24-bit format. There is no color table, and the
// pixels are stored in 3-byte pairs. Oddly, all windows bitmaps are
// stored upside-down - the bottom line is stored first.

    protected static void readRGB24(int width, int height, int pixels[],
        DataInputStream in)
    throws IOException
    {

// Start storing at the bottom of the array
        for (int h = height-1; h >= 0; h--) {
         int pos = h * width;
            for (int w = 0; w < width; w++) {

// Read in the red, green, and blue components
             int red = in.read();
             int green = in.read();
             int blue = in.read();

// Turn the red, green, and blue values into an RGB color with
// an alpha value of 255 (fully opaque)
                pixels[pos++] = 0xff000000 + (red << 16) +
               (green << 8) + blue;
            }
        }
    }
```


The `readRGB` method is a good example of how to extract bits that have been packed into a byte. It computes the number of pixels stored in a byte by dividing 8 by the number of bits per pixel. When you extract bits from a byte, you have to shift the byte to the right and mask out everything but the bits you are interested in. For example, if you want the leftmost 2 bits in a byte, you shift the byte 6 bits to the right, then AND the byte with 3 (3 is the bit mask for 2 bits). The general formula for an n-bit bit mask is `(1 << n) - 1`. For instance, for a 2-bit mask, it's `(1 << 2) - 1`, which is 4–1, or 3. The `readRGB` method computes an array of shift values indicating how many bits to shift for each pixel stored in the byte. For instance, if you are storing 4 pixels per byte (i.e., 2-bit pixels), you will have 4 shift values which are 6, 4, 2, and 0. That is, for the first pixel value, you shift the byte 6 bits to the right. For the second pixel, you shift 4 bits to the right. Note that these shifts are not cumulative. You are always starting with the original byte.

Listing 4.4 Source Code for *BMPReader.java* (continued)

```
// readRGB reads in pixels values that are stored uncompressed.
// The bits represent indices into the color table.

    protected static void readRGB(int width, int height, int colorTable[],
        int bitCount, int pixels[], DataInputStream in)
    throws IOException
    {

// How many pixels can be stored in a byte?
        int pixelsPerByte = 8 / bitCount;

// A bit mask containing the number of bits in a pixel
        int bitMask = (1 << bitCount) - 1;

// The shift values that will move each pixel to the far right
        int bitShifts[] = new int[pixelsPerByte];

        for (int i=0; i < pixelsPerByte; i++) {
            bitShifts[i] = 8 - ((i+1) * bitCount);
        }

        int whichBit = 0;

// Read in the first byte
        int currByte = in.read();

// Start at the bottom of the pixel array and work up
        for (int h=height-1; h >= 0; h--) {
            int pos = h * width;
            for (int w=0; w < width; w++) {

// Get the next pixel from the current byte
                pixels[pos] = colorTable[
                    (currByte >> bitShifts[whichBit]) &
                    bitMask];
          pos++;
                whichBit++;

// If the current bit position is past the number of pixels in
// a byte, we advance to the next byte
                if (whichBit >= pixelsPerByte) {
                    whichBit = 0;
                    currByte = in.read();
                }
            }
        }
    }


// readRLE reads run-length encoded data in either RLE4 or RLE8 format.

    protected static void readRLE(int width, int height, int colorTable[],
        int bitCount, int pixels[], DataInputStream in,
        int imageSize, int pixelSize)
    throws IOException
```

```
    {
        int x = 0;
        int y = height-1;

// You already know how many bytes are in the image, so only go
// through that many.

        for (int i=0; i < imageSize; i++) {

// RLE encoding is defined by two bytes
            int byte1 = in.read();
            int byte2 = in.read();
            i += 2;

// If byte 0 == 0, this is an escape code
            if (byte1 == 0) {

// If escaped, byte 2 == 0 means you are at end of line
                if (byte2 == 0) {
                    x = 0;
                    y--;

// If escaped, byte 2 == 1 means end of bitmap
                } else if (byte2 == 1) {
                    return;

// if escaped, byte 2 == 2 adjusts the current x and y by
// an offset stored in the next two words
                } else if (byte2 == 2) {
                    int xoff = (char) intelShort(
                        in.readUnsignedShort());
                    i+= 2;
                    int yoff = (char) intelShort(
                        in.readUnsignedShort());
                    i+= 2;
                    x += xoff;
                    y -= yoff;

// If escaped, any other value for byte 2 is the number of bytes
// that you should read as pixel values (these pixels are not
// run-length encoded)
                } else {
                    int whichBit = 0;

// Read in the next byte
                    int currByte = in.read();

                    i++;
                    for (int j=0; j < byte2; j++) {

                        if (pixelSize == 4) {
// The pixels are 4-bits, so half the time you shift the current byte
// to the right as the pixel value
                            if (whichBit == 0) {
                                pixels[y*width+x] = colorTable[(currByte >> 4)
                                    & 0xf];
                            } else {
```

continues

Listing 4.4 Continued

```
// The rest of the time, you mask out the upper 4 bits, save the pixel
// value, then read in the next byte
                              pixels[y*width+x] = colorTable[currByte & 0xf];
                              currByte = in.read();
                              i++;
                          }
                      } else {
                          pixels[y*width+x] = colorTable[currByte];
                          currByte = in.read();
                          i++;
                      }
                      x++;
                      if (x >= width) {
                          x = 0;
                          y--;
                      }
                  }
// The pixels must be word-aligned, so if you read an uneven number of
// bytes, read and ignore a byte to get aligned again.
                  if ((byte2 & 1) == 1) {
                      in.read();
                      i++;
                  }
              }


// If the first byte was not 0, it is the number of pixels that
// are encoded by byte 2
          } else {
              for (int j=0; j < byte1; j++) {

                  if (pixelSize == 4) {
// If j is odd, use the upper 4 bits
                      if ((j & 1) == 0) {
                          pixels[y*width+x] = colorTable[(byte2 >> 4) & 0xf];
                      } else {
                          pixels[y*width+x+1] = colorTable[byte2 & 0xf];
                      }
                  } else {
                      pixels[y*width+x+1] = colorTable[byte2];
                  }
                  x++;
                  if (x >= width) {
                      x = 0;
                      y--;
                  }
              }
          }
      }
  }
// intelShort converts a 16-bit number stored in intel byte order into
// the local host format
```

```
        protected static int intelShort(int i)
        {
            return ((i >> 8) & 0xff) + ((i << 8) & 0xff00);
        }

    // intelInt converts a 32-bit number stored in intel byte order into
    // the local host format

        protected static int intelInt(int i)
        {
            return ((i & 0xff) << 24) + ((i & 0xff00) << 8) +
                ((i & 0xff0000) >> 8) + ((i >> 24) & 0xff);
        }
    }
```


The `intelShort` and `intelInt` methods in Listing 4.4 are extremely handy methods that really belong in their own class. They convert numbers from little-endian to big-endian byte order. You can actually use these methods to convert both ways. If you use `intelInt` on a big-endian number, it returns a little-endian number. The same holds true for `intelShort`.

Manipulating Images

Java's producer-consumer model makes it simple to create filters that provide many interesting image effects. Just to refresh your memory, an image producer provides the data for an image. An image consumer takes the image data and displays it. When you create an image from an URL, the data read from that URL serves as the image producer. When you create an image from an in-memory array, the `MemoryImageSource` is the image producer. To display an image, you connect an image producer to an image consumer and the image consumer displays the image. An image filter works like both a producer and a consumer. It acts like a consumer when it receives pixel data from the producer; then it acts like a producer when it sends the pixel data on to the consumer. Depending on the image effect you are creating, you may have to create a complete in-memory copy of the image before passing it on to the consumer. Other times, you may be able to take the array of pixels passed to you, manipulate it, and pass it on to the consumer. For example, if you want to rotate an image 90 degrees, you do not have to create an in-memory image. You only need to recompute the position of the pixels you receive. Listing 4.5 shows a filter that performs a 90-degree rotation of an image.

Listing 4.5 Source Code for *RotateFilter.java*

```
import java.awt.image.*;

// This filter rotates an image 90 degrees by reversing the horizontal
// coordinates and then exchanging the x and y coordinates of each
// pixel.

public class RotateFilter extends ImageFilter
{
     public RotateFilter()
     {
     }

// Since you flip the image, if the image is delivered in either
// complete scan lines or top-down, left-right order, you won't be
// passing the data to the consumer that way, so filter out those
// flags from the hints.

     public void setHints(int hints)
     {
          consumer.setHints(hints & ~(ImageConsumer.COMPLETESCANLINES +
               ImageConsumer.TOPDOWNLEFTRIGHT));
     }

// Because you exchange x and y coordinates, width is now height and
// height is now width.
     public void setDimensions(int width, int height)
     {
          consumer.setDimensions(height, width);
     }

// To rotate the pixels, create a new array and copy over the
// pixels, reversing the horizontal pixels and then swapping
// x and y.

     public void setPixels(int x, int y, int width, int height,
          ColorModel model, byte[] pixels, int offset, int scansize)
     {
// Create a new array for the pixels

          byte[] rotatePixels = new byte[pixels.length];

          for (int ry=0; ry < height; ry++) {
               for (int rx=0; rx < width; rx++) {

// copy in the pixels with reversed x and y
                    rotatePixels[rx*height + ry] =
                         pixels[(ry+1)*scansize-rx-1+offset];
               }
          }
          consumer.setPixels(y, x, height, width, model, rotatePixels,
               0, height);
     }

// To rotate the pixels, create a new array and copy over the
// pixels, reversing the horizontal pixels and then swapping
// x and y.
```

```
     public void setPixels(int x, int y, int width, int height,
          ColorModel model, int[] pixels, int offset, int scansize)
     {
// Create a new array for the pixels

          int[] rotatePixels = new int[pixels.length];

          for (int ry=0; ry < height; ry++) {
               for (int rx=0; rx < width; rx++) {

// copy in the pixels with reversed x and y
                    rotatePixels[rx*height + ry] =
                         pixels[(ry+1)*scansize-rx-1+offset];
               }
          }
          consumer.setPixels(y, x, height, width, model, rotatePixels,
               0, height);
     }
}
```


Listing 4.6 shows an applet that uses this filter to display an image and a rotated version of the image.

Listing 4.6 Source Code for *RotateApplet.java*

```
import java.applet.Applet;
import java.awt.Graphics;
import java.awt.Image;
import java.awt.MediaTracker;
import java.awt.image.*;

// This applet displays an image rotated 90 degrees using the
// RotateFilter image filter.

public class RotateApplet extends Applet
{
     Image image;
     Image origImage;

     public void init()
     {

          String imageName = getParameter("image");
          if (imageName == null) imageName = "samantha.gif";

// Get the original image
          origImage = getImage(getDocumentBase(), imageName);

// Need to wait on the image for this one. The image filters
// get upset if you try to filter an image that hasn't been
// loaded yet. You should really display alternate information
// rather than just waiting for the image, though.
```

continues

Listing 4.6 Continued

```
            MediaTracker mt = new MediaTracker(this);
            mt.addImage(origImage, 0);
            try {
                mt.waitForAll();
            } catch (Exception e) {
            }
// Now filter the image
            image = createImage(new FilteredImageSource(
                origImage.getSource(), new RotateFilter()));
        }

        public void paint(Graphics g)
        {
            g.drawImage(origImage, 10, 10, this);
            g.drawImage(image, 240, 10, this);
        }
}
```

Figure 4.5 shows a plain image and an image rotated 90 degrees by this filter.

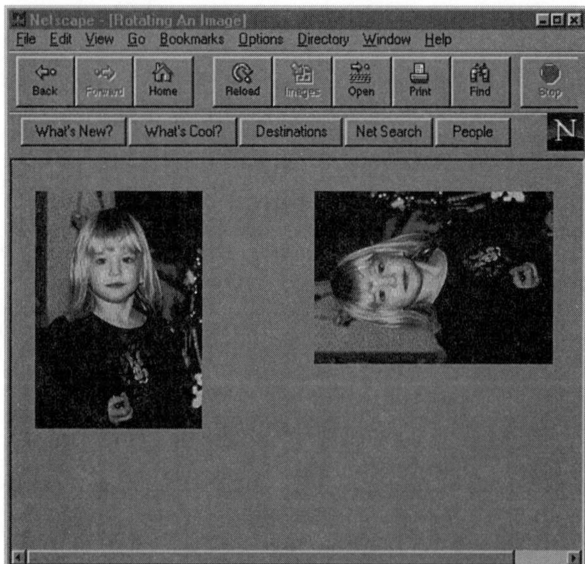

Fig. 4.5
Image filters enable you to perform effects such as rotation.

Performing Image-Processing Algorithms

Sometimes the changes you need to make to an image require that you have a complete copy of the image first. You can set up a filter to do this by saving all the pixels you receive in the `setPixels` call. Unlike the other image filters, your `setPixels` method will not invoke the `setPixels` method in the consumer. When the `imageComplete` method is called, you know that you have all the pixels and can process your pixel data. Once you have performed your image processing, you can invoke the `setPixels` method in the consumer and pass it your modified pixels, then call `imageComplete` in the consumer. When you are building your own copy of the image, keep in mind that the pixels in the `setPixels` call are not necessarily RGB values. You should use the image's color model to convert them to RGB first. When you call `setPixels` in the consumer, you can use `ColorModel.getRGBdefault()` as the color model because you will have converted all your pixel values to RGB.

Listing 4.7 shows an abstract image effects class. It implements the ImageObserver interface and gets all the pixels in the image. Once all the pixels have been delivered, it calls the `performEffect` method to manipulate the image. After the effect has been performed, it calls `deliverPixels` to send the pixels to its consumers.

Listing 4.7 Source Code for *EffectFilter.java*

```
import java.awt.image.*;

/**
 * Abstract class for implementing image effects on the
 * whole image. This class loads in an image and then calls
 * the performEffect method to perform the image effect, then
 * it delivers the pixels to the consumer.
 * @author Mark Wutka
 */

// This class is an example of a filter that requires all the
// pixels to be present before it can operate.

public abstract class EffectFilter extends ImageFilter
{
// Storage area for image info
      int width;
      int height;
      int pixels[];

      public EffectFilter()
      {
      }

// Filter the COMPLETESCANLINES hint out of the hints. You know you won't be
// presenting complete scan lines.

      public void setHints(int hints)
      {
            consumer.setHints(hints & ~ImageConsumer.COMPLETESCANLINES);
      }
```

continues

Listing 4.7 Continued

```
// When you find out the dimensions of the image, you can create the holding
// area for the pixels.

     public void setDimensions(int width, int height)
     {
             this.width = width;
             this.height = height;
             this.pixels = new int[width*height];

             consumer.setDimensions(width, height);
     }

// An image filter has two different versions of setPixels. This one
// takes an array of bytes as the pixel values. This implies that the
// color model is an indexed color model. Because this filter needs pixels
// in RGB format, you just get the RGB value from the color model and put
// it into our array of pixels.

     public void setPixels(int x, int y, int width, int height,
           ColorModel model, byte[] pixels, int offset, int scansize)
     {

// Process every row in the source array
           for (int i=0; i < height; i++) {

// Shortcuts to save some computation time
                 int destLineOffset = (y+i)*width;
                 int srcLineOffset = i*scansize+offset;

// Process every pixel in the row
                 for (int j=0; j < width; j++) {

// Get the pixel value, make sure it is unsigned (the &0xff does this)
                       int pixel = pixels[srcLineOffset+j]&0xff;

// Get the RGB value
                       this.pixels[destLineOffset+x+j] =
                             model.getRGB(pixel);
                 }
           }
     }

// You don't actually know if the color model here is the RGB color
// model or not, so just treat it like it might be an indexed model.

     public void setPixels(int x, int y, int width, int height,
           ColorModel model, int[] pixels, int offset, int scansize)
     {
// Process every row in the source array
           for (int i=0; i < height; i++) {

// Shortcuts to save some computation time
                 int destLineOffset = (y+i)*width;
                 int srcLineOffset = i*scansize+offset;
```

```
// Process every pixel in the row
                for (int j=0; j < width; j++) {

// Get the pixel value, make sure it is unsigned (the &0xff does this)
                        int pixel = pixels[srcLineOffset+j];

// Get the RGB value
                        this.pixels[destLineOffset+x+j] =
                            model.getRGB(pixel);
                }
            }
        }

// When the image producer is finished sending us pixels it calls
// imageComplete. You take this opportunity to perform the effect
// and then send all the pixels to our consumer before passing on
// the imageComplete call to the consumer. Up to this point the consumer
// doesn't know anything about our pixels. It's about to learn!

        public void imageComplete(int status)
        {
// Do the effect
            performEffect();

// Send the pixels to the consumer
            deliverPixels();

// You're done now!
            super.imageComplete(status);
        }

        public abstract void performEffect();

// deliverPixels sends the whole array of pixels to the consumer in one shot

        protected void deliverPixels()
        {
            consumer.setPixels(0, 0, this.width, this.height,
                ColorModel.getRGBdefault(),
                this.pixels, 0, this.width);
        }
}
```

Listing 4.8 shows an image effect that performs an imaging algorithm called an emboss. The emboss filter looks rather confusing, but it is actually fairly simple. It assumes that you are shining a light from the upper-left corner of the image, and that a light pixel is typically higher (closer to the front) than a dark pixel. Given these two conditions, it looks at each pixel and examines the 8 surrounding pixels. The emboss algorithm applies a weighting matrix to the surrounding pixels. The upper left pixel is given a weight of –2, the top and left pixels are given a weight of –1. The lower right pixel is given a weight of 2, and the bottom and right pixels are given a weight of 1. You multiply the color values of these pixels by their weights, add the values together, and divide by 8. This creates a weighted average. What this really does is compute a slope. If you were walking from the upper left pixel to the lower right pixel, it would decide whether you were going uphill or downhill. If the weighted average is negative, you would be walking downhill, because the upper and left pixels would be lighter (they have higher pixel values) than the lower-right pixels.

This slope is then used to either lighten or darken the current pixel. If it is an uphill slope, it would catch more light, so the pixel is lightened. If it is a downhill slope, it would catch less light, so it is darkened. Rather than lightening and darkening the existing pixel, the algorithm starts with a uniform gray value for each pixel. This essentially transfers the slopes of the original image onto a plain gray image without transferring the colors themselves. The end result is an interesting emboss effect that gives the image a 3-D look.

Listing 4.8 Source Code for *EmbossFilter.java*

```
public class EmbossFilter extends EffectFilter
{
      public EmbossFilter()
      {
      }

// This is where the actual emboss effect is performed. It uses an
// edge-detection matrix and maps the edge value onto a field of
// all gray. When it does this, it is essentially "bending" the gray
// by adding shadows where all the edges are. This creates a neat
// embossing effect.

      public void performEffect()
      {
// newPixels holds the new embossed image
               int newPixels[] = new int[width*height];

// For each pixel, compute the embossing values. You start one pixel down
// and in because the edge-detection needs to look one pixel in every
// direction and this keeps us from running off the edge.

              for (int y=1; y < height-1; y++) {
                    int lineOffset = y * width;
                    for (int x = 1; x < width-1; x++) {
                          int pointOffset = lineOffset+x;
                          int redSum = 0;
                          int greenSum = 0;
                          int blueSum = 0;

// Perform the edge detection - the matrix used is:
// -2 -1 0
// -1  0 1
//  0  1 2
```

```
// These values are applied individually to the red, green and blue
// components, then the values are normalized and added to the plain
// gray image to "bend" or "crinkle" it.

                        redSum -= 2*((pixels[pointOffset-width-1]
                              >> 16)&0xff);
                        greenSum -= 2*((pixels[pointOffset-width-1]
                              >> 8)&0xff);
                        blueSum -= 2*(pixels[pointOffset-width-1]
                              &0xff);

                        redSum -= ((pixels[pointOffset-width]
                              >> 16)&0xff);
                        greenSum -= ((pixels[pointOffset-width]
                              >> 8)&0xff);
                        blueSum -= (pixels[pointOffset-width]
                              &0xff);

                        redSum -= ((pixels[pointOffset-1]
                              >> 16)&0xff);
                        greenSum -= ((pixels[pointOffset-1]
                              >> 8)&0xff);
                        blueSum -= (pixels[pointOffset-1]
                              &0xff);

                        redSum += 2*((pixels[pointOffset+width+1]
                              >> 16)&0xff);
                        greenSum += 2*((pixels[pointOffset+width+1]
                              >> 8)&0xff);
                        blueSum += 2*(pixels[pointOffset+width+1]
                              &0xff);

                        redSum += ((pixels[pointOffset+width]
                              >> 16)&0xff);
                        greenSum += ((pixels[pointOffset+width]
                              >> 8)&0xff);
                        blueSum += (pixels[pointOffset+width]
                              &0xff);

                        redSum += ((pixels[pointOffset+1]
                              >> 16)&0xff);
                        greenSum += ((pixels[pointOffset+1]
                              >> 8)&0xff);
                        blueSum += (pixels[pointOffset+1]
                              &0xff);

// Normalize the values
                        redSum >>= 3;
                        greenSum >>= 3;
                        blueSum >>= 3;

// Add these sums to medium-gray
                        redSum += 0x7f;
                        greenSum += 0x7f;
                        blueSum += 0x7f;

// Make sure the values are within the 0-255 range
```

continues

Listing 4.8 Continued

```
                    if (redSum < 0) redSum = 0;
                    if (redSum > 255) redSum = 255;
                    if (greenSum < 0) greenSum = 0;
                    if (greenSum > 255) greenSum = 255;
                    if (blueSum < 0) blueSum = 0;
                    if (blueSum > 255) blueSum = 255;

// Compute the final gray value as the maximum of red, green, and blue
                    int gray = Math.max(greenSum,
                          Math.max(redSum, blueSum));
// Store the new value in the array (since you want the gray value for
// red, green and blue, multiplying by 0x010101 will fill all 3 components
// with the gray value.
                    newPixels[pointOffset] = 0xff000000 +
                          0x010101 * gray;
                }
            }
            this.pixels = newPixels;
        }
}
```

Figure 4.6 shows an example of image embossing.

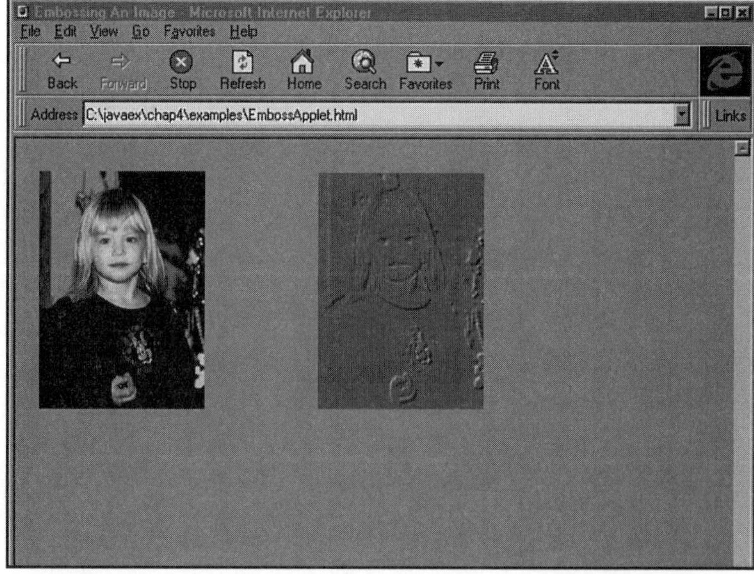

Fig. 4.6
Image embossing is one of the many imaging algorithms you can perform.

Filtering Image Colors

Many image effects involve the simple changing of colors. Rather than filtering the individual image pixels, you can filter the pixel colors instead. If the pixel's x and y coordinates do not have any effect on a pixel's filtered color, you should set the `canFilterIndexColorModel` variable to `true`. This greatly speeds up the filtering process if the image uses an index color model, because you filter only the index and not the entire image. Listing 4.9 shows an image filter that creates a photo negative of an image by XOR-ing the red, green, and blue components with 255.

Listing 4.9 Source Code for *NegativeFilter.java*

```
import java.awt.image.*;

// This class is a simple RGB filter that inverts
// colors by XORing the color components with
// 0xff, which makes black become white and vice versa.

public class NegativeFilter extends RGBImageFilter
{
      public NegativeFilter()
      {
            canFilterIndexColorModel = true;
      }

      public int filterRGB(int x, int y, int rgb)
      {
            return
                  (rgb & 0xff000000) +      // preserve transparency
                  (rgb & 0xffffff) ^ 0xffffff; // xor the components
      }
}
```

Figure 4.7 shows an image along with its negative counterpart.

Filtering Based on Pixel Position

Some image filters require you to know the x and y components of the pixel to determine its coloring. For example, if you want to perform a lighting effect in which the pixels farther from the light are darker, you need to compute the distance of the pixel from the light source. The distance calculation uses the old standard square root of the x distance squared plus the y distance squared. In other words, given two points x1,y1 and x2,y2, the distance between them is sqrt((x1–x2)×(x1–x2)+(y1-y2)×(y1-y2)). Listing 4.10 shows an image filter that performs a lighting effect using the pixel's position.

Fig. 4.7
The RGBImageFilter modifies the colors of an image.

Listing 4.10 Source Code for *LightingFilter.java*

```
import java.awt.image.*;

/**
 * Simulates the presence of a white light source shining
 * down on an image. When you create the filter, you supply
 * the X,Y coordinates for the center of the light, the radius
 * of the light, the intensity of the light, and a fading factor
 * for the light. An intensity of 1.0 gives you at most the same
 * brightness as the original image, higher than 1.0 causes white
 * washout near the light (really bright light), and less than 1 means
 * it's pretty dark. The fade factor indicates how much the light fades
 * as you get farther from it. A fade of 0.0 means it doesn't fade at all.
 * The formula for the intensity of light is the distance from the circle
 * of light * the fade. If the intensity is 1 and the fade is 0.01, any point
 * that is 100 pixels or more away from the light will be black (since by
 * the intensity formula, the intensity is 1.0 - (100 * 0.01), or 0).
 *
 * @author Mark Wutka
*/

public class LightingFilter extends RGBImageFilter
{

/** the center x coordinate of the circle of light */
     public int centerX;

/** the center y coordinate of the circle of light */
     public int centerY;
```

```
/** the radius of the circle of light */
     public int radius;

/** the intensity of the light */
     public double intensity;

/** How quickly the intensity fades as you go away from the light */
     public double fade;

/**
 * Creates an instance of a lighting filter which shines a circle
 * of light on an image.
 *
 * @param centerX the X coordinate of the center of the light circle
 * @param centerY the Y coordinate of the center of the light circle
 * @param radius the radius of the light circle
 * @param intensity the intensity of the light, > 1.0 whitens the colors
 *          within the circle (it's brighter).
 * @param fade how quickly the light fades as you leave the circle. If fade
 *           is >= 1.0, it is pitch black outside the circle.
 */
     public LightingFilter(int centerX, int centerY, int radius,
          double intensity, double fade)
     {
          this.centerX = centerX;
          this.centerY = centerY;
          this.radius = radius;
          this.intensity = intensity;

// Can't have an intensity less than 0, an intensity of 0 is total darkness
// How much blacker could it be? The answer is "none more black". - N. Tufnel
          if (intensity < 0.0) intensity = 0.0;

          this.fade = fade;

// Because the lighting is position dependent, this filter
// cannot filter an index color model;
          canFilterIndexColorModel = false;
     }

     public int filterRGB(int x, int y, int rgb)
     {
// Save the pixel's transparency value
          int trans = rgb & 0xff000000;

// Compute the distance from the edge of the circle (distance from center
// - radius).
          double dist = Math.sqrt((x-centerX)*(x-centerX) +
               (y-centerY)*(y-centerY)) - radius;
          if (dist < 0.0) dist = 0.0;

// Compute the intensity based on distance and fade
          double intense = intensity - dist * fade;

// Again, none more black than 0.0
          if (intense < 0.0) intense = 0.0;
```

continues

Listing 4.10 Continued

```
// Adjust the colors based on the new intensity
        int red = (int)(((rgb >> 16) & 0xff) * intense);
// Max color value for each component is 255
        if (red > 255) red = 255;

        int green = (int)(((rgb >> 8) & 0xff) * intense);
        if (green > 255) green = 255;

        int blue = (int)((rgb & 0xff) * intense);
        if (blue > 255) blue = 255;

// Return the new color
        return trans + (red << 16) + (green << 8) + blue;
    }
}
```

Figure 4.8 shows the output from the lighting filter.

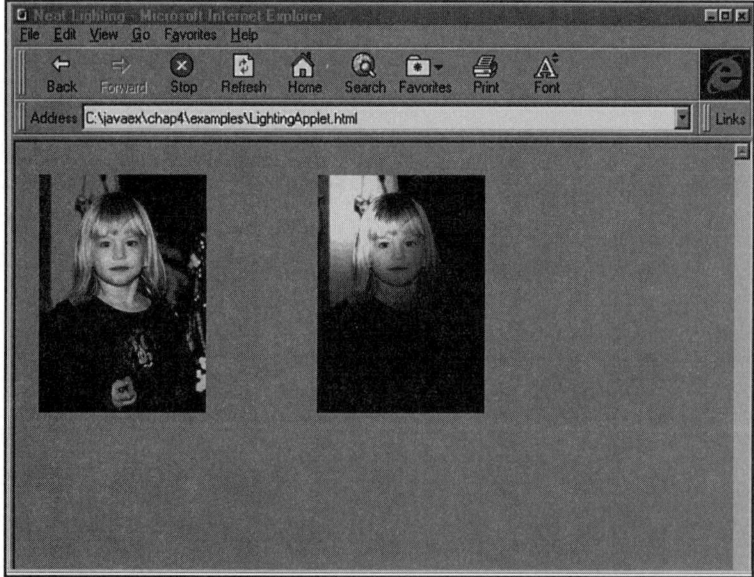

Fig. 4.8
Filters based on pixel position can create neat effects.

Downloading Images

When your applet starts up and begins downloading its images, you shouldn't wait for all the images to be loaded before your applet really starts. The `MediaTracker` class is nice for this, but you must be careful when using it. The media tracker allows you to wait for your images to be downloaded. Many times, this is acceptable to you. If you are creating an applet for a commercial Web page, however, you should avoid any possible delay. One option you have with the media tracker is to spawn a thread that waits for images and calls repaint when all the images have been loaded. Of course, that requires you to set up a special thread, which you also may not want to do.

If your applet is not already runnable, you can create a `run` method and use the media tracker in the `run` method. If your applet already has a run method, you must set up another class that is responsible for running the media tracker. By the time you create another runnable class that uses the media tracker, you might as well just use the `ImageObserver` interface.

The `Component` class, of which `Applet` is a subclass, contains everything you need to start downloading images and check on their progress. Your applet can implement the `ImageObserver` interface so it can be notified as your images are downloaded successfully. When you use the `ImageObserver` interface, you implement the `imageUpdate` method, which is called whenever there is more information available about the image. Your `imageUpdate` method should check the `flags` parameter to see when the `ImageObserver.ALLBITS` flag is set. When this flag is set, the image has finished loading. You can then repaint the screen using the full image. Listing 4.11 shows an applet that implements the `ImageObserver` interface to see when all its images have finished downloading.

Listing 4.11 Source Code for *DownloadApplet.java*

```
import java.awt.*;
import java.awt.image.*;
import java.applet.*;

// This applet acts as an image observer to watch for images
// to be ready. While applets are being loaded, it displays
// a message where the applet will be drawn. Once the image is
// loaded, it displays the image. If there is an error loading
// an image, it prints an error message in place of the image.

public class DownloadApplet extends Applet implements ImageObserver
{
// The three images we are loading

     protected Image moe;
     protected Image larry;
     protected Image curly;

     public DownloadApplet()
     {
     }

     public void init()
     {
```

continues

Listing 4.11 Continued

```
// get the images, this doesn't necessarily start download them, however
        moe = getImage(getDocumentBase(), "moe2.gif");
        larry = getImage(getDocumentBase(), "larry2.gif");
        curly = getImage(getDocumentBase(), "curly2.gif");

// start downloading the images
        prepareImage(moe, this);
        prepareImage(larry, this);
        prepareImage(curly, this);
    }

// Show image checks the flags associated with an image. If the image
// is still loading, it displays the loadingMessage string. If the image
// had an error loading, it displays the errorMessageString. Otherwise,
// it displays the fully-loaded image.

    protected void showImage(Graphics g, int x, int y, Image image,
        String loadingMessage, String errorMessage)
    {
// Get the status of the image
        int flags = checkImage(image, this);

// If the image aborted or had an error, print the error message
        if ((flags & (ImageObserver.ABORT+ImageObserver.ERROR)) != 0)
        {
            g.drawString(errorMessage, x, y+30);
            return;

// If the image has been loaded fully, display it
        } else if ((flags & ImageObserver.ALLBITS) != 0) {
            g.drawImage(image, x, y, this);

// If the image is still loading, display the loading message
        } else {
            g.drawString(loadingMessage, x, y+30);
            return;
        }
    }

    public void paint(Graphics g)
    {
        showImage(g, 10, 10, moe, "Moe's coming!",
            "Moe can't make it.");
        showImage(g, 200, 10, larry, "Larry's coming!",
            "Larry can't make it.");
        showImage(g, 390, 10, curly, "Curly's coming!",
            "Curly can't make it.");
    }

    public boolean imageUpdate(Image img, int flags, int x, int y,
        int width, int height)
    {
// Whenever an image's status changes, imageUpdate gets called. If the
// image aborts, has an error, or is complete, we call repaint to redraw
```

```
// the image with the updated information.

          if ((flags & ImageObserver.ALLBITS+ImageObserver.ABORT+
               ImageObserver.ERROR) != 0)
          {
               repaint();
          }
// Otherwise, if we just got more pixels or something else, there's
// no need to repaint, we don't need to change the current message.

          return true;
     }
}
```

Figure 4.9 shows the output of the applet while it is waiting for the image to be downloaded.

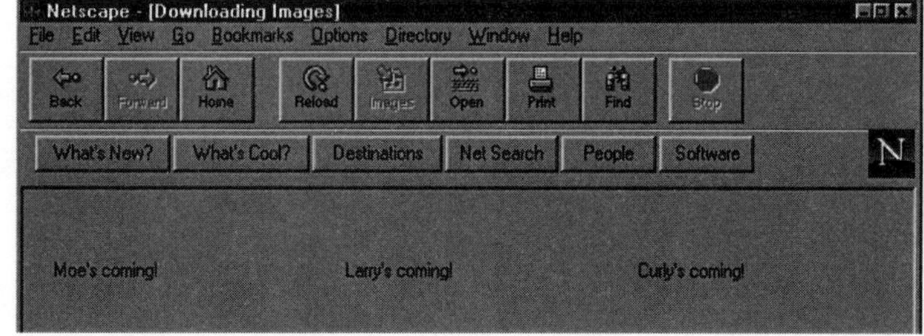

Fig. 4.9
You should display alternate information while waiting for an image to download.

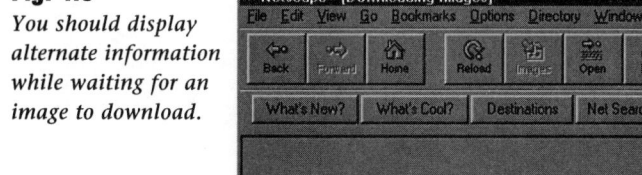

chapter 5

Animating Images

5

by Mark Wutka

In this chapter

- **Animating whole and partial images**
  You can create interesting animation effects by displaying images in a sequence, similar to a film. Unlike a film, where you display a series of whole images, you can animate just a small portion of an image.
- **Using filters to change animation frames**
  You don't have to use pre-built frames for animation. You can create various image filters that change the image frames each time. By filtering either the image itself or the colors in the image, you can create interesting animation sequences from a single image.
- **Animating graphics**
  Instead of animating images, you may want to animate figures drawn with the AWT Graphics class. This style of animation is very common in video games.
- **Eliminating flicker**
  Flicker is the nemesis of many animation programs. There are some simple steps you can take to eliminate flicker from any animation program you write.

Animation

Animation involves changing a picture over and over to simulate movement of some sort. There are several different types of animation you can perform in a Java applet. You can display a sequence of images, or you can display a single image while changing a portion of it. You can change an image by running it through a filter or by changing the colors in the image. You can also perform animation with the basic graphics classes.

Animation is a powerful technique for applets. Having a portion of your display that moves can make your application or your Web page much livelier. There are far more uses for animation that just sprucing up a Web page, however.

Animation is frequently used in video games. In fact, it's probably one of the most common factors in computer games. Modern adventure games often use sequences of real-life images to give the game a modern feel. Arcade games frequently employ graphical animation, although some have begun to integrate images into the games as well.

Beyond gaming, animation is an excellent tool for computer-assisted learning. Rather than describing a technique with plain old text, you can demonstrate it through animation. This type of animation is often done with images but not necessarily. You may be demonstrating a technique that requires a graphical representation that is computed while the program is running.

An Animation Driver

To perform animation, you have to create a thread that repeatedly changes the animation sequence and repaints the picture. Because the different animation techniques all use this same method, you can use the same mechanism to trigger the next animation sequence. The idea here is that you create a timer class that calls a method at specific intervals. Ideally, you would like the timer class to be able to invoke different methods in your applet, allowing you to run multiple timers in a single applet. You can do this in Java, but it takes a little extra work.

The first thing you need to do in setting up this timer class is to define the method the timer will call each time. Listing 5.1 shows the `TimerCallback` interface that defines this method.

Listing 5.1 Source Code for *TimerCallback.java*

```
// This interface defines a callback for the Timer class

public interface TimerCallback
{
     public void tick();
}
```

Once you have this interface defined, you can create a `Timer` class that repeatedly calls the `tick` method at some fixed interval. You should keep track of the amount of time that elapses during the call to the `tick` method and only sleep for the amount of time remaining before the next tick. This makes your animation much smoother and helps minimize the effects of garbage collection. Obviously, if the `tick` method takes longer than the interval, your animation will be slower than you desire.

Listing 5.2 shows a reusable timer class that repeatedly calls the `tick` method in a `TimerCallback` interface at a certain interval. You can set the interval when you create the `Timer` object, and you may change it at any time.

Listing 5.2 Source Code for *Timer.java*

```
/**
 * This class implements an interval timer. It calls
 * the tick method in the callback interface after
 * a fixed number of milliseconds (indicated by the
 * interval variable). It measures the amount of time spent
 * in the tick method and adjusts for it.
 * To start up a timer with this class, create it with
 * a callback and the number of milliseconds in the interval
 * and then call the start method:
 * <PRE>
 *
 *    Timer timer = new Timer(this, 2000);      // 2 second interval
 *    timer.start();
 *
 * </PRE>
 *
 * @author Mark Wutka
 */

public class Timer extends Object implements Runnable
{

     protected Thread timerThread;

/** The number of milliseconds in the interval*/
     protected long interval;

/** The callback interface containing the tick method */
     protected TimerCallback callback;

     public Timer()
     {
     }

     public Timer(TimerCallback callback)
     {
          this.callback = callback;
     }

     public Timer(long interval)
     {
          this.interval = interval;
     }

     public Timer(TimerCallback callback, long interval)
```

continues

5

Listing 5.2 Continued

```
    {
        this.callback = callback;
        this.interval = interval;
    }

/** returns the number of milliseconds in the interval */
    public long getInterval()
    {
        return interval;
    }

/** sets the number of milliseconds in the interval
 * @param newInterval the new number of milliseconds
 */
    public void setInterval(long newInterval)
    {
        interval = newInterval;
    }

/** returns the callback interface */
    public TimerCallback getCallback()
    {
        return callback;
    }

/** changes the callback interface
 * @param callback the new callback
 */
    public void setCallback(TimerCallback callback)
    {
        this.callback = callback;
    }

/** starts the timer */
    public void start()
    {
        timerThread = new Thread(this);
        timerThread.start();
    }

/** stops the timer */
    public void stop()
    {
        timerThread.stop();
        timerThread = null;
    }

    public void run()
    {
        while (true)
        {
// Check the current time
```

```
                long startTime = System.currentTimeMillis();

// If there is a callback, call it
                if (callback != null)
                {
                     callback.tick();
                }

// Check the time again
                long endTime = System.currentTimeMillis();

// The amount of time to sleep is the interval minus the time spent
// in the tick routine
                long sleepTime = interval - (endTime - startTime);

// If you've passed the next interval, hurry up and call the next tick
                if (sleepTime <= 0) continue;

                try {
                     Thread.sleep(sleepTime);
                } catch (Exception insomnia) {
                     // might as well ignore this exception
                }
           }
      }
}
```

Now, you can only have one tick method, so how can you support multiple timers in a single application? The answer lies in a design pattern called the `Command` pattern. An object that implements the `tick` method is considered a command object. If you want to have multiple timers that call different methods in your class, you create a number of intermediate objects. Suppose you have the following object:

```
public class DualTimers extends Object
{
     public DualTimers()
     {
     }

     public void timer1Tick()
     {
          System.out.println("Tick!");
     }

     public void timer2Tick()
     {
          System.out.println("Tock!");
     }
}
```

To set up timers to call each of these methods, create small intermediate classes to invoke each of these methods:

```
public class Timer1Callback extends Object implements TimerCallback
{
     protected DualTimers whichTimer;

     public Timer1Callback(DualTimers timer)
     {
          whichTimer = timer;
     }

     public void tick()
     {
          whichTimer.timer1Tick();
     }
}
```

Notice that this `Timer1Callback` class can be passed to a `Timer` object, and when its `tick` method is called, it will call the `timer1Tick` method in the `DualTimer` class. Similarly, you can create a `Timer2Callback` object:

```
public class Timer2Callback extends Object implements TimerCallback
{
     protected DualTimers whichTimer;

     public Timer2Callback(DualTimers timer)
     {
          whichTimer = timer;
     }

     public void tick()
     {
          whichTimer.timer2Tick();
     }
}
```

Figure 5.1 shows the relationship between a `Timer` object and a `TimerCallback` object.

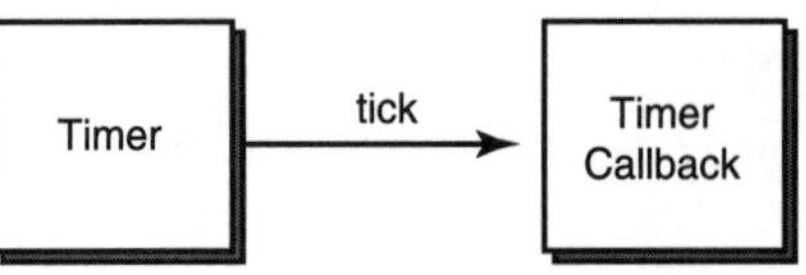

Fig. 5.1
In the simple configuration, a `Timer` object invokes the `tick` method in a `TimerCallback` object.

Figure 5.2 shows how the relationship between these two objects changes when you use intermediate objects.

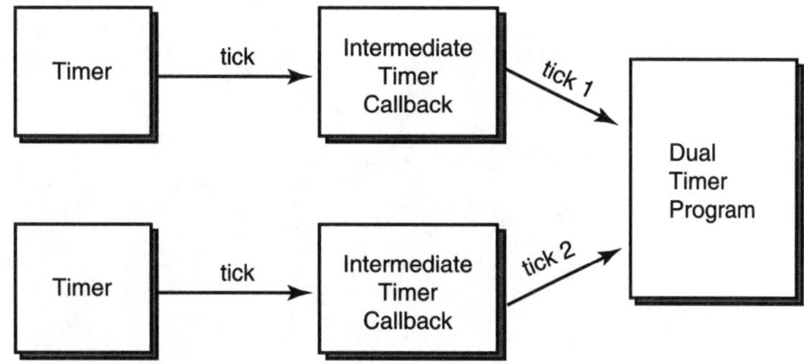

Fig. 5.2
Intermediate timer callbacks allow a single object to have multiple timer callbacks.

5

Now that you have these command objects, you can create two timers that call methods in the `DualTimer` object:

```
public class TestDualTimers extends Object
{
     public static void main(String[] args)
     {
          DualTimers dual = new DualTimers();
          Timer1Callback tc1 = new Timer1Callback(dual);
          Timer2Callback tc2 = new Timer2Callback(dual);

          Timer timer1 = new Timer(tc1, 1000);
          Timer timer2 = new Timer(tc2, 2000);

          timer1.start();
          timer2.start();
     }
}
```

In the previous example, you create only a single instance of the `DualTimers` object but two different timers that eventually trigger methods in `DualTimers`. If you only need to invoke a single method in an object, you don't need to create this extra layer of objects. Figure 5.3 shows this test program in operation.

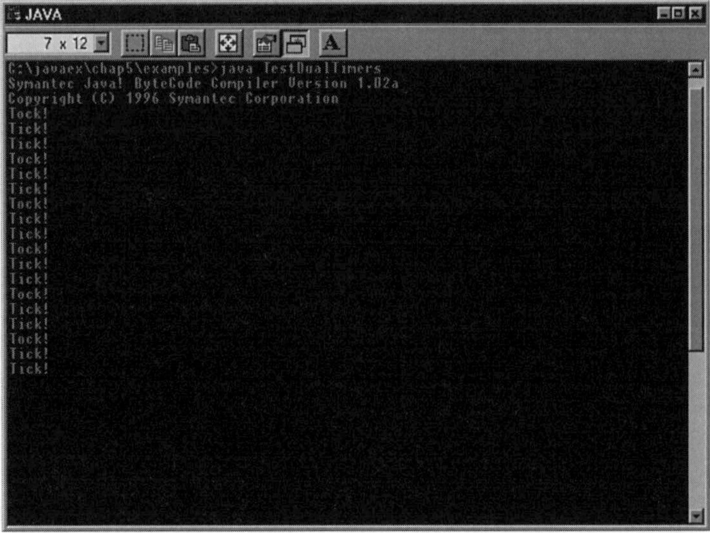

Fig. 5.3
Timer 1, triggered every second, prints `tick`*, while timer 2, triggered every two seconds, prints* `tock`.

Animating Image Sequences

Performing animation by rapidly changing a series of images is one of the oldest forms of animation. It is the same method that movies use; however, your applet will only have a fraction of the number of frames that a movie has. The `Timer` class that was just discussed is a great help in creating image sequence animation. You simply need to load the images you want and then set up a timer. Every time the timer ticks, decide which image you want to display next and call `repaint`.

When you are first loading the images for an animation sequence, you should print some text in your applet or even some of the images from the animation—just to keep your viewers from getting impatient. You can use the `ImageObserver` interface to track which images have been loaded.

Listing 5.3 shows an applet that cycles a set of six images using the `Timer` class to trigger the next change. It displays a text message when it first comes up, and when the first image has been loaded, it displays it. Then, when the rest of the images have been loaded, it starts the animation.

Listing 5.3 Source Code for *CycleAnimation.java*

```
import java.applet.*;
import java.awt.*;
import java.awt.image.*;
```

```
// This applet demonstrates several useful techniques in dealing
// with animating images.
// 1. It uses the Timer class to trigger the next animation frame
// 2. It displays a "teaser" while the images are being loaded
// 3. It does not use the MediaTracker to wait for images, but
//    knows when all the images are ready.

public class CycleAnimation extends Applet implements TimerCallback,
     ImageObserver
{
     protected Image[] images;
     int whichImage;

// This applet cycles from 0-5 and then cycles back down from 5-0
// You won't need imageDirection if you only cycle one way.
     int imageDirection;

// have we started the animation or not?
     boolean animationStarted;

     Timer timer;

     public CycleAnimation()
     {
          timer = null;
          animationStarted = false;
     }

     public void init()
     {
          images = new Image[6];
          for (int i=0; i < 6; i++) {
// Get images named mark1.gif - mark6.gif
               images[i] = getImage(getDocumentBase(),
                    "mark"+(i+1)+".gif");

// Start downloading the images, but don't wait for them
               prepareImage(images[i], this);
          }
// Animation will start at image 0, and go up to 5
          whichImage = 0;
          imageDirection = 1;
     }

// This update method prevents a minor flickering that occurs because
// the default update method clears the screen before drawing
     public void update(Graphics g)
     {
          paint(g);
     }

     public void paint(Graphics g)
     {

// If we haven't started the animation, display a "teaser"
          if (!animationStarted)
          {
// If image 0 has been loaded go ahead and display it
```

continues

Listing 5.3 Continued

```
                int flags = checkImage(images[0], this);
                if ((flags & ImageObserver.ALLBITS) != 0) {
                     g.drawImage(images[0], 10, 10, this);
                } else {

// If we haven't even gotten image 0, just display text
                     g.drawString("Watch this space", 10, 30);
                     g.drawString("For neat animation", 10, 50);
                }
           } else {

// If we're in the animation, draw the current image in the sequence
                g.drawImage(images[whichImage], 10, 10, this);
           }
     }

// imageUpdate is called when there is an update to any of the images
// that are being loaded.

     public boolean imageUpdate(Image img, int flags, int x, int y,
           int width, int height)
     {

// If this update isn't telling us that an image has been loaded
// completely, we don't want to hear about it
           if ((flags & ImageObserver.ALLBITS) == 0) {
                return true;
           }

// If we've gotten the first image, go ahead and repaint
           if (img == images[0]) {
                repaint();
           }

// Check to see if all the images have been loaded (ALLBITS set in
// all of them)
           for (int i=0; i < images.length; i++) {
                int iflags = checkImage(images[i], this);

// Uh oh, we found one that isn't finished
                if ((iflags & ImageObserver.ALLBITS) == 0) {
                     return true;
                }
           }

// all right, we're ready to roll!

           startAnimation();
           return true;
     }

     public void tick()
     {
// Change the image - if we are counting from 0 to 5, which direction
// will be 1, if we are going from 5 to 0, whichDirection will be -1
```

```
            whichImage += imageDirection;

// If we've gone past the first image, change direction
            if (whichImage < 0) {
                 whichImage = 0;
                 imageDirection = 1;

// If we've gone past the last image, change direction
            } else if (whichImage >= images.length) {
                 whichImage = images.length-1;
                 imageDirection = -1;
            }
            repaint();
       }

       protected void startAnimation()
       {
            animationStarted = true;
            timer = new Timer(this, 500);
            timer.start();
       }
  }
```


Figures 5.4 and 5.5 show consecutive frames of this animation.

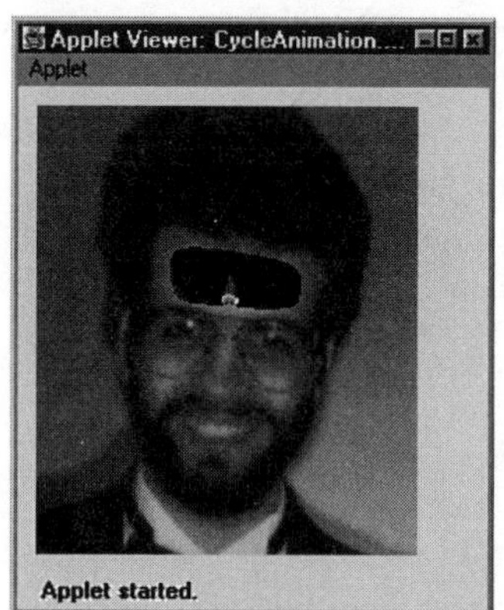

Fig. 5.4
You can create an animation sequence by cycling through different images.

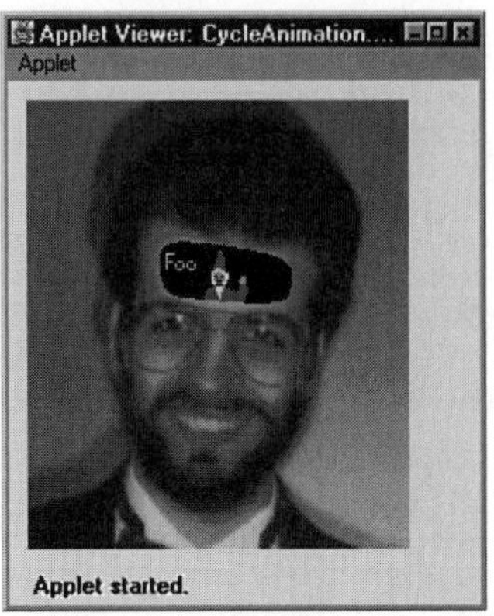

Fig. 5.5
Animation sequences often have only minor changes between frames.

Animating Portions of an Image

You will often find that the area that changes from one animation frame to the next is very small compared to the size of the entire area. This is not as true for images taken from a real video sequence because real-life motions are seldom restricted to one little area. If you can define a small rectangle that encloses the changed area from one image to the next, you can simply download one full image and then the different versions of the smaller rectangle. This could mean a huge difference in the time it takes to download your images. You aren't limited to changing just one portion of an image, of course. If there are multiple areas that change, you can download different rectangles for the different changed areas. The main idea here is that you work with one big image and a small set of changed areas.

For example, you might be doing a Monty Python-style animation on a picture of some celebrity in which his or her mouth is moving in an obviously fake manner. You only need to load the picture once and then load various small images of the mouth region.

Listing 5.4 shows an applet very similar to the full-frame animation applet, except that it loads a single base image and a set of smaller frames.

Listing 5.4 Source Code for *AnimatePortion.java*

```
import java.applet.*;
import java.awt.*;
import java.awt.image.*;

// This applet performs animation by loading in a whole image
// and then successive versions of a much smaller potion of the
// image.

public class AnimatePortion extends Applet implements TimerCallback,
```

```
    ImageObserver
{
    protected Image baseImage;
    protected Image[] images;
    int whichImage;

// This applet cycles from 0-5 and then cycles back down from 5-0
// You won't need imageDirection if you only cycle one way.
    int imageDirection;

// Have we started the animation or not?
    boolean animationStarted;

    Timer timer;

    public AnimatePortion()
    {
        timer = null;
        animationStarted = false;
    }

    public void init()
    {
        images = new Image[6];

// Load the base (whole) image
        baseImage = getImage(getDocumentBase(), "mark1.gif");

        for (int i=0; i < 6; i++) {
// Get partial images named animprt1.gif - animprt6.gif
            images[i] = getImage(getDocumentBase(),
                "animprt"+(i+1)+".gif");

// Start downloading the images, but don't wait for them
            prepareImage(images[i], this);
        }
// Animation will start at image 0, and go up to 5
        whichImage = 0;
        imageDirection = 1;
    }

// This update method prevents a minor flickering that occurs because
// the default update method clears the screen before drawing
    public void update(Graphics g)
    {
        paint(g);
    }

    public void paint(Graphics g)
    {

// If we haven't started the animation, display a "teaser"
        if (!animationStarted)
        {
// If base image has been loaded go ahead and display it
            int flags = checkImage(baseImage, this);
            if ((flags & ImageObserver.ALLBITS) != 0) {
                g.drawImage(baseImage, 10, 10, this);
```

5

continues

Listing 5.4 Continued

```
                } else {

// If we haven't even gotten the base image, just display text
                    g.drawString("Watch this space", 10, 30);
                    g.drawString("For neat animation", 10, 50);
                }
            } else {

// If we're in the animation, draw the base image and the current
// smaller animated portion.
                g.drawImage(baseImage, 10, 10, this);
                g.drawImage(images[whichImage], 70, 70, this);
            }
        }

// imageUpdate is called when there is an update to any of the images
// that are being loaded.

        public boolean imageUpdate(Image img, int flags, int x, int y,
            int width, int height)
        {

// If this update isn't telling us that an image has been loaded
// completely, we don't want to hear about it
            if ((flags & ImageObserver.ALLBITS) == 0) {
                return true;
            }

// If we've gotten the base image, go ahead and repaint
            if (img == baseImage) {
                repaint();
                return true;
            }

// Check to see if all the images have been loaded (ALLBITS set in
// all of them)
            for (int i=0; i < images.length; i++) {
                int iflags = checkImage(images[i], this);

// Uh oh, we found one that isn't finished
                if ((iflags & ImageObserver.ALLBITS) == 0) {
                    return true;
                }
            }

// all right, we're ready to roll!

            startAnimation();
            return true;
        }

        public void tick()
        {
// Change the image - if we are counting from 0 to 5, which direction
// will be 1, if we are going from 5 to 0, whichDirection will be -1
```

```
            whichImage += imageDirection;

// If we've gone past the first image, change direction
            if (whichImage < 0) {
                whichImage = 0;
                imageDirection = 1;

// If we've gone past the last image, change direction
            } else if (whichImage >= images.length) {
                whichImage = images.length-1;
                imageDirection = -1;
            }
            repaint();
        }

        protected void startAnimation()
        {
            animationStarted = true;
            timer = new Timer(this, 500);
            timer.start();
        }
    }
```

Figures 5.6 and 5.7 show the portions of the overall image that actually change. The overall animation is identical to the one in Figures 5.4 and 5.5.

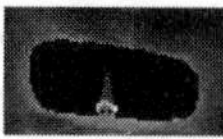

Fig. 5.6
It is often better to animate images by animating only the section that changes.

Fig. 5.7
Only the changed sections are redrawn when painting the next frame.

Animating with a Filter

Filters make wonderful devices for animation. Instead of downloading a sequence of images, you download a single image and use a filter to change the image from one frame to the next. Once you create the filter, you can either generate a complete set of animation frames up-front, or you can generate new frames on-the-fly as the applet is running. The choice between pre-generating the frames and generating them on-the-fly is a classic speed versus size tradeoff. The pregenerated frames require a lot of memory, but you can do faster animation because you don't take the time to generate the frames each time. The on-the-fly method requires only enough memory for the original frame and the current generated frame but runs much slower because it takes time to generate an image. If your filter is quick, you can get away with the on-the-fly method.

Filter animation requires a few interesting tricks. First, when you create new images over and over, you consume memory in the windowing system. This memory isn't always released when you might expect. You can't always rely on the garbage collection system to clean it up as fast as you need it to. Normally, when you create a filtered image, you use a statement such as the following:

```
image = createImage(new FilteredImageSource(
        originalImage.getSource(), imageFilter));
```

If you do this statement over and over in an animation loop, you may consume too many system resources. Rather than creating a new image, you should reinitialize the image. In other words, put the image back to a state where it hasn't produced any pixels. This causes it to either reuse its current system resources or free up the resources it has allocated already. You reinitialize an image using the `flush` method:

```
image.flush()
```

Another thing to consider when filtering images is that even though the original image may be completely loaded, you also need to make sure that the filtered image has been generated completely before drawing it. This is not as big a deal when displaying an image once, but when you get into a loop and start flushing out pixels over and over, you can really slow things down trying to display a filtered image before it is ready. This is one of the places in which the `MediaTracker` class comes in handy. After you flush out an image, you should set up a `MediaTracker` class to wait for the image to be rebuilt. Here is an example that rebuilds an image after the call to `flush`:

```
image.flush();

MediaTracker tracker = new MediaTracker(this);
tracker.addImage(image, 0);
try {
     if (!tracker.waitForID(0)) {     // If there's an error, don't repaint
          return;
     }
} catch (Exception waitingError) {
     return;           // Again, if there's an error, don't repaint
}
repaint();      // Draw the newly-loaded image
```

Listing 5.5 shows a simple filter that changes the transparency value of an image, causing it to fade in and out. It is quite suitable for animation.

Listing 5.5 Source Code for *TransFilter.java*

```
import java.awt.image.*;

// This filter fades an image by moving the RGB values towards
// the background color.
// The transValue variable controls the amount of transparency
// for the image. A level of 255 means fully opaque, while 0 means
// fully transparent. The formula for a color component is
// (background * (255 - transValue) + component * transValue) / 255
// Notice that when transValue is 0, the component isn't part of
// the final color, instead the background is the whole color
// when transValue is 255, the background isn't used at all, and the
// full color component is the new color.

public class TransFilter extends RGBImageFilter {
      private int transValue;
      private int bgRed;
      private int bgGreen;
      private int bgBlue;

      public TransFilter(int tV, int backgroundRGB)
      {
            canFilterIndexColorModel = true;
            transValue = tV;
            bgRed = (backgroundRGB >> 16) & 255;
            bgGreen = (backgroundRGB >> 8) & 255;
            bgBlue = backgroundRGB & 255;
      }

// Changes the transparency value

      public void setTransValue(int newValue)
      {
            transValue = newValue;
      }

// Retrieves the transparency value
      public int getTransValue()
      {
            return transValue;
      }

// Adjusts the transparency value of an RGB value, essentially
// multiplying the transparency by transValue / 255

      public int filterRGB(int x, int y, int rgb)
      {
// Compute the new red, green and blue components

            int red = (bgRed * (255 - transValue) +
                  ((rgb >> 16) &0xff) * transValue) / 255;

            int green = (bgGreen * (255 - transValue) +
                  ((rgb >> 8) & 0xff) * transValue) / 255;
```

continues

Listing 5.5 Continued

```
            int blue = (bgBlue * (255 - transValue) +
                 (rgb & 0xff) * transValue) / 255;

// Combine the components back into a single RGB value, preserving the
// original transparency value from the RGB component.

            return (rgb & 0xff000000) + (red << 16) + (green << 8) +
                 blue;
      }
}
```

Figure 5.8 shows an image in the process of fading. The applet that produces this image uses the `TransFilter` image filter to produce the fading effect. This applet is included on the CD-ROM that comes with this book.

Fig. 5.8
You can produce neat effects by filtering the colors in an image.

Cycling the Color Palette

Color palette cycling has traditionally been a "poor man's animation." The color palette is essentially an indexed color model. Since the advent of indexed colors, programmers have been performing a cheap method of animation by repeatedly changing sections of the color palette. This technique is often used to show flowing water or motion between two points. If you want to perform palette cycling on an existing image, you may have to do a bit of work with the image to set up the palette order. If you generate the image from a memory image source, you can create your own index color model that is easy to cycle.

Unlike other color filters, you don't change the colors in the `getRGB` method in a color palette cycler. Instead, you override the `filterIndexColorModel` method, which creates a new index color model based on the existing one. Listing 5.6 shows an implementation of a color palette cycler. Its constructor takes three parameters—the location of the first palette entry to be cycled, the number of consecutive entries to cycle, and the direction of the cycle. If the direction is positive, the colors are cycled from left to right. If the direction is negative, they are cycled from right to left. The direction also indicates the number of positions a color moves during each cycle. Normally, direction should be 1 or –1, to move each color over by 1 position. You may want to move sets of colors, however. For instance, if you need to shift colors in pairs, set the direction to 2 or –2. The `cycleComponent` method cycles the palette every time it is called.

Listing 5.6 Source Code for *CycleFilter.java*

```
import java.awt.*;
import java.awt.image.*;

//
// This class cycles the colors in an index color model.
// When you create a CycleFilter, you give the offset in
// the index color model and also the number of positions
// you want to cycle. Then every time you call cycleColors,
// it increments the cycle position. You then need to re-create
// your image and its colors will be cycled.
//
// This filter will only work on images that have an indexed
// color model.

public class CycleFilter extends RGBImageFilter {

// The offset in the index to begin cycling
     protected int cycleStart;

// How many colors to cycle
     protected int cycleLen;

// The current position in the cycle
     protected int cyclePos;

// The cycle direction and length
     protected int direction;

// A temporary copy of the color components being cycled
     protected byte[] tempComp;

     public CycleFilter(int cycleStart, int cycleLen, int direction)
     {
          this.cycleStart = cycleStart;
          this.cycleLen = cycleLen;
          this.direction = direction;
          tempComp = new byte[cycleLen];

          cyclePos = 0;

// Must set this to true to allow the shortcut of filtering
// only the index and not each individual pixel

          canFilterIndexColorModel = true;
     }

// cycleColorComponent takes an array of bytes that represent
// either the red, green, blue, or alpha components from the
```

continues

Listing 5.6 Continued

```
// index color model, and cycles them based on the cyclePos.
// It leaves the components that aren't part of the cycle intact.

     public void cycleColorComponent(byte component[])
     {

// If there aren't enough components to cycle, leave this alone
          if (component.length < cycleStart + cycleLen) return;

// Make a temporary copy of the section to be cycled
          System.arraycopy(component, cycleStart, tempComp,
               0, cycleLen);

// Now for each position being cycled, shift the component over
// by cyclePos positions.
          for (int i=0; i < cycleLen; i++) {
               component[cycleStart+(cyclePos+i)%cycleLen] =
                    tempComp[i];
          }
     }

// cycleColors moves the cyclePos by <direction> locations.
// If direction is positive, the colors move from left to
// right. If direction is negative, they move from right
// to left.

     public void cycleColors()
     {
          cyclePos = (cyclePos + direction) % cycleLen;
          if (cyclePos < 0) cyclePos += cycleLen;
     }

// Can't really filter direct color model RGB this way, because you have
// no idea what rgb values get cycled, so just return the original
// rgb values.

     public int filterRGB(int x, int y, int rgb)
     {
          return rgb;
     }

// filterIndexColorModel is called by the image filtering mechanism
// whenever the image uses an indexed color model and the
// canFilterIndexColorModel flag is set to true. This allows you
// to filter colors without filtering each and every pixel
// in the image.

     public IndexColorModel filterIndexColorModel(IndexColorModel icm)
     {

// Get the size of the index color model
          int mapSize = icm.getMapSize();

// Create space for the red, green, and blue components
          byte reds[] = new byte[mapSize];
          byte greens[] = new byte[mapSize];
```

```
            byte blues[] = new byte[mapSize];

// Copy in the red components and cycle them
            icm.getReds(reds);
            cycleColorComponent(reds);

// Copy in the green components and cycle them
            icm.getGreens(greens);
            cycleColorComponent(greens);

// Copy in the blue components and cycle them
            icm.getBlues(blues);
            cycleColorComponent(blues);

// See if there is a transparent pixel. If not, copy in the alpha
// values, just in case the image should be partially transparent.

            if (icm.getTransparentPixel() == -1) {

// Copy in the alpha components and cycle them
                 byte alphas[] = new byte[mapSize];
                 icm.getAlphas(alphas);
                 cycleColorComponent(alphas);

                 return new IndexColorModel(icm.getPixelSize(),
                      mapSize, reds, greens, blues, alphas);
            } else {

// If there was a transparent pixel, ignore the alpha values and
// set the transparent pixel in the new filter
                 return new IndexColorModel(icm.getPixelSize(),
                      mapSize, reds, greens, blues,
                      icm.getTransparentPixel());
            }
       }
}
```

Listing 5.7 shows an applet that displays a .GIF image with a customized color palette. The image contains several figures colored with consecutive color palette entries. As the palette cycles, the colors of the figures change.

Listing 5.7 Source Code for *Cycler.java*

```
import java.awt.*;
import java.awt.image.*;
import java.applet.*;

// This applet creates a series of moving
// lines by creating a memory image and cycling
// its color palette.

public class Cycler extends Applet implements TimerCallback
{
     protected Image origImage; // the image before color cycling
     protected Image cycledImage;     // image after cycling
```

continues

Listing 5.7 Continued

```
     protected CycleFilter colorFilter;     // performs the cycling

     public void init()
     {

// Create the uncycled image
          origImage = getImage(getDocumentBase(), "cycleme.gif");
          MediaTracker mt = new MediaTracker(this);
          mt.addImage(origImage, 0);
          try {
               mt.waitForID(0);
          } catch (Exception hell) {
          }

// Create the filter for cycling the colors
          colorFilter = new CycleFilter(1, 5, 1);

// Create the first cycled image
          cycledImage = createImage(new FilteredImageSource(
               origImage.getSource(),
               colorFilter));

          Timer t = new Timer(this, 1000);
          t.start();
     }

// Paint simply draws the cycled image
     public synchronized void paint(Graphics g)
     {
          g.drawImage(cycledImage, 0, 0, this);
     }

// Flicker-free update
     public void update(Graphics g)
     {
          paint(g);
     }

// Cycles the colors and creates a new cycled image. Uses media
// tracker to ensure that the new image has been created before
// trying to display. Otherwise, we can get bad flicker.

     public synchronized void tick()
     {
// Cycle the colors
          colorFilter.cycleColors();

// Flush clears out a loaded image without having to create a
// whole new one. When we use waitForID on this image now, it
// will be regenerated.

          cycledImage.flush();

          MediaTracker myTracker = new MediaTracker(this);
          myTracker.addImage(cycledImage, 0);
          try {
```

```
// Cause the cycledImage to be regenerated
                myTracker.waitForID(0);
            } catch (Exception ignore) {
            }
// Now that we have reloaded the cycled image, ask that it
// be redrawn.
            repaint();
        }
}
```

Figure 5.9 shows an image whose colors are being cycled.

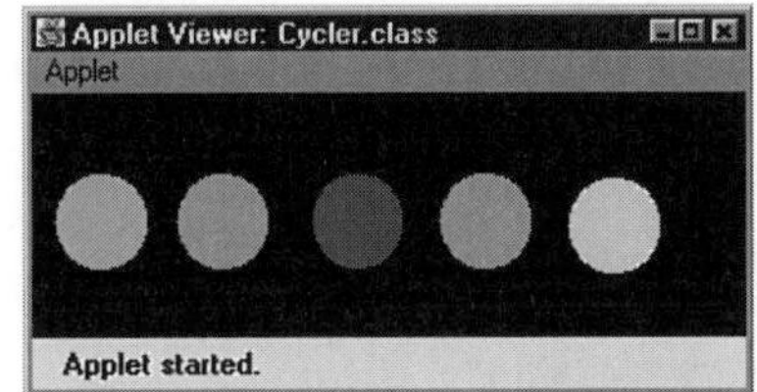

Fig. 5.9
Cycling colors in the color palette creates neat animation effects.

5

Animating Graphics

In addition to animating images, you can perform animation with the graphics drawing functions. There are two ways to animate graphical figures. You can create each frame anew, clearing the screen and drawing the new figure, or you can use the XOR drawing function to move a figure without redrawing the rest of the screen.

Redrawing the Entire Screen

Redrawing the entire screen is the easiest way to perform animation, because when the `paint` method is called, the drawing area has already been cleared. All you need to do is draw the new frame. Listing 5.8 shows an applet that moves a ball back and forth on the screen using this simple technique. As usual, it uses the `Timer` class to trigger the next frame.

Listing 5.8 Source Code for *BallAnim1.java*

```
import java.awt.*;
import java.applet.*;

// This applet moves three balls around the screen by repainting
// the entire scene every time.

public class BallAnim1 extends Applet implements TimerCallback
{
```

continues

Listing 5.8 Continued

```
     int ballX[] = { 0, 200, 0 }; // Current X coord of each ball
     int ballY[] = { 0, 0, 100 }; // Current Y coord
     int ballXSpeed[] = { 1, 0, 1 }; // Current X speed
     int ballYSpeed[]= { 1, 1, 0 }; // Current Y Speed

     Timer timer;

     Color ballColor[] = { Color.red, Color.yellow, Color.blue };

     int numBalls = ballX.length;

     public void init()
     {
     }

// Repaint the entire scene (i.e. draw each ball)

     public void paint(Graphics g)
     {
          for (int i=0; i < numBalls; i++) {
               g.setColor(ballColor[i]);
               g.fillOval(ballX[i], ballY[i], 30, 30);
          }
     }

// For each timer tick, move the balls. If they go off the edge anywhere,
// change their direction.

     public void tick()
     {
          for (int i=0; i < numBalls; i++) {

// Move the ball
               ballX[i] += ballXSpeed[i];
               ballY[i] += ballYSpeed[i];

// See if it goes off the edge anywhere
               if ((ballX[i] < 0) || (ballX[i] >= size().width)) {
                    ballXSpeed[i] = -ballXSpeed[i];
               }
               if ((ballY[i] < 0) || (ballY[i] >= size().height)) {
                    ballYSpeed[i] = -ballYSpeed[i];
               }
          }
          repaint();
     }

     public void start()
     {
          Timer timer = new Timer(this, 100);
          timer.start();
     }
```

```
        public void stop()
        {
            timer.stop();
            timer = null;
        }
}
```

Using this method, the figures you draw have a notion of depth. The first figure drawn is on the bottom, while the last figure drawn is on the top. Being on top means that if a figure shares any screen area with another figure, the figure on top covers the other figure. This makes sense—if you draw one figure and then draw another figure on top of it, the second figure would obscure the first one.

Figure 5.10 shows the BallAnim1 applet in action.

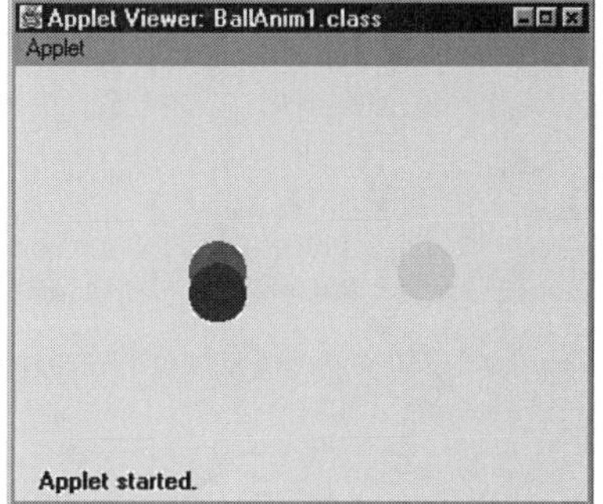

Fig. 5.10
By redrawing all figures in a particular sequence, you create a sense of depth.

Doing Animation with XOR

XOR animation is not as pretty as other animation, but it has the advantage of speed. This technique relies on the fact that when you draw a figure in XOR mode, you can erase it again by just drawing it again in XOR mode. There is no restriction in drawing order in XOR mode because whenever figures overlap in XOR mode, they always look the same, no matter which figure is drawn first. Of course, the figures don't look as nice, either. When two figures overlap in XOR mode, the overlapped portion is a combination of the two figures, meaning it is a different color from either figure. If you are drawing in black and white, the overlapped portion of two white figures will be black. When you draw XOR figures with a direct color model, the colors are XORed together. When you use an index color model, the index values are XORed together. This can give the overlapping regions some really funky colors, but it works. XOR animation isn't used very often, but it can come in handy if it is too costly to redraw an entire frame and you are only moving a few objects on the screen.

When you draw in XOR mode, you create your own `update` method that does not clear the drawing area before calling the `paint` routine. Otherwise, you might as well not use XOR mode. Your `update` method should look like this:

```
public void update(Graphics g)
{
     paint(g);
}
```

Listing 5.9 shows an example of XOR animation, with three shapes moving in different directions. Notice the interesting color combinations when the figures collide.

Listing 5.9 Source Code for *BallAnim2.java*

```
import java.awt.*;
import java.applet.*;

// This applet moves 3 balls around the screen using XOR animation.

public class BallAnim2 extends Applet implements TimerCallback
{
     int ballX[] = { 0, 200, 0 };      // X coords of each ball
     int ballY[] = { 0, 0, 100 };      // Y coords
     int ballXSpeed[] = { 1, 0, 1 }; // Speed in X direction
     int ballYSpeed[]= { 1, 1, 0 };  // Speed in Y direction

     boolean drewFirst = false;     // Have we drawn anything yet?

     Timer timer;

     Color ballColor[] = { Color.red, Color.yellow, Color.blue };

     int numBalls = ballX.length;

     public void init()
     {
     }

// special version of update that doesn't erase the screen

     public void update(Graphics g)
     {
          paint(g);
     }

     public void paint(Graphics g)
     {

// Go into XOR mode with white as the XOR color
          g.setXORMode(Color.white);

// redraw the old balls, causing them to be erased. Don't try to erase anything
// if we haven't drawn the first time, otherwise there will be garbage
// left on the screen.
```

```
          if (drewFirst) {
               for (int i=0; i < numBalls; i++) {
                    g.setColor(ballColor[i]);
                    g.fillOval(ballX[i], ballY[i], 30, 30);
               }
          }

// Now move the balls. In our repaint, we erase the old, move, and then
// draw the new.
          moveBalls();

// Draw the balls in their new position
          for (int i=0; i < numBalls; i++) {
               g.setColor(ballColor[i]);
               g.fillOval(ballX[i], ballY[i], 30, 30);
          }
          drewFirst = true;
     }

     public void moveBalls()
     {
          for (int i=0; i < numBalls; i++) {

// Move the ball
               ballX[i] += ballXSpeed[i];
               ballY[i] += ballYSpeed[i];

// See if it has gone off the edge
               if ((ballX[i] < 0) || (ballX[i] >= size().width)) {
                    ballXSpeed[i] = -ballXSpeed[i];
               }
               if ((ballY[i] < 0) || (ballY[i] >= size().height)) {
                    ballYSpeed[i] = -ballYSpeed[i];
               }
          }
     }

// Rather than moving the balls in the tick method, we move them in the
// paint method. All tick needs to do is trigger a repaint.

     public void tick()
     {
          repaint();
     }

     public void start()
     {
          Timer timer = new Timer(this, 100);
          timer.start();
     }

     public void stop()
     {
          timer.stop();
          timer = null;
     }
}
```

Figure 5.11 shows the BallAnim2 applet in action.

Fig. 5.11 *XOR animation produces strange results when objects collide.*

Eliminating Flicker

You may have noticed a lot of flicker in some of your animation applets. Flicker is actually just a very quick change on the drawing area. If you use the standard `update` method, the screen is cleared before your `paint` method is called. Your eye picks up that momentary clearing, making it look like the screen flickers. Fortunately, there are simple ways to eliminate flicker.

First, you can override the `update` method that doesn't clear the screen before calling `paint`:

```
public void update(Graphics g)
{
     paint(g);
}
```

If your `paint` method relies on the screen being cleared, this may give you trouble. You can counter this, however, by using the second technique, which, when used in conjunction with the above `update` method, should eliminate flicker from your applet completely. This method is called "double-buffering."

Double-Buffering

The technique of double-buffering involves drawing to an off-screen image and then drawing the off-screen in a single method call. To perform double-buffering, you need to declare an instance variable to hold the off-screen image:

```
Image offscreenImage;
```

Next, in your `init` method, you need to create the image:

```
offscreenImage = createImage(size().width, size().height);
```

Finally, you can create an `update` method that draws to this off-screen image. By clearing the off-screen image before calling `paint`, you can add double-buffering to any applet without changing the applet's `paint` method.

Listing 5.10 shows one of the animation examples with a flicker-free `update` method. The changes made to accommodate the flicker-free `update` are the addition of the `offscreenImage` variable, its initialization in the `init` method, and a new `update` method.

Listing 5.10 Source Code for *BallAnim3.java*

```
import java.awt.*;
import java.applet.*;

// This applet moves three balls around the screen by repainting
// the entire scene every time.
// It has a flicker-free update method.

public class BallAnim3 extends Applet implements TimerCallback
{

     int ballX[] = { 0, 200, 0 }; // Current X coord of each ball
     int ballY[] = { 0, 0, 100 }; // Current Y coord
     int ballXSpeed[] = { 1, 0, 1 }; // Current X speed
     int ballYSpeed[]= { 1, 1, 0 }; // Current Y Speed

     Timer timer;

     Color ballColor[] = { Color.red, Color.yellow, Color.blue };

     int numBalls = ballX.length;

     Image offscreenImage;

     public void init()
     {
          offscreenImage = createImage(size().width, size().height);
     }

     public void update(Graphics g)
     {
// Get a graphics context for the offscreen area
          Graphics offscreenG = offscreenImage.getGraphics();

// Clear the offscreen area to the background color
          offscreenG.setColor(getBackground());
          offscreenG.fillRect(0, 0, size().width, size().height);

// Paint on the offscreen image
          paint(offscreenG);

// Copy the offscreen image to the screen
          g.drawImage(offscreenImage, 0, 0, this);
     }
```

continues

Listing 5.10 Continued

```
// Repaint the entire scene (i.e. draw each ball)

     public void paint(Graphics g)
     {
          for (int i=0; i < numBalls; i++) {
               g.setColor(ballColor[i]);
               g.fillOval(ballX[i], ballY[i], 30, 30);
          }
     }

// For each timer tick, move the balls. If they go off the edge anywhere,
// change their direction.

     public void tick()
     {
          for (int i=0; i < numBalls; i++) {

// Move the ball
               ballX[i] += ballXSpeed[i];
               ballY[i] += ballYSpeed[i];

// See if it goes off the edge anywhere
               if ((ballX[i] < 0) || (ballX[i] >= size().width)) {
                    ballXSpeed[i] = -ballXSpeed[i];
               }
               if ((ballY[i] < 0) || (ballY[i] >= size().height)) {
                    ballYSpeed[i] = -ballYSpeed[i];
               }
          }
          repaint();
     }

     public void start()
     {
          Timer timer = new Timer(this, 100);
          timer.start();
     }

     public void stop()
     {
          timer.stop();
          timer = null;
     }
}
```

chapter 6

Communicating with a Web Server

6

by Mark Wutka

In this chapter

- **Getting data from a Web server**
  You can read data from a Web server using built-in Java classes, or using sockets to implement the HTTP protocol. You can use these methods to read files from the Web server.
- **Sending queries to a Web server**
  In addition to serving files, many Web servers allow you to perform queries. Your applets can send queries to a Web server very easily.
- **Storing data on a Web server**
  There are a few techniques you can use to store files on a Web server. Some of them require very little extra programming, while some others require a little more work.
- **Keeping track of cookies**
  The Cookie protocol is a mechanism that some Web servers use to store data on the client side. If you want your applet to support cookies, you have to add some code to perform the cookie protocol.

Java and Web Servers

The Web server is the home of a Java applet. Not only does the applet live there, it must rely on the Web server for any information or files it wants to download. As some of the applet security restrictions are lifted and replaced with a better security mechanism, this will not be the case. For now, however, the Web server is the only place an applet can count on being able to access. Applications, on the other hand, may access data in countless ways, but still find Web servers to be a wonderful source of information.

Getting Files Using the *URL* Class

The URL class allows you to access any URL on the World Wide Web, as long as your browser or Java environment supports the protocol for the URL. You can safely assume that your environment supports the HTTP protocol. Other protocols such as FTP may not be available, however. Keep in mind that if you open an URL and read it yourself, there is no way to take the data you read and display it as a fully-formatted HTML page unless you do it yourself. If you want to open an URL and have your browser display it, you should use the showDocument method in the Applet class, which is discussed in the section, "Loading Another URL from an Applet," in Chapter 7, "Creating Smarter Forms."

The URL class is really just a class for naming resources on the World Wide Web, much like the File class represents file names, but not the contents of a file. In order to get the contents of an URL, you need to open an input stream to the URL. You can do this one of two ways. The simplest way is to call the openStream method in the URL class:

```
URL someURL = new URL("http://abcdef.com/mydocument.html");
InputStream inStream = someURL.openStream();
```

This input stream will provide you with the contents of the file named by the URL. This method is most useful when you are only concerned with the file contents and not with any of the HTTP headers associated with the file. To get these, you need to use the URLConnection class.

The URLConnection class represents a network connection to a WWW resource. When you open an input stream on an URL, it really opens an URLConnection and then calls the getInputStream in the URLConnection object. The following code fragment is the equivalent of the previous example:

```
URL someURL = new URL("http://abcdef.com/mydocument.html");
URLConnection urlConn = someURL.openConnection();
InputStream inStream = urlConn.getInputStream();
```

The advantage of the URLConnection class is that it gives you much finer control over an URL connection. For example, you can retrieve the headers associated with the file. The two header fields that you will probably be most interested in are the content type and content length. You can fetch these with the getHeaderField and getHeaderFieldInt methods:

```
String contentType = urlConn.getHeaderField("content-type");
int contentLength = urlConn.getHeaderFieldInt(
"content-length", -1); // returns -1 if length isn't specified
```

These header fields are so popular, in fact, that they have their own special methods that do the equivalent of the above code—getContentType and getContentLength:

```
String contentType = urlConn.getContentType();
int contentLength = urlConn.getContentLength();
```

Listing 6.1 shows a sample applet that uses an `URL` class to read its own .class file.

Listing 6.1 Source Code for *FetchURL.java*

```
import java.applet.*;
import java.awt.*;
import java.net.*;
import java.io.*;

// This applet demonstrates the use of the URL and URLConnection
// class to read a file from a Web server. The applet reads its
// own .class file, because you can always be sure it exists.

public class FetchURL extends Applet
{
     byte[] appletCode; // Where to store the contents of the .class file

     public void init()
     {
          try {

// Open a URL to this applet's .class file. You can locate it by
// using the getCodeBase method and the applet's class name.
               URL url = new URL(getCodeBase(),
                    getClass().getName()+".class");

// Open a URLConnection to the URL
               URLConnection urlConn = url.openConnection();

// See if you can find out the length of the file. This allows you to
// create a buffer exactly as large as you need.

               int length = urlConn.getContentLength();

// Because you can't be sure of the size of the .class file, use a
// ByteArrayOutputStream as a temporary container. Once you are finished
// reading, you can convert it to a byte array.

               ByteArrayOutputStream tempBuffer;

// If you don't know the length of the .class file, use the default size
               if (length < 0) {
                    tempBuffer = new ByteArrayOutputStream();
               } else {
                    tempBuffer = new ByteArrayOutputStream(length);
               }

// Get an input stream to this URL
               InputStream instream = urlConn.getInputStream();

// Read the contents of the URL and copy it to the temporary buffer
               int ch;
               while ((ch = instream.read()) >= 0) {
```

continues

Listing 6.1 Continued

```
                    tempBuffer.write(ch);
                }

// Convert the temp buffer to a byte array (you don't do anything with
// the array in this applet other than take its size).
                appletCode = tempBuffer.toByteArray();
            } catch (Exception e) {
                e.printStackTrace();
            }
        }

        public void paint(Graphics g)
        {
            g.setColor(Color.black);

            if (appletCode == null) {
                g.drawString("I was unable to read my .class file",
                    10, 30);
            } else {
                g.drawString("This applet's .class file is "+
                    appletCode.length+" bytes long.", 10, 30);
            }
        }
}
```

Figure 6.1 shows the output from the FetchURL applet.

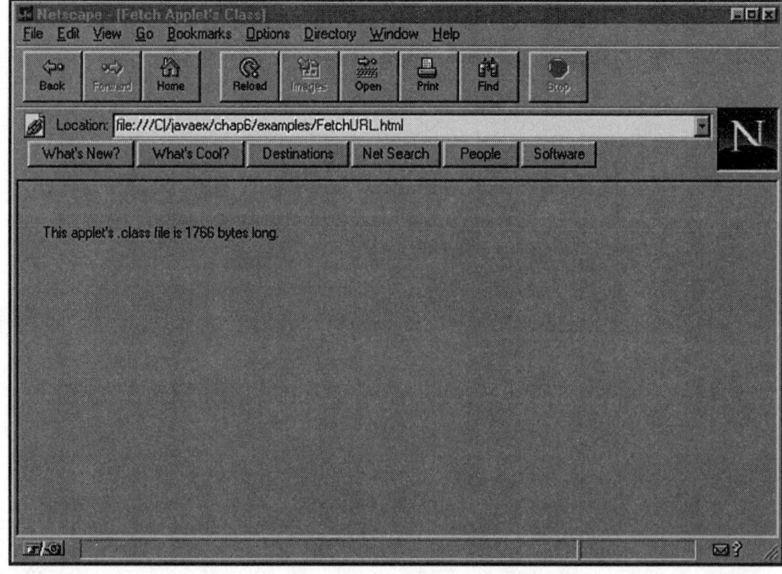

Fig. 6.1
An applet can perform an HTTP GET using the `URL` *class.*

The FetchURL applet is a typical example of an applet that opens an URL and reads data from it. For example purposes, the applet reads its own .class file. There is no advantage to reading a .class file, but for example purposes it is quite handy, because you know for sure that the .class file must be there. If the .class file wasn't there, the applet wouldn't run in the first place.

The applet first opens the URL, and then gets an input stream for the URL. It tries to get the content length, which indicates how much data there is to retrieve. This value isn't always available, however, so the applet uses `ByteArrayOutputStream` as a temporary storage mechanism.

Tip

Vectors and byte array output streams are extremely handy storage containers when you don't know the size of the data you are storing. You should use a vector whenever you need to store an unknown number of objects. The byte array output stream is a handy alternative to the vector when you are storing bytes.

Once the applet has read its .class file, it simply displays a message telling how many bytes it read.

Getting Files Using Sockets

If, for some reason, you decide that you want to bypass the URL and URLConnection classes and speak HTTP directly over a socket, you are probably a glutton for punishment or just a genuine bit-head. Actually, the HTTP protocol is very simple, so it isn't that big a deal to open up a socket and fetch information. All you need to do is open the socket, send a GET message, and start reading.

When you read data from an HTTP server directly over a socket, you'll get all the header information first. Each line in the header is terminated by a carriage return and then a line feed (in Java, "\r\n"). The end of the header section is marked by a blank line. After that comes the data, in whatever form the server sends it. The "content-type" header tells you what type of data to expect. If you're just reading a text file, it should be "text/plain."

Listing 6.2 shows an applet that uses a socket connection to fetch a file from a Web server. Like the example in Listing 6.1, this applet fetches its own .class file.

```
import java.applet.*;
import java.awt.*;
```

Listing 6.2 Source Code for *FetchSockURL.java*

```
import java.net.*;
import java.io.*;

// This applet shows you how to open up a socket to an HTTP server
// and read a file. The applet reads its own .class file, because
// you can always be sure it exists.

public class FetchSockURL extends Applet
{
     byte[] appletCode; // Where to store the contents of the .class file

     public void init()
     {
          try {

// If the port number returned for the code base is -1, use the
// default http port of 80.

               int port = getCodeBase().getPort();
               if (port < 0) port = 80;

// Open up a socket to the Web server where this applet came from
               Socket sock = new Socket(getCodeBase().getHost(),port);

// Get input and output streams for the socket connection
               DataInputStream inStream = new DataInputStream(
                    sock.getInputStream());
               DataOutputStream outStream = new DataOutputStream(
                    sock.getOutputStream());

// Send the GET request to the server
// The request is of the form: GET filename HTTP/1.0
// In this case, the filename will be the applet's filename as returned
// by the getCodeBase method. Notice that you send two \r\n's
// The first one terminates the request line, the second indicates the
// end of the request header.

               outStream.writeBytes("GET "+
                    getCodeBase().getFile()+getClass().getName()+
                    ".class HTTP/1.0\r\n\r\n");

// Just to show you how it's done, look through the headers for
// the content length. First, assume it's -1.

               int length = -1;

               String currLine;

// Read the next line from the header, quit if you hit EOF
```

```
                while ((currLine = inStream.readLine()) != null)
                {

// if the length of the line is 0, you just hit the end of the header
                     if (currLine.length() == 0) break;

// See if it's the content-length header
                     if (currLine.toLowerCase().startsWith(
                          "content-length:")) {

// "content-length:" is 15 characters long, so parse the length starting at
// offset 15 (the 16th character). Catch any exceptions when parsing
// this number - it's not so important that you have to quit.
                          try {
                               length = Integer.valueOf(
                                    currLine.substring(15)).
                                    intValue();
                          } catch (Exception ignoreMe) {
                          }
                     }
                }
// Because you can't be sure of the size of the .class file, use a
// ByteArrayOutputStream as a temporary container. Once you are finished
// reading, you can convert it to a byte array.

                ByteArrayOutputStream tempBuffer;

// If you don't know the length of the .class file, use the default size
                if (length < 0) {
                     tempBuffer = new ByteArrayOutputStream();
                } else {
                     tempBuffer = new ByteArrayOutputStream(length);
                }

// Read the contents of the URL and copy it to the temporary buffer
                int ch;
                while ((ch = inStream.read()) >= 0) {
                     tempBuffer.write(ch);
                }

// Convert the temp buffer to a byte array (you don't do anything with
// the array in this applet other than take its size.
                appletCode = tempBuffer.toByteArray();
           } catch (Exception e) {
                e.printStackTrace();
           }
      }

      public void paint(Graphics g)
      {
           g.setColor(Color.black);

           if (appletCode == null) {
                g.drawString("I was unable to read my .class file",
                     10, 30);
           } else {
```

6

continues

Listing 6.2 Continued

```
                g.drawString("This applet's .class file is "+
                    appletCode.length+" bytes long.", 10, 30);
            }
        }
    }
```

Like the FetchURL applet, the FetchSockURL applet reads its own .class file from the Web server. FetchSockURL doesn't use the built-in URL class, however. Instead, it creates a socket connection to the Web server. Once this connection is made, the applet sends a GET request to the Web server to retrieve the .class file. The `GET` request usually looks something like this:

```
GET /classes/FetchSockURL.class HTTP/1.0
```

This line is followed by a blank line, indicating the end of the HTTP headers. You can send your own headers immediately after the `GET` request if you like. Just make sure they appear before the blank line. The FetchSockURL applet actually writes out the blank line in the same statement where it writes out the `GET` request, so you'll need to remove the \r\n from the end of the `writeBytes` statement if you add your own headers. If you do that, don't forget to write out a blank line after your headers.

Once the GET request has been sent to the server, the applet begins reading lines from the socket connection. The server will send a number of header lines, terminated by a blank line. This will be followed by the actual content of the page.

The FetchSockURL applet scans through the headers looking for the content length header field, which usually looks like this:

```
Content-length: 1234
```

Like the FetchURL applet, the FetchSockURL applet can handle situations where the content length is unknown. It uses the same technique of writing the data to a byte array output stream as it reads it. You can tell when you have reached the end of the content because you'll hit the end of file on the socket (the `read` method will return -1).

Performing a Query with *GET*

Many Web servers allow you to get information based on a query. In other words, you don't just ask for a file, you ask for a file and pass some query parameters. This determines the information you get back. This is most often used in Web search engines. Most Web servers support an interface called CGI—Common Gateway Interface. While you don't really need to know the intricacies of CGI to write queries, you do need to know how it expects queries to look.

A CGI query looks like a regular URL except it has extra parameters on the end. The query portion starts with a "?" and is followed by a list of parameters. Each parameter in the query is separated by a "&", and parameter values are specified in a "name=value" format. Parameters are not required to have values. A CGI query to run a script called find-people, taking parameters called `name`, `age`, and `occupation`, would look like this:

```
http://localhost/cgi-bin/find-people?occupation=engineer&age=30&name=smith
```

Knowing this, you can easily write a class that takes an URL and a set of parameters and generates a query URL. Listing 6.3 shows just such a class.

Listing 6.3 Source Code for *URLQuery.java*

```
import java.net.*;
import java.util.*;

// This class provides a way to create an URL to perform a query
// against a Web server. The query takes the base URL of the
// the program you are sending the query to, and a set of properties
// that will be converted into a query string.

public class URLQuery extends Object
{
     public static URL createQuery(URL originalURL, Properties parameters)
     throws MalformedURLException
     {

// Queries have the file name followed by a ?
          String newFile = originalURL.getFile()+"?";

// Now append the query parameters to the filename
          Enumeration e = parameters.propertyNames();

          boolean firstParameter = true;

          while (e.hasMoreElements()) {
               String propName = (String) e.nextElement();

// Parameters are separated by &'s, if this isn't the first parameter
// append a & to the current query string (file name)

               if (!firstParameter) newFile += "&";

// Add the variable name to the query string
               newFile += URLEncoder.encode(propName);

// Get the variable's value
               String prop = parameters.getProperty(propName);

// If the variable isn't null, append "=" followed by the value
               if (prop != null) {
                    newFile += "="+URLEncoder.encode(prop);
               }
```

continues

Listing 6.3 Continued

```
                firstParameter = false;
            }

// Return the full URL consisting of the original protocol, host, and port
// and the new, enhanced filename, which contains all the query parameters.
// This URL is suitable for opening with showDocument or any other URL
// operation.
            return new URL(originalURL.getProtocol(),
                originalURL.getHost(), originalURL.getPort(), newFile);
        }
}
```

You retrieve the results of a query just like you retrieve any other file on the Web. You can open up a stream directly from the URL, you can get a `URLConnection` object, or you can open up a socket and speak directly to the server. Because queries frequently return Web pages, you may want to use the `openDocument` method in the `Applet` class. This enables you to see the results of the query all neatly formatted by the Web browser instead of the raw HTML codes that you get from an input stream. Listing 6.4 shows an applet that submits a query to the Lycos search engine (**http://www.lycos.com**) and displays the results using `showDocument`.

Listing 6.4 Source Code for *LycosQuery.java*

```
import java.applet.*;
import java.util.*;
import java.net.*;
import java.io.*;

// This applet performs a query against the Lycos search engine
// and opens up the results as a new document.

public class LycosQuery extends Applet
{
    public void init()
    {
        try {

// Create the base URL to the lycos query

            URL url = new URL(
                "http://www.lycos.com/cgi-bin/pursuit");

            Properties queryProps = new Properties();

// Fill in the query variables. These were determined by looking
// at the Lycos query form. You search on the terms "java" and "cgi"
// requesting a maximum of 20 entries. The minscore value of .5 is
// what Lycos calls a "good match".
```

```
            queryProps.put("query", "java cgi");
            queryProps.put("matchmode", "and");
            queryProps.put("maxhits", "20");
            queryProps.put("minscore", ".5");
            queryProps.put("terse", "standard");

// Create the query URL
               URL fullURL = URLQuery.createQuery(url, queryProps);

// Open up the results as a new document
               getAppletContext().showDocument(fullURL);

           } catch (Exception e) {
               e.printStackTrace();
           }
       }
}
```

Figure 6.2 shows the results of the Lycos query generated by the LycosQuery applet.

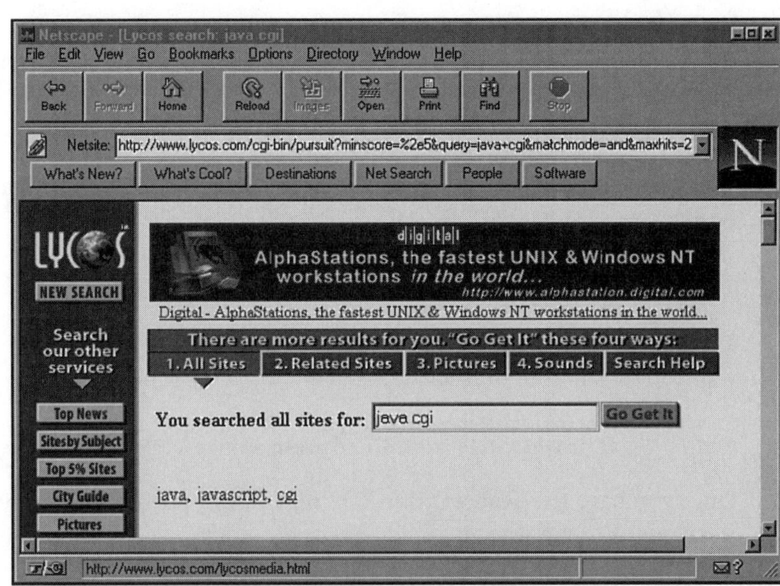

Fig. 6.2
You can create a query and then use showDocument to display the results.

Posting Data with the *URL* Class

Web queries are actually something of a hack. They use the HTTP GET message, which was originally intended to retrieve files. A query actually sends data to the Web server embedded in the name of the file it is requesting. One of the problems you can encounter with Web queries is that they are limited in size. You can't use a query to send back a large block of text like an e-mail message or a problem report. The HTTP POST message can handle large blocks of data. In fact, that's what it was intended for. Most query programs, at least the well-written ones, can handle requests either as a GET or a POST message.

A GET method sends only an HTTP header in its message. A POST, on the other hand, has both a header and content. In this way, the POST message is very similar in structure to an HTTP response. You are required by the HTTP protocol to include a Content-length: field in a POST message.

You have to do a number of extra things when sending a POST message with the `URLConnection` class. First, you must enable output on the connection by calling `setDoOutput`:

```
myURLConnection.setDoOutput(true);
```

For good measure, you should also call `setDoInput`:

```
myURLConnection.setDoInput(true);
```

Next, you should disable caching. You want to make sure that your information goes all the way to the server, and that the response you receive is really from the server and not from the cache:

```
myURLConnection.setUseCaches(false);
```

You should set a content type for the data you are sending. A typical content type would be `application/octet-stream`:

```
myURLConnection.setRequestProperty("Content-type",
"application/octet-stream");
```

You are required to send a content length in a POST message. You can set this the same way you set the content type:

```
myURLConnection.setRequestProperty("Content-length",
     ""+stringToSend.length()); // cheap way to convert int to string
```

Once you have the headers taken care of, you can open up an output stream and write the content to the stream:

```
DataOutputStream outStream = new DataOutputStream(
     myURLConnection.getOutputStream());
outStream.writeBytes(stringToSend());
```

Make sure that the string you send is terminated with `\r\n`.

Once you have sent the information for the post, you can open up an input stream and read the response back from the server just as you did with a GET. Listing 6.5 shows an application that sends a POST message to one of the NCSA's example CGI programs.

Listing 6.5 Source Code for *URLPost.java*

```
import java.net.*;
import java.io.*;

public class URLPost extends Object
{
    public static void main(String args[])
    {
        try {
            URL destURL = new URL(
                "http://hoohoo.ncsa.uiuc.edu/cgi-bin/test-cgi/foo");

// The following request data mimics what the NCSA example CGI
// form for this CGI program would send.

            String request = "button=on\r\n";
            URLConnection urlConn = destURL.openConnection();

            urlConn.setDoOutput(true);    // we need to write
            urlConn.setDoInput(true);    // just to be safe...
            urlConn.setUseCaches(false);    // get info fresh from server

// Tell the server what kind of data you are sending - in this case,
// just a stream of bytes.

            urlConn.setRequestProperty("Content-type",
                "application/octet-stream");

// Must tell the server the size of the data you are sending. This also
// tells the URLConnection class that you are doing a POST instead
// of a GET.

            urlConn.setRequestProperty("Content-length", ""+request.length());

// Open an output stream so you can send the info you are posting

            DataOutputStream outStream = new DataOutputStream(
                urlConn.getOutputStream());

// Write out the actual request data

            outStream.writeBytes(request);
            outStream.close();

// Now that you have sent the data, open up an input stream and get
// the response back from the server

            DataInputStream inStream = new DataInputStream(
                urlConn.getInputStream());

            int ch;

// Dump the contents of the request to System.out

            while ((ch = inStream.read()) >= 0) {
                System.out.print((char) ch);
```

6

continues

Listing 6.5 Continued

```
                }

                inStream.close();

            } catch (Exception e) {
                e.printStackTrace();
            }
        }
    }
```

Figure 6.3 shows the working of this application.

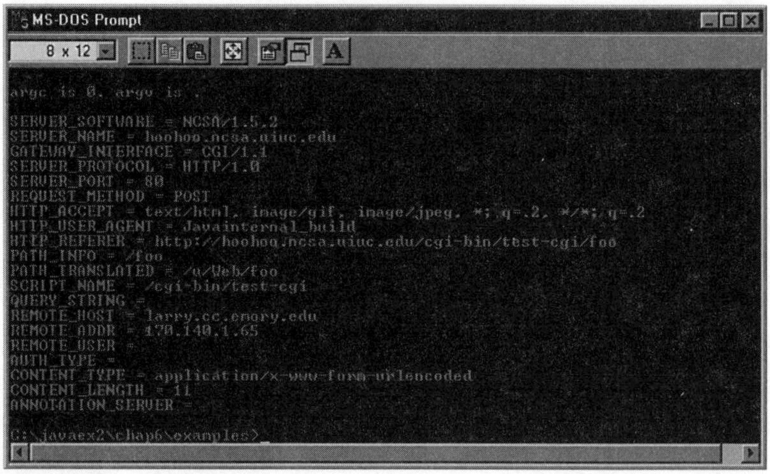

Fig. 6.3
A Java applet or application can use the `URL` *class to perform an HTTP POST.*

Posting Data Using Sockets

You have already seen the basic differences between the `GET` and the `POST` messages. If you want to perform a `POST` with a raw socket connection, rather than using the `URLConnection` class, you don't have to do a whole lot. It is basically the same method you used when you wrote a socket-based HTTP `GET`, but in addition to sending the `GET` command, you must also send the "Content-type," and "Content-length" messages, as well as the request data.

Listing 6.6 shows the socket-based equivalent of the example program in Listing 6.5.

Listing 6.6 Source Code for *PostSockURL.java*

```
import java.net.*;
import java.io.*;

// This applet shows you how to open up a socket to an HTTP server
// and post data to a server. It posts information to one of the
// example CGI programs set up by the NCSA.

public class PostSockURL extends Object
{
     public static void main(String args[])
     {
          try {

// Open up a socket to the Web server where this applet came from
               Socket sock = new Socket("hoohoo.ncsa.uiuc.edu", 80);

// Get input and output streams for the socket connection
               DataInputStream inStream = new DataInputStream(
                    sock.getInputStream());
               DataOutputStream outStream = new DataOutputStream(
                    sock.getOutputStream());

// This request is what is sent by the NCSA's example form

               String request = "button=on\r\n";

// Send the POST request to the server
// The request is of the form: POST filename HTTP/1.0

               outStream.writeBytes("POST /cgi-bin/test-cgi/foo "+
                    " HTTP/1.0\r\n");

// Next, send the content type (don't forget the \r\n)
               outStream.writeBytes(
                    "Content-type: application/octet-stream\r\n");

// Send the length of the request
               outStream.writeBytes(
                    "Content-length: "+request.length()+"\r\n");

// Send a \r\n to indicate the end of the header
               outStream.writeBytes("\r\n");

// Now send the information you are posting

               outStream.writeBytes(request);


// Dump the response to System.out

               int ch;

               while ((ch = inStream.read()) >= 0) {
                    System.out.print((char) ch);
               }
```

continues

Listing 6.6 Continued

```
// We're done with the streams, so close them
                inStream.close();
                outStream.close();

            } catch (Exception e) {
                e.printStackTrace();
            }
        }
    }
```

Supporting the Cookie Protocol

One of the early problems that plagued Web page designers was how to give information to the client browser for it to remember. If you had one million people accessing your Web server, you don't want to keep information for each one of them on your server if their browsers could just as easily store the information. Fortunately, Netscape noticed this problem fairly early and came up with the notion of a cookie.

A cookie is really just a piece of information that has a name, a value, a domain, and a path. Whenever you open up an URL to the cookie's domain and access any files along the cookie's path, the cookie's name and value are passed to the server when you open the URL. A typical use of this might be an access count or a user name. Netscape defined a request header tag called "Cookie:" that is used to pass cookie name-value pairs to the server. A server can set cookie values in a browser by sending a `Set-cookie` tag in the response header.

You should now be able to create Java applications that can open up URLs directly, without the interference of a browser, so you may want to support the cookie protocol. It would be nice if this protocol could be built right into the `URL` and `URLConnection` classes. You are welcome to tackle this problem. At first, it would seem like a simple thing to do, but you will find that the URLConnection class, although it has methods to set the desired fields in a request header, will not actually pass these fields to the server. This means that you can call `setRequestProperty("Cookie", "Something=somevalue")` all day long and the server will never see it. If you want to speak cookies, you'll have to speak HTTP over a socket. Luckily for you, this chapter contains code to do just that.

Listing 6.7 shows a Cookie class that represents the information associated with a cookie. It doesn't actually send or receive cookies; it is more like a Cookie data type. One interesting feature is that its constructor can create a cookie from the string returned by the cookie's toString method, making it easy to store cookies in a file and retrieve them.

Tip

It is often useful to create a string representation of an object that can be used to re-create the object at a later time. While you can use object serialization to read and write objects to a file, a string representation can be edited with a simple text editor.

Listing 6.7 Source Code for *Cookie.java*

```
import java.net.*;
import java.util.*;

// This class represents a Netscape cookie. It can parse its
// values from the string from a Set-cookie: response (without
// the Set-cookie: portion, of course). It is little more than
// a fancy data structure.

public class Cookie
{
// Define the standard cookie fields

     public String name;
     public String value;
     public Date expires;
     public String domain;
     public String path;
     public boolean isSecure;

// cookieString is the original string from the Set-cookie header.
// Just save it rather than trying to regenerate for the toString
// method. Note that since this class can initialize itself from this
// string, it can be used to save a persistent copy of this class!

     public String cookieString;

// Initialize the cookie based on the origin URL and the cookie string

     public Cookie(URL sourceURL, String cookieValue)
     {
          domain = sourceURL.getHost();
          path = sourceURL.getFile();

          parseCookieValue(cookieValue);
     }

// Initialize the cookie based solely on its cookie string
     public Cookie(String cookieValue)
     {
          parseCookieValue(cookieValue);
     }
```

continues

6

Listing 6.7 Continued

```
// Parse a cookie string and initialize the values

     protected void parseCookieValue(String cookieValue)
     {
          cookieString = cookieValue;

// Separate out the various fields, which are separated by ;'s

          StringTokenizer tokenizer = new StringTokenizer(
               cookieValue, ";");

          while (tokenizer.hasMoreTokens()) {

// Eliminate leading and trailing white space
               String token = tokenizer.nextToken().trim();

// See if the field is of the form name=value or if it is just
// a name by itself.
               int eqIndex = token.indexOf('=');

               String key, value;

// If it is just a name by itself, set the field's value to null
               if (eqIndex == -1) {
                    key = token;
                    value = null;

// Otherwise, the name is to the left of the '=', value is to the right
               } else {
                    key = token.substring(0, eqIndex);
                    value = token.substring(eqIndex+1);
               }

               isSecure = false;

// convert the key to lowercase for comparison with the standard field names

               String lcKey = key.toLowerCase();

               if (lcKey.equals("expires")) {
                    expires = new Date(value);
               } else if (lcKey.equals("domain")) {
                    if (isValidDomain(value)) {
                         domain = value;
                    }
               } else if (lcKey.equals("path")) {
                    path = value;
               } else if (lcKey.equals("secure")) {
                    isSecure = true;

// If the key wasn't a standard field name, it must be the cookie's name
// You don't use the lowercase version of the name here.
               } else {
                    name = key;
                    this.value = value;
               }
```

```
        }
    }

// isValidDomain performs the standard cookie domain check. A cookie
// domain must have at least two portions if it ends in
// .com, .edu, .net, .org, .gov, .mil, or .int. If it ends in something
// else, it must have 3 portions. In other words, you can't specify
// .com as a domain, it has to be something.com, and you can't specify
// .ga.us as a domain, it has to be something.ga.us.

    protected boolean isValidDomain(String domain)
    {

// Eliminate the leading period for this check
        if (domain.charAt(0) == '.') domain = domain.substring(1);

        StringTokenizer tokenizer = new StringTokenizer(domain, ".");
        int nameCount = 0;

// just count the number of names and save the last one you saw
        String lastName = "";
        while (tokenizer.hasMoreTokens()) {
            lastName = tokenizer.nextToken();
            nameCount++;
        }

// At this point, nameCount is the number of sections of the domain
// and lastName is the last section.

// More than 2 sections is okay for everyone
        if (nameCount > 2) return true;

// Less than 2 is bad for everyone
        if (nameCount < 2) return false;

// Exactly two, you better match one of these 7 domain types

        if (lastName.equals("com") || lastName.equals("edu") ||
            lastName.equals("net") || lastName.equals("org") ||
            lastName.equals("gov") || lastName.equals("mil") ||
            lastName.equals("int")) return true;

// Nope, you fail - bad domain!
        return false;
    }

// Use the cookie string as originally set in the Set-cookie header
// field as the string value of this cookie. It is unique, and if you write
// this string to a file, you can completely regenerate this object from
// this string, so you can read the cookie back out of a file.

    public String toString()
    {
        return cookieString;
    }
}
```

6

The `Cookie` class is basically a holder for cookie data. The only methods in the `Cookie` class deal with converting strings into cookies and vice versa. The `parseCookieValue` method in the `Cookie` class implements a crucial part of the cookie protocol. It takes a string containing the settings for a cookie. The settings are of the form `name=value` and are separated by semicolons. The settings include the name of the cookie, the cookie's value, its expiration date, and the path name for the cookie.

The domain setting for a cookie specifies which hosts should receive the cookie. Whenever a URL in the cookie's domain is opened and the URL is in the cookie's path, the server for that URL is passed the cookie. For example, if you set the domain to **mydomain.com** and the path to **/me/stuff**, then the URL **http://mydomain.com/me/stuff/mycgi** will receive the cookie. An URL of **http://mydomain.com/you/files** would not receive the cookie, because the paths don't match.

There are some restrictions on the cookie's domain, too. If the domain ends in **.com**, **.edu**, **.org**, **.net**, **.gov**, **.mil**, or **.int**, you only need two components in the domain. In other words, you need one other name in addition to the ending. For example, **mydomain.com** is a valid domain.

If the domain ends with any other name, you must have at least three components in the domain. For example, **mydomain.au** would not be a valid cookie domain, but **mydomain.outback.au** would be valid.

Because cookies are supposed to be persistent, you need a class to manage your cookies—preferably by storing them in a file or a database. Listing 6.8 presents a portion of the `CookieDatabase` class that maintains a table of known cookies. The full source to the class is available on the CD-ROM that comes with this book. It has methods to store the table in a file and retrieve the table from a file. It can also examine an URL and return a string of cookie values for that URL.

The `CookieDatabase` class does not actually read cookies from a Web server or write them to the server. It simply keeps a table of known cookies. If presented with a host name and path name, the `CookieDatabase` class will determine which cookies are valid for that host name and path name and will return the appropriate cookie string.

The `getCookieString` method from the `CookieDatabase` class, shown in Listing 6.8, performs the matching between an URL and a cookie. It decides what cookies should be sent for a particular URL and creates a string containing all the cookie values that need to be sent.

Listing 6.8 *getCookieString* Method from *CookieDatabase*

```
// getCookieString does some rather ugly things. First, it finds all the
// cookies that are supposed to be sent for a particular URL. Then
// it sorts them by path length, sending the longest path first (that's
// what Netscape's specs say to do - I'm only following orders).

     public static String getCookieString(URL destURL)
     {
          if (cookies == null) {
               cookies = new Vector();
          }

// sendCookies will hold all the cookies you need to send
          Vector sendCookies = new Vector();

// currDate will be used to prune out expired cookies as we go along

          Date currDate = new Date();

          for (int i=0; i < cookies.size();) {
               Cookie cookie = (Cookie) cookies.elementAt(i);

// See if the current cookie has expired. If so, remove it

               if ((cookie.expires != null) && (currDate.after(
                    cookie.expires))) {
                    cookies.removeElementAt(i);
                    continue;
               }

// You only increment i if you haven't removed the current element
               i++;

// If this cookie's domain doesn't match the URL's host, go to the next one
               if (!destURL.getHost().endsWith(cookie.domain)) {
                    continue;
               }

// If the paths don't match, go to the next one
               if (!destURL.getFile().startsWith(cookie.path)) {
                    continue;
               }

// Okay, you've determined that the current cookie matches the URL, now
// add it to the sendCookies vector in the proper place (i.e. ensure
// that the vector goes from longest to shortest path).

               int j;
               for (j=0; j < sendCookies.size(); j++) {
                    Cookie currCookie = (Cookie) sendCookies.
                         elementAt(j);

// If this cookie's path is longer than the cookie[j], you should insert
// it at position j.
                    if (cookie.path.length() <
                         currCookie.path.length()) {
```

6

continues

Listing 6.8 Continued

```
                    break;
               }
          }

// If j is less than the array size, j represents the insertion point
          if (j < sendCookies.size()) {
               sendCookies.insertElementAt(cookie, j);

// Otherwise, add the cookie to the end
          } else {
               sendCookies.addElement(cookie);
          }
     }

// Now that the sendCookies array is nicely initialized and sorted, create
// a string of name=value pairs for all the valid cookies

     String cookieString = "";

     Enumeration e = sendCookies.elements();
     boolean firstCookie = true;

     while (e.hasMoreElements()) {
          Cookie cookie = (Cookie) e.nextElement();

          if (!firstCookie) cookieString += "; ";
          cookieString += cookie.name + "=" + cookie.value;
          firstCookie = false;
     }

// Return null if there are no valid cookies
     if (cookieString.length() == 0) return null;
     return cookieString;
  }
```

Finally, Listing 6.9 shows you an example application that fetches a Web page that contains a cookie. Whenever the application runs, it loads its cookie table from a file called cookies.dat. After you run the program, you can look at the cookies.dat file. It is printable text. The program accesses a Web page called "Andy's Netscape HTTP Cookie Page" (**http://www.illuminatus.com/cookie**), which is a great resource for learning about cookies and seeing them in action.

Since the CookieDatabase class does not automatically look for cookies in a response from a Web server, and does not automatically send cookie data, you have to do that yourself. Cookies are sent to the server in the header portion of an HTTP command.

Note

You can set only a few specific header values in the `URL` class, and the cookie string is not one of them. This means that you have to use sockets to perform a `GET` or `POST` that supports cookies.

Whenever you open an URL, you can get the cookie string for the URL by calling `getCookieString` in the `CookieDatabase` class. When reading the response from the Web server, you must scan the header results for the Set-cookie command. Whenever you find this command, you pass the cookie string from the `Set-cookie` command to the `addCookie` method in the `CookieDatabase` class. The method will extract all the important information from the cookie string.

Listing 6.9 Source Code for *TestCookie.java*

6

```
import java.net.*;
import java.io.*;

// This application demonstrates the CookieDatabase and Cookie
// classes. It first loads the cookie database from cookies.dat,
// then it opens up Andy's Netscape HTTP Cookie Page, which happens
// to assign you a cookie.
// Because the Java URL classes do not let you set arbitrary header
// strings (GRR!!!), you have to do cookie stuff MANUALLY (double-GRR!!)
//
// Much of this code was taken from the example of doing a GET with
// raw sockets.

public class TestCookie extends Object
{
     public static void main(String args[])
     {
          try {
               CookieDatabase.loadCookies("cookies.dat");
          } catch (IOException ignore) {
          }

          try {

// URL to Andy's Netscape HTTP Cookie Page, it's quite helpful
               URL url = new URL("http://www.illuminatus.com/cookie");

               int port = url.getPort();
               if (port < 0) port = 80;

// Open a socket to the server
               Socket socket = new Socket(url.getHost(), port);
```

continues

Listing 6.9 Continued

```
// Create an output stream so you can write out the request header
               DataOutputStream outStream = new DataOutputStream(
                    socket.getOutputStream());

// Write the GET command
               outStream.writeBytes(
                    "GET "+url.getFile()+" HTTP/1.0\r\n");

// See if there are any valid cookies for this URL
               String cookieString = CookieDatabase.
                    getCookieString(url);

// If so, write out a cookie header
               if (cookieString != null) {
                    outStream.writeBytes("Cookie: "+
                         cookieString+"\r\n");
               }

// Write out \r\n for the end of the header area
               outStream.writeBytes("\r\n");

// Now read the response from the server
               DataInputStream inStream = new DataInputStream(
                    socket.getInputStream());

               String line;

// Read the header strings scanning for a set-cookie tag, which
// means you have to update the cookie database

               while ((line = inStream.readLine()) != null) {
                    if (line.length() == 0) break;

// if you got a set-cookie, create a new cookie and add it to the database
                    if (line.toLowerCase().startsWith(
                         "set-cookie: ")) {

                         CookieDatabase.addCookie(
                              new Cookie(url,
                              line.substring(12)));
                    }
               }

// Now that you've finished with the header, just dump out the
// contents of the page. This won't look too pretty, it's all pure
// HTML.
               int ch;

               while ((ch = inStream.read()) >= 0) {
                    System.out.print((char) ch);
               }

// Save the cookie database for later use

               CookieDatabase.saveCookies("cookies.dat");
```

```
        } catch (Exception e) {
            e.printStackTrace();
        }
    }
}
```

chapter 7

Creating Smarter Forms

by Mark Wutka

In this chapter

- **Creating forms with Java**
  Using Java's AWT, you can create the same kinds of forms that you can create with HTML.
- **Handling errors locally**
  You can save the user a lot of time and cut down on server usage if you can trap errors in form entries before the form is sent to the server.
- **Providing better help**
  When you create forms in Java, you can add context-sensitive help, since you know what the user is currently doing.
- **Creating context-sensitive forms**
  Like paper forms, HTML forms have a fixed format that does not change while you enter data. With Java, you can create forms that adjust themselves to the input, enabling and disabling sections based on previous selections.
- **Providing Web links**
  You can open up other Web URLs from a Java applet and ask the browser to display them. This allows you to create interesting new forms of Web links.
- **Creating lively image maps**
  You don't have to settle for the same old boring image maps, where you simply click a region. You can create image maps that detect mouse movement and change when the mouse passes over a particular area.

Smarter Forms

In the beginning, Web pages were not very lively. You could read information, click certain words and pictures, and view other unlively pages. Then, the forms interface came along and added some degree of interaction with a page. You were able to enter data and then click a button and send your information to a server, which would analyze what you sent and return the results. Unfortunately, these forms were also lacking a certain "lively" quality. All the error checking was left up to the server, as was any other form of interaction such as context-sensitive help. Java enables you to spice up your old Web forms. You can perform error checking before you ever send data to the server, drastically improving response time to the user and cutting down on server usage. You can also add context-sensitive help. You can even create dynamic forms that change depending on the other information added.

Creating Forms with the AWT

Java's AWT toolkit contains a set of GUI components that are very useful for constructing forms suitable for a Web page. All the form components provided in HTML have equivalent AWT components, so you can simulate any existing HTML form.

Listing 7.1 shows just such a form, a query entry form for the Lycos Web searching engine (**http://www.lycos.com**). It enables you to enter the keywords to search for, and some other search parameters, and then it sends the query to the Lycos server just as if you had used, the Lycos page.

Note

This applet is meant for demonstration purposes only. While it will function with the real Lycos server, it does not display the advertisements from the normal Lycos search page. Although you may consider this a plus, it really isn't. Advertisements keep companies like Lycos in business and allow them to provide these wonderful services to you at no cost. Please do not use this applet or any other program to thwart a company's advertising displays. It hurts everyone in the long run.

Listing 7.1 Source Code for *LycosForm.java*

```
import java.awt.*;
import java.applet.*;
import java.net.*;
import java.util.*;

// This applet demonstrates the use of AWT components as an
// alternative to the HTML forms interface. It creates a query
// for the Lycos search engine and displays the results using
// the showDocument method.

public class LycosForm extends Applet
{
```

```
protected TextField queryString; // the terms to search for

protected Choice matchTerms; // how many terms to match
String matchTermValues[] = { "and", "or", "2", "3", "4",
     "5", "6", "7" };

protected Choice matchStrength; // how good a match
String matchStrengthValues[] = { ".1", ".3", ".5", ".7", ".9" };

protected Choice resultCount; // how many matches to show
String resultCountValues[] = { "10", "20", "30", "40" };

protected Choice resultType;  // how much information to display
String resultTypeValues[] = { "terse", "standard", "verbose" };

protected Button searchButton; // perform the query

public void init()
{
// Arrange the query form as a 3 horizontal grid elements
     setLayout(new GridLayout(3, 0));

// Create the element with the query string and submit button
     add(createQueryPanel());

// Create the element containing search options
     add(createSearchOptionsPanel());

// Create the element containing display options
     add(createDisplayOptionsPanel());

}
```


The AWT layout managers provide a reasonable way to place components on the screen without putting them in fixed positions. This allows your applet to adapt to different screen sizes. Unfortunately, it is often difficult to arrange the components the way you want them. The `GridBagLayout` class provides the most flexible way to arrange components, but it is often rather cumbersome to use. As an alternative to the `GridBagLayout` class, or even in conjunction with it, you can use different panels to group your components, nesting some panels within others. The `LycosQuery` class uses this technique. It creates a main panel that uses a grid layout with three rows. The first row is another panel that uses a flow layout, while the last two rows use two-column grid layouts.

Tip

Grid layouts expand components to fill all available space. If you want to maximize a component's size, the grid layout is a good choice. Flow layouts, on the other hand, don't adjust the component size, so they tend to use the minimum required space. Grid bag layouts let you choose either of these options.

Listing 7.1 Source Code for LycosForm.java (continued)

```
// createQueryPanel creates a panel containing a text field
// for query terms and the button used to send the query to Lycos

     protected Panel createQueryPanel()
     {
          Panel panel = rEw Panel();
          panel.setLayout(new FlowLayout(FlowLayout.LEFT));

          panel.add(new Label("Query: "));

          queryString = new TextField(30);
          panel.add(queryString);

          searchButton = new Button("Search");
          panel.add(searchButton);

          return panel;
     }

// createSearchOptionsPanel creates a panel containing the
// choices for the number of terms to match and the strength
// of the matches.

     protected Panel createSearchOptionsPanel()
     {
          Panel panel = new Panel();
          panel.setLayout(new GridLayout(0, 3));
          panel.add(new Label("Search Options:"));

          matchTerms = new Choice();
          matchTerms.addItem("match all terms (AND)");
          matchTerms.addItem("match any term (OR)");
          matchTerms.addItem("match 2 terms");
          matchTerms.addItem("match 3 terms");
          matchTerms.addItem("match 4 terms");
          matchTerms.addItem("match 5 terms");
          matchTerms.addItem("match 6 terms");
          matchTerms.addItem("match 7 terms");

          matchTerms.select(1);     // default on the OR option
          panel.add(matchTerms);

          matchStrength = new Choice();
          matchStrength.addItem("loose match");
          matchStrength.addItem("fair match");
          matchStrength.addItem("good match");
          matchStrength.addItem("close match");
          matchStrength.addItem("strong match");

          matchStrength.select(0); // default on the loose match
          panel.add(matchStrength);

          return panel;
     }
```

```
// createDisplayOptionsPanel creates a panel containing the choices for
// the number of matches returned and the amount of detail to return.

     protected Panel createDisplayOptionsPanel()
     {
          Panel panel = new Panel();
          panel.setLayout(new GridLayout(0, 3));
          panel.add(new Label("Display Options:"));

          resultCount = new Choice();
          resultCount.addItem("10 results per page");
          resultCount.addItem("20 results per page");
          resultCount.addItem("30 results per page");
          resultCount.addItem("40 results per page");

          resultCount.select(0);     // Default to 10 results per page
          panel.add(resultCount);

          resultType = new Choice();
          resultType.addItem("Summary Results");
          resultType.addItem("Standard Results");
          resultType.addItem("Detailed Results");

          resultType.select(1);     // Default to Standard Results
          panel.add(resultType);

          return panel;
     }
```


The URLQuery class used in this next part of the LycosQuery class was introduced in the section, "Performing a Query with GET," in Chapter 6, "Communicating with a Web Server." It allows you to create an HTTP query from an URL and a properties table containing the query parameters. It would be nice if you could examine the data coming back from the query and still let the browser display the actual HTML codes returned, but on most browsers you can't. You can either examine the data coming back and display it yourself from the Java program, or use showDocument to display the data directly.

Listing 7.1 Source Code for LycosForm.java (continued)

```
// sendRequest uses the URLGet class to create a CGI Query to Lycos.

     protected void sendRequest()
     {
          Properties queryProps = new Properties();

          queryProps.put("query", queryString.getText());
          queryProps.put("matchmode", matchTermValues[
               matchTerms.getSelectedIndex()]);
          queryProps.put("minscore", matchStrengthValues[
               matchStrength.getSelectedIndex()]);
          queryProps.put("maxhits", resultCountValues[
               resultCount.getSelectedIndex()]);
          queryProps.put("terse", resultTypeValues[
```

continues

Listing 7.1 Continued

```
                resultType.getSelectedIndex()]);

            try {
                URL lycosURL = new URL(
                    "http://www.lycos.com/cgi-bin/pursuit");

                URL fullURL = URLQuery.createQuery(lycosURL,
                    queryProps);

                getAppletContext().showDocument(fullURL);
            } catch (Exception e) {
                e.printStackTrace();
            }
        }

        public boolean action(Event evt, Object whichAction)
        {

// If someone pressed the button, send the request

            if (evt.target == searchButton) {
                sendRequest();
                return true;
            }
            return false;
        }
}
```

Figure 7.1 shows the original version of the Lycos query form.

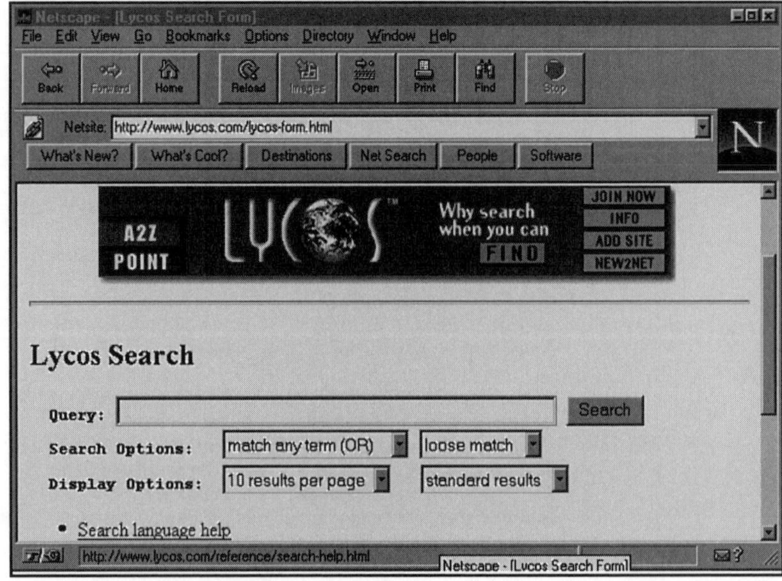

Fig. 7.1
The Lycos search engine is a popular Web search tool.

Figure 7.2 shows a mimic of an HTML form.

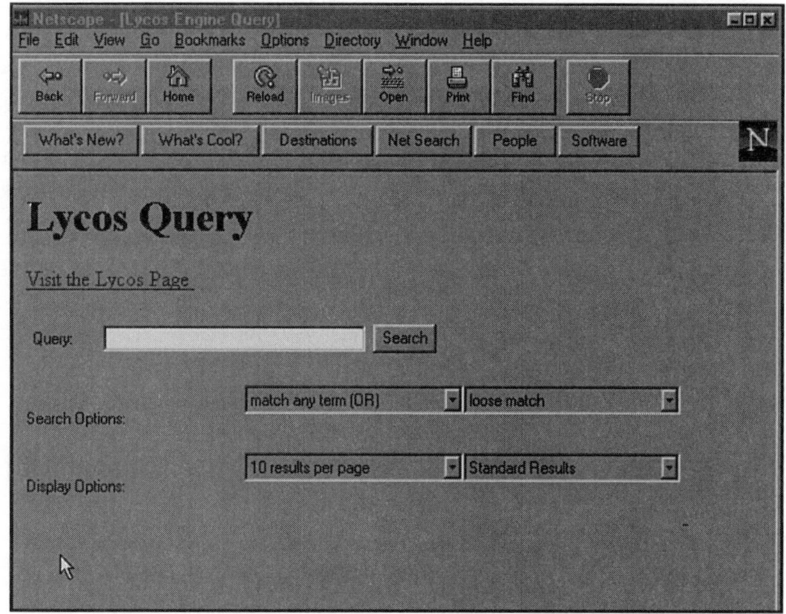

Fig. 7.2
You can mimic any HTML form in Java.

You may be wondering why you should go through the trouble of creating a Java applet that presents a form when it is easier to define one in HTML. If you are simply presenting a form, with no help facility and no error checking, go ahead and do it in HTML. The real advantage of Java comes when you need to do things beyond the basic form facilities in HTML.

Checking for Errors on the Client Side

You can increase the response time of your forms and lessen the load on your server if you put error checking into your Java forms. When you do forms in HTML, there is no way to check to make sure the data is correct before you send it off to the server. You put all the responsibility for error checking on the server's shoulders. This also means that the user has to wait for the request to go out to the server, and a response to come back, before he knows that there was something wrong.

If you use Java to do error checking, you will make the user happier because he will know instantly that he has entered incorrect data. You will also decrease the load on your server because it is no longer handling any incorrect data (hopefully). As your forms become more and more complex, the need for error checking grows dramatically.

In the example of the Lycos query form, the only place in which you can make an error entering data is in the query string itself. If you fail to enter any keywords, the search engine has nothing to look for. While Lycos normally just presents you with another form, this Java version of the query form pops up a dialog box reminding you that you need to enter keywords in the query entry area. The only place you need to change the old `LycosForm` class is in the `action` method. You make it call a `checkRequest` method instead of `sendRequest`. The `checkRequest` method verifies the form, and if everything is correct, it calls `sendRequest`. Here are the updated `action` and `sendRequest` methods:

```
        public boolean action(Event evt, Object whichAction)
        {
// If someone pressed the button, send the request

                if (evt.target == searchButton) {
                        checkRequest();
                        return true;
                }
                return false;
        }

        protected void checkRequest()
        {
                if (queryString.getText().length() == 0) {
                        OKDialog.createOKDialog(
                                "Please enter a list of terms to search for");
                        return;
                }

                sendRequest();
        }
```

This is actually a pretty minor form of error checking. On more advanced forms, you may need to check to see that information entered in one section is consistent with information entered in another area. For example, you might have a "sex" field on your form and a "maiden name" field somewhere else. If sex was "male," the maiden name doesn't apply. Your error checking routine would check to make sure that if you entered something under "maiden name," you had better be female. You can avoid some situations such as this one by creating dynamic forms, which are discussed later in this chapter.

Adding Context-Sensitive Help

Context-sensitive help is an incredibly useful feature, especially on the day when a software product comes with a 500-page manual. While you should strive towards making your program completely intuitive, requiring no special training or documentation, that isn't always possible. Context-sensitive help can lessen the need for other documentation and is much more timely and relevant than an online user's manual.

In case you are unclear about what "context-sensitive help" is, it is simply help on what you are currently doing. For example, if you are entering text in a field and you suddenly press the help key, you should expect to get help for the text field you are entering. Many software products require that you pop up the online manual and skip to the page discussing the field you want information on. If you know what the user is currently doing, you know what to tell them when they ask for help.

The way you present context-sensitive help is up to you. One very useful method, which is also quite passive, is to display a one-line message at the bottom of the screen giving a quick description of the area where the mouse is. For example, when you are looking at a Web page and pass the mouse over a link, your browser may display the destination URL for that link at the bottom of the page. This is a form of context-sensitive help. You can also define a particular key to be the "help" key. Tell the user to press that key any time he needs help. The F1 key in many software packages is the help key; you should seriously consider making it the help key in your applets, too. Remember that you want to give all your applets and applications a similar feel in the same way that most cars have a similar feel. It doesn't take long to figure out how to drive a car you've never seen before. It should be that way with software.

Listing 7.2 shows a `HelpDialog` class that is useful for popping up screens containing help text. The help dialog is a simple OK dialog box—it displays a text message and a button labeled "OK" which, when clicked, makes the dialog box disappear. One thing to keep in mind when you want to create dialog boxes is that you must have a parent frame for the dialog box. When you are running an applet, you can't normally access the applet's parent frame. The `HelpDialog` class addresses this problem by creating its own frame. It saves the frame in a static variable so it doesn't have to create a new frame the next time it needs to create a dialog window.

You can actually access the parent frame for an applet. Sometimes it will work exactly like you want. It usually works for dialogs, but it fails miserably on some platforms when you try to create a menu for the parent frame. You can use the `getParent` method from the component class to trace back up through the component hierarchy to find the applet's parent frame. The following code fragment finds an applet's parent frame:

```
Component parentFrame = getParent();
while ((parentFrame != null) &&
      !(parentFrame instanceof Frame)) {
      parentFrame = parentFrame.getParent();
}
Frame myFrame = (Frame) parentFrame;
```

At this point, `myFrame` would either contain the parent frame of the applet, or `null` if it couldn't find the parent frame.

Listing 7.2 Source Code for *HelpDialog.java*

```
import java.awt.*;

// The HelpDialog class is a variation on the OKDialog class.
// It allows you to create an OK dialog with a textarea instead
// of a label. You can use this to display help text.

public class HelpDialog extends Dialog
{
     protected Button okButton;
     protected static Frame createdFrame;

     public HelpDialog(Frame parent, String message)
     {
          super(parent, false);     // Must call the parent's constructor

// Create the OK button and the message to display
          okButton = new Button("OK");
          TextArea helpInfo = new TextArea(message, 10, 40);
          helpInfo.setEditable(false);

          setLayout(new BorderLayout());

          add("Center", helpInfo);

          add("South", okButton);

          resize(500, 300);
     }

// The action method just waits for the OK button to be clicked;
// when it is, it hides the dialog, causing the show() method to return
// back to whoever activated this dialog.

     public boolean action(Event evt, Object whichAction)
     {
          if (evt.target == okButton)
          {
               hide();
               if (createdFrame != null)
               {
                    createdFrame.remove(this);
                    createdFrame.hide();
                    dispose();
                    return true;
               }
          }
          return true;
     }

// Shortcut to create a frame automatically, the frame is a static variable
// so all dialogs in an applet or application can use the same frame.

     public static void createHelpDialog(String helpText)
     {
```

```
// If the frame hasn't been created yet, create it
          if (createdFrame == null)
          {
               createdFrame = new Frame("Help");
          }
// Create the dialog now
          HelpDialog helpDialog = new HelpDialog(createdFrame, helpText);

// Shrink the frame to nothing
          createdFrame.resize(0, 0);

// Show the dialog
          createdFrame.show();
          helpDialog.show();
     }
}
```

In addition to the HelpDialog class, you need a way to assign help information directly to your AWT components. It would have been nice if Sun had built that right into the AWT, and maybe they will in the future, but for now you have to do it yourself. You could subclass all the AWT components to support help if you really had nothing better to do for a month or two, but there are easier ways. One simple way is just to store the components and their corresponding help text in a hash table. Whenever someone requests help from within an AWT component, look in the table and see if you have defined any help for that component. Listing 7.3 shows the HelpSystem class that enables you to assign help text to AWT components. It also contains a method to display the help for a component, but it makes no assumptions on how you actually request the help in the first place.

Listing 7.3 Source Code for *HelpSystem.java*

```
import java.awt.*;
import java.util.*;

// Help system is a container for help strings. You can add
// and remove help strings for components. It also provides
// a doHelp method that actually pops up the help dialog.

public class HelpSystem extends Object
{
     Hashtable helpTable;

     public HelpSystem()
     {
          helpTable = new Hashtable();
     }

     public void addHelp(Component comp, String text)
     {
          helpTable.put(comp, text);
```

continues

Listing 7.3 Continued

```
        }

        public void removeHelp(Component comp)
        {
             helpTable.remove(comp);
        }

        public boolean doHelp(Component comp)
        {
             if (comp == null) return false;

             String helpString = (String) helpTable.get(comp);

             if (helpString == null) {
                  return false;
             }

             HelpDialog.createHelpDialog(helpString);

             return true;
        }
   }
```

Now that you have a way to display help and a way to map help strings to components, you need to add some sort of help key to your applet. Going back to the Lycos search form applet, you can modify it to use F1 as the help key. The AWT components are polite enough to ignore `keyDown` events for keys they do not recognize, and they all leave the F1 key alone. You can trap the F1 key in your applet and display the appropriate help text. To add context-sensitive help to the `LycosForm` class, you need to create an instance of the help system. Since there are several methods that actually use the help system, you declare it as an instance variable:

```
protected HelpSystem helpSystem = new HelpSystem();
```

Next, for each component that will have a help screen, you add the component to the help system. For example, once you create the `queryString` text field, you can add a help string for it with the following code fragment:

```
helpSystem.addHelp(queryString,
"QUERY HELP\nEnter the words you want to search\n"+
"for separated by spaces. Avoid common words like\n "+
"\"the\" or \"and\".");
```

The trickiest part of implementing the help system is grabbing the F1 key and figuring out which component the user wants help on. When you receive keyboard events, you are given an x and y coordinate where the keystroke occurred. Unfortunately, this does not really indicate where the mouse was when you pressed the key. The x and y coordinates are bounded by the component that currently has the keyboard focus. For context-sensitive help, you don't want the user to have to move the keyboard focus to another component before requesting help. If this were the case, they would have to click a button before they could get help for that button. What you must do, instead, is track the movement of the mouse all the time. You can do this very simply by creating two instance variables in your class, `mouseX` and `mouseY`:

```
protected int mouseX;  // the current X coord of the mouse
protected int mouseY;  // the current Y coord of the mouse
```

Next, you override the mouseMove method. This method is called whenever the mouse moves. You simply copy the x and y coordinates of the mouse and return:

```
public boolean mouseMove(Event evt, int x, int y)
{
mouseX = x;
mouseY = y;
return false;
}
```

Notice that you `return false` from the `mouseMove` method. This indicates that you haven't actually handled the mouse movement event, allowing the event to be passed to another component. If you do not want another component to see the mouse movement event, you should return `true` instead.

7

The hardest part of implementing this context-sensitive help system is determining which component the user wants help on. The problem here is that you have to take the x and y coordinates of the mouse and locate the component at those coordinates.

The `locate` method does this, sort of. The `locate` method takes an x and y coordinate and returns the component at those coordinates. It only looks one level deep in the component hierarchy, however. If you are using nested panels, as the LycosForm applet does, the `locate` method will only return the panel enclosing the component you really want.

The solution for this problem is simple. If the `locate` method returns a container, you use the `locate` method in that container. You keep repeating the process until `locate` returns a component that is not a container.

There is one additional little sticking point here. The `locate` method expects the x and y coordinates to be relative to the container you are searching. The first time you call `locate`, everything is fine, since the mouse x and y coordinates are relative to your applet. After that, you have to adjust them to be relative to the container returned by `locate`. For example, suppose you had mouse coordinates of 100, 50 and the `locate` method returned an instance of the `Panel` class for those coordinates. Suppose that the panel's upper-left corner was at 65, 45. You would subtract the panel's coordinates from the original mouse coordinates, giving a new location of 35,5. Now you call the `locate` method in the panel with the new coordinates. You can use the `location` method to get the coordinates of the upper-left corner of any component. Listing 7.4 shows a keyDown method for the LycosForm applet that uses this technique to identify the component where the F1 key was pressed.

Listing 7.4 Source Code for the *keyDown* Method in *LycosForm3.java*

```
public boolean keyDown(Event evt, int ch)
{
      if (ch == Event.F1) {
                int x = mouseX;
                int y = mouseY;

// Find out which component this x,y is inside
                Component whichComp = locate(x, y);

// If the component is a container, descend into the container and
// find out which of its components contains this x,y

                while (whichComp instanceof Container) {

// If you have to search within a container, adjust the x,y to be relative
// to the container.
                         x -= whichComp.location().x;
                         y -= whichComp.location().y;
                         Component nextComp = whichComp.locate(x, y);

// if locate returns the component itself, you're done
                         if (nextComp == whichComp) break;
                         whichComp = nextComp;
                }

// Display any available help on the component
                helpSystem.doHelp(whichComp);
      }
      return false;
}
```

Figure 7.3 shows the LycosForm3 applet in action with a Help dialog box displayed.

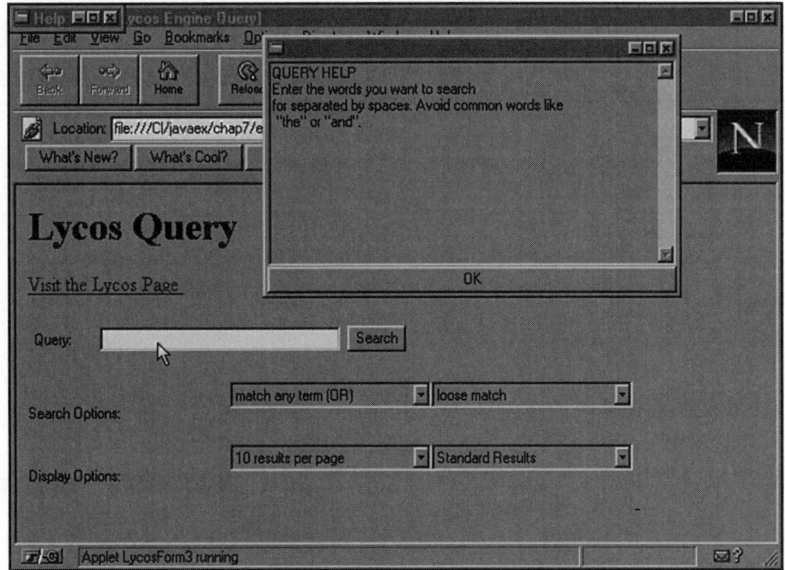

Fig. 7.3
Context-sensitive help screens make your applets easier to use.

Creating Dynamic Forms

It's funny that with all the advanced technology running on the desktop today, the methods of recording information haven't really changed. Most online forms are just electronic versions of printed forms. This is really a shame because we now have the ability to create forms that adapt to the information you are entering.

For example, suppose you are creating a personal information form containing all the typical pieces of information associated with a person. If you look at a typical form of this type, you'll see many sections with instructions such as "Fill in this section only if married." No computerized form should have instructions such as that—not when there are so many ways to avoid it.

If you really must have your form look exactly the same, no matter what information is being entered, consider selectively enabling and disabling components if they apply. Listing 7.5 shows a very brief example of this technique.

Listing 7.5 Source Code for *DynamicDisable.java*

```
import java.awt.*;
import java.applet.*;

// This applet demonstrates the technique of enabling and
// disabling components based on the values of other components.
// Specifically, it has a choice for sex of "Male" or "Female".
// It also has a maiden name field that is enabled only if sex is
// "Female".

public class DynamicDisable extends Applet
{
     TextField maidenName;
     Choice sex;

     public void init()
     {

// Create the sex choice
          sex = new Choice();
          sex.addItem("Male");
          sex.addItem("Female");

// Default to male
          sex.select(0);

          add(sex);

// Create maiden name and disable it because sex defaults to male

          maidenName = new TextField(20);
          maidenName.disable();

          add(maidenName);
     }

     public boolean action(Event evt, Object whichAction)
     {

// If you get an action event on sex, look at the current
// value and enable or disable maiden name accordingly

          if (evt.target == sex)
          {
// If the index is 0, "male" has been selected, so disable maiden name
               if (sex.getSelectedIndex() == 0) {
                    maidenName.disable();

// otherwise, enable maiden name
               } else {
                    maidenName.enable();
               }
               return true;
          }
          return false;
     }
}
```

This technique doesn't provide much of an improvement over paper forms, however. You could still be looking at a huge document full of components, some of which are enabled and some which are disabled. It would be a lot kinder to the user to show him only the items he actually needs to fill in. In other words, rather than just disabling a component, hide it—make it invisible. Hiding has its drawbacks, however. When you hide a component, the layout manager will change the layout of the components. If you aren't using a layout manager, this won't be a problem. If you are using a layout manager, pay special attention to how the form changes when you show and hide various components. You may want to perform a mixture of disabling and hiding. Listing 7.6 shows a very brief example of how to hide and show components dynamically, using the same components as the example in Listing 7.5. Notice that you must call the `validate` method after hiding or showing a component. This causes the layout manager to recompute the component positions.

Listing 7.6 Source Code for *DynamicHide.java*

```
import java.awt.*;
import java.applet.*;

// This applet demonstrates the technique of hiding and
// showing components based on the values of other components.
// Specifically, it has a choice for sex of "Male" or "Female".
// It also has a maiden name field that is visible only if sex is
// "Female".

public class DynamicHide extends Applet
{
     TextField maidenName;
     Choice sex;

     public void init()
     {

// Create the sex choice
          sex = new Choice();
          sex.addItem("Male");
          sex.addItem("Female");

// Default to male
          sex.select(0);

          add(sex);

// Create maiden name and hide it because sex defaults to male

          maidenName = new TextField(20);
          maidenName.hide();

          add(maidenName);
```

continues

Listing 7.6 Continued

```
    }

    public boolean action(Event evt, Object whichAction)
    {

// If you get an action event on sex, look at the current
// value and show or hide maiden name accordingly

        if (evt.target == sex)
        {
// If the index is 0, "male" has been selected, so hide maiden name
            if (sex.getSelectedIndex() == 0) {
                maidenName.hide();
                validate();

// otherwise, show maiden name
            } else {
                maidenName.show();
                validate();
            }
            return true;
        }
        return false;
    }
}
```

The CardLayout layout manager is another good tool for dynamic form construction. It lets you create a stack of different containers (usually panels), only one of which is displayed at any time. By using a card layout, you can create all your panels ahead of time and add them to the card layout. Then, whenever you want to display a specific panel, you tell the card which panel to display. For example, you may have panels that display information on Moe, Larry, and Curly. Listing 7.7 shows a simple example program that uses a card layout and some buttons to select the specific card.

Listing 7.7 Source Code for *CardExample.java*

```
import java.applet.*;
import java.awt.*;

// This applet demonstrates how a card layout can be used to
// display different panels. The panels are given names when
// added to the card layout. There are buttons at the bottom of
// the screen with names corresponding to the panel names. When
// you press a button, it tells the card layout to display the
// card with the same name as the button.

public class CardExample extends Applet
{
```

```
    CardLayout cards;
    Panel stoogePanel;

    public void init()
    {

// Need a border layout to have the stooge panel in the center and
// the buttons at the bottom.

            setLayout(new BorderLayout());

// Create the main display panel
            stoogePanel = new Panel();

// Give the main display panel a card layout
            cards = new CardLayout();
            stoogePanel.setLayout(cards);

// Create the panels for the different cards. For demo purposes, each
// panel just has a label on it.

            Panel moePanel = new Panel();
            moePanel.add(new Label("Moe"));

            Panel larryPanel = new Panel();
            larryPanel.add(new Label("Larry"));

            Panel curlyPanel = new Panel();
            curlyPanel.add(new Label("Curly"));

// Add the separate panels to the stoogePanel giving them their
// own card names.

            stoogePanel.add("Moe", moePanel);
            stoogePanel.add("Larry", larryPanel);
            stoogePanel.add("Curly", curlyPanel);

// Put the stoogePanel in the middle of the applet's border layout

            add("Center", stoogePanel);

// Now create a row of buttons for selecting the different cards. The
// button names must match the names used above.

            Panel selectorPanel = new Panel();
            selectorPanel.add(new Button("Moe"));
            selectorPanel.add(new Button("Larry"));
            selectorPanel.add(new Button("Curly"));

// Put the row of buttons at the bottom part of the border layout
            add("South", selectorPanel);
    }

    public boolean action(Event evt, Object whichAction)
    {
```

7

continues

Listing 7.7 Continued

```
// If the action event is for a button, whichAction is the button's
// label, which is also the name of a card in this program. We just
// tell the card layout to show the appropriate card.

                if (evt.target instanceof Button) {
                        cards.show(stoogePanel, (String) whichAction);
                        return true;
                }
                return false;
        }
}
```

Figure 7.4 shows the CardExample applet in action. The buttons along the bottom select the different card, which simply contain a single label.

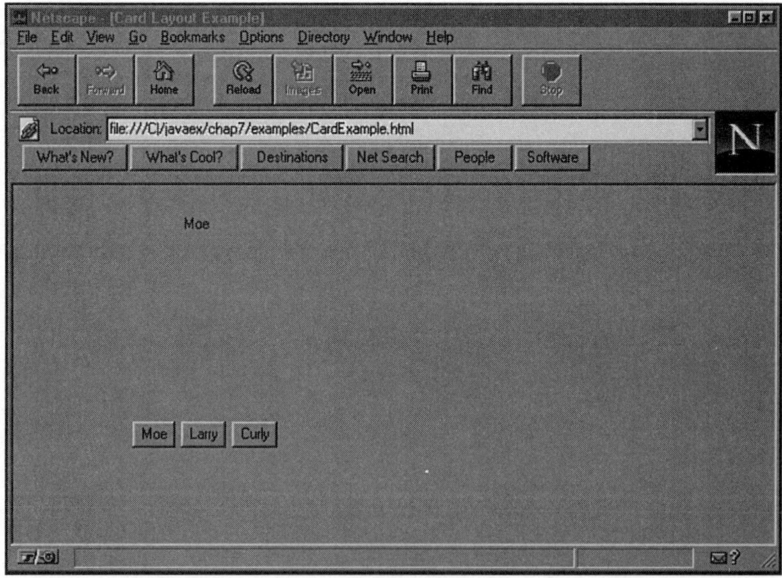

Fig. 7.4
A card layout enables you to display one of several panels.

When you are creating dynamic forms, you can group sections of your forms onto different cards. You can create different methods for going from one card to the next, like having a master index of the different cards, or putting Next and Prev buttons on each card. If you want to disable a section of the form, don't make that section's card available.

For example, suppose you have a part of the form for entering marriage information—date, place, witnesses, and so on. If a person is single, you don't want to present that part. You can remove it from the set of cards in your card layout.

Loading Another URL from an Applet

You may have noticed that several applets in the last two chapters actually open up URLs on the Web and display their contents in the browser. They all use the `showDocument` method in the `AppletContext` class. You can use the `showDocument` class to give your Java applets the same connectivity to the rest of the Web that any Web page has. This also enables you to create new and unique ways to access Web pages.

The `showDocument` method can take a second parameter, which is the target frame for the URL. Your Java applet can open up an URL in its own frame, its parent frame, the top-most frame, a brand new frame, or a particular named frame. You can use this ability to create interesting Web page layouts. For instance, you can create an index applet in Java that provides some neat new way of listing URLs. You could run this applet in a narrow frame on the left side of the page, leaving the rest of the page for the frame where the selected URL will be loaded.

Note

One of the major features lacking in Java is the ability for a Java program to generate HTML data that is displayed by the browser. The `showDocument` method in Netscape bypasses the `URLConnection` class and goes straight to a native method to load an URL. You should be able to generate your own HTML data in HotJava if you create a special `URLConnection` class and define a protocol type for it. We can only hope there will soon be a way to do this in all browsers.

Creating Image Maps with Hot Spots

Image maps were a neat addition to the Web a few years ago. Rather than a list of textual links, you could open up an URL by clicking a particular part of an image. These image maps still have limitations, however, because they are not very interactive. You can create a Java image map, however, that contains hotspots—areas that light up when the mouse passes over them. You can also add context-sensitive help, which is always a nice thing to have.

To create an image map with hot spot, you need a way to define what a "hot spot" is. You could simply create a class that represented an area of the image. This class would also be responsible for displaying whatever should appear when the mouse passes over the hot spot. Listing 7.8 shows an abstract class that defines the methods necessary to implement such a class.

Listing 7.8 Source Code for *ImageRegion.java*

```
import java.awt.*;

// ImageRegion is an abstract definition of the region
// area supported by the ImageMap class.
public abstract class ImageRegion extends Object
{
     public ImageRegion()
     {
     }

// select is called when you click the mouse within a region
     public void select()
     {
     }

// mouseEnter is called when the mouse enters a region
     public void mouseEnter()
     {
     }

// mouseLeave is called when the mouse leaves a region
     public void mouseLeave()
     {
     }

// getBoundingBox should return the smallest rectangle that
// completely encloses this region.

     public abstract Rectangle getBoundingBox();

// inside returns true if x,y is within this region

     public abstract boolean inside(int x, int y);

// paint is used to draw any hotspot popup information
     public void paint(Graphics g)
     {
     }
}
```

Because the `ImageRegion` class is an abstract class, you need something concrete to actually implement a region. You will almost certainly need to define a rectangular region at some point. Actually, it is trivial to extend a rectangular region to be a polygon region. Listing 7.9 shows an implementation of `ImageRegion` that supports polygon regions.

Listing 7.9 Source Code for *ImageRegionPoly.java*

```
import java.awt.*;

// ImageRegionPoly implements a rectangular region for
// use with the ImageMap class.
```

```
public class ImageRegionPoly extends ImageRegion
{
     Polygon boundary;

     public ImageRegionPoly()
     {
          boundary = new Polygon();
     }

     public ImageRegionPoly(Polygon p)
     {
          boundary = p;
     }

     public Rectangle getBoundingBox()
     {
          return boundary.getBoundingBox();
     }

     public boolean inside(int x, int y)
     {
          return boundary.inside(x, y);
     }
}
```

You may also have a need for a circular region. The `ImageRegionCircle` class in Listing 7.10 implements a circular region.

Listing 7.10 Source Code for *ImageRegionCircle.java*

```
import java.awt.*;

// ImageRegionCircle defines a circular region for use
// with the ImageMap class.

public class ImageRegionCircle extends ImageRegion
{
     Point center;
     int radius;

     public ImageRegionCircle()
     {
          center = new Point(0, 0);
          radius = 0;
     }

     public ImageRegionCircle(Point center, int radius)
     {
          this.center = center;
          this.radius = radius;
     }

     public Rectangle getBoundingBox()
     {
```

continues

Listing 7.10 Continued

```
            return new Rectangle(center.x - radius, center.y - radius,
                2*radius, 2*radius);
        }

    // Use the distance formula to determine if a point is inside or not.
    // If the distance between x,y and the center of the region is <= the
    // radius of the circle, the point is within the region.

        public boolean inside(int x, int y)
        {
            int xd = center.x - x;
            int yd = center.y - y;

            int dist = (int) Math.sqrt(xd*xd+yd*yd);

            return dist <= radius;
        }
    }
```

Now that you have a method for defining a region in an image, you need a way to display an image, add these regions to it, and track the mouse to see when it hits a region. The `ImageMap` class in Listing 7.11 does just that. It also shows you how to define a canvas that displays an image.

Listing 7.11 Source Code for *ImageMap.java*

```
    import java.awt.*;
    import java.util.*;

    // The image map is a canvas that displays an image and supports
    // hotspots. The hotspots are defined by subclasses of ImageRegion.
    // There can only be one hotspot active at a time. Whenever a hotspot
    // is active, its paint method is called so it can paint any popup
    // information. You could display a little box of text saying what
    // the hotspot does, for instance. The default paint method for a
    // hotspot does nothing.

    public class ImageMap extends Canvas
    {
        Image image;
        Vector regions;
        ImageRegion selectedRegion;
        boolean moved;

        public ImageMap(Image image)
        {
            this.image = image;
            regions = new Vector();
            moved = true;
        }

    // The size of the Canvas is defined by the size of the image.
```

```
    public Dimension minimumSize()
    {
        return new Dimension(image.getWidth(this),
            image.getHeight(this));
    }

    public Dimension preferredSize()
    {
        return minimumSize();
    }

    public Dimension size()
    {
        return minimumSize();
    }

    public void addRegion(ImageRegion region)
    {
        regions.addElement(region);
    }

    public void removeRegion(ImageRegion region)
    {
        regions.removeElement(region);
        if (region == selectedRegion) {
            selectedRegion = null;
        }
    }

// To repaint this canvas, redraw the image. Then, if there is a hotspot
// active, call that hotspot's paint method.

    public void paint(Graphics g)
    {
// Draw the image
        g.drawImage(image, 0, 0, this);

        if (selectedRegion != null) {

// Find the bounding box for the current region (hotspot)
            Rectangle r = selectedRegion.getBoundingBox();

// Create a graphics context for the bounding box
            Graphics regionGraphics = g.create(r.x, r.y,
                r.width, r.height);

// Let the region paint its little area
            selectedRegion.paint(regionGraphics);
        }
    }

// Flicker-free update

    public void update(Graphics g)
    {
        paint(g);
    }
```

The next section of the `ImageMap` class demonstrates a very important concept in object-oriented design. The `ImageMap` class implements a framework that allows you to plug in different `ImageRegion` objects. You can add many new types of `ImageRegion` objects without changing the `ImageMap` class itself. It is very important to correctly assign class responsibilities in your design. In this case, the `ImageMap` class is responsible for displaying the master image, or background image. It is also responsible for tracking mouse movements and passing them on to affected regions. The `ImageRegion` class is responsible for displaying itself on the map if necessary, and for responding to a mouse click.

> **Tip**
> When designing classes for an application, you want to be able to add functionality by adding new classes, and not by changing existing classes. Try to identify things that may change and let those things be implemented by a separate class.

Listing 7.11 Source Code for *ImageMap.java* (continued)

```
// Need to watch the mouse movement to see if the mouse hits
// a hotspot or not.

    public boolean mouseMove(Event evt, int x, int y)
    {
         moved = true;     // kludge to handle mouse-click problem

// Quick shortcut here, see if you're still in the current region
         if ((selectedRegion != null) &&
              selectedRegion.inside(x, y)) {
              return true;
         }

// If there's a current region and you're not in it, tell the old
// region that the mouse left it.

         if (selectedRegion != null) {
              selectedRegion.mouseLeave();
              selectedRegion = null;
         }

// Check all the regions to see if the mouse is within any of them.
// If two overlap, it's on a first come, first served basis - that is,
// the first region that was added has priority.

         Enumeration e = regions.elements();
         while (e.hasMoreElements()) {
              ImageRegion r = (ImageRegion) e.nextElement();

// See if the mouse's x,y is within the region's area
              if (r.inside(x, y)) {
```

```
                    selectedRegion = r;
                    r.mouseEnter();
                    break;
               }
          }

          repaint();
          return true;
     }

// Mouse down handles mouse clicks, and also will keep track
// of mouse movement

     public boolean mouseDown(Event evt, int x, int y)
     {
// The moved flag is a kludge. Sometimes you'll get more than
// one mouse click. Assume that if the mouse doesn't move
// between clicks, the user doesn't want more than one click.

          if (!moved) return true;
          moved = false;

// Quick shortcut here
          if ((selectedRegion != null) &&
               selectedRegion.inside(x, y)) {
               selectedRegion.select();
               return true;
          }

          if (selectedRegion != null) {
               selectedRegion.mouseLeave();
               selectedRegion = null;
          }

          Enumeration e = regions.elements();
          while (e.hasMoreElements()) {
               ImageRegion r = (ImageRegion) e.nextElement();
               if (r.inside(x, y)) {
                    selectedRegion = r;
                    r.mouseEnter();
                    r.select();
                    break;
               }
          }
          repaint();
          return true;
     }
}
```

You may have noticed that the implementations of the image regions were incredibly small and didn't really seem to do anything. You are correct on both counts. To get any benefit out of the regions, you have to create subclasses that actually do something.

Suppose you want to create a map that has a set of circular hotspots that light up with the name of the city in that section of the map. You need to keep track of the name of the city and also implement a paint method that displays the city name. Because an image map isn't very useful if you can't select items, your city hotspot should also do something when you click it. Listing 7.12 shows a circular region that represents a city. When you click the region, it pops up an OK dialog box telling you which city you clicked.

Listing 7.12 Source Code for *CityRegion.java*

```
import java.awt.*;

// This class implements a special version of the
// ImageRegionCircle class to represent cities on a map.
// When the mouse gets within range of a city, the city name
// is displayed. When you click the city, it pops up a dialog
// box telling you what city you clicked.

public class CityRegion extends ImageRegionCircle
{
     String name;

     public CityRegion()
     {
     }

// You can specify either x,y to create a CityRegion or a Point

     public CityRegion(String name, int x, int y)
     {

// Set up the region as a circle with a radius of 30 pixels

          super(new Point(x, y), 30);     // radius of 30
          this.name = name;
     }

     public CityRegion(String name, Point p)
     {

// Set up the region as a circle with a radius of 30 pixels
          super(p, 30);     // radius of 30
          this.name = name;
     }

// Paint is called when the mouse is within this city's bounding
// area - for this class, defined as a circle of radius 30
// We just draw the city's name in blue. Note that the graphics
// area is bounded by the bounding box for the region (actually, the
// smallest rectangle that will enclose the area because the regions
// can be non-rectangular).

     public void paint(Graphics g)
     {
          g.setColor(Color.blue);
          g.drawString(name, 0, 35);
     }

// If you click a city, you'll get a dialog box
```

```
     public void select()
     {
          OKDialog.createOKDialog("You selected the city of "+name);
     }
}
```

Now that all the pieces of the puzzle are in, you can create an the image map for displaying these cities. Listing 7.13 shows the `CityApplet` class.

Listing 7.13 Source Code for *CityApplet.java*

```
import java.awt.*;
import java.applet.*;

// This applet demonstrates the use of the ImageMap class
// It loads a map of the U.S.A. and creates a set of regions
// for the map. The regions are implemented in the CityRegion class.
// The numbers for the city coordinates are approximate, and were
// determined through ocular analysis (I eyeballed the map).

public class CityApplet extends Applet
{
     public void init()
     {

// Load the map image
          Image usaImage = getImage(getDocumentBase(), "usa.gif");

// Be naughty and use the MediaTracker to make sure the map is loaded
          MediaTracker mt = new MediaTracker(this);
          mt.addImage(usaImage, 0);

          try {
               mt.waitForAll();
          } catch (Exception ignore) {
          }

// Create an image map object for the image
          ImageMap imageMap = new ImageMap(usaImage);

// Add city regions to the image map
          imageMap.addRegion(new CityRegion("Atlanta", 323, 202));
          imageMap.addRegion(new CityRegion("New York", 377, 118));
          imageMap.addRegion(new CityRegion("L.A.", 45, 196));
          imageMap.addRegion(new CityRegion("San Fran", 34, 164));
          imageMap.addRegion(new CityRegion("Seattle", 52, 74));
          imageMap.addRegion(new CityRegion("Dallas", 218, 236));
          imageMap.addRegion(new CityRegion("Chicago", 277, 123));
          imageMap.addRegion(new CityRegion("Miami", 367, 270));
          imageMap.addRegion(new CityRegion("Denver", 102, 143));

// Add the image map to the applet
          add(imageMap);
     }
}
```

Figure 7.5 shows the output from this applet.

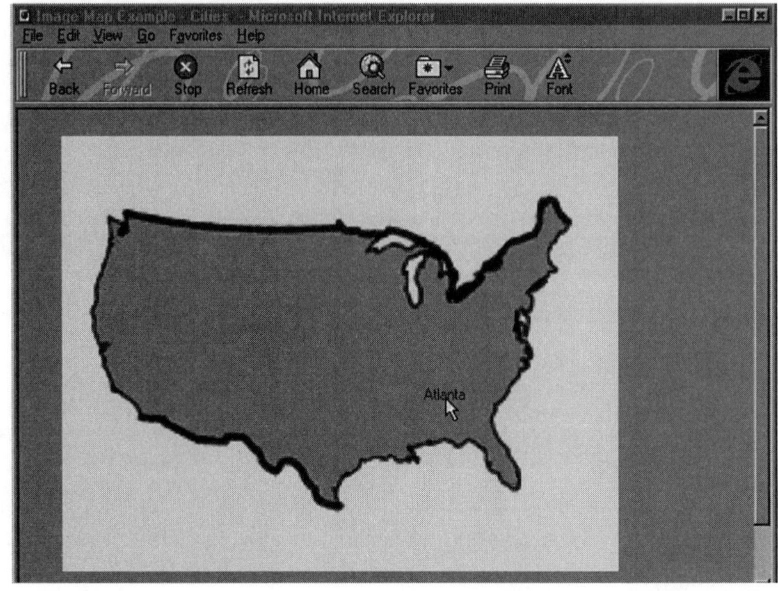

Fig. 7.5
Image maps in Java can implement hot spots.

chapter 8

Reading and Writing Files from an Applet

by Mark Wutka

8

In this chapter

- **Using JFS to expand an applet's capabilities**
  The Java File System package provides an easy way for applets to read and write files, as well as other things normally forbidden by security restrictions.
- **Saving files on a Web server**
  Since your applet can't write files on the local filesystem, you can store your files on your Web server using the HTTP `Post` *command.*
- **Using FTP for file access**
  The File Transfer Protocol (FTP) gives you another way to send files to a server and retrieve them again. You can also perform other file maintenance tasks using FTP.

Applets and Files

Because of security restrictions, an applet may not read or write files on the local system. This is to protect you from a malicious applet storing a virus on your computer or deleting all your files. Even if you could only read files on the local system, someone could snoop around on your computer and retrieve private information.

Before you start exploring the various methods of storing files from an applet, ask yourself first whether you want your applet manipulating files directly. If you are designing a system where you have an applet presenting the user interface for an application running on a server, you should consider doing all the file access from the application. The more code you put on the applet, the longer it takes for it to start up. Even if you have designed your application this way, you may still have reasons to directly read and write files from the applet. For example, you might want to save configuration information for the user interface (colors, fonts). It wouldn't make sense to make this part of the main application, because separating the user interface from the application also means separating the application from the user interface. In other words, the application shouldn't know anything about the user interface, except how it interacts with the applet.

Using the JFS Filesystem for Applets

The JFS filesystem, by Jamie Cameron, is one of the most useful sets of Java classes to come along. It provides NFS-like file and print services for applets. You can get this wonderful product on the Internet at **http://www.ncs.com.sg/java/jfs**.

JFS solves a number of pesky problems for applets. It provides a way to read and write files, create and delete files and directories, print files, and open URLs and socket connections to hosts other than the ones the applets came from. JFS isn't some sort of cheap hack around Java's security model; it is a full-featured server system. This means, of course, that you have to run the JFS server, which is written in Java, to use JFS.

The `JFSclient` class is the applet's interface to the JFS server. You create an instance of `JFSclient` by passing the host name of the JFS server to the constructor. If you are doing this from an applet, the host must be the host that the applet was loaded from, which means your Web server has to run JFS.

Once you create a `JFSclient`, you must send a user name and password to the JFS server. JFS has its own set of user names and passwords; these are not the operating system's user names. This is quite important because the applet must contain the user name and password in order to perform the logon. Anyone with evil intentions and a little patience can find out the user name and password that the applet sends. If these were logon IDs for your Web server, it would be simple for someone to log on to your Web server and wreak all kinds of havoc. If you forget to send the authentication information, the other methods in the `JFSclient` will simply hang, which may not be quite the result you were looking for.

Listing 8.1 shows a very simple example that retrieves a file stored in the JFS file system.

Listing 8.1 Source Code for *JFSGet.java*

```
import java.applet.*;

// This program demonstrates the use of the JFSclient
// class to fetch a file.

public class JFSGet extends Object
{
```

```
    public static void main(String args[])
    {
        try {

// Create a JFS client to host 192.0.0.3
            JFSclient jfs = new JFSclient("192.0.0.3");

// Log on as root, with no password
            jfs.auth("root", "");

// Fetch the file called "volcano"
            byte[] volcfile = jfs.get("/home/root/volcano", 0);

// Dump it to the screen
            for (int i=0; i < volcfile.length; i++) {
                System.out.print((char)volcfile[i]);
            }
            System.out.println();

        } catch (Exception e) {
            e.printStackTrace();
        }
    }
}
```

The JFSGet program is very straightforward. It creates a `JFSclient` object that is connected to a JFS server whose IP address is **192.0.0.3**, then it authenticates itself using the name `root` with no password. Next, it uses the `get` method to retrieve a file as an array of bytes. Finally, it loops through the array of bytes and prints them to the `System.out`.

Caution
This example does not use an authentication password. In practice, you should always use a password in JFS authentication. Otherwise, you may open your system up to possible corruption from other people on the Internet.

Printing Files Using JFS

Under most of the current browser implementations, you may not print Java applets within a Web page. You will usually find an unfortunate blank space on your printout where the applet should be. There aren't even any methods or classes within Java to perform printing functions. While JFS can't quite deal with rendering the output from your applet on a printer, it does allow you to send text data to a printer. If you have a PostScript printer, you could sent PostScript codes to the printer and get graphical output. Printer access in JFS is done through a special device called "/dev/Printer." This one device file represents all the printers on your system. You choose the printer when you send a message to this device. Unlike UNIX, in which you use the same functions to write to devices or files, JFS uses special methods named devput and devget to communicate with the special devices. When you want to send data to a printer, you can pass the printer name to the device driver using the devput method. The following code fragment sends an array of bytes to a printer named myprinter:

```
JFSclient myClient = new JFSClient(getDocumentBase().getHost());
byte databytes[] =  (some way of getting data bytes)
Message deviceInfo = new Message();
deviceInfo.add("Printer", "myprinter");
myClient.devput("/dev/Printer", databytes, deviceInfo);
```

The printers are defined in a file called /etc/printers within the JFS filesystem. If you are running UNIX, you don't need to be concerned about all these /dev and /etc files. JFS maintains its own filesystem structure, the root of which can be in any directory on the system. What JFS calls /etc/printers may really be /home/mark/jfs/root/etc/printers. The /etc/printers file contains multiple lines that each contain four fields separated by colons:

```
printer name:printer type:printer description:print command
```

The default /etc/printers that comes with JFS contains the single line:

```
default:Postscript:The Default Printer:lpr
```

Accessing Other Web Servers from JFS

One of the other problems that JFS solves for applets is the nasty restriction of not being able to access any other servers other than the one the applet came from. The /dev/Web device in JFS is a URL redirection device that enables you to retrieve data from any URL on the Net. Use the devget method to tell the /dev/Web device where to get the data from:

```
JFSclient myClient = new JFSClient(getDocumentBase().getHost());
Message deviceInfo = new Message();
deviceInfo.add("URL", "http://www.mcp.com");
Message response = myClient.devget("/dev/Web", deviceInfo);
byte[] responseData = response.getdata();
```

Saving Files Using HTTP Post

If you don't want the overhead of JFS, you have some alternatives. You can take advantage of the existing classes that are able to post data to a Web server. Remember that when you post data to a Web server, you are essentially sending it a file. The only thing you have to do is create something to take the posted data and store it in a file. This turns out to be a trivial task under UNIX. The following shell script enables you to store data in a file:

```
#!/bin/sh
echo "Content-type: text/plain"
echo
dd ibs=1 count=$CONTENT_LENGTH of=$QUERY_STRING 2>/dev/null
echo $?
```

This script probably requires a bit of explanation. First of all, the filename that you are storing into is encoded in the URL and not in the posted data. If you were to call this script `putfile` and put it in the `cgi-bin` directory of your Web server, the following URL would try to post to a file called putme:

```
http://mywebhost/cgi-bin/putfile?putme
```

The shell script kicks into action by first printing response data that is required by every CGI program, namely the "Context-type" information. Next, it prints a blank line, signifying the end of the header information. Now comes the key to this script—the `dd` command. This command is similar to the `cat` command, except that it has the ability to read and write a fixed number of records. The `ibs=1` option tells `dd` to use an input block size of 1 byte, meaning that the `count` option will tell how many bytes to read. Because the http server stores the number of bytes you posted in an environment variable called `CONTENT_LENGTH`, you use this variable as the `count` parameter for `dd`. Finally, the `of` parameter is the name of the output file you are writing to. Any error messages are sent to `/dev/null`, but the numeric exit code is printed as the final line of the response generated by the script. If the `dd` command is successful, the `echo $?` line will echo a 0.

Listing 8.2 shows a class that uses the `POST` command to send data to this script.

Listing 8.2 Source Code for *PostPutFile.java*

```
import java.net.*;
import java.io.*;

// This class provides a static method to post a file to the
// putfile script, which takes a filename as a parameter passed
// in the POST request itself, and then receives the bytes as
// the posted data.

public class PostPutFile extends Object
{
// Put sends the named file to a specific URL. The URL should
// contain the path name of the putfile script. This method
// will append the ?filename to the script name.
// It returns 0 if the put was successful, or a non-zero number
// if it failed for some reason.

    public static int put(URL url, String filename, byte[] bytes)
    throws IOException, MalformedURLException
    {
```

continues

Listing 8.2 Continued

```
// Run the putfile script and ask it to store the data in a file called "putme"

        URL destURL = new URL(url.getProtocol(), url.getHost(),
          url.getPort(), url.getFile()+"?"+filename);

// Define the data that you want stored in the file.

        URLConnection urlConn = destURL.openConnection();

        urlConn.setDoOutput(true);     // we need to write
        urlConn.setDoInput(true);     // just to be safe...
        urlConn.setUseCaches(false);     // get info fresh from server

// Tell the server what kind of data we are sending - in this case,
// just a stream of bytes.

        urlConn.setRequestProperty("Content-type",
            "application/octet-stream");

// Must tell the server the size of the data we are sending. This also
// tells the URLConnection class that we are doing a POST instead
// of a GET.

        urlConn.setRequestProperty("Content-length", ""+bytes.length);

// Open an output stream so we can send the info we are posting

        OutputStream outStream = urlConn.getOutputStream();

// Write out the actual request data

        outStream.write(bytes);

        outStream.close();

// Now that we have sent the data, open up an input stream and get
// the response back from the server

        DataInputStream inStream = new DataInputStream(
            urlConn.getInputStream());

        String line = inStream.readLine();

        inStream.close();

        try {
            int result = Integer.valueOf(line).intValue();
            return result;
        } catch (Exception parseError) {
            return -1;
        }
    }
}
```

Listing 8.3 shows a simple example applet that stores a file using the `PostPutFile` class.

Listing 8.3 Source Code for *TestPutFile.java*

```
import java.net.*;
import java.applet.*;

public class TestPutFile extends Applet
{
     public void init()
     {
          try {
               URL destURL = new URL(getDocumentBase(),
                    "/cgi-bin/putfile");

// Define a string we want to send

               String dataToSend = "This is a string that I want \n"+
                    "to store in the file.\n";

// The PostPutFile class wants a byte array, however, so we convert
// the string to a byte array.

               byte[] bytes = new byte[dataToSend.length()];

               dataToSend.getBytes(0, dataToSend.length(), bytes, 0);

               PostPutFile.put(destURL, "/home/mark/putme", bytes);

          } catch (Exception e) {
               e.printStackTrace();
          }
     }
}
```


Note

The new version of HTTP (HTTP 1.1) includes a `PUT` command that allows you to store a file without creating a separate CGI program to save the file. Some HTTP servers already support this new option. If you have a server that supports `PUT` and you want to save files from Java, you won't be able to use the `URL` class to send the file (until the `URL` class supports `POST`). You can, however, use the `PostSockURL` class from Chapter 6, "Communicating with a Web Server," with a little modification (change `POST` to `PUT` when it sends the HTTP command).

Storing and Retrieving Files with FTP

As its name implies, the File Transfer Protocol is useful for sending files back and forth between an applet and a server. You just need to make sure that your server supports FTP. If you are running UNIX or Windows NT, it should come with the operating system. The FTP protocol is defined in Internet RFC 959.

The FTP protocol requires you to use two different connections between client and server. The control connection is used by the client to send commands to the server. The server sends responses over the control connection. Whenever the client or server needs to send a large block of data, a data connection must be established. Figure 8.1 illustrates the connections between a client and an FTP server.

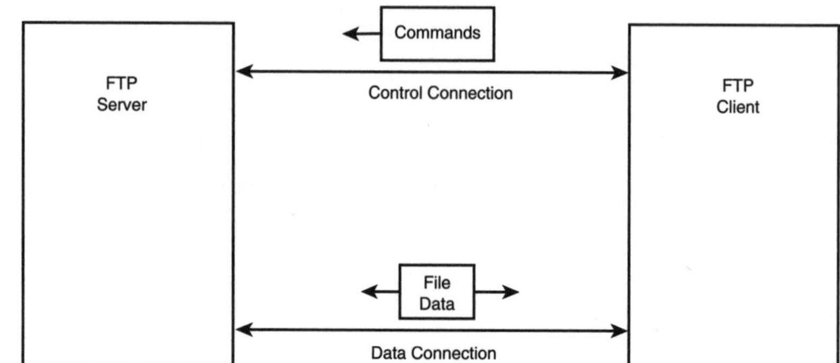

Fig. 8.1
A client uses two different connections to communicate with an FTP server.

Sending FTP Commands

The control connection used in FTP is an ASCII, line-oriented connection, similar to SMTP (Simple Mail Transfer Protocol). A client sends a command to the server as a line terminated by carriage. The response from the server is one or more ASCII lines containing a 3-digit return code and a text response. For example, when you send the `USER` command to tell the FTP server that you want to log in as **mark**, you send:

```
USER mark
```

The FTP server would respond with a line like:

```
331 Password required for mark
```

The response codes from FTP are grouped into five categories, based on the first digit in the response code:

- `1xx` means that the command has been started successfully, and is in the process of running. You will get another response when the command completes. When the server starts transmitting a file it sends a `1xx` response, and then sends a `2xx` response when the file has been sent.

- `2xx` indicates that the command has been completed successfully.
- `3xx` is sent when the server accepts your command, but needs more information from you in order to proceed. This often occurs when you send a `USER` command and the system wants you to send a password.
- `4xx` means that the command cannot be completed due to some temporary problem. If you send the same command again, it may be accepted.
- `5xx` indicates that the command cannot be completed. If you try the same command again, it will be rejected again.

FTP responses can span more than one line. Whenever the server sends a multiline response, each line begins with the response code followed by a dash (-). The last line of the response does not contain a dash. All you have to do when reading responses is look for a dash as the fourth character. If there is a dash, you need to read another line. Listing 8.4 shows the `doCommand` and `getResponse` methods from the `FTPSession` class which are included on the CD for this book. These methods are responsible for sending commands and receiving responses. The `getResponse` method checks for a dash to see if the response is a multiline response. You could use these same methods for other Internet protocols that use this same request-response format, like SMTP.

Note

The `FTPSession` class uses `DataInputStream` and `DataOutputStream` filters on top of the normal socket input and output streams. This allows `FTPSession` to send and receive whole lines of data rather than reading and writing one character at a time.

Listing 8.4 *doCommand* and *getResponse* Methods from *FTPSession.java*

```
// Send a command and wait for a response

     public String doCommand(String commandString)
     throws IOException
     {
          outStream.writeBytes(commandString+"\n");
          String response = getResponse();
          return response;
     }

// Get a response back from the server. Handles multi-line responses
// and returns them as part of the string.
```

continues

Listing 8.4 Continued

```
     public String getResponse()
     throws IOException
     {
          String response = "";

          for (;;) {
               String line = inStream.readLine();

               if (line == null) {
                    throw new IOException(
                         "Bad response from server.");
               }

// FTP response lines should at the very least have a 3-digit number

               if (line.length() < 3) {
                    throw new IOException(
                         "Bad response from server.");
               }
               response += line + "\n";

// If there isn't a '-' immediately after the number, we've gotten the
// complete response. ('-' is the continuation character for FTP responses)

               if ((line.length() == 3) ||
                    (line.charAt(3) != '-')) return response;
          }
     }
```

Tip

If you already had a class that implemented the SMTP protocol, you might consider moving the methods for sending and receiving commands into a new superclass for the SMTP class. Then the FTP and SMTP classes would be subclasses of this new class. This kind of situation occurs often in object-oriented programming. You discover that there are parts of a class that can be used by other classes, so you split out the reusable parts into a separate class. Obviously, it would have been better if you could have anticipated that the parts would need to be reused, but you don't always realize these things ahead of time.

Establishing an FTP Session

The first step in establishing an FTP session is creating the connection to the FTP server. FTP connections are normal TCP socket connections. The default FTP port is 21, but you should allow for other port numbers, since you may be running a special version of FTP for another reason.

Once you have established a connection, the FTP server will send you a response, which is really just a greeting from the server. It is very important that you be prepared to read this response once you have connected to the server. If you don't read the response and just go on and send a USER command to begin your login, you will be confused and think that the greeting is the response from the USER command, and you will probably remain confused for the rest of the session. The greeting usually looks something like this:

```
220 flamingo FTP server (Version wu-2.4(1) Wed May 10 21:00:32 CDT 1995) ready
```

Once you connect to the server, you have to log on. At the minimum, you must send a USER command. This command is in the format:

```
USER username
```

For example, for you to sign on as **mark**, you would use the command line:

```
USER mark
```

Since most user names on an FTP server have a password (if they don't, there's a security risk), the server will most likely respond with a command like:

```
331 Password required for mark
```

You would then be required to send a password with the PASS command:

```
PASS password
```

If mark's password is **Shh!!!!!**, the appropriate PASS command is:

```
PASS Shh!!!!!
```


The response to the PASS command is usually something like this:

```
230 User mark logged in.
```

The FTP protocol allows for a third login parameter called the account, which is sent using the ACCT command. If you get a response with a response code of 332 (need account for login) after sending the PASS command, you need to send an ACCT command:

```
ACCT account
```

The account parameter is rarely used on UNIX systems, and is not restricted to the login sequence. You could receive a 332 response code for any operation, meaning that you must supply an account parameter when performing that operation. For instance, your server may password-protect files, and could require you to send the password to a file with the ACCT command before you can retrieve the file.

Sending Simple FTP Commands

The FTP protocol supports many useful commands that allow you to perform most important file operations. Some of the simple FTP commands are shown in Table 8.1.

Table 8.1 Some Common FTP Commands

Command	Function
CWD *directory*	Changes the working directory
CDUP	Changes directory to the parent of the current directory (like cd .. in UNIX or Windows)
DELE *filename*	Deletes a file
MKD *directory*	Creates a new directory
RMD *directory*	Deletes a directory
RNFR *old-filename*	Renames *old-filename* (must be followed by RNTO, which gives the new name)
RNTO *new-filename*	Sets the new name of a file being renamed by a RNFR command

A simple command is one that does not require a data connection. Some FTP commands require you to set up a second connection, either to send raw data to the server, or receive raw data from the server. Table 8.2 shows you the commands that require a data connection.

Table 8.2 FTP Commands that Require a Data Connection

Command	Function
LIST	Gets a list of all the files in the current directory
LIST *directory*	Gets a list of all the files in a specific directory
RETR *filename*	Retrieves a file from the FTP server
STOR *filename*	Sends a file to the FTP server

Establishing a Data Connection

Whenever an FTP server needs to transfer raw data to or from a client, it uses a separate data connection for the transfer. Normally, the client sets up a listen socket (in Java, a ServerSocket) to accept an incoming connection from the FTP server. The client then sends the host address and port number of the listen socket to the server using the PORT command. The format of the PORT command is:

```
PORT h1,h2,h3,h4,p1,p2
```

The h1-h4 parameters are the individual bytes in the client's host address. If the client's host address was **192.0.0.1**, the bytes would be 192,0,0,1. The p1 and p2 parameters are the upper and lower bytes of the listen socket's port number. The following code fragment extracts p1 and p2 from a port number:

```
int p1 = (portNumber >> 8) & 0xff;
int p2 = portNumber & 0xff;
```

An example PORT command for a host with an address is **192.0.0.3** and a port number of 1234 is:

```
PORT 192,0,0,3,4,210
```

You can verify that the port bytes of 4 and 210 are indeed port 1234 by computing (p1*256) + p2, or (4*256) + 210.

Once you send the PORT command, you can issue a command that requires a data connection like RETR, STOR, or LIST. Once you issue a command that requires a data connection, the server will connect to the listen socket and either send or receive data, depending on the command. Figure 8.2 shows the typical interaction sequence between an FTP server and a client performing a RETR command.

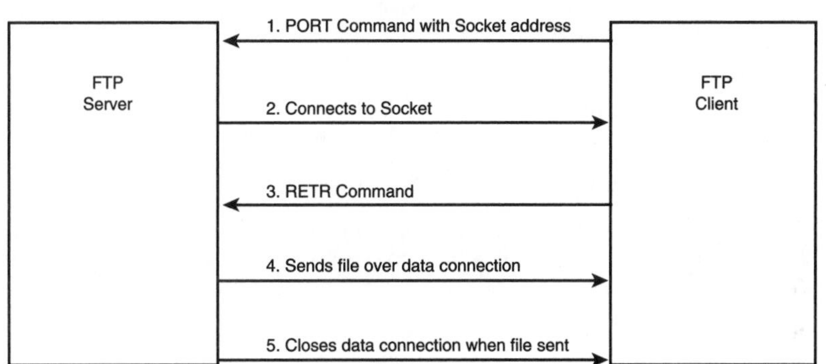

Fig. 8.2
A server connects to a client to establish a data connection.

The normal method of data connection will not work for Java applet because an applet may not accept an incoming socket connection. Fortunately, the FTP protocol gives you another option for establishing a data connection—the PASV command.

The PASV command is similar to the PORT command, except that it causes the server to create the listen socket. The response from the PASV command gives the host address and port number for the listen socket in the same h1,h2,h3,h4,p1,p2 format as used in the PORT command. Here is an example PASV command and the response from the server:

```
PASV
227 Entering Passive Mode (127,0,0,1,6,114)
```

Once the server returns the response, the client can establish the data connection. Figure 8.3 shows the typical interaction sequence between an FTP server and a client performing a STOR command, using PASV to set up the data connection.

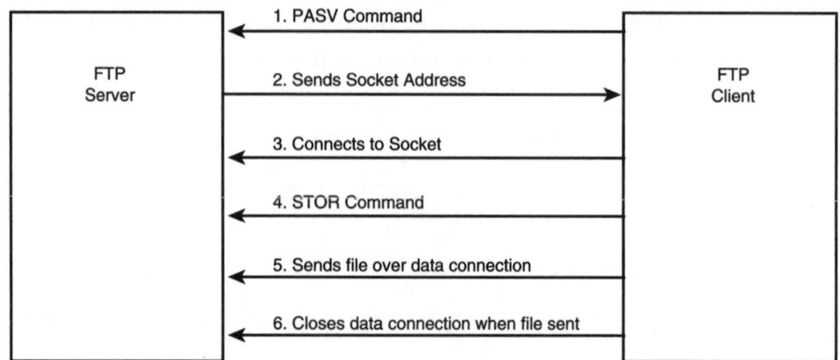

Fig. 8.3
The PASV *command forces the server to create the listen socket for the data connection.*

Listing 8.5 shows the `doPasvPort` method from the `FTPSession` class. It sends a `PASV` command, parses the response, and then establishes a socket connection with the server.

Listing 8.5 ***doPasvPort*** **Method from** ***FTPSession.java***

```
protected synchronized Socket doPasvPort()
     throws IOException
     {

// Send the PASV command
          String response = doCommand("PASV");

// If it wasn't in the 200s, there was an error

          if (response.charAt(0) != '2') {
               throw new IOException(response);
          }

// The pasv response looks like:
// 227 Entering Passive Mode (127,0,0,1,4,160)
// We'll look for the ()'s at the end first

          int parenStart = response.lastIndexOf('(');
          int parenEnd = response.lastIndexOf(')');

// Make sure they're both there and that the ) comes after the (
          if ((parenStart < 0) || (parenEnd < 0) ||
               (parenStart >= parenEnd)) {
               throw new IOException("PASV response format error");
          }

// Extract the address bytes
          String pasvAddr = response.substring(parenStart+1, parenEnd);

// Create a tokenizer to parse the bytes
          StringTokenizer tokenizer = new StringTokenizer(pasvAddr, ",");

// Create the array to store the bytes
          int[] addrValues = new int[6];
```

```
// Parse each byte
          for (int i=0; (i < 6) && tokenizer.hasMoreTokens(); i++) {
               try {
                    addrValues[i] = Integer.valueOf(
                         tokenizer.nextToken()).intValue();
               } catch (Exception e) {
                    throw new IOException(
                         "PASV response format error");
               }
          }

// We ignore the host addresses, assuming that the host address is
// the same as the host address we used to connect the first time.

          Socket newSock = new Socket(host, (addrValues[4] << 8) +
               addrValues[5]);

          return newSock;
     }
```

Listing 8.6 shows the put method from the FTPSession class. It uses the doPasvPort command to set up a data connection, then sends a STOR command to the FTP server. The STOR command should return a response code in the 100–199 range, indicating that the STOR may proceed. When you finish sending the file to the FTP server, you must close down the data connection. This tells the server that you have finished. You should then receive another response from the server over the command connection, which should have a response code in the 200–299 range.

8

Listing 8.6 *put* Method from *FTPSession.java*

```
public synchronized void put(String remoteFile, byte[] data,
          boolean doBinary)
     throws IOException
     {

// If transferring in binary mode, send a type command for type I (IMAGE)
          if (doBinary) {
               String response = doCommand("TYPE I");
               if (response.charAt(0) != '2') {
                    throw new IOException(response);
               }

// If transferring in ASCII mode, send a type command for type A (ASCII)
          } else {
               String response = doCommand("TYPE A");
               if (response.charAt(0) != '2') {
                    throw new IOException(response);
               }
          }

// Open up a data connection
          Socket putSock = doPasvPort();
```

continues

Listing 8.6 Continued

```
// Tell the server where we want it to store the data we are sending

          String response = doCommand("STOR "+remoteFile);

// If the request is successful, the server should send a response
// in the 100s and then start receiving the bytes. Once the data
// connection is closed, it should send a response in the 200s.

          if (response.charAt(0) != '1') {
               putSock.close();
               throw new IOException(response);
          }

// If binary mode, just write all the bytes
          if (doBinary) {
               OutputStream out = putSock.getOutputStream();

               out.write(data);

// If ASCII mode, write the data a line at a time

          } else {
               DataInputStream in = new DataInputStream(
                    new ByteArrayInputStream(data));
               DataOutputStream out = new DataOutputStream(
                    putSock.getOutputStream());

               String line;

               while ((line = in.readLine()) != null) {
                    out.writeBytes(line+"\r");
               }
          }

          putSock.close();

          response = getResponse();

// Make sure we got a 200 response

          if (response.charAt(0) != '2') {
               throw new IOException(response);
          }
     }
```

The `FTPSession` class is quite simple to use. You just create an instance of `FTPSession` by passing the destination host name, the user name, and the password to the constructor, and then using the `get` and `put` methods to retrieve and send files, respectively. Listing 8.7 shows an example applet that copies a file by retrieving it and then storing it under a new name.

Listing 8.7 Source Code for *TryFTP.java*

```
import java.applet.*;
import java.io.*;

// This applet demonstrates the use of the FTPSession class.
// It copies a file called "volcano" to a file called "vol.ftp"
// by fetching the file and then storing it with a new name.

public class TryFTP extends Applet
{
     public void init()
     {
          try {
// Create the session to host 192.0.0.3, using a user name of anonymous
// and a password of mark@localhost

               FTPSession sess = new FTPSession(
                    "192.0.0.3",
                    "anonymous", "mark@localhost");

// Fetch the file
               byte[] file = sess.get("/home/mark/volcano", true);

// Store the file
               sess.put("/home/mark/vol.ftp", file, true);


          } catch (Exception e) {
               e.printStackTrace();
          }
     }
}
```

Caution

Be extremely careful when using the `FTPSession` class with respect to the user name and password. Even though your applet is compiled, it is fairly trivial to look through the code and find the user name and password that are sent. You should either use anonymous FTP, or set up a user account that is not allowed to log on to your system and is allowed to use only FTP. Otherwise, you are broadcasting a free user account all over the Internet whenever you put your applet out there.

chapter 9

Creating Reusable Graphics Components

9

by Mark Wutka

In this chapter

- **Using the Command pattern**
  The Command design pattern is very useful when creating reusable graphics components. It enables you to create graphical components that you can use in your application without creating subclasses of them.
- **Creating a custom component**
  You may need a common graphical component that Java doesn't support. You might also need to create a specialized graphical component that is specific to your application. You can use the `Canvas` *class to create a custom component, like an image button.*
- **Using the model-view-controller paradigm**
  The model-view-controller paradigm is a common approach to user interface design that separates the application, the input, and the output. By designing your applications this way, you can take advantage of reusable components.

Reusable Components

Amid all the excitement and debate over Java's cross-platform abilities, Java's features as an object-oriented programming language tend to get lost. Java falls somewhere between C++ and Smalltalk on the object-oriented scale. The general structure of Java's classes are similar to C++, but it adds a few more capabilities that are closer to Smalltalk. For example, the interface mechanism allows you to invoke methods in an object without knowing the object's class hierarchy. In C++, you must have a reference to the object's class or one of its superclasses to invoke a method. Smalltalk, of course, allows you the ultimate freedom of invoking any method in any object. This gives Smalltalk GUI designers a huge advantage in creating reusable components.

In Smalltalk, when you add a button to your application, you can tell the button to invoke a specific method in a specific object whenever the button is pressed. If you were allowed to do this in Java, it would look something like this:

```
public class MyClass extends Applet
{
     public void handleButtonPress()
     {
          // code to handle a button being pressed
     }

     public void init()
     {
          Button myButton = new Button("Press Me", this,
               handleButtonPress);
     }
}
```

Unfortunately, you can't do this in Java because it doesn't support pointers or references to functions. You can't even do it effectively in C++, and it supports function pointers. This problem is solved in C++ by something called a functor, also known as the Command pattern in design pattern lingo.

The Command Pattern

The Command pattern addresses the problem of invoking arbitrary methods in an object. The basic mechanism of the Command pattern is that you create small objects that implement a specific interface—each object is responsible for invoking a different method.

Suppose you want to create buttons for your applet and have each button invoke a different method in your applet. You could create your own `action` method in the applet and handle the `action` events for the buttons, but that would turn out to be too much work in a larger applet. Instead, you define an interface like the one shown in Listing 9.1:

Listing 9.1 Source Code for *Command.java*

```
public interface Command
{
     public void doCommand();
}
```

Now, to be able to use this interface with a button, you need a subclass of `Button` that invokes `doCommand` whenever the button is pressed. Listing 9.2 shows an implementation of a CommandButton object that does this.

Listing 9.2 Source Code for *CommandButton.java*

```
import java.awt.Button;
import java.awt.Event;

// This class implements a Button that supports the
// Command interface. When the button is pressed, it
// invokes the doCommand method in the Command interface.

public class CommandButton extends Button
{

// The interface where we will invoke doCommand

     protected Command buttonCommand;

// It's always polite to implement the empty constructor if
// you can get away with it.

     public CommandButton()
     {
     }

// Allow a CommandButton with a command but no label

     public CommandButton(Command command)
     {
          buttonCommand = command;
     }

// Allow a CommandButton to use the typical Button constructor

     public CommandButton(String label)
     {
          super(label);
     }

// The most useful constructor allows a label and a command

     public CommandButton(String label, Command command)
     {
          super(label);

          buttonCommand = command;
     }

// When we get an action event, invoke doCommand in buttonCommand

     public boolean action(Event evt, Object which)
     {
```

9

continues

Listing 9.2 Continued

```
// Make sure the action event is for this object
          if (evt.target != this) return false;

// Make sure we have a buttonCommand defined!
          if (buttonCommand == null) return false;

          buttonCommand.doCommand();

          return true;
     }

// Since you can create a CommandButton without passing it a
// Command interface, you need to be able to set the command later.

     public void setCommand(Command command)
     {
          buttonCommand = command;
     }
}
```

Now, suppose you want to pass parameters when the command is invoked. For example, suppose you want to assign numbers to buttons and pass the number as part of the command. You do not need to change the `Command` interface or the `CommandButton` class for this. The key to the Command pattern is the creation of small command objects that invoke the real methods. Listing 9.3 shows a small command object implementation whose `doCommand` method turns around and invokes `changeNumber` in a `NumberApplet` object.

Listing 9.3 Source Code for *ChangeNumberCommand.java*

```
// This class implements a simple command object
// that invokes a method called changeNumber in a
// NumberApplet object whenever doCommand is called

public class ChangeNumberCommand extends Object implements Command
{
     protected NumberApplet applet;
     protected int number;

     public ChangeNumberCommand(NumberApplet applet, int number)
     {
          this.applet = applet;
          this.number = number;
     }

     public void doCommand()
     {
          applet.changeNumber(number);
     }
}
```

The ChangeNumberCommand object illustrates the key feature of the Command pattern. It acts as an intermediary between the CommandButton and the NumberApplet. The CommandButton says doCommand(), the NumberApplet wants to hear changeNumber(5), the ChangeNumberCommand object performs the translation. Listing 9.4 shows the implementation of the NumberApplet class.

Listing 9.4 Source Code for *NumberApplet.java*

```
import java.applet.Applet;
import java.awt.Label;

// This applet displays a label containing a number,
// followed by three buttons which change the number.
// It uses the ChangeNumberCommand to translate the
// doCommand method in the CommandButton to the
// changeNumber method in this object.

public class NumberApplet extends Applet
{
     Label number;

     public void init()
     {
// Start the label out at 0
          number = new Label("0");

          add(number);

// Create the object to change the label to 1
          add(new CommandButton("1",
               new ChangeNumberCommand(this, 1)));

// Create the object to change the label to 2
          add(new CommandButton("2",
               new ChangeNumberCommand(this, 2)));
// Create the object to change the label to 3
          add(new CommandButton("3",
               new ChangeNumberCommand(this, 3)));
     }

// changeNumber actually performs the change

     public void changeNumber(int newNumber)
     {
          number.setText(""+newNumber);
     }
}
```

Figure 9.1 shows the NumberApplet applet in action.

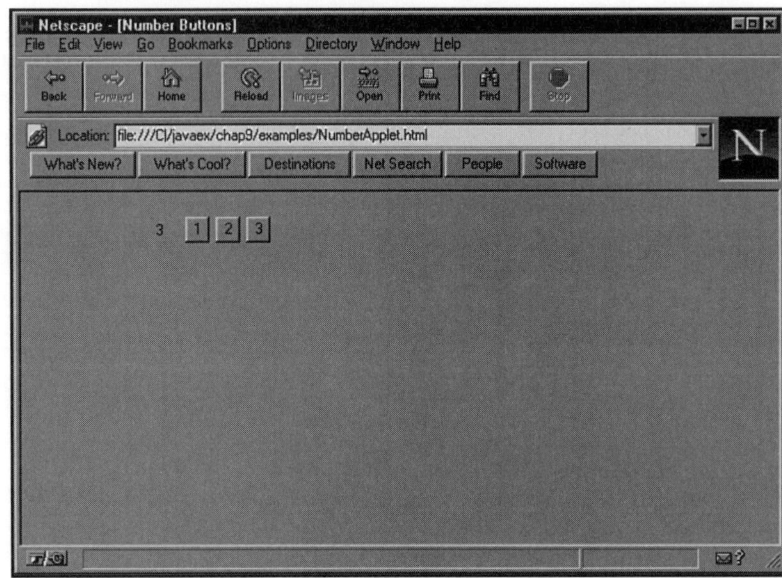

Fig. 9.1
The Command pattern makes it easy to use components without subclassing them.

You can also cascade commands, creating command objects that translate from one command into another. For example, the `ChangeNumberCommand` object invokes a `changeNumber` method in a NumberApplet that takes a number. It is a shame that the object is restricted to `NumberApplets`. You will probably have many situations where you want to do a numeric command—a command that takes a number. You should go ahead and define a `NumberCommand` interface to handle such situations, as shown in Listing 9.5:

Listing 9.5 Source Code for *NumberCommand.java*

```
public interface NumberCommand
{
     public void doCommand(int number);
}
```

Now, because you have already seen an example where you want to take an object that invokes a regular `Command` and turn that into a `NumberCommand`, you can feel pretty confident that an object that converts from one to the other will get a lot of use. Listing 9.6 shows the class to do this.

Listing 9.6 Source Code for *CommandToNumberCommand.java*

```
// This class translates a Command.doCommand() method into
// a NumberCommand.doCommand(int) method.
```

```
public class CommandToNumberCommand extends Object implements Command
{
     protected NumberCommand numberCommand;
     protected int number;

     public CommandToNumberCommand(NumberCommand command, int number)
     {
          this.numberCommand = command;
          this.number = number;
     }

     public void doCommand()
     {
          numberCommand.doCommand(number);
     }
}
```

You will soon end up with a library of commands and command conversions, such as `StringCommand`, `StringCommandToNumberCommand`, `BooleanCommandToStringCommand`, etc. You'll also have new components that invoke these commands, like `CommandTextField`, which would invoke a `doCommand` method in a `StringCommand` object. These objects take only minutes to write, but they can save you hours of coding. Figure 9.2 illustrates how some of these objects might be connected.

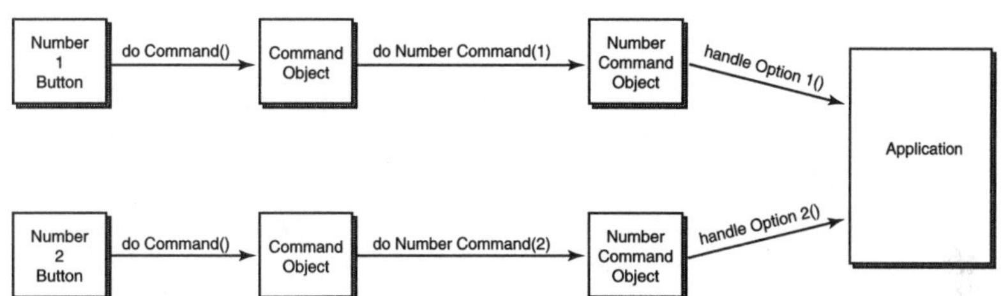

Fig. 9.2
Different command objects can be linked together like building blocks.

Invoking Commands from a Menu

Buttons and menu items are very similar in their usage. In fact, you can think of a menu as a hierarchy of buttons. Both of the components represent an action without any parameters. Components like a choice or an option button have an additional parameter associated with them. For example, with a choice, the parameter is the new item chosen. For an option button, the parameter is whether the button is now selected or deselected. Because of the similarity between Buttons and MenuItems, you can use the same `Command` interface for both menu items and buttons. This means that you can create buttons that are shortcuts for menu items, both sharing the same instance of a `Command` object. Listing 9.7 shows an implementation of a `CommandMenuItem`.

Listing 9.7 Source Code for *CommandMenuItem.java*

```
import java.awt.*;

// This is a menu item that supports the command
// interface. Whenever an ACTION_EVENT is posted
// to it, it invokes the doCommand method.

public class CommandMenuItem extends MenuItem
{
// The Command interface to invoke

     protected Command whichCommand;

     public CommandMenuItem(String label, Command whichCommand)
     {
          super(label);
          this.whichCommand = whichCommand;
     }

     public boolean postEvent(Event evt)
     {

// If we get an ACTION_EVENT event, call doCommand
          if (evt.id == Event.ACTION_EVENT)
          {
               whichCommand.doCommand();
               return true;
          }

// Otherwise, let the super class handle the postEvent
          return super.postEvent(evt);
     }
}
```

Creating a Reusable Image Button

The AWT `Button` class does not allow you to display an image in the button, only text. This is really annoying for people who would like to make toolbars and other useful GUI components. You can implement an image button pretty easily by creating a subclass of `Canvas`.

When creating a custom component using the `Canvas` class, there are basically two things you have to do—draw the component and handle input events. For an image button, you also have the added burden of waiting for the image to be downloaded.

Setting the Size of a Canvas

The `ImageButton` class, included on the CD with this book, implements an image button as a subclass of `Canvas`. It does not require that the image be completely downloaded before the button can be displayed. Because you don't always know what size a component needs to be, thanks to the wonder of layout managers, your image button class needs to be flexible enough to fit into any layout. You have a choice of keeping the image the same size all the time and putting some kind of border around the image, or of resizing the image itself to match the new button size.

Note

Whenever you create your own subclass of `Canvas`, you must set the canvas size either by calling the `resize` method or by implementing your own `minimumSize` and `preferredSize` methods.

The `ImageButton` class computes its preferred size from the size of the image. The minimum size is the size of the button when there is no image (4x4, which leaves room for the shadowing effects). The `ImageButtonClass` also implements its own `size` method. The `size` method is used when the button size is fixed. In other words, you can specify a fixed size for the button that will never be changed by the layout manager. Listing 9.8 shows the sizing methods for the `ImageButton` class.

Listing 9.8 Image Sizing Methods from *ImageButton.java*

```
// The minimum size is the amount of space for the shading around the
// edges, plus one pixel for the image itself.

     public Dimension minimumSize()
     {
          return new Dimension(4, 4);
     }

// We'd prefer to have just enough space for the shading (shading takes
// 3 pixels in each direction) plus the size of the image.

     public Dimension preferredSize()
     {
          return new Dimension(buttonImage.getWidth(this)+3,
               buttonImage.getHeight(this)+3);
     }

     public Dimension size()
     {

// If the sized isn't fixed, just say super-size it! (har har)

          if (!fixedSize) return super.size();
          return preferredSize();
     }
```

9

Caution

If an image hasn't been downloaded yet, the getWidth and getHeight methods will return –1. This can cause unpleasant exceptions if you use these values to set the width or height of a canvas. The ImageButton class does not have that problem because it leaves space on either size of the image. If the image hasn't been downloaded, the preferredSize method will return a dimension of 2×2. If it hadn't added 3 to both width and height, it would be returning a dimension of –1×–1, which would surely cause an error.

Handling Input Events

The ImageButton class is concerned only with mouse movements. It needs to know when someone selects the button. You might think that you would only need to look for a MOUSE_DOWN event, but it is not that simple. On most systems, if you hold the mouse down and then move the mouse away from the button before releasing the mouse, the button pops up as if you had never clicked it. You often use this functionality if you start to click the wrong button. The ImageButton class needs to handle that case.

In order to allow you to move the mouse away from the button while it is down, you can't trigger the button's action on a mouse click. Instead, you must trigger it when the mouse is released. That way, you need to have the mouse pointer on the button, click the mouse, and release it before you actually perform the button's action.

If you were to only implement the mouseDown and mouseUp events, you'd still have one problem. You need to make the button pop back up when the mouse leaves the button area. This means that the ImageButton class must also implement the mouseExit method. If it did not implement this method, whenever you moved the mouse away from the button, the button would appear to be stuck in the down position.

It would be really nice if you could watch for the mouse entering the button's area and have the button notice whether the mouse was up or down and adjust accordingly. Unfortunately, the MOUSE_ENTER and MOUSE_EXIT events do not give any indication of whether the mouse is up or down. The reason this is nice is that most buttons will automatically pop down if you move the mouse over them while you are holding the mouse button down. If you try this with the image button, you'll see that it does not do this.

Listing 9.9 shows the mouse event handlers for the image button class. The mouse event handlers manipulate a Boolean variable called isDown, which keeps track of whether the button is currently up or down. This value is then used by the paint method to determine whether the button should be drawn up or down.

Listing 9.9 Mouse Handling Methods from *ImageButton.java*

```
// If we get a mouse click, make a note it and push the button down

     public boolean mouseDown(Event evt, int x, int y)
     {
          isDown = true;
          repaint();
          return true;
     }

// If we get mouseUp, see if we thought the mouse was down. If so,
// the button has been clicked. Generate an action event so this button
// behaves just like a real button.

     public boolean mouseUp(Event evt, int x, int y)
     {
          if (isDown) {
               Event newEvt = new Event(this, evt.when,
                    Event.ACTION_EVENT, x, y, 0, 0, buttonImage);
               this.postEvent(newEvt);
          }
          isDown = false;
          repaint();
          return true;
     }

// If the mouse leaves the area, move the button up.

     public boolean mouseExit(Event evt, int x, int y)
     {
          if (isDown) {
               isDown = false;
               repaint();
          }
          return true;
     }
```


Painting the Canvas

The `paint` method is the one method that you should always see in a subclass of `Canvas`. You may not handle mouse events or anything else, but you need to paint the canvas. Otherwise, you'll just get a blank space. For the image button, the painting is interesting.

Most window systems use the same basic effect for creating 3-D effects. You imagine that there's a light shining from the upper-left corner of the screen. Anything on the screen that is raised (coming off the screen towards you) would catch the light on its upper left side, and the lower left side would be in shadow. Anything that is lowered (going inside the screen, away from you) would catch light on the lower-right corner, and the upper-left would be in shade. Also, when a button is lowered, the image or text in the image is usually shifted a small amount to the right and down.

Figure 9.3 shows the image button in the raised position. Notice that the top and left edges are lighter, while the bottom and right edges are darker.

Fig. 9.3
By lightening the upper-left side of an image, and darkening the lower-right, you create a raised effect.

Figure 9.4 shows the image button in the lowered position. Notice that the top and left edges are now darker and the bottom and right edges are lighter.

Fig. 9.4
By darkening the upper-left side of an image, and lightening the lower-right, you create a lowered effect.

Listing 9.10 shows the `paint` method for the `ImageButton` class. It draws the shading for the upper-left part of the button, then draws the image before adding the shading for the lower-right.

Listing 9.10 *paint* Method from *ImageButton.java*

```
// paint displays the shading and the image

     public void paint(Graphics g)
     {
          Dimension currSize = size();
          int width = currSize.width;
          int height = currSize.height;

          int imgHeight = buttonImage.getHeight(this);
          int imgWidth = buttonImage.getWidth(this);
```

```
// Display the shading in the upper left. If the button is up, the
// upperleft shading is white, otherwise it's black

          if (isDown) {
               g.setColor(Color.black);
          } else {
               g.setColor(Color.white);
          }
          g.drawLine(0, 0, width-1, 0);
          g.drawLine(0, 0, 0, height-1);

// If the button is up, we draw the image starting at 1,1

          int imgX = 1;
          int imgY = 1;

// If the button is down, move the image right and down one pixel and
// draw gray shading at 1,1

          if (isDown) {
               g.setColor(Color.gray);
               g.drawLine(1, 1, width-2, 1);
               g.drawLine(1, 1, 1, height-2);
               imgX++;
               imgY++;

// If the button is up, draw gray shading just inside the bottom right shading
          } else {
               g.setColor(Color.gray);
               g.drawLine(1, height-2, width-1, height-2);
               g.drawLine(width-2, 1, width-2, height-2);
          }

// Compare the width of the button to the width of the image, if
// the button is wider, move the image over to make sure it's centered.

          int xDiff = (width - 3 - imgWidth) / 2;
          if (xDiff > 0) imgX += xDiff;

// Compare the height of the button to the height of the image, if
// the button is taller, move the image down to make sure it's centered.

          int yDiff = (height - 3 - imgHeight) / 2;
          if (yDiff > 0) imgY += yDiff;

          g.drawImage(buttonImage, imgX, imgY, this);

// Draw the bottom right shading. If the button is up, the shading is
// black, otherwise it's white.

          if (isDown) {
               g.setColor(Color.white);
          } else {
               g.setColor(Color.black);
          }
          g.drawLine(1, height-1, width-1, height-1);
          g.drawLine(width-1, 1, width-1, height-1);

     }
```

Watching for Image Updates

Rather than requiring that images be completely loaded, the `ImageButton` class redraws itself when an image finishes loading. To do this, it implements the `ImageObserver` interface. If you only need to know that an image has finished downloading, you only need to examine the `flags` parameter to see if the `ImageObserver.ALLBITS` flag has been set.

When the `ImageButton` class learns that the image has finished downloading, it resizes itself and calls `repaint` to redraw itself with the completed image. Listing 9.11 shows the `imageUpdate` method for the `ImageButton` class.

Listing 9.11 *imageUpdate* Method from *ImageButton.java*

```
public boolean imageUpdate(Image img, int flags, int x, int y,
        int width, int height)
    {

// If we have a complete image, resize the button and ask the parent
// to recompute all the component positions. Good thing this only
// gets called once!

        if ((flags & ImageObserver.ALLBITS) != 0) {
            resize(img.getWidth(this)+3, img.getHeight(this)+3);
            getParent().validate();
        }

// Let the canvas class handle any other information it was looking for
        return super.imageUpdate(img, flags, x, y, width, height);
    }
```

Tip

Any time a component resizes itself, it should call the `validate` method in the `parent` container. This causes the container to reposition its components based on the updated size.

Creating a *CommandImageButton*

Now that you have created your own custom component, you can see how easily you can fit it into the Command interface scheme. You only need to create a subclass of `ImageButton` called `CommandImageButton`. Listing 9.12 shows you how to do this.

Listing 9.12 Source Code for *CommandImageButton.java*

```
import java.awt.Event;
import java.awt.Image;

// This class implements a ImageButton that supports the
// Command interface. When the button is pressed, it
// invokes the doCommand method in the Command interface.

public class CommandImageButton extends ImageButton
{

// The interface where we will invoke doCommand

     protected Command buttonCommand;

// Allow a CommandButton to use the typical ImageButton constructor

     public CommandImageButton(Image image)
     {
          super(image);
     }

// Allow a CommandButton to use the typical ImageButton constructor

     public CommandImageButton(Image image, boolean fixedSize)
     {
          super(image, fixedSize);
     }

// The most useful constructor allows an Image and a command

     public CommandImageButton(Image image, Command command)
     {
          super(image);

          buttonCommand = command;
     }

// The most useful constructor allows an Image and a command

     public CommandImageButton(Image image, boolean fixedSize,
          Command command)
     {
          super(image, fixedSize);

          buttonCommand = command;
     }

// When we get an action event, invoke doCommand in buttonCommand

     public boolean action(Event evt, Object which)
     {

// Make sure the action event is for this object
          if (evt.target != this) return false;
```

9

continues

Listing 9.12 Continued

```
// Make sure we have a buttonCommand defined!
          if (buttonCommand == null) return false;

          buttonCommand.doCommand();

          return true;
     }

// Since you can create a CommandImageButton without passing it a
// Command interface, you need to be able to set the command later.

     public void setCommand(Command command)
     {
          buttonCommand = command;
     }
}
```

Now you can use the `CommandImageButton` in all your applications where you were using the CommandButton. The number button application earlier in this chapter needs only a few changes. Listing 9.13 shows a version of the number applet that uses image buttons instead of regular buttons and also uses the `CommandToNumberCommand` object to convert from a `Command` to a `NumberCommand` interface.

Listing 9.13 Source Code for *NumberApplet2.java*

```
import java.applet.Applet;
import java.awt.Label;
import java.awt.Color;

// This applet displays a label containing a number,
// followed by three buttons which change the number.
// It uses the ChangeNumberCommand to translate the
// doCommand method in the CommandButton to the
// changeNumber method in this object.

public class NumberApplet2 extends Applet implements NumberCommand
{
     Label number;

     public void init()
     {
          setBackground(Color.gray);

// Start the label out at 0
          number = new Label("0");

          add(number);

// Create the object to change the label to 1
          add(new CommandImageButton(
```

```
                getImage(getDocumentBase(), "one.gif"),
                new CommandToNumberCommand(this, 1)));

// Create the object to change the label to 2
          add(new CommandImageButton(
                getImage(getDocumentBase(), "two.gif"),
                new CommandToNumberCommand(this, 2)));

// Create the object to change the label to 3
          add(new CommandImageButton(
                getImage(getDocumentBase(), "three.gif"),
                new CommandToNumberCommand(this, 3)));
     }

// changeNumber actually performs the change

     public void doCommand(int newNumber)
     {
          number.setText(""+newNumber);
     }
}
```

Figure 9.5 shows the `NumberApplet2` applet in action.

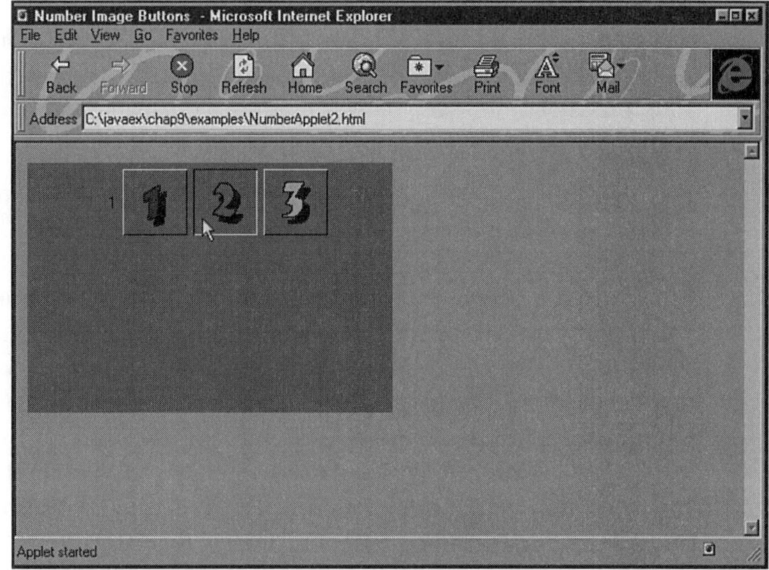

Fig. 9.5
It is much easier to integrate new components when you use the Command pattern.

9

Using the *Observer* Interface

The `Observer` interface and `Observable` class implement another design pattern called the `Observer` pattern. While you may not have used these two classes yet, you have seen a similar system in the form of the `ImageObserver` interface used when dealing with images. The idea behind the `Observer` interface is that you may have an object that wants to know when another object changes. For instance, you may be displaying a car's speed and need to know when the speed changes. Rather than creating a loop that constantly asks the car how fast it's going, you simply ask the car to tell you when its speed changes. It's a simple mechanism, but it can have a huge impact on your design.

The Model-View-Controller Paradigm

The reason the `Observer` interface is so effective is that it uses the Model-View-Controller (MVC) paradigm. The idea behind MVC is that an application really consists of three things—a model, some views of the model, and some controllers.

The model is the part of the application that contains the actual application logic. It does the database access, it computes numbers, it manipulates data structures. It is really the heart of your application. When we talk about separating the user interface from the application, the model is the application.

If the model represents the application, then the view and controller represent the user interface. The user interface is conceptually split into input components and output components. A controller is an input component. It supplies information to the model. A view is an output component—it displays information from the model. MVC is not some brand new, untested theory—it is the way Smalltalk applications have been written for many years.

Pay close attention to the interfaces between the model and your views and controllers. It is very easy to let a model perform things that should rightly be part of a view or a controller. For example, suppose you are doing an aircraft tracking system and you are getting flight positions from the FAA over a modem. These positions are in the form of a text message that contains the aircraft identification and current information about it. You would have some code reading these messages from the modem and passing them to another routine that parses the information out of the message. It is very easy to think of the code that reads the messages as the controller, and put the parsing mechanism in the model. It is also wrong. The parsing routine is also part of the controller. The model should have absolutely no dependence on the external representation of information. This is an extremely important point, because it greatly affects the reusability of your code. You should be able to change input sources and change output formats without touching the model. In other words, the model deals with pure information that has no external meaning attached to it.

Figure 9.6 shows the conceptual relationship between the model, the view, and the controller. It also shows how the aircraft tracking system fits into this model.

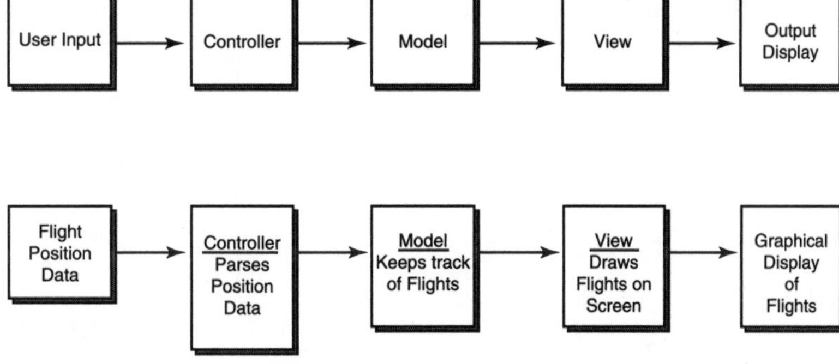

Fig. 9.6
The model-view-controller paradigm is a good, object-oriented way of designing applications.

Observables and the Model-View-Controller Paradigm

The `Observer` interface and the `Observable` class make it easier for you to create views of data in the model by creating a notification system to let your view know when data in the model has changed. The mechanism is very simple. You create some object in your model that is a subclass of `Observable`. Anytime this class changes, it calls `setChanged` to flag itself as having changed, and then calls `notifyObservers`. The reason for the separation is that you may run through a series of checks in your model, any one of which might change the data. When you have finished, you call `notifyObservers` one time, rather than notifying the observers after every check. Whether to notify every time or periodically is a design decision.

Listing 9.14 shows an example `ObservableInt` class which is an `Observable` version of an integer.

9

Listing 9.14 Source Code for *ObservableInt.java*

```
import java.util.*;

//
// ObservableInt - an integer Observable
//
// This class implements the Observable mechanism for
// a simple int variable.
// You can set the value with setValue(int)
// and int getValue() returns the current value.

public class ObservableInt extends Observable
{
     int value;     // The value everyone wants to observe

     public ObservableInt()
     {
          value = 0;     // By default, let value be 0
```

continues

Listing 9.14 Continued

```
     }

     public ObservableInt(int newValue)
     {
          value = newValue;      // Allow value to be set when created
     }

     public synchronized void setValue(int newValue)
     {
//
// Check to see that this call is REALLY changing the value
//
          if (newValue != value)
          {
               value = newValue;

// Mark this class as "changed"
               setChanged();

// Tell the observers about it, pass the new value as an Integer object
// This saves the observers time because they don't have to ask what
// the new value is.
               notifyObservers(new Integer(value));
          }
     }

     public synchronized int getValue()
     {
          return value;
     }
}
```

On the `Observer` side of things, you can create components that redisplay themselves when the `Observable` changes. Listing 9.15 shows an `IntLabel` class that observes an `ObservableInt` and displays its current value.

Listing 9.15 Source Code for *IntLabel.java*

```
import java.awt.*;
import java.util.*;

// IntLabel - a Label that displays the value of
// an ObservableInt.

public class IntLabel extends Label implements Observer
{
     private ObservableInt intValue;      // The value we're observing

     public IntLabel(ObservableInt theInt)
     {
          intValue = theInt;
```

```
// Tell intValue we're interested in it

          intValue.addObserver(this);

// Initialize the label to the current value of intValue

          setText(""+intValue.getValue());
     }

// Update will be called whenever intValue is changed, so just update
// the label text.

     public void update(Observable obs, Object arg)
     {
          setText(((Integer) arg).toString());
     }
}
```

Listing 9.16 shows an `IntTextField` that allows you to change the value of an `ObservableInt`. It will also act as an `Observer` in case another object changes the value.

Listing 9.16 Source Code for *IntTextField.java*

```
import java.awt.*;
import java.util.*;

// IntTextField - a TextField that reads in integer values and
// updates an Observable int with the new value.  This class
// is both a "view" of the Observable int, since it displays
// its current value, and a "controller" since it updates the
// value.

public class IntTextField extends TextField implements Observer
{
     private ObservableInt intValue;

     public IntTextField(ObservableInt theInt)
     {
// Initialize the field to the current value, allow 3 input columns

          super(""+theInt.getValue(), 3);
          intValue = theInt;
          intValue.addObserver(this);     // Express interest in value
     }

// The action for the text field is called whenever someone presses "return"
// We'll try to convert the string in the field to an integer, and if
// successful, update the observable int.

     public boolean action(Event evt, Object whatAction)
     {
          Integer intStr;          // to be converted from a string
```

continues

9

Listing 9.16 Continued

```
          try {     // The conversion can throw an exception
               intStr = new Integer(getText());

// If we get here, there was no exception, update the observable

               intValue.setValue(intStr.intValue());
          } catch (Exception oops) {
// We just ignore the exception
          }
          return true;
     }

// The update action is called whenever the observable int's value changes.
// We just update the text in the field with the new int value

     public void update(Observable obs, Object arg)
     {
          setText(((Integer)arg).toString());
     }
}
```

Putting these objects together in a working applet is trivial. Listing 9.17 shows an applet that demonstrates these objects.

Listing 9.17 Source Code for *ObservableApplet.java*

```
import java.applet.*;

// This class demonstrates the ObservableInt, IntTextField
// and IntLabel classes.

public class ObservableApplet extends Applet
{
     public void init()
     {
          ObservableInt intValue = new ObservableInt(0);

          add(new IntTextField(intValue));
          add(new IntLabel(intValue));
     }
}
```

Using *Observables* for Other Classes

The `Observer` interface is useful in non-graphical applications, too. It allows you to create more modular software by reducing the direct interconnection of components. The `Observer` interface is sort of a one-way interaction. The `Observers` usually know what kind of object they're watching, but the `Observables` usually just know that there are `Observers` watching.

Caution

When you use the `Observer` interface, you gain a lot of flexibility, because objects no longer have to know what objects are watching them. An observed object just sends out a notification that it has changed. You now have a lot of objects that are acting completely on their own, responding to updates and performing their own tasks. You must pay close attention to your object model here. Make sure each object is only performing the tasks it is responsible for. Try to make each object's roles and responsibilities as clear as possible. Otherwise, debugging a system like this will be a nightmare.

Listing 9.18 shows an example `Observable` class that represents an aircraft for a flight tracking system. Notice that none of its instance variables are public. You need to be able to notice when a variable changes value. If your instance variables are all public, any object can come along and change the value without you being notified. By restricting all the variable manipulation to accessor functions (`get`/`set` functions), you maintain the ability to notice when a variable changes.

Tip

When you call `notifyObservers`, you may pass it an object that will be passed to the `update` method in all observers. You can use this object to pass specific information about the update. If you plan to handle multiple types of updates, you should create an event class, similar to the AWT's `Event` class, which tells the `update` method what kind of update it is and which objects are involved.

9

Listing 9.18 Source Code for *Aircraft.java*

```
import java.util.*;

// This class demonstrates an observable object with multiple
// values that can change. If an individual value is changed,
// it calls notifyObservers. You can also change the values in
// bulk using setAll.
//
```

continues

Listing 9.18 Continued

```
// When you create observable classes like this, you can't have
// public variables if you need to know when those varables change.
// Otherwise, if altitude was public, anyone could say:
// aircraft.altitude = 10000;
// and no observers would be notified.

public class Aircraft extends Observable
{
     protected String id;

     protected double latitude;
     protected double longitude;
     protected double altitude;
     protected double speed;

     public Aircraft(String id)
     {
          this.id = id;
     }

     public Aircraft(String id, double lat, double lon, double alt,
          double speed)
     {
          this.id = id;
          this.latitude = lat;
          this.longitude = lon;
          this.altitude = alt;
          this.speed = speed;
     }

     public String getID() { return id; }

     public double getAltitude() { return altitude; }

     public void setAltitude(double newAlt)
     {
          altitude = newAlt;
          setChanged();
          notifyObservers(this);
     }

     public double getLatitude() { return latitude; }

     public void setLatitude(double newLat)
     {
          latitude = newLat;
          setChanged();
          notifyObservers(this);
     }

     public double getLongitude() { return longitude; }

     public void setLongitude(double newLon)
     {
          longitude = newLon;
```

```
            setChanged();
            notifyObservers(this);
        }

        public double getSpeed() { return speed; }

        public void setSpeed(double newSpeed)
        {
            speed = newSpeed;
            setChanged();
            notifyObservers(this);
        }

        public void setAll(double lat, double lon, double alt, double speed)
        {
            this.latitude = lat;
            this.longitude = lon;
            this.altitude = alt;
            this.speed = speed;

            setChanged();
            notifyObservers(this);
        }
}
```

Listing 9.19 shows an example module that watches an `Aircraft` for changes and prints a warning when the altitude is too high.

Listing 9.19 Source Code for *AltitudeMonitor.java*

```
import java.util.*;

// This class demonstrates how you can add new features to an
// application without rewriting a lot of code. In this case,
// this is a module that monitors aircraft altitudes and prints
// out a warning if one gets too high. The aircraft class doesn't
// know anything about this class, their only interaction is
// through the Observer-Observable interface.

public class AltitudeMonitor extends Object implements Observer
{
        double maxAltitude;

        public AltitudeMonitor(double maxAlt)
        {
            this.maxAltitude = maxAlt;
        }

// Somewhere in your application you will have to add code
// to tell this object about new aircraft.

        public void addAircraft(Aircraft newAircraft)
        {
```

9

continues

Listing 9.19 Continued

```
            newAircraft.addObserver(this);
        }

        public void update(Observable obs, Object arg)
        {

// Make sure this update is for an aircraft
            if (!(obs instanceof Aircraft)) return;

            Aircraft ac = (Aircraft) obs;

            if (ac.getAltitude() > maxAltitude) {
                System.out.println("Warning! Aircraft too high!");
                return;
            }
        }
}
```

Figure 9.7 shows the relationship between an altitude monitor and an aircraft.

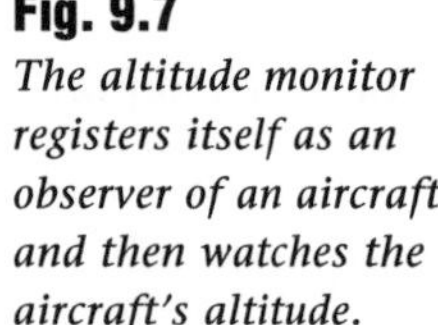

Fig. 9.7
The altitude monitor registers itself as an observer of an aircraft and then watches the aircraft's altitude.

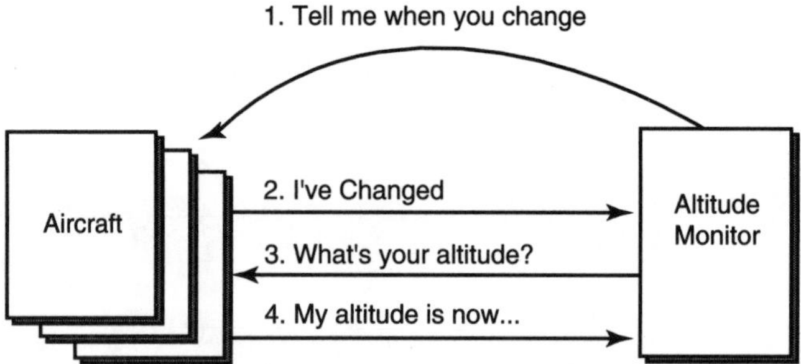

One of the advantages of designing things this way is that `AltitudeMonitor` could be an add-on feature to your tracking system. You could create whole sets of monitors similar to this that your customer could pick from. Notice, however, there's still one little flaw here. When you add a new aircraft, you have to call `addAircraft` in the `AircraftMonitor` object. If you wanted to add new types of monitors, you'd have to call a similar method in the new monitor. This is not good. You want to be able to add a new monitor without adding even one line of code. You can do it, too!

You can create an `AircraftRegistry` class that is an `Observable`. Its job in life is to notify its observers whenever a new aircraft is added. Instead of calling `addAircraft` for each different monitor you have in your system, you just call `addAircraft` in the registry, and it notifies its observers of the new aircraft. Listing 9.20 shows an implementation of an `AircraftRegistry` class. It is implemented as a `singleton` class, which means there is only one in the entire system. A `singleton` class is implemented by keeping a protected static pointer to the lone instance of the class. You also hide the constructor so no one can create their own instance. Then, you create a `static` method that returns the lone instance of the class, creating a new one if there wasn't one already.

Listing 9.20 Source Code for *AircraftRegistry.java*

```
import java.util.*;


// This class provides a way for aircraft monitors to find out
// about new aircraft. It is implemented as a singleton class, which
// means there is only one. Its constructor is protected, so you
// can't create a new AircraftRegistry manually. Any time you need
// the registry, you access it through: AircraftRegistry.instance()

public class AircraftRegistry extends Observable
{

// reference to the single instance of AircraftRegistry in the system

     protected static AircraftRegistry registry;

     protected AircraftRegistry()
     {
     }

// Return the lone instance of this class. If there isn't one, create it.

     public synchronized static AircraftRegistry instance()
     {
          if (registry == null) {
               registry = new AircraftRegistry();
          }

          return registry;
     }

// When an aircraft is added to the system, notify all the interested parties

     public void addAircraft(Aircraft aircraft)
     {
          setChanged();

// Pass the new aircraft to the interested parties
          notifyObservers(aircraft);
     }
}
```

Now, the `AltitudeMonitor` class no longer needs the `AddAircraft` method. Instead, its `update` method has to be smart enough to know whether the update came from an `Aircraft` or from the `AircraftRegistry`. Listing 9.21 shows the updated `AltitudeMonitor` class.

Listing 9.21 Source Code for *AltitudeMonitor2.java*

```
import java.util.*;

// This class demonstrates how you can add new features to an
// application without rewriting a lot of code. In this case,
// this is a module that monitors aircraft altitudes and prints
// out a warning if one gets too high. The aircraft class doesn't
// know anything about this class, their only interaction is
// through the Observer-Observable interface.
//
// This class uses the AircraftRegistry to learn about new aircraft.

public class AltitudeMonitor2 extends Object implements Observer
{
     double maxAltitude;

     public AltitudeMonitor2()
     {
          maxAltitude = 40000.0;
          AircraftRegistry.instance().addObserver(this);
     }

     public AltitudeMonitor2(double maxAlt)
     {
          this.maxAltitude = maxAlt;
          AircraftRegistry.instance().addObserver(this);
     }

     public void update(Observable obs, Object arg)
     {

// See if this update is for an aircraft

          if (obs instanceof Aircraft) {

               Aircraft ac = (Aircraft) obs;

               if (ac.getAltitude() > maxAltitude) {
                    System.out.println(
                         "Warning! Aircraft too high!");
                    return;
               }

// If this update is from the registry, it is telling us about
// a new aircraft, so start observing the new aircraft

          } else if (obs instanceof AircraftRegistry) {
               Aircraft ac = (Aircraft) arg;
               ac.addObserver(this);
          }
     }
}
```

This may seem like a lot of fuss to you, but it makes your software much more modular. The `AircraftRegistry` class provides just the extra level of abstraction to really make this system modular. Now you can add new monitors without changing a line of code anywhere in the program. You can dynamically load new monitors on-the-fly, thanks to Java's class loading interface.

Figure 9.8 shows the relationship between an aircraft, the aircraft registry, and the altitude monitor.

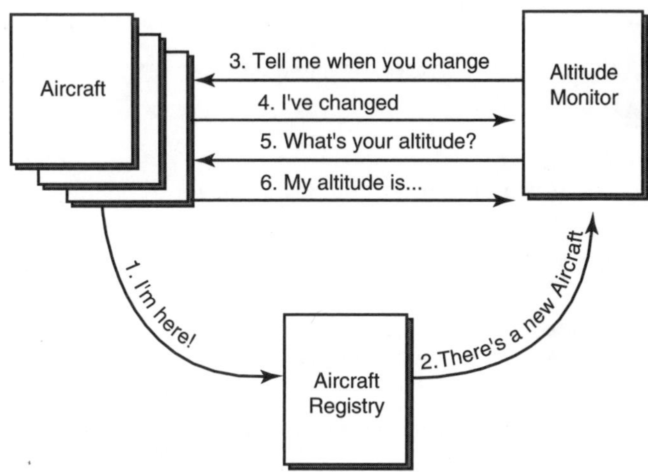

Fig. 9.8
The aircraft registry sends out updates when a new aircraft is created.

Listing 9.22 shows a simple program that tests the interaction between an `Aircraft`, the `AircraftRegistry`, and the `AltitudeMonitor` classes. The `monitors` array contains a list of the aircraft monitors to be loaded, currently just the `AltitudeMonitor2` class. This list could be read in from a file just as easily, so you wouldn't have to recompile even the test program to add new monitors; however, for this demonstration, a static array is sufficient.

9

Listing 9.22 Source Code for *TestMonitor.java*

```
// This class demonstrates the highly dynamic nature of the
// Aircraft, AircraftRegistry, and AltitudeMonitor classes.

public class TestMonitor extends Object
{

// The list of monitors to dynamically load.
     static String monitors[] = { "AltitudeMonitor2" };

// Load the monitors dynamically

     public static void createMonitors()
     {
          for (int i=0; i < monitors.length; i++) {
```

continues

Listing 9.22 Continued

```
                try {

// Use the class loader. If the load fails, print an error message, but
// keep running.
                    Class monClass = Class.forName(monitors[i]);
                    monClass.newInstance();
                } catch (Exception e) {
                    System.err.println("Got error creating class "+
                        monitors[i]);
                    System.err.println(e);
                }
            }
        }

        public static void main(String[] args)
        {

// Dynamically load the aircraft monitors
            createMonitors();

// Create a dummy aircraft
            Aircraft ac = new Aircraft("MW1234NA",
                0.0, 0.0, 10000.0, 400.0);

// Add the dummy aircraft to the system
            AircraftRegistry.instance().addAircraft(ac);

// Play with the altitudes and see if the monitor catches it.

            System.out.println("Setting to 12000");
            ac.setAltitude(12000.0);

            System.out.println("Setting to 48000");
            ac.setAltitude(48000.0);
        }
}
```

The only disadvantage of this program dynamically loading the monitors is that the dynamic loading process can only call the empty constructor for the monitor. You would have to find alternate means of the monitors getting their configuration. Although these examples are fairly specific to a particular application, the concepts apply to a wide range of applications. Use the `Observer-Observable` interface to separate components as much as possible. You will find that it is much easier to plug in new components.

chapter 10

Inter-Applet Communication

10

by Mark Wutka

In this chapter

- **Letting applets interact**
  Applets don't really exist in their own little world. Instead, all the applets on a page run in the same Java virtual machine. This means that applets can communicate with each other, allowing you to create flexible user interfaces.
- **Communicating with pipes**
  The pipe stream classes in Java allow two objects to exchange data using the classes in the `java.io` *package.*
- **Broadcasting data over multiple pipes**
  Using stream filters, you can create a way for an object to send data over many streams at once without having to perform multiple writes.
- **Creating a registry for applets**
  You don't have to use the browser to locate other applets. You can create a central registry where applets, and other objects, can identify themselves by name and be located by other objects.

This chapter deals with the communication between applets running within the same browser. It does not address the problem of sending information between applets running in separate browsers. The two problems are completely different. When two applets are in the same browser, they can communicate using any form of inter-object communication, including direct method calls. Communication between applets in different browsers requires some form of networking and usually an intermediate server. One common form of network communication is Remote Method Invocation (RMI), which is discussed in Chapter 16, "Creating 3-Tier Distributed Applications with RMI."

Locating Other Applets

You will occasionally need to allow two or more applets on a Web page to communicate with each other. Because the applets all run within the same Java context—that is, they are all in the same virtual machine together—applets can invoke each other's methods. The one tricky part is getting the applets in touch with each other. The `AppletContext` class has methods for locating another applet by name, or retrieving all the applets in the current runtime environment. Listing 10.1 shows an applet that examines all the applets in the runtime environment and displays them in a scrolling list.

Listing 10.1 Source Code for *ListApplets.java*

```
import java.applet.*;
import java.awt.*;
import java.util.*;

// This applet demonstrates the use of the getApplets method to
// get an enumeration of the current applets.

public class ListApplets extends Applet
{
     public void init()
     {

// Get an enumeration all the applets in the runtime environment
          Enumeration e = getAppletContext().getApplets();

// Create a scrolling list for the applet names
          List appList = new List();

          while (e.hasMoreElements()) {

// Get the next applet
               Applet app = (Applet) e.nextElement();

// Store the name of the applet's class in the scrolling list
               appList.addItem(app.getClass().getName());
          }

          add(appList);
     }
}
```

Figure 10.1 shows the ListApplets applet on a page with a number of other applets.

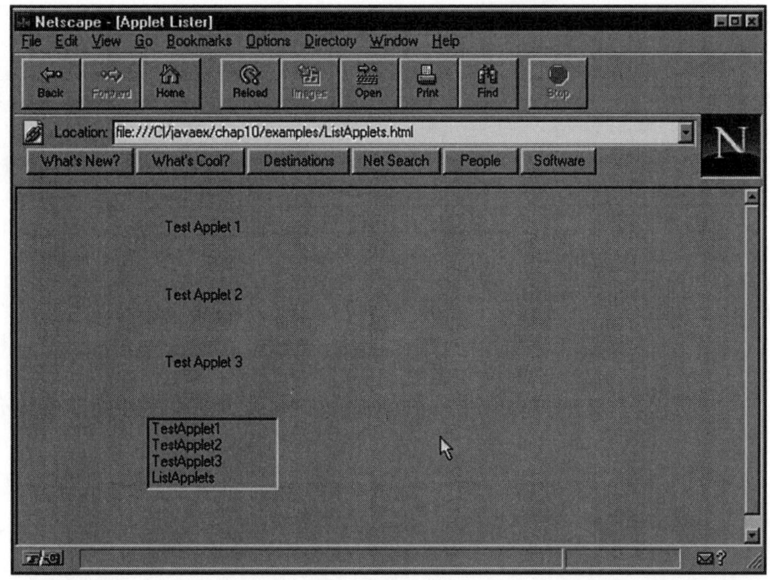

Fig. 10.1
An applet can see what other applets are running on the same page.

> **Note**
> Be prepared to check for an applet again if you can't find it the first time. Your browser may not load applets all at once, or you might dynamically load an applet. You may receive a `NullPointerException` if you try to get an applet that doesn't exist—be prepared to catch it. You may have difficulty distinguishing when an applet hasn't been loaded yet from error situations in which it can't be loaded. Try picking a maximum amount of time you'll wait for an applet to be loaded, and then assume that there's a problem if the applet you want hasn't been loaded after that time.

10

If you already know the name of the applet you want to access, you can locate it with the `getApplet` method. The following code fragment locates an applet named `findme`:

```
Applet findme = getAppletContext().getApplet("findme");
if (findme != null) {
// do something with findme
}
```

You might think that the applet name you use in `getApplet` is the class name of the applet. This is not the case. You set the applet's name in your `<APPLET>` HTML tag. For example, here is the `<APPLET>` tag for an applet class called `FindMe`, which has an applet name of `findme`:

```
<APPLET codebase="." code="FindMe.class" name="findme">]
```

Tip

Only use lowercase names for applets. Some versions of Netscape convert the applet name to lowercase. The name of the applet is separate from the name of the applet's class, so you can still use uppercase letters in the class name.

Exchanging Data Using Piped Streams

Once two applets have located each other, their means of communication is the same as for any two objects in the system. This means they can invoke each other's methods, share common arrays between them, or send data over stream pipes.

A stream pipe is a pair of streams: One is an input stream; the other is an output stream. Any data written to the input stream can be read from the output stream it is connected to. You can use this mechanism to pass data between two applets or any two objects in the system. One object creates both a `PipedInputStream` and a `PipedOutputStream` class, and then passes one end of the pipe to the other object. Whichever object has the output end of the pipe can then start writing to the pipe, while the object that has the input side can start reading.

Tip

Since stream pipes are subclasses of `FileInputStream` and `FileOutputStream`, you can use the existing stream filters to pass different kinds of data. The `DataInputStream` and `DataOutputStream` classes are good for passing simple data types over pipes, while the `ObjectInputStream` and `ObjectOutputStream` are excellent for passing whole objects.

Stream pipes are useful for doing sequenced messaging between objects. Sometimes one object needs to tell another object to perform several tasks in sequence. If some of the tasks take a long time, you don't want the requesting object to have to wait for all the tasks to be performed, yet you want to ensure that they are done in the proper sequence. If the requests are made by sending messages over a stream pipe, the sequencing problem is solved, as is the waiting problem. The requesting object can write all its requests to the `PipedOutputStream` and continue on. The object performing the tasks reads each message from its `PipedInputStream`, performs the requested task, and then reads the next message from the pipe. The messages are guaranteed to be read in the same sequence they were written.

Listing 10.2 shows an applet that creates a stream pipe and passes one end of the pipe to another applet. It demonstrates how to create a pipe and how to wait for an applet to appear. The `SenderApplet` first looks for its companion applet—`ReaderApplet`. Since the sender may be loaded before the reader, it must retry the search if it can't find the reader the first time it checks. It tries once every second for 30 seconds before deciding that the reader isn't going to be loaded.

Once the sender finds the reader, it passes one end of the stream pipe to the reader through a simple method call. If you find that you frequently need to pass stream pipes this way, you should define an interface line this:

```
public interface StreamPipeClient
{
      public void setInputStream(InputStream);
}
```

This frees the sender from having to know the exact class name of the reader. As you can see in Listing 10.2, the sender knows that the reader is an instance of `ReaderApplet`.

Listing 10.2 Source Code for *SenderApplet.java*

```
import java.applet.*;
import java.io.*;

// This applet creates a stream pipe and uses it to pass
// data to another applet. It waits for the other applet to
// be loaded, then invokes a method on that applet to pass it
// the input side of the pipe.

public class SenderApplet extends Applet implements Runnable
{
     protected PipedInputStream inStream;
     protected PipedOutputStream outStream;

     Thread appletThread;

     public void init()
     {
// Create the pipe. It doesn't matter which end you create first, you just
// pass the first end to the constructor of the other end.
          try {
               inStream = new PipedInputStream();
               outStream = new PipedOutputStream(inStream);
          } catch (Exception e) {
               e.printStackTrace();
          }
     }

     public void run()
     {
          Applet app = null;
```

continues

Listing 10.2 Continued

```
        AppletContext context = getAppletContext();

        int tries = 0;     // how many times we've looked

// Start looking for the reader applet

        while (app == null) {

// Try to locate an applet named "reader"

            try {
                app = context.getApplet("reader");

// If we get here and app isn't null, we've found it, break out
// of this while loop
                if (app != null) break;
            } catch (Exception e) {
            }

// We couldn't find the applet. If we've tried 30 times (at once per second)
// we assume it isn't coming up.

            tries++;
            if (tries > 30) {
                return;     // time out after 30 seconds
            }

// Sleep for a second before looking again
            try {
                Thread.sleep(1000);
            } catch (Exception insomnia) {
            }
        }

// Now that we found the applet, cast it to a ReaderApplet so
// we can invoke setInputStream

        ReaderApplet reader = (ReaderApplet) app;

// Give the ReaderApplet the input end of the stream

        reader.setInputStream(inStream);


        while (true) {

// Write byte values of 0-9 to the stream pipe over and over

            for (int i=0; i < 10; i++) {
                try {
                    outStream.write(i);

                    Thread.sleep(1000);

                } catch (Exception ignore) {
                }
```

```
            }
        }
    }

    public void start()
    {
        appletThread = new Thread(this);
        appletThread.start();
    }

    public void stop()
    {
        appletThread.stop();
        appletThread = null;
    }
}
```

Listing 10.3 shows the reader portion of the pipe demonstration. The sender applet had to perform a loop to wait for the reader to become active. The reader has a similar problem—it has to wait for the sender to give it the input end of the pipe. It looks at the input stream once every second, and once the input stream is no longer null, it starts reading data.

Tip

Rather than continually polling to see when the input stream is no longer `null`, the reader could use the wait/notify mechanism. Basically, if the input stream is `null`, the `run` method calls `wait`, which puts its thread to sleep. Then, the `setInputStream` method could call `notify` to wake the `run` method back up so it can start reading again.

Listing 10.3 Source Code for *ReaderApplet.java*

```
import java.applet.*;
import java.awt.*;
import java.io.*;

// This applet is the companion to the SenderApplet. It receives
// an input stream from the sender and begins reading one byte at
// a time, changing a label on the screen to the string representation
// of each byte read so you can see it in action.

public class ReaderApplet extends Applet implements Runnable
{
     protected InputStream inStream;
     protected Thread appletThread;
     protected Label label;
```

continues

Listing 10.3 Continued

```
     public void init()
     {
          label = new Label("X");
          add(label);
     }

// This method will be called by the SenderApplet when it locates this
// applet.

     public void setInputStream(InputStream inStream)
     {
          this.inStream = inStream;
     }

     public void run()
     {

// Wait for the input stream
          while(inStream == null)
          {
               try {
                    Thread.sleep(1000);
               } catch (Exception insomnia) {
               }
          }

// Start reading bytes
          while (true) {

               try {
                    int ch = inStream.read();

// If ch < 0, we hit EOF, indicating some type of shutdown

                    if (ch < 0) return;

// Update the label with the byte we just read
                    label.setText(""+ch);
               } catch (Exception e) {
                    return;
               }
          }
     }

     public void start()
     {
          appletThread = new Thread(this);
          appletThread.start();
     }

     public void stop()
     {
          appletThread.stop();
          appletThread = null;
     }
}
```

Creating Multi-Client Pipes

One of the problems you occasionally run into when doing inter-process communication with streams is that sometimes you need to send the same message to a number of clients. It would be nice if you had a stream that would write a message to a set of streams rather than making you do multiple writes. All you need to do is create an output stream that keeps track of the output streams it needs to copy data to, and then create a write method that writes the same byte to every connected stream.

Listing 10.4 shows a `MultiClientOutputStream` class that enables you to connect up multiple output streams to a single output stream. Whenever you write to it, it copies the data you write to every stream that has been connected.

Listing 10.4 Source Code for *MultiClientOutputStream*

```
import java.io.*;
import java.util.*;

// This class implements an output stream that sends its output
// to any number of client output streams. It allows an object to
// make one write request that gets forwarded to all streams
// connected to this one.

public class MultiClientOutputStream extends OutputStream
{
     protected Vector clients; // The streams connected to this one

     public MultiClientOutputStream()
     {
          clients = new Vector();
     }

     public synchronized void write(int ch)
     {
          Enumeration e = clients.elements();

// It is bad medicine to remove elements from a vector while you are
// still enumerating through it, but we need to remove output streams
// from the client vector when we get write errors on them. We create
// a vector of outputstreams that need to be removed, but it only
// gets created if at least one stream needs to be removed.
// Once we finish iterating through the output streams, we remove the
// dead ones.

          Vector deadElements = null;

          while (e.hasMoreElements()) {

               OutputStream out = (OutputStream) e.nextElement();

               try {
```

continues

10

Listing 10.4 Continued

```
                    out.write(ch);

               } catch (IOException deadStream) {

// If we haven't created the deadElements vector yet, do it now
                    if (deadElements == null) {
                         deadElements = new Vector();
                    }
// Flag this stream as needing to be deleted
                    deadElements.addElement(out);
               }
          }

// If we had any dead elements, remove them from the vector of clients

          if (deadElements != null) {
               e = deadElements.elements();
               while (e.hasMoreElements()) {
                    clients.removeElement(e.nextElement());
               }
          }
     }

// addOutputStream connects a new stream up to the set of clients

     public void addOutputStream(OutputStream out)
     {
          if (!clients.contains(out)) {
               clients.addElement(out);
          }
     }

// removeOutputStream removes a stream from the set of clients (we no
// longer send output to it).

     public void removeOutputStream(OutputStream out)
     {
          clients.removeElement(out);
     }
}
```

Listing 10.5 shows a small test program that illustrates the use of the `MultiClientOutputStream` class.

Listing 10.5 Source Code for *TestMulti.java*

```
import java.io.*;

// This class demonstrates the use of the multi-client output stream.
// It hooks both System.out and System.err to the multi-client stream.
// It then writes information to the multi-client stream, which causes
// the information to appear twice - once when it is copied to System.out,
// the other time when it is copied to System.err.

public class TestMulti extends Object
{
     public static void main(String[] args)
     {
          try {

// Create the multi-client stream
               MultiClientOutputStream out =
                    new MultiClientOutputStream();

// Connect System.out and System.err to the multi-client stream

               out.addOutputStream(System.out);
               out.addOutputStream(System.err);

// Use a PrintStream to write so we can use print and println

               PrintStream printme = new PrintStream(out);

// Write out some test data, it should appear twice

               printme.println("Hello there!");
               printme.println("Is there an echo in here?");

// Test out the fact that if you add a duplicate streams, it still
// only gets one copy of the data.

               out.addOutputStream(System.out);
               printme.println("You should still be seeing double");

// Test the disconnection of an output stream (stop writing to System.err)

               out.removeOutputStream(System.err);
               printme.println("You should only be seeing single");

          } catch (Exception e) {
               e.printStackTrace();
          }
     }
}
```

Figure 10.2 shows the output from the TestMulti application.

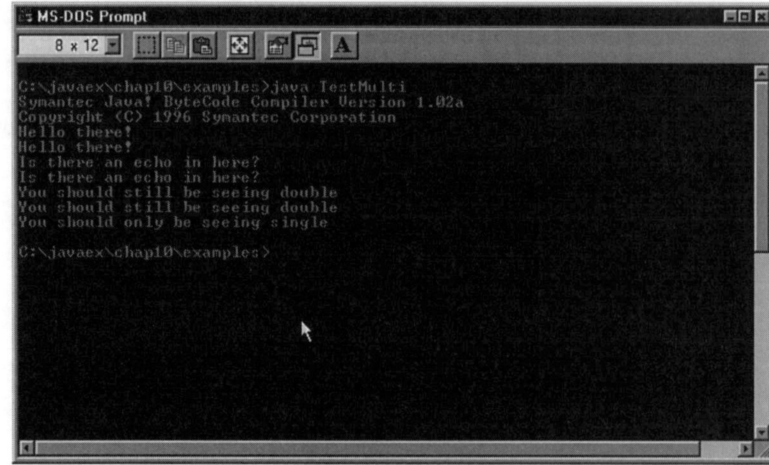

Fig. 10.2
Using the `MultiClient OutputStream`*, you can write data on multiple streams with a single write call.*

Sharing Information with Singleton Objects

If you want to do inter-applet communications, you can take advantage of the fact that because all the applets run in the same instance of the virtual machine, all static class variables are shared between applets. This means you can implement singleton classes that are shared by all the applets. As you recall from Chapter 9, a singleton is a class that has only one unique instance. Its constructor is hidden so classes cannot create new instances. You access the one instance of the class through a static method in the class such as `instance()`. You can create a singleton class that acts as a registry for all the applets in the runtime environment. If the registry is implemented as an observable, you can watch for new applets to become available. This allows two applets to sync up without having to constantly poll the `getApplet` method to see when the applet becomes available.

Listing 10.6 shows an implementation of the `AppletRegistry` class. The applet registry uses a hash table to store applets by name. Whenever you want to find an applet, you call `findApplet` with the name of the applet you're looking for:

```
Applet findit = AppletRegistry.instance().findApplet("FindMeApplet");
```

When an applet starts up, it calls `addApplet`:

```
AppletRegistry.instance().addApplet("FindMeApplet", this);
```

The `AppletRegistry` is observable. Whenever an applet is added or removed, it sends an update to its observers. This allows any object implementing the `Observer` interface to find out whenever an applet is added to the registry. This is a nice alternative to polling the registry for particular applets.

Since the registry sends a notification when applets are added or removed, it uses a simple event mechanism when it sends the notification. The object passed to the update method in the observers is an instance of `AppletRegistryEvent`. This object, in turn, contains the information specific to the event (the name of the applet, the applet itself, and whether it is being added or removed).

Listing 10.6 Source Code for *AppletRegistry.java*

```
import java.applet.Applet;
import java.util.*;

// This class implements an applet registry where applets
// can locate each other. It is an observable, so if you want
// to wait for a particular class, you can be an observer. This
// is better than the polling you have to do with getApplet.
//
// This class is implemented as a singleton, which means there
// is only one. The single instance is kept in a protected
// static variable and returned by the instance() method.

public class AppletRegistry extends Observable
{

// The single copy of the registry
     protected static AppletRegistry registry;

// The table of applets
     protected Hashtable applets;

// Used for generating unique applet names
     protected int nextUnique;

     protected AppletRegistry()
     {
          applets = new Hashtable();
          nextUnique = 0;
     }

// Returns the long instance of the registry. If there isn't a registry
// yet, it creates one.

     public synchronized static AppletRegistry instance()
     {
          if (registry == null) {
               registry = new AppletRegistry();
          }
          return registry;
     }

// Adds a new applet to the registry - stores it in the table and
// sends a notification to its observers.

     public synchronized void addApplet(String name, Applet newApplet)
```

continues

10

Listing 10.6 Continued

```
     {
          applets.put(name, newApplet);
          setChanged();
          notifyObservers(new AppletRegistryEvent(
               AppletRegistryEvent.ADD_APPLET,
               name, newApplet));
     }

// Adds a new applet to the registry - stores it in the table and
// sends a notification to its observers. If uniqueName is false, the
// applet's name is non-unique. Store the applet in a table with a
// unique version of the name (appends <#> to the name where # is
// a constantly increasing number).

     public synchronized void addApplet(String name, Applet newApplet,
          boolean uniqueName)
     {
          if (!uniqueName && (applets.get(name) != null)) {
               name = name + "<"+nextUnique+">";
               nextUnique++;
          }

          applets.put(name, newApplet);
          setChanged();
          notifyObservers(new AppletRegistryEvent(
               AppletRegistryEvent.ADD_APPLET,
               name, newApplet));
     }

// removes an applet from the table and notifies the observers

     public synchronized void removeApplet(Applet applet)
     {
          Enumeration e = applets.keys();

          while (e.hasMoreElements()) {
               Object key = e.nextElement();

               if (applets.get(key) == applet) {
                    applets.remove(key);
                    setChanged();
                    notifyObservers(new AppletRegistryEvent(
                         AppletRegistryEvent.REMOVE_APPLET,
                         (String)key, applet));
                    return;
               }
          }
     }

// removes an applet from the table and notifies the observers

     public synchronized void removeApplet(String name)
     {
          Applet applet = (Applet) applets.get(name);
          if (applet == null) return;
```

```
            applets.remove(name);

            setChanged();
            notifyObservers(new AppletRegistryEvent(
                AppletRegistryEvent.REMOVE_APPLET,
                name, applet));
        }

// finds an applet by name, or returns null if not found

        public Applet findApplet(String name)
        {
            return (Applet) applets.get(name);
        }

// lets you see all the applets in the registry

        public Enumeration getApplets()
        {
            return applets.elements();
        }
}
```

Listing 10.7 shows the implementation of the `AppletRegistryEvent` object used by the `AppletRegistry`. This is an example of how to set up an event that is passed to the `update` method in an observable's observers.

Listing 10.7 Source Code for *AppletRegistryEvent.java*

```
import java.applet.Applet;

public class AppletRegistryEvent extends Object
{
        public final static int ADD_APPLET = 1;
        public final static int REMOVE_APPLET = 2;

        public int id;
        public String appletName;
        public Applet applet;

        public AppletRegistryEvent()
        {
        }

        public AppletRegistryEvent(int id, String appletName, Applet applet)
        {
            this.id = id;
            this.appletName = appletName;
            this.applet = applet;
        }
}
```

Figure 10.3 shows the relationship between applets, the applet registry, and the observers of the registry.

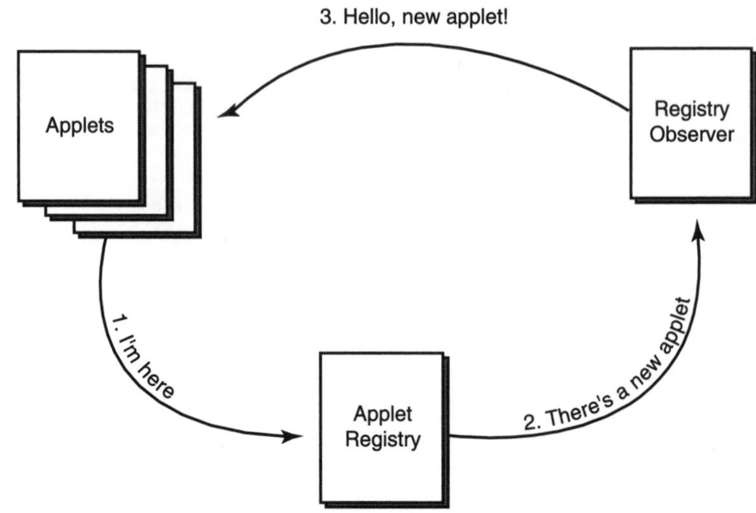

Fig. 10.3
Applets add themselves to the registry, which tells its observers about the new applets.

To take advantage of the `AppletRegistry`, a new applet must register itself by calling the `addApplet` method. Listing 10.8 shows a new version of the `SenderApplet` example from earlier in this chapter. The corresponding `ReaderApplet` only needs to call `addApplet("reader", this)` in its `init` method to support the registry.

Because the new sender applet uses the applet registry, it doesn't have to continually check to see when the reader is loaded. Instead, it waits until it receives an `AppletRegistryEvent` that tells it that the reader applet has been added. Once it learns that the reader has been added, it passes one end of the pipe stream to the reader and starts a thread that writes data to the pipe.

Listing 10.8 Source Code for *SenderApplet2.java*

```
import java.applet.*;
import java.io.*;
import java.util.*;

// This applet creates a stream pipe and uses it to pass
// data to another applet. It waits for the other applet to
// be loaded, then invokes a method on that applet to pass it
// the input side of the pipe.

// Rather than using the standard getApplet method to check
// for the other applet being loaded, it uses the AppletRegistry.
// Also, it doesn't start its thread until the applet has been
// started and an update has been received stating that the
// other applet has been added.

public class SenderApplet2 extends Applet implements Runnable, Observer
{
```

```
    protected PipedInputStream inStream;
    protected PipedOutputStream outStream;

    protected boolean started = false;

    Thread appletThread = null;

    public synchronized void init()
    {
// Create the pipe. It doesn't matter which end you create first, you just
// pass the first end to the constructor of the other end.
        try {
            inStream = new PipedInputStream();
            outStream = new PipedOutputStream(inStream);
        } catch (Exception e) {
            e.printStackTrace();
        }

// Add this applet to the registry
        AppletRegistry.instance().addApplet("sender", this);

// Start watching the registry
        AppletRegistry.instance().addObserver(this);

// If the reader applet is already in the registry, set it up

        Applet applet = AppletRegistry.instance().findApplet("reader");

        if (applet != null) {
            initReader(applet);
        }
    }

// update is called by the registry whenever an applet is added or removed.

    public synchronized void update(Observable obs, Object ob)
    {
        if (!(ob instanceof AppletRegistryEvent)) return;

        AppletRegistryEvent evt = (AppletRegistryEvent) ob;

        if (evt.appletName.equals("reader")) {

            initReader(evt.applet);
        }
    }

    public void initReader(Applet applet)
    {
// Now that we found the applet, cast it to a ReaderApplet so
// we can invoke setInputStream

        ReaderApplet2 reader = (ReaderApplet2) applet;

// Give the ReaderApplet the input end of the stream

        reader.setInputStream(inStream);
```


continues

Listing 10.8 Continued

```
          appletThread = new Thread(this);

          if (started) {
               appletThread.start();
          }
     }

     public void run()
     {
          while (true) {

// Write byte values of 0-9 to the stream pipe over and over

               for (int i=0; i < 10; i++) {
                    try {
                         outStream.write(i);

                         Thread.sleep(1000);

                    } catch (Exception ignore) {
                    }
               }
          }
     }

     public synchronized void start()
     {
          started = true;

// If the applet thread has already been created, start it. This is
// done to synchronize with the update method. We don't know if start
// or update will be called first. This method sets the started flag to
// true, but only starts the thread if it has been created.
// The update method creates the thread, but only starts it if the
// started flag is true.

          if (appletThread != null) {
               appletThread.start();
          }
     }

     public void stop()
     {
          appletThread.stop();
          appletThread = null;
      }
}
```

The reader applet that corresponds to `SenderApplet2` is not too different from the original reader applet. The main difference is that it now adds itself to the applet registry. It still uses a polling mechanism to wait for its input stream. Again, you could use the wait/notify mechanism to keep from polling. Listing 10.9 shows the `ReaderApplet2` applet.

Listing 10.9 Source Code for *ReaderApplet2.java*

```
import java.applet.*;
import java.awt.*;
import java.io.*;

// This applet is the companion to the SenderApplet. It receives
// an input stream from the sender and begins reading one byte at
// a time, changing a label on the screen to the string representation
// of each byte read so you can see it in action.

public class ReaderApplet2 extends Applet implements Runnable
{
	protected InputStream inStream;
	protected Thread appletThread;
	protected Label label;

	public void init()
	{
		label = new Label("X");
		add(label);

		AppletRegistry.instance().addApplet("reader", this);
	}

// This method will be called by the SenderApplet when it locates this
// applet.

	public void setInputStream(InputStream inStream)
	{
		this.inStream = inStream;
	}

	public void run()
	{

// Wait for the input stream
		while(inStream == null)
		{
			try {
				Thread.sleep(1000);
			} catch (Exception insomnia) {
			}
		}

// Start reading bytes
		while (true) {

			try {
				int ch = inStream.read();

// If ch < 0, we hit EOF, indicating some type of shutdown

				if (ch < 0) return;

// Update the label with the byte we just read
```

10

continues

Listing 10.9 Continued

```
                        label.setText(""+ch);
                } catch (Exception e) {
                        return;
                }
        }
    }

    public void start()
    {
        appletThread = new Thread(this);
        appletThread.start();
    }

    public void stop()
    {
        appletThread.stop();
        appletThread = null;
    }
}
```

chapter 11

Sending E-Mail from an Applet

11

by Mark Wutka

In this chapter

- **Sending e-mail from an applet**
  Sometimes, the only way an applet may send information back to a server is via e-mail. Many Internet service providers allow you to create a Web page, but they don't give you a way to run CGI scripts, or any other kind of server-side code. Almost all of them, however, will allow you to send e-mail.
- **Reading your e-mail remotely**
  The Post Office Protocol version 3 (POP3) is a handy Internet protocol that lets you read your mail remotely. You can use this protocol to implement a mail-reader applet, or to programmatically retrieve e-mail sent from applets.

Sending E-Mail

One of the problems you may encounter when designing an application is not being able to run server-side applications. Many Web providers have a limited set of features available for processing form data. If you can't post data to a Web server, you may still be able to receive data from a client applet by sending e-mail.

This solution is not useful if you need to create a form that provides instant feedback. It is useful for creating things like a guest book or an order form.

The idea here is that instead of using an HTTP POST to send data to a server, you e-mail the information instead. This is far less desirable than the post mechanism because you have to write something that goes through your mailbox and extracts the information.

Sending E-Mail Using the SMTP Protocol

The simple mail transfer protocol (SMTP) is surprisingly simple for sending mail messages. A client delivers a mail message to a server by opening a socket connection (a TCP socket) to port 25 on the server. Once the connection is made, the client sends a series of commands, delivers the message, then disconnects.

Tip

The SMTP protocol, like other Internet protocols, is defined in a document called an RFC (Request For Comment). The Internet RFCs are available from a number of sites, and many are in hypertext format. Beware that many of the RFCs are very dry and do not make for good leisure reading. The SMTP protocol is defined in RFC 821.

All commands and responses are terminated by CRLF (in Java, \r\n). For each command the client sends, the server responds with a text response that starts with a 3-digit return code. Return codes in the `200-299` range indicate a successful command. A return code in the `300-399` range indicates that the command was initially successful but that it needs more information to complete. Commands in the `400-499` and `500-599` range indicate errors. An error in the `400-499` range indicates that there was an error on the server (server down, file system full), while errors in the `500-599` range indicate an error on the client side (invalid password, unknown command). This pattern of error codes is used in many Internet protocols.

The format of the return codes is like that of the FTP protocol. If a return code is followed immediately by a '-', the response is multiline (the '-' character is a continuation character). The sequence of messages sent by the client to the server is:

1. "HELO"—a simple greeting from the client to the server. This can also include the host name the client would like to be known by. For example: "HELO mail-o-matic.com". Many servers ignore the alternative host name if it is not a valid name for your host.
2. "MAIL FROM: sender's address"—identifies the user account that is sending this mail. It does not have to be a valid account on the client machine. In other words, you could say that the mail was from an account halfway around the world.

   In case you think this would be a neat way to fake messages from someone, remember that the mail header contains a detailed path of where a message came from, so fake messages can be traced. An example "MAIL FROM" line would be: "MAIL FROM: wutka@netcom.com."

3. "RCPT TO: recipient address"—identifies the address where this mail will be sent. Many mail servers do not need this address to be on the server itself. This allows you to bounce messages from one server to another.

Specifically, if your Web server has a mail server but you want to receive mail from your applets at an account on another host, you should be able to send mail to your alternative account. The format of the address is the same as in the "MAIL FROM" line: "RCPT TO: wutka@netcom.com".

"DATA"—tells the mail server that the client is ready to start sending the body of the mail message. The server should respond with a code in the `300-399` range if this command is successful, indicating that it wants more input—namely, the mail message.

After the `DATA` command, the client sends the mail message one line at a time. When it is finished sending the message, the client sends a "." on a line by itself. If any other line in the message starts with a ".", the client adds an extra "." before the start of the line.

Note

If you want to experiment with the SMTP protocol and see what the responses look like, you can pretend to be a mail server client by using a telnet program and telnetting to port 25 on some mail server. Just enter the SMTP commands manually and hit return after each one.

You should see a response. If you want to abort the message, just disconnect the telnet session sometime before you send the "." to end a message.

Listing 11.1 shows a transcript from an SMTP session performed using the telnet command.

Listing 11.1 An SMTP Telnet Session

```
220-flamingo Sendmail 8.6.12/8.6.9 ready at Sun, 22 Sep 1996 21:26:28 -0400
220 ESMTP spoken here
HELO
250 flamingo Hello contessa [192.0.0.1], pleased to meet you
MAIL FROM: elvis
250 elvis... Sender ok
RCPT TO: mark
250 mark... Recipient ok
DATA
354 Enter mail, end with "." on a line by itself
Subject: Well hey there
```

11

continues

Listing 11.1 Continued

```
Uh huh huh. Thank yuh. Thank yuh very much.
   The King
.
250 VAA07236 Message accepted for delivery
```

Listing 11.2 shows a class that implements a session with an SMTP server. The `sendMessage` method actually sends the message. It automatically closes down the connection if the message is sent correctly, but you need to close it down manually if you get an exception.

Listing 11.2 Source Code for *SMTPSession.java*

```
import java.io.*;
import java.net.*;
import java.util.*;

public class SMTPSession extends Object
{
     public String host;     // Host name we connect to
     public int port;     // port number we connect to, default=25

     public String recipient;
     public String sender;
     public String[] message;

     protected Socket sessionSock;

     protected DataInputStream inStream;
     protected DataOutputStream outStream;

     public SMTPSession()
     {
     }

     public SMTPSession(String host, String recipient,
          String sender, String[] message)
     throws IOException
     {
          this.host = host;
          this.port = 25;     // default SMTP port is 25

          this.recipient = recipient;
          this.message = message;
          this.sender = sender;
     }

     public SMTPSession(String host, int port, String recipient,
          String sender, String[] message)
     throws IOException
     {
```

```
            this.host = host;
            this.port = port;
            if (this.port <= 0) this.port = 25;

            this.recipient = recipient;
            this.message = message;
            this.sender = sender;
        }

// Close down the session

        public void close()
        throws IOException
        {
            sessionSock.close();
            sessionSock = null;
        }

// Connect to the server

        protected void connect()
        throws IOException
        {
            sessionSock = new Socket(host, port);
            inStream = new DataInputStream(
                sessionSock.getInputStream());
            outStream = new DataOutputStream(
                sessionSock.getOutputStream());

        }

// Send a command and wait for a response

        protected String doCommand(String commandString)
        throws IOException
        {
            outStream.writeBytes(commandString+"\n");
            String response = getResponse();
            return response;
        }

// Get a response back from the server. Handles multi-line responses
// and returns them as part of the string.

        protected String getResponse()
        throws IOException
        {
            String response = "";

            for (;;) {
                String line = inStream.readLine();

                if (line == null) {
                    throw new IOException(
                        "Bad response from server.");
                }
```

11

continues

Listing 11.2 Continued

```
// FTP response lines should at the very least have a 3-digit number

               if (line.length() < 3) {
                    throw new IOException(
                         "Bad response from server.");
               }
               response += line + "\n";

// If there isn't a '-' immediately after the number, we've gotten the
// complete response. ('-' is the continuation character for FTP responses)

               if ((line.length() == 3) ||
                    (line.charAt(3) != '-')) return response;
          }
     }


// Sends a message using the SMTP protocol

     public void sendMessage()
     throws IOException
     {
          connect();

// After connecting, the SMTP server will send a response string. Make
// sure it starts with a '2' (reponses in the 200's are positive
// responses.

          String response = getResponse();
          if (response.charAt(0) != '2') {
               throw new IOException(response);
          }

// Introduce ourselves to the SMTP server with a polite "HELO"
          response = doCommand("HELO");

          if (response.charAt(0) != '2') {
               throw new IOException(response);
          }

// Tell the server who this message is from

          response = doCommand("MAIL FROM: " + sender);

          if (response.charAt(0) != '2') {
               throw new IOException(response);
          }


// Now tell the server who we want to send a message to

          response = doCommand("RCPT TO: " + recipient);

          if (response.charAt(0) != '2') {
               throw new IOException(response);
          }
```

```
// Okay, now send the mail message

          response = doCommand("DATA");

// We expect a response beginning with '3' indicating that the server
// is ready for data.

          if (response.charAt(0) != '3') {
               throw new IOException(response);
          }

// Send each line of the message

          for (int i=0; i < message.length; i++) {

// Check for a blank line
               if (message[i].length() == 0) {
                    outStream.writeBytes("\n");
                    continue;
               }

// If the line begins with a ".", put an extra "." in front of it.

               if (message[i].charAt(0) == '.') {
                    outStream.writeBytes("."+message[i]+"\n");
               } else {
                    outStream.writeBytes(message[i]+"\n");
               }
          }

// A "." on a line by itself ends a message.

          response = doCommand(".");

          if (response.charAt(0) != '2') {
               throw new IOException(response);
          }

          close();
     }
}
```

Listing 11.3 shows a sample guest book applet that e-mails its information to a server. As you can see, the bulk of the applet just deals with setting up the screen components. The portion that sends e-mail is fairly small. Notice that the `GuestBookApplet` class uses a grid bag layout to arrange the input fields. When you are creating a simple form with labeled fields, this form of the grid bag works very well. The form is essentially a set of right-justified labels and left-justified input fields. You use the `GridBagConstraints.EAST` anchor value to right-justify a component, and the `GridBagConstraings.WEST` anchor to left-justify a component. Since the left-justified components (the input fields, in this case) are the last components in their respective rows, they will all line up with each other. If you were to do this form as a series of nested panels, you wouldn't be able to guarantee that the input fields would line up.

If you want to set up a completely automated guest book registration, you will also need to write a program to read the guest book e-mail messages and store them somewhere. You could write such a program using the POP3 protocol, which is discussed in the next section. The program could scan through your mail messages looking for those messages with a subject heading that matches the guest book heading (in the case of the `GuestBookApplet` program, it's "GUESTBOOK REGISTRATION").

Listing 11.3 Source Code for *GuestBookApplet.java*

```
import java.applet.*;
import java.awt.*;

// This applet demonsrates the use of the SMTPSession class to
// send e-mail information from an applet. It implements a simple
// guest book that reads a name and e-mail address.

public class GuestBookApplet extends Applet
{
     protected TextField nameField;
     protected TextField emailField;
     protected Button submitButton;

     public void init()
     {

// in order to lay the applet out where there are labels to the
// left of the text fields in a reasonable format, we use the
// GridBagLayout layout manager.

          GridBagLayout layout = new GridBagLayout();
          GridBagConstraints c = new GridBagConstraints();

          setLayout(layout);

          c.weightx = 1.0;
          c.weighty = 1.0;

// Set up a label that is right-justified (anchored EAST) and
// is the second to the last element in a row (RELATIVE)

          Label nameLabel = new Label("Name:");
          c.anchor = GridBagConstraints.EAST;
          c.gridwidth = GridBagConstraints.RELATIVE;
          layout.setConstraints(nameLabel, c);
          add(nameLabel);

// Set up a left-justified text field that is the last element on the row
          nameField = new TextField(30);
          c.anchor = GridBagConstraints.WEST;
          c.gridwidth = GridBagConstraints.REMAINDER;
          layout.setConstraints(nameField, c);
          add(nameField);
```

```
// Again, right-justifies label, second-to last in row
        Label emailLabel = new Label("E-Mail address:");
        c.anchor = GridBagConstraints.EAST;
        c.gridwidth = GridBagConstraints.RELATIVE;
        layout.setConstraints(emailLabel, c);
        add(emailLabel);

// Text field, left justified, last in row
        emailField = new TextField(30);
        c.anchor = GridBagConstraints.WEST;
        c.gridwidth = GridBagConstraints.REMAINDER;
        layout.setConstraints(emailField, c);
        add(emailField);

// Now create a centered Submit button that is the only thing in its row
        submitButton = new Button("Submit");
        c.anchor = GridBagConstraints.CENTER;
        c.gridwidth = GridBagConstraints.REMAINDER;
        layout.setConstraints(submitButton, c);
        add(submitButton);

    }

    public boolean action(Event evt, Object whichAction)
    {

// If someone hits the button, send the registration e-mail
        if (evt.target == submitButton) {
             sendRegistration();
             return true;
        }
        return false;
    }

    protected void sendRegistration()
    {
        String[] emailMessage = new String[3];

// emailMessage contains the text of the message. You have to
// generate your own subject line in SMTP. Use the name and
// the email address as the only two lines in the message body.

        emailMessage[0] = "Subject: GUESTBOOK REGISTRATION";
        emailMessage[1] = nameField.getText();
        emailMessage[2] = emailField.getText();

        try {

// We use dummy e-mail names here, the first one is the name of
// the recpient, the second is the name of the sender. Fill in
// your specific addresses for this applet.

             SMTPSession mailSession = new SMTPSession(
                  getDocumentBase().getHost(),
                  "recipient@somewhere.xxx",
                  "sender@.someplace.yyy",
                  emailMessage);
```

continues

Listing 11.3 Continued

```
// Send the mail message
                mailSession.sendMessage();

// This applet SHOULD display some sort of positive response to
// say that the entry has been submitted, but it doesn't.

            } catch (Exception e) {

// This is a REALLY bogus way to flag an error. You should pop up a
// dialog box or something.

                e.printStackTrace();
            }
        }
}
```

Figure 11.1 shows the guest book in action.

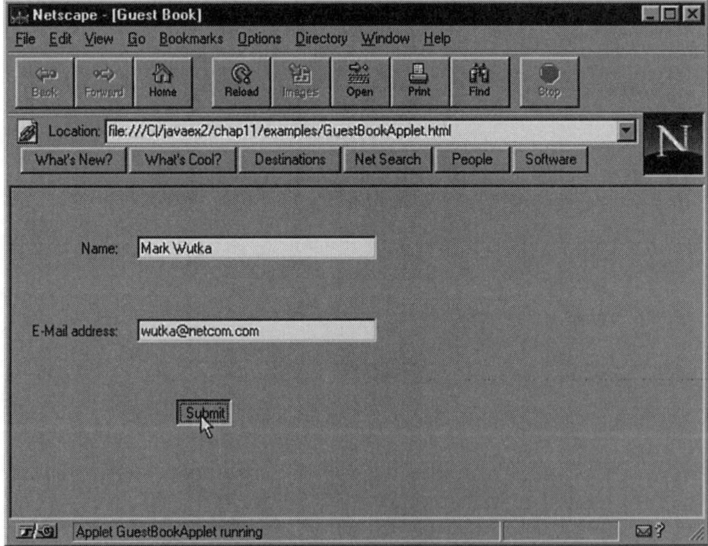

Fig. 11.1
A guest book applet can register guests by sending e-mail.

Accessing Your Mailbox with the POP3 Protocol

The Post Office Protocol version 3 (POP3) allows you to access your mailbox remotely. If you subscribe to an Internet provider and your e-mail is stored on a server, you can read the mail using POP3 without having to copy your entire mailbox down to your local machine. POP3 is defined in RFC 1725.

Unlike some of the other Internet protocols, the POP3 protocol does not use numeric responses. Instead, its responses start with a plus for a successful command or a minus in the case of an error. Also, there are only a few specific circumstances when POP3 returns multiline responses.

These are in the form of multiple lines terminated by a line containing only a period (exactly the same form that is used by the SMTP DATA command). When you connect to a POP3 server, usually at port 110, you send a USER command with the user name of the mailbox you are reading, followed by a PASS command containing the user's password.

Caution

Some mail servers store mail in a different place when you use POP3 to read your mail. If you read your mail using the POP3 protocol, and then you go back to using your normal mail reader, you may suddenly find that your mailbox is completely empty. Don't panic. Your mail has probably been copied to another file. For example, if you have a Netcom shell account, your mail is normally stored in .mailbox/inbox. If you read your mail with POP3, however, your mail is moved to .mailbox/inbox.pop.

Once you have logged on to the POP3 server, you can do the following:

- Retrieve a message count using the STAT command.
- Get a list of active message numbers with the LIST command.
- Examine the beginning of a message with the TOP command (this command is optional according to the standard but should be available on most servers).
- Read an entire message with the RETR command.
- Delete a message with the DELE command.

Listing 11.4 shows a POP3 session performed using telnet. It reads the message sent by the telnet session in Listing 11.1.

Listing 11.4 Telnet Log of POP3 Session

```
+OK flamingo POP3 Server (Version 1.004) ready.
USER mark
+OK please send PASS command
PASS Shhh!!!!
+OK 1 messages ready for mark in /usr/spool/mail/mark
LIST
```

continues

Listing 11.4 Continued

```
+OK 1 messages; msg# and size (in octets) for undeleted messages:
1 461
.
RETR 1
+OK message 1 (461 octets):
X-POP3-Rcpt: mark@flamingo
Return-Path: elvis
Received: from  (contessa [192.0.0.1]) by flamingo (8.6.12/8.6.9)
 with SMTP id VAA07236 for mark; Sun, 22 Sep 1996 21:26:34 -0400
Date: Sun, 22 Sep 1996 21:26:34 -0400
From: elvis@contessa
Message-Id: <199609230126.VAA07236@flamingo>
Subject: Well hey there
Apparently-To: mark@flamingo

Uh huh huh. Thank yuh. Thank yuh very much.
   The King

.
DELE 1
+OK message 1 marked for deletion
LIST
+OK 1 messages; msg# and size (in octets) for undeleted messages:
.
QUIT
+OK flamingo POP3 Server (Version 1.004) shutdown.
```

As you can see, the POP3 protocol has all the ingredients that enable you to make a nice e-mail reader. All you need is a Java class to do the POP3 protocol. Listing 11.3 shows an excerpt from the `POP3Session` class, which uses all of the POP3 commands mentioned above (there are a few more optional ones that haven't been covered). The complete source to the `POP3Session` class is available on the CD that comes with this book. The only part that has been omitted is the section that sets up the host name, port number, user name, and password for the session. The first part of the `POP3Session` class implements the normal `POP3` commands. Each POP3 command is implemented by a separate method. The actual sending and receiving of commands is handled by a small set of methods that understand the format of the methods.

As you will see, most of the methods that implement the POP3 commands are very similar. They all send a command and retrieve a response. Some of them return a string response, some of them return no response, and some of them return an array of strings for commands that give a multiline response. Listing 11.5 gives the source code for the `POP3Session` class.

Listing 11.5 Source Code for *POP3Session.java*

```
import java.io.*;
import java.net.*;
import java.util.*;

// This class implements a POP3 (Post Office Protocol 3) session
// with a mail server. It allows you to create remote mail readers.
// You create a POP3 session by providing a host name and a username/password
// combination for the user whose mailbox you are reading.
// After creating an instance of this class, you must call the connect
// method to actually connect to the server. You must always close the
// connection manually with the close method.

public class POP3Session extends Object
{
     protected Socket pop3Sock;
     protected DataInputStream inStream;
     protected DataOutputStream outStream;

// The host name and port we connect to. Default POP3 port is 110
     public String host;
     public int port;

// The user name and password of the mailbox we want
     public String userName;
     public String password;

     public POP3Session()
     {
     }

     public POP3Session(String host, String userName, String password)
     {
          this.host = host;
          this.port = 110;
          this.userName = userName;
          this.password = password;
     }

     public POP3Session(String host, int port, String userName,
          String password)
     {
          this.host = host;
          this.port = port;
          this.userName = userName;
          this.password = password;
     }

// POP3 positive responses start with a '+', negative responses start with '-'
// isErrorResponse returns true if a response does not start with a '+'

     protected boolean isErrorResponse(String str)
     {
          return str.charAt(0) != '+';
     }
```

11

continues

Listing 11.5 Continued

```
// fetches the current number of messages using the POP3 STAT commant

     public int getMessageCount()
     throws IOException
     {

// Send the command
          String response = doCommand("STAT");

// Check for error
          if (isErrorResponse(response)) {
               throw new IOException(response);
          }

// The format of the response is +OK # other text, we are interested in the
// number after the OK, but we need to stop parsing before the other text.
// We take the substring from offset 4 (the start of the number) and go
// up to the first space, then convert that string to a number.

          try {
               int count = Integer.valueOf(response.substring(4,
                    response.indexOf(' ', 4))).
                    intValue();
               return count;
          } catch (Exception e) {
               throw new IOException("Invalid response - "+response);
          }
     }

// Get headers returns a list of message numbers along with some sizing
// information, and possibly other information depending on the server.

     public String[] getHeaders()
     throws IOException
     {
          String response = doCommand("LIST");

          if (isErrorResponse(response)) {
               throw new IOException(response);
          }

          return getData();
     }

// Get header returns the message number and message size for
// a particular message number. It may also contain other information

     public String getHeader(int messageNumber)
     throws IOException
     {
          String response = doCommand("LIST "+messageNumber);

          if (isErrorResponse(response)) {
               throw new IOException(response);
          }
```

```
          return response;
     }

// Retrieves the entire text of a message using the POP3 RETR command

     public String[] getMessage(int messageNumber)
     throws IOException
     {
          String response = doCommand("RETR "+messageNumber);

          if (isErrorResponse(response)) {
               throw new IOException(response);
          }

          return getData();
     }

// Retrieves the first <linecount> lines of a message using the POP3 TOP
// command. Note: this command may not be available on all servers. If
// it isn't available, you'll get an exception.

     public String[] getMessageHead(int messageNumber, int lineCount)
     throws IOException
     {
          String response = doCommand("TOP "+messageNumber+" "+
               lineCount);

          if (isErrorResponse(response)) {
               throw new IOException(response);
          }

          return getData();
     }

// deletes a particular message

     public void deleteMessage(int messageNumber)
     throws IOException
     {
          String response = doCommand("DELE "+messageNumber);

          if (isErrorResponse(response)) {
               throw new IOException(response);
          }
     }

// Undoes any pending deletions

     public void reset()
     throws IOException
     {
          String response = doCommand("RSET");

          if (isErrorResponse(response)) {
               throw new IOException(response);
          }
     }
```


continues

Listing 11.5 Continued

```
// Initiates a graceful exit

     public void quit()
     throws IOException
     {
          String response = doCommand("QUIT");

          if (isErrorResponse(response)) {
               throw new IOException(response);
          }
     }

// Connects to the POP2 server and logs on with the USER and PASS commands

     public void connect()
     throws IOException
     {

// Make the connection
          pop3Sock = new Socket(host, port);
          inStream = new DataInputStream(pop3Sock.getInputStream());
          outStream = new DataOutputStream(pop3Sock.getOutputStream());

// Send a logon (USER) command
          String response = doCommand("USER "+userName);
          if (isErrorResponse(response)) {
               throw new IOException(response);
          }

// Send a PASS command
          response = doCommand("PASS "+password);
          if (isErrorResponse(response)) {
               throw new IOException(response);
          }
     }
```

Notice that there is a lot of repetition in the methods that perform the different POP3 commands. These methods all use the `doCommand` method to send a command and then use `isErrorResponse` to see if the command resulted in an error. You could combine these steps into a single method. In addition, the POP3 commands either return a string, an array of strings, an integer, or no value. You could create command methods that execute POP3 commands and return each of these result types. In general, you do this kind of grouping if you have a large number of each command type. If you only have one or two, it may not be worth the effort, unless you think that there may be more in the future.

The rest of the `POP3Session` class deals with establishing a connection and the sending and receiving of data. For most Internet protocols, you use the same format, or a small group of formats for all commands. You take advantage of this fact by writing methods that send commands in the format that the protocol expects.

In the case of the POP3 protocol, every command returns a one-line response. The `doCommand` method sends a command string and waits for the response line. You can determine whether a response line is an error response by using the `isErrorResponse` method.

Several POP3 commands also return multiple lines after the initial response. When you receive a '.' by itself on a line, you have reached the end of the response. Since a mail message might contain a '.' on a line by itself, POP3 specifies that any line beginning with a '.' will have an extra '.' at the beginning. The POP3 method handles these multi-line responses and returns an array of strings containing the lines in the response as shown in Listing 11.5.

Listing 11.5 Source Code for *POP3Session.java*

```
// Connects to the POP2 server and logs on with the USER and PASS commands

    public void connect()
    throws IOException
    {

// Make the connection
        pop3Sock = new Socket(host, port);
        inStream = new DataInputStream(pop3Sock.getInputStream());
        outStream = new DataOutputStream(pop3Sock.getOutputStream());

// Send a logon (USER) command
        String response = doCommand("USER "+userName);
        if (isErrorResponse(response)) {
            throw new IOException(response);
        }

// Send a PASS command
        response = doCommand("PASS "+password);
        if (isErrorResponse(response)) {
            throw new IOException(response);
        }
    }
// Shuts down the connection immediately. You should call this if you
// get an exception.

    public void close()
    throws IOException
    {
        pop3Sock.close();
        pop3Sock = null;
    }

// Sends a POP3 command and retrieves the response
    protected String doCommand(String command)
    throws IOException
    {
        outStream.writeBytes(command+"\n");
        String response = inStream.readLine();
        return response;
    }
```

11

continues

Listing 11.5 Continued

```
// Retrieves a multi-line POP3 response. If a line contains "." by itself,
// it is the end of the response. If a line starts with a ".", it should
// really have two "."'s We strip off the leading "."

     protected String[] getData()
     throws IOException
     {

// Don't know how many lines we're getting, so put them in a vector first
          Vector lines = new Vector();

          String line;

// Read lines from the server
          while ((line = inStream.readLine()) != null) {

// If we get a "." on a line by itself, that's the end of the multi-line
// response. Create a string array and copy the lines of the response
// into it.
               if (line.equals(".")) {

// Create the array to return
                    String response[] = new String[
                         lines.size()];

// Copy the strings from the vector into the array
                    lines.copyInto(response);
                    return response;
               }

// If a line starts with a ".", strip it off.

               if ((line.length() > 0) && (line.charAt(0) == '.')) {
                    line = line.substring(1);
               }
               lines.addElement(line);
          }
          throw new IOException("Connection closed.");
     }
}
```

Note

Remember that applets are usually restricted to making socket connections only to the host they were loaded from. This means that your applet must be loaded from the POP3 server for you to use the `POP3Session` class in an applet. This is not unreasonable, however, since many Web servers also run the POP3 service for local e-mail accounts.

Listing 11.6 shows a very simple application that tests the features of the `POP3Session` class. Remember to replace `YourPOP3Server`, `YourUserName`, and `YourPassword` with your own values.

Listing 11.6 Source Code for *TestPOP3.java*

```
public class TestPOP3 extends Object
{
     public static void main(String[] args)
     {
          try {
               POP3Session pop3 = new POP3Session("YourPOP3Host",
                    "YourUserName", "YourPassword");
// Connect to the server
               pop3.connect();

// Get a message count
               System.out.println("There are "+pop3.getMessageCount()+
               " messages.");

// Get a list of messages (the results look pretty boring)
               String[] headers = pop3.getHeaders();

               System.out.println("Message headers:");

               for (int i=0; i < headers.length; i++) {
                    System.out.println(headers[i]);
               }

// Try fetching message #1, hopefully there will be one

               String[] message = pop3.getMessage(1);
               System.out.println("Message #1");

               for (int i=0; i < message.length; i++) {
                    System.out.println(message[i]);
               }

// Try fetching message #99. Unless your mailbox is really full, there won't
// be one. We are expecting that and we try to cetch the exception.

               try {
                    String header = pop3.getHeader(99);
               } catch (Exception e) {
                    System.out.println("Got error getting message #99, good!");
               }

// Tell the server we're through
               pop3.quit();

// Close down the socket
               pop3.close();
          } catch (Exception e) {
```

11

continues

Listing 11.6 Continued

```
// If we get any error at all, just print a stack trace

                e.printStackTrace();
            }
        }
}
```

chapter 12

Protecting Applet Code

12

by Mark Wutka

In this chapter

- **Why protect your code?**
  While the overall spirit of the Internet involves the free exchange of information and ideas, there are times when you want to protect your code.
- **Copyrighting your code**
  In addition to the normal steps you can take in filing for a copyright, you should also put copyrights in your code. There are a number of ways you can do this.
- **Locking your applet to a site**
  If your applet should be run only from a particular Web server, you can put checks in your code to make sure that the applet was loaded from the correct Web server.
- **Hiding information**
  The techniques of hiding information in a program are almost a science. Because of the way Java stores programs, it is harder to hide information in a Java program.

Protecting Your Code from Unauthorized Use

Although many people put their applets out on the Web for free, you may not want someone else to take your applet and use it on their own Web page. Some people are critical of protective attitudes but it is completely your choice.

You may have put in a lot of hard work and you don't want someone else taking advantage of your work for free. Or you may be developing a commercial applet that your customers will be paying for. They don't want to pay a lot of money only to have a competitor use the same applet for free.

The downloadable aspect of Java makes copyright protection much harder. With traditional software packages, you can protect your software from unauthorized use through authorization keys, license servers, and other means. This doesn't work so well for Java, however, because the people who end up running your applet may not be the people who paid for its development.

If you developed a cool applet for some big corporation's Web page, they probably paid for it. But the people who run the applet are the people who visit the Web page. They have to be able to run the applet unrestricted.

Caution
If you intend to take legal recourse if your code is stolen or misused, be sure to consult a lawyer before making the software available on the Web. Many firms specialize in copyright and intellectual property laws, and can advise you on the best ways to protect yourself.

Embedding Copyrights in Your Code

The first step to take in protecting your code is to embed a copyright statement in your code warning against unauthorized redistribution. Try to make it as plain as possible. Also, put a notice in the source for your Web page.

Note
If you don't want your code misused, make that point very plain. If someone has to go digging through your code or through a lengthy license agreement just to find out that they can't use it, they probably won't take the time to look. They'll use it anyway.

Many people who use others' applets don't steal them intentionally. They just assume that the applets can be reused freely, since so many on the Web can be.

You might include a copyright statement in your code this way:

```
char copyright = "Copyright (c) 1996 by Mark Wutka - "+
      "Unauthorized distribution is forbidden. For questions "+
      "about licensing this code, send mail to wutka@netcom.com.";
```

You should also include a similar copyright on your Web page:

```
<! Copyright (c) 1996 blah blah blah >
```

If you want to ensure that the copyright notice has been retained on the Web page, you can turn the copyright into a parameter and make the applet check for it. For example:

```
<APPLET codebase="." code="VerifyCopyright.class width=200 height=200>
<PARAM name="copyright" value="Copyright (c) 1996 by Mark Wutka - All Rights
➥Reserved">
```

Your applet then checks for the `copyright` parameter:

```
import java.applet.*;

public class VerifyCopyright extends Applet
{
     public String copyright =
          "Copyright (c) 1996 by Mark Wutka - All Rights Reserved";

     public void init()
     {
          String copyrightParam = getParameter("copyright");
          if ((copyrightParam == null) || !copyrightParam.equals(
               copyright)) {
               throw new SecurityException("Invalid Copyright");
          }

     }
}
```

This doesn't stop someone who's clever enough to change the copyright statement in your code, however. But it does remind someone to include the copyright on their Web page if they use your applet.

Verifying the Origin of the Applet

One very effective way of ensuring that your applet isn't misappropriated accidentally is to check the location from which the applet was loaded. In your `init` method, call `getDocumentBase` and check to see that the host name is the host name of your Web page.

If you use a public Web provider, you may also want to check the file name since someone else on your Web provider could be using your applet. The following code fragment verifies the origin of the applet:


```
public void init()
{
     if (!getDocumentBase().getHost().equals("www.webcom.com")) {
          throw new SecurityException("Unauthorized Applet Use!");
     }
```

Although this will protect you from someone accidentally using your code without your permission, it does not help when someone intentionally reuses your applet. A code thief could easily disassemble your program and either change the host name in the check, or remove the check completely. To protect yourself against intentional misuse, you can try hiding the security checks in your code.

Hiding Information in Your Applet

If someone wants to hack into your applet to get around your security or figure out one of your complex algorithms, they will. Accept that fact right now and you'll save yourself a lot of disappointment later.

The best you can do is to make it more costly to get around the security than to write the applet in the first place. One of the most popular techniques for doing this is called *obfuscation.*

Obfuscation is intentional misdirection in your code. It is like encryption except that the code is never decrypted.

Typical forms of obfuscation include meaningless loops, tests, computations, function names that have nothing to do with the function, very long functions that do a lot of unnecessary things or are interspersed with unnecessary things, and strange interactions between variables and functions.

There is a market for good code obfuscators, because obfuscation by hand frequently leads to bigger, slower programs. An ideal obfuscator would make your program terribly confusing while not increasing the size, the speed, or the correctness of the program. Keep your eye out for such obfuscators if you are worried about someone stealing your code.

Note

There is no such thing as security by obscurity. Don't think that you can hide a password in your code without someone figuring it out. Just because you can come up with a function that you wouldn't be able to unravel doesn't mean someone else can't figure it out. You would be amazed at the things people can figure out when deciphering code.

If you need secure transactions, such as banking funds transfers, don't even think about obfuscation. Use a secure, encrypted protocol and a signed applet. This is discussed later in this book.

Obfuscating a Working Program

Although you can't absolutely protect information in your code without some form of encryption, you can make it hard to unravel. In lieu of an object-code obfuscator or an obfuscating compiler, you can use some techniques on your code to make it harder to read.

Tip

Don't try to build obfuscation into your program from the start. It will take you forever to debug. Start with a good, easy-to-read program, get it working, and then start applying obfuscation techniques.

Make All Your Function and Variable Names Meaningless

Variable names like `extraShips` or `maxMissiles` are easy targets for someone who wants to hack your game program to make it easier to play. This shouldn't be a concern if the game is a stand-alone game.

If someone wants to cheat, that's their concern. However, if you are writing a networked game or you have a central repository for the high scores of your game, you want to make it harder to cheat.

You can do this by changing all your variable and method names to things like `xx1y` and `zzqb`. You can make a simple editing script to go through and change the real names to the obfuscated ones before you compile the release version of your program. You must, however, always keep a real copy available.

No one wants to debug obfuscated source code. Some of us have trouble figuring out why we did something in a plainly readable source file!

Perform Occasional Useless Computations or Loops

If someone is trying to unravel a complex algorithm, you may want to throw garbage into the middle. Just make sure that you aren't killing your applet's performance. When you do useless computations, you might take advantage of various mathematical properties.

For example, shifting a value left 1 bit is the same as multiplying by two. Shifting 1 bit to the right is the same as dividing by 1. You can multiply a number by any value using a combination of adds and bit shifts.

Suppose you want to multiply a number by 12. Find all the powers of 2 that add together to make 12—in this case, 4 and 8. Every number will have exactly one combination like this. Now, to multiply a number by 4, you shift it left 2 bits. To multiply by 8, you shift it left by 3 bits. Thus, `x * 12` can be written as `(x << 3) + (x << 2)`.

To use this for obfuscation, take the simple equation

```
int c = a + b;
```

You can rewrite `b` as `(13*b)-(12*b)`, then replace the `12*b` with some bit shifts, leading to:

```
int c = a + (13*b) - (b << 4) - (b << 2);
```

You can also use the principle that the sum of the numbers between 0 and n (including n) is `n * (n + 1) / 2`. The following example illustrates how this might add to the confusion:

```
int sum = 0;
for (int i=0; i<= n; i++) {
      sum += i * n;
}
sum /= (n * (n + 1)) >> 1;
```

Would you have guessed that this is the equivalent of the following statement:

```
int sum = n;
```

Remember that this kind of obfuscation increases the size of your code and makes it slower. Don't add loops like this when you have to do the computation many times.

Hide Small Numbers in Strings

Suppose you have written a shoot-em-up space game in which each player gets five ships. No matter how you change your variables, if users see something like

```
static int fdkj = 5;
```

they are going to try to change that value and see if it changes the number of ships. For small values, you can hide the values inside strings. For example, you might have a string like

```
static String alert = "Exception in computation.";
```

which looks like an unobfuscated error message. The letter 'E' has an ASCII value of 69, meaning that you can use `'E' - 64` as the number of ships:

```
int ships = alert.charAt(0) - (1 << 6); // ('E' - 64 or 5)
```

Of course, you would obscure the variable name of `ships`.

Create Large Methods

This may be one of the hardest parts of code obfuscation since you tend to create a lot of small, specialized methods. If someone is trying to unravel your code, they may pick one method at a time, figure out what it does, then assign it a meaningful name wherever it is used.

You can discourage this by "unrolling" your methods where they are called. In other words, take the code that is in the method and insert it in place of the method call. For example, if you originally had the following method:

```
public int computeAverage(int values[])
{
     int sum = 0;
     for (int i=0; i < values.length; i++) {
          sum += values[i];
     }
     return sum / values.length;
}
```

You would replace every occurrence of the call to `computeAverage` with the code from the method, preferably with an obfuscated name for the `sum` variable.

Spread Methods Out Among Subclasses

Rather than grouping all your methods into one object, you can split the object using inheritance and implement methods in different classes. This makes it much harder to find a particular method when you are trying to trace the code. As with several other obfuscation methods, this tends to slow the code down and uses up more memory, since the runtime must now keep track of several classes.

 **Note**

The problem of code obfuscation is a hot topic. It has been rumored that Sun may start building an obfuscator into the Java compiler that ships with the Java Development Kit. This has yet to come about, however.

Using a Commercial Obfuscator

There was a flurry of debate on the Internet after the introduction of a very successful Java decompiler called Mocha. It was able to take a .class file and turn it into a very readable Java source file. It didn't always reproduce the original source code exactly, and comments were missing, of course, but the program worked well enough to cause great concern among Java developers.

You can try Mocha for yourself. It is available for free at **http://web.inter.nl.net/users/H.P.van.Vliet/mocha.htm**. Keep in mind, however, that many source code licenses, including those from Sun, prohibit you from decompiling or disassembling any of their code. The purpose of such a restriction is usually to prevent code theft. Many times, a company won't mind if you are doing the disassembly just to find out how something works or even to fix a crucial bug.

While Mocha was causing a storm in the Java community, its author was busy working on the counterpart to Mocha, which is called Crema. The Crema program is a code obfuscator, and does a very good job at jumbling up a .class file. Unlike Mocha, Crema is not free, but you can download it for evaluation purposes. The Crema Web page is located at **http://web.inter.nl.net/users/H.P.van.Vliet/crema.html**. Obfuscating your code may be a very tough thing for you to do. Hopefully you won't have to do it very often. After all, the Internet fosters a spirit of information sharing, not hiding.

PART II

Java Applications

chapter 13

Running Applets as Applications

by Mark Wutka

In this chapter

- **Applets versus applications**
  Every Java programmer is familiar with the fact that applets usually run within a browser, and applications run as stand-alones. The actual differences between the two is not as well known. Once you know what differentiates an applet from an application, you can see how an applet could run as a stand-alone application.
- **Allowing an applet to run as an application**
  If you have a very simple applet, you may not need to provide a full-featured environment in order to run it stand-alone. In many cases, the only applet features you are using are those common to all AWT containers.
- **The applet's runtime environment**
  An applet relies on certain parts of its environment to be present. The browser usually supplies these elements, which are accessed through the `java.applet` *package.*
- **Creating an applet context**
  The applet context is the key to running applets as stand-alone applications. Once you can create your own working applet context, you have an environment where you can run any applet.

Differences Between Applets and Applications

Although there are many differences between the capabilities of applets and of applications in terms of security restrictions, there are very few environmental differences between the two. You can actually run an applet as a stand-alone application with just a few minor additions.

Applets automatically have a parent frame when they are loaded. When you run a stand-alone application, however, you have to create your own frame.

Applets also have the notion of document-base and code-base URLs, as well as an application context. This context represents the browser itself and supplies methods to load sound files, fetch images, and open other documents.

One of the biggest differences between an applet and an application is something that you might never think of. An applet has a network-aware class loader. When an applet needs to load a class, its class loader goes over the network to get it. The system class loader that is used by applications does not do this. If you want a stand-alone application to load classes over a network, you must write your own class loader to do it. The section "A Zipfile Class Loader" in Chapter 21, "Download Strategies," shows you how to write your own class loader.

Applets are, of course, intended to run inside Web browsers. In fact, you cannot run a stand-alone application in a Web browser, only an applet. You can, however, run an applet outside of a Web browser. You simply have to implement the same kind of framework that the browser provides automatically.

There are some benefits to being able to run an applet as a stand-alone application. If you always write your user interfaces as applets, you can run them inside of a browser or stand-alone without changing your code. This means that you never have to go in and change your code to run inside a browser, or to run stand-alone. Each time you write a new user interface, it is automatically ready to run wherever it is needed.

Note

The term application, when used in conjunction with Java, usually indicates a program running stand-alone. The term applet always refers to a program running within a browser. Unfortunately, this separation implies that the two are always separate things. A distributed application, in the traditional sense, is made up of many components. In the Java world, some of these components may be applets, and some may be stand-alone applications, but they all fit together to make a distributed application.

Allowing an Applet to Run as an Application

You can run almost any applet as an application but some are easier than others. If your applet does not use the `getDocumentBase`, `getCodeBase`, or any of the `AppletContext` methods, you may be able to get away with creating a frame and launching the applet in the frame. In these cases, the applet is little more than a typical AWT container (remember, the `Applet` class is a subclass of `java.awt.Panel`).

Applets are first initialized by the `init` method, then started by the `start` method. Applications, on the other hand, are initialized and started with a static method called `main`. Fortunately, these methods can peacefully coexist in the same class.

By adding a `main` method that automatically creates a frame and adds the applet to the frame, you make your applet run either as an applet or as an application. Listing 13.1 shows a simple applet that will also run as an application.

Listing 13.1 Source Code for *StandaloneApplet.java*

```
import java.awt.*;
import java.applet.*;

// StandaloneApplet is an applet that runs either as
// an applet or a standalone application.  To run
// standalone, it provides a main method that creates
// a frame, then creates an instance of the applet and
// adds it to the frame.

public class StandaloneApplet extends Applet
{
     public void init()
     {
          add(new Button("Standalone Applet Button"));
     }

     public static void main(String args[])
     {
// Create the frame this applet will run in
          Frame appletFrame = new Frame("Some applet");

// The frame needs a layout manager, use the GridLayout to maximize
// the applet size to the frame.
          appletFrame.setLayout(new GridLayout(1,0));

// Have to give the frame a size before it is visible
          appletFrame.resize(300, 100);

// Make the frame appear on the screen. You should make the frame appear
// before you call the applet's init method. On some Java implementations,
// some of the graphics information is not available until there is a frame.
// If your applet uses certain graphics functions like getGraphics() in the
// init method, it may fail unless there is a frame already created and
// showing.
          appletFrame.show();

// Create an instance of the applet
          Applet myApplet = new StandaloneApplet();

// Add the applet to the frame
          appletFrame.add(myApplet);

// Initialize and start the applet
          myApplet.init();
```


continues

Listing 13.1 Continued

```
            myApplet.start();

      }
  }
```

Figure 13.1 shows `StandaloneApplet` running within a Web browser, while Figure 13.2 shows it running as a stand-alone application.

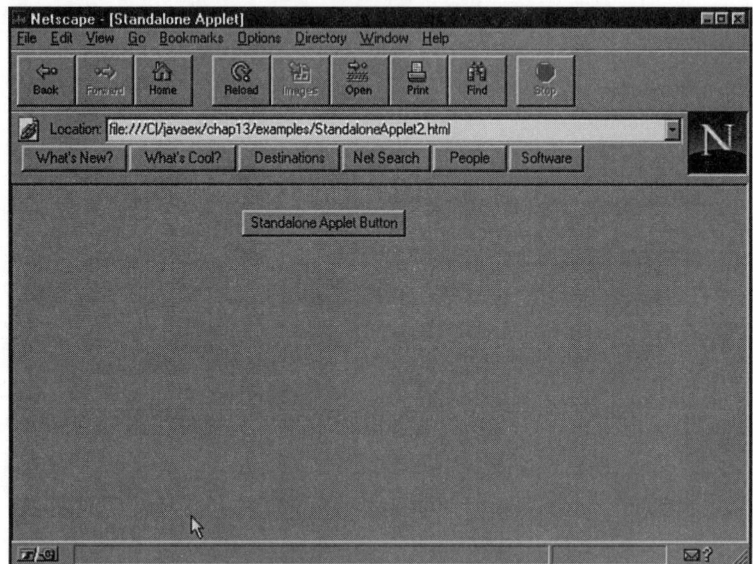

Fig. 13.1
Many applets act as simple AWT containers.

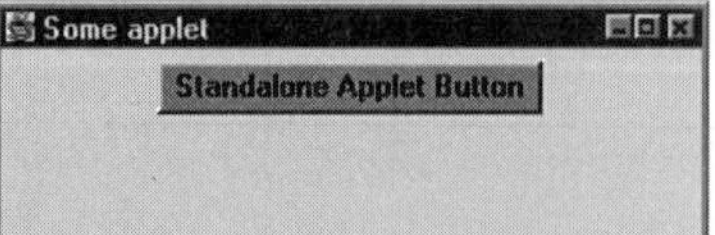

Fig. 13.2
Sometimes a simple frame is all you need to run an applet stand-alone.

The Applet's Runtime Environment

An applet is itself just an AWT container with a few extra methods for interacting with its runtime environment. Most of the applet's other methods are really implemented by three interfaces—`AppletStub`, `AppletContext`, and `AudioClip`.

The `AppletStub` interface is used by a browser or other applet environment to give the `Applet` class access to its environment. The applet stub defines methods for determining the applet's document base and code base (the URLs from which the applet's parent document and .class file were loaded), the applet's parameters (usually specified by the `<PARAM>` HTML tag), and the applet's context.

The `AppletContext` interface provides an applet with methods for loading images and audio clips, as well as opening up new URLs in the browser, and finding out what other applets are running in the current environment. Each browser has its own `AppletContext` class that knows how to perform specific tasks within the browser. When a browser loads an applet, it calls `setStub` in the `Applet` object, which sets the applet's stub (as you might guess). This stub, in turn, has a method called `getAppletContext`, which returns the applet's `AppletContext` object. If you want to implement your own `AppletContext` object, you must also create your own `AppletStub` object. Otherwise, there would be no way to associate your `AppletContext` object with an applet—there's no `setAppletContext` method in the `Applet` class.

Note

As an applet programmer, you never access the `AppletContext` and `AppletStub` interfaces directly. The `Applet` class presents all the methods available in the `AppletContext` and `AppletStub` interfaces. The methods in the `Applet` class simply call the corresponding methods in the `AppletContext` and `AppletStub` interfaces. This technique is called *delegation*.

Figure 13.3 shows the relationship between the `Applet`, the `AppletStub`, and the `AppletContext`.

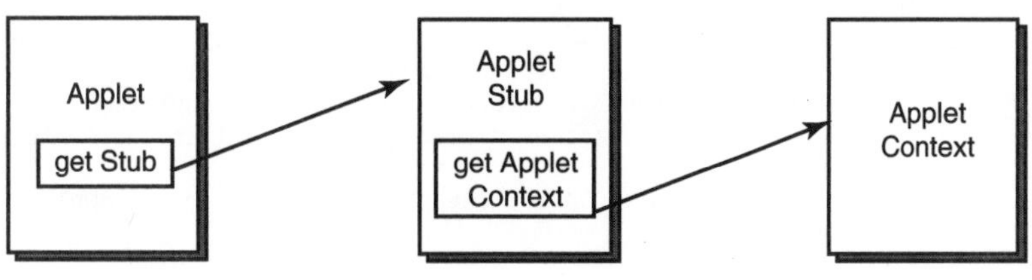

Fig. 13.3
The applet stub is directly associated with the applet, and provides access to the applet context.

If you look at the `Applet` class, you'll notice that it has methods for playing audio clips. Like most of the other methods provided by the `Applet` class (with the exception of the AWT container methods), the audio methods simply call methods in the `AudioClip` interface.

Creating an Applet Context

When you create an applet manually and add it to a frame, the applet is missing some key information that it may rely on. Many applets make use of the `getDocumentBase` and `getCodeBase` methods, as well as some methods in the `AppletContext` class. If you want to run an applet stand-alone that uses these methods, you have to create an applet stub and an applet context for the applet.

The applet stub interface defines a set of methods that an applet uses to get information about where it was loaded from. The `getCodeBase`, `getDocumentBase`, and `getParameter` methods in the applet class actually go to the applet's stub to get these pieces of information.

In addition, the applet stub is responsible for finding the `AppletContext` object for the applet. The `AppletContext` object has methods for fetching images and sound clips, opening up URLs in the browser, and displaying status messages in the browser's status window area (on Netscape, this is at the bottom of the browser). The `AppletContext` also provides methods to locate other applets running within the browser.

Listing 13.2 shows the `RunAppletContext`, which implements an `AppletContext` that can be used to run almost any applet in a stand-alone application.

Listing 13.2 Source Code for *RunAppletContext.java*

```
import java.applet.*;
import java.util.*;
import java.awt.*;
import java.net.*;

// This class provides a generic applet context for standalone
// applications. It is implemented as a singleton object, which
// means that there is only one instance of this class within the
// runtime environment. It stores all the loaded applets in a
// hash table so it can provide working getApplet and getApplets methods.

public class RunAppletContext extends Object implements AppletContext,
     AudioClip
{

// The pointer to the lone instance of this class
     protected static RunAppletContext context;

// The table of all the known applets in the runtime environment.
     protected Hashtable applets;

     protected RunAppletContext()
     {
          applets = new Hashtable();
     }
```

```
// Returns the lone instance of the RunAppletContext. If there isn't
// an instance, it creates a new one.

     public synchronized static RunAppletContext instance()
     {
          if (context == null) {
               context = new RunAppletContext();
          }
          return context;
     }

// Adds an applet to the table of known applets

     public void addApplet(Applet applet, String name)
     {
          applets.put(name, applet);
     }

// Locates an applet in the table

     public Applet getApplet(String name)
     {
          return (Applet) applets.get(name);
     }

// Returns an enumeration of all the known applets

     public Enumeration getApplets()
     {
          return applets.elements();
     }

// Tries to load an audio clip using Sun's AppletAudioClip
// which is distributed with the JDK. This class may not be
// available in all Java implementations since it is not a
// documented part of the JDK.

     public AudioClip getAudioClip(URL url)
     {
          try {
               return new sun.applet.AppletAudioClip(url);
          } catch (Exception e) {
               return this;
          }
     }

// Uses the AWT Toolkit class to fetch an image from a URL

     public Image getImage(URL url)
     {
          return Toolkit.getDefaultToolkit().getImage(url);
     }

// Since we aren't running in a browser and there aren't really
// any classes to render HTML in Java, we have to wimp out with
// the showDocument method and just print a message that the
// applet wanted to load a URL.
```


continues

Listing 13.2 Continued

```
     public void showDocument(URL url)
     {
          System.out.println("Wanted to show document on: "+url);
     }

     public void showDocument(URL url, String target)
     {
          System.out.println("Wanted to show document on: "+url+
               " in frame "+target);
     }

// Just print to System.out for showStatus.

     public void showStatus(String status)
     {
          System.out.println(status);
     }

// If we can't create an instance of sun.applet.AppletAudioClip, we
// return a pointer to this same object, which happens to also implement
// the AudioClip interface, but it doesn't do anything with them.
// The following three methods are the methods for AudioClip:

     public void play() {};
     public void loop() {};
     public void stop() {};
}
```

To use a custom applet context, you need a custom applet stub since the stub is the class that returns the applet context. The stub contains the very useful `getDocumentBase`, `getCodebase`, and `getParameter` methods.

Listing 13.3 shows a handy `RunAppletStub` that allows you to customize the code and document bases as well as the applet parameters by using the system properties. It also returns an instance of `RunAppletContext` for the applet's context.

Listing 13.3 Source Code for *RunAppletStub.java*

```
import java.applet.*;
import java.net.*;
import java.awt.*;

// This class provides an applet stub for applets running
// as standalone applications. You can set the document base
// by setting the "docbase" system property. Likewise, you can set
// the code base through the "codebase" property.
// You can provide applet parameters by setting system properties
// with the applet's name followed by the parameter. For example:
// <PARAM name="stooge" value="moe">
// for an applet named MyApplet, could be set in this stub
// with by setting the system property "MyAppletstooge" to "moe".
```

```
// You can also just set the "stooge" property, but it will try
// using the appletname in front first. This allows you to run
// multiple applets at once that have the same parameter names.


public class RunAppletStub extends Object implements AppletStub
{
     Frame appletFrame;
     Applet applet;
     String appletName;
     String startDir;

     public RunAppletStub()
     {
     }

// startDir is the local directory where this applet is started, or
// another directory if you prefer. If you don't specify a code base
// or a document base, the startDir is used for those. The directory
// separators must be '/' and not '\' or the URL class gets confused.

     public RunAppletStub(Frame appletFrame, Applet applet, String name,
          String startDir)
     {
          this.appletFrame = appletFrame;
          this.applet = applet;
          this.appletName = name;
          this.startDir = startDir;

          RunAppletContext.instance().addApplet(applet, name);
     }

     public void setParams(Frame appletFrame, Applet applet, String name,
          String startDir)
     {
          this.appletFrame = appletFrame;
          this.applet = applet;
          this.appletName = name;
          this.startDir = startDir;

          RunAppletContext.instance().addApplet(applet, name);
     }

     public boolean isActive() { return true; }

// Return the document base URL. Try getting the docbase system parameter.
// If that isn't available, use the startDir directory.

     public URL getDocumentBase()
     {
          String docbase = System.getProperty("docbase");

          try {
               if (docbase == null) {
                    return new URL("file://"+startDir);
               } else {
                    return new URL(docbase);
               }
```

13

continues

Listing 13.3 Continued

```
            } catch (MalformedURLException e) {
                return null;
            }
        }

    // Return the code base URL. Try getting the codebase system parameter.
    // If that isn't available, use the startDir directory.

        public URL getCodeBase()
        {
            String codebase = System.getProperty("codebase");

            try {
                if (codebase == null) {
                    return new URL("file://"+startDir);
                } else {
                    return new URL(codebase);
                }
            } catch (MalformedURLException e) {
                return null;
            }
        }

    // fetch a parameter for the applet from the system properties. First
    // try the applet name followed by the param name. If that's null,
    // try just the param name.

        public String getParameter(String paramName)
        {
            String prop = System.getProperty(appletName+paramName);
            if (prop != null) return prop;
            return System.getProperty(paramName);
        }

        public AppletContext getAppletContext()
        {
            return RunAppletContext.instance();
        }

    // appletResize is the only reason we need a reference to the applet's
    // frame. If the applet wants to resize, we resize the frame, then
    // the applet.

        public void appletResize(int width, int height)
        {
            appletFrame.resize(width+10, height+20);
            applet.resize(width, height);
        }
    }
```

All you have to do in your applet to use the `RunAppletStub` is create the stub and call the `setStub` applet method. Listing 13.4 shows the stand-alone applet updated to use the `RunAppletStub` class.

Listing 13.4 Source Code for *Standalone2.java*

```
import java.awt.*;
import java.applet.*;

// StandaloneApplet is an applet that runs either as
// an applet or a standalone application.  To run
// standalone, it provides a main method that creates
// a frame, then creates an instance of the applet and
// adds it to the frame.

public class Standalone2 extends Applet
{
     public void init()
     {
          add(new Button("Standalone Applet Button"));
     }

     public static void main(String args[])
     {
// Create the frame this applet will run in
          Frame appletFrame = new Frame("Some applet");

// The frame needs a layout manager, use the GridLayout to maximize
// the applet size to the frame.
          appletFrame.setLayout(new GridLayout(1,0));

// Have to give the frame a size before it is visible
          appletFrame.resize(300, 100);

// Make the frame appear on the screen. You should make the frame appear
// before you call the applet's init method. On some Java implementations,
// some of the graphics information is not available until there is a frame.
// If your applet uses certain graphics functions like getGraphics() in the
// init method, it may fail unless there is a frame already created and
// showing.
          appletFrame.show();

// Create an instance of the applet
          Applet myApplet = new Standalone2();

// Add the applet to the frame
          appletFrame.add(myApplet);

// Now try to get an applet stub for this class.

          RunAppletStub stub = new RunAppletStub(appletFrame,
               myApplet, "standalone-applet", "http://localhost/");
          myApplet.setStub(stub);

// Initialize and start the applet
          myApplet.init();
          myApplet.start();

     }
}
```

13

You have to write this special `main` method only a few times before you start wondering whether you couldn't create a loader that automatically did all that stuff for you. The `RunApplet` class, included on the CD with this book, can load multiple applets.

When you start an applet, you can specify the applet's width, height, name, and starting directory. For example, the following command line starts the applet `Applet1` with a size of 400×300, a name of `myapplet`, and a starting directory of /home/mark:

```
java RunApplet Applet1,width=400,height=300,name=myapplet,startDir=/home/mark
```

Make sure there are no spaces in the parameters for a single applet; otherwise, they will be confused with parameters for another applet. You can run multiple applets by putting them all on the same command line. The following command runs applets named `Applet1` and `Applet2`:

```
java RunApplet Applet1 Applet2
```

Notice that the `width`, `height`, `name`, and `startDir` parameters are optional.

The `RunApplet` class is arranged slightly differently from the preceding `Standalone2` class. Most of the work that is done in the `main` method in `Standalone2` is now in a method called `StartApplet`. Listing 13.5 shows the `startApplet` method for the `RunApplet` class.

Listing 13.5 *startApplet* Method from *RunApplet.java*

```
// Creates the frame, sets the stub, starts the applet

    public static void startApplet(Applet applet, int width, int height,
        String name, String startDir)
    {

// Create the applet's frame
        Frame appletFrame = new Frame(name);

// Allow room for the frame's borders
        appletFrame.resize(width+10, height+20);

// Use a grid layout to maximize the applet's size
        appletFrame.setLayout(new GridLayout(1, 0));

// Add the applet to the frame
        appletFrame.add(applet);

// Show the frame, which makes sure all the graphics info is loaded
// for the applet to use.

        appletFrame.show();

// Create and set the stub
        AppletStub stub = new RunAppletStub(appletFrame, applet, name,
            startDir);
        applet.setStub(stub);
```

```
// initialize the applet
        applet.init();

// Make sure the frame shows the applet
        appletFrame.validate();

// Start up the applet
        applet.start();
```

The bulk of the `RunApplet` class is taken up by the `main` method, which spends all its time parsing command-line arguments. For each command-line argument, the `main` method creates a `StringTokenizer` object that uses a comma as the separator. For each token, the method checks to see whether it contains any of the allowable parameters, and, if so, parses the parameter. The applet's `startDir` parameter is used by the applet stub to return the document base and code base URLs. The `URL` class requires all directories to use the forward slash (/), as opposed to the backward slash (\) used by Windows and OS/2. The `main` method has to scan through the `startDir` parameter and replace any backward slashes with forward slashes. It uses a `StringBuffer` object to do this. The `StringBuffer` class allows you to build and edit strings more efficiently than using the `String` class, because you can directly change the characters in a `StringBuffer` object.

The main method simply turns the `startDir` parameter into a `StringBuffer` object, scans through the buffer replacing \s with /s, and then converts the `StringBuffer` object back into a `String`. Listing 13.6 shows the source code for the `main` method.

Tip

The technique of using a `StringBuffer` object to manipulate a `String` object is used very often by Java, but you don't always know it. Whenever you combine an integer and a string, like `"Count: "+5`, the Java compiler actually generates calls to the `StringBuffer` class to create the new string.

Listing 13.6 *main* Method from *RunApplet.java*

```
public static void main(String[] args)
    {
        if (args.length < 1) {
            System.err.println("Please supply the applet name.");
        }

// For each arg, parse out the applet class name and other params

        for (int i=0; i < args.length; i++) {
            StringTokenizer tokenizer = new StringTokenizer(
```

13

continues

Listing 13.6 Continued

```
            String className = null;

// default to 300x200 frame
            int width = 300;
            int height = 200;

            String name = null;
            String startDir = null;

            while (tokenizer.hasMoreTokens()) {
                String token = tokenizer.nextToken();

// Look for width= parameter, if found, get the integer. If there's
// an error parsing the int, just ignore it

                if (token.startsWith("width=")) {
                    try {
                        width = Integer.valueOf(
                            token.substring(6)).
                            intValue();
                    } catch (Exception ignore) {
                    }

// Look for the height parameter, ignore if there's an error
                } else if (token.startsWith("height=")) {
                    try {
                        height = Integer.valueOf(
                            token.substring(7)).
                            intValue();
                    } catch (Exception ignore) {
                    }

// Look for the optional applet name
                } else if (token.startsWith("name=")) {
                    name = token.substring(5);

// Normally, you just give the applet's class name in the parameter
// list, but if you like, you can be more specific and say
// applet=xxx.
                } else if (token.startsWith("applet=")) {
                    className = token.substring(7);

// Set the home directory for the applet. If not set, will
// use the current directory (from System property "user.dir")

                } else if (token.startsWith("startdir=")) {
                    startDir = token.substring(9);
                } else {
                    if (className == null) {
                        className = token;
                    } else {
                        System.err.println(
                            "Invalid parameter - "+
                            token);
                    }
```

```
                }
            }

            if (className == null) {
                System.err.println(
                    "No class name specified in: "+
                    args[i]);
            }
            if (name == null) name = className;

// If no startDir set, use the "user.dir" property

            if (startDir == null) {
                startDir = System.getProperty("user.dir")+"//";
            }

// This little piece of bogosity changes any \'s in the start dir
// to /'s, since the URL classes require /'s.

            StringBuffer buff = new StringBuffer(startDir);
            for (int j=0; j < buff.length(); j++) {
                if (buff.charAt(j) == '\\') {
                    buff.setCharAt(j, '/');
                }
            }

// Convert the string buffer back to a string.
            startDir = new String(buff);

// Load the applet's class
            try {
                Class appletClass = Class.forName(className);
                Applet runme = (Applet) appletClass.
                    newInstance();

// Start the applet
                startApplet(runme, width, height, name,
                    startDir);
            } catch (Exception e) {

// If there's an error, just say which applet had the problem,
// but don't quit.

                System.err.println("Error starting applet - "+
                    args[i]);
                System.err.println(e);
            }
        }
    }
```

chapter 14

Creating Your Own Class Archive Files

by Mark Wutka

In this chapter

- **Using Info-ZIP to create archive files**
  The Info-ZIP program is a free utility to create zip archives on a wide variety of platforms. You can use it to create .zip files containing Java classes.
- **Viewing classes stored in a zip archive**
  It is a fairly simple procedure to extract a .class file from a zip archive file. Once you extract a file, you can use the javap utility to disassemble the class file so you can see what it does.
- **Updating a browser's class library**
  While it is a risky procedure, you have the ability to update the zip archive used by a Web browser. This allows you to add your own classes to the browser without loading them over the network.
- **Using other class archivers**
  There are other zip archivers available. Some work better than others for creating archives for Java. Microsoft has introduced an alternative to the zip archive called a cabinet. Java 1.1 also features a similar feature called a JAR (Java ARchive).

Class Archive Files

Java classes are sometimes packaged together in special archive files. To date, the only officially allowed format for these files is the zip format.

When you install the JDK, or almost any Java-enabled browser, you will notice a .zip file somewhere in the files you have installed. This file is sometimes but not always called classes.zip.

Netscape, for instance, stores its files in moz2_0.zip or moz3_0.zip. (The numbers indicate version numbers; they might also be 2_01, 3_01, and so on.)

These zip files hold Java .class files in uncompressed format. The Java runtime environment can't read a class file from a zip file if it has been compressed. Since compression is one of the major features of zip archiving programs, you must explicitly turn off compression when you create the archive.

Sun will soon add another archive format to the mix: the JAR format (Java ARchive). Instead of using the current method in which each class is downloaded individually, you should be able to package your classes in JAR files and download them in one large bundle. And you should not have to add any code to your programs to allow JAR packaging.

Creating Your Own Archive File with Info-ZIP

The first thing you need to create a class archive, other than the classes themselves, is a zip archiver. The Info-ZIP is an excellent archiver for creating zip files since it is free, available on a variety of platforms, and can store files in uncompressed format.

The main home page for Info-ZIP is located at **http://quest.jpl.nasa.gov/Info-ZIP** and at a number of mirror sites. Info-ZIP is available in both source and binary form, with binaries available for Windows, OS/2, VMS, most major UNIX platforms, and more. Just follow the instructions on the Info-ZIP Web page for downloading and installing for your platform. Figure 14.1 shows the Info-ZIP Web page.

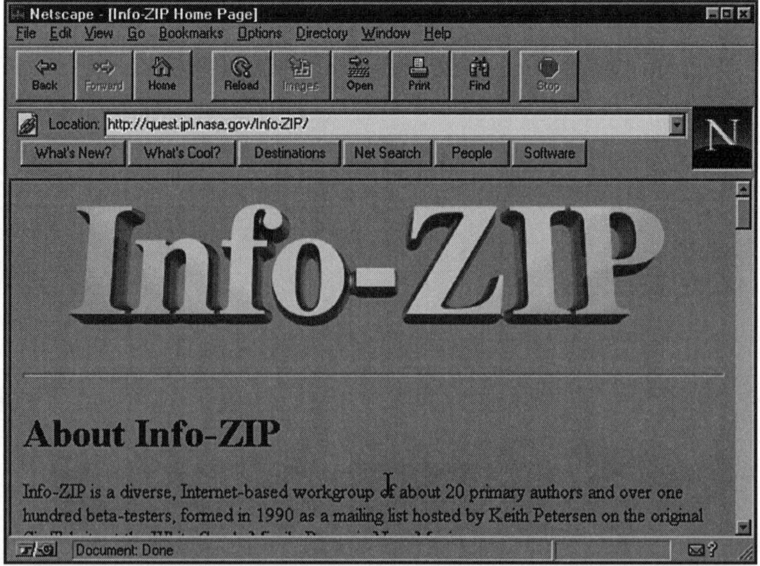

Fig. 14.1
The Info-ZIP program is available for a wide variety of systems.

If the classes in your archive belong to a package, the path name of each class must have the package name. For each subpackage name, you must also have a directory.

For instance, if you have a class that belongs to a package called: `mylib.awtstuff.interfaces`, you must have a directory called `mylib` holding a subdirectory called `awtstuff`, which itself must hold a directory called `interfaces`. Your class must then be stored in the `interfaces` directory.

Tip
Once you've unpacked the zip program, don't forget to add it to your command path.

To archive the entire `mylib` package into a file called `mylib.zip`, go to the parent directory of `mylib` and type:

```
zip -r -0 mylib.zip mylib
```

The `-r` argument tells zip to include subdirectories in the archive. Without this argument, you would have to include the full path name of every file in the `mylib` directory.

The `-0` option is extremely important because it stores the files with no compression. If you don't use the `-0` option, you still create a zip file but Java can't use it, because zip compresses files by default.

Tip
When you create a zip archive, remember to add the full path name of the zip file to your CLASSPATH variable. Although class files are picked up when their directory name is in the CLASSPATH, .zip files must be mentioned explicitly. For example, if you created a file called `myclasses.zip`, your CLASSPATH under Windows might look like: `CLASSPATH=C:\mystuff\myclasses.zip;C:\JAVA\LIB\CLASSES.ZIP`.

Viewing the Contents of a Zip Archive

Once you have become familiar with the known Java classes, you might want to start exploring the hidden classes in the various browsers and Java environments. Begin by finding out what files are stored in the browser's class library. Use the unzip program from Info-ZIP.

The following command displays the contents of a class archive named `classes.zip`:

```
unzip -v classes.zip
```

These class archives typically hold hundreds of .class files, so be prepared for many pages of output. Suppose you are browsing through the `classes.zip` file from the JDK and notice a class file called `sun/net/www/protocol/http/HttpURLConnection.class`. You can get a copy of this class with the command:

```
unzip classes.zip sun/net/www/protocol/http/HttpURLConnection.class
```

This extracts the file and creates a nice chain of subdirectories off your current directory. From your current directory, assuming that "." is in your `CLASSPATH` variable, you can examine the method and variable names in this class with the `javap` command:

```
javap sun.net.www.protocol.http.HttpURLConnection
```

Tip

Notice the relationship between package names and subdirectories. For each "." in the class name, there is a "/" (under UNIX) or a "\" (under Windows and OS/2) in the .class file path.

If you are really daring, you can use `javap -c` to disassemble the code in the .class file:

```
javap -c sun.net.www.protocol.http.HttpURLConnection
```

Caution

Before disassembling any code that comes with a license agreement, look over the license agreement closely. Many vendors explicitly forbid the disassembling of their code. Although they are probably more worried about you stealing their trade secrets than just seeing what their code does, you are still breaking the law if you disassemble their code without permission.

Adding Classes Directly to the Browser's Library

Your browser loads classes from the local filesystem if they are included in its `CLASSPATH` variable. Sometimes, however, you may want to add classes directly to the browser's zip library.

Caution

Changing a browser's own class archive is dangerous. You could accidentally introduce a class that bypasses the applet security restrictions.

You could also accidentally overwrite a necessary class and cause your browser to stop working. Always make a backup copy of the original zip file before making any changes, and make sure you know what you are doing.

Adding classes to a zip file is no different from creating a new zip file. To add the `mylib` package to a class archive named `classes.zip`, use the following command:

```
zip -0 classes.zip mylib
```

You can also replace classes in a class archive. For instance, you may want to insert a dummy security manager that removes any restrictions on applets and applications.

The security manager for each browser is in a different package, so you need to adjust your dummy security manager and the zip command for each browser. To insert a dummy security manager into Netscape, for instance, you need to replace `netscape.applet.AppletSecurity`.

The following command does that for Netscape version 2:

```
zip -0 moz2_0.zip netscape/applet/AppletSecurity.class
```

You need to have copied `AppletSecurity.class` into the `netscape/applet` (`netscape\applet` under Windows) subdirectory. Again, this is a dangerous thing to play with. You could open up your entire company's network to malicious hacking just by replacing classes in your own browser.

Creating Class Archives with Other Zip Archivers

You can use any archiver to create zip archives for use with Java as long as you can turn off the file compression. For example, the PKZIP 2.04 command-line option to turn off compression is `-e0`. Unfortunately, PKZIP does not support long filenames, so its use in archiving Java classes is limited.

The WinZip utility provides a nice graphical interface for creating zip files. You can find WinZip on the Web at **http://www.winzip.com**. WinZip is a shareware program, so you may try it out for a period of time before deciding to buy it. You will probably discover that it is well worth the price.

One of the advantages of WinZip is that you may view a zip archive in a window, and view any single file stored in the archive, without having to unpack it first. Since WinZip recognizes the Windows file types, when you double-click a file, WinZip brings up the appropriate viewer for that file.

When you create a zip archive with WinZip, you can switch off compression from the screen where you enter file names. Figure 14.2 shows the WinZip screen on which you can switch off compression.

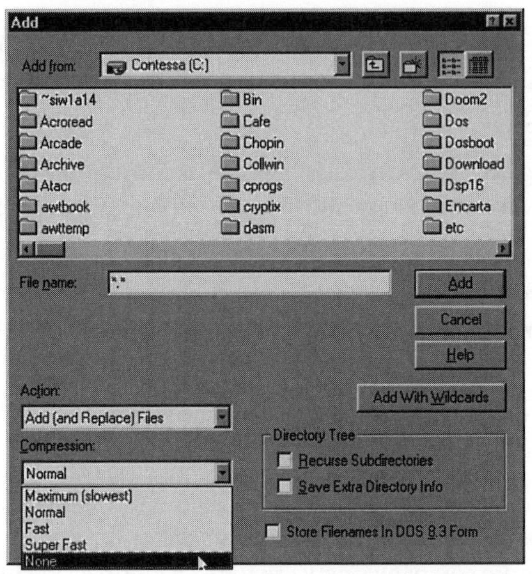

Fig. 14.2
Select "None" for compression type in WinZip.

Creating Cabinet Files for Internet Explorer

Microsoft Internet Explorer supports an alternative to zip files called cabinets. Cabinets can include .class files, images, and audio clips. Cabinets are not limited to Java files, however. IE supports many other kinds of executable content, and any of them may be packaged in a cabinet file. Cabinets may also contain compressed data, allowing you to download code quickly.

The data compression, along with the fact that you can group many different file types in a cabinet, make cabinets an attractive alternative to zip files. The biggest disadvantage to cabinets is that they are currently available only under Internet Explorer.

In order to store files in a cabinet, you need the Cabinet Development Kit (CDK) from Microsoft. This is available from Microsoft's Web site at **http://www.microsoft.com/workshop/java/cab-f.htm.**

Once you have downloaded and unpacked the CDK, you can use the cabarc program to create cabinets. Make sure that your PATH setting includes the directory where you unpacked the CDK. The command-line for the cabarc program is very similar to that of a zip archiver:

```
cabarc n cabfilename files
```

For example, to pack all the .class files and all the .gif files in the current directory into a cabinet file called mycabinet.cab, you would use the following command:

```
cabarc n mycabinet.cab *.class *.gif
```

If you want to include a whole directory tree, add the -r and -p options to cabarc. For instance, to package the current directory, including all subdirectories, and store them in a file called mycab.cab, you would use the following command:

```
cabarc -r -p n mycab.cab *.*
```

Once you have created a cabinet file, you can use it in a Web page by including the following applet parameter:

```
<PARAM name="cabbase" value="cabfilename">
```

The following example .html file loads an applet called MyApplet from a cabinet file called mycab.cab:

```
<HTML>
<HEAD>
<TITLE>Cabinet Example</TITLE>
</HEAD>
<BODY>
<APPLET codebase="." code="MyApplet.class" width=250 height=250>
<PARAM name="cabbase" value="mycab.cab">
You need a Java enabled browser to see this program.
</APPLET>
</BODY>
</HTML>
```

You don't have to do anything special to access images and audio clips that are stored in cabinet files. Just access them via the codebase or document base URLs as you normally would. The IE browser will take care of the rest.

Note

For Java 1.1, Sun has defined an archive format called JAR (Java ARchive) that is very similar to the cabinet format. It also supports data compression and can store multiple types of files. Since the JAR format will be part of future releases of Java, it will be available on any Java-compliant platform.

chapter 15

Accessing Databases with JDBC

15

by Krishna Sankar

In this chapter

- **Organizing your data for a relational database**
  Java Database Connectivity (JDBC) brings the power of the relational database model to Java programs. The relational database concepts that are the foundations of modern databases, such as SQL, tables, and joins, are discussed.
- **Designing client/server database applications**
  This chapter discusses some of the mission-critical database system concepts, such as two-tier, three-tier, and multi-tier systems, transaction processing, cursors, and replication.
- **Accessing databases with JDBC**
  You will learn the history, progression, and the current status of the JDBC specification, and be introduced to the inner working of JDBC and an explanation of the JDBC security model.
- **Handling JDBC connections, SQL statements, and retrieving results**
  You will find in-depth coverage of how to handle connections, SQL statements, result sets, warnings and exceptions, date, time, and so on.

Standard relational data access is very important for Java programs because the Java applets by nature are not monolithic, all-consuming applications. As applets by nature are modular, they need to read persistent data from data stores, process the data, and write the data back to data stores for other applets to process. Monolithic programs could afford to have their own proprietary schemes of data handling. But as Java applets cross operating system and network boundaries, you need published open data access schemes.

The Java Database Connectivity (JDBC) of the Java Enterprise API's JavaSoft is the first of such cross-platform, cross-database approaches to database access from Java programs. From a developer's point of view, JDBC is the first standardized effort to integrate relational databases with Java programs. JDBC has opened all the relational power that can be mustered to Java applets and applications. In this chapter, you will see how JDBC can be effectively used to develop database programs using Java.

First, you will look at some basics applicable to databases in general.

Organizing Your Data for a Relational Database

Databases, as you know, contain organized data. A database can be as simple as a flat file (a single computer file with data usually in a tabular form) containing names and telephone numbers of one's friends, or as elaborate as the worldwide reservation system of a major airline. Many of the principles discussed in this chapter are applicable to a wide variety of database systems.

Structurally, there are three major types of databases:

- Hierarchical
- Relational
- Network

During the 1970s and 1980s, the hierarchical scheme was very popular. This scheme treats data as a tree-structured system with data records forming the leaves. Examples of the hierarchical implementations are schemes like b-tree and multi-tree data access. In the hierarchical scheme, to get to data, users need to traverse up and down the tree structure. The most common relationship in a hierarchical structure is a one-to-many relationship between the data records, and it is difficult to implement a many-to-many relationship without data redundancy.

The network data model solved this problem by assuming a multi-relationship between data elements. In contrast to the hierarchical scheme where there is a parent-child relationship, in the network scheme, there is a peer-to-peer relationship. Most of the programs developed during those days used a combination of the hierarchical and network data storage and access model.

During the 90s, the relational data access scheme came to the forefront. The relational scheme views data as rows of information. Each row contains columns of data, called fields. The main concept in the relational scheme is that the data is uniform. Each row contains the same number of columns. One such collection of rows and columns is called a *table*. Many such tables (which can be structurally different) form a *relational database*.

Figure 15.1 shows a sample relational database schema (or table layout) for an enrollment database. In this example, the database consists of three tables: the Students Table that contains student information, the Courses Table that has the courses information, and the StudentCourses Table that has the student course relation. The Students Table has student ID, name, address, and so on; the Courses Table contains the course ID, subject name or course title, term offered, location, and so on.

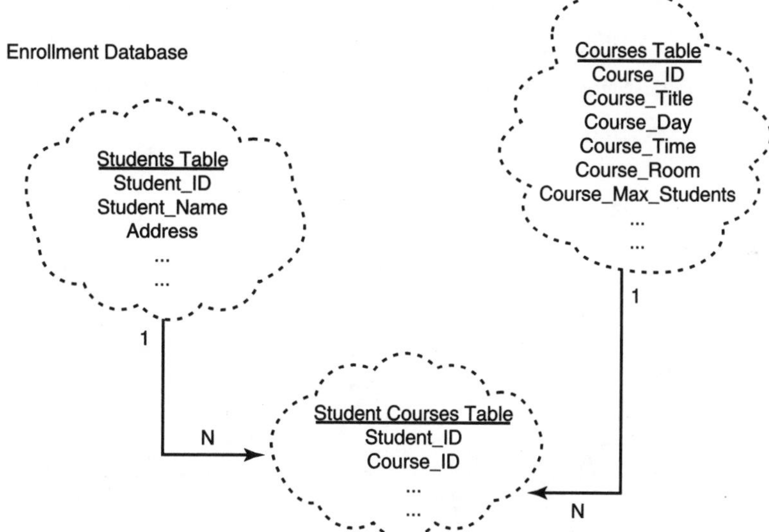

Fig. 15.1
A sample relational database schema for the Enrollment Database.

Now that you have the student and course tables of data, how do you relate the tables? That is where the relational part of the relational database comes in the picture. To relate two tables, either the two tables will have a common column, or you will need to create a third table with two columns, one from the first table and the second from the second table.

Take a look at how this is done. In this example, to relate the Students Table with the Courses Table, you need to make a new StudentCourses Table which has two columns: Student_ID and Course_ID. Whenever a student takes a course, make a row in the StudentCourses Table with the Student_ID and the Course_ID. Thus, the table has the student and course relationship. If you want to find a list of students and the subjects they take, go to the Student Courses Table, read each row, find the student name corresponding to the Student_ID, from the Courses Table find the course title corresponding to the Course_ID, and select the Student_Name and the Course_Title columns.

Using SQL

Once relational databases started becoming popular, database experts wanted a universal database language to perform actions on data. The answer was *SQL*, or *Structured Query Language*. The SQL existed before the relational concepts but the association of SQL and relational database concepts made SQL grow into a mainstream database language.

SQL has constructs for:

1. Data manipulation, such as create, update, and delete.
2. Data definition, such as create tables and columns.
3. Security for restricting access to data elements and creating users and groups.
4. Data management, including backup, bulk copy, and bulk update.
5. Most importantly, transaction processing—SQL is used along with programming languages like Java, C++, and others.

SQL is used for data handling and interaction with the back-end database management system.

Tip

Each database vendor has their own implementation of the SQL. In the Microsoft SQL server, which is one of the client/server relational DMBS, the SQL is called the Transact/SQL, while the Oracle SQL is called the PL/SQL. The different vendors have different extensions to the common X/Open and ANSI X3H2 standard. For the most part, SQL = SQL on any platform. The differences come in framework additions designed to take advantage of a particular database's functionality or capabilities.

Note

SQL became an ANSI (American National Standards Institute) standard in 1986 and later was revised to become SQL-92. JDBC is SQL-92-compliant.

Combining Data from Multiple Tables Using Joins

Just because a database consists of tables with rows of data does not mean that you are limited to view the data in the fixed tables in the database. A *join* is a process in which two or more tables are combined to form a single table. The join can be dynamic, where two tables are merged to form a virtual table, or static, where two tables are joined and saved for future reference. A static join is usually a stored procedure which can be invoked to refresh and then query the saved table. Joins are performed on tables that have a column of common information. Conceptually, there are many types of joins, which are discussed later in this section.

Before you dive deeper into joins, look at the following example, where you fill the tables of the database schema in Figure 15.1 with a few records as shown in Tables 15.1, 15.2, and 15.3. In these tables, I show only the relevant fields or columns.

Table 15.1 Students Table

Student_ID	Student_Name
1	John
2	Mary
3	Jan
4	Jack

Table 15.2 Courses Table

Course_ID	Course_Title
S1	Math
S2	English
S3	Computer
S4	Logic

Table 15.3 StudentCourses Table

Student_ID	Course_ID
2	S2
3	S1
4	S3

Inner Join

A simple join called the inner join with the Students and StudentCourses Tables will give you a table like the one shown in Table 15.4. That is, you get a new table which combines the Students and StudentCourses Tables by adding the Student_Namecolumn to the StudentCourses Table.

Table 15.4 Inner Join Table

Student_ID	Student_Name	Course_ID
2	Mary	S2
3	Jan	S1
4	Jack	S3

Just because you are using the Student_ID to link the two tables does not mean that you should fetch that column. You can exclude the key field from the result table of an inner join. The SQL statement for this inner join is as follows:

```
SELECT Students.Student_Name, StudentCourses.Course_ID
FROM Students, StudentCourses
WHERE Students.Student_ID = StudentCourses.Student_ID
```

Outer Join

An outer join between two tables (say Table1 and Table2) occurs when the result table has all the rows of the first table and the common records of the second table. (The first and second table are determined by the order in the SQL statement.) If you assume a SQL statement with the "FROM Table1,Table2" clause, in a left outer join, all rows of the first table (Table1) and common rows of the second table (Table2) are selected. In a right outer join, all records of the second table (Table2) and common rows of the first table (Table1) are selected. A left outer join with the Students Table and the StudentCourses Table creates Table 15.5.

Table 15.5 Outer Join Table

Student_ID	Student_Name	Course_ID
1	John	<null>
2	Mary	S2
3	Jan	S1
4	Jack	S3

This join is useful if you want the names of all students, regardless of whether they are taking any subjects this term, and the subjects taken by the students who have enrolled in this term. Some people call it an if-any join, as in, "Give me a list of all students and the subjects they are taking, if any."

The SQL statement for this outer join is as follows: (`oj` = Outer Join)

```
SELECT Students.Student_ID,Students.Student_Name,StudentCourses.Course_ID
FROM {
oj c:\enrol.mdb Students
LEFT OUTER JOIN c:\enrol.mdb
StudentCourses ON Students.Student_ID = StudentCourses .Student_ID
}
```

The full outer join, as you may have guessed, returns all the records from both the tables merging the common rows, as shown in Table 15.6.

Table 15.6 Full Outer Join Table

Student_ID	Student_Name	Course_ID
1	John	<null>
2	Mary	S2
3	Jan	S1
4	Jack	S3
<null>	<null>	S4

Subtract Join

What if you want only the students who haven't enrolled in this term or the subjects who have no students (the tough subjects or professors)? Then, you resort to the subtract join. In this case, the join returns the rows that are not in the second table. Remember, a subtract join has only the fields from the first table. By definition, there are no records in the second table. The SQL statement looks like the following:

```
SELECT Students.Student_Name
FROM {
oj c:\enrol.mdb Students
LEFT OUTER JOIN c:\enrol.mdb
StudentCourses ON Students.Student_ID = StudentCourses .Student_ID
}
WHERE (StudentCourses.Course_ID Is Null)
```

General Discussion on Joins and SQL Statements

There are many other types of joins, such as the self join, which is a left outer join of two tables with the same structure. An example is the assembly/parts explosion in a Bill of

Materials application for manufacturing. But usually the join types that we have discussed so far are enough for normal applications. As you gain more expertise in SQL statements, you will start developing exotic joins.

In all of these joins, you were comparing columns that have the same values; these joins are called *equi-joins*. Joins are not restricted to comparing columns of equal values. You can join two tables based on column value conditions (such as the column of one table being greater than the other).

One more point: For equi-joins, as the column values are equal, you retrieved only one copy of the common column. Then, the joins are called *natural joins*. When you have a non equi-join, you might need to retrieve the common columns from both tables.

Once a SQL statement reaches a database management system, the DBMS parses the SQL statement and translates the SQL statements to an internal scheme called a query plan to retrieve data from the database tables. This internal scheme generator, in all the client/server databases, includes an *optimizer module*. This module, which is specific to a database, knows the limitations and advantages of the database implementation.

In many databases—for example, the Microsoft SQL Server—the optimizer is a cost-based query optimizer. When given a query, this optimizer generates multiple query plans, computes the cost estimates for each (knowing the data storage schemes, page I/O, and so on), and then determines the most efficient access method for retrieving the data, including table join order and index usage. This optimized query is converted into a binary form called the *execution plan*, which is executed against the data to get the result. There are known cases where straight queries take hours to perform that when run through an optimizer have resulted in an optimized query, which is performed in minutes. All the major client/server databases have the query optimizer module built in, which processes all the queries. A database system administrator can assign values to parameters such as cost, storage scheme, and so on, and fine-tune the optimizer.

Designing Client/Server Database Applications

A typical client/server system is at least a department-wide system, and most likely an organizational system spanning many departments in an organization. *Mission-critical* and *line-of-business systems*, such as brokerage, banking, manufacturing, and reservation systems, fall into this category. Most systems are internal to an organization, and also span the customers and suppliers. Almost all such systems are on a local area network (LAN), plus they have wide area network (WAN) connections and dial-in capabilities. With the advent of the Internet/intranet and Java, these systems are getting more and more sophisticated and are capable of doing business in many new ways.

Take the case of Federal Express. Their Web site can now schedule package pickups, track a package from pickup to delivery, and get delivery information and time. You are now on the threshold of an era where online commerce will be as common as shopping malls. Now, look at some of the concepts that drive these kinds of systems.

Client/Server System Tiers

Most of the application systems will involve modules with functions for a front-end GUI, business rules processing, and data access through a DBMS. In fact, major systems like online reservation, banking and brokerage, and utility billing involve thousands of business rules, heterogeneous databases spanning the globe, and hundreds of GUI systems. The development, administration, maintenance, and enhancement of these systems involve handling millions of lines of code, multiple departments, and coordinating the work of hundreds if not thousands of personnel across the globe. The multi-tier system design and development concepts are applied to a range of systems from departmental systems to such global information systems.

Tip

In the two- and three-tier systems, an application is logically divided into three parts:

- GUI Graphical User Interface, which consists of the screens, windows, buttons, list boxes, and so on.
- Business Logic The part of the program that deals with the various data element interactions. All processing is done based on values of data elements. A good example is the logic for determining the credit limit depending on the annual income. Another business logic is the calculation of income tax based on the tax tables (even though some people consider it illogical!). In manufacturing systems, a reorder point calculation logic based on the material usage belongs in the business logic category.
- DBMS The Database Management System that deals with the actual storage and retrieval of data.

Two-Tier Systems

On the basic level, a *two-tier system* involves the GUI and business logic, directly accessing the database. The GUI can be on a client system, and the database can be on the client system or on a server. Usually, the GUI is written in languages like C++, Visual Basic, PowerBuilder, Access Basic, and Lotus Script. The database systems typically are Microsoft Access, Lotus Approach, Sybase "SQL Anywhere," or Watcom DB Engine and Personal Oracle.

Three-Tier Systems

Most of the organizational and many of the departmental client/server applications today follow the *three-tier strategy,* where the GUI, business logic, and the DBMS are in logically three layers. Here, the GUI development tools are Visual Basic, C++, and PowerBuilder. The middle-tier development tools also tend to be C++ or Visual Basic, and the back-end databases are Oracle, Microsoft SQL Server, or Sybase SQL Server. The three-tier concept gave rise to an era of database servers, application servers, and GUI client machines. Operating systems such as UNIX, Windows NT, and Solaris rule the application server and database server world. Client operating systems like Windows are popular for the GUI front end.

Multi-Tier Systems

Now with Internet and Java, the era of "network is the computer" and "thin client" paradigm shifts have begun. The Java applets with their own objects and methods created the idea of the multi-tiered client/server systems. Theoretically, a Java applet can be a business rule, GUI, or DBMS interface. Each applet can be considered a layer. In fact, the Internet and Java were not the first to introduce the object-oriented, multi-tiered systems concept. OMG's CORBA architecture and Microsoft's OLE (now ActiveX) architectures are all proponents of modular object-oriented, multi-platform systems. With Java and the Internet, these concepts became much easier to implement.

In short, the systems' design and implementation progressed from two-tiered architecture to three-tiered architecture to the current inter-networked, Java applet-driven multi-tier architecture.

Handling Transactions

The concept of transactions is an integral part of any client/server database. A *transaction* is a group of SQL statements that update, add, and delete rows and fields in a database. Transactions have an all or nothing property—either they are committed if all statements are successful, or the whole transaction is rolled back if any of the statements cannot be executed successfully. Transaction processing assures the data integrity and data consistency in a database.

Note

JDBC supports transaction processing with the `commit()` and `rollback()` methods. Also, JDBC has the `autocommit()` which, when on, all changes are committed automatically and, if off, the Java program has to use the `commit()` or `rollback()` methods to effect the changes to the data.

Transaction ACID Properties

The characteristics of a transaction are described in terms of the Atomicity, Consistency, Isolation, and Durability (ACID) properties.

A transaction is atomic in the sense that it is an entity. All the components of a transaction happen or do not happen. There is no partial transaction. If only a partial transaction can happen, then the transaction is aborted. The atomicity is achieved by the `commit()` or `rollback()` methods.

A transaction is consistent because it does not perform any actions that violate the business logic or relationships between data elements. The consistent property of a transaction is very important when you develop a client/server system, because there will be many transactions to a data store from different systems and objects. If a transaction leaves the data store inconsistent, all other transactions also would potentially be wrong, resulting in a system-wide crash or data corruption.

A transaction is isolated because the results of a transaction are self-contained. They do not depend on any preceding or succeeding transaction. This is related to a property called *serializability*, which means the sequence of transactions are independent; in other words, a transaction does not assume any external sequence.

Finally, a transaction is durable, meaning the effects of a transaction are permanent even in the face of a system failure. That means some form of permanent storage should be a part of a transaction.

Distributed Transaction Coordinator

A related topic in transactions is the coordination of transactions across heterogeneous data sources, systems, and objects. When the transactions are carried out in one relational database, you can use the `commit()`, `rollback()`, `beginTransaction()`, and `endTransaction()` statements to coordinate the process. But what if you have diversified systems participating in a transaction? How do you handle such a system? As an example, look at the Distributed Transaction Coordinator (DTC) available as a part of Microsoft SQL Server 6.5 database system.

In the Microsoft DTC, a transaction manager facilitates the coordination. *Resource managers* are clients that implement resources to be protected by transactions—for example, relational databases and ODBC data sources.

An application begins a transaction with the transaction manager, and then starts transactions with the resource managers, registering the steps (enlisting) with the transaction manager.

The transaction manager keeps track of all enlisted transactions. The application, at the end of the multi-data source transaction steps, calls the transaction manager to either commit or abort the transaction.

When an application issues a commit command to the transaction manager, the DTC performs a two-phase commit protocol:

1. It queries each resource manager if it is prepared to commit.
2. If all resources are prepared to commit, DTC broadcasts a commit message to all of them.

The Microsoft DTC is an example of very powerful next generation transaction coordinators from the database vendors. As more and more multi-platform, object-oriented Java systems are being developed, this type of transaction coordinators will gain importance. Already, many middleware vendors are developing Java-oriented transaction systems.

Dealing with Cursors

A relational database query normally returns many rows of data. But an application program usually deals with one row at a time. Even when an application can handle more than one row—for example, by displaying the data in a table or spreadsheet format—it can still handle only a limited number of rows. Also, updating, modifying, deleting, or adding data is done on a row basis.

This is where the concept of cursors come in the picture. In this context, a cursor is a pointer to a row. It is like the cursor on the CRT—a location indicator.

Note

Different types of multi-user applications need different types of data sets in terms of data concurrency. Some applications need to know as soon as the data in the underlying database is changed. Such as the case with reservation systems, the dynamic nature of the seat allocation information is extremely important. Others such as statistical reporting systems need stable data; if data is in constant change, these programs cannot effectively display any results. The different cursor designs support the need for the various types of applications.

A cursor can be viewed as the underlying data buffer. A fully scrollable cursor is one where the program can move forward and backward on the rows in the data buffer. If the program can update the data in the cursor, it is called a *scrollable, updatable cursor*.

Caution

An important point to remember when you think about cursors is the transaction isolation. If a user is updating a row, other users might be viewing the row in a cursor of their own. Data consistency is important here. Worse, the other users also might be updating the same row!

Tip

The `ResultSet` in JDBC API is a cursor. But it is only a forward scrollable cursor—this means you can move only forward using the `getNext()` method.

ODBC Cursor Types

ODBC cursors are very powerful in terms of updatability, concurrency, data integrity, and functionality. The ODBC cursor scheme allows positioned delete and update and multiple row fetch (called a rowset) with protection against lost updates.

ODBC supports static, keyset-driven, and dynamic cursors.

In the static cursor scheme, the data is read from the database once, and the data is in the snapshot recordset form. Because the data is a snapshot (a static view of the data at a point of time), the changes made to the data in the data source by other users are not visible. The dynamic cursor solves this problem by keeping live data, but this takes a toll on network traffic and application performance.

The keyset-driven cursor is the middle ground where the rows are identified at the time of fetch, and thus changes to the data can be tracked. Keyset-driven cursors are useful when you implement a backward scrollable cursor. In a keyset-driven cursor, additions and deletions of entire rows are not visible until a refresh. When you do a backward scroll, the driver fetches the newer row if any changes are made.

Note

ODBC also supports a modified scheme, where only a small window of the keyset is fetched, called the *mixed cursor*, which exhibits the keyset cursor for the data window and a dynamic cursor for the rest of the data. In other words, the data in the data window (called a `RowSet`) is keyset-driven, and when you access data outside the window, the dynamic scheme is used to fetch another keyset-driven buffer.

Cursor Applications

You might be wondering where these cursor schemes are applied and why we need such elaborate schemes. In short, all the cursor schemes have their place in information systems.

Static Cursors

Static cursors provide a stable view of the data, because the data does not change. They are good for data mining and data warehousing types of systems. For these applications, you want the data to be stable for reporting executive information systems or for statistical or analysis purposes. Also, the static cursor outperforms other schemes for large amounts of data retrieval.

Dynamic Cursors

On the other hand, for online ordering systems or reservation systems, you need a dynamic view of the system with row locks and views of data as changes are made by other users. In such cases, you will use the dynamic cursor. In many of these applications, the data transfer is small, and the data access is performed on a row-by-row basis. For these online applications, aggregate data access is very rare.

Bookmark

Bookmark is a concept related to the cursor model, but is independent of the cursor scheme used. *Bookmark* is a placeholder for a data row in a table. The application program requests a bookmark for a row from the underlying database management system. The DBMS usually returns a 32-bit marker which can be later used by the application program to get to that row of data. In ODBC, you will use the `SQLExtendedFetch` function with `SQL_FETCH_BOOKMARK` option to get a bookmark. The bookmark is useful for increasing performance of GUI applications, especially the ones where the data is viewed through a spreadsheet-like interface.

Positioned Update/Delete

This is another cursor-related concept. If a cursor model supports positioned update/delete, then you can update/delete the current row in a result set without any more processing, such as a lock, read, or fetch.

In SQL, a positioned update or delete statement is in the form of:

```
UPDATE/DELETE <Field or Column values etc.> WHERE CURRENT OF <cursor name>
```

The positioned update statement to update the fields in the current row is

```
UPDATE <table> SET <field> = <value> WHERE CURRENT OF <cursor name>
```

The positioned `delete` statement to delete the current row takes the form of:

```
DELETE <table> WHERE CURRENT OF <cursor name>
```

Generally, for this type of SQL statement to work, the underlying driver or the DBMS has to support updatability, concurrency, and dynamic scrollable cursors. But there are many other ways of providing the positioned update/delete capability at the application program level. Presently, JDBC does not support any of the advanced cursor functionalities. However, as the JDBC driver development progresses, I am sure there will be very sophisticated cursor management methods available in the JDBC API.

Replication

Data replication is the distribution of corporate data to many locations across the organization, and it provides reliability, fault-tolerance, data-access performance due to reduced communication, and, in many cases, manageability as the data can be managed as subsets.

As you have seen, the client/server systems span an organization, possibly its clients and suppliers, most probably in a wide geographic locations. Systems spanning the entire globe are not uncommon when you're talking about mission-critical applications, especially in today's global business market. If all the data is concentrated in a central location, it would be almost impossible for the systems to effectively access data and offer high performance. Also, if data is centrally located, in the case of mission-critical systems, a single failure will bring the whole business down. Using replicated data across an organization at various geographic locations is a sound strategy.

Different vendors handle replication differently. For example, the Lotus Notes groupware product uses a replication scheme where the databases are considered peers, and additions/updates/deletions are passed between the databases. Lotus Notes has replication formulas that can select subsets of data to be replicated based on various criteria.

The Microsoft SQL server, on the other hand, employs a publisher-subscriber scheme where a database or part of a database can be published to many subscribers. A database can be a publisher *and* a subscriber. For example, the western region can publish its slice of sales data while receiving (subscribing to) sales data from other regions.

There are many other replication schemes from various vendors to manage and decentralize data. Replication is a young technology that is slowly finding its way into many other products.

Now it is time for you to dive deep into the main topic, JDBC.

Accessing Databases with JDBC

JDBC is Java Database Connectivity—a set of relational database objects and methods for interacting with data sources. The JDBC APIs are part of the Enterprise APIs specified by JavaSoft, and thus they will be a part of all Java Virtual Machine (JVM) implementations.

Tip

Even though the objects and methods are based on the relational database model, JDBC makes no assumption about the underlying data source or the data storage scheme. You can access and retrieve audio or video data from many sources and load into Java objects using the JDBC APIs! The only requirement is that there should be a JDBC implementation for that source.

JavaSoft introduced the JDBC API specification in March 1996 as draft Version 0.50 and was open for public review. The specification went from Version 0.50 to 0.60 to 0.70 and now is at Version 1.01, dated August 8, 1996. The JDBC Version 1.01 specification available at **http://splash.javasoft.com/jdbc/** (jdbc-0101.ps or jdbc-0101.pdf) includes all of the improvements from the four months of review by vendors, developers, and the general public. Most probably, by the time you are reading this chapter, JDBC Version 1.1 or even 2.0 might be available !

Now, look at the origin and design philosophies. The JDBC designers based the API on X/Open SQL Call Level Interface (CLI). It is not coincidental that ODBC is also based on the X/Open CLI. The JavaSoft engineers wanted to gain leverage from the existing ODBC implementation and development expertise, thus making it easier for Independent Software Vendors (ISVs) and system developers to adopt JDBC. But ODBC is a C interface to DBMSs and thus is not readily convertible to Java. So JDBC design followed ODBC in spirit as well in its major abstractions and implemented the SQL CLI with "a Java interface that is consistent with the rest of the Java system," as it is described in Section 2.4 of the JDBC specification. For example, instead of the ODBC `SQLBindColumn` and `SQLFetch` to get column values from the result, JDBC used a simpler approach (which you see later).

How Does JDBC Work?

As we have discussed, JDBC is designed upon the CLI model. JDBC defines a set of API objects and methods to interact with the underlying database. A Java program first opens a connection to a database, makes a statement object, passes SQL statements to the underlying DBMS through the statement object, and retrieves the results as well as information about the result sets. Typically, the JDBC class files and the Java applet/application reside in the client. They could be downloaded from the network also. To minimize the latency during execution, it is better to have the JDBC classes in the client. The Database Management System and the data source are typically located in a remote server.

Figure 15.2 shows the JDBC communication layer alternatives. The applet/application and the JDBC layers communicate in the client system, and the driver takes care of interacting with the database over the network.

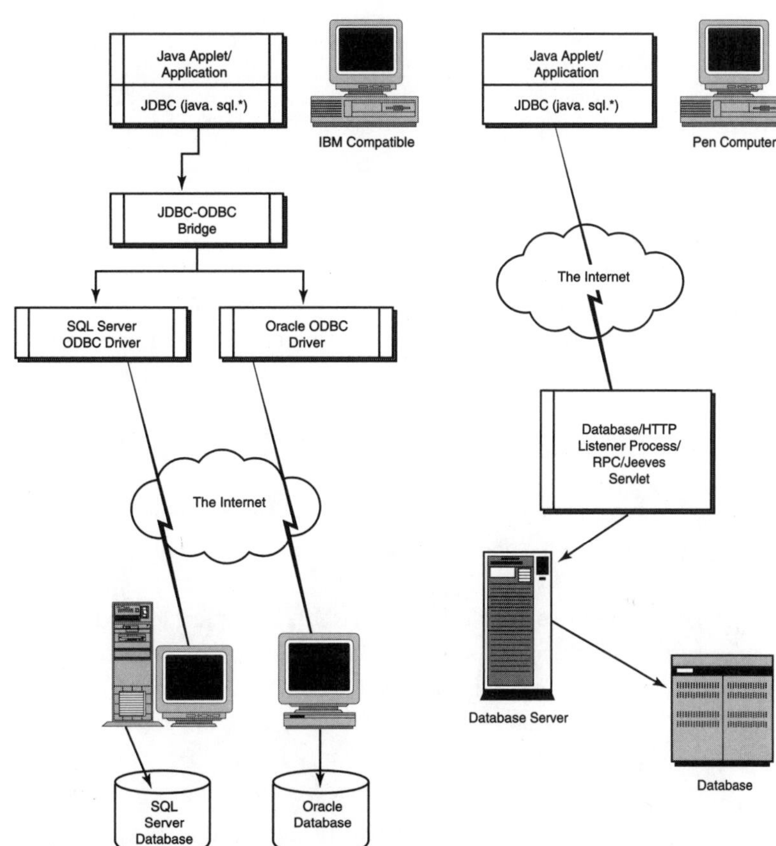

Fig. 15.2
JDBC database communication layer alternatives. The JDBC driver can be a native library, like the JDBC-ODBC Bridge, or a Java class talking across the network to an RPC or Jeeves Servlet or HTTP listener process in the database server.

The JDBC classes are in the java.sql package, and all Java programs use the objects and methods in the java.sql package to read from and write to data sources. A program using the JDBC will need a driver for the data source with which it wants to interface. This driver can be a native module (like the JDBCODBC.DLL for the Windows JDBC-ODBC Bridge developed by Sun/Intersolv), or it can be a Java program that talks to a server in the network using some RPC or Jeeves Servlet or an HTTP talker-listener protocol. Both schemes are shown in Figure 15.2.

Note

As you can see from Figure 15.2, JDBC can be implemented as a native driver or as a gateway to an RPC. Which implementation is better is a question that will be answered as the JDBC architecture matures.

One reason to implement a native library is the advantage of speed. Also, local databases could be handled using native libraries more easily than gateways.

On the other hand, for a handheld device or a network computer, "network is the system." For these devices, a full Java implementation of JDBC that talks to an RPC type of system or a Jeeves servlet on the database server is a good solution.

It is conceivable that an application will deal with more than one data source—possibly heterogeneous data sources. (A database gateway program is a good example of an application that accesses multiple heterogeneous data sources.) For this reason, JDBC has a DriverManager whose function is to manage the drivers and provide a list of currently loaded drivers to the application programs.

Note

Even though the word *Database* is in the name JDBC, the form, content, and location of the data is immaterial to the Java program using JDBC, so long as there is a driver for that data. Hence, the notation data source to describe the data is more accurate than Database, DBMS, DB, or just file. In the future, Java devices such as televisions, answering machines, or network computers will access, retrieve, and manipulate different types of data (audio, video, graphics, time series, and so on) from various sources that are not relational databases at all! And much of the data might not even come from mass storage. For example, the data could be video stream from a satellite or audio stream from a telephone.

ODBC also refers to data sources, rather than databases when being described in general terms.

JDBC Security Model

Security is always an important issue, especially when databases are involved. As of the writing of this book, JDBC follows the standard security model in which applets can connect only to the server from where they are loaded; remote applets cannot connect to local databases. Applications have no connection restrictions. For pure Java drivers, the security check is automatic, but for drivers developed in native methods, the drivers must have some security checks.

Note

With Java 1.1 and the Java Security API, you will have the ability to establish "trust relationships," which will allow you to verify trusted sites. Then, you could give applets downloaded from trusted sources more functionality by giving them access to local resources.

Accessing ODBC Databases with the JDBC-ODBC Bridge

As a part of JDBC, JavaSoft also will deliver a driver to access ODBC data sources from JDBC. This driver is jointly developed with Intersolv and is called the JDBC-ODBC bridge. The JDBC-ODBC bridge is implemented as the JdbcOdbc.class and a native library to access the ODBC driver. For the Windows platform, the native library is a DLL (JDBCODBC.DLL).

As JDBC is close to ODBC in design, the ODBC bridge is a thin layer over JDBC. Internally, this driver maps JDBC methods to ODBC calls, and thus interacts with any available ODBC driver. The advantage of this bridge is that now JDBC has the capability to access almost all databases, as ODBC drivers are widely available. You can use this bridge (Version 1.0105) to run the example programs in this chapter.

JDBC Classes—Overview

When you look at the class hierarchy and methods associated with it, the topmost class in the hierarchy is the `DriverManager`. The `DriverManager` keeps the driver information, state information, and so on. When each driver is loaded, it registers with the `DriverManager`. The `DriverManager`, when required to open a connection, selects the driver depending on the JDBC URL.

Note

True to the nature of the Internet, JDBC identifies a database with an URL. The URL is of the form:

jdbc:<subprotocol>:<subname related to the DBMS/Protocol>

For databases on the Internet/intranet, the subname can contain the Net URL **//hostname:port/...** The `<subprotocol>` can be any name that a database understands. The `odbc` subprotocol name is reserved for ODBC-style data sources. A normal ODBC database JDBC URL looks like:

jdbc:odbc:<*ODBC DSN*>;User=<*username*>;PW=<*password*>

If you are developing a JDBC driver with a new subprotocol, it is better to reserve the subprotocol name with JavaSoft, which maintains an informal subprotocol registry.

The `java.sql.Driver` class is usually referred to for information such as PropertyInfo, version number, and so on. So the class could be loaded many times during the execution of a Java program using the JDBC API.

Looking at the `java.sql.Driver` and `java.sql.DriverManager` classes and methods, as listed in Table 15.9, you see that the `DriverManager` returns a `Connection` object when you use the `getConnection()` method.

Other useful methods include the `registerDriver()`, `deRegister()`, and `getDrivers()` methods. Using the `getDrivers()` method, you can get a list of registered drivers. Figure 15.3 shows the JDBC class hierarchy, as well as the flow of a typical Java program using the JDBC APIs.

In the next subsection, follow the steps required to access a simple database access using JDBC and the JDBC-ODBC driver.

Anatomy of a JDBC Application

To handle data from a database, a Java program implements the following general steps. Figure 15.3 shows the general JDBC objects, the methods, and the sequence. First, the program calls the `getConnection()` method to get the `Connection` object. Then, it creates the `Statement` object and prepares a `SQL` statement.

A SQL statement can be executed immediately (`Statement` object), or can be a compiled statement (`PreparedStatement` object) or a call to a stored procedure (`CallableStatement` object). When the method `executeQuery()` is executed, a `ResultSet` object is returned. SQL statements such as update or delete will not return a `ResultSet`. For such statements, the `executeUpdate()` method is used. The `executeUpdate()` method returns an integer which denotes the number of rows affected by the SQL statement.

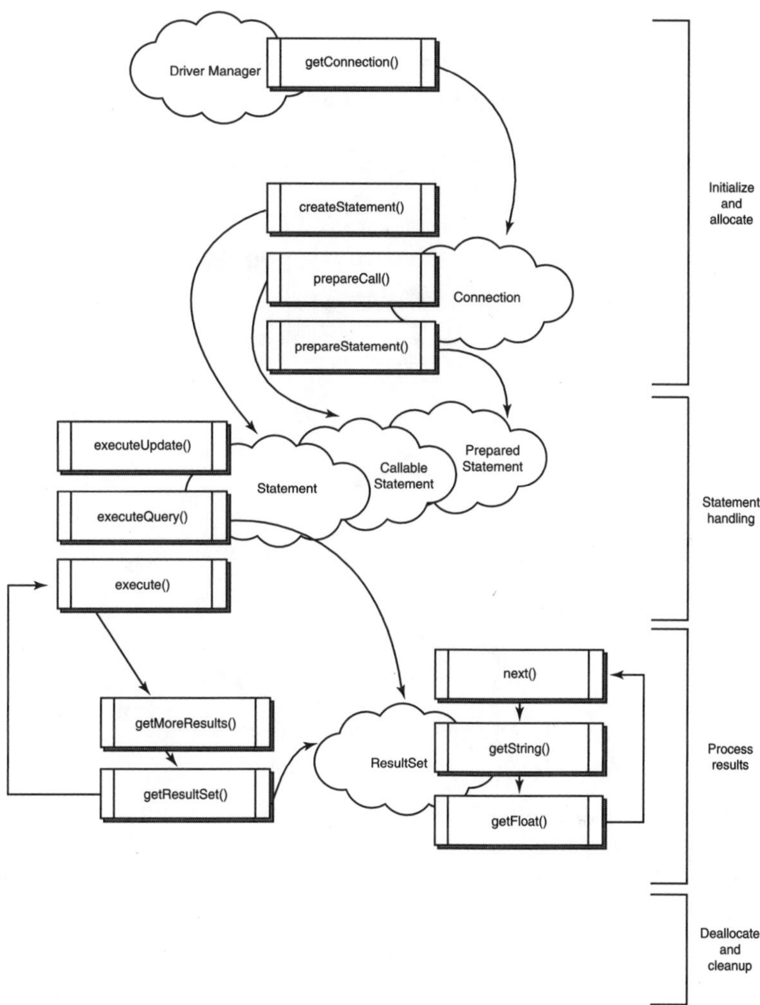

Fig. 15.3
JDBC class hierarchy and a JDBC API flow.

The `ResultSet` contains rows of data that is parsed using the `next()` method. In case of a transaction processing application, methods such as `rollback()` and `commit()` can be used either to undo the changes made by the SQL statements or permanently affect the changes made by the SQL statements.

JDBC API Examples

These examples access the Student database, the schema of which is shown in Figure 15.4. The tables in the examples that you are interested in are the Students Table, Classes

Table, Instructors Table, and Students_Classes Table. This database is a Microsoft Access database. The full database and sample data are generated by the Access Database Wizard. You access the database using JDBC and the JDBC-ODBC bridge.

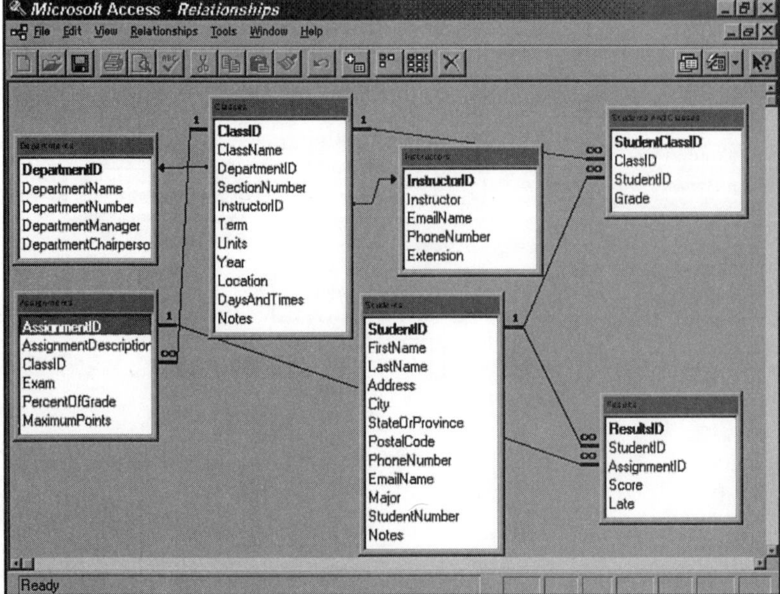

Fig. 15.4 *JDBC example database schema.*

Before you jump into writing a Java JDBC program, you need to configure an ODBC data source. As you saw earlier, the `getConnection()` method requires a data source name (DSN), user ID, and password for the ODBC data source. The database driver type or subprotocol name is `odbc`. So the driver manager finds out from the ODBC driver the rest of the details.

But wait, where do you put the rest of the details? This is where the ODBC setup comes into the picture. The ODBC Setup program runs outside the Java application from the Microsoft ODBC program group. The ODBC Setup program allows you to set up the data source so that this information is available to the ODBC Driver Manager, which, in turn, loads the Microsoft Access ODBC driver. If the database is in another DBMS form—say, Oracle—you configure this source as Oracle ODBC driver. In Windows 3.x, the Setup program puts this information in the ODBC.INI file. With Windows 95 and Windows NT 4.0, this information is in the Registry. Figure 15.5 shows the ODBC setup screen.

Querying a Database with JDBC

In Listing 15.1, you will list all of the students in the database by a SQL SELECT statement. The steps required to accomplish this task using the JDBC API are iterated as follows. For each step, the Java program code with the JDBC API calls follows the description of the steps.

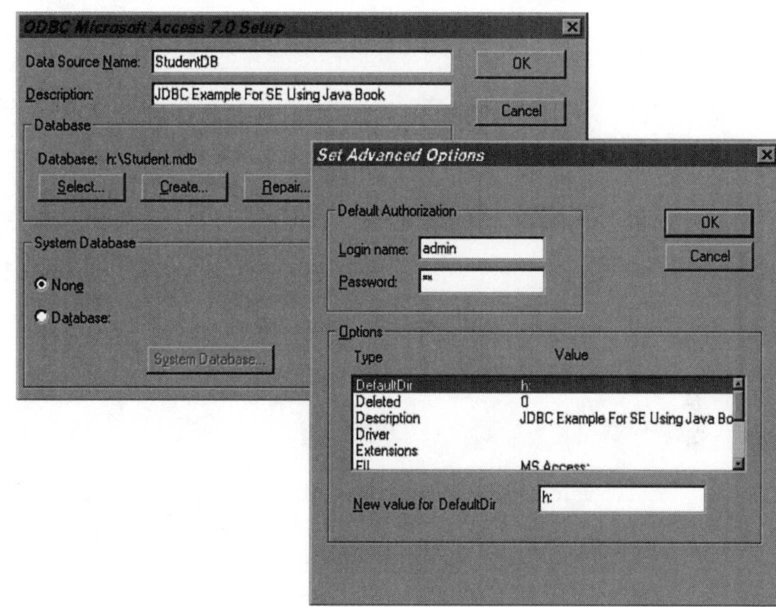

Fig. 15.5 *ODBC setup for the example database. After this setup, the example database URL is **jdbc:odbc: StudentDB;uid= "admin";pw="sa".***

Listing 15.1 Using a SQL *SELECT* Statement

```
     //Declare a method and some variables.
     public void ListStudents() throws SQLException {
int i, NoOfColumns;
String StNo,StFName,StLName;
          //Initialize and load the JDBC-ODBC driver.
Class.forName ("jdbc.odbc.JdbcOdbcDriver");
          //Make the connection object.
Connection Ex1Con = DriverManager.getConnection(
"jdbc:odbc:StudentDB;uid="admin";pw="sa");
//Create a simple Statement object.
Statement Ex1Stmt = Ex1Con.createStatement();
//Make a SQL string, pass it to the DBMS, and execute the SQL statement.
ResultSet Ex1rs = Ex1Stmt.executeQuery(
 "SELECT StudentNumber, FirstName, LastName FROM Students");
//Process each row until there are no more rows.
          // Displays the results on the console.
System.out.println("Student Number        First Name      Last Name");
while (Ex1rs.next()) {
// Get the column values into Java variables
StNo = Ex1rs.getString(1);
StFName = Ex1rs.getString(2);
StLName = Ex1rs.getString(3);
```

continues

Listing 15.1 Continued

```
System.out.println(StNo,StFName,StLName);
}
}
```

The program illustrates the basic steps that are needed to access a table and lists some of the fields in the records.

Updating a Database with JDBC

In Listing 15.2, you update the `FirstName` field in the Students Table by knowing the student's `StudentNumber`. As in the last example, the code follows the description of the step.

Listing 15.2 Updating the *FirstName* Field

```
     //Declare a method and some variables and parameters.
public void UpdateStudentName(String StFName, String StLName,
 String StNo) throws SQLException {
int RetValue;
         // Initialize and load the JDBC-ODBC driver.
Class.forName ("jdbc.odbc.JdbcOdbcDriver");
// Make the connection object.
Connection Ex1Con = DriverManager.getConnection(
"jdbc:odbc:StudentDB;uid="admin";pw="sa");
// Create a simple Statement object.
Statement Ex1Stmt = Ex1Con.createStatement();
//Make a SQL string, pass it to the DBMS, and execute the SQL statement
String SQLBuffer = "UPDATE Students SET FirstName = "+
StFName+", LastName = "+StLName+
" WHERE StudentNumber = "+StNo
RetValue = Ex1Stmt.executeUpdate( SQLBuffer);
System.out.println("Updated " + RetValue + " rows in the Database.");
}
```

In this example, you execute the SQL statement and get the number of rows affected by the SQL statement back from the DBMS.

The previous two examples show how you can do simple yet powerful SQL manipulation of the underlying data using the JDBC API in a Java program. In the following sections, you examine each JDBC class in detail.

The *Connection* Class

The `Connection` class is one of the major classes in JDBC. It packs a lot of functionality, ranging from transaction processing to creating statements, in one class.

As you saw earlier, the connection is for a specific database that can be interacted with in a specific subprotocol. The `Connection` object internally manages all aspects about a connection, and the details are transparent to the program. Actually, the `Connection` object is a pipeline into the underlying DBMS driver. The information to be managed includes the data source identifier, the subprotocol, the state information, the DBMS SQL execution plan ID or handle, and any other contextual information needed to interact successfully with the underlying DBMS.

 **Note**

The data source identifier could be a port in the Internet database server that is identified by the `//<server name>:port/...` URL, just a data source name used by the ODBC driver, or a full path name to a database file in the local computer. For all you know, it could be a pointer to a data feed of the stock market prices from Wall Street!

Another important function performed by the `Connection` object is transaction management. The handling of transactions depends on the state of an internal autocommit flag that is set using the `setAutoCommit()` method, and the state of this flag can be read using the `getAutoCommit()` method. When the flag is `true`, the transactions are automatically committed as soon as they are completed. There is no need for any intervention or commands from the Java application program. When the flag is `false`, the system is in the manual mode. The Java program has the option to commit the set of transactions that happened after the last commit or to rollback the transactions using the `commit()` and `rollback()` methods.

 **Note**

JDBC also provides methods for setting the transaction isolation modularity. When you are developing multi-tiered applications, there will be multiple users performing concurrently interleaved transactions that are on the same database tables. A database driver has to employ sophisticated locking and data-buffering algorithms and mechanisms to implement the transaction isolation required for a large-scale JDBC application. This is more complex when there are multiple Java objects working on many databases that could be scattered across the globe! Only time will tell what special needs for transaction isolation there will be in the new Internet/intranet paradigm.

Once you have a successful `Connection` object to a data source, you can interact with the data source in many ways. The most common approach from an application developer standpoint is the objects that handle the `SQL` statements.

Handling SQL Statements

The `Statement` object does all of the work to interact with the Database Management System in terms of SQL statements. You can create many `Statement` objects from one `Connection` object. Internally, the `Statement` object would be storing the various data needed to interact with a database, including state information, buffer handles, and so on. But these are transparent to the JDBC application program.

Note

When a program attempts an operation that is not in sync with the internal state of the system (for example, a `next()` method to get a row when no SQL statements have been executed), this discrepancy is caught and an exception is raised. This exception, normally, is probed by the application program using the methods in the `SQLException` object.

JDBC supports three types of statements:

- `Statement`
- `PreparedStatement`
- `CallableStatement`

The `Connection` object has the `createStatement()`, `prepareStatement()`, and `prepareCall()` methods to create these `Statement` objects.

Before you explore these different statements, see the steps that a SQL statement goes through.

A Java application program first builds the SQL statement in a string buffer and passes this buffer to the underlying DBMS through some API call. A SQL statement needs to be verified syntactically, optimized, and converted to an executable form before execution. In the Call Level Interface (CLI) Application Program Interface (API) model, the application program passes the SQL statement to the driver which, in turn, passes it to the underlying DBMS. The DBMS prepares and executes the SQL statement.

After the DBMS receives the SQL string buffer, it parses the statement and does a syntax check run. If the statement is not syntactically correct, the system returns an error condition to the driver, which generates a `SQLException`. If the statement is syntactically correct, depending on the DBMS, then many query plans usually are generated that are run through an optimizer (often a cost-based optimizer). Then, the optimum plan is translated into a binary execution plan. After the execution plan is prepared, the DBMS usually returns a handle or identifier to this optimized binary version of the SQL statement back to the application program.

The three JDBC statement (viz., `Statement`, `PreparedStatement`, and `CallableStatement`) types differ in the timing of the SQL statement preparation and the statement execution. In the case of the simple `Statement` object, the SQL is prepared and executed in one step (at least from the application program point of view. Internally, the driver might get the identifier, command the DBMS to execute the query, and then discard the handle). In the case of a `PreparedStatement object`, the driver stores the execution plan handle for later use. In the case of the `CallableStatement object`, the SQL statement is actually making a call to a stored procedure that is usually already optimized.

Note

As you know, stored procedures are encapsulated business rules or procedures that reside in the database server. They also enforce uniformity across applications, as well as provide security to the database access. Stored procedures last beyond the execution of the program. So the application program does not spend any time waiting for the DBMS to create the execution plan.

Now, look at each type of statement more closely and see what each has to offer a Java program.

Creating and Using Direct SQL Statements

A `Statement` object is created using the `createStatement()` method in the `Connection` object. Table 15.7 shows all methods available for the `Statement` object.

Table 15.7 Statement Object Methods

Return Type	Method Name	Parameter
`ResultSet`	`executeQuery`	`(String sql)`
`int`	`executeUpdate`	`(String sql)`

continues

Table 15.7 Continued

Return Type	Method Name	Parameter
Boolean	execute	(String sql)
Boolean	getMoreResults	( )
void	close	( )
int	getMaxFieldSize	( )
void	setMaxFieldSize	(int max)
int	getMaxRows	( )
void	setMaxRows	(int max)
void	setEscapeProcessing	(boolean enable)
int	getQueryTimeout	( )
void	setQueryTimeout	(int seconds)
void	cancel	( )
java.sql.SQLWarning	getWarnings	( )
void	clearWarnings	( )
void	setCursorName	(String name)
ResultSet	getResultSet	( )
int	getUpdateCount	( )

The most important methods are `executeQuery()`, `executeUpdate()`, and `execute()`. As you create a `Statement` object with a `SQL` statement, the `executeQuery()` method takes a SQL string. It passes the SQL string to the underlying data source through the driver manager and gets the `ResultSet` back to the application program. The `executeQuery()` method returns only one `ResultSet`. For those cases that return more than one `ResultSet`, the `execute()` method should be used.

Caution

Only one `ResultSet` can be opened per `Statement` object at one time.

For `SQL` statements that do not return a `ResultSet` such as the `UPDATE`, `DELETE`, and `DDL` statements, the `Statement` object has the `executeUpdate()` method that takes a SQL string and returns an integer. This integer indicates the number of rows that are affected by the SQL statement.

Note

The JDBC processing is synchronous; that is, the application program must wait for the SQL statements to complete. But because Java is a multithreaded platform, the JDBC designers suggest using threads to simulate asynchronous processing.

The `Statement` object is best suited for ad hoc SQL statements or SQL statements that are executed once. The DBMS goes through the syntax run, query plan optimization, and the execution plan generation stages as soon as this SQL statement is received. The DBMS executes the query and then discards the optimized execution plan. So, if the `executeQuery()` method is called again, the DBMS goes through all of the steps again.

The following example program shows how to use the `Statement` class to access a database (The database schema is shown in Figure 15.4 earlier in this chapter). In this example, you will list all of the subjects (classes) available in our enrollment database and their location and day and times. The SQL statement for this is `"SELECT ClassName, Location, DaysAndTimes FROM Classes"`. You will create a `Statement` object and pass the SQL string during the `executeQuery()` method call to get this data.

```
     //Declare a method and some variables.
     public void ListClasses() throws SQLException {
int i, NoOfColumns;
String ClassName,ClassLocation, ClassSchedule;
          //Initialize and load the JDBC-ODBC driver.
Class.forName ("jdbc.odbc.JdbcOdbcDriver");
          //Make the connection object.
Connection Ex1Con = DriverManager.getConnection(
"jdbc:odbc:StudentDB;uid="admin";pw="sa");
//Create a simple Statement object.
Statement Ex1Stmt = Ex1Con.createStatement();
//Make a SQL string, pass it to the DBMS, and execute the SQL statement.
ResultSet Ex1rs = Ex1Stmt.executeQuery(
 "SELECT ClassName, Location, DaysAndTimes FROM Classes");
//Process each row until there are no more rows.
// And display the results on the console.
System.out.println("Class         Location      Schedule");
while (Ex1rs.next()) {
// Get the column values into Java variables
ClassName = Ex1rs.getString(1);
ClassLocation = Ex1rs.getString(2);
ClassSchedule = Ex1rs.getString(3);
System.out.println(ClassName,ClassLocation,ClassSchedule);
}
}
```

As you can see, the program is very straightforward. You do the initial connection and so on, and create a `Statement` object. Pass the SQL along with the method `executeQuery()` call. The driver will pass the SQL string to the DBMS, which will perform the query and return the results. After the statement is done, the optimized execution plan is lost.

Creating and Using Compiles SQL Statements (*PreparedStatement*)

In the case of a `PreparedStatement` object, as the name implies, the application program prepares a SQL statement using the `java.sql.Connection.prepareStatement()` method. The `prepareStatement()` method takes a SQL string, which is passed to the underlying DBMS. The DBMS goes through the syntax run, query plan optimization, and the execution plan generation stages but does not execute the SQL statement. Possibly, the DBMS returns a handle to the optimized execution plan that the JDBC driver stores internally in the `PreparedStatement` object.

The methods of the `PreparedStatement` object are shown in Table 15.8. Notice that the `executeQuery()`, `executeUpdate()`, and `execute()` methods do not take any parameters. They are just calls to the underlying DBMS to perform the already optimized SQL statement.

Table 15.8 *PreparedStatement* Object Methods

Return Type	Method Name	Parameter
`ResultSet`	`executeQuery`	`()`
`int`	`executeUpdate`	`()`
`Boolean`	`execute`	`()`

One of the major features of a `PreparedStatement` is that it can handle `IN` types of parameters. The parameters are indicated in a `SQL` statement by placing the **?** as the parameter marker instead of the actual values. In the Java program, the association is made to the parameters with the `setXXXX()` methods, as shown in Table 15.9. All of the `setXXXX()` methods take the parameter index, which is 1 for the first "?," 2 for the second "?," and so on.

Table 15.9 *java.sql.PreparedStatement*—Parameter-Related Methods

Return Type	Method Name	Parameter
`void`	`clearParameters`	`()`
`void`	`setAsciiStream`	`(int parameterIndex, java.io.InputStream x, int length)`
`void`	`setBinaryStream`	`(int parameterIndex, java.io.InputStream x, int length)`
`void`	`setBoolean`	`(int parameterIndex, boolean x)`

Return Type	Method Name	Parameter
void	setByte	(int parameterIndex, byte x)
void	setBytes	(int parameterIndex, byte x[ ])
void	setDate	(int parameterIndex, java.sql.Date x)
void	setDouble	(int parameterIndex, double x)
void	setFloat	(int parameterIndex, float x)
void	setInt	(int parameterIndex, int x)
void	setLong	(int parameterIndex, long x)
void	setNull	(int parameterIndex, int sqlType)
void	setNumeric	(int parameterIndex, Numeric x)
void	setShort	(int parameterIndex, short x)
void	setString	(int parameterIndex, String x)
void	setTime	(int parameterIndex, java.sql.Time x)
void	setTimestamp	(int parameterIndex, java.sql. Timestamp x)
void	setUnicodeStream	(int parameterIndex, java.io. InputStream x, int length)
Advanced Features—Object Manipulation		
void	setObject	(int parameterIndex, Object x, int targetSqlType, int scale)
void	setObject	(int parameterIndex, Object x, int targetSqlType)
void	setObject	(int parameterIndex, Object x)

In the case of the `PreparedStatement`, the driver actually sends only the execution plan ID and the parameters to the DBMS. This results in less network traffic and is well-suited for Java applications on the Internet. The `PreparedStatement` should be used when you need to execute the SQL statement many times in a Java application. But remember, even though the optimized execution plan is available during the execution of a Java program, the DBMS discards the execution plan at the end of the program. So, the DBMS must go through all of the steps of creating an execution plan every time the program runs. The `PreparedStatement` object achieves faster SQL execution performance than the simple `Statement` object, as the DBMS does not have to run through the steps of creating the execution plan.

The following example program shows how to use the `PreparedStatement` class to access a database. (The database schema is shown in Figure 15.4 earlier in this chapter.) In this example, you will be a little more aggressive and optimize the example you developed in the `Statement` example. The simple `Statement` example can be improved in a couple of major ways. First, the DBMS will go through building the execution plan every time. So you will make it a `PreparedStatement`. Secondly, the query will list all courses which could scroll away. You will improve this situation by building a parameterized query as follows:

```
     //Declare class variables
Connection Con;
PreparedStatement PrepStmt;
boolean Initialized = false;
     private void InitConnection() throws SQLException {
          //Initialize and load the JDBC-ODBC driver.
Class.forName ("jdbc.odbc.JdbcOdbcDriver");
          //Make the connection object.
Con = DriverManager.getConnection( "jdbc:odbc:StudentDB;uid="admin";pw="sa");
//Create a prepared Statement object.
PrepStmt = Ex1Con.prepareStatement(
 "SELECT ClassName, Location, DaysAndTimes FROM Classes WHERE ClassName = ?");
Initialized = True;
}
     public void ListOneClass(String ListClassName) throws SQLException {
int i, NoOfColumns;
String ClassName,ClassLocation, ClassSchedule;
          if (! Initialized) {
InitConnection();
}
// Set the SQL parameter to the one passed into this method
PrepStmt.setString(1,ListClassName);
ResultSet Ex1rs = PrepStmt.executeQuery()
//Process each row until there are no more rows and
// display the results on the console.
System.out.println("Class         Location      Schedule");
while (Ex1rs.next()) {
// Get the column values into Java variables
ClassName = Ex1rs.getString(1);
ClassLocation = Ex1rs.getString(2);
ClassSchedule = Ex1rs.getString(3);
System.out.println(ClassName,ClassLocation,ClassSchedule);
}
}
```

Now, if a student wants to check the details of one subject interactively, the above example program can be used. You will save execution time and network traffic from the second invocation onwards because you are using the `PreparedStatement` object.

Calling Stored Procedures (*CallableStatement*)

For a secure, consistent, and manageable multi-tier client/server system, the data access should allow the use of stored procedures. Stored procedures centralize the business logic in terms of manageability and also in terms of running the query. Java applets running on clients with limited resources cannot be expected to run huge queries. But the results are important to those clients. JDBC allows the use of stored procedures by the `CallableStatement` class and with the escape clause string.

A `CallableStatement` object is created by the `prepareCall()` method in the `Connection` object. The `prepareCall()` method takes a string as the parameter. This string, called an *escape clause*, is of the form

```
{[? =] call <stored procedure name> [<parameter>,<parameter> ...]}
```

The `CallableStatement` class supports parameters. These parameters are of the `OUT` kind from a stored procedure or the `IN` kind to pass values into a stored procedure. The parameter marker (question mark) must be used for the return value (if any) and any output arguments, because the parameter marker is bound to a program variable in the stored procedure. Input arguments can be either literals or parameters. For a dynamic parameterized statement, the escape clause string takes the form:

```
{[? =] call <stored procedure name> [<?>,<?> ...]}
```

The `OUT` parameters should be registered using the `registerOutparameter()` method—as shown in Table 15.10— before the call to the `executeQuery()`, `executeUpdate()`, or `execute()` methods.

Table 15.10 *CallableStatement—OUT* Parameter Register Methods

Return Type	Method Name	Parameter
void	registerOutParameter	(int parameterIndex, int sqlType)
void	registerOutParameter	(int parameterIndex, int sqlType, int scale)

After the stored procedure is executed, the DBMS returns the result value to the JDBC driver. This return value is accessed by the Java program using the methods in Table 15.11.

Table 15.11 *CallableStatement* Parameter Access Methods

Return Type	Method Name	Parameter
Boolean	getBoolean	(int parameterIndex)
byte	getByte	(int parameterIndex)
byte[]	getBytes	(int parameterIndex)
java.sql.Date	getDate	(int parameterIndex)

continues

Table 15.11 Continued

Return Type	Method Name	Parameter
double	getDouble	(int parameterIndex)
float	getFloat	(int parameterIndex)
int	getInt	(int parameterIndex)
long	getLong	(int parameterIndex)
Numeric	getNumeric	(int parameterIndex, int scale)
Object	getObject	(int parameterIndex)
short	getShort	(int parameterIndex)
String	getString	(int parameterIndex)
java.sql.Time	getTime	(int parameterIndex)
java.sql.Timestamp	getTimestamp	(int parameterIndex)
Miscellaneous		
boolean	wasNull	()

If a student wants to find out the grades for a subject in the database schema shown in Figure 15.4, you need to do many operations on various tables such as find all assignments for the student, match them with class name, calculate grade points, and so on. This is a business logic (academics is also a business and the concepts apply here, too !) well-suited for a stored procedure. In this example, we give the stored procedure a student ID, class ID, and it will return the grade! Your client program becomes simple, and all the processing is done at the server. This is where you will use a `CallableStatement`.

The stored procedure call is of the following form:

```
studentGrade = getStudentGrade(StudentID,ClassID).
```

In the JDBC call, you will create a `CallableStatement` object with the `?` symbol as placeholders for parameters and then connect Java variables to the parameters as shown in the following example:

```
public void DisplayGrade(String StudentID, String ClassID) throws SQLException {
➥int Grade;
          //Initialize and load the JDBC-ODBC driver.
Class.forName ("jdbc.odbc.JdbcOdbcDriver");
          //Make the connection object.
Connection Con = DriverManager.getConnection(
"jdbc:odbc:StudentDB;uid="admin";pw="sa");
//Create a Callable Statement object.
```

```
CallableStatement CStmt = Con.prepareCall({?=call getStudentGrade[?,?]});
// Now tie the placeholders with actual parameters.
// Register the return value from the stored procedure
// as an integer type so that the driver knows how to handle it.
// Note the type is defined in the java.sql.Types.
CStmt.registerOutParameter(1,java.sql.Types.INTEGER);
// Set the In parameters (which are inherited from the PreparedStatement class)
CStmt.setString(1,StudentID);
CStmt.setString(2,ClassID);
// Now we are ready to call the stored procedure
int RetVal = CStmt.executeUpdate();
// Get the OUT parameter from the registered parameter
// Note that we get the result from the CallableStatement object
Grade = CStmt.getInt(1);
// And display the results on the console.
System.out.println(" The Grade is : ");
System.out.println(Grade);
}
```

As you can see, JDBC has minimized the complexities of getting results from a stored procedure. It still is a little involved, but is simpler. Maybe in the future, these steps will become simpler.

Now that you have seen how to communicate with the underlying DBMS with SQL, see what you need to do to process the results sent back from the database as a result of the SQL statements.

Retrieving Results in JDBC

The `ResultSet` object is actually a tubular data set; that is, it consists of rows of data organized in uniform columns. In JDBC, the Java program can see only one row of data at one time. The program uses the `next()` method to go to the next row. JDBC does not provide any methods to move backwards along the `ResultSet` or to remember the row positions (called *bookmarks* in ODBC). Once the program has a row, it can use the positional index (1 for the first column, 2 for the second column, and so on) or the column name to get the field value by using the `getXXXX()` methods. Table 15.12 shows the methods associated with the `ResultSet` object.

Table 15.12 *java.sql.ResultSet* Methods

Return Type	Method Name	Parameter
boolean	next	( )
void	close	( )
boolean	wasNull	( )

continues

Table 15.12 Continued

Return Type	Method Name	Parameter
Get Data by Column Position		
java.io.InputStream	getAsciiStream	(int columnIndex)
java.io.InputStream	getBinaryStream	(int columnIndex)
boolean	getBoolean	(int columnIndex)
byte	getByte	(int columnIndex)
byte[]	getBytes	(int columnIndex)
java.sql.Date	getDate	(int columnIndex)
double	getDouble	(int columnIndex)
float	getFloat	(int columnIndex)
int	getInt	(int columnIndex)
long	getLong	(int columnIndex)
java.sql.Numeric	getNumeric	(int columnIndex, int scale)
Object	getObject	(int columnIndex)
short	getShort	(int columnIndex)
String	getString	(int columnIndex)
java.sql.Time	getTime	(int columnIndex)
java.sql.Timestamp	getTimestamp	(int columnIndex)
java.io.InputStream	getUnicodeStream	(int columnIndex)
Get Data by Column Name		
java.io.InputStream	getAsciiStream	(String columnName)
java.io.InputStream	getBinaryStream	(String columnName)
boolean	getBoolean	(String columnName)
byte	getByte	(String columnName)
byte[]	getBytes	(String columnName)
java.sql.Date	getDate	(String columnName)
double	getDouble	(String columnName)
float	getFloat	(String columnName)
int	getInt	(String columnName)
long	getLong	(String columnName)
java.sql.Numeric	getNumeric	(String columnName, int scale)
Object	getObject	(String columnName)

Return Type	Method Name	Parameter
short	getShort	(String columnName)
String	getString	(String columnName)
java.sql.Time	getTime	(String columnName)
java.sql.Timestamp	getTimestamp	(String columnName)
java.io.InputStream	getUnicodeStream	(String columnName)
int	findColumn	(String columnName)
SQLWarning	getWarnings	( )
void	clearWarnings	( )
String	getCursorName	( )
ResultSetMetaData	getMetaData	( )

As you can see, the `ResultSet` methods—even though there are many—are very simple. The major ones are the `getXXX()` methods. The `getMetaData()` method returns the meta data information about a `ResultSet`. The `DatabaseMetaData` also returns the results in the ResultSet form. The `ResultSet` also has methods for the silent `SQLWarnings`. It is a good practice to check any warnings using the `getWarning()` method that returns a null if there are no warnings.

Handling Exceptions in JDBC—*SQLException* Class

The `SQLException` class in JDBC provides a variety of information regarding errors that occurred during a database access. The `SQLException` objects are chained so that a program can read them in order. This is a good mechanism, as an error condition can generate multiple errors and the final error might not have anything to do with the actual error condition. By chaining the errors, you can actually pinpoint the first error. Each `SQLException` has an error message and vendor-specific error code. Also associated with a `SQLException` is a `SQLState` string that follows the `XOPEN` `SQLstate` values defined in the SQL specification. Table 15.13 lists the methods for the `SQLException` class.

Table 15.13 *SQLException* Methods

Return Type	Method Name	Parameter
SQLException	SQLException	(String reason, String SQLState, int vendorCode)
SQLException	SQLException	(String reason, String SQLState)

continues

Table 15.13 Continued

Return Type	Method Name	Parameter
SQLException	SQLException	(String reason)
SQLException	SQLException	( )
String	getSQLState	( )
int	getErrorCode	( )
SQLException	getNextException	( )
void	setNextException	(SQLException ex)

Handling Exceptions in JDBC—*SQLWarnings* Class

Unlike the `SQLExceptions` that the program knows have happened because of raised exceptions, the `SQLWarnings` do not cause any commotion in a Java program. The `SQLWarnings` are tagged to the object whose method caused the `Warning`. So you should check for `Warnings` using the `getWarnings()` method that is available for all objects. Table 15.14 lists the methods associated with the `SQLWarnings` class.

Table 15.14 SQLWarnings Methods

Return Type	Function Name	Parameter
SQLWarning	SQLWarning	(String reason, String SQLstate, int vendorCode)
SQLWarning	SQLWarning	(String reason, String SQLstate)
SQLWarning	SQLWarning	(String reason)
SQLWarning	SQLWarning	( )
SQLWarning	getNextWarning	( )
void	setNextWarning	(SQLWarning w)

Handling Date and Time

Now that you have seen all of the main database-related classes, look at some of the supporting classes that are available in JDBC. These classes include `Date`, `Time`, `TimeStamp`,

`Numeric`, and so on. Most of these classes extend the basic Java classes to add the capability to handle and translate data types that are specific to SQL.

java.sql.Date

This package gives a Java program the capability to handle SQL DATE information with only year, month, and day values. This package contrasts with the `java.util.Date`, where the time in hours, minutes, and seconds is also kept (see Table 15.15).

Table 15.15 *java.sql.Date* Methods

Return Type	Method Name	Parameter
`Date`	`Date`	`(int year, int month, int day)`
`Date`	`valueOf`	`(String s)`
`String`	`toString`	`()`

java.sql.Time

As seen in Table 15.16, the `java.sql.Time` adds the `Time` object to the `java.util.Date` package to handle only hours, minutes, and seconds. `java.sql.Time` is also used to represent SQL `TIME` information.

Table 15.16 *java.sql.Time* Methods

Return Type	Method Name	Parameter
`Time`	`Time`	`(int hour, int minute, int second)`
`Time`	`Time`	`valueOf(String s)`
`String`	`toString`	`()`

java.sql.Timestamp

The `java.sql.Timestamp` package adds the `Timestamp` class to the `java.util.Date` package. It adds the capability of handling nanoseconds. But the granularity of the subsecond timestamp depends on the database field as well as the operating system (see Table 15.17).

Table 15.17 *java.sql.Timestamp* Methods

Return Type	Method Name	Parameter
Timestamp	Timestamp	(int year, int month, int date, int hour, int minute, int second, int nano);
Timestamp	valueOf	(String s)
String	toString	( )
int	getNanos	( )
void	setNanos	(int n)
boolean	equals	(Timestamp ts)

Handling SQL Types

In JDBC, the SQL types are defined in the `java.sql.Types` class and the different numeric types are handled in the `java.sql.Numeric` class.

java.sql.Types

This class defines a set of `XOPEN` equivalent integer constants that identify SQL types. The constants are final types. Therefore, they cannot be redefined in applications or applets. Table 15.18 lists the constant names and their values.

Table 15.18 *java.sql.Types* Constants

Constant Name	Value
BIGINT	-5
BINARY	-2
BIT	-7
CHAR	1
DATE	91
DECIMAL	3
DOUBLE	8
FLOAT	6
INTEGER	4

Constant Name	Value
LONGVARBINARY	-4
LONGVARCHAR	-1
NULL	0
NUMERIC	2
OTHER	1111
REAL	7
SMALLINT	5
TIME	92
TIMESTAMP	93
TINYINT	-6
VARBINARY	-3
VARCHAR	12

JDBC in Perspective

In this chapter, you saw how JDBC has ushered in an era of simple yet powerful database access for Java programs. JDBC is an important step in the right direction to elevate the Java language to the Java platform. The Java APIs—including the Enterprise APIs (JDBC, RMI, Serialization, and IDL), Security APIs, and the Server APIs—are the essential ingredients for developing enterprise-level, distributed, multi-tier client/server applications.

The JDBC specification life cycle happened in the speed of the Net—one Net year is widely clocked as equaling seven normal years. The version 1.01 JDBC specification is fixed, so the developers and driver vendors are not chasing a moving target.

Another factor in favor of JDBC is its similarity to ODBC. JavaSoft made the right decision to follow ODBC philosophy and abstractions, thus making it easy for ISVs and users to leverage their ODBC experience and existing ODBC drivers. In the JDBC specification, this goal is described as "JDBC must be implementable on top of common database interfaces."

By making JDBC a part of the Java language, you received all of the advantages of the Java language concepts for database access. Also, as all implementers have to support the Java APIs, JDBC has become a universal standard. This philosophy, stated in the JDBC specification as "provide a Java interface that is consistent with the rest of the Java system," makes JDBC an ideal candidate for use in Java-based database development.

Another good design philosophy is the driver independence of the JDBC. The underlying database drivers can either be native libraries—such as a dynamic link lbrary (.dll) for the Windows system or Java routines connecting to listeners. The full Java implementation of JDBC is suitable for a variety of Network and other Java OS computers, thus making JDBC a versatile set of APIs.

Note

In my humble opinion, the most important advantage of JDBC is its simplicit and versatility. The goal of the designers was to keep the API and common cases simple and "support the weird stuff in separate interfaces." Also, they wanted to use multiple methods for multiple functionality. They have achieved their goals even in this first version. For example, the `statement` object has the `executeQuery()` method for SQL statements returning rows of data, and it has the `executeUpdate()` method for statements without data to return. Also, uncommon cases, such as statements returning multiple `ResultSets`, have a separate method—`execute()`.

As more applications are developed with JDBC and as the Java platform matures, more and more features will be added to JDBC. One of the required features, especially for client/server processing, is a more versatile cursor. The current design leaves the cursor management details to the driver. I would prefer more application-level control for scrollable cursors, positioned update/delete capability, and so on. Another related feature is the bookmark feature, which is useful especially in a distributed processing environment such as the Internet.

PART III

Creating 3-Tier Distributed Applications

chapter 16

Creating 3-Tier Distributed Applications with RMI

by Mark Wutka

In this chapter

- **Designing 3-tier applications**
  There are many advantages to creating 3-tier applications instead of 2-tier. To fully realize the benefits of 3-tier applications, you must put in a lot of up-front design work.
- **Invoking methods remotely with RMI**
  The Remote Method Invocation package allows an object to invoke methods in another object over the network. This makes it much easier to design distributed applications.
- **Implementing remote methods**
  There are just a few simple steps you need to take to create methods that can be invoked remotely. Aside from some extra setup, the actual remote method implementation is no different from local methods.
- **Invoking remote methods**
  There is very little difference between invoking methods locally and invoking methods remotely. Once you create a connection to a remote server, the only extra thing you need to be aware of is that remote methods can throw a special remote exception.
- **Performing peer-to-peer method invocations**
  You aren't restricted to a pure client/server model when using RMI. Objects can invoke methods on one another, where both objects act like servers and clients.

There are many ways that objects can communicate with one another over a network. Traditionally, objects would communicate with one another using sockets and a custom protocol. Remote procedure calls have also been a popular communication mechanism for the past few years. Java provides two additional mechanisms for remote object-to-object communication. Java provides an interface into the CORBA-distributed object architecture, which is discussed in

Chapter 17, "Creating CORBA Clients." Remote Method Invocation (RMI) provides a very simple method for one Java object to invoke a method in another Java object across a network with very little extra work. Unlike many remote communication systems that require you to describe the remote methods in a separate file, RMI works right off existing objects, providing seamless integration.

Creating 3-Tier Applications

The 2-tier model for applications is the most common model in use today. Many application designers think only in terms of the database and the application.

The availability of 2-tier application builders has helped perpetuate this philosophy. The 2-tier model is not a "bad thing," but there are cases in which the 3-tier model would be a better choice.

Just to review, the 2-tier model consists of an application and a database. A 3-tier model consists of an application, a layer of business logic, and a database. Once you break out of the 2-tier mold, you often start adding multiple tiers. Figure 16.1 illustrates the difference between a 2-tier and 3-tier application design.

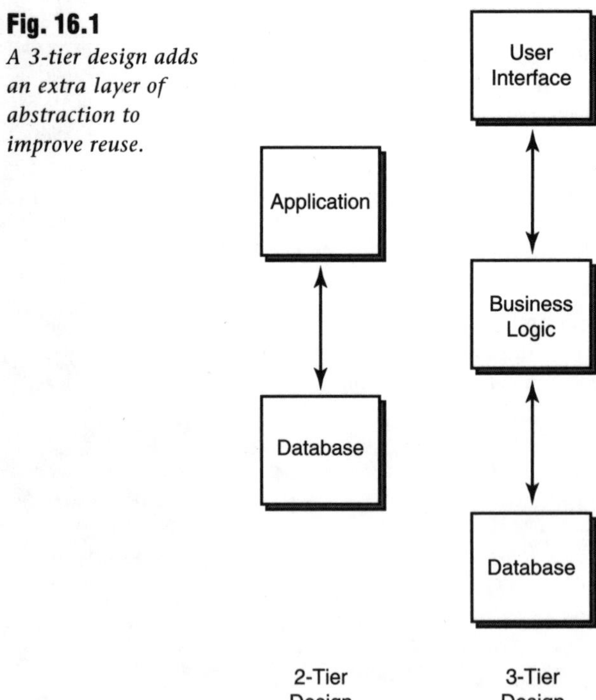

Fig. 16.1
A 3-tier design adds an extra layer of abstraction to improve reuse.

You can also divide your application into an application logic tier and a presentation tier (the user interface). In a 2-tier model, the business logic is part of the application. In smaller applications, this is not a problem because there may be only one application implementing a particular business process.

In larger systems, however, many applications use the same areas of business logic. In a 2-tier environment, this means that the business logic is replicated across every application. If you change the business logic, you must change every application.

Durable software systems are designed from the ground up with change in mind. A good designer creates modular components with well-defined interfaces so that any single component can be changed without affecting the rest of the system. The 3-tier and multi-tier models are simply the results of modular design.

Before you go off thinking that creating 3-tier designs is simple, think again. Identifying business processes in a large company and reducing them to a set of methods is not a task for the fainthearted.

Many companies do not have their business logic documented as a series of processes. Instead, it is only implied in the code of the applications. The identification of business processes and business logic is a subject for another book, however.

In practice, the line between 2-tier and 3-tier is often rather fuzzy. You may have what is essentially a 2-tier application whose user interface is broken out into a separate module.

The application logic and the business logic are still intermixed, but a portion of the application is distributed. Just because you can't get a handle on the actual business logic doesn't mean you can't still work at making your software more modular and add the benefits of distributed computing.

RMI is very useful for separating an application from its user interface. You define the methods that comprise the interactions between the user interface and the client, and then make these interactions through remote method invocation (RMI). This allows an applet to implement the user interface for an application running on a server somewhere, without developing a custom communications system.

RMI Features

RMI is like a remote procedure call (RPC) mechanism in other languages. One object makes a method call into an object on another machine and gets a result back. Like most RPC systems, RMI requires that the object whose method is being invoked (the server) must already be up and running.

Remote methods are defined by remote interfaces. That is, a remote interface defines a set of methods that can be called remotely. Any object that wants some of its methods to be called remotely must use one or more remote interfaces.

An object that uses a remote interface is called a *server*. An object that calls a remote method is called a *client*. An object can be both a client and a server: These names indicate only who is calling in a particular instance and who is being called.

Once you define a remote interface and create an object that uses the interface, you still need a way for the client to invoke methods on the server. Unfortunately, it is not quite as easy as instantiating a server object.

You need to create a *stub* for the client. An object's stub is a remote view of that object in that it contains only the remote methods of the object. The stub runs on the client side and is the representative of the remote object in the client's data space.

The client invokes methods on the stub and the stub then invokes the methods on the remote object. This allows any client to invoke remote methods through normal Java method invocation. A stub is also called a *proxy*. Figure 16.2 shows the relationship between a client, a server, and a stub.

Fig. 16.2
A stub invokes remote methods on behalf of a client.

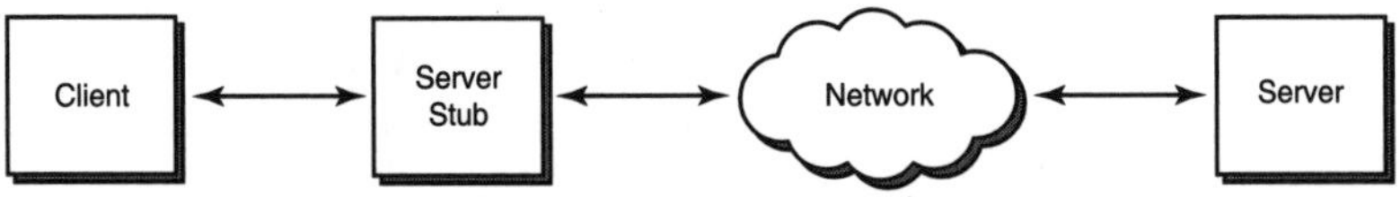

RMI adds an extra feature that most RPC systems do not have. Remote objects can be passed as parameters in remote method calls. When you pass a remote object as a parameter, you actually pass a stub for the object.

The real object always stays on the machine where it was originally started. The stub that is passed then invokes methods back to the original object. Stubs can also be passed as parameters and work the same way. Figure 16.3 illustrates how a client passes a stub to a server so that the server can invoke methods on the client.

In a distributed system, you need a way for clients to find the servers they need. RMI provides a simple name lookup object that allows a client to get a stub for a particular server based on the server's name. The naming service that comes with the RMI system is fairly simplistic but is useful for most cases. Figure 16.4 shows how a client uses the naming service to find a server.

Fig. 16.3
A client can pass a stub to a server so the server can invoke methods on the client.

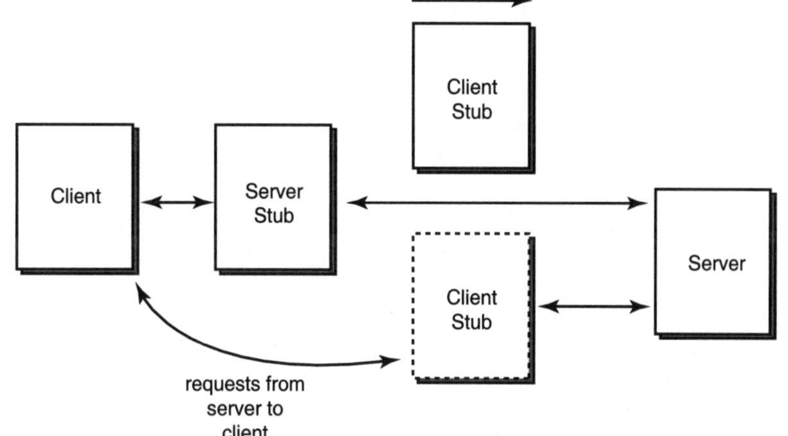

Fig. 16.4
The naming service allows a client to locate a server by name.

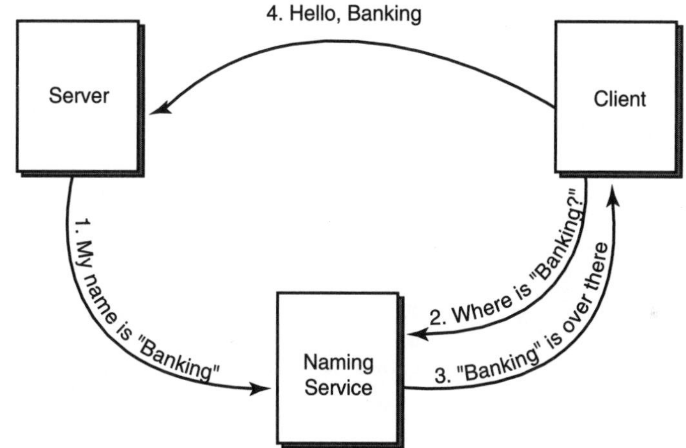

Creating an RMI Server

To create an object whose methods can be called remotely (a server object), you need to create a remote interface. All remote interfaces must extend the `java.rmi.Remote` interface.

Defining a Remote Interface

When you define a remote interface, pay special attention to the interaction between the objects. Remote invocations carry much heavier penalties than local invocations. Try to minimize the number of method invocations needed to get the job done.

Ideally, you want to do things with a single method call. Every method in a remote interface can throw a `java.rmi.RemoteException`. This exception is thrown by the underlying RMI system whenever there is an error in sending or receiving information.

Listing 16.1 shows a sample remote interface for a simple banking application.

Listing 16.1 Source Code for *Banking.java*

```
package banking;

// This interface represents a set of remote methods for a
// banking service. All money amounts are given in cents, so
// one dollar is represented as 100.

public interface Banking extends java.rmi.Remote
{

// getBalance returns the current balance in the account
     public int getBalance(Account account)
          throws java.rmi.RemoteException, BankingException;

// withdraw subtracts an amount from an account
     public void withdraw(Account account, int amount)
          throws java.rmi.RemoteException, BankingException;

// deposit adds an amount to the account
     public void deposit(Account account, int amount)
          throws java.rmi.RemoteException, BankingException;

// transfer subtracts an amount from one account and
// adds it to another.
     public void transfer(Account fromAccount, Account toAccount,
          int amount)
          throws java.rmi.RemoteException, BankingException;
}
```

Notice that the account information is encapsulated in an `Account` object. This allows you to change the way you represent accounts without modifying the interface. Of course, you may have to change the client and server to understand the new account format.

Tip

Try to encapsulate related parameters into a single object, especially if they are subject to change. If a position is given by an x,y coordinate, encapsulate it in a `Position` object so you can later change the position to be x,y,z or even polar coordinates. This allows you to keep the remote interface the same.

Listing 16.2 shows the `Account` object used in the `Banking` interface.

Listing 16.2 Source Code for *Account.java*

```
package banking;

// This class contains the information that defines
// a banking account.

public class Account extends Object
{
// Flags to indicate whether the account is savings or checking
     public static final int CHECKING = 1;
     public static final int SAVINGS = 2;

     public String id;     // Account id, or account number
     public String password;     // password for ATM transactions
     public int which;     // is this checking or savings

     public Account()
     {
     }

     public Account(String id, String password, int which)
     {
          this.id = id;
          this.password = password;
          this.which = which;
     }

     public String toString()
     {
          return "Account { "+id+","+password+","+which+" }";
     }

// Tests equality between accounts.
     public boolean equals(Object ob)
     {
          if (!(ob instanceof Account)) return false;
          Account other = (Account) ob;

          return id.equals(other.id) &&
               password.equals(other.password) &&
               (which == other.which);
     }

// Returns a hash code for this object

     public int hashCode()
     {
          return id.hashCode()+password.hashCode()+which;
     }
}
```

Tip

When encapsulating similar data into an object, always define the `equals` and `hashCode` methods. You may occasionally want to store the objects in hash tables and other structures, and without these methods, two objects containing identical data look like two separate objects.

Listing 16.3 shows the `BankingException` class for the `Banking` interface.

Listing 16.3 Source Code for *BankingException.java*

```
package banking;

// Defines a generic banking exception for the banking interface.

public class BankingException extends Exception
{
     public BankingException()
     {
     }

     public BankingException(String problem)
     {
          super(problem);
     }
}
```

Tip

Don't lump all your exceptions into one big exception, hiding the specific information in a string. Create exceptions specifically for each separate case. You don't want to parse the exception string to find out what kind of exception it was. Instead, you should be using `instanceof`.

For a simple interface like the `Banking` interface, there are only two specific exceptions defined: `InvalidAccountException` and `InsufficientFundsException`. Listings 16.4 and 16.5 show these exceptions.

Listing 16.4 Source Code for *InvalidAccountException.java*

```
package banking;

// Defines an exception for an invalid account and indicates
// which account was invalid. Also allows an error string.

public class InvalidAccountException extends BankingException
{
      public Account account;           // which account was invalid

      public InvalidAccountException()
      {
      }

      public InvalidAccountException(String str)
      {
              super(str);
      }

      public InvalidAccountException(Account account)
      {
              this.account = account;
      }

      public InvalidAccountException(Account account, String str)
      {
              super(str);
              this.account = account;
      }
```

Listing 16.5 Source Code for *InsufficientFundsException.java*

```
package banking;

// Defines a simple Insufficent Funds exception for the
// Banking interface.

public class InsufficientFundsException extends BankingException
{
     public InsufficientFundsException()
     {
     }

     public InsufficientFundsException(String problem)
     {
          super(problem);
     }
}
```

Creating the Server Implementation

The remote interface defines only which methods in an object are remote methods. You must still implement the remote object itself.

The implementation of the remote methods is straightforward: It is no different from implementing normal methods. Apart from the implementation of the methods, you need some startup code to create a security manager, create the remote objects, and register them with the `Naming` service.

When a server registers itself to the `Naming` service, it can call either the `bind` or `rebind` methods. The `bind` method throws an `AlreadyBoundException` if you try to bind an existing name to an object. The `rebind` method simply forgets about the old name association and binds the name to the new object.

Caution

It is possible for a client or server to send you malicious objects. You should exercise extreme caution when interacting with clients or servers that you did not write.

The RMI system includes a `StubSecurityManager` that implements some security measures to help protect your applications. If you run RMI servers or clients as stand-alone programs and you don't have your own security manager, make sure you set `StubSecurityManager`. The default for stand-alone programs is to have no security manager.

Listing 16.6 shows a sample implementation of a remote banking object.

Listing 16.6 Source Code for *BankingImpl.java*

```
package banking;

import java.rmi.Naming;
import java.rmi.server.UnicastRemoteServer;
import java.rmi.server.StubSecurityManager;

import java.util.*;

// This class implements a remote banking object. It sets up
// a set of dummy accounts and allows you to manipulate them
// through the Banking interface.
//
// Accounts are identified by the combination of the account id,
// the password and the account type. This is a quick and dirty
// way to work, and not the way a bank would normally do it, since
```

```
// the password is not part of the unique identifier of the account.

public class BankingImpl extends UnicastRemoteServer implements Banking
{
     public Hashtable accountTable;

// The constructor creates a table of dummy accounts.

     public BankingImpl()
     throws java.rmi.RemoteException
     {
          accountTable = new Hashtable();

          accountTable.put(
               new Account("AA1234", "1017", Account.CHECKING),
               new Integer(50000));     // $500.00 balance

          accountTable.put(
               new Account("AA1234", "1017", Account.SAVINGS),
               new Integer(148756));     // $1487.56 balance

          accountTable.put(
               new Account("AB5678", "4456", Account.CHECKING),
               new Integer(7742));     // $77.32 balance

          accountTable.put(
               new Account("AB5678", "4456", Account.SAVINGS),
               new Integer(32201));     // $322.01 balance
     }

// getBalance returns the amount of money in the account (in cents).
// If the account is invalid, it throws an InvalidAccountException

     public int getBalance(Account account)
     throws java.rmi.RemoteException, BankingException
     {

// Fetch the account from the table
          Integer balance = (Integer) accountTable.get(account);

// If the account wasn't there, throw an exception
          if (balance == null) {
               throw new InvalidAccountException(account);
          }

// Return the account's balance
          return balance.intValue();
     }

// withdraw subtracts an amount from the account's balance. If
// the account is invalid, it throws InvalidAccountException.
// If the withdrawal amount exceeds the account balance, it
// throws InsufficientFundsException.

     public synchronized void withdraw(Account account, int amount)
     throws java.rmi.RemoteException, BankingException
     {
```

continues

Listing 16.6 Continued

```
// Fetch the account
        Integer balance = (Integer) accountTable.get(account);

// If the account wasn't there, throw an exception
        if (balance == null) {
             throw new InvalidAccountException(account);
        }

// If we are trying to withdraw more than is in the account,
// throw an exception

        if (balance.intValue() < amount) {
             throw new InsufficientFundsException();
        }

// Put the new balance in the account

        accountTable.put(account, new Integer(balance.intValue() -
             amount));
   }

// Deposit adds an amount to an account. If the account is invalid
// it throws an InvalidAccountException

   public synchronized void deposit(Account account, int amount)
   throws java.rmi.RemoteException, BankingException
   {

// Fetch the account
        Integer balance = (Integer) accountTable.get(account);

// If the account wasn't there, throw an exception
        if (balance == null) {
             throw new InvalidAccountException(account);
        }

// Update the account with the new balance
        accountTable.put(account, new Integer(balance.intValue() +
             amount));
   }

// Transfer subtracts an amount from fromAccount and adds it to toAccount.
// If either account is invalid it throws InvalidAccountException.
// If there isn't enough money in fromAccount it throws
// InsufficientFundsException.

   public synchronized void transfer(Account fromAccount,
        Account toAccount, int amount)
   throws java.rmi.RemoteException, BankingException
   {

// Fetch the from account
        Integer fromBalance = (Integer) accountTable.get(fromAccount);

// If the from account doesn't exist, throw an exception
```

```
            if (fromBalance == null) {
                throw new InvalidAccountException(fromAccount);
            }

// Fetch the to account
            Integer toBalance = (Integer) accountTable.get(toAccount);

// If the to account doesn't exist, throw an exception
            if (toBalance == null) {
                throw new InvalidAccountException(toAccount);
            }

// Make sure the from account contains enough money, otherwise throw
// an InsufficientFundsException.

            if (fromBalance.intValue() < amount) {
                throw new InsufficientFundsException();
            }


// Subtract the amount from the fromAccount
            accountTable.put(fromAccount,
                new Integer(fromBalance.intValue() - amount));

// Add the amount to the toAccount
            accountTable.put(toAccount,
                new Integer(toBalance.intValue() + amount));
        }

        public static void main(String args[])
        {

// Need a security manager to prevent malicious stubs
            System.setSecurityManager(new StubSecurityManager());

            try {
// Create the bank
                BankingImpl bank = new BankingImpl();

// Register the bank with the naming service.
                Naming.rebind("NetBank", bank);

            } catch (Exception e) {
                System.out.println("Got exception: "+e);
                e.printStackTrace();
            }
        }
}
```

Creating the Stub Class

You don't have to create the stub class for your remote object by hand. The RMI system provides a special utility to automatically generate the stub class for you.

To generate the stubs for the `BankingImpl` class, the `BankingImpl.class` file should be stored in a directory called `banking` somewhere on your system. Go to the parent directory of the `banking` directory and type:

```
rmic -d . banking.BankingImpl
```

This creates the stubs for the `BankingImpl` class and also puts them in the `banking` directory.

Creating an RMI Client

Creating an RMI client is a simple task. When you need to access a remote object, you call the `lookup` method in the `Naming` service (also called the *registry*).

The `lookup` method returns a stub for the remote object. The contains all the remote methods defined for that object. If the stub is not on the client system, the RMI system tries to download the stubs from the remote object's host or from wherever the remote object was loaded.

Listing 16.7 shows a very simple application that remotely invokes methods in the `BankingImpl` object.

Listing 16.7 Source Code for *BankingClient.java*

```
import java.rmi.server.StubSecurityManager;
import java.rmi.Naming;

import banking.*;

// This program tries out some of the methods in the BankingImpl
// remote object.

public class BankingClient
{

     public static void main(String args[])
     {

// Always set up a security manager when running RMI
          System.setSecurityManager(new StubSecurityManager());

// Create an Account object for the account we are going to access.

          Account myAccount = new Account(
               "AA1234", "1017", Account.CHECKING);

          try {

// Get a stub for the BankingImpl object (the stub implements the
```

```
// Banking interface).

                Banking bank = (Banking)Naming.lookup("NetBank");

// Check the initial balance
                System.out.println("My balance is: "+
                     bank.getBalance(myAccount));

// Deposit some money
                bank.deposit(myAccount, 50000);

// Check the balance again
                System.out.println("Deposited $500.00, balance is: "+
                     bank.getBalance(myAccount));

// Withdraw some money
                bank.withdraw(myAccount, 25000);

// Check the balance again
                System.out.println("Withdrew $250.00, balance is: "+
                     bank.getBalance(myAccount));

           } catch (Exception e) {
                System.out.println("Got exception: "+e);
                e.printStackTrace();
           }
      }
}
```

Creating Peer-to-Peer RMI Applications

Distributed systems that support only a pure client/server model sometimes give system designers fits. In many applications, such as banking, the pure client/server model fits quite well, since the client always initiates requests, and the server handles them and passes the data back until the transaction is completed.

In other applications, you need the server to be able to invoke methods in the client as well. This is called peer-to-peer since both objects take on the role of client and server.

The observer-observable model is often needed in distributed systems. The interaction in the model occurs in both directions. Consequently, you need the observer to behave as a client to register itself with the observable and then behave as a server so the observable can invoke the `update` method in the observer.

If an object can only be a client or a server and not both, you can still implement the observer-observable model but the methods are ugly. The observer could periodically poll the observable to see whether it changes. But this would put a tremendous burden on the observable, since it spends a lot of time telling the observers that it hasn't changed.

The observable could also set up a `waitForChange` method that blocks until the observable changes. This could result in a large number of threads on the observable just sitting around waiting for a change.

It consumes less network resources than the polling method because there are no "have you changed?" "No." messages flying back and forth. This is still a less-than-optimal solution, however.

For one thing, suppose the observable changes in the time that it takes the observer to call `waitForChange` again. Should it keep track of whether things have changed since the last call? If so, that's extra work. If not, the observer may miss changes.

The RMI system allows an object to be both a client and a server, relieving you of many of these headaches. Typically, one object starts out as the server and one starts out as the client. At some point, the client invokes a method on the server and passes a stub back to the client, and the client also becomes a server.

You might, for example, have a server that sends periodic updates of information. A client registers with the server telling it what information it wants and passes the client's stub to the server. Whenever the server has new information, it invokes a method in what was originally the client via the stub. Figure 16.5 shows the relationship between two objects in a peer-to-peer stock-quoting system.

Fig. 16.5
The stock-quote server uses RMI to send quotes to its clients.

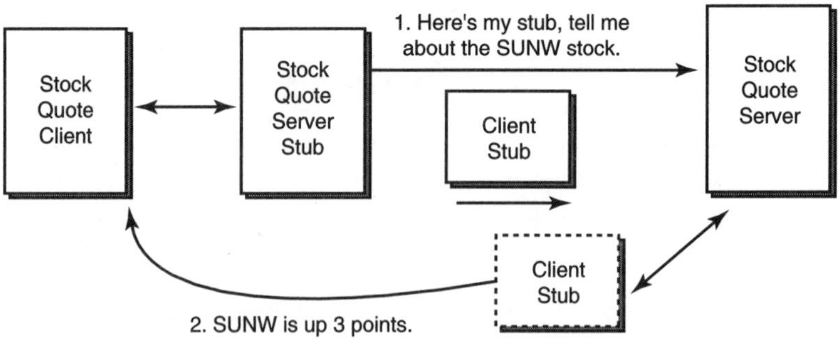

Listing 16.8 shows a remote interface for a stock-quoting system that invokes a method in its clients to deliver stock quotes.

Listing 16.8 Source Code for *StockQuoteServer.java*

```
package stocks;

// Defines a remote interface for a stock quoting system.
// Stock quotes are delivered to remote objects through the
// StockQuoteClient interface.
```

```
public interface StockQuoteServer extends java.rmi.Remote
{

// addWatch tells the server that the client wants quotes for
// a certain stock.

     public void addWatch(StockQuoteClient client, String stock)
          throws java.rmi.RemoteException, StockQuoteException;

// removeWatch tells the server that the client no longer wants
// to watch a certain stock.

     public void removeWatch(StockQuoteClient client, String stock)
          throws java.rmi.RemoteException, StockQuoteException;

// removeClient tells the server that the client no longer wants
// to watch any stocks.

     public void removeClient(StockQuoteClient client)
          throws java.rmi.RemoteException, StockQuoteException;

// getStockList returns an array of all the stocks that can be watched

     public String[] getStockList()
          throws java.rmi.RemoteException;
}
```

Listing 16.9 shows the `StockQuoteClient` interface that the `StockQuoteServer` uses to notify its clients of new quotes.

Listing 16.9 Source Code for *StockQuoteClient.java*

```
package stocks;

// Defines a callback interface for the StockQuoteServer so
// it can notify its clients of new stock quotes.

public interface StockQuoteClient extends java.rmi.Remote
{
     public void quote(StockQuote quote)
     throws java.rmi.RemoteException;
}
```

Rather than putting the individual elements of a stock quote into the method definition, the stock quotes are passed around in a `StockQuote` object. If the system expands the information in the stock quote, it still works with the existing clients, as long as it doesn't remove or rename any fields.

This lets you build an extensible system without having to change all your existing clients at once. If you change the `quote` method, however, all the clients have to change. Listing 16.10 shows the `StockQuote` object.

Listing 16.10 Source Code for *StockQuote.java*

```
package stocks;

// Defines the information contained in a stock quote for the
// StockQuoteClient interface.

public class StockQuote
{
     public String stock;     // the stock name
     public double amount;     // the last price
     public double change;     // the last change

     public StockQuote()
     {
     }

     public StockQuote(String stock, double amount, double change)
     {
          this.stock = stock;
          this.amount = amount;
          this.change = change;
     }
}
```

The stock-quote system defines its own exceptions. You should always do this for your systems if you intend to throw any exceptions outside the standard ones in Java.

`StockQuoteException` serves as the base class for all specific exceptions in the stock-quote system. There is only one specific exception defined: `UnknownStockException`.

Again, if you can define a specific exception, do it. Don't heap everything into one generic exception. Listings 16.11 and 16.12 show `StockQuoteException` and `UnknownStockException`.

Listing 16.11 Source Code for *StockQuoteException.java*

```
package stocks;

// Defines a generic exception for the stock quoting system

public class StockQuoteException extends Exception
{
     public StockQuoteException()
     {
     }

     public StockQuoteException(String str)
     {
          super(str);
     }
}
```

Listing 16.12 Source Code for *UnknownStockException.java*

```
package stocks;

// Defines an exception for an unknown stock.

public class UnknownStockException extends StockQuoteException
{
     public UnknownStockException()
     {
     }

     public UnknownStockException(String str)
     {
          super(str);
     }
}
```

Distributed systems have their own unique little problems. When you invoke a method on an object locally, you don't worry about whether or not the method will be invoked. If you get an exception, you know that there was an error within the method and not a problem invoking the method.

There are, however, many things in a distributed system that can stand between a client and the remote method it is invoking. When you get a `RemoteException`, you don't know what the problem is. The network could have had a temporary failure, the server program could have died, or the machine the server was running on could have died.

Listing 16.13 shows the `addWatch` method from the `StockQuoteServerImpl` class included on the CD for this book. This method is invoked by clients to subscribe to stock quotes. The first parameter to the `addWatch` method is a reference to the client (actually, a stub for communicating with the client). The server saves this reference for later use when it goes to publish new stock quotes. The `StockQuoteServerImpl` keeps a table of clients for each stock, because a stock can have multiple clients (a client of a stock receives quotes for that stock).

Listing 16.13 *addWatch* Method for *StockQuoteServerImpl.java*

```
// addWatch adds a client to the list of clients watching a stock

     public void addWatch(StockQuoteClient client, String stock)
     throws java.rmi.RemoteException, StockQuoteException
     {

// If we don't know about the stock, throw an exception

          if (stocks.get(stock) == null) {
               throw new UnknownStockException(stock);
          }
```

continues

Listing 16.13 Continued

```
// Get the container of clients watching this stock
        Vector clients = (Vector) stockClients.get(stock);

// If no clients are watching, create the container
        if (clients == null) {
            clients = new Vector();
            clients.addElement(client);
            stockClients.put(stock, clients);

// Only add the client if it isn't already there. We don't want to
// double-update clients.

        } else if (!clients.contains(client)) {
            clients.addElement(client);
        }
    }
```

One of the most important things you must handle when performing callbacks is figuring out when a client has disconnected. The `StockQuoteServerImpl` class uses a very simple technique—when the server sends a stock quote to a client that results in an exception, the server disconnects the client. Listing 16.14 shows the `publishQuote` method from the `StockQuoteServerImpl`. Notice that when the `publishQuote` method catches an exception when publishing the quote, it does not immediately remove the client. Instead, it stores the reference to the client in a separate vector. This is necessary because an enumeration can become confused if you remove elements from a vector while you are enumerating through it.

Listing 16.14 *publishQuote* Method from *StockQuoteServerImpl.java*

```
// publishQuote sends a stock quote to every client who is watching

    protected void publishQuote(StockQuote quote)
    {

// Get the list of clients for the stock
        Vector v = (Vector) stockClients.get(quote.stock);

// If there are no clients, we're done
        if (v == null) return;

        Enumeration e = v.elements();

// When we get an exception sending a notification to a client, we
// remove the client. We don't do it until we've sent all the
// notifications however. We store them in badClients until then.

        Vector badClients = null;
```

```
            while (e.hasMoreElements()) {

                StockQuoteClient client = (StockQuoteClient)
                    e.nextElement();

// send the quote to the client
                try {
                    client.quote(quote);

// If we get an error, add the client to the list of bad clients

                } catch (java.rmi.RemoteException oops) {
                    if (badClients == null) {
                        badClients = new Vector();
                    }
                    badClients.addElement(client);
                }
            }

// If there were any bad clients, remove them

            if (badClients != null) {
                e = badClients.elements();
                while (e.hasMoreElements()) {
                    clearClient(
                        (StockQuoteClient) e.nextElement());
                }
            }
        }
```

To do peer-to-peer RMI from an applet, you have to create another object to be the server for method invocations to the applet. You can't remotely call methods in a subclass of `Applet` because you must inherit from `RemoteServer`.

Since Java doesn't allow multiple inheritance, you must define another object to handle the incoming remote method invocations. If you really want to invoke methods in the applet, the special object you create can just turn around and invoke methods in the applet.

Listing 16.15 shows a simple stock-quote client that receives all stock quotes from the stock-quote server.

Listing 16.15 Source Code for *StockQuoter.java*

```
package stocks;

import java.rmi.server.UnicastRemoteServer;
import java.rmi.server.StubSecurityManager;

// This class is a client of the StockQuoteServer. It acts as a
// server too, since the StockQuoteServer invokes the update method
// in this object.
```

continues

Listing 16.15 Continued

```
public class StockQuoter extends UnicastRemoteServer
implements StockQuoteClient
{
     public StockQuoter()
     throws java.rmi.RemoteException
     {
     }

// When we receive a stock quote, just print out the information

     public void quote(StockQuote stockQuote)
     throws java.rmi.RemoteException
     {
          System.out.println(stockQuote.stock+": "+stockQuote.amount+
               "("+stockQuote.change+")");
     }

     public static void main(String[] args)
     {
// Always use a security manager for RMI.
          System.setSecurityManager(new StubSecurityManager());

          try {

// Get a stub to the stock quoting system
               StockQuoteServer server = (StockQuoteServer)
                    java.rmi.Naming.lookup("StockQuotes");

// Create an instance of this object to receive the incoming stock quotes
               StockQuoter quoter = new StockQuoter();

// Get a list of all the stock we can watch
               String[] stocks = server.getStockList();

// Subscribe to each stock
               for (int i=0; i < stocks.length; i++) {
                    server.addWatch(quoter, stocks[i]);
               }

          } catch (Exception e) {
               System.out.println("Got exception: "+e);
               e.printStackTrace();
          }
     }
}
```

Garbage Collection, Remote Objects, and Peer-to-Peer

RMI has a reference-count, garbage-collection system that works with Java's garbage collection. RMI keeps track of the number of remote references to an object and prevents it from being collected by the Java garbage collector. When an object has no more references, it can be collected by the Java garbage collector but only if it has no local references, either.

If you are familiar with garbage collection, you know that reference-count garbage collection does not work when you can have circular references. That is, if A has a reference to B and B has a reference to A, neither is ever collected because they each always have at least one active reference.

For a straight client/server model, you won't have a problem since the references are one-way. Problems can occur whenever an object is acting both as a client and a server.

It might be as simple as two objects holding references to each other. But it might also be a more complex chain in which A refers to B, which refers to C, which refers to D, which refers back to A. All of these objects would always have at least one reference, even if they were not in use.

If you have this kind of setup, you may have to do a little nudging to get objects collected. You can break this uncollectable chain by explicitly setting a client reference to null rather than hoping the whole object will be collected.

The stock-quoting system takes a good approach in that it allows the client to tell the quote server to remove any references to the client. When the client shuts down, it should disconnect itself from the client by calling `removeClient`. That breaks the circular reference chain.

chapter 17

Creating CORBA Clients

by Ken Cartwright

In this chapter

- **How to use a server's CORBA IDL interface definition file to develop an ORB-enabled Java applet**
  A CORBA server defines the API to its services using CORBA's Interface Definition Language (IDL). An IDL compiler is used to generate the code necessary to support CORBA based client/server connectivity.

- **How the design of an IDL interface affects client design and implementation**
  The nature of a server's IDL interface has a large impact on the character of the interaction between client and server, and drives some significant client-side design decisions. This chapter will describe some approaches to IDL interface definition and their impact on client applets.

- **How to use the basic CORBA services to enable client/server connectivity**
  The ability to connect to a distant CORBA-enabled server (possibly written in another programming language), obtain a reference to an object in that server, and invoke a function on that object is a straightforward but powerful capability. This chapter will illustrate these basic services.

- **How CORBA-based client/server connectivity differs from the combination of *Java.net.**, *Java.io.**, and CGI**
  In many cases CORBA based client/server connectivity is more appropriate than the commonly used combination of the Java connectivity libraries and CGI programs. This chapter compares the differences between these mechanisms.

- **How and when to use CORBA's dynamic invocation interface**
  CORBA's dynamic invocation interface (DII) supports some interesting functionality which is particularly suited to some situations. This chapter describes the functionality of the DII and illustrates its utility with a particular type of distributed application.

- **How Java and CORBA services support or hamper various client/server architectures**
  The combination of Java and CORBA is a big step forward in client/server applications. This chapter will look at various distributed architectures and discuss how Java and CORBA affect them.

The combination of Java and CORBA is a very positive development for client/server systems. While CORBA is the leading heterogeneous distributed system standard, Java provides an extremely portable and powerful mechanism for the development of client-side functionality. And, due to the marriage of these two technologies, many client/server applications that were previously cost-prohibitive are now cost-effective. This situation results from the simple fact that Java and CORBA solve technical problems and simplify many aspects of client/server development and deployment. More specifically, Java and CORBA provide standards-based heterogeneous inter-process communication, client-side deployment, flexible decoupling of clients and servers, portable client-side functionality, and abstraction of some of the more time-consuming aspects of programming in general. This chapter highlights and illustrates some of the ways that CORBA enhances the client/server capabilities of Java-based client applications.

Defining IDL Interfaces

Although this is a chapter on writing CORBA-enabled Java clients rather than servers, a few words about the definition of IDL interfaces are appropriate in order to convey the context of CORBA client interoperability. CORBA's Interface Definition Language (IDL) is a declarative language used to define the interfaces that may be called by a client process. The nature of an IDL interface may vary dramatically from one distributed application to the next. IDL interfaces will vary from very coarse and generic to very fine-grained and specific. Where an interface lies in this continuum will likely depend on some variation of the following factors:

- Are the clients and servers being developed independently?
- Will there be many different clients and/or many servers which must cooperate?
- Is the server intended to provide a wide variety of services?

If the answer to any two of the above questions is yes, then look into the possibility of defining your server's interface(s) in a more coarse and generic fashion. This can significantly enhance the extensibility and longevity of your distributed system. As new servers and clients are introduced to your distributed system there will be much less likelihood that existing clients and servers will need to change. An example of a coarse and generic interface is one that has a comparatively small number of IDL interfaces defined, uses some of the more generic IDL types as function parameters (for example, `NameValuePairs`, `any`), and has functions that are not specific to the services provided by the server. An example of a rather specific interface is the one following. This IDL interface describes the server functionality invoked by the client applet which forms the basis for the examples in this chapter.

Listing 17.1 CHAPT17LISTINGS.TXT—Notebook Server IDL Interface

```
interface NotebookIF
{
   typedef sequence<string> stringListType;  //resizeable list of strings
   typedef exception AccessNotAuthorizedExc;  // user access denied
   typedef exception NoSuchBookExc{string bookName;};  // no such notebook
   typedef exception NoSuchPageExc{string pageName;};  //no such page

   //each user must provide a user name and password
   short authorizeUser(in string userName, in string password)
                     raises(AccessNotAuthorizedExc);
   //the list of existing notebooks is returned
   stringListType getBooks(in string userName, in string password)
                         raises(AccessNotAuthorizedExc);
   //the list of existing notebook pages is returned
   stringListType  getPages(in string bookName,
                          in string userName,
                          in string password)
                          raises(AccessNotAuthorizedExc, NoSuchBookExc);
   //retrieves the contents of a notebook page
   string retrievePage(in string bookName, in string pageName,
                     in string userName, in string password)
                     raises(AccessNotAuthorizedExc,
                            NoSuchPageExc,
                            NoSuchBookExc);
   //saves the contents of a notebook page
   short savePage(in string bookName,
                in string pageName,
                in string pageContent,
                in string userName,
                in string password)
                raises(AccessNotAuthorizedExc, NoSuchBookExc);
};
```

Note

As a footnote, it has become a popular convention to arrive at the name of the class which implements an IDL interface by taking the name of the interface to be implemented and suffixing it with an abbreviation of the word "implementation." Using the Web-based notebook server as an example, this convention would result in an IDL interface named "`Notebook`" and an implementation class called "`Notebook_impl`". While this seems reasonable on the surface, the fact that this is an ORB-centric convention can present a problem as the server evolves through the development process. The problem arises when it becomes necessary to change the classes or services which are ORB-enabled (have IDL interfaces), or when it becomes necessary to alter the way in which classes implement the IDL interfaces. If a service that has not been previously ORB-enabled must become so, it will then be necessary to change the name of the class implementing that service to add the "impl" suffix. Worse yet, a change to the class's file name is also likely. A better convention is to suffix the name of the IDL interface with characters indicating that it is an interface (such as `IF` or `_if`), and apply no suffix to the implementation class. In this example, the IDL interface is then `"NotebookIF"` while the implementation class name is simply `"Notebook"`. This way, if you wish to support the implementation of the `NotebookIF` interface with another, pre-existing class, neither the `Notebook` class nor the additional implementation classes need have their names changed.

Tip

When defining IDL functions use `oneway` where possible. CORBA provides the ability to classify IDL functions as `oneway` (as long as they do not have a return value or user defined exceptions). A `oneway` function results in a non-blocking call for the client process. The effect is that a client invoking a `oneway` call will continue processing immediately after the ORB call is made. There is not a wait for the called function to complete. The performance gains on the client side can be significant. There is also less likelihood for deadlock in the event that a server attempts to call back the client as part of its response to call from the client.

The client applet is a simplified Web-based Notebook allowing a user to create, store, retrieve, and display notebooks and notebook pages. The core of the applet is the free form drawing pallet on which the user types or draws whatever information is necessary. All persistent information about the authorized users, notebooks, and the contents of their pages is accessed and stored on the server's host.

The services of the notebook server are invoked by the client applet, depicted in Figure 17.1, using ORB calls from the applet's host back to the server's host. The Java-enabled ORB product used for the examples in this chapter was `OrbixWeb`. It is important to recognize that `OrbixWeb` adheres to the security restrictions imposed on Java applets executing within Web browsers by only allowing ORB calls back to the host from which the applet was dynamically downloaded. As a consequence, the Notebook server must reside on the same machine as the Web server. This restriction has architectural ramifications which will be discussed later in the chapter. A side effect of the necessity to select a specific Java-enabled ORB product to create and compile the examples in this chapter is that some of the client-side syntax presented may be specific to the chosen ORB. However, most, if not all, of the points and concepts presented here will apply to all reasonably capable Java-enabled ORBs.

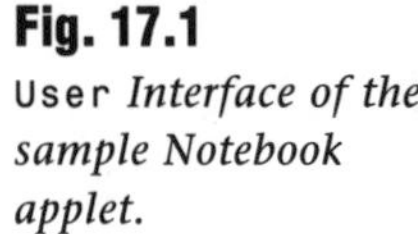

Fig. 17.1
User *Interface of the sample Notebook applet.*

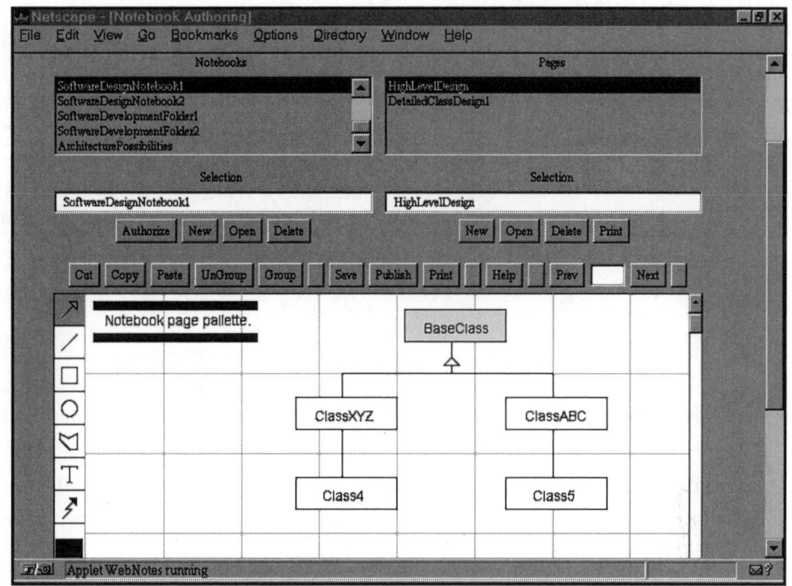

Compiling IDL Interfaces for Java Clients

In order to write an applet that communicates with a server application by way of a CORBA-compliant ORB, clearly there must be a server which is CORBA-enabled (for example, a server whose external interface is defined using IDL). If the client applet intends to use the static invocation interface (SII) to make calls to the target server (the dynamic invocation interface, or DII, is discussed later in this chapter), then the server's IDL interface definition file(s) must be parsed by a Java-capable IDL compiler. This is not a minor point, particularly if the server portion of the application is not written in Java. For instance, the server for the Notebook example is implemented in C++. Clearly the C++ proxy classes generated when the server was compiled are useless to the Java client.

When the IDL interface definition file is parsed by the Java IDL compiler, one or more Java interface and class source files will be generated. These files should be compiled along with the other Java applet files and loaded on the Web server. At runtime, the resulting ORB support classes will act as proxies, or intermediaries, between the client objects and the server's ORB objects. These proxies forward all ORB calls made by the client applet to the server process and un-marshall all return values.

As indicated in Figure 17.2, the existence of the proxy object insulates the user-defined classes from the process of actually making the distributed function call. In fact, the reason that making an ORB call from a user-defined class is so syntactically similar to making a local call is that the user's call is actually a call to a local proxy object.

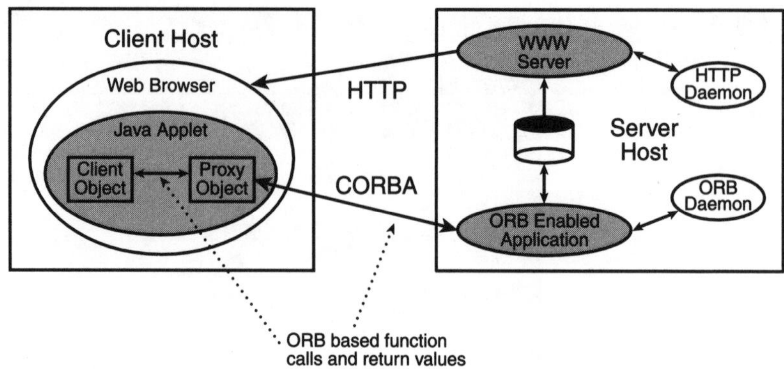

Fig. 17.2
Client-side proxy objects mediate between local client objects and the target server.

When deploying the applet on your Web server, be sure to place all necessary ORB related files in their proper directory hierarchies. As the applet is loaded and the ORB-related classes are imported, the Java-enabled Web browser will look in the directories indicated by the standard Java "dot" notation. Listing 17.2 provides an example of this statement.

Listing 17.2 CHAPT17LISTINGS.TXT—*SystemException* Import Statement

```
import IE.Iona.Orbix2.CORBA.SystemException;
```

This statement tells the class loader to retrieve the file in IE/Iona/Orbix2/CORBA/SystemException.class relative to the CODEBASE of the applet.

Loading these additional .class files from the Web server to support the necessary ORB functionality can consume a significant amount of time, many seconds in some cases. And because the Java loader is "lazy" (it does not load a class until its services are needed by the applet), the applet user may be surprised when there is a significant delay in response to a possibly minor input event. One reasonable solution is to force the loader to load all the necessary ORB-related class files when the applet is initialized. This can be accomplished by making a call from the applet's `init()` function to one or more functions in the ORB classes to be imported. It may also be effective to spawn a lower priority thread which performs some operations in the background resulting in the loading of the necessary ORB support classes.

Writing a Client Applet

The basic functionality of an ORB is all that is necessary to create a very nice client/server application using Java and an ORB. The steps to utilize an ORB's basic functionality are really pretty simple:

1. Implement code to connect to the server object(s).
2. Implement function calls to the server.
3. Implement exception handling.

The third step here is of heightened importance in a distributed application. As suggested by the exception handling requirements of the Java.net classes, failure is much more likely when distributed interprocess communication is involved than when all object-to-object communication occurs in local memory. You will look a bit closer at ORB exception handling later in this chapter, but suffice it to say that ORB exception handling is not conceptually or syntactically different than standard Java exception handling. As a footnote, it is likely that Java programmers will more readily adjust to the idiosyncrasies of ORB-based programming as a result of their exposure to the Java.net classes.

As suggested above, before a call can be invoked on one of the ORB-enabled objects in the server, the client must connect or otherwise get access to one of these objects. A client can get access to a server object in various ways. The most common way to initially establish a connection is to *bind* to the target object. In order to accomplish this, the client must provide sufficient information to the object request broker to determine the target host, server, and object. The function below establishes connectivity to the only object in the Notebook server. Because there is only one object of type `NotebookIF` (the interface type generated by the IDL compiler) in the server, you need not specify a specific target object. Providing the host name and the server name is sufficient.

Listing 17.3 CHAPT17LISTINGS.TXT—Function to Bind to the Notebook Server Object

```
NotebookIF.Ref notebookRef;

public boolean bindObject ()
{
   String hostName = new String("xxx.xxx.xxx.xxx"); // host name of the target server
   String markerServer = new String(":notebookServer"); // name of the target server

   if(notebookRef!=null)                    // if the server object has not already been
                                               ➥bound
      return true;
   else
   {
```

continues

Listing 17.3 Continued

```
        // bind to the server object
        try {notebookRef = NotebookIF._bind(markerServer, hostName);}
        catch (SystemException sysExc) {
           showStatus("ORB Connect failed." + sysExc.toString ());
           return false;}
     }
     showStatus("ORB Connect succeeded.");
     return true;
  }
```

The primary purpose of the `bindObject()` function here is to set the value of `notebookRef`. This is the reference to the object in our notebook server. Syntactically, this object reference is used just as any other Java object reference is used. And, because your `bindObject()` function returns a `boolean` flag indicating whether `notebookRef` has been set, this function can be called prior to making any ORB call. In the event-handling function of the Notebook applet, the following function is called as part of the event-handling process when you click the Save button.

Listing 17.4 CHAPT17LISTINGS.TXT—Client Applet Function to Save Notebook Page

```
public void savePage(String bookName, String pageName,
                     String pageContent, String userName,
                     String password)
{
   if(bindObject())  //verify that the server object has been bound
   {
      try{notebookRef.savePage(bookName,
                               pageName,
                               pageContent,
                               userName,
                               password);}  // make the ORB call
      catch(SystemException sysExc) {
         showStatus("ORB Call to savePage failed");return;}
      //...handle other exceptions ...
      showStatus("Notebook Page Saved");   // indicate that the page has been saved
   }
   else
   {
      showStatus("Error in ORB Connection.");
   }
}
```

Similarly, in the event-handling function of the Notebook applet, the following function is called as part of the event-handling process when the Open Page button is pressed.

The ability shown in Listing 17.5 to bind to a server-side ORB object and to use the resulting object reference to make a heterogeneous, interprocess ORB call is the fundamental functionality provided to a CORBA-enabled client. While most object request brokers provide a greate deal of functionality, you can use this basic "bind and call" functionality to perform most client-side operations

Listing 17.5 CHAPT17LISTINGS.TXT—Client Applet Function to Open a Notebook Page

```
public void openPage(String pageName, String bookName, String userName, String
password)
{
    String content;
    if(bindObject())  //verify that the server object has been bound
    {
       try{content = notebookRef.retrievePage(bookName,
                                              pageName,
                                              userName,
                                              password);}  // make the ORB call
       catch(SystemException exc) {
          showStatus("ORB Call to retrievePage failed");return;}
       //...handle other exceptions ...
       notepad.openPage(content);  // open the Page on the Canvas
    }
    else
    {
       showStatus("Error in ORB Connection.");
    }
}
```

Handling Exceptions

Not surprisingly, most Java IDL compilers generate exception classes which inherit from `java.lang.Exception`. It is this inheritance which enables any ORB exception to be handled in the same manner as any other Java exception. Recall that one of the functions in the `NotebookIF` IDL interface is the `retrievePage()` function that can generate three user-defined exceptions. The IDL shown in Listing 17.6 is a restatement of that function definition.

Listing 17.6 CHAPT17LISTINGS.TXT—IDL Definition of *retrievePage* Function with Exceptions

```
string retrievePage(in string bookName, in string pageName,
                    in string userName, in string password)
```

continues

Listing 17.6 Continued

```
                    raises(AccessNotAuthorizedExc,
                           NoSuchPageExc,
                           NoSuchBookExc);
```

The IDL compiler generates the Java code shown in Listing 17.1 for the definition of this function, as shown in Listing 17.7.

Listing 17.7 CHAPT17LISTINGS.TXT—Java Code Generated from IDL Definition of *savePage* Function

```
public String retrievePage(String bookName, String pageName,
                           String userName, in string password)
                           throws NotebookIF.AccessNotAuthorizedExc,
                                  NotebookIF.NoSuchPageExc,
                                  NotebookIF.NoSuchBookExc,
                                  IE.Iona.Orbix2.CORBA.SystemException;
```

Notice that the generated Java function definition has an additional exception defined, `CORBA.SystemException`. This is necessary due to the various CORBA-defined exceptions which may be thrown by an attempt to make a CORBA ORB call. For a complete list of these exceptions, refer to the documentation for your ORB and the CORBA specification.

In order to pass compilation, your code must handle all potential exceptions. Therefore, the complete code for your client's `openPage()` function is shown in Listing 17.8.

Listing 17.8 CHAPT17LISTINGS.TXT—Client Applet *openPage* Function with all Exceptions Handled

```
public void openPage(String pageName, String bookName, String userName, String
password)
{
    String content;
    if(bindObject())  //verify that the server object has been bound
    {
       try{content = notebookRef.retrievePage(bookName,
                                             pageName,
                                             userName,
                                             password);}  // make the ORB call
       catch(NotebookIF.AccessNotAuthorizedExc noAccess) {
          showStatus("User access denied.  Page Note Retrieved");return;}
       catch(NotebookIF.NoSuchPageExc noPage) {
          showStatus("No such notebook page:  " + noPage.pageName");return;}
       catch(NotebookIF.NoSuchBookExc noBook) {
          showStatus("No such notebook:  " + noBook.bookName");return;}
       catch(SystemException sysExc) {
```

```
            showStatus("ORB Call to retrievePage failed");return;}

         notepad.openPage(content);  // open the Page on the Canvas
      }
      else
      {
         showStatus("Error in ORB Connection.");
      }
   }
```

17

If you have experience handling Java exceptions, the above exception-handling code will look very familiar. Each of the four possible exceptions is handled. For each exception, a status message is sent to the browser. Where the exception populates an exception attribute, that attribute is concatenated to the status message.

Note

As noted earlier in this chapter, it is advantageous to define IDL functions `oneway` (non-blocking). This is due to the performance gains resulting from the client processes' ability to continue processing immediately following an ORB call. An unfortunate side effect of defining one or more exceptions for an IDL function is that you then lose the option to make it `oneway`. An IDL function that may raise a user-defined exception cannot be non-blocking. Therefore, if client-side responsiveness is of particular importance to your application, it may be advantageous to define an `exception callback` IDL interface in your client, remove all exceptions from your server's IDL function definitions, and make them `oneway`. Then, code your server such that if the need arises to raise a user-defined exception, it calls the client's exception callback interface to asynchronously notify it of the problem.

CGI Programs, *Java.net.**, and *Java.io.** May Not Be the Best Choices

CGI programs have formed an invaluable function in bringing information and functionality to the Web. CGI programs, in concert with several of the Java.net classes (`URL`, `URLConnection`, `DataInputStream`, and `DataOutputStream`), are one of the primary mechanisms many Java developers use to communicate with a server. However, in many instances, an object-request broker provides a much more flexible and efficient solution to server-side connectivity than the combination of `Java.net.*/Java.io.*` and CGI.

The advantages of CORBA over CGI and `Java.net.*` for server communication center around the simplicity of basic CORBA-based client/server interactions and the wide applicability of a CORBA-based server. This is in contrast to the cumbersome nature of CGI and `Java.net.*` client/server interactions and the limited applicability of a CGI-based server. More specifically, because the CGI protocol only supports input and output parameters by way of environment variables and standard input/output, all parameters must be packaged into and out of string form. Of course, CORBA has no such limitation. Parameters may be passed as any of the basic IDL types (short, float, string, sequence, and so on), or as any complex type defined in the server's interface definition. The CGI protocol does not inherently support the invocation of a specific function. As a result, the Web site designer must build and manage several CGI programs, each specifically designed either to perform a single function or write one or more multipurpose CGI programs. In the latter case, the invoked CGI program must parse the string-based input parameters passed to it in order to determine the desired function.

CORBA allows a Web client to make a very specific function call to a very specific object in a server program using a very natural syntax. Additionally, most existing server applications were not written to support CGI access, and modifying a server application to support CGI access seems to be an unnecessarily narrow and cumbersome solution to the broader problem of supporting client interactions with a given server. On the other hand, many existing server applications already provide client access via a CORBA layer. But even where a server application is not CORBA-enabled, CORBA is a much more generic, extensible, and efficient solution to providing client/server access to data and functionality. The final benefit of CORBA over CGI and `Java.net.*` is that making a CORBA call in Java is simply less problematic than the corresponding `Java.net.*` calls. There is no need for the use of the `URL`, `URLConnection`, `DataInputStream`, and `DataOutputStream` classes.

Consider the example of passing a user name and password to a server program and getting back a list of notebook names to support your notebook applet. Listing 17.9 uses the `Java.net.*` and `Java.io.*` classes to establish a connection with a CGI program on the server, pass the user name and password to the CGI, and read the CGI output. Once the string containing the list of books is read from the input stream, the string must be unpacked (tokenized) to display each notebook name in a Java ListItem.

Listing 17.9 CHAPT17LISTINGS.TXT—Using *Java.net. and *Java.io.** to Pass Data to and Read from a CGI**

```
String books;
String userInfo = new String(userName + "¦" + password);
URLEncoder.encode(userInfo);
```

```
try{

   booksURL = new URL(this.getDocumentBase(),"CGIToGetListOfNotebooks");
   conn = booksURL.openConnection();
   conn.setUseCaches(false);
   outStream = new PrintStream(conn.getOutputStream());
   outStream.println("string="+userInfo);
   outStream.close();
   inData=new DataInputStream(conn.getInputStream());
   books= new String(inData.readLine());inData.close();

} catch (MalformedURLException mExc) {
System.err.println("MalformedURLException: " + mExc.toString());
} catch (IOException ioExc) {
System.err.println("IOException: " + ioExc.toString());

if(books !=null)
   if(books.length()>0)
   {
      StringTokenizer tzr = new StringTokenizer(temps,"¦");
      while(tzr.hasMoreTokens())
         bookList.addItem(tzr.nextToken(),-1);
   }
```


The same task accomplished in Listing 17.9 is accomplished in Listing 17.10 using an ORB call to a CORBA-based server. Differences of note are the comparative simplicity of establishing a server connection (just bind) and getting the result of the server call (the list of books is set as the return value of the ORB call).

Listing 17.10 CHAPT17LISTINGS.TXT—Code to Make an ORB Call and Get the Return Value

```
StringListType books = null;  //Define the ORB sequence of notebook names

try {notebookRef = NotebookIF._bind(markerServer, hostName);}
catch (SystemException sysExc) {
   showStatus("ORB Connect failed. " + sysExc.toString ()); return true;}

try{books = notebookRef.getNotebooks(userName,password);} //get the list of notebooks
catch(SystemException sysExc) {
   showStatus("ORB Call to getNotebooks failed"); return true;}
//...handle other exceptions ...

if(books != null)  //verify that the ORB sequence has been set
   if(books.length>0)  //verify that there is at least one notebook
   {
      for(int j = 0;j<books.length;j++)
         bookList.addItem(books[j],-1); //Add the notebook name to the ListItem
   }
```

Consider the example of reading a character string from the applet's server. The code segment shown in Listing 17.11 uses the `Java.net.*` and `Java.io*` classes to establish a connection with a preexisting file on the server and to read the file's content, a character string.

Listing 17.11 CHAPT17LISTINGS.TXT—Code Using *Java.net and *Java.io** to Read from a File on the Server Host**

```
try{saveFile = new URL(this.getDocumentBase(),"docs/pagefile1");}
catch (Exception exc) {
   showStatus("Error in URL creation."); return true;}

try{conn = saveFile.openConnection();}
catch (Exception exc) {
   showStatus("Error in URL connection.");return true;}
conn.setUseCaches(false);

try{inData=new DataInputStream(conn.getInputStream());}
catch(Exception exc) {
   showStatus("Error getting input stream"); return true;}

try{s= new String(inData.readLine());inData.close();}
catch(Exception exc) {
   showStatus("Error reading data input stream"); return true;}
```

The code segment shown in Listing 17.12 uses an ORB call to a CORBA-based server to accomplish the same task.

Listing 17.12 CHAPT17LISTINGS.TXT—Code to Make an ORB Call to Read Data from the Server

```
try {notebookRef = NotebookIF._bind(markerServer, hostName);}
catch (SystemException sexc) {
   showStatus("ORB Connect failed. " + sexc.toString ()); return true;}

try{s = notebookRef.retrievePage(encodedPageName,encodedBookName);}
catch(SystemException exc) {
   showStatus("ORB Call to savePage failed"); return true;}
```

As you can see, even setting aside the code to define variables, significantly fewer lines of Java code are necessary to make the corresponding ORB call. And, more importantly, there are fewer points of failure.

The above discussions and code segments highlight the advantages of writing Java applets as CORBA-based clients rather than clients based on `Java.net.*`, `Java.io.*`, and CGI. However, the intention here is not that a CORBA solution is always the best solution. It may be that the necessary server-side functionality is not sufficiently complex to warrant purchasing an ORB product and writing a CORBA server. Another meaningful consideration is a developer's exposure to CORBA technology. Development time is very valuable, and it may be that the time necessary to come up to speed on a given ORB is prohibitive given specific development goals and deadlines.

A final consideration is firewall interoperability. It may be the case that an applet will be downloaded from a server to a client host residing behind the firewall set up by the client's organization. If this is the case, it is possible that the TCP/IP-based ORB connection attempts back to the originating host will raise a Java security exception. This results from the fact that the communication protocol your ORB uses may not support the ability to account for firewall proxies. On the other hand, `Java.net.URLConnection` does. Use of the `Java.net.URLConnection` to establish connections back to a host outside a firewall will have a greater likelihood of success.

Using the Dynamic Invocation Interface and the Interface Repository

With the plethora of software applications in existence, it is becoming increasingly common for sophisticated users to request the ability to mix and match suites of software tools and applications into larger, loosely coupled "mega-programs." The capabilities of CORBA's Dynamic Invocation Interface (DII) and the Interface Repository (IR) are intended to meet this type of requirement. While not the only solution to such a requirement, the interface repository allows a client application to discover the specific makeup of a server's IDL interface. The client may then use this information to construct and invoke a call on that server using the dynamic invocation interface. The key point here is that the client need not have any prior knowledge of the server's interface definition in order to discover its content and make an ORB call to it.

As an example, consider the requirement that your notebook applet support the definition and execution of workflows, where a workflow definition is created by a sophisticated user/modeler and is comprised of a mapped-out sequence of dependent simulations or other applications. In general, these workflow definitions must be entirely modifiable at the will of the user in the event that a different simulation is more appropriate for a given iteration of the workflow. The facilities of the IR and DII can be used to meet these requirements.

Unfortunately, the DII and IR do not perform enough magic to obviate the need to CORBA-enable simulations and applications which may potentially participate in the workflow. As a result, a precursor to this solution is the creation of a CORBA interface to each participating application. A second precondition to this solution is the necessity for the client application to obtain on ORB reference to a target object in the server.

There are at least two approaches to obtaining this reference. The first is to use the `object_from_string()` function to create the object reference using a string obtained from another server or from a persistent store, while the second is to enforce a naming convention on the interface defined in the participating servers. An example of the second approach would be that simulation servers, potentially participating in the workflow, must define and implement an IDL interface that has the same name as the simulation server itself. This interface must contain all the operations the workflow tool may invoke on it. Example IDL interfaces for two possible workflow simulations are shown in Listing 17.13.

Listing 17.13 CHAPT17LISTINGS.TXT—IDL Interfaces for Two Possible Workflow Simulation Servers

```
// Simulation server called SimpleTrafficSimulator
interface SimpleTrafficSimulator
{
    short determineNumberOfLanes(in long numberVehiclesPeak,
                                 in long numberVehiclesAvgPerHour);
    short determineAverageSpeed(in short numberOfLanes,
                                in short numberOfVehicles,
                                in short weatherCondition);
};

// Simulation server called SimpleHighwayCostCalculator
interface SimpleHighwayCostCalculator
{
    long determineConstructionCost(in short numberOfLanes,
                                   in short numberofHighwayMiles);
    long determineAnnualMaintenanceCost(in long constructionCost,
                                        in short numberofHighwayMiles,
                                        in short numberOfVehiclesPerMonth,
                                        in short averageWeatherCondition);
};
```

To support the new workflow requirements of the Notebook applet, you will need to add two functions to the Notebook IDL interface: one to register a candidate simulation with the notebook server, and another to retrieve a list of these candidate simulations. This is the code for the IDL functions that support the new workflow requirement:

```
oneway void registerSimulation(in string serverName);
stringListType getAvailableSimulations();
```

Once the traffic simulator and highway cost simulations have been registered with the Notebook server through the `registerSimulation()` function call, the client applet may call the `getAvailableSimulations()` function to ask for all candidate simulations and display the simulation names to the user. Once the user has selected a simulation for inclusion in a workflow, the name of the selected simulation server is used as a parameter to the `_bind() operation` to obtain an object reference to the target server object. Providing the simulation name informs the server-side ORB daemon which server should be "bound," that is, which server process the client application wants to connect with (see Listing 17.14).

Listing 17.14 Binding to a Server Discovered at Runtime

```
Object.Ref objectRef = null;
String markerServer = new String(":" + userSelectedSimulationName);
try {objectRef = Object._bind(markerServer, hostName);}
catch (SystemException sysExc) {
   showStatus("ORB Connect failed. " + sysExc.toString ()); return true;}
```

Once the applet has a reference to the target object in the chosen simulation server, the interface repository can be queried to discover the list of operations supported by the interface, as well as the signature of each of the operations (see Listing 17.15).

Listing 17.15 Interrogate the Server's Interface Repository

```
IE.Iona.Orbix2.InterfaceDef.Ref interfaceRef;
// Get the complete interface definition
try {interfaceRef = objRef._get_interface();}
//... Handle any exceptions ...

IE.Iona.Orbix2.InterfaceDef.FullInterfaceDescription entireInterface;
try {entireInterface = interfaceRef.describe_interface();}
// ...Handle any exceptions ...
```

The struct obtained from the call to `Ref.describe_interface()` includes all necessary information to construct and invoke an operation on the chosen interface. The struct is defined in Listing 17.16

Listing 17.16 Definition of CORBA's Interface Definition Struct

```
struct FullInterfaceDescription {
          Identifier name;
          RepositoryId id;
          RepositoryId defined_in;
          OpDescriptionSeq operations;
          AttrDescriptionSeq attributes;
       };
```

As you can see, the interface description struct contains two sequences. The first is a sequence of structs, each of which describes an operation that you may invoke once you use the DII to build the call. This is actually a sequence of `OperationDescription` structs. For further details about the content of these structs, peruse the documentation for your

ORB or the CORBA specification. But the content of the `OperationDescription` struct and its components tells you all you need to know in order to describe the interface of each invocable function to the workflow modeler. The modeler then selects the function to invoke and inputs the necessary function parameters. The DII is then used to dynamically build and invoke the function on the target server. Using these same mechanisms you can dynamically connect applications by obtaining the output parameters from a DII call and feeding them to another function in another server as defined by the user's workflow, again using the IR and DII. With your traffic simulator and highway cost calculator servers, it makes sense to model a workflow link between the `SimpleTrafficSimulator::determineNumberOfLanes()` function and the `SimpleHighwayCostCalculator::determineConstructionCost()` function. The results of a DII call to the first function will be captured and used as one of the DII input parameters to the second function.

While the workflow example presents a compelling use for the IR and the DII, the Java code necessary to implement it is far too complex to present here. So the code segments presented later in the chapter use the IR and the DII to build and invoke one of the more simple operations in the `NotebookIF` IDL interface. Listing 17.17 is a restatement of the Notebook server's IDL interface.

Listing 17.17 Notebook Server IDL Interface

```
interface NotebookIF
{
   typedef sequence<string> stringListType;
   typedef exception AccessNotAuthorizedExc;
   typedef exception NoSuchBookExc{string bookName;};
   typedef exception NoSuchPageExc{string pageName;};

   short authorizeUser(in string userName, in string password)
                       raises(AccessNotAuthorizedExc);
   stringListType getBooks(in string userName, in string password)
                           raises(AccessNotAuthorizedExc);
   stringListType  getPages(in string bookName,
                            in string userName,
                           in string password)
                            raises(AccessNotAuthorizedExc, NoSuchBookExc);
   string retrievePage(in string bookName, in string pageName,
                       in string userName, in string password)
                       raises(AccessNotAuthorizedExc,
                              NoSuchPageExc,
                              NoSuchBookExc);
   short savePage(in string bookName, in string pageName,
                  in string pageContent, in string userName,
                 in string password)
                  raises(AccessNotAuthorizedExc, NoSuchBookExc);
};
```

As with the workflow example, create an object reference to the target server and use it to query the interface repository for the available operations and their corresponding arguments, as shown in Listing 17.18.

Listing 17.18 Binding to the Server and Querying Its Interface Repository

```
NotebookIF.Ref notebookRef = null;
String hostName = new String("xxx.xxx.xxx.xxx"); // host name of the target server
String markerServer = new String(":notebookServer"); // name of the target server

try {notebookRef = NotebookIF._bind(markerServer, hostName);}
catch (SystemException sysExc) {
   showStatus("ORB Connect failed. " + sysExc.toString ()); return;}

// Get the complete interface definition
IE.Iona.Orbix2.InterfaceDef.Ref interfaceRef;
try {interfaceRef = notebookRef._get_interface();}
catch (SystemException sysExc) {
   showStatus("IR call to get interface failed. " + sysExc.toString ()); return;}

IE.Iona.Orbix2.InterfaceDef.FullInterfaceDescription entireInterface;
try {entireInterface = interfaceRef.describe_interface();}
catch (SystemException sysExc) {
   showStatus("IR call to describe interface failed. " + sysExc.toString ());
return;}
```

In Listing 17.19, the operation and operation argument information is used to create and populate a CORBA "request" object. A request object houses the information necessary to communicate to the ORB what function should be invoked and the value of each of the function's input arguments.

Listing 17.19 Construct and Populate a CORBA Request Object

```
Request req = null;
String operationName = new String(entireInterface.attributes.buffer[0].name);
try{req = notebookRef._request(operationName);}
catch (SystemException sysExc) {
   showStatus("Add Request argument failed. " + sysExc.toString ()); return;}

//Since we know here that the first operation is authorizeUser(string,string)
//we can simply add the two arguments to the request without looking
//at the content of the OperationDescription struct .
try{(req.arguments().add(new Flags(_CORBA.ARG_IN)).value()).insertString(userName);}
catch (SystemException sysExc) {
   showStatus("Add Request argument failed. " + sysExc.toString ()); return;}
catch (IE.Iona.Orbix2.CORBA.CORBAException cExc) {
   showStatus("Add Request argument failed. " + cExc.toString ()); return;}

try{(req.arguments().add(new Flags(_CORBA.ARG_IN)).value()).insertString(password);}
catch (SystemException sysExc) {
   showStatus("Add Request argument failed. " + sysExc.toString ()); return;}
catch (IE.Iona.Orbix2.CORBA.CORBAException cExc) {
   showStatus("Add Request argument failed. " + cExc.toString ()); return;}
```

Listing 17.19 includes this line of code:

```
try{(req.arguments().add(new Flags(_CORBA.ARG_IN)).value()).insertString(password);}
```

This deserves a bit of explanation. Clearly, it could be broken down into many more lines of function calls and attribute definitions, but as a single line of code, it very succinctly adds an argument value to the DII request object. Broken down, this line of code gets the list of arguments from the request object, adds a new `in` argument to the list of arguments, gets the `value` object for the new argument, and finally, sets the argument value with a string containing the password entered by the user.

Once the parameters are inserted, the request can be invoked using the DII's `invoke` function, as shown in Listing 17.20.

Listing 17.20 Invoke the *request* Object

```
try{req.invoke();}
catch (SystemException sysExc) {
   showStatus("Attempt to invoke Request failed. " + sysExc.toString ()); return;}
catch(IE.Iona.Orbix2.CORBA.CORBAException cExc) {
   showStatus("Attempt to invoke Request failed. " + cExc.toString ()); return;}
```

And very simply, the return value is retrieved by calling it, as shown in Listing 17.21.

Listing 17.21 Extract the Returned *NamedValue* Object from the *request* Object

```
NamedValue returnValue = null;
try{returnValue = req.result();}
catch (SystemException sysExc) {
   showStatus("Attempt to extract Request result failed. " + sysExc.toString ());
return;}
```

However, the return value is of type `NamedValue`. This is a CORBA type which contains an optional name and a value. But to further complicate the matter, the value is of type `Any`. `Any` is a CORBA type which is comprised of a type indicator and the value itself. In Listing 17.22, you know that the `return` value of the function `authorizeUser(...)` is a short.

Listing 17.22 Extract the *return* Value from the Returned *NamedValue* Object

```
short authorizationResult = 0;
try{authorizationResult = (returnValue.value()).extractShort();}
catch (SystemException sysExc) {
   showStatus("Attempt to extract Request return value failed. " + sysExc.toString
());
   return;}
```

Clearly, the process of creating, invoking, and getting the result(s) of a DII call is significantly more involved than making the same call using the SII (Static Invocation Interface). Given this fact, you would probably want to use the DII only when absolutely necessary. However, as the workflow example suggests, it can come in handy when runtime program discovery and interaction are functional requirements.

Using Filters

For security purposes, each function in your `NotebookIF` IDL interface requires that a user name and password be included as two of the function parameters. But suppose that the need for this information was just an afterthought, and that your original interface definition did not require these parameters for every call. Depending on the number and complexity of the clients dependent on your server, it could be problematic to recode each client applet and the server functions to provide and accept the user name and password with every call. The functionality provided by filters can simplify this problem (not all available ORBs provide filter-type functionality).

The idea behind filters is that they intercept outgoing and incoming ORB calls at various points in the ORB's request marshalling and unmarshalling process. At each of these interception points, data can be added to or removed from the ORB request. There are various imaginable uses for the utility of filters (encryption, bookkeeping, and so on), but, for your notebook applet and server, the new necessity to verify access on each ORB call can be addressed using a client-side and server-side filter without requiring a change to any preexisting client or server code. What your client-side filter will need to do is piggyback each outgoing ORB call with a user name and password. A server-side filter will then be written to extract them and assess authorization, raising a system exception if authorization does not succeed.

Your Java-enabled ORB supports filtering functionality by enabling the implementation of a user-defined filter class. This class must inherit from the ORB's built-in filter class. The point in the marshalling process where your authorization data is added to the ORB request is dictated by the filter function which you choose to override in the filter class (see Figure 17.3). In the filter class defined in Listing 17.23, the user name and passwords are added to any outgoing ORB request prior to the marshalling and creation of the outgoing request packet. Because the outgoing request object is passed to the filtering functions, the functionality of the `DII::Request` class, as described earlier in this chapter, can be used to add the user name and passwords to the outgoing ORB call.

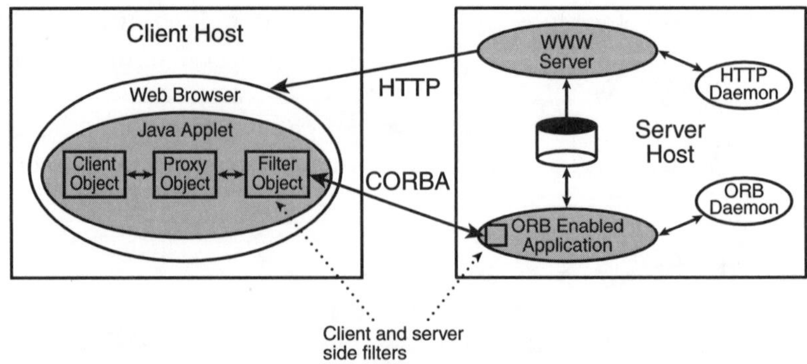

Fig. 17.3
User defined filters enable examination and modification of function parameter values during the marshalling and unmarshalling of ORB function calls.

Listing 17.23 Implementation of *PiggybackFilter* Class

```
import IE.Iona.Orbix2.CORBA.SystemException;
import IE.Iona.Orbix2.CORBA.Request;
import java.io.*;

public class PiggybackFilter extends IE.Iona.Orbix2.CORBA.Filter
{
   public boolean outRequestPreMarshal(Request request)
   {
      try{request.insertString(userName);}
      catch(IE.Iona.Orbix2.CORBA.SystemException ex)
      {System.out.println("Outgoing filter failure"); return false;}
      try{request.insertString(password);}
      catch(IE.Iona.Orbix2.CORBA.SystemException ex)
      {System.out.println("Outgoing filter failure"); return false;}

      return true;
   }
};
```

To register the filter object with the client ORB, the filter's constructor should be called prior to the first ORB call.

Some Points About Distributed System Architecture

When developing a distributed application, one of the early tasks is to settle on an overall software architecture. While this is not a book on distributed system architecture, an exploration of some of the architectural possibilities and how they relate to and can be addressed by the combination of Java and CORBA is appropriate. The architecture of your notebook client and server system, illustrated in Figure 17.4, is straightforward. As a matter of fact, if it were not for the possible use of client- and server-side filters to support authorization and maybe encryption, there could not be a more simplistic Web/Java/CORBA-based architecture.

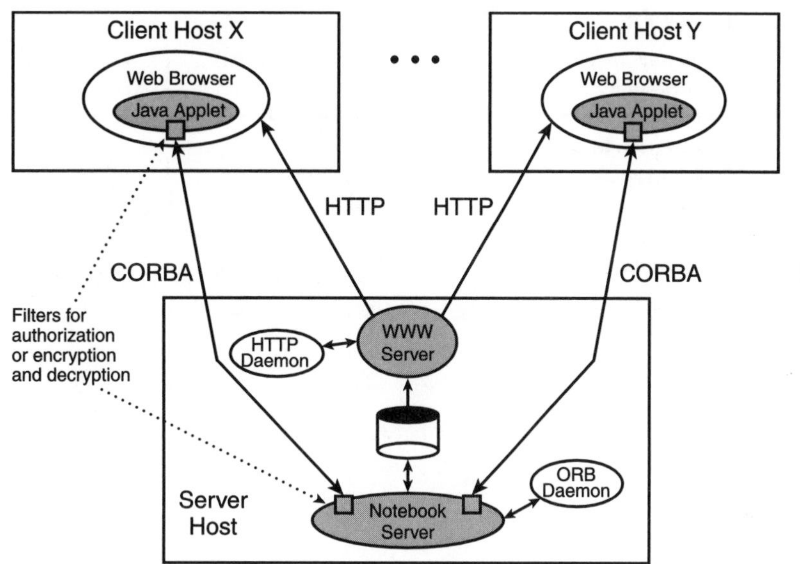

Fig. 17.4
The two-tier, distributed architecture of your Notebook application supports multiple clients and has collocated Web server and ORB server processes to adhere to the Java applet client/server connectivity restrictions.

The only potential point of complexity here is the necessity for the notebook server to support multiple concurrent client applets. But this point of complexity is standard issue for any client/server application. The solutions here vary depending on the client's need to support read-write and read-only control over information accessed from the server, or whether a simple first-come/first-served approach will suffice. Of particular note in your notebook system architecture is the collocation of the Web server application and the ORB-based application. Because Java's security model prefers that client applets make network connections only back to the host from which they originated, it may be an architectural necessity to collocate the Web server and the ORB-based application. This does not present a problem for your simple notebook application, but with more sophisticated applications, it may be a problem which must be worked around. (Some ORB vendors have developed client-side Java libraries that work with this aspect of the Java security model to obviate this issue.)

Figure 17.5 is an example of an application architecture which works with, but around, the inability to access only a single host from a Java/ORB-based applet. This architecture is applicable when there is a need for client applets to request the services of multiple ORB-based servers residing on multiple hosts. The primary difference with this architecture is the existence of an application proxy server. This ORB-enabled server is called by all client applets for any server request. The parameters sent with each client request are examined by the application proxy to determine which host and server it should forward the call to. It then forwards the call to the target host and server, returning any output parameters to the originating client.

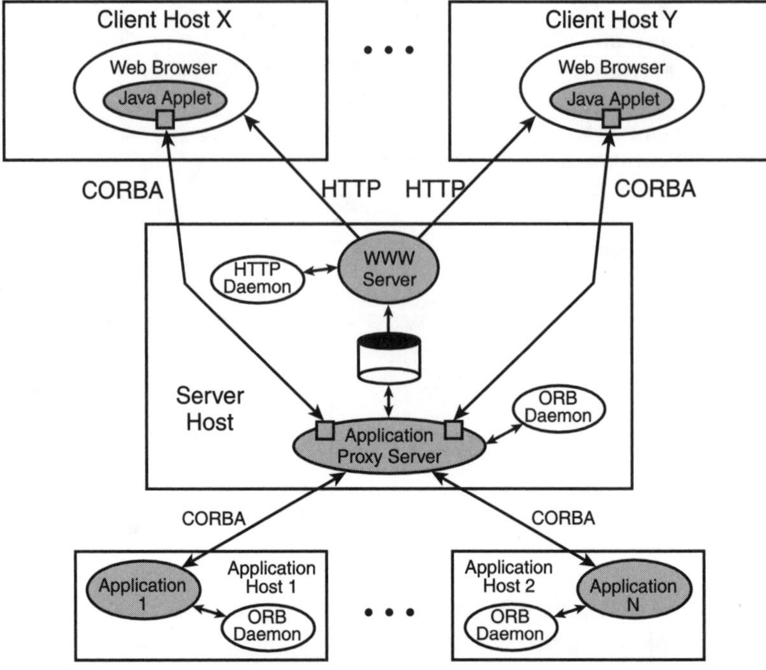

Figure 17.5
Distributed architecture with an application proxy server to indirectly support multi-host applet connectivity while adhering to the Java applet client/server connectivity restrictions.

There are a few important ramifications of this architecture. As discussed earlier in this chapter, IDL interfaces can be very fine-grained and specific or more coarse and general purpose. The notebook server example has a very specific IDL interface. Because the notebook server is rather simplistic and because the server's client applet is likely to be the only client application, having a less generic interface is not likely to present a problem. In contrast, however, the application proxy server in Figure 17.5 must be able to forward function calls to multiple-target applications and potentially support many different clients. So it is preferable that its IDL interface be very generic and inherently extensible. It would not be good if each introduction of a new target application resulted in the need to significantly change the IDL interface and the implementation code of the application proxy. Given this, the application proxy server, in its simplest form, could have a single function capable of handling a call targeted for any function in any of the target applications. The IDL definition of this function could take the form shown in Listing 17.24.

Listing 17.24 IDL Definition of a Generic Application *proxy* Function

```
NVPairListType performOperation(in string targetApp,
                                in string targetInterface,
                                in string targetFunction,
                                in NVPairListType inParameters);
```

Using the `proxy` function, the client provides the names of the target application (a CORBA-enabled server), IDL interface, and function to indicate where the application proxy should forward the call. Any input and output parameters are provided and returned using a list of name/value pairs. There are several variations on the specific signature of this function, but the intent is always the same: To provide a single generic interface to one or more specific services in support of client/server extensibility.

As you have probably ascertained, an additional ramification of this architecture is the requirement that client applets be able to deal with the generic nature of the application proxy interface. More specifically, each client ORB call requires creation and population of a name/value pair list, and examination of the returned name/value pair list. While this process can be simplified using the various DII and IR facilities of the ORB, it is an unfortunate reality of generic IDL interfaces. The advantages of loose coupling of clients and servers do not come without a price. It is worth pointing out that your application proxy server is just one example of the need to decouple client and servers by defining generic IDL interfaces. This architectural technique is not specific to the marriage of Java applets and CORBA servers. Many existing distributed systems were built on this very paradigm.

There are certainly other architectural possibilities which may provide a more appropriate solution to a given problem. For example, a downfall of both previously described architectures is the lack of scalability in the face of high client demand on the servers. In both cases, there is a single host supporting the throughput demands of all clients, a classic shortcoming of 2-tier client/server architectures. As illustrated in Figure 17.6, one architectural solution is to create a 3-tier architecture by pushing the server's persistent data store to a commonly accessible host and establishing two or more server hosts, each having resident Web-server and ORB-server applications.

The complexity to manage with this solution is concurrent data access attempts from the now multiple ORB servers. However, most of the more capable object and relational database products provide mechanisms to support multiple concurrent clients. The notebook server referred to in this chapter, for example, uses an object-oriented database for its persistent storage mechanism. It is certainly feasible to implement the notebook server such that it utilizes the distribution, transaction, and locking mechanisms provided by the OODBMS to support multiple notebook servers accessing the single persistent store of notebook information.

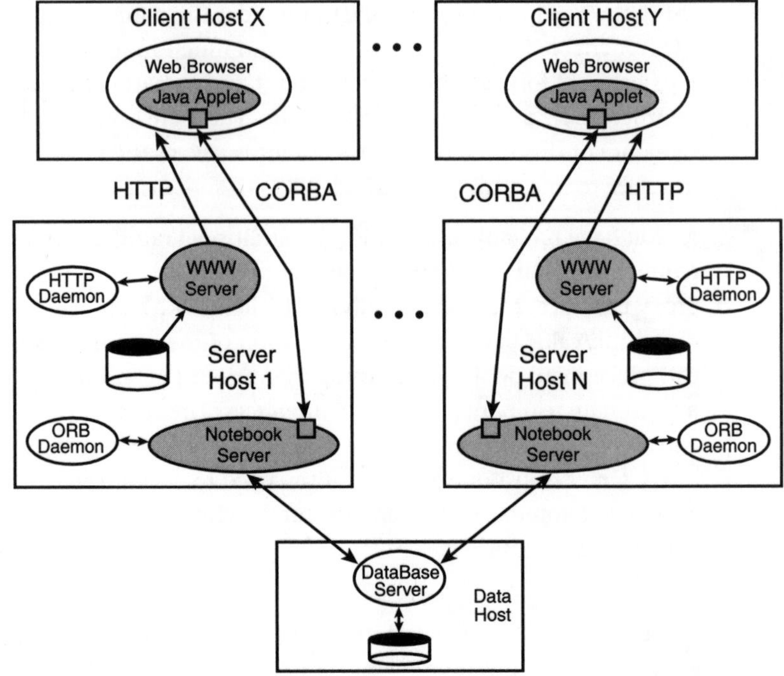

Fig. 17.6
A distributed architecture with three tiers and multiple ORB server processes can support greater scalability.

chapter 18

Using CORBA IDL with Java

By Mark Wutka

In this chapter

- **A brief introduction to CORBA**
  CORBA is still a young architecture, and many people are unfamiliar with it. Once you realize what CORBA provides, you will see what enormous potential it has.
- **Mapping IDL to Java**
  Since CORBA's Interface Definition Language (IDL) is language-independent, you need to know how to convert from IDL to Java. While there are automated tools to perform this conversion, you still need to know how the conversion is performed.
- **Accessing CORBA servers from an Applet**
  CORBA enables programs in one language to communicate with programs written in another language. You can create applets that invoke methods in non-Java applications using CORBA.
- **Creating JavaIDL clients**
  JavaIDL is Sun's CORBA framework that is part of Java 1.1. You can create CORBA clients in JavaIDL that communicate with other CORBA applications, whether they are written in Java or not.
- **Creating VisiBroker clients**
  VisiBroker, formerly called Black Widow, is another CORBA framework that is written entirely in Java. Netscape has licensed VisiBroker for future versions of the Netscape Navigator browser. While VisiBroker is very similar to JavaIDL, there are a few key differences.

What Is CORBA?

In Chapter 17, "Creating CORBA Clients," you learned how to create a CORBA client using the OrbixWeb client. If this is your first exposure to CORBA, you may not realize what CORBA actually is.

The Common Object Request Broker Architecture (CORBA) is a tremendous vision of distributed objects interacting without regard to their location or operating environment. CORBA is still in its infancy, with some standards still in the definition stage, but the bulk of the CORBA infrastructure is defined. Many software vendors are still working on some of the features that have been defined.

CORBA consists of several layers. The lowest layer is the Object Request Broker, or ORB. The ORB is essentially a remote method invocation facility. The ORB is language-neutral, meaning you can create objects in any language and use the ORB to invoke methods in those objects. You can also use any language to create clients that invoke remote methods through the ORB. There is a catch to the "any language" idea. You have to define a language mapping between the implementation language and CORBA's Interface Definition Language (IDL).

When you go from IDL to your implementation language, you generate a stub and a skeleton in the implementation language. The stub is the interface between the client and the ORB; the skeleton is the interface between the ORB and the object (or server). Figure 18.1 shows the relationship between the ORB, an object, and a client wishing to invoke a method on the object.

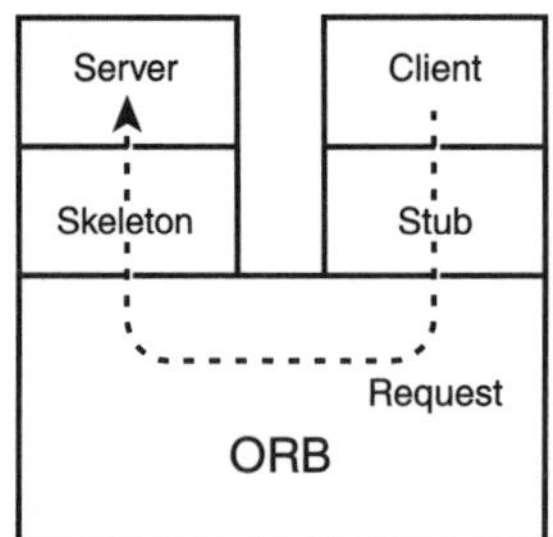

Fig. 18.1
CORBA clients use the ORB to invoke methods on a CORBA server.

While the ORB is drawn conceptually as a separate part of the architecture, it is often just part of the application. A basic ORB implementation might include a naming service (see the following discussion) and a set of libraries that facilitate communications between clients and servers. Once a client locates a server, it communicates directly with that server, not going through any intermediate program. This permits efficient CORBA implementations.

The ORB is both the most visible portion of CORBA and the least exciting. CORBA's big benefit comes in all the services that it defines. Among the services defined in CORBA are

- Lifecycle
- Naming

- Persistence
- Events
- Transactions
- Querying
- Properties

These services are a subset of the full range of services defined by CORBA. The Lifecycle and the Naming services crystallize Sun's visionary phrase, "The network is the computer." These services allow you to instantiate (create) new objects without knowing where the objects reside. You might be creating an object in your own program space, or you might be creating an object halfway around the world, and your program will never know it.

The Lifecycle service enables you to create, delete, copy, and move objects on a specific system. As an application programmer, you would prefer not to know where an object resides. As a systems programmer, you need the Lifecycle service to implement this location transparency for the application programmer. One of the hassles you frequently run into in remote procedure call systems is that the server you are calling must already be up and running before you can make the call. The Lifecycle service removes that hassle; you can create an object, if you need to, before invoking a method on it.

The Naming service enables you to locate an object on the network by name. You want the total flexibility of being able to move objects around the network without having to change any code. The Naming service gives you that ability by associating an object with a name instead of a network address.

The Persistence service lets you save objects somewhere and retrieve them later. This might be in a file, or it might be on an object database. The CORBA standard doesn't specify which. That is left up to the individual software vendors.

The Event service is a messaging system that allows more complex interaction than a simple message call. You could use the Event service to implement a network-based Observer-Observable model, for instance. There are event suppliers that send events, and event consumers that receive them. A server or a client is either push or pull. A push server sends events out when it wants to (it pushes them out), while a push client has a push method and automatically receives events through this method. A pull server doesn't send out events until it is asked; you have to pull them out of the server. A pull client does not receive events until it asks for them. It might help to use the term poll in place of pull. A pull server doesn't deliver events on its own; it gives them out when it is polled. A pull client goes out and polls for events.

The Transaction service is one of the most complex services in the CORBA architecture. It enables you to define operations across multiple objects as a single transaction. This kind of transaction is similar to a database transaction. It handles concurrency, locking, and even rollbacks in case of a failure. A transaction must comply with a core set of requirements that are abbreviated ACID:

- Atomicity A transaction is a single event. Everything in the transaction is either done as a whole or undone. You don't perform a transaction partially.
- Consistency When you perform a transaction, you do not leave the system in an inconsistent state. For example, if you have an airline flight with one seat left, you don't end up assigning that seat to two different people if their transactions occur at the same time.
- Isolation No other objects see the results of a transaction until that transaction is committed. Even if transactions are executing simultaneously, they have a sequential order with respect to the data.
- Durability If you commit a transaction, you can be sure that the change has been made and stored somewhere. It doesn't get lost.

The transaction service usually relies on an external Transaction Processing (TP) system.

The Object Querying service lets you locate objects based on something other than name. For instance, you could locate all ships registered in Liberia, or all Krispy Kreme donut locations in Georgia. This feature is usually used when your objects are stored in an object database.

The Properties service lets objects store information on other objects. A property is like a sticky-note. An object writes some information down on a sticky-note and slaps it on another object. This has tremendous potential because it lets information be associated with an object without the object having to know about it.

The beauty of the whole CORBA system is that all of these services are available through the ORB interface, so once your program can talk to the ORB, you have these services available. Of course, your ORB vendor may not have implemented all of these services yet.

Sun's IDL to Java Mapping

In order to use Java in a CORBA system, you need a standard way to convert attributes and methods defined in IDL into Java attributes and methods. Sun has proposed a mapping and released a program to generate Java stubs and skeletons from an IDL definition.

Defining interfaces in IDL is similar to defining interfaces in Java, since you are defining only the signatures (parameters and return values) of the methods and not the implementation of the methods.

IDL Modules

A module is the IDL equivalent of the Java package. It groups sets of interfaces together in their own namespace. Like Java packages, IDL modules can be nested.

Here is an example IDL module definition (shown without any definitions, which are discussed later in this chapter):


```
module MyModule {
     // insert your IDL definitions here, you must have at least
     // one definition for a valid IDL module
};
```

This module would be generated in Java as a package called `MyModule`:

```
package MyModule;
```

When you nest modules, the Java packages you generate are also nested. For example, consider the following nested module definition:

```
module foo {
     module bar {
          module baz {
// insert definitions here
          };
     };
};
```

Tip

Don't forget to put a semicolon (;) after the closing brace (}) of a module definition. Unlike Java, C, and C++, you are *required* to put a semicolon after the brace in IDL.

The Java package definition for interfaces within the `baz` module is

```
package foo.bar.baz;
```

IDL Constants

As in Java, you can define constant values in IDL. The format of an IDL constant definition is

```
const type variable = value;
```

The type of a constant is limited to `boolean`, `char`, `short`, `unsigned short`, `long`, `unsigned long`, `float`, `double`, and `string`.

Constants are mapped into Java in an unusual way. Each constant is defined as a class with a single, static, final, public variable, called `value`, that holds the value of the constant. This is done because IDL lets you define constants within a module, but Java requires that constants belong to a class.

Here is an example IDL constant definition:

```
module ConstExample {
     const long myConstant = 123;
};
```

This IDL definition produces the following Java definition:

```
package ConstExample;
public final class myConstant {
     public static final int value = (int) (123L);
}
```

IDL Data Types

IDL has roughly the same set of primitive data types as Java except for a few exceptions:

- The IDL equivalent of the Java `byte` data type is the `octet`.
- IDL supports the `String` type, but it is called `string`.
- Characters in IDL can only have values between 0 and 255. The JavaIDL system checks your characters to make sure they fall within this range, including characters stored in strings.
- IDL supports 16, 32, and 64-bit integers, but the names for the 32 and 64-bit types are slightly different. In IDL, the 32-bit value is called a `long`, while in Java it is called an `int`. The IDL equivalent of the Java `long` is the `long long`.
- IDL supports unsigned `short`, `int`, and `long` values. In Java, these values are stored in signed variables. You must be very careful when dealing with large unsigned values, since they may end up negative when represented in Java.

Enumerated Types

Unlike Java, IDL lets you create enumerated types that represent integer values. The JavaIDL system turns the enumerated type into a class with public, static, final values.

Here is an example IDL enumerated type:

```
module EnumModule {
     enum Medals { gold, silver, bronze };
};
```

This definition produces the Java class shown in Listing 18.1:

Listing 18.1 Java Definition of Enumerated Types

```
package EnumModule;
public class Medals {
 public static final int gold = 0,
               silver = 1,
               bronze = 2;
 public static final int narrow(int i) throws sunw.corba.EnumerationRangeException {
     if (gold <= i && i <= bronze) {
      return i;
     }
     throw new sunw.corba.EnumerationRangeException();
 }
}
```


Since you can also declare variables of an enumerated type, JavaIDL creates a holder class that is used in place of the data type. The holder class contains a single instance variable called `value` that holds the enumerated value. The holder for the `Medals` enumeration looks like the definition in Listing 18.2:

Listing 18.2 Java Definition of Holder Class for Enumerated Types

```
package EnumModule;
public class MedalsHolder
{
 //     instance variable
 public int value;
 //     constructors
 public MedalsHolder() {
     this(0);
 }
 public MedalsHolder(int __arg) {
     value = EnumModule.Medals.narrow(__arg);
 }
}
```

You can create a `MedalsHolder` by passing an enumerated value to the constructor:

```
MedalsHolder medal = new MedalsHolder(Medals.silver);
```

The `narrow` method performs range checking on values and throws an exception if the argument is outside the bounds of the enumeration. It returns the value passed to it, so you can use it to perform passive bounds checking. For example:

```
int x = Medals.narrow(y);
```

assigns y to x only if y is in the range of enumerated values for `Medals`, otherwise it throws an exception.

Structures

An IDL struct is like a Java class without methods. In fact, JavaIDL converts an IDL struct into a Java class whose only methods are a null constructor and a constructor that takes all the structure's attributes.

Here is an example IDL struct definition:

```
module StructModule {
     struct Person {
          string name;
          long age;
     };
};
```

This definition produces the Java class declaration shown in Listing 18.3 (with some JavaIDL-specific methods omitted):

Listing 18.3 Java Definition of IDL Struct

```
package StructModule;
public final class Person {
 //     instance variables
 public String name;
 public int age;
 //     constructors
 public Person() { }
 public Person(String __name, int __age) {
     name = __name;
     age = __age;
 }
}
```

Like the enumerated type, a struct also produces a holder class that represents the structure. The holder class contains a single instance variable called `value`. Listing 18.4 shows the holder for the `Person` structure:

Listing 18.4 Java Definition of Holder Class for IDL Struct

```
package StructModule;
public final class PersonHolder
{
 //     instance variable
 public StructModule.Person value;
 //     constructors
 public PersonHolder() {
     this(null);
 }
 public PersonHolder(StructModule.Person __arg) {
```

```
        value = __arg;
    }
  }
```

Unions

The union is another C construct that didn't survive the transition to Java. The IDL union actually works more like the variant record in Pascal, since it requires a *discriminator* value. An IDL union is essentially a group of attributes, only one of which can be active at a time. The discriminator indicates which attribute is in use at the current time. A short example should make this a little clearer. Listing 18.5 shows an IDL union declaration:

Listing 18.5 An IDL Union Declaration

```
module UnionModule {
     union MyUnion switch (char) {
          case 'a':      string aValue;
          case 'b':     long bValue;
          case 'c':      boolean cValue;
          default:     string defValue;
     };
};
```

The character value in the switch, known as the discriminator, indicates which of the three variables in the union is active. If the discriminator is `'a'`, the `aValue` variable is active. Because Java doesn't have unions, a union is turned into a class with accessor methods for the different variables and a variable for the discriminator. The class is fairly complex. Listing 18.6 shows a subset of the definition for the `MyUnion` union:

Listing 18.6 Subset of Java Definition for an IDL Union

```
package UnionModule;
public class MyUnion {
//     constructor
 public MyUnion() {
//     only has a null constructor
 }
 //     discriminator accessor
 public char discriminator()
     throws sunw.corba.UnionDiscriminantException {
//     returns the value of the discriminator
 }
 //     branch constructors and get and set accessors
 public static MyUnion createaValue(String value) {
//     creates a MyUnion with a discriminator of 'a'
```

continues

Listing 18.6 Continued

```
    }
    public String getaValue()
        throws sunw.corba.UnionDiscriminantException {
//      returns the value of aValue (only if the discriminator
//      is 'a' right now)
    }
    public void setaValue(String value) {
//      sets the value of aValue and set the
//     discriminator to 'a'
    }
    public void setdefValue(char discriminator, String value)
        throws sunw.corba.UnionDiscriminantException {

//      Sets the value of defValue and sets the discriminator.
//     Although every variable has a method in this form, it
//     is only useful when you have a default value in the
//     union.
    }
}
```

The holder structure should be a familiar theme to you by now. JavaIDL generates a holder structure for a union. The holder structure for `MyUnion` would be called `MyUnionHolder` and would contain a single instance variable called `value`.

Sequences and Arrays

IDL sequences and arrays both map very neatly to Java arrays. Sequences in IDL can be either unbounded (no maximum size) or bounded (a specific maximum size). IDL arrays are always of a fixed size. Since Java arrays have a fixed size, but the size isn't known at compile-time, the JavaIDL system performs runtime checks on arrays to make sure they fit within the restrictions defined in the IDL module.

Here is a sample IDL definition containing an array, a bounded sequence and an unbounded sequence:

```
module ArrayModule {
     struct SomeStructure {
          long longArray[15];
          sequence <boolean> unboundedBools;
          sequence <char, 15> boundedChars;
     };
};
```

The arrays are defined in Java as:

```
public int[] longArray;
public boolean[] unboundedBools;
public char[] boundedChars;
```

Exceptions

CORBA has the notion of exceptions. Unlike Java, however, exceptions are not just a type of object, they are separate entities. IDL exceptions cannot inherit from other exceptions. Otherwise, they work like Java exceptions and may contain instance variables.

Here is an example IDL exception definition:

```
module ExceptionModule {
     exception YikesError {
          string info;
     };

};
```

18

This definition creates the Java file shown in Listing 18.7 (with some JavaIDL-specific methods removed):

Listing 18.7 Java Definition of IDL Exception

```
package ExceptionModule;
public class YikesError
     extends sunw.corba.UserException {
 //     instance variables
 public String info;
 //     constructors
 public YikesError() {
     super("IDL:ExceptionModule/YikesError:1.0");
 }
 public YikesError(String __info) {
     super("IDL:ExceptionModule/YikesError:1.0");
     info = __info;
 }
}
```

Interfaces

Interfaces are the most important part of IDL. An IDL interface contains a set of method definitions, just like a Java interface. Like Java interfaces, an IDL interface can inherit from other interfaces. Here is a sample IDL interface definition:

```
module InterfaceModule {
     interface MyInterface {
          void myMethod(in long param1);
     };
};
```

IDL classifies method parameters as being either `in`, `out`, or `inout`. An `in` parameter is identical to a Java parameter; it is a parameter passed by value. Even though the method can change the value of the variable, the changes are discarded when the method returns.

An `out` variable is an output-only variable. The method is expected to set the value of this variable, which is preserved when the method returns, but no value is passed in for the variable (it is uninitialized).

An `inout` variable is a combination of the two; you pass in a value to the method. If the method changes the value, the change is preserved when the method returns.

The fact that Java parameters are `in`-only poses a small challenge when mapping IDL to Java. Sun has come up with a reasonable approach, however. For any out or inout parameters, you pass in a holder class for that variable. The CORBA method can then set the `value` instance variable with the value that is supposed to be returned.

Attributes

IDL lets you define variables within an interface. These translate into `get` and `set` methods for the attribute. An attribute can be specified as `readonly`, which prevents the generation of a `set` method for the attribute. For example, if you defined an IDL attribute as

```
attribute long myAttribute;
```

your Java interface would then contain the following methods:

```
int getmyAttribute() throws omg.corba.SystemException;
void setmyAttribute() throws omg.corba.SystemException;
```

Using CORBA in Applets

Although the full CORBA suite represents a huge amount of code, the requirements for a CORBA client are fairly small. All you really need for a client is the ORB itself. You can access the CORBA services from another location on the network. This enables you to have very lightweight CORBA clients. In other words, you can create applets that are CORBA clients.

The only real restriction on applets using CORBA is that an applet can only make network connections back to the server it was loaded from. This means that all the CORBA services must be available on the Web server (or there must be some kind of proxy set up).

Since an applet cannot listen for incoming network connections, an applet cannot be a CORBA server in most cases. You might find an ORB that gets around this restriction by using connections made by the applet. Most Java ORBs available today have the ability to run CORBA servers on an applet for a callback object. For a callback, an applet might create a server object locally and then pass a reference for its server object to a CORBA server running on another machine. That CORBA server could then use the reference to invoke methods in the applet as a client. Figure 18.2 illustrates how an applet might act as a CORBA server.

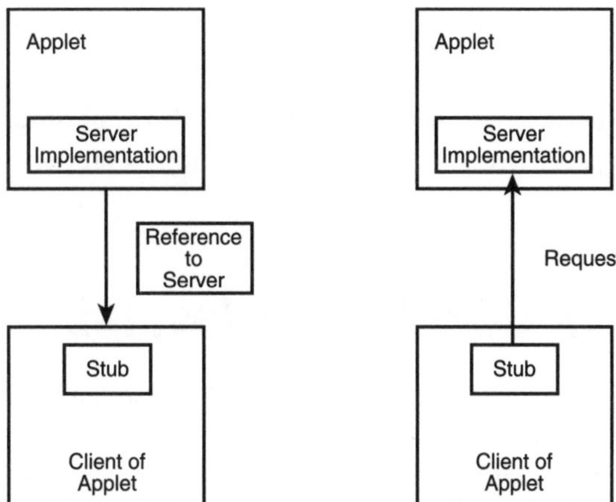

Fig. 18.2
An applet can act as a server by passing a reference to a local CORBA server.

Choosing Between CORBA and RMI

CORBA and RMI each has its advantages and disadvantages. RMI will be a standard part of Java on both the client and server side, making it a good, cheap tool. Since it is a Java-only system, it integrates cleanly with the rest of Java. RMI is really only a nice remote procedure call system, however.

CORBA defines a robust, distributed environment, providing almost all the necessary features for distributed applications. Not all of these features have been implemented by most vendors, yet. Most CORBA clients are offered free, but you must pay for the server software. This is the typical pricing model for most Internet software nowadays. If you don't need all the neat features of CORBA and don't want to spend a lot of money, RMI might be the right thing for you.

Your company may feel that Java is not yet ready for prime time. If this is the case, but you believe that Java is the environment of the future, you should start working CORBA into your current development plans, if possible.

CORBA is a language-independent system. You can implement your applications in C++ today using many of the Java design concepts. Specifically, keep the application and the user interface separated and make the software as modular as possible. If you use CORBA between the components of your system, you can migrate to Java by slowly replacing the various components with CORBA-based Java software.

If you are a programmer trying to convince your skeptical management about the benefits of Java, use CORBA to make a distributed interface into one of your applications (hopefully you have a CORBA product for the language your application is written in). Next, write a Java applet that implements the user interface for your application using CORBA to talk to the real application. You have instantly ported part of your application to every platform that can run a Java-enabled browser. Hopefully, your applet will perform as well as the old native interface to the application.

This same technique opens up your existing CORBA applications to non-traditional devices like cell-phones and PDAs. If you aren't ready to support those devices yet, at least you now have a pathway.

Creating CORBA Clients with JavaIDL

The JavaIDL system consists of an IDL-to-Java converter, a lightweight ORB, and a simple naming service. The JavaIDL interface is intended to be an interface to multiple ORBs, much the same way that JDBC interfaces with multiple databases.

There are two simple steps in creating a CORBA client in JavaIDL:

1. Create a reference to a stub using the `createRef` method in the particular stub.
2. Use the `sunw.corba.Orb.resolve` method to create a connection between the stub and a CORBA server.

For example, suppose you had the IDL definition for a banking interface, as shown in Listing 18.8.

Listing 18.8 Source Code for *Banking.idl*

```
module banking {

     enum AccountType {
          CHECKING,
          SAVINGS
     };

     struct AccountInfo {
          string id;
          string password;
          AccountType which;
     };

     exception InvalidAccountException {
          AccountInfo account;
     };

     exception InsufficientFundsException {
     };
```

```
        interface Banking {

            long getBalance(in AccountInfo account)
                raises (InvalidAccountException);

            void withdraw(in AccountInfo account, in long amount)
                raises (InvalidAccountException,
                    InsufficientFundsException);

            void deposit(in AccountInfo account, in long amount)
                raises (InvalidAccountException);

            void transfer(in AccountInfo fromAccount,
                in AccountInfo toAccount, in long amount)
                raises (InvalidAccountException,
                    InsufficientFundsException);
        };
    };
```


You create a reference to a stub for the banking interface with the following line:

```
BankingRef bank = BankingStub.createRef();
```

Next, you must create a connection between the stub and a CORBA server by *resolving* it. Since JavaIDL is meant to be the standard Java interface for all ORBs, it requires an ORB-independent naming scheme. Sun decided on a URL-type naming scheme of the format

`idl:`*`orb_name`*`://`*`orb_parameters`*

The early versions of JavaIDL shipped with an ORB called the Door ORB, which is a very lightweight ORB containing little more than a naming scheme. To access a CORBA object using the Door ORB, you must specify the host name and port number used by the CORBA server you are connecting to and the name of the object you are accessing. The format of this information is

`hostname``:`*`port`*`/`*`object_name`*

If you want to access an object, named Bank, via the Door ORB, running on a server at port 5150 on the local host, you resolve your stub this way:

```
sunw.corba.Orb.resolve(
      "idl:sunw.door://localhost:5150/Bank",
      bank);
```

Remember that the `bank` parameter is the `BankingRef` returned by the `BankingStub.createRef` method. Once the stub is resolved, you can invoke remote methods in the server using the stub.

Listing 18.9 shows the full JavaIDL client for the banking interface. As you can see, once you have connected the stub to the server, you can invoke methods on the stub just like it was a local object.

Listing 18.9 Source Code for *BankingClient.java*

```
import banking.*;

// This program tries out some of the methods in the BankingImpl
// remote object.

public class BankingClient
{

     public static void main(String args[])
     {

// Create an Account object for the account we are going to access.

          Account myAccount = new Account(
               "AA1234", "1017", AccountType.CHECKING);

          AccountInfo myAccountInfo = myAccount.toAccountInfo();
          try {

// Get a stub for the BankingImpl object

               BankingRef bank = BankingStub.createRef();
               sunw.corba.Orb.resolve(
                    "idl:sunw.door://localhost:5150/Bank",
                    bank);

// Check the initial balance
               System.out.println("My balance is: "+
                   bank.getBalance(myAccountInfo));

// Deposit some money
               bank.deposit(myAccountInfo, 50000);

// Check the balance again
               System.out.println("Deposited $500.00, balance is: "+
                    bank.getBalance(myAccountInfo));

// Withdraw some money
               bank.withdraw(myAccountInfo, 25000);

// Check the balance again
              System.out.println("Withdrew $250.00, balance is: "+
                    bank.getBalance(myAccountInfo));

               System.out.flush();
               System.exit(0);

          } catch (Exception e) {
               System.out.println("Got exception: "+e);
               e.printStackTrace();
          }
     }
}
```

Creating CORBA Clients with VisiBroker

VisiBroker, formerly known as Black Widow, is very similar to JavaIDL in its mapping from IDL to Java. Both JavaIDL and VisiBroker map the IDL data types and data structures the same way, and both handle `inout` and `out` parameters the same way.

Note

Netscape and VisiBroker recently announced that future versions of the Netscape Navigator would contain the VisiBroker CORBA client. You will soon be able to write applets for Netscape that don't have to download the ORB software before they run.

The only difference between the two ORBs on the client side is in the way you connect a stub to a server.

Under VisiBroker, you must first initialize the ORB with the following line:

```
CORBA.ORB orb = CORBA.ORB.init();
```

You only need to initialize the ORB once, no matter how many stubs you create. Next, you connect the stub to the server using the `bind` method. For example, to connect your stub to an object named `Bank`, you would use the following call:

```
Banking bank = Banking_var.bind("Bank");
```

Tip

You'll often see the terms *bind* and *resolve* used in network programming. Bind refers to attaching two things together, like you bind a port number to a socket, meaning you assign that port number to the socket. In the VisiBroker context, you bind a stub to a server object, meaning you connect them together. Resolve is another word for lookup. When you resolve a name, you find the object the name refers to. When you resolve a stub, you find the named object the stub should be connected to.

chapter 19

Creating CORBA Servers

19

by Mark Wutka

In this chapter

- **Creating servers with CORBA**
  A CORBA server makes a nice alternative to a Web server. You can invoke methods on a CORBA server rather than encoding information in an HTTP request.
- **Implementing peer-to-peer communications with callbacks**
  The typical client/server model doesn't always work well for all applications. Sometimes you need the server to invoke methods on its client. You can create a callback mechanism with CORBA that allows the server to call a client's methods.
- **Using CORBA with non-CORBA objects**
  If you have an existing object that isn't CORBA-aware, you can create a wrapper that provides a CORBA interface to that object. This technique allows you to turn existing applications into distributed applications with a minimum amount of work.

A CORBA server has objects whose methods are invoked remotely by its clients. A single server can have any number of objects, and can activate and deactivate objects at any time. An active object is visible to the clients, whereas an inactive object cannot be accessed by clients.

Creating a Basic CORBA Server

The interface between the ORB and the implementation of a server is called a *skeleton*. A skeleton for an IDL interface gets information from the ORB, invokes the appropriate server method, and sends the results back to the ORB.

You normally don't have to write the skeleton itself; you just supply the implementation of the remote methods. Figure 19.1 illustrates the flow of a method invocation through a skeleton to your implementation.

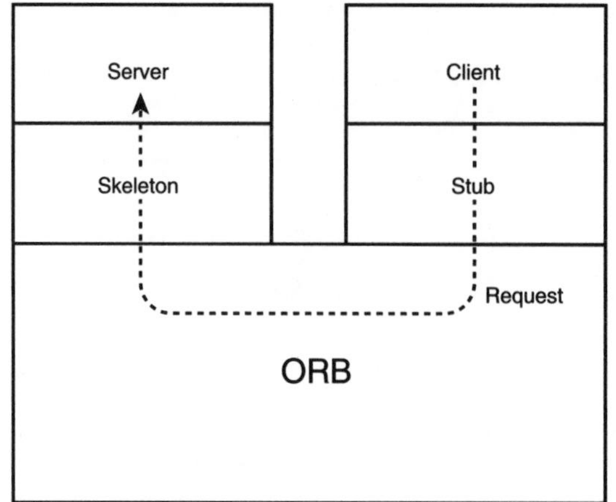

Fig 19.1
The `Skeleton` *class translates CORBA requests into method invocation.*

Listing 19.1 shows an IDL definition of a simple banking interface. You will see how to create a server for this interface in both JavaIDL and VisiBroker.

Listing 19.1 Source Code for *Banking.idl*

```
module banking {

     enum AccountType {
          CHECKING,
          SAVINGS
     };

     struct AccountInfo {
          string id;
          string password;
          AccountType which;
     };

     exception InvalidAccountException {
          AccountInfo account;
     };

     exception InsufficientFundsException {
     };

     interface Banking {

          long getBalance(in AccountInfo account)
               raises (InvalidAccountException);

          void withdraw(in AccountInfo account, in long amount)
               raises (InvalidAccountException,
                    InsufficientFundsException);
```

```
            void deposit(in AccountInfo account, in long amount)
                raises (InvalidAccountException);

            void transfer(in AccountInfo fromAccount,
                in AccountInfo toAccount, in long amount)
                raises (InvalidAccountException,
                    InsufficientFundsException);
        };
    };
```

Using Classes Defined by IDL Structs

When an IDL struct is turned into a Java class, it does not have custom `hashCode` and `equals` methods. This means that two instances of this class having identical data are not equal.

If you want to add custom methods to these structs, you have to create a separate class and define methods to convert from one class to the other.

In Chapter 16, "Creating 3-Tier Distributed Applications with RMI," the RMI-based banking application defines an `Account` class that has its own `hashCode` and `equals` methods. This allows it to be stored in a hash table.

The following code shows the two methods that need to be added to the `Account` class to convert to and from `AccountInfo` objects.

```
// Allow this object to be created from an AccountInfo instance

        public Account(AccountInfo acct)
        {
                this.id = acct.id;
                this.password = acct.password;
                this.which = acct.which;
        }

// Convert this object to an AccountInfo instance

        public AccountInfo toAccountInfo()
        {
                return new AccountInfo(id, password, which);
        }
```

VisiBroker Skeletons

VisiBroker implements skeletons in a traditional way. When you generate your skeletons and stubs for an IDL module, it generates an abstract skeleton class.

This class has all the code to communicate with the ORB and to invoke the remote methods. It leaves the remote methods themselves as abstract methods.

When you use the remote methods, you create a subclass of the skeleton class and use those abstract methods. The name of the skeleton class generated for an IDL interface, at least for VisiBroker, is the name of the interface, prefaced by `_sk_`.

Every object that uses a CORBA interface in VisiBroker must identify itself by a name. The constructor for the skeleton class sends this name to the ORB itself.

When you create a subclass of the skeleton, you must create a constructor that passes a name up to the superclass, for example:

```
public class BankingImpl extends _sk_Banking
{
     public BankingImpl(String bankingObjectName)
     {
          super(bankingObjectName);
     // other initialization code here
     }
```

The implementation of the skeleton methods is straightforward. In fact, you can use the implementation of the `BankingImpl` class from Chapter 16, changing only the `java.rmi.RemoteException` exceptions to `CORBA.SystemException`.

The following code fragment is an example of one of the methods from the `BankingImpl` for VisiBroker:

```
// getBalance returns the amount of money in the account (in cents).
// If the account is invalid, it throws an InvalidAccountException

     public int getBalance(AccountInfo accountInfo)
     throws CORBA.SystemException, InvalidAccountException
     {

// Fetch the account from the table
          Integer balance = (Integer) accountTable.get(
               new Account(accountInfo));

// If the account wasn't there, throw an exception
          if (balance == null) {
               throw new InvalidAccountException(accountInfo);
          }

// Return the account's balance
          return balance.intValue();
     }
```

Once you create an object that uses a remote interface, you need a program that creates instances of these objects so the clients can use them. To do this, you must first initialize the VisiBroker ORB with the following line:

```
CORBA.ORB orb = CORBA.ORB.init();
```

Next, you must create an instance of the Basic Object Adapter, or BOA. The BOA is a standard CORBA object used to communicate with the ORB.

It was intended for systems where the ORB and the server are separate programs or even on separate machines. The BOA has methods for activating and deactivating objects, and for activating and deactivating the entire server.

You create an instance of a BOA with the following line:

```
CORBA.BOA boa = orb.BOA_init();
```

Next, create an instance of your implementation object. In this case, the implementation object is the `BankingImpl` object.

While you are instantiating a `BankingImpl` object, you want to refer to it as an instance of the `Banking` object, as far as the BOA is concerned, so you should store the new object in a variable of type `Banking`.

Also, when you create the implementation, you must give it the name that the other clients will use to access it. In this case, the name is `Bank`. You create the instance with the following line:


```
Banking banking = new BankingImpl("Bank");
```

Even though you have created an implementation object, the ORB still does not know about it. You must identify the object to the BOA by calling the `obj_is_ready` method:

```
boa.obj_is_ready(banking);
```

If you have more than one implementation object, you should identify them all to the BOA at this point. Once all the objects have been identified, call the BOA's `impl_is_ready` to tell the ORB that everything is ready to go:

```
boa.impl_is_ready();
```

When you have called `impl_is_ready`, your server is ready to go, and clients can begin connecting to it.

Listing 19.2 shows a startup object that initializes the ORB, creates an instance of the `BankingImpl` class, and activates it using the BOA.

Listing 19.2 Source Code for *BankingServer.java*

```
package banking;

// This class creates a BankingImpl object and activates
// it through the BOA (Basic Object Adaptor).

public class BankingServer
{

     public static void main(String[] args)
     {
```

continues

Listing 19.2 Continued

```
        try {

// Initialize the ORB
            CORBA.ORB orb = CORBA.ORB.init();

// Create a BOA
            CORBA.BOA boa = orb.BOA_init();

// Create the banking service implementation. Clients will
// request access to the object by the name "Bank".
            Banking banking = new BankingImpl("Bank");

// Tell the BOA about the banking object
            boa.obj_is_ready(banking);

// Activate all the objects in the BOA
            boa.impl_is_ready();

        } catch (Exception e) {
            System.out.println("Got exception: "+e);
            e.printStackTrace();
        }
    }
}
```

Using the VisiBroker TIE Interface

The traditional approach of using an abstract skeleton class with an implementation subclass works well for many situations. In fact, in C++ you may never have any problems with it, since C++ allows multiple inheritance.

In Java, however, you can run into some hairy problems using this method. You may want to create a remote object that is a subclass of a non-CORBA object. Using the normal skeleton class provided by VisiBroker uses up your one permitted inheritance.

The VisiBroker TIE interface addresses this problem. The concept of the TIE is common in several ORBs and is sometimes called *delegation.*

TIE doesn't stand for anything. It refers to the idea that it ties a CORBA object to a non-CORBA object, providing remote access to the non-CORBA object.

In the regular skeleton implementation, the skeleton *is* the implementation. In the TIE implementation, the skeleton and the implementation are separate objects.

VisiBroker's implementation of the TIE in Java is quite simple. When you create Java files from IDL, VisiBroker creates a Java interface for each interface you define in IDL. The name of the Java interface is the name of the IDL interface with the word Operations appended to it.

For instance, the IDL interface `Banking` would generate a Java interface called `BankingOperations`. VisiBroker also generates a skeleton TIE implementation, whose name is the name of the IDL interface, prefaced by _tie_, like `_tie_Banking`.

Unlike the normal skeleton class, the TIE skeleton class is not an abstract class. Instead, it uses the methods in the IDL interface.

All these methods do, however, is invoke identical methods in an instance of `BankingOperations`. In other words, the TIE skeleton class works like a pass-thru.

Figure 19.2 illustrates the relationship between a TIE skeleton and an object using the `BankingOperations` interface.

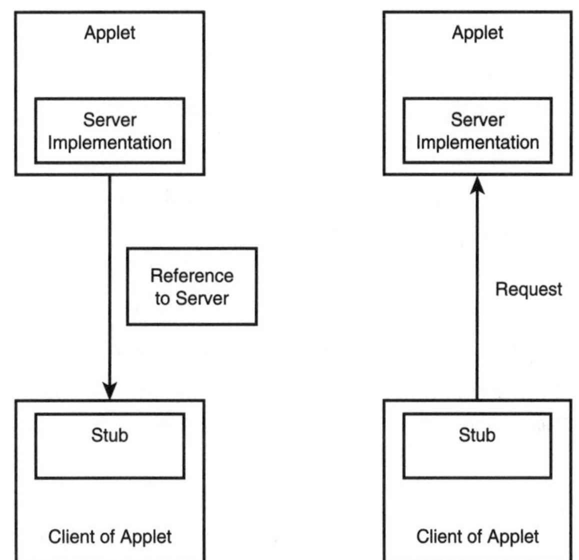

Fig. 19.2
The TIE skeleton invokes implementation methods in another object.

When you create an implementation object for a TIE interface, it does not have to be a subclass of the skeleton. In fact, it shouldn't be.

Instead, it must use an `Operations` interface (`BankingOperations`, for example). The only link that the implementation has to CORBA is that each method in the `Operations` interface can throw the `CORBA.SystemException` exception.

Unlike the regular skeleton implementation, the constructor for the TIE implementation object does not have to accept the object's name. You can use the empty constructor if you like.

The only difference in start-up between the regular skeleton implementation and the TIE implementation is that for the TIE implementation, you first create the TIE implementation object, and then you create an instance of the TIE skeleton, passing it the implementation object.

The following code fragment creates a TIE implementation of the `Banking` interface, followed by the TIE skeleton for that interface:

```
BankingTieImpl impl = new BankingTieImpl();
Banking banking = new _tie_Banking(impl, "Bank");
```

As you can see, the object's name is passed to the constructor for the TIE skeleton, not to the TIE implementation.

JavaIDL Skeletons

JavaIDL doesn't even bother with an abstract skeleton class. Instead, it always generates a TIE interface for every class, although the JavaIDL specification never uses the term *TIE*.

Like VisiBroker, JavaIDL creates an `Operations` interface that has Java versions of the methods defined in the IDL interface. The only difference between the interface created by JavaIDL and the interface created by VisiBroker is the name of the CORBA system exception. JavaIDL calls it `sunw.corba.SystemException.`

The implementation object you create does not use the `Operations` interface directly. Instead, it uses the `Servant` interface, which extends the `Operations` interface. For example, your implementation for the `Banking` interface might be declared as

```
public class BankingImpl implements BankingServant
```

Although JavaIDL is intended to be Sun's recommendation for mapping IDL into Java, it was released with a lightweight ORB called the Door ORB. This ORB provides just enough functionality to get clients and servers talking to each other, but not much more.

Depending on the ORB, the initialization varies, as does the activation of the objects. For the Door ORB distributed with JavaIDL, you initialize the ORB with the following line:

```
sunw.door.Orb.initialize(servicePort);
```

The `servicePort` parameter you pass to the ORB is the port number it should use when listening for incoming clients. It must be an integer value. Your clients must use this port number when connecting to your server.

After you initialize the orb, you can instantiate your implementation object. For example:

```
BankingImpl impl = new BankingImpl();
```

Next, you create the skeleton, passing it the implementation object:

```
BankingRef server = BankingSkeleton.createRef(impl);
```

Finally, you activate the server by publishing the name of the object:

```
sunw.door.Orb.publish("Bank", server);
```

Listing 19.3 shows the complete JavaIDL startup program for the banking server.

Listing 19.3 Source Code for *BankingServer.java*

```
package banking;

public class BankingServer
{

// Define the port that clients will use to connect to this server
     public static final int servicePort = 5150;

     public static void main(String[] args)
     {

// Initialize the orb
          sunw.door.Orb.initialize(servicePort);

          try {

               BankingImpl impl = new BankingImpl();
// Create the server
               BankingRef server =
                    BankingSkeleton.createRef(impl);

// Register the object with the naming service as "Bank"
               sunw.door.Orb.publish("Bank", server);

          } catch (Exception e) {
               System.out.println("Got exception: "+e);
               e.printStackTrace();
          }
     }
}
```


Creating Callbacks in CORBA

Callbacks are a handy mechanism in distributed computing. You use them whenever your client wants to be notified of some event but doesn't want to sit and poll the server to see if the event has occurred yet.

In a regular Java program, you'd just create a callback interface and pass the server an object that uses the callback interface. When the event occurs, the server invokes a method in the callback object.

As it turns out, callbacks are just that easy in CORBA. You define a callback interface in your IDL file and then create a method in the server's interface that takes the callback interface as a parameter. The following IDL file defines a server interface and a callback interface:

```
module callbackDemo
{
     interface callbackInterface {
          void doNotify(in string whatHappened);
     };

     interface serverInterface {
          void setCallback(in callbackInterface callMe);
     };
};
```

Under JavaIDL, the `setCallback` method would be defined as:

```
void setCallback(callbackDemo.callbackInterfaceRef callMe)
    throws sunw.corba.SystemException;
```

Once you have the `callbackDemo.callbackInterfaceRef` object, you can invoke its `whatHappened` method at any time. At this point, the client and server are on a peer-to-peer level. They are each other's client and server.

Wrapping CORBA Around an Existing Object

When you create CORBA implementation objects, you are tying that object to a CORBA implementation. Even if you use the TIE interface in your ORB, your methods still can throw the CORBA `SystemException` exception.

This is not the ideal situation. Even though JavaIDL and VisiBroker are similar, you still have to make minor changes when going from one to the other. If the conversion is a one-time thing, that may not be a big deal.

If, on the other hand, you have to maintain multiple versions of a complex object, you don't want to keep multiple copies of the actual implementation code.

You can solve this problem, but it takes a little extra work up front. First, concentrate on using the object you want, without using CORBA, RMI, or any other remote interface mechanism.

This is the one copy you use across all your implementations. This object, or set of objects, can define its own types, exceptions, and interfaces.

Next, to make this object available remotely, define an IDL interface that is as close to the object's interface as you can get. There may be cases where they won't match exactly, but you can take care of that.

Once you generate the Java classes from the IDL definition, create an implementation that simply invokes methods on the real implementation object. This is essentially the same as a TIE interface, with one major exception: the implementation class has no knowledge of CORBA.

You can even use this technique to provide multiple ways to access a remote object. Figure 19.3 shows a diagram of the various ways you might provide access to your implementation object.

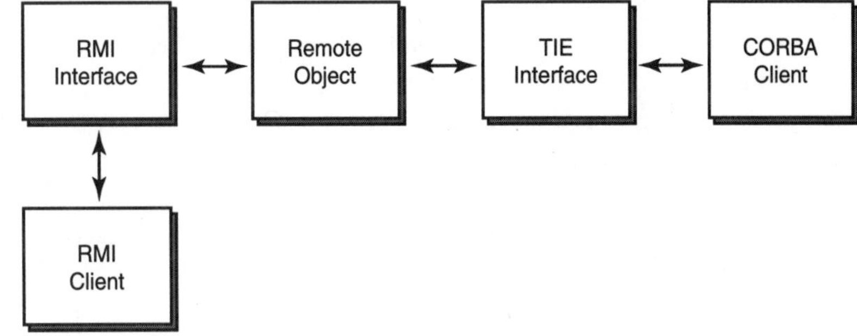

Fig. 19.3
A single object can be accessed by many types of remote object systems.

Although this may sound simple, it has some additional complexities that you must address. If your implementation object defines its own exceptions, you must map those exceptions to CORBA exceptions. You must also map between Java objects and CORBA-defined objects.

Once again, the banking interface is a good starting point for illustrating the problems and solutions in separating the application from CORBA.

The original banking interface is defined with a hierarchy of exceptions, a generic `BankingException`, with `InsufficientFundsException` and `InvalidAccountException` as subclasses. This poses a problem in CORBA, since exceptions aren't inherited.

You must define a `BankingException` exception in your IDL file, this way:

```
exception BankingException {};
```

In addition, since you probably want the banking application itself to be in the banking package, change the IDL module name to `remotebanking`.

The implementation for the `Banking` interface in the remotebanking module must do two kinds of mapping. First, it must convert instances of the `Account` object to instances of the `AccountInfo` object.

This may seem like a pain and, frankly, it is, but it's a necessary pain. If you start to intermingle the classes defined by CORBA with the real implementation of the application, you end up having to carry the CORBA portions along with the application, even if you don't use CORBA.

Mapping to and from CORBA-Defined Types

You can define static methods to handle the conversion from the application data types to the CORBA-defined data types. For example, the banking application defines an `Account` object.

The remotebanking module defines this object as `AccountInfo`. You can convert between the two with the following methods:

```
// Create a banking.Account from an AccountInfo object

public static banking.Account makeAccount(AccountInfo info)
{
        return new banking.Account(info.id, info.password,
                info.which);
}

// Create an AccountInfo object from a banking.Account object

public static AccountInfo makeAccountInfo(banking.Account account)
{
        return new AccountInfo(account.id, account.password,
                account.which);
}
```

Your remote implementation of the banking interface needs access to the real implementation, so the constructor for the `RemoteBankingImpl` object needs a reference to the `banking.BankingImpl` object:

```
protected banking.BankingImpl impl;

public RemoteBankingImpl(banking.BankingImpl impl)
{
        this.impl = impl;
}
```

Creating Remote Method Wrappers

Now all your remote methods have to do is convert any incoming `AccountInfo` objects to `banking.Account` objects, catch any exceptions, and throw the proper remote exceptions. Here is the implementation of the remote `withdraw` method:

```
// call the withdraw function in the real implementation, catching
// any exceptions and throwing the equivalent CORBA exception

public synchronized void withdraw(AccountInfo accountInfo, int amount)
throws sunw.corba.SystemException, InvalidAccountException,
        InsufficientFundsException, BankingException
{

        try {

// Call the real withdraw method, converting the accountInfo object
// to a banking.Account object first
```

```
                impl.withdraw( makeAccount(accountInfo), amount);

        } catch (banking.InvalidAccountException excep) {

// The banking.InvalidAccountException contains an Account object.
// Convert it to an AccountInfo object when throwing the CORBA exception

                throw new InvalidAccountException(
                        makeAccountInfo(excep.account));

        } catch (banking.InsufficientFundsException nsf) {
                throw new InsufficientFundsException();
        } catch (banking.BankingException e) {
                throw new BankingException();
        }
}
```

Although it would be nice if you could get the IDL-to-Java converter to generate this automatically, it has no way of knowing exactly how the real implementation looks.

Implementing Wrapped Callbacks

The notion of the callback is particularly nasty, since you can't just encapsulate the CORBA calls going to the server. The server has to make CORBA calls back to the client.

The stock quote system introduced in Chapter 16 has a good example of a callback system. Unfortunately, there's one feature in the stock quote system that needs to be changed.

Whenever you create a callback system, leave room for the callback to throw an exception. You may never use it, but it makes it much easier to create a distributed version of the application.

Figure 19.4 illustrates the relationship between the real implementation and the CORBA wrappers in a callback system.

The revised version of the `StockQuoteClient` interface is shown in Listing 19.4.

Listing 19.4 Source Code for *StockQuoteClient.java*

```
package stocks;

// Defines a callback interface for the StockQuoteServer so
// it can notify its clients of new stock quotes.

public interface StockQuoteClient
{
     public void quote(StockQuote quote) throws
          StockQuoteClientException;
}
```

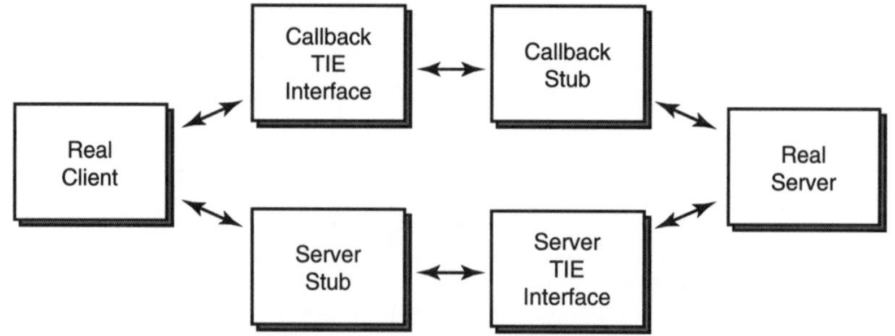

Fig. 19.4
Callbacks need special handling in a CORBA system.

The `StockQuoteClientException` is a simple subclass of `Exception` with no extra parameters. The stock-quote server likes to know when it can no longer send quotes to a client. If an error occurs, it removes the client from its tables.

The trick to wrapping CORBA around a callback system is that you have to create a wrapper for the callback as well as for the server. The wrapper uses the methods that the non-CORBA server defines for its callback and then invokes the corresponding method in the CORBA client.

Listing 19.5 shows the implementation of the `RemoteStockCallback` object, which does the distributed callback.

Listing 19.5 Source Code for *RemoteStockCallback.java*

```
package remotestocks;

public class RemoteStockCallback implements stocks.StockQuoteClient
{

// Client is the CORBA client whose methods we want to invoke
     protected StockQuoteClientRef client;

// Server is the CORBA-wrapper for the stock quote server. If there
// is an error sending a quote to the client, we tell the wrapper
// about it so it can remove this client from its tables.
     protected RemoteStockQuoteImpl server;

// makeRemoteStockQuote converts a stocks.StockQuote object (the Non-CORBA
// object) into a remotestocks.StockQuote object (the CORBA version of
// the stock quote).

     protected static StockQuote makeRemoteStockQuote(
          stocks.StockQuote quote)
     {
          return new StockQuote(quote.stock, quote.amount,
               quote.change);
     }

     public RemoteStockCallback(StockQuoteClientRef client,
```

```
            RemoteStockQuoteImpl server)
        {
            this.client = client;
            this.server = server;
        }

// quote is invoked by the real stock quote server implementation, not
// the CORBA server.

        public void quote(stocks.StockQuote quote) throws
             stocks.StockQuoteClientException
        {
// Try to invoke the remote method, converting the stocks.StockQuote
// to the CORBA version, remotestocks.StockQuote
            try {
                client.quote(makeRemoteStockQuote(quote));
            } catch (Exception e) {

// If there was an error, remove this client from the server, then
// throw an exception to the real implementation server.

                try {
                    server.removeCallback(client);
                } catch (Exception ignore) {
                }
                throw new stocks.StockQuoteClientException();
            }
        }
}
```

19

Now in the normal implementation of the stock quote system, the client calls the `addWatch` method in the server, passing it the reference to the client and the name of the stock to watch. The server adds this client to its tables and invokes the `quote` method in the client every time the stock's value changes.

With a CORBA front-end on the server, things change slightly. When the request comes into the CORBA wrapper, it creates an instance of `RemoteStockCallback`, passing to its constructor the client stub that was passed in the `addWatch` call.

The wrapper then calls the `addWatch` method in the real server implementation, passing it the `RemoteStockCallback`. Here is the implementation of the `addWatch` method in the CORBA wrapper:

```
// addWatch adds a client to the list of clients watching a stock

public void addWatch(StockQuoteClientRef client, String stock)
throws sunw.corba.SystemException, UnknownStock
{

// See if we have already created a callback object for this client.
        RemoteStockCallback callback = (RemoteStockCallback)
                stockClients.get(client);
```

```
// If we didn't already have a callback, create one and add it
// to the table.
        if (callback == null) {
                callback = new RemoteStockCallback(client, this);

                stockClients.put(client, callback);
        }

// Now call the addWatch method in the real implementation
        try {
                impl.addWatch(callback, stock);
        } catch (stocks.UnknownStockException e) {
                throw new UnknownStock(stock);
        }
}
```

Now when the real stock quote server publishes a stock quote, it ends up calling the `quote` method in the `RemoteStockCallback` object. This callback object, in turn, calls the `quote` method in the distributed client.

Figure 19.5 illustrates the sequence of events for publishing a stock quote.

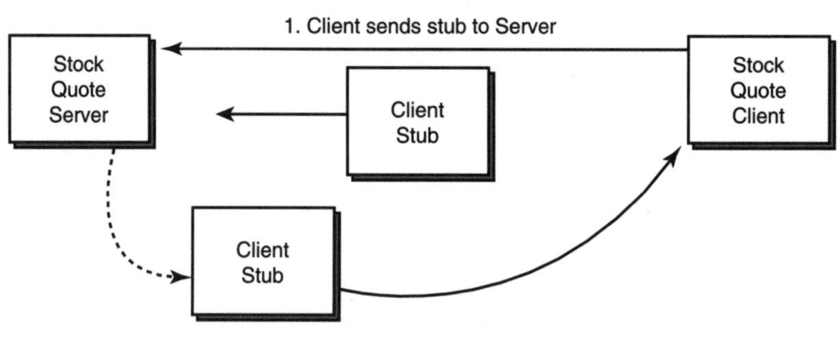

Fig. 19.5
`RemoteStockCallback` *acts as a proxy for a distributed client.*

PART IV

Speeding Up Java

chapter 20

Increasing Graphics Performance

20

by Mark Wutka

In this chapter

- **Double-buffering to speed up drawing**
  The technique of writing to an off-screen buffer instead of directly to the screen, usually called double-buffering, can speed up the graphics performance on some systems. Of course, it can also slow down the graphics performance on other systems. Your applet can take a short amount of time at startup and determine whether double-buffering is a help or a hindrance for drawing.
- **Performing selective updates**
  You can speed up your graphics performance by repainting only the areas of the screen that have changed. This results in fewer actual updates to the underlying graphics system, which often consumes the most time.
- **Redrawing changed areas**
  Sometimes it is not so easy to do all your drawing in the `paint` *method. You may prefer to update the screen immediately, without waiting for a repaint. If you use double-buffering, you can always draw to the off-screen buffer.*

If you are just doing simple animation sequences in Java, the performance you get from most Java environments is probably fine. If you are trying to write a video game or some other graphics-intensive program, you may find that you have to squeeze out every bit of performance from Java. Sometimes you are able to make some basic assumptions about the graphics environment you are running on, but that is not the case with Java. You don't know if your program will be running on a laptop with a simple VGA card, or on a Silicon Graphics system with extremely fast graphics.

On the PC platform alone, you have a wide variety of graphics capabilities. A simple system may have an old VGA card with an ISA bus interface, or an accelerated graphics card running on a PCI bus Pentium system. The approach used by many graphics vendors is to detect the system type either at installation time or at runtime. Once a program knows how well the graphics perform, it can adjust itself to accommodate a slower system. You can do this in Java, as well. In fact, it is even more important in Java since Java runs on so many different platforms.

Aside from adjusting to the capabilities of the local system, you can also reduce the amount of drawing your program has to do. If you redraw only the parts of a screen that need to be redrawn, you have more time to perform other tasks, or to create more animation frames.

Double-Buffering to Speed Up Drawing

Double-buffering, which was introduced in Chapter 5, "Animating Images," is typically used to prevent flicker when you are doing animation. Under some graphics systems, however, it can also increase the graphics drawing speed.

This happens when the native drawing routines in the operating system have a lot of overhead when drawing to a visible area. The operating system often does far less work when you are writing to an off-screen area.

Just to refresh your memory, when you do double-buffering, you create an image that is the same size as the screen. You then use the `getGraphics` method to get a graphics context for the image, which you pass to your `paint` method. When the `paint` method does its drawing, it is really drawing on the image you created and not the actual screen. Once the `paint` method is finished, the `update` method copies the off-screen image to the screen.

Detecting the Best Drawing Method at Runtime

Unfortunately, some Java systems draw faster when they are drawing off-screen, whereas others draw faster when they are drawing to the visible area. If you don't mind taking a short delay when your applet starts up, you can do a quick benchmark to choose between double-buffering and straight drawing.

Note

There are many reasons for the speed differences between double-buffering and straight drawing. Sometimes the way the graphics system is implemented makes a difference. Some graphics systems can draw bitmaps to the screen much faster than they can draw individual pixels. In these cases, it is often better to write to a buffer and then draw the whole buffer. Other times, the graphics system may copy things to a buffer anyway, and if you draw to your own off-screen buffer, you waste time copying from one buffer to another.

To autodetect the graphics speed, do a simple series of drawings on an off-screen image and record the number of milliseconds it takes to complete the drawing. Then, do the same series of drawings to the screen and compare the results.

If you want the test to be invisible, do all the drawings in the applet's background color. Instead of doing the drawings invisibly, you can make a neat design that is just a normal part of the applet's startup.

Listing 20.1 shows an autodetect method that tries doing double-buffering and direct drawing. It tries to draw a series of images as many times as it can for approximately 500 milliseconds. Normally, you would just use whichever method is able to draw more frames in 500 milliseconds. If they happen to come up with the same number of frames, this autodetect method compares the total time used by each test. It is possible that one of the tests was allowed more drawing time than the other. If that is the case, and the tests each drew the same number of frames, the test that took less time to run is the faster method.

Listing 20.1 *doAutoDetect* Method from *AutoDetect.java*

```
// doAutoDetect performs tries drawing to the screen and to a
// buffer. Whichever one takes the least time (actually, whichever
// one it can do the most times within a set time constraint) is
// the one that is best.

     protected void doAutoDetect(Graphics g)
     {

// Create the off-screen drawing area

          offscreenImage = createImage(size().width, size().height);
          offscreenGraphics = offscreenImage.getGraphics();

          long start;
          long end;

// Tally the number of times we were able to draw direct and buffered
          int directCount = 0;
          int bufferedCount = 0;

// Draw in the applet's background color, makes the autodetection invisible.

          g.setColor(getBackground());
```

continues

Listing 20.1 Continued

```
// Mark what time we started
          start = System.currentTimeMillis();
          end = start;

// Paint patterns directly to the screen, but only for 500 milliseconds

          while ((end-start) < 500) {
               paintDetectDesign(g);
               end = System.currentTimeMillis();
               directCount++;
          }
          g.setColor(getForeground());

// record the total time spent drawing directly
          long directTime = end - start;

          start = System.currentTimeMillis();
          end = start;

// Paint patterns to the offscreen graphics, but only for 500 milliseconds

          while ((end-start) < 500) {
               paintDetectDesign(offscreenGraphics);
               end = System.currentTimeMillis();
               bufferedCount++;
          }

          long bufferedTime = end - start;

// If we were able to draw more times using the buffered graphics,
// or if the drawing counts are the same, but the total time for
// the buffering was less, buffering is faster.

          if ((bufferedCount > directCount) ||
               ((bufferedCount == directCount) &&
                (bufferedTime < directTime))) {
               drawDirect = false;
          } else {

// If we want to draw direct, free the space taken up by the
// offscreen image and graphics context.
               offscreenImage.flush();
               offscreenImage = null;
               offscreenGraphics = null;
               drawDirect = true;
          }
          detected = true;
     }
```

The `doAutoDetect` method does not do any drawing itself. Instead, it calls another method called `paintDetectDesign`. This allows you to change the pattern you draw to perform the test. One of the things you might do when performing your test is to simulate the kind of drawing you plan to do. If you plan to draw a lot of images, your drawing test should draw some images. Listing 20.2 shows a sample `paintDetectDesign` that performs some basic graphics operations.

Listing 20.2 ***paintDetectDesign*** **Method from** ***AutoDetect.java***

```
// paintDetectDesign performs some graphical operations to gauge the time
// it takes to paint either directly or to an offscreen area. It just draws
// some lines, boxes and ovals a number of times and then returns.

     protected void paintDetectDesign(Graphics g)
     {
          for (int i=0; i < 10; i++) {
               g.drawLine(0, 0, 100, 100);
               g.fillRect(0, 0, 100, 100);
               g.fillOval(0, 0, 100, 100);
          }
     }
```


Creating an Autodetecting *update* Method

The trick with running the autodetection method is that you must run it from your `update` method. You can also run it from your `paint` method, but only if your `update` method isn't already doing double-buffering. You can create an `update` method that can be reused again and again, and can adapt to either direct screen drawing or double-buffered drawing.

The `update` method first checks to see if it has already performed the autodetection, and if not, calls `doAutoDetect`. Next, if the autodetection decided that it is faster to do double-buffering, the `update` method clears the drawing area in the off-screen buffer and then calls the `paint` method, making `paint` draw to the off-screen buffer.

If it is faster to draw directly to the screen, the `update` method simply calls `super.update`, which will clear the screen and call the `paint` method. Listing 20.3 shows an `update` method that performs all of these functions and works in conjunction with the `doAutoDetect` method.

Listing 20.3 ***update*** **Method from** ***AutoDetect.java***

```
     public void update(Graphics g)
     {

// If we haven't run auto-detection yet, do it now
          if (!detected) {
               doAutoDetect(g);
          }
```

continues

Listing 20.3 Continued

```
// If we draw direct, go ahead and call the parent update. This will
// clear the drawing area and then call paint. If you don't want the
// drawing area cleared, just change the super.update(g);
// to paint(g);

          if (drawDirect) {
               super.update(g);
          } else {

// If we're doing buffered drawing, simulate the effects of the
// default update method by clearing the offscreen drawing area.
// If you don't want the drawing area cleared, remove the calls
// to setColor and fillRect.

// Clear the offscreen drawing area and set the drawing
// color back to foreground.

               offscreenGraphics.setColor(getBackground());
               offscreenGraphics.fillRect(0, 0, size().width,
                    size().height);
               offscreenGraphics.setColor(getForeground());

// Paint to the offscreen image

               paint(offscreenGraphics);

// Copy the offscreen image to the screen

               g.drawImage(offscreenImage, 0, 0, this);
          }
     }
```

The doAutoDetect and update methods from the AutoDetect class require some other variables to be present. You will find the complete source to the AutoDetect class on the CD that comes with this book.

Performing Selective Updates

Normally, when you want to redraw the screen you call the repaint method. This in turn calls update, which calls paint, which redraws the entire screen. If you are redrawing a complex scene, you could spend a lot of time redrawing things that never changed.

If you can keep track of which part of the screen actually changed and just redraw that part, you will save a lot of time. Unfortunately, it isn't always so easy to redraw only a portion of the screen.

Graphics systems like to deal with rectangles when it comes to repainting. Some systems allow you to create a list of rectangles describing the changed regions.

Java does not permit this, however. You can either repaint the entire screen or repeatedly call the `repaint` method for each rectangular region of the screen that needs to be changed.

Your ability to override the `update` method gives you a third option. If you create an `update` method that does not clear the screen, you can call `repaint` for the entire drawing area. Then, in your `paint` routine, examine only the changed areas and redraw them.

Listing 20.4 shows an applet that calls `repaint` to redraw only portions of the drawing area. The applet draws several rectangles, but will redraw only a rectangle if it touches the part of the screen that is being repainted. You can find out the part of the screen that is being repainted by calling the `getClipRect` method in the `Graphics` object that is passed to the `paint` method. The `getClipRect` method returns a `Rectangle` object that describes the area being repainted. One of the handy features about the `Rectangle` class is that it contains a method to tell whether two rectangles intersect. The `UpdateRects` applet uses this capability to see which of its rectangles intersect with the drawing area. If a rectangle doesn't intersect with the current drawing area, it doesn't repaint that rectangle.

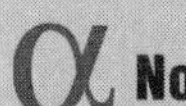

Note

If you want to see if a `Polygon` object intersects with the drawing area, you can use the `getBoundingRect` method in the `Polygon` class to get the rectangle that encloses the polygon. You can then use the `intersects` method in the enclosing rectangle to see if it intersects with the drawing area. There are cases where this technique might cause you to redraw a polygon when it really didn't need to be redrawn, but the amount of work it would take to prevent these cases probably won't save you any time overall.

Listing 20.4 Source Code for *UpdateRects.java*

```
import java.awt.*;
import java.applet.*;

// This applet demonstrates the use of selective updates, calling
// repaint specifically for the areas that change.

public class UpdateRects extends Applet implements TimerCallback
{

// colors contains the colors we cycle through for each shape we draw
     Color colors[] = {
          Color.red, Color.green, Color.blue, Color.yellow
     };
```

continues

Listing 20.4 Continued

```
// rects contains the rectangles for each area we want to draw

     Rectangle rects[] = {
          new Rectangle(0, 0, 50, 50),
          new Rectangle(100, 0, 50, 50),
          new Rectangle(0, 100, 50, 50),
          new Rectangle(100, 100, 50, 50)
     };

// We cycle each rectangle through a set of colors. Start them off
// with different colors.

     int rectColor[] = { 0, 1, 2, 3 };

     Timer timer;

// paint assumes that it is only painting a portion of the screen.
// It examines the area it is supposed to repaint by calling
// getClipRect, then it uses the intersects method in the Rectangle
// class to see which rectangles intersect with the repainted area.
// If a rectangle doesn't intersect, it doesn't need to be redrawn.

     public void paint(Graphics g)
     {

// Get the area we are painting
          Rectangle clipRect = g.getClipRect();

          for (int i=0; i < rects.length; i++) {

// If this rectangle doesn't intersect with the clipping area,
// we don't need to repaint it, so just go on to the next rectangle

               if (!clipRect.intersects(rects[i])) continue;

// For each rectangle we just call fillOval and use the dimensions of
// the rectangle.
               g.setColor(colors[rectColor[i]]);
               g.fillOval(rects[i].x, rects[i].y,
                    rects[i].width, rects[i].height);
          }
     }

// For every timer tick we change the colors of each rectangle and
// call repaint for each area we change, rather than calling one
// big repaint.

     public void tick()
     {
          for (int i=0; i < rects.length; i++) {

// Change the rectangle's color
               rectColor[i] = (rectColor[i] + 1) %
                    colors.length;
```

```
// Call repaint just for this rectangle

                repaint(rects[i].x, rects[i].y, rects[i].width,
                     rects[i].height);
           }
      }

      public void start()
      {
// Timer tick every 250 milliseconds (4 times a second)
           timer = new Timer(this, 250);
           timer.start();
}

      public void stop()
      {
           timer.stop();
           timer = null;
      }
}
```

Alternatively, you can create a rectangle that represents the changed area and enlarge the rectangle to encompass newly changed areas. The `Rectangle` class contains an `add` method that returns the smallest rectangle that encloses two other rectangles.

When you determine the rectangle that encloses a changed area, you add that rectangle to the current changed area, producing a new changed-area rectangle. You have to be careful with this approach. If you start adding all your rectangles together, you may end up with one big rectangle that is as large as the drawing area.

This method is useful when you are moving an object around in fairly small increments. If the rectangular area holding the object's old area intersects with the new area, you might be better off adding the rectangles together. The closer the areas are to each other, the better it is to add the rectangles. If they are far apart, the sum of the rectangles holds a lot more unaffected space.

This might cause you to spend a lot of time repainting areas that haven't changed. Adding rectangles is a trade-off. You have to balance the redrawing of areas that may not need redrawing against the reduced number of repaints you actually do.

Redrawing Changed Areas

Rather than updating changed rectangular regions, you can simply redraw the changed areas. You create an `update` method that does not clear the drawing area. Instead, you assume that everything should stay the same and just redraw the changed parts.

This is most useful when you don't need to move objects around to arbitrary locations. Instead, you have fixed positions that can change and you just need to keep track of which ones have changed. It becomes more difficult to do this when you have overlapping objects that move frequently. Every time you update a portion of the screen, you have to figure out which objects are even partially visible in the changed section of screen, and you must repaint each object.

A Tetris game is a perfect example of this kind of selective updating. The game board is a grid. No grid cells overlap and you don't move any objects across the cells. All you need to do when redrawing a Tetris board is paint the grid cells that have changed since the last time you repainted.

The big snag with this technique is that it doesn't work well for direct screen painting, only for off-screen drawing. The reason is that the drawing area can be erased by the windowing system at any time, and your `paint` method is responsible for restoring it. In other words, you may be keeping track of the sections of the screen that you change, but the screen can be changed by external programs, as well. For instance, someone could open up another application that obscures your drawing area, and then close down that application again. At that point, you would need to update the entire screen.

If you are updating only specific areas of the screen, you will lose the rest if the screen gets erased. This doesn't happen with off-screen drawing because you control the drawing surface completely. It doesn't get erased unless you erase it.

If you are drawing off-screen (double-buffering), you can take advantage of the fact that the drawing area is available at any time and can't be accidentally erased. You can do your drawing from anywhere in your program, not just in the `paint` method. Of course, the off-screen picture won't be shown on the screen until your `paint` method is called.

This can be a huge advantage, since you don't have to keep track of what needs to be drawn when the `paint` method finally gets called. If you decide something needs to be changed, you change it immediately.

Listing 20.5 shows a series of methods from a Tetris-like applet that drops blocks on the screen. There are several methods for drawing blocks that actually draw on the off-screen drawing area. After a drawing method has drawn its blocks, it calls repaint to redraw the screen.

Listing 20.5 Partial Listing of *BlockDrop.java*

```
// paintBlock colors in a single grid block on a graphics object

    public void paintBlock(Graphics g, int x, int y)
    {
        g.setColor(colors[blockGrid[y][x]]);
```

```
            g.fillRect(x * blockSize, y * blockSize,
                 blockSize, blockSize);
       }

// drawNewBlock paints a new block on the off-screen image, then calls
// repaint for just that block's area

       public void drawNewBlock(int x, int y)
       {
            paintBlock(offscreenGraphics, x, y);

            repaint(x * blockSize, y * blockSize, blockSize, blockSize);
       }

// drawBlockPair paints a block and the block below, then calls repaint
// for the 2-block area.

       public void drawBlockPair(int x, int y)
       {
            paintBlock(offscreenGraphics, x, y);
            paintBlock(offscreenGraphics, x, y+1);

            repaint(x * blockSize, y * blockSize, blockSize, blockSize*2);
       }

// drawAllBlocks draws all the blocks in the grid to the off-screen area,
// then calls repaint for the entire screen.

       public void drawAllBlocks()
       {
            for (int y=0; y < gridHeight; y++) {
                 for (int x=0; x < gridWidth; x++) {
                      paintBlock(offscreenGraphics, x, y);
                 }
            }
            repaint();
       }

       public void paint(Graphics g)
       {
            g.drawImage(offscreenImage, 0, 0, this);
       }

       public void update(Graphics g)
       {
            paint(g);
       }
```

20

Note

Notice that the `drawBlock` and `drawBlockPair` methods in `BlockDrop.java` call `repaint` with a specific region. Even though the `paint` method assumes it is redrawing the entire screen, it really updates just a tiny portion of the screen. This technique does make a difference, even when `paint` still tries to draw the whole area. The reason it makes a difference is that you aren't using the low-level graphics routines to update every pixel on the screen, which does take some time.

The whole reason for this exercise of drawing to an off-screen buffer is that you are no longer constrained to doing all your drawing in the `paint` method. As soon as you decide that something on the screen needs to change, you can change it. Of course, you have to repaint the screen before the change is visible.

The `BlockDrop` applet drops blocks from the top of the screen by using a timer. It is able to redraw blocks from within the `tick` method (called by the timer) because it is drawing to an off-screen buffer. If it were drawing directly to the screen, it would have to make a note of which items had changed and then repaint the area for those items. The `paint` method would have to look at what had changed and repaint only those areas of the screen. Listing 20.6 shows the `tick` method from the `BlockDrop` applet. Notice that once it decides to add a new block or change a block, it immediately calls the methods to redraw the blocks.

Listing 20.6 *tick* Method from *BlockDrop.java*

```
// Every time tick is called, either move the current block down, or
// start a new block

     public void tick()
     {
// If there isn't a block falling, create a new one

          if (!blockFalling) {
               blockX = (int)(gridWidth * Math.random());
               blockY = 0;

// Put the block into the grid with a random color (adjust the random color
// to start at 1 and not 0).

               blockGrid[blockY][blockX] = 1+(int)((colors.length-1) *
                    Math.random());
               blockFalling = true;

               drawNewBlock(blockX, blockY);
          } else {

// See if we can still move the block down. If the block's Y is still above
// the bottom, and the color of the grid element below it is 0, the block
// is allowed to move.
```

```
                if ((blockY < gridHeight-1) &&
                     (blockGrid[blockY+1][blockX]) == 0) {

// Copy the block's color to the grid element below
                     blockGrid[blockY+1][blockX] =
                          blockGrid[blockY][blockX];
// Clear out the current grid element
                     blockGrid[blockY][blockX] = 0;
                     blockY++;

// Draw both the newly empty element and the block's new location
                     drawBlockPair(blockX, blockY-1);
                } else {
// If we can't move the block, need to check the next time
                     blockFalling = false;
                }
// See if the bottom is full
                checkGridFloor();
           }
       }
```

Figure 20.1 shows the `BlockDrop` applet in action. The complete source code to `BlockDrop.java` is on the CD that comes with this book.

20

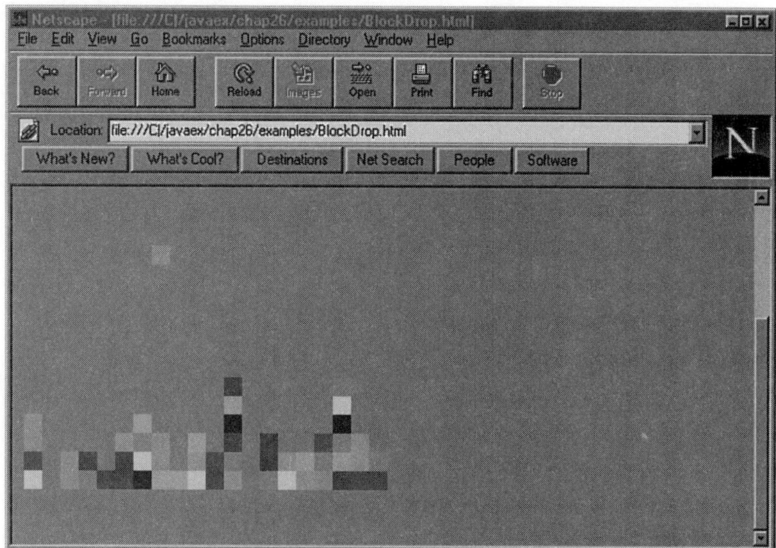

Fig. 20.1
The `BlockDrop` applet calls drawing routines from outside the paint method.

You can convert the `BlockDrop` applet to do direct screen writes very easily. Simply comment out the calls to `paintBlock` in `drawNewBlock`, `drawBlockPair`, and `drawAllBlocks`, and insert the following `update` method:

```
public void update(Graphics g)
{
```

```
        Rectangle clipRect = g.getClipRect();

// Compute the starting X and ending X of the area to be repainted

        int blockStartX = clipRect.x / blockSize;
        int blockEndX = (clipRect.x + clipRect.width) / blockSize;
        if (blockEndX >= gridWidth) blockEndX = gridWidth - 1;

// Compute the starting Y and ending Y of the area to be repainted

        int blockStartY = clipRect.y / blockSize;
        int blockEndY = (clipRect.y + clipRect.height) / blockSize;
        if (blockEndY >= gridHeight) blockEndY = gridHeight - 1;

// Repaint only the blocks that need to be repainted

        for (int y=blockStartY; y <= blockEndY; y++) {
                for (int x=blockStartX; x <= blockEndX; x++) {
                        paintBlock(g, x, y);
                }
        }
}
```

Some of these issues may be less important as the Java graphics system is improved. One of the features to be added is sprite animation, which allows you to define objects that can move around the screen. The graphics system would then take care of updating the changed areas. You would no longer have to keep track of them by hand.

chapter 21

Download Strategies

21

by Mark Wutka

In this chapter

- **Downloading in the background**
  When you run a Java program, you don't have to load every class that the program is going to use. Sometimes, you may run a program and never make use of certain classes. It doesn't make sense to load them if you aren't going to use them. If you know you will need a class, but not immediately, you can download the class in the background, allowing the applet to start up quickly.
- **Providing local libraries**
  There may be cases where it is advantageous to ship a library to the users so that they install it in their browsers. This may be because of the size of the library, or because of security restrictions, which are relaxed for locally installed classes.
- **Downloading classes in zipped format**
  Normally, when you download classes, the applet class loader creates a separate network connection for each class. Many times, it takes longer to establish the connection than it does to download the class. If you package all your classes into one file, you can shorten the download time considerably.
- **Storing classes in jars and cabinets**
  There are other alternatives to zip archives. Sun's JAR format and Microsoft's Cabinet format are two of the most recent additions.

Waiting for an applet to finish downloading can be annoying at times, especially for a big applet. A quote like, "Great applet, but it takes five minutes to download," does not inspire people to run out and try it.

Although there aren't any tricks to shove bits through the network any faster, you can make your applets aware that things may take a while and give the user something to do while they wait.

It would certainly be a boon to many users, but the ability to download classes in compressed form does not necessarily give a big speed boost to everyone. In fact, maybe not at all for the people who need it the most—the modem users.

Most modems these days are able to do data compression by themselves. This saves you some time when downloading text files and other uncompressed data at rates faster than the modem's communication speed.

For compressed zip files and to some extent GIF files, however, you transfer data only at the modem's normal speed. Data compression removes the redundancy in a file. The more redundant the file, the better it compresses.

Note

Since images usually contain a high amount of redundancy, the GIF and JPEG standards also include data compression. This is why you don't get much speed gain by transmitting images over a compressing modem.

Text data compresses very well because it is fairly redundant. Binary data does not usually compress as well as text, but certain types of binary data do. Once you compress a file and remove that redundancy, you cannot compress it any more.

When a compressing modem is trying to send a compressed file, it can't find anything to compress: All the redundant information has already been removed.

Although you probably won't have to write your own compression or decompression routines, it is helpful to have an idea of how a data compression routine goes about compressing data. This may give you a better idea of why some things compress better than others. The most common form of compression today is actually a combination of two popular compression algorithms—Huffman coding and Lempel-Ziv (LZ) compression.

Huffman Coding and Lempel-Ziv Compression

The idea behind Huffman coding is that you use different length bit patterns to encode different pieces of data. The patterns that occur most often are given the shortest bit patterns, while the patterns that occur more frequently are given longer bit patterns. If you were encoding 8-bit bytes with Huffman coding, you would have many Huffman codes that were less than 8 bits in length, and probably some that were more than 8 bits. When a compression program performs Huffman encoding, it builds a lookup tree. Figure 21.1 shows a sample Huffman tree.

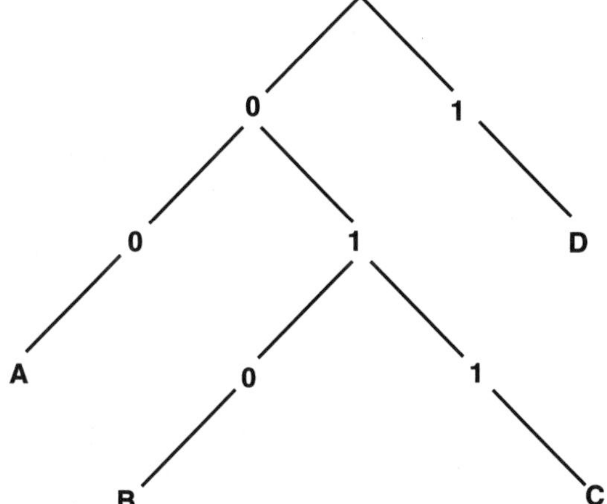

Fig. 21.1
A Huffman tree stores the bit patterns for pieces of data.

By looking at this Huffman tree, you can see that the letter D was the most frequently occurring letter in the original data file. The way you can tell this is that it has the shortest bit sequence. The letter A, which has a sequence length of 2, is the second most frequent letter. B and C have bit lengths of 3, and are the least frequent characters. You can get a better understanding of how this tree works by watching how a Huffman decoder uncompresses a stream of data. Suppose you had the Huffman tree in Figure 21.1 and the following stream of bits:


```
1001100010011
```

The Huffman decoder would look at the first bit in the sequence, which is 1, and start at the top of the tree and take the branch labeled 1, which goes directly to D. This means that the first letter in the decompressed data is D. The next bit in the sequence is 0. Taking the 0 branch in the Huffman tree, you see that you need another bit in order to make a decision. The next bit is 0, which leads you to A, which has a bit pattern of 00. The decoded sequence is DA so far. Next comes two more 1s. You already know that a 1 by itself is a D, so the next two letters are both D, making the decoded sequence DADD. Another two 0s mean that the next letter is A, so you are up to DADDA. Next comes 0 followed by a 1. You can see on the tree that 0-1 leads you to another branch, so you look at the third bit, which is 0. This leads you to B (whose code is 010). The next sequence, 0-1-1, leads you to C, making the final decompressed string DADDABC.

If you had written this string using normal 8-bit ASCII characters, you would have used 56 bits (7 characters of 8 bits each). The more unbalanced the Huffman tree is, the more compression you get, because the most frequent characters have very short encoding sequences. If you are encoding binary data, where the bytes are more spread out, the

Huffman tree is more balanced. If you had a tree that covered all 256 bytes and each byte occurred at roughly the same frequency, you would end up with 8-bit sequences for every byte, which would mean that you couldn't really compress the data with Huffman coding. This is one reason why text tends to compress better than binary data. In addition, text generally uses less than half of the 256 ASCII characters, meaning that even if every text character occurred an identical number of times, they would still have bit sequences of only 7 bits (maybe 6 if there were few enough characters).

The Lempel-Ziv (LZ) compression algorithm goes a step beyond Huffman coding. Whereas Huffman coding usually looks at only single characters, LZ compression looks for repeating patterns within a stream of bytes. Whenever there is a repeating pattern, LZ compression removes the repeated copies and inserts a pointer to the original pattern. For example, suppose you had the original DADDABC pattern. The LZ compression would take DA and call it sequence 1. Then, the next D would be replaced with a code for "repeat sequence 1 for 1 character." The next two characters, DA again, would be replaced with "repeat sequence 1." And, then, BC would stay by itself. For a short sequence like this, it would probably take longer to encode the repeat information than it would to encode the original sequence. LZ compression programs tend to look for longer patterns, though. Some of them look at patterns that are 12 characters, often even more than that. This is another way to eliminate the redundancy. Where Huffman coding gets rid of extra bits in characters, LZ compression shortens the repetition of patterns. If you combine these two features together, you get a powerful form of compression. Most of the common compression programs use this combination in the form of an algorithm called `Deflate`.

If you were to compress a file that had already been compressed, the Huffman coding would not be able to come up with a better sequence of bits, since it had already generated the optimal set. Chances are, it would come up with a balanced tree resulting in no compression. The LZ compression would not be able to find any repeating sequences because they had already been eliminated the first time. This is why you don't get a performance boost when you download a compressed file with a compressing modem.

Delayed Downloading

One of the many nice features of Java is that it can load classes while a program is running. There are some limits on this, however.

If a method references a class, that class must be loaded before the method is executed. Java uses a one-time lookup mechanism for efficiency.The first time an instruction referencing another class is executed, the Java runtime does a lookup on the referenced class. Once the class is found, the instruction is changed to refer directly to the referenced class, bypassing the lookup. If you never execute the lookup instruction, the instruction is never changed. You cannot count on this exact behavior, however.

Some Just-In-Time (JIT) compilers resolve all the references when a method is executed. This means that all the referenced classes must be loaded before the method is called.

Once a method is compiled, any unresolved references remain unresolved, even if the referenced class is loaded later.

Note
Almost any operation involving an object of a particular class will cause that class to be loaded. If you declare an object of a particular class, that class is not immediately loaded. You can even safely test that object to see if it is `null` without causing a load. Almost anything else, however, will trigger a load. Some of the things that require a load are using `instanceof`, invoking a method, or passing the object as a parameter to a method. In the last case, you may not need to load the class if the parameter type is the same class as the object. If they are different classes, the object's class must be loaded to determine if that object is an instance of the parameter's class.

Delayed Instantiation

If you know that you won't be needing an object until a certain time, you can delay the instantiation of that object. For example, suppose you have a spreadsheet applet that can create nice graphs of the data. The graphing class may be fairly large.

Someone who just wants to enter data in the spreadsheet doesn't want to wait for the graphing class to be downloaded before they can begin. Rather than instantiating the `graphing` class in the `init` method, you wait until someone really wants to do graphing before downloading the graphing code.

Your applet might look something like this:

```
public class SpreadsheetApplet extends Applet
{
     SpreadsheetGraphing graphing;     // will be loaded later

     public void init()
     {
          // perform setup
     }

     public void createGraph()
     {
```

```
        if (graphing == null) {
            graphing = new SpreadsheetGraphing();
        }
        .
        .
        .
```

If the `createGraph` method is never called, the graphing software is never loaded. Much of the early excitement about Java was over this very feature.

The idea that you grab only the code you need as you need it is a refreshing alternative to the huge pieces of software on the market today with millions of bytes dedicated to features used only by a small percentage of people.

Downloading in the Background

While delayed instantiation allows an applet to start running quickly, you still have to wait for a class to be instantiated when you go to use it. You may have saved users the five-minute hit up front by not loading the graphing software. But when they go to create a graph, they'll have to wait.

You can alleviate this problem by downloading classes in a background thread. Basically, you create a thread that takes a list of classes and loads them into the runtime environment.

By running this in the background, you can keep your main applet going while loading in extra features that are likely to be needed. You might even keep track of the features a particular user favors and download the code for those features first.

This is an interesting trade-off between a big, do-everything software package and a load-as-you-go system. It starts off as a bare-bones system but gradually grows.

Listing 21.1 shows a class that loads other classes in the background. It uses the `Class.forName()` method to load the class so that it doesn't have to create an instance.

Listing 21.1 Source Code for *BackgroundLoader.java*

```
// This class loads other classes in the background so they
// are ready for you when you need them. It supports a callback
// mechanism to let you know when a class has been loaded.

public class BackgroundLoader extends Object implements Runnable
{
    Thread loaderThread;

    String[] classes;      // the classes to load

    LoaderCallback callback;     // who to notify
```

```
// This constructor just loads one class with no notification
// The loading doesn't take place until you call the start method.

     public BackgroundLoader(String oneClass)
     {
          this.classes = new String[1];
          this.classes[0] = oneClass;
     }

// This constructor loads a single class, and performs a callback
// when the class is loaded. It doesn't start loading until start is called.

     public BackgroundLoader(String oneClass, LoaderCallback callback)
     {
          this.classes = new String[1];
          this.classes[0] = oneClass;
          this.callback = callback;
     }

// This constructor loads a whole set of classes with no callback.
// Again, it doesn't start loading until start is called.

     public BackgroundLoader(String[] classes)
     {
          this.classes = classes;
     }

// This constructor loads a whole set of classes and performs a callback
// It doesn't start loading until start is called.

     public BackgroundLoader(String[] classes, LoaderCallback callback)
     {
          this.classes = classes;
          this.callback = callback;
     }

     public void run()
     {
// If there's nothing to load, we're done
          if (classes == null) return;

          for (int i=0; i < classes.length; i++) {

               try {

// Class.forname will initiate the loading of a class
                    Class.forName(classes[i]);

// If there's a callback, call it.
                    if (callback != null) {
                         callback.classLoaded(classes[i]);
                    }
               } catch (Exception e) {
// Ignore any errors in loading the class. Let the error occur when
// the program tries to instantiate the class. You never know, it
// might not try.
```

continues

21

Listing 21.1 Continued

```
            }
        }
    }

    public void start()
    {
        loaderThread = new Thread(this);
        loaderThread.start();
    }

    public void stop()
    {
        loaderThread.stop();
        loaderThread = null;
    }
}
```

Listing 21.2 shows the `LoaderCallback` interface used by the `BackgroundLoader` class.

Listing 21.2 Source Code for *LoaderCallback.java*

```
public interface LoaderCallback
{
    public void classLoaded(String className);
}
```

Listing 21.3 shows a sample applet that uses the background loader. It doesn't start the downloading until you click a button.

Listing 21.3 Source Code for *TestLoadApplet.java*

```
import java.net.*;
import java.applet.*;
import java.awt.*;

// This class tests the use of the BackgroundLoader. It presents
// a button that, when pressed, initiates the downloading of
// a class called "Fooble". When the class is successfully loaded,
// it presents a new button that lets you use the Fooble class.
//
// It uses the LoaderCallback mechanism to detect when the Fooble
// class has been loaded.

public class TestLoadApplet extends Applet implements LoaderCallback
{
    Button loadButton;
    Button useButton;
```

```
    Fooble foo;

    public void init()
    {
         loadButton = new Button("Push to start loading");
         add(loadButton);
    }

// classLoaded is called when a class is loaded successfully.

    public void classLoaded(String className)
    {
         useButton = new Button("Push to use fooble");
         remove(loadButton);     // remove the old button
         add(useButton);          // add the new button
         validate();         // update the layout
    }

    public boolean action(Event evt, Object which)
    {
         if (evt.target == loadButton) {
// Start loading "Fooble" in the background, and use this class
// as the callback
              BackgroundLoader bl = new BackgroundLoader(
                   "Fooble", this);

// Start the loader (most important!)
              bl.start();
         } else if (evt.target == useButton) {

// If useButton exists and is pushed, we know the Fooble has been loaded
// so we can now instantiate it and invoke methods on it
              foo = new Fooble();

              foo.bar();
         }

         return true;
    }
  }
```

Listing 21.4 shows the `Fooble` class used by the `TestLoadApplet` applet.

Listing 21.4 Source Code for *Fooble.java*

```
public class Fooble
{
     public void bar()
     {
          System.out.println("Fooble sez: Bar!");
     }
  }
```

21

Providing Local Libraries

Admittedly, this next trick violates the concept of downloaded code. If you have a large library of Java code that you don't want someone to have to download every time they go to run your applets, you can provide them with a library they can install in their local system. Although you may want to zip the library up into a single file, it may have to be unzipped on the user's file system if you use data compression when you create the zip archive.

The procedure for installing local libraries varies from browser to browser. For this example, assume you have a class named `Graphing` in a package called `spreadsheet`.

To create a zip file to export to users, create a directory called `spreadsheet` and copy the `Graphing.class` file into the directory. Next, go to the parent directory of the spreadsheet directory and type

```
zip -0 graphing.zip spreadsheet/Graphing.class
```

Now, you have a zipped archive file that you can distribute to your users. You can put as many classes into the zip archive as you like.

By using the `-0` option, you store the classes in uncompressed form. This allows Hotjava and Appletviewer users to use the archive without unzipping it.

Caution
Although Java's security model reduces the danger of malicious programs, you should be wary when installing local libraries, and only install libraries from sites, companies, or people you trust. Security restrictions are more relaxed for locally installed classes.

Installing Local Libraries for Hotjava and Appletviewer

For the Hotjava and Appletviewer browsers, you can choose to leave the archive file in zipped format, or you can unpack it. You can put the file anywhere you like, either packed or unpacked.

All you have to do is set your CLASSPATH environment variable to include either the directory where you unpacked the zip file or the full pathname of the zip file.

To change your CLASSPATH variable on Windows 95, you need to edit the autoexec.bat file. There may already be an entry that sets the class path.

If you put the .zip file in C:\Spreadsheet\lib, but did not unpack it, you need to add C:\Spreadsheet\lib\graphing.zip to the class path. If you unpacked the zip file in that directory, just add C:\Spreadsheet\lib to the class path.

Under Windows 95 and Windows NT, the class path entries are separated by semicolons. Here is an example entry for a CLASSPATH setting under Windows 95:

```
set CLASSPATH=.;C:\JAVA\LIB\CLASSES.ZIP;C:\Spreadsheet\lib
```

The philosophy is the same for Windows NT but instead of editing autoexec.bat, you go to your control panel, select the System icon, and enter or change the CLASSPATH environment variable there.

If you use Symantec Café, there is yet a third place to set the CLASSPATH (Café does not recognize the CLASSPATH environment variable). You must edit the CLASSPATH setting in C:\Café\bin\sc.ini (assuming you installed Café into C:\Café).

For UNIX systems, the unpacking procedure is the same, but the format and location of the CLASSPATH variable is slightly different. Under UNIX, the class path entries are separated by colons instead of semicolons.

The command to set an environment variable depends on your login shell. If you use the Korn shell (ksh) or the Bourne shell (sh), the command looks like this (assuming graphing.zip was unpacked in /home/mark/spreadsheet/lib, and Java is in /usr/local/java):


```
export CLASSPATH=.:/usr/local/java/lib/classes.zip:/home/mark/spreadsheet/lib
```

This variable is probably set in your .profile file. If you use C-shell (csh) or its variants, the command is:

```
setenv CLASSPATH .:/usr/local/java/lib/classes.zip:/home/mark/spreadsheet/lib
```

It is probably set in your .login or .cshrc file (or maybe .tcshrc if you use tcsh). Different UNIX sites set things up differently, which is why these file names are not as definite as you might like.

If you can't find the CLASSPATH variable anywhere and you are successfully running Java already, it has to be there somewhere. If you are the one who installed your Java system, look back at the installation instructions for your Java system. They will probably refresh your memory. If someone else installed Java for you, you need to either find them or find the installation instructions.

Installing Local Libraries for Netscape

If you are running Netscape on a UNIX system, follow the preceding instructions for setting the CLASSPATH variable, but make sure you include Netscape's class archive in your class path.

Under Netscape version 2, the class file is called moz2_0.zip and is in the directory where you unpacked Netscape. Under Netscape 3, it is either in the file moz3_0.zip or java3_0.zip.

These files may also have other version numbers like 2_01 or 2_02. You can leave the archive zipped for the UNIX version of Netscape.

To install a set of classes locally for the Windows NT/95 Netscape Navigator, you must unpack the archive in Netscape's class library directory. If your Netscape is installed in C:\Netscape\Navigator, you need to unpack the zip file in the directory called C:\Netscape\Navigator\Program\Java\Classes.

When you have unpacked the graphing.zip file, you should end up with a directory called C:\Netscape\Navigator\Program\Java\Classes\spreadsheet.

Installing Local Libraries for Internet Explorer

Microsoft's Internet Explorer treats Java as a separate package and already anticipates the use of locally stored class files. When you install the package, it creates a directory called C:\WINDOWS\JAVA, where it stores Java-related files.

You will find the CLASSES.ZIP file in the CLASSES subdirectory. To install the graphing.zip file in C:\WINDOWS\JAVA, create a subdirectory called ISVCLASS (that is, C:\WINDOWS\JAVA\ISVCLASS), then unpack graphing.zip in the ISVCLASS directory.

When you're done, you should have a directory called C:\WINDOWS\JAVA\ISVCLASS\spreadsheet that was created when you unpacked the zip file. Now when you run Internet Explorer, it can use classes from the ISVCLASS directory.

Tip

The Java environment installed by Internet Explorer also contains a stand-alone Java interpreter called JVIEW, which is installed in C:\WINDOWS. JVIEW is the equivalent of the java command that comes with the Java Development Kit.

Downloading Classes in Zipped Format

Since Java classes are normally packaged in zip files, it would be nice if an applet could load in a single zip file holding the classes it needs, rather than download them one at a time.

The use of zip downloading is fairly new in browsers. If your browser doesn't use it, you still have an option.

Zip Downloading in Netscape Navigator Version 3

Netscape Navigator Version 3 allows you to specify a zip archive in the `<APPLET>` tag, which it uses to get classes before trying to download them one at a time.

If you package all the classes for myapplet.class into the file myclasses.zip, your `<APPLET>` tag would look like this:

```
<APPLET codebase="." archive="myclasses.zip" code="myapplet.class" width=100
height=100>
```

The `archive` parameter is the new addition for zip use. It should be in the same directory as your other .class files. You should use both zipped and unzipped classes, since not everyone has Netscape.

A Zipfile Class Loader

You can use the loading of zip files in any browser by creating a special class loader that understands zip files. The only trick is that the class loader has to be installed on the local machine.

21

You cannot download a class loader over the network because of security restrictions. Since not everyone who runs your applet has the zip class loader installed, your applet should check to see if it is available before using it.

Writing a zip class loader is fairly simple once you know the format of zip files. Since Java zip files cannot use compression, you don't have to worry about all the messy code involved with decompression.

A zip archive is actually a collection of data blocks. There are three types of blocks in a zip file—a local block, a central directory block, and an end block. At the beginning of each block is a 4-byte signature value that identifies what type of block it is. If you just want to read files from the zip file, you are really interested only in local blocks. The only thing you have to pay attention to in the other blocks is their size. Each block has its own header that contains the important information about the block, including its size. If you read a block's header and want to skip the block, you have to look at the header to figure out how many bytes to skip.

Listing 21.5 shows the `readZipStream` method from the `ZipClassLoader` class. The full source to the `ZipClassLoader` is on the CD that comes with this book. Since you won't be using compression in the zip files, it is fairly simple to scan through the zip file looking for local blocks. Whenever the `readZipStream` method finds a local block, it grabs the block's filename and the actual bytes in the block and sticks them in a hash table for later use.

Listing 21.5 *readZipStream* Method from *ZipClassLoader.java*

```
// readZipStream is the heart of this class. It reads the class files from
// an input stream in zip format. It only pays attention to the local blocks
// and ignores the central and end blocks (if you know about the zip format).
// Once it reads in a class it stores it in a hash table, but does NOT load
// the classes automatically. You must call loadClass to do this.

     protected void readZipStream(DataInputStream zipStream)
     throws IOException
     {
          byte[] localHeader = new byte[LOCALLEN];
          byte[] centralHeader = new byte[CENTRALLEN];
          byte[] endHeader = new byte[ENDLEN];
          byte[] signature = new byte[SIGLEN];
           try
                while (true)

// Figure out what type of block we are readin
                     zipStream.readFully(signature)

// Convert the signature to an intege
                     int sig = getInt(signature, 0)

// If it's a central block, skip the whole bloc
                     if (sig == CENTRALSIG)

// Read in the central header byte
                          zipStream.readFully(centralHeader)

// Figure out how many extra bytes follow the central heade
                          int skipLen
                               getShort(centralHeader, 24)
                               getShort(centralHeader, 26)
                               getShort(centralHeader, 28)

// Skip those extra byte
                          zipStream.skipBytes(skipLen)

// Go process the next bloc
                          continue

// If this is an end block, skip the block and process the next on
                     } else if (sig == ENDSIG)

// read the full end block heade
                          zipStream.readFully(endHeader)
```

```
// figure out how many extra bytes there are
                        int skipLen = getShort(endHeader, 16);
// skip the extras
                        zipStream.skipBytes(skipLen);
                        continue;

// If we get any other signature other than local, there's an error
                    } else if (sig != LOCALSIG) {
                        throw new IOException(
                            "Invalid Block Signature");
                    }
// read the local heade
                    zipStream.readFully(localHeader)

// get the length of the data for this fil
                    int dataLen = getInt(localHeader, 14)

// get the length of the file nam
                    int nameLen = getShort(localHeader, 22)

// Figure out how many extra bytes there ar
                    int skipLen = getShort(localHeader, 24)

// Read in the file nam
                    byte[] nameBuf = new byte[nameLen]
                    zipStream.readFully(nameBuf)

// Convert the file name to a strin
                    String className = new String(nameBuf, 0)

// Skip any extra byte
                    zipStream.skipBytes(skipLen)

// If this is an empty file, just go to the next bloc
                    if (dataLen == 0) continue


// Read in the actual bytes for the file
                    byte[] dataBytes = new byte[dataLen];
                    zipStream.readFully(dataBytes);

// Add the class to the hash table
                    classData.put(className, dataBytes);
                }
            } catch (EOFException e) {
                return;
            }
        }
```

21

Since the Zip format originated on the PC platform, all numbers in a zip file are stored in Intel byte order (also known as little-endian). The `readZipFile` method uses the methods `getShort` and `getInt` to read little-endian numbers from a byte array. Listing 21.6 shows these methods.

Listing 21.6 *getShort* and *getInt* Methods from *ZipClassLoader.java*

```
// getShort reads two bytes from a byte array starting at offset <offset>
// and converts them to an integer using Intel byte ordering.

     protected int getShort(byte[] bytes, int offset)
     {
          return ((bytes[offset+1]&255) << 8) + (bytes[offset+0]&255);
     }
// getInt reads four bytes from a byte array starting at offset <offset
// and converts them to an integer using Intel byte ordering

      protected int getInt(byte[] bytes, int offset

     {
          return ((bytes[offset+3]&255) << 24) + ((bytes[offset+2]&255) << 16) +
               ((bytes[offset+1]&255) << 8) + (bytes[offset+0]&255);
       }
```

Tip

If you do enough work with different byte orders, it won't take you long to realize that you need a utility class for converting to and from little-endian byte order. If you write such a class, you might consider methods to transfer to and from byte arrays, as well as just rearranging the bytes within a short or integer number.

The `readZipStream` method reads only the individual .class files from a zip archive and stores them in a hash table. It doesn't actually do any class loading. For that, you must call the `loadClass` method in the class loader. Normally, the `loadClass` method in a class loader is a protected method. In this case, however, you need to tell the class loader to begin loading a class, and the only way to do that is to expose the `loadClass` method. Listing 21.7 shows the `loadClass` method from the `ZipClassLoader` class. It expects the classes to have been loaded into a hash table called `classData`. Once it loads a class, it caches the loaded class in a table called `loadedClasses`. If the class loader is asked to load a class that it doesn't know about, it calls the system class loader to see if it is a local class.

Listing 21.7 *loadClass* Method from *ZipClassLoader.java*

```
public synchronized Class loadClass(String className,
          boolean resolve) throws ClassNotFoundException
     {
          Class newClass = (Class) loadedClasses.get(className);

// If the class was in the loadedClasses table, we don't
// have to load it again, but we better resolve it, just
// in case.
```

```
          if (newClass != null)
          {
               if (resolve) // Should we resolve?
               {
                    resolveClass(newClass);
               }
               return newClass;
          }

// The classes are stored in the classData table by their original filename
// which will be the class name followed by ".class"

          byte[] classBytes = (byte[]) classData.get(className+".class");
          if (classBytes != null) {
// Define the new class
               newClass = defineClass(classBytes, 0,
                    classBytes.length);
          } else {
// Before we throw an exception, see if the system already know
// about this clas
                try
                     newClass = findSystemClass(className)
                     return newClass
                } catch (Exception any)
                     throw new ClassNotFoundException(className)


// Store the class in the table of loaded classe
           loadedClasses.put(className, newClass)

// If we are supposed to resolve this class, do i
           if (resolve

                resolveClass(newClass)


           return newClass

        }
```

Listing 21.8 shows a modified version of the QuickLoader applet from Chapter 2. The ZipLoader applet tries to load a class from a zip archive. In addition to the `applet` parameter that tells it which applet to run, it accepts the `zipfile` parameter that tells it the name of the zip file to use.

Also notice that there are no method calls to the zip class loader from inside the `run` method. If the class doesn't exist and you run your applet with a JIT, the JIT may choke on the `run` method if the zip class loader isn't installed locally.

If you isolate the references to the zip class loader, the `run` method is able to function in the absence of the zip class loader.

To see why this could happen, imagine that you did make direct references to the class loader from the run method. Before the run method is called, the JIT compiles the run method into native code, resolving any class references. Since the run method directly references the ZipClassLoader class, the JIT is unable to resolve all the references and it refuses to execute the method. Even if it executed the method, and the method loaded the ZipClassLoader class successfully, it would still not be able to invoke methods in `ZipClassLoader`, because all the method calls had already been compiled by the JIT.

Listing 21.8 Source Code for *ZipLoader.java*

```
import java.applet.Applet;
import java.applet.AppletStub;
import java.awt.Graphics;
import java.awt.GridLayout;
import java.awt.Label;
import java.net.URL;

// This applet is responsible for loading another applet in the
// background and displaying the applet when it finishes loading.
// The name of the applet to load is supplied by a <PARAM> tag.
// For example:
// <PARAM name="applet" value="RealApplet">
// which would load an applet class called RealApplet
// It uses the ziploader.ZipClassLoader, if available, to load
// in the classes. The "zipfile" param supplies the name of the
// zip file to read. For example:
// <PARAM name="zipfile" value="real.zip">
public class ZipLoader extends Applet implements Runnable, AppletStu

      String appletToLoad
      String zipArchive
      Label label
      Thread appletThread

      ziploader.ZipClassLoader loader

      public void init(

// Get the name of the applet to loa
           appletToLoad = getParameter("applet")

// Get the name of the zip archiv
           zipArchive = getParameter("zipfile")

// If there isn't one, print a messag
           if (appletToLoad == null)
                label = new Label("No applet to load.")
           } else
                label = new Label("Please wait - loading applet "
                     appletToLoad)

           add(label)

      }
```

```
// Have to do this in a method separate from the run method, otherwise
// some JITs get upset if the ziploader package isn't installed.
// This method check to see if the ZipClassLoader exists, and if so,
// instantiates it.
     public void tryLoader(String zipArchive

          try
// See if the class exist
               Class.forName
                    "ziploader.ZipClassLoader")
// Try to load the zip loade
               loader = new ziploader.ZipClassLoader
                    new URL(getCodeBase(), zipArchive))
          } catch (Exception ignore)



// This method loads a class that is stored in the ZipClassLoader
// It must be a separate method from run to keep some JITs fro
// getting upset when the loader isn't installed

     public Class loadZipClass(String className
     throws ClassNotFoundException, InstantiationException
          IllegalArgumentExceptio

          return loader.loadClass(className, true)


     public void run(

// If there's no applet to load, don't bother loading it
          if (appletToLoad == null) return

          Class appletClass = null

          try

// See if the zip class loader is installe

               if (zipArchive != null)
                    tryLoader(zipArchive)


               if (loader != null)
// Try loading the class from the zip fil
                    appletClass = loadZipClass(appletToLoad)


// If the class wasn't created from the zip loader, try a regular loa
               if (appletClass == null)
                    appletClass = Class.forName(appletToLoad)


// Create an instance of the apple
               Applet realApplet = (Applet)appletClass.newInstance()
```

21

continues

Listing 21.8 Continued

```
// Set the applet's stub - this will allow the real applet to use
// our document base, code base, and applet context.
            realApplet.setStub(this);
// Remove the old message and put the applet u

             remove(label)

// The grid layout maximizes the components to fill the screen area - w
// want the real applet to be maximized to our size

             setLayout(new GridLayout(1, 0))

// Add the real applet as a child componen
             add(realApplet)

// Crank up the real apple
             realApplet.init()
             realApplet.start()
         } catch (Exception e)

// If we got an error anywhere, print i
             label.setText("Error loading applet.")
             e.printStackTrace()


// Make sure our screen layout is redraw
         validate()

    }
    public void start(

         appletThread = new Thread(this)

        appletThread.start();
    }
    public void stop(

         appletThread.stop()
         appletThread = null


// appletResize is the one method in the AppletStub interface tha
// isn't in the Applet class. We'll just use the applet resiz
// method and hope it works

    public void appletResize(int width, int height

         resize(width, height)

    }
  }
```

Packaging Classes in Jars and Cabinets

With coffee metaphors running out, Sun and other vendors have branched out into a more general kitchen motif. For Java 1.1, Sun has created an alternative to a zip archive called a JAR (Java ARchive). Unlike the current zip archive constraints under Java, a JAR can contain compressed data. Because the JAR format is a part of the core Java 1.1 specification, you can expect all Java-enabled browsers to support this format when they become Java 1.1 compliant.

Microsoft has also created an alternative to the zip archive called a cabinet. Chapter 14, "Creating Your Own Class Archive Files," tells you everything you need to know about packaging classes and other files into cabinets. Like the JAR format, the Cabinet format supports data compression, allowing you to download your classes faster if you aren't already compressing your download with a compressing modem.

chapter 22

Faster Image Downloads

22

by Mark Wutka

In this chapter

- **Reducing image size**
  One of the easiest ways to shorten the download time of an image is to make the image smaller. You can often do this by using a different image format, making a smaller image, or reducing the image quality.
- **Combining images onto image strips**
  It is often advantageous to download a single image strip containing all the images you need. Every time you download a different image, you take a slight hit in performance since you have to create a new network connection. If you have to download only a single image, you make only one network connection.
- **Storing only parts on an image strip**
  When you create animated images, you often reuse large portions of an image between frames. If you can break up your image into the separate parts that change, you can store only the parts that change instead of storing whole images.

Images often account for a large amount of an applet's download time. Even though both the GIF and JPEG formats used by Java involve data compression, the images can still be rather large.

Since these images are already compressed, you won't realize much benefit from additional data compression, either. You need to find ways of either reducing the original image size or getting the images in a more efficient fashion.

Reducing Image Size

One of the easiest techniques for quicker downloads isn't part of Java at all. If you are willing to accept a reduction in image quality, you can often drastically reduce the size of an image.

The two formats used by Java are GIF (Graphics Interchange Format) and JPEG (Joint Photographic Experts Group—the creators of the format). Each has its own advantages and disadvantages, and frequently, one or the other provides a distinct size advantage.

The GIF format is geared toward 8-bit images or at least images with fewer colors. The GIF format works better when storing noncomplex images.

When an image is complex, as in a photograph, GIF does not store images as well as other formats. It works very well for storing patterns like a checkerboard or your Web page background.

The JPEG format was created with photography in mind. It allows 24-bit color and can store images with varying image quality.

JPEG has a number of optimizations that assume that it is storing photograph-type images. So when it goes to store something as mundane as a checkerboard, the resulting file can be several times as large as the equivalent GIF file.

Since JPEG allows you to store images with varying quality, you can reduce the size of a JPEG just by storing it as a lower-quality image. The quality of an image is actually determined by the amount of image compression.

The compression is given as a percentage ranging from 0 to 100. The higher the amount of compression, the lower the quality. You don't have to use 0 percent compression all the time when storing high-quality images.

Many images can be stored with 20 percent or even 40 percent compression with no loss of quality. On the other side, 100 percent compression does not reduce a file to nothing.

The variations in file size are not always in direct proportion to the change in compression factor. Figure 22.1 shows a 24-bit image stored with 40 percent compression, whereas Figure 22.2 shows an image stored with 80 percent compression.

Even though the compression of the second figure is twice the amount of the first figure, the reduction in file size is much greater. The file size for the first figure is approximately 96K, whereas the file size for the second figure is about 16K.

If you are really concerned with image size, try storing the image in both GIF and JPEG formats and see which is smaller. If JPEG is the way you want to go, try varying amounts of compression to see how much quality you are willing to lose in exchange for a smaller file.

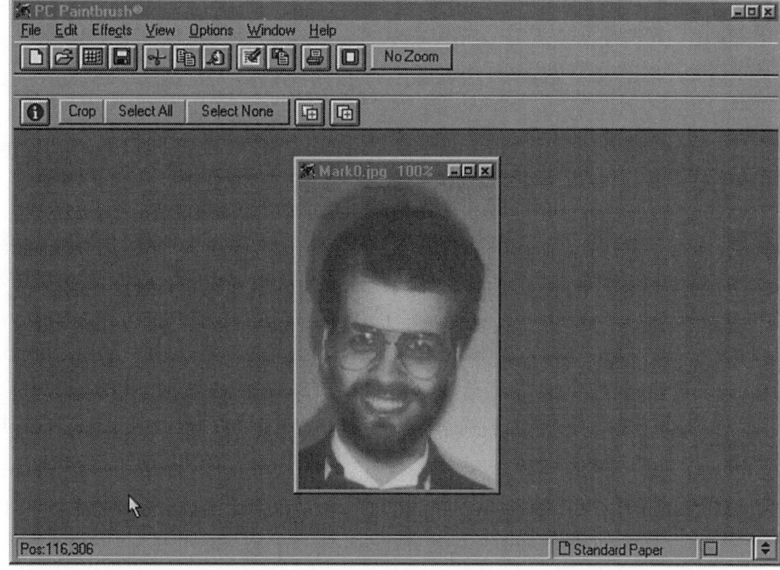

Fig. 22.1
JPEG can compress many images with no loss of quality.

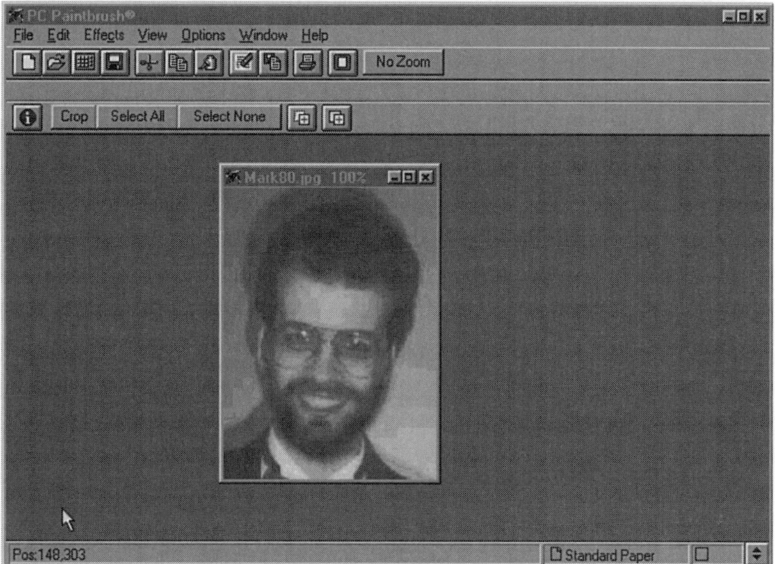

Fig. 22.2
JPEG images tend to get grainier the more they are compressed.

Image Strips

Every time you download a file over the network, a certain amount of overhead is involved in setting up the network connection, no matter how small the file. If you have to download a large number of files, you lose a lot of time in the connection overhead alone.

To compound the problem, if you download a large number of files simultaneously, you can't predict which file will be loaded first. This may not be so bad when you are downloading data files but if you are doing animation, it can be a pain.

You want to present something to the user as quickly as possible, preferably immediately, even if it's just a "Please wait..." message. Depending on the animation, you might want to grab the first frame and display it while waiting for the rest.

You might also build up the animation gradually, showing the frames in order as you get them. For instance, if you have the first two frames, loop through them, adding the third frame to the loop when it is loaded.

You can save yourself a lot of time if you just combine your images onto a single, larger image and download it. Although it's true it takes longer than downloading a single frame, the overall time to download the single image is less than the time it would take to download 12 frames individually.

The image containing all your animation frames is called an *image strip*.

Tip
You don't have to be doing animation to use this technique. It works any time you need to load several images into your applet.

Figure 22.3 shows an image strip consisting of multiple views of a person with a real head and cartoon body.

You can create an image strip with almost any paint program, as long as it works with a GIF or JPEG format. One thing to look for, however, is the ability to determine pixel coordinates. You need to know exactly where on the image strip each image is located.

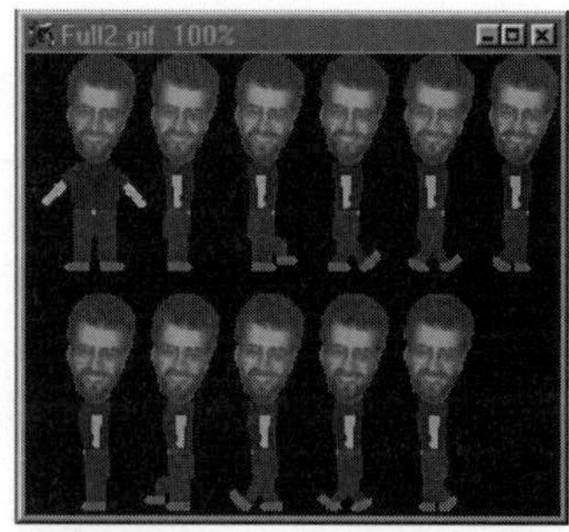

Fig. 22.3
Combining multiple images onto one image strip can save you time when downloading.

Many paint programs show you the current cursor location somewhere on the screen, which helps tremendously. If the program has a zoom feature, it really takes the guesswork out of finding the images.

The trick to displaying images from an image strip is that you make use of clipping. Although you could use the `CropImageFilter` class to view just a portion of the image, the class adds a lot of unnecessary overhead. The clipping functions built into the AWT do the same function only much, much faster.

When you draw an image from an image strip, you are essentially viewing the image strip through a lens the size of the image you want to draw. You move the image strip around underneath the lens to view a different image.

It's like using a microscope. The microscope lens is in a fixed position. If you want to see a different part of the microscope slide, you have to move the slide around.

Since the lens is fixed and you must move the image, you have to move the image in the opposite direction from the direction you would move the lens. In other words, if you normally move the lens 50 pixels to the right and 20 pixels down, you must move the image 50 pixels to the left and 20 pixels up.

Figure 22.4 shows the relative positioning of the lens and the image.

In Java lingo, the lens you use to view the image strip is called the *clipping area*. A clipping area is the area in which you can draw.

You may have noticed that Java doesn't give you an error when you try to draw images that are way outside the bounds of your applet but it also doesn't draw outside the bounds. This is because all your drawing is done within a clipping region.

The default clipping region for your applet is the entire area of the applet. You can change the clipping area, however, with the `Graphics.clipRect` method.

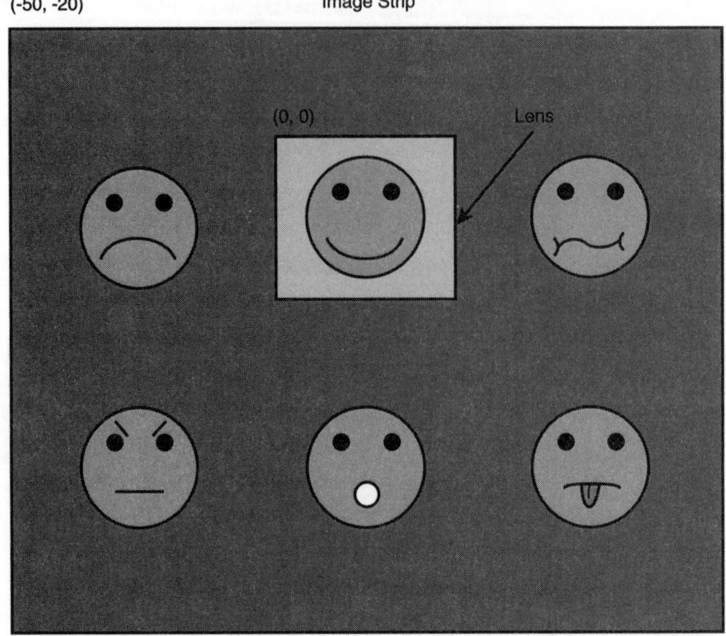

Fig. 22.4
You must draw an image strip relative to the lens.

Using the *Graphics.clipRect* Method

The `clipRect` method in the `Graphics` class allows you to change the clipping region of your drawing area. The only restriction is that you can never enlarge the clipping area.

To draw an image from an image strip, you first set the clipping area to the location and size of the image you are drawing. For example, suppose you want to draw an 80×60 image at location 40,30.

The corresponding `clipRect` call, assuming the variable `g` is an instance of `Graphics`, would be:

```
g.clipRect(40, 30, 80, 60);
```

Once you have created the clipping region, you still draw the image relative to the whole graphics area. In other words, the clipping region creates something like a graphics stencil that protects the rest of the graphics area from being painted, but you act like you are still painting the entire graphics area.

Remember that when you use image strips, you really draw the entire image strip every time; you just create a small window on top of the image strip so you see only one image at a time. Once you create a clipping region, you still have to figure out the x and y coordinates where the image strip should be drawn. The formula for the image strip's x and y coordinates is:

```
int imageStripX = clippingRegionX - imageX;
int imageStripY = clippingRegionY - imageY;
```

The `imageX` and `imageY` variables are the x and y coordinates of the image you want to draw relative to the image strip. In other words, if you want to draw an image from an image strip that is at location 50,10 on the strip, you would use 50 for the `imageX` and 10 for the `imageY` variables.

For the example of a clipping region at 40,30 and an image location of 50,10, you would draw the image strip at -10, 20 (that's 40-50, 30-10). To see why this is so, think of what would happen if you drew the image strip at 0,0. The image you really want is over at 50,10. Now, shift the image 50 pixels to the left and 10 pixels up (draw it at -50,-10). Now the image you want to draw is at location 0,0 on the screen. You really want it at 40,30, however, so you add 40 to the x coordinate and 30 to the y coordinate, moving the image you want over to location 40,30. Now if you look at what you did to the actual x,y of the full image strip, you moved the x coordinate left 50 and right 40, for a total movement of left 10, making its x coordinate -10. You shifted the y coordinate up 10 spaces and down 30 spaces, making a total movement of 20 pixels down, giving a y coordinate of 20.

Note

Since you can't enlarge the clipping area, once you reduce the clipping area to the size of the image, you can't draw anything outside of that boundary. If you need to draw multiple things in your `paint` method, do the image strip drawing last. This becomes a real problem if you do offscreen drawing. Normally, when you do offscreen drawing, you create an offscreen graphics context one time, just after you create the offscreen image. Once you change the clipping region on the offscreen graphics context, it stays changed. If you want to reset it, you have to create another offscreen graphics context by calling the `getGraphics` method in the offscreen image. You should probably also call the `dispose` method in the old graphics context first to free up its resources.

Creating Another Graphics Context

As you now know, the `clipRect` method has a serious drawback in that it can only shrink, effectively limiting you to drawing one image-strip image in a `paint` method. This may be acceptable in many cases, but you need an alternative.

Instead of changing the clipping region, you can create a new graphics drawing area that is a portion of the current drawing area. Then, instead of calling the `drawImage` method in your current drawing area, you call the same method in the subarea.

The `create` method in the `Graphics` class creates a subarea within the main drawing area. If you change the clipping region in the subarea, it doesn't affect the main area.

You don't need to clip the subarea, however, because you can just create it to be the size of the clipping area you want. To create a subarea at location 40,30 that is 80×60 pixels, you would do this:

```
Graphics subArea = g.create(40, 30, 80, 60);
```

You could then draw your image in this subarea:

```
subArea.drawImage(imageStrip, -75, -25, this);
```

Once you are done with the subarea, you should free up its resources by calling the `dispose` method:

```
subArea.dispose();
```

Note

When you draw images on a subarea, you do not add the x and y locations of the subarea to the coordinates for the image strip. In other words, if you use a subarea to draw an image that is at location 75,25 on an image strip, you always draw the image strip at location -75,-25, no matter where you create the subarea. This is different from the method where you just create a clipping region. The coordinates of the upper-left corner of a clipping region are the coordinates relative to the drawing area. The coordinates of the upper-left corner of a subarea are 0,0.

You can use the following method in your programs to draw images from an image strip without doing all the clipping yourself:

```
public void drawStripImage(Graphics g, Image imageStrip,
     int drawX, int drawY, int stripX, int stripY,
     int imageWidth, imageHeight)
{
     Graphics subArea = g.create(drawX, drawY, imageWidth,
          imageHeight);
```

```
        subArea.drawImage(imageStrip, -stripX, -stripY, this);
        subArea.dispose();
    }
```

In the preceding method, `g` is the original Graphics object from your `paint` method, `imageStrip` is the image strip you are drawing from, `drawX,drawY` are the coordinates where you want to draw the image, `stripX,stripY` is the location of the image on the image strip, and `imageHeight` and `imageWidth` are the width and height of the image.

Storing Only Parts on an Image Strip

You can save a great deal of additional time in downloading if you put whole frames in an image strip. The animation you are doing often has pieces that don't change from one frame to the next.

When that is the case, you can save space by storing the common parts only once. When you draw each animation frame, you put the parts together to make a whole image.

The images in Figure 22.3 have many common pieces. In fact, they were designed by using some common pieces. Every image has an identical head, and there are only three different body positions.

The only things that change consistently from frame to frame are the legs. This kind of partitioning takes a little bit of work up front, although it actually makes it easier to create multiple frames on your image strip since you don't have to redraw the entire frame each time.

Figure 22.5 shows a reduced image strip that contains only pieces of the images.

Fig. 22.5
Storing only pieces of images that are put together later can save even more time.

The file holding the image pieces is about one-fourth the size of the full set of images. When you piece together images, it is a good idea to use the GIF format and use a transparent pixel.

The image in Figure 22.5 uses black as the transparent pixel. This means that whenever pieces from the image strip are drawn, any area that is black is not drawn. This allows you to overlay pieces on top of one another.

Figure 22.6 shows an applet that puts these pieces together to form an animated sequence of a silly person walking back and forth. Notice that you don't see any of the black area from the image strip, even against the white background. This is because of the transparency.

Fig. 22.6
By using transparent pixels, you can piece images together seamlessly.

Note

Of the two image formats currently understood by Java, only GIF images may be transparent. The JPEG format does not support transparent images.

There are several tools available on the Internet for creating transparent GIFs. On the Windows platform, one of the most popular tools is PaintShop Pro, available as a shareware program from **http://www.jasc.com/pspdl.html**. Remember that shareware programs are not free. If you use it, you should pay for it.

The GIFTOOL program, from **http://www.homepages.com/tools/giftool**, is available on a wide variety of platforms and is also a shareware program. GIFTOOL is a little tougher to use since it is a command-line tool, but its availability on many platforms is appealing.

The idea behind transparent GIFs is that you mark one of the colors in the GIF color table as being a transparent pixel. Obviously, you must be using an indexed color model to create a transparent image. This is why JPEG cannot support transparent pixels—JPEG always uses 24-bit color, which never needs a color index.

When you draw images based on pieces, you must pay special attention to the relative positions of the different parts. When you draw a multipart figure at a particular location, how do you decide exactly where to draw the pieces?

For the animated figure in Figure 22.6, you might say that the figure's location is determined by the upper left corner of the head. In other words, if you want to draw the figure at location 40,20, you draw the head so that the head part of the image is drawn at 40,20. You must then determine the position of the other parts relative to the head.

For example, in Figure 22.6, the body portion is drawn 48 pixels down and 6 to the right from the upper left corner of the head. These locations are determined by using a paint program or other tools. Once you determine the relative positions of the pieces, you can store them in the following class:

Listing 22.1 Source Code for *ImageStripImage.java*

```
public class ImageStripImage
{

// distFromXOrigin and distFromYOrigin give the position where
// this image should be drawn relative to the location, or origin,
// of the multi-part image.

     public int distFromXOrigin;
     public int distFromYOrigin;

// stripX,StripY give the location of this image on the image strip
     public int stripX;
     public int stripY;


     public int width;     // the width of this image
     public int height;     // the height of this image

     public ImageStripImage(int distX, int distY, int stripX,
          int stripY, int width, int height)
     {
          this.distFromXOrigin = distX;
          this.distFromYOrigin = distY;

          this.stripX = stripX;
          this.stripY = stripY;

          this.width = width;
          this.height = height;
     }
   }
```


Once you have a piece of an image defined by this structure, you can draw it using this variation of the `drawStripImage` method:

```
public void drawStripImage(Graphics g, Image imageStrip,
     int drawX, int drawY, ImageStripImage imageInfo)
{
     Graphics subArea = g.create(drawX + imageInfo.distFromXOrigin,
drawY + imageInfo.distFromYOrigin, imageInfo.width,
          imageInfo.height);
     subArea.drawImage(imageStrip, -imageInfo.stripX, -imageInfo.stripY, this);
     subArea.dispose();
}
```

This variation of the `drawStripImage` method adjusts the location of the image piece by that piece's relative position to the overall position of the image.

There is a full example of an image strip animation available on the CD that comes with this book. It is called ImageStripApplet.java.

PART

V

Java Web Servers

chapter 23

Creating Web Services in Java

by Mark Wutka

In this chapter

- **Using Java objects instead of CGI**
  A Java object that resides in the same runtime environment as the Web server gives you a big performance advantage over CGI. In addition, a Java Web service stays running instead of terminating like a CGI program.
- **Using the Web server as a computing server**
  You can use a Java Web server to perform computational services for users. This is handy if you happen to have a very fast machine and want to make its computing resources available over the Internet.
- **Adding Web access to your Java applications**
  You can create a Web interface into an existing application while still allowing others to use the application as it was designed.
- **Migrating off the Web server in the future**
  If you design your Web applications well, you will be able to take advantage of other communications methods as they become more prevalent. Eventually, you may abandon HTTP altogether.

Several Web servers now allow you to create Java applets that use Web services. This allows you use Java instead of some of the popular languages like C++ and Perl.

If you are developing applications in Java, you can provide Web access to these applications without complicated, native method calls. As the Web servers improve, they will eventually be able to get Java programs from their clients and run them, turning the Web server into a computing server.

Although Web servers are very popular right now, the limitations of the HTTP protocol will become more of a hindrance than a help as the world of distributed objects takes shape.

Your application may get away with HTML forms this year but it may need to use CORBA or RMI to communicate with a complex applet next year.

You can design your applications right now with the possibility of CORBA or RMI in the future.

Using Java Objects Instead of CGI

Java objects provide some distinct advantages over CGI-based Web programs. They have less start-up cost, they continue to run, and they can be used on any software platform that supports Java.

Whenever the server gets a request that is handled by a CGI program, it must start the CGI program, which has some fixed amount of overhead. After the CGI program finishes processing a request, it terminates.

If a CGI program needs to maintain information across requests, it must store the information in a database or a file, and read it in again the next time it starts up. These start-up costs can be very high if the CGI program has to establish a session with a database every time.

FastCGI is an improvement over CGI. Instead of running a new program every time, FastCGI programs are always running. When a new request comes in, the Web server passes information to a FastCGI program via an interface protocol. Although this is certainly faster than regular CGI, the communication between the Web server and the FastCGI program can still be rather slow.

The most desirable option so far is to run the request handler as part of the Web server. Some commercial Web servers have hooks that allow you to add request handlers directly to the server. These hooks, or plug-ins, give you the speed you need.

Of course, when you want to run the same service on a different hardware platform or a different operating system, you have to create another version of the plug-in.

Figure 23.1 illustrates the relationship between the Web server and the request handling code for CGI, FastCGI, and plug-in modules.

Java is an ideal platform for using Web services. It runs on multiple platforms, it can be dynamically loaded, and it has a good security system.

In a Java Web server, the objects that handle requests are written entirely in Java. These request-handling objects are called *servlets*.

Unlike traditional CGI request handlers, servlets do not go away when they finish processing a request. This eliminates the heavy start-up overhead.

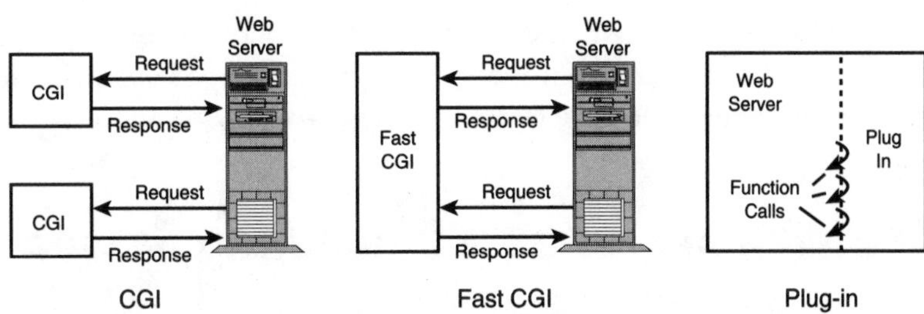

Fig. 23.1 *Traditional Web servers have evolved from simple, slow CGI to high-speed plug-ins.*

Unlike FastCGI, servlets run within the Web server itself, eliminating the communications overhead incurred when the server passes a request to the handler. And unlike plug-ins, servlets can run on any platform that supports Java.

Servlets can also take advantage of Java's security framework, allowing different levels of security for different servlets. For instance, you could define a security policy that allowed a servlet to access only certain directories on your file system. In addition, you could limit other Java features, like network access.

This feature is ideal for Web-space providers who have been unable to provide CGI access to their customers for fear of a malicious CGI program destroying the system. Now they can provide a Java Web server and allow their customers to write servlets that can only access the customer's files, and not those belonging to other customers.

If you get the same old story from your Web provider about why they can't give you CGI, suggest to them that they set up a Java Web server. If they won't, find a provider who will.

The Servlet API

Sun has defined an API for writing servlets and has used the API in the Jeeves server. The core of the API is, of course, the `Servlet` class.

The two most important methods in the `Servlet` class are `init` and `service`. The `init` method is called when the servlet is first created and is responsible for initializing the servlet. It is like the `init` method in the `Applet` class.

The `service` method takes two parameters, an object using the `ServletRequest` interface and an object using the `ServletResponse` interface. The `service` is responsible for handling an HTTP request, which is in the `ServletRequest` object, and returning a response, which is transmitted in the `ServletResponse` object.

The API also includes `ServletStub` and `ServletContext` classes. The `ServletStub`, like the `AppletStub`, is not normally used for `Servlet` programming.

The `ServletContext` class has information about the server in which the servlet is running, as well as information about other servlets on the server. The Servlet API is discussed in greater detail in Chapter 24, "Writing Web Services in Jeeves."

The Web Server as a Computing Server

Java Web servers open up new possibilities for Web-based services. Since Java can dynamically load new code and execute it, what's to stop you from downloading servlets over the network the same way a browser downloads an applet?

You could set up a high-performance computing Web service, running a Java Web server on a mainframe-class machine. Customers who had to perform computations that might take hours on their own systems could send servlets to your computing server. Your mainframe could crunch their numbers in a shorter time and return the results.

If you have some large, numerical non-Java application, for instance, you could provide access to the application via native methods. A customer would send you a servlet that makes various calls to your numerical application. This is discussed in more detail in Chapter 33, "Web-Enabling Legacy Systems."

Adding Web Access to Your Java Applications

As you write new Java applications, you may want to provide access to these applications via the Web. If you design your application well, adding new interfaces to the application should not be a problem.

As this book has stressed from the beginning, you should strive to separate your application logic from your user interface. Once the interface to the application is well-defined, you can add new ways to access your application without changing the application.

In the case of a Web server, the servlet acts as a proxy for the user interface. In other words, the servlet acts like a user as far as the application is concerned and then passes information back to the Web browser, which implements the real user interface.

Figure 23.2 illustrates the relationship between the servlet, the application, and the user, as compared to a typical user interface.

The interface between the servlet and the application objects can take a number of different forms. The application could run in the same Java environment as the Web server. The servlets would then make normal Java method calls to the application. Figure 23.3 illustrates this relationship.

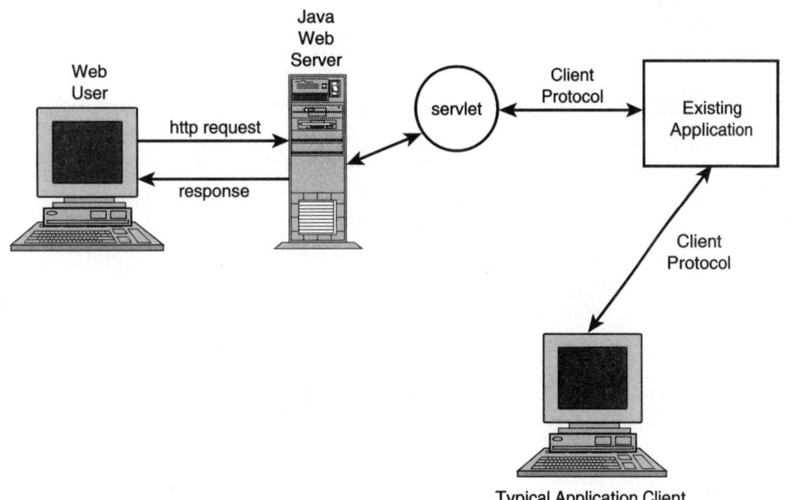

Fig. 23.2
A servlet can act as a user interface proxy to an application.

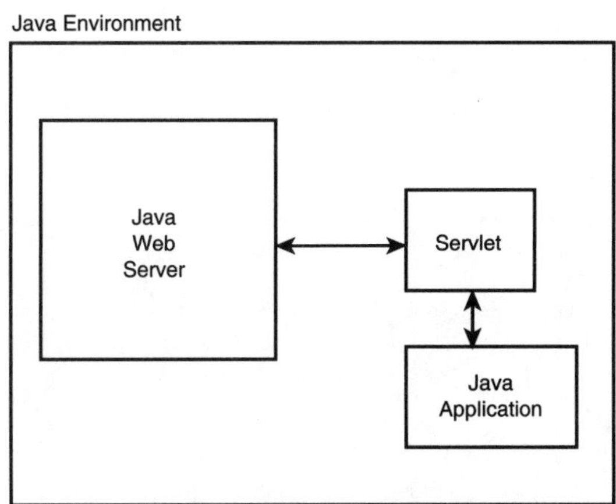

Fig. 23.3
A Java application can run in the same Java environment as the Java Web server.

The application and the Web server could also be running on the same physical host but running in separate Java environments. The servlet would need to use RMI, CORBA, or some other form of interprocess communication to access the application, as illustrated in Figure 23.4.

Once a servlet uses RMI or CORBA to communicate with the application, there is no need to keep the application and the Web server on the same physical host. Figure 23.5 illustrates a possible configuration.

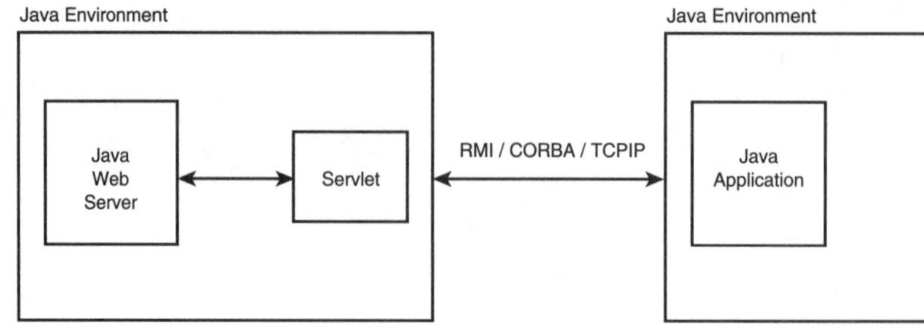

Fig. 23.4
A servlet can use RMI or CORBA to communicate with the real application.

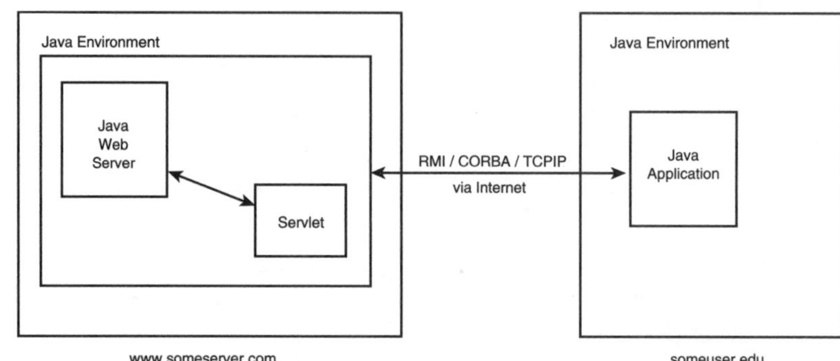

Fig. 23.5
The server can access the application across the network.

Note

Two of the factors for deciding whether to put the servlet and the application on two different hosts are the amount of computation performed by the application and the amount of interaction between the application and the servlet.

If the application needs a lot of CPU time, it would be better off on a separate host. If the application and the servlet exchange large volumes of data or pass many messages between them, they would be better off on the same host.

Suppose you want to add Web access to the banking application from Chapter 18, "Using CORBA IDL with Java." You could create a servlet to handle each of the four operations in the banking interface. Each servlet would have a pointer to a banking object, possibly even the same object, if you want to use the banking object as a singleton object.

A banking servlet could create an instance of the banking implementation in its `init` method:

```
public void init()
{
```

```
        bank = new banking.BankingImpl();
    }
```

Then the `service` method, which handles incoming requests, would translate the incoming HTTP request to a method call to the `BankingImpl` object as shown in Listing 23.1.

Listing 23.1 Method Call to *BankingImpl* Object

```
public void service(ServletRequest req, ServletResponse resp)
{
// Get the table of request paramaters
     Hashtable params = req.getQueryParameters();

// Get the account number, account password, and account type
     String account = params.get("account");
     String password = params.get("password");
     String accountTypeName = params.get("accountType");

// Convert the account type name into one of the allowable
// account types, or return an error if it's an illegal type
     int accountType;
     if (accountTypeName.equals("checking")) {
          accountType = banking.Account.CHECKING;
     } else if (accountTypeName.equals("savings")) {
          accountType = banking.Account.SAVINGS;
     } else {
          res.writeErrorResponse(SC_BAD_REQUEST,
"Invalid account type");
          return;
     }

// Get the balance using the BankingImpl object
     try {
          int balance = bank.getBalance(
               new Account(account, password, accountType);

// Store the resulting information in the response/
          res.setStatus(SC_OK);
          res.setContentType("text/html");
          res.writeHeaders();

// Get a print stream for writing the HTML for the response
          PrintStream out = new PrintStream(
res.getOutputStream());

// Generate an HTML response containing the balance
          out.println("<HTML><HEAD>");
          out.println("<TITLE>Bank Account Balance</TITLE>");
          out.println("</HEAD><BODY>");
          out.println("<H1>Current Account Balance:</H1>");

// The BankingImpl object stores balances in cents, we have
// to convert it to dollars manually.
```

23

continues

Listing 23.1 Continued

```
            out.println("<P>$"+balance/100+"."+balance%100);
            out.println("</BODY></HTML>");
            out.flush();
        } catch (banking.InvalidAccountException) {
// If there was an invalid account exception, pass this on
// to the client
            res.writeErrorResponse(SC_UNAUTHORIZED,
                "Invalid account");
            return;
        } catch (Exception e) {

// If there was any other exception, something's wrong internally
            res.writeErrorResponse(SC_INTERNAL_SERVER_ERROR,
                "Got error performing request");
            return;
        }
}
```

As you can see, the servlet makes use of the existing `BankingImpl` object without actually doing any of the banking operations itself. In this configuration, the `BankingImpl` object must be running in the same Java environment as the Web server. You could also replace the `BankingImpl` object with a CORBA or RMI stub, and make `remote` method invocations to a banking object running somewhere else.

Migrating off the Web Server in the Future

You may be completely focused on writing Web-server-based solutions right now, but that doesn't mean that you will still be doing that a year from now. Web browsers are becoming much more intelligent and some of them are starting to use more protocols than just HTTP.

Netscape, for instance, has announced that a future version of their browser will include a CORBA client. You don't want to write all these applications right now, only to turn around next year and have to rewrite them again from scratch.

The secret to migrating your Web applications is quite simple: *Don't write Web applications*. Instead, write applications and then provide Web access to them.

That may sound like a contradiction but it is just a reiteration of the separation of user interface from application idea. When you write Web server applications, you tend to think of them only in terms of the Web server.

You may take certain shortcuts that you will regret later or you may intermingle the handling of Web documents with the real function of your application. Don't do that.

First, think of the task your application is really trying to do and write the application without any mention of servlets or HTTP. Finally, when you have a working application, write the servlet or servlets that link the application to the Web.

As always, you will find that it takes more effort to develop a Web service by splitting it into two parts. You will save time in the long run, however, because you can add new ways to access your application without changing the application at all.

chapter 24

Writing Web Services for Jeeves

by David Edgar Liebke

In this chapter

- **What is Jeeves?**
  Jeeves is both a fully functional Web server and a collection of class libraries used to develop and extend it, and other, Internet servers.
- **Using the Jeeves HTTP server**
  The basic HTTP server architecture serves as the foundation for learning the processes of administering and securing your Jeeves Web site.
- **Extending Jeeves' functionality with servlets**
  Servlets conform to a standard application programming interface (API) that will soon be supported by other Web servers. Using the servlet API, along with the Jeeves class libraries, you will extend the functionality of the basic Web server.
- **Building a database servlet**
  You will extend Jeeves' functionality with a servlet that connects it to a database. This will make it possible to search for or enter data from any Web browser.
- **Building a simple autonomous agent system**
  Servlets can provide the foundation for a system of roaming agents that act on their users' behalf. You will develop a simple agent system that includes an agent capable of searching for or entering data into a remote database, later to return home with the results.

Jeeves is a Java-based Web server development toolkit that includes a fully functional HTTP Web server. This chapter describes how to write servlets that extend the function of the HTTP server using the Web server toolkit.

The chapter begins by introducing the HTTP server's architecture. You will go through the process of administering the server. This background knowledge lays the foundation for the rest of the chapter.

In the second part of the chapter, you learn how to write servlets that extend Jeeves' functions. This section begins with an introduction to the servlet API, which is at the heart of Jeeves' functionality and extensibility. You then learn about Jeeves' rich collection of tools that enhance servlet development.

Finally, two examples show you what can be done with servlets and Jeeves. The first is a database servlet that puts a Web front end on any database that supports the Java Database Connectivity (JDBC) interface. The second takes advantage of Java's object serialization to create a simple example of an autonomous agent system.

What Is Jeeves?

Jeeves is often described simply as a Java Web server, but it is much more. Jeeves is a server development toolkit. At the center of the Jeeves toolkit is a package of generic server classes. With these classes, any developer can quickly build connection-oriented servers.

Another important component of the toolkit is the *servlet*. Servlets are Java objects that comply with the servlet API and are used to add functions to Web servers. The servlet API is Sun's proposed standard for extending Web server functions with Java.

Note
In addition to Jeeves, Acme Serve is a basic Web server that complies with the servlet API. It is available at **http://www.acme.com/**.

In addition to the servlet API and the generic server classes, the Jeeves toolkit includes security classes, administrative classes, utility classes, and a set of servlets that provide basic Web server functions.

The Jeeves HTTP server was developed from this toolkit and is a fully functioning Web server that provides all the features common to other Web servers.

Tip
For more information about Jeeves, check out **http://www.javasoft.com/products/jeeves**.

The Jeeves HTTP Server

This part of the chapter introduces you to the Jeeves HTTP server. It begins with an architectural overview and then moves on to basic server installation and administration.

By the end of this section, you'll have a basic understanding of the server architecture and administrative design. This lays the foundation for extending the server with servlets, which you will learn how to do in the second part of this chapter.

Architectural Overview

The Jeeves HTTP server is built on the framework provided by the generic server classes discussed earlier. This framework is the core of the Jeeves server development toolkit. Here is a brief description of the workings of a generic Jeeves server, followed by a description of the specific workings of the HTTP server.

An object of the `sun.server.Server` class waits in a loop for connection requests. Connections are placed on a queue while the server determines if there are handler objects of the `sun.server.ServerHandler` class available in the handler thread pool.

If none are available and the maximum number of handler threads has not been reached, the server starts a new handler thread. If, on the other hand, the number of handlers exceeds the minimum needed, and some have been idle for a period longer than the specified timeout parameter, the idle handlers expire.

In the case of the HTTP server, once the server receives an HTTP request, it is queued for servicing by the pool of HTTP server handler threads. The HTTP handler then authorizes and applies name translation rules to the request, and passes the request on to the appropriate servlet.

Servlets provide the core function of the Jeeves HTTP server, as well as providing a means for extending that function. The HTTP server includes a set of core servlets that provide common Web server functions.

For instance, the `FileServlet` fulfills HTTP `GET` requests, returning the requested file to the client. The `Invoker` servlet is used to dynamically invoke servlets that have been explicity requested by a client using an URL of the form:

http://ServerHostName/servlet/<servletName>

The `Invoker` supports only local servlets but will soon be able to dynamically load servlets from across a network. The `SSInclude` servlet parses server-side include files (files with an .shtml extension) and calls any servlet that was referenced.

The `CgiServlet` provides backward compatibility for the large body of existing CGI programs. The `ImageMapServlet` uses server-side image maps. Finally, there is the `Admin` Servlet that works together with the Admin applet to help with administrative tasks (you'll learn more about this in the next section).

Installing and Running the Jeeves HTTP Server

First, you need a host that has the Java runtime installed. Once you have an appropriate host, installing Jeeves is simply a matter of unzipping the distribution and running the httpd program found in the bin directory under the main installation directory. You can test whether the server is up by pointing a Web browser at the following URL:

http://ServerHostName:8888/

The server's default port is 8888; you will learn how to change this and other defaults in this chapter.

Tip

You must have at least version 1.0.2 of the JDK to run Jeeves.

Caution

If you are running Jeeves on a Windows 95 machine, you must make sure that the logs directory is under the main installation directory. Unzip tends not to extract directories that have no files, as is the case with the logs directory.

Administering the Jeeves Web Server

There are two ways to administer the Jeeves Web server. You can use the administration Web page, which includes an applet that enables you to modify many of the server's parameters dynamically. Or you can change the configuration files, listed in Table 24.1, by hand.

You can adjust many parameters. Some of these changes take effect immediately and others do not take effect until the server is restarted. In the following section, you will proceed step-by-step through the administration process, using both the administration Web page and the configuration files.

Note

Some properties can be changed only by hand. For instance, the server allows you to change the welcome page property from the default of index.html but you cannot do this from the administration Web page. You must change the httpd.properties file using a text editor.

Table 24.1 Jeeves Configuration Files

File Name	Properties
httpd.properties	Server name, port number, minimum threads, maximum threads, timeout, ramcache, keepalive, keepalive timeout, and location of other property files
rules.properties	Translation rules for invoking servlets
alias.properties	Translation rules for path aliases
servlet.properties	Servlet codebase, servlet code, and initArgs
mime.properties	MIME configuration
acl.properties	Access control file

Administering Jeeves from a Java-Enabled Browser

You can manage the Jeeves Web server remotely using any Java-enabled Web browser. Once the server is running, you can access the administration Web page by pointing your browser at the following URL:

http://ServerHostName:8888/admin/admin.html

You are prompted for a user name and password. The default administration account name and password are **admin**. Once authorized, you see the page shown in Figure 24.1.

The window on the left includes a list of administrative tasks, including HTTP configuration, log configuration, file aliasing, servlet aliasing, servlet loading, MIME configuration, user configuration, group configuration, access control list (ACL) configuration, and resource protection.

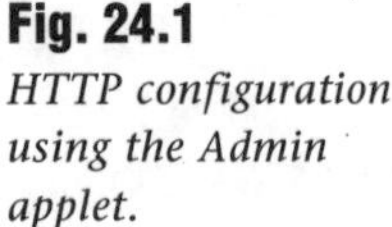

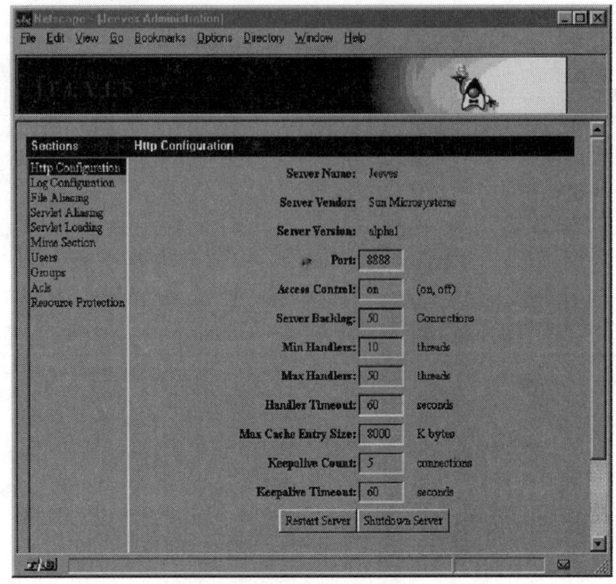

Fig. 24.1
HTTP configuration using the Admin applet.

Modifying Basic Web Server Parameters

Jeeves has many tunable parameters. Figure 24.1 shows the parameters you can modify from the administration Web page. There are other properties, such as the server user (UNIX version only) and server host name, that can be changed only from the httpd.properties file.

Jeeves lets you set the number of handler threads that are started and how long an idle thread remains before being destroyed. In the httpd.properities file, you'll find the following thread properties: `server.min.threads`, `server.max.threads`, and `server.timeout`.

Jeeves uses connection `keepalive` to improve performance by keeping the connections to client browsers open even after the request has been fulfilled. This reduces the overhead of bringing the connection up and down for multiple requests from the same client.

The `keepalive` count property determines the number of hits from a single client that are received before the connection is brought down. The `keepalive` timeout determines the time in seconds the connection stays up after a request has been fulfilled.

Configuring Web Server Logging

You can specify where log files are stored and the level of logging detail for the Access, Error, and Event logs. These changes are made from the Log Configuration screen (see Figure 24.2) or the httpd.properties file.

The Access log is in Common Log format, which lets you use existing log-analyzing scripts on them. All the log files reside in the $JEEVES-HOME/logs directory.

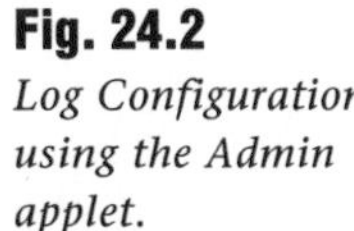

Fig. 24.2
Log Configuration using the Admin applet.

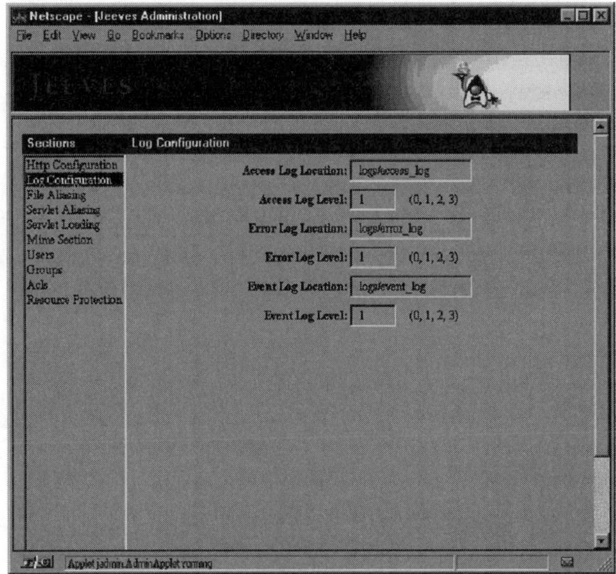

Creating File Aliases

You can map virtual paths in the requested URL to an arbitrary real path name on the server's disk. These changes take effect immediately if done from the File Aliasing screen (see Figure 24.3); otherwise, you can make the changes to the alias.properties file.

Fig. 24.3
File aliasing using the Admin applet.

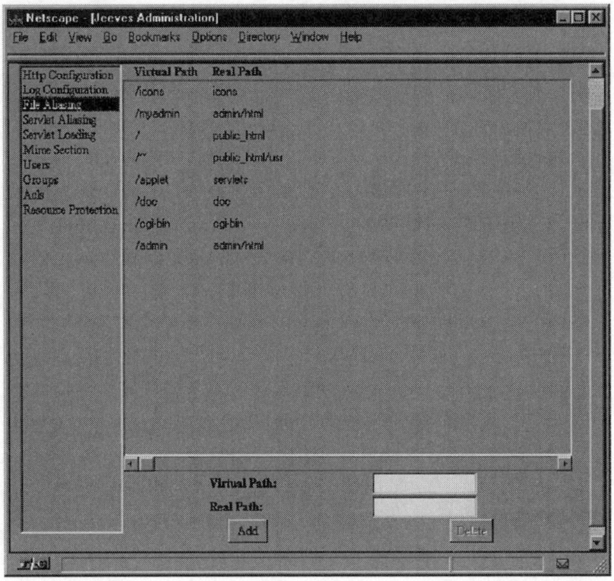

24

Configuring MIME

The mime.properties file and the Mime Section of the administration Web page allows you to map Mime types to file extensions. This information is sent from the server to the client browser.

The browser uses this information to figure out what to do with the file it is about to receive from the server. For example, in the case of a file with a .mov extension, the browser should start up a QuickTime viewer. You can also change the mime.properties file by hand.

Loading Servlets into the Web Server

To execute servlets, you must map the servlet name to a class that lies somewhere in the server's `CLASSPATH` environment variable. You can do this from the Servlet Loading screen of the administration Web page (see Figure 24.4).

Remote servlets can also be loaded by specifying their URL to the location field of the administration page.

When you use the Web page, the changes take effect immediately. When you use the servlets.properties file, you can map the servlet called `myservlet` to the `MyServlet` class in the `mypackage` package with the following entry:

```
myservlet.code=mypackage.MyServlet
```

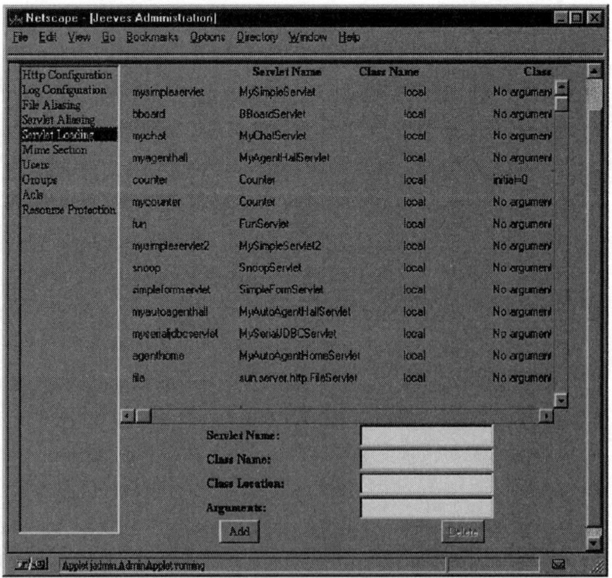

Fig. 24.4
Servlet loading using the Admin applet.

When you change the servlet.properties file, the changes do not take effect until the server is restarted. You can now invoke `myservlet` with the following URL:

http://<server_host>/servlet/myservlet

The virtual path **/servlet** is mapped to the Invoker, which then calls the referenced servlet.

Creating Servlet Aliases

Servlets can also be mapped to arbitrary document names. When you use the Servlet Aliasing screen (see Figure 24.5), all changes are dynamic. Otherwise, change the rules.properties file. Again, changes to the configuration files take effect after the server has been restarted.

To map `myservlet` to `myservlet.html`, put the following line into the rules.properties file:

```
/myservlet.html=myservlet
```

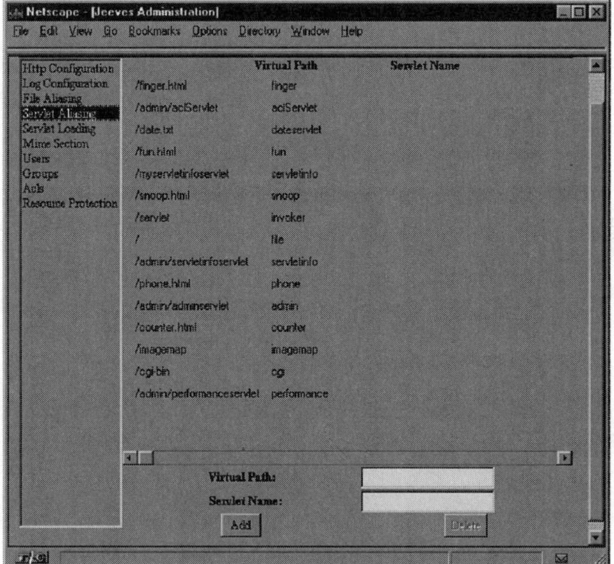

Fig. 24.5
Servlet aliasing using the Admin applet.

HTTP Server Security

Jeeves uses an extensible, access-control list framework for controlling requests for files and servlets. Only the Basic HTTP authentication scheme is allowed, but Jeeves accepts the configuration of different authentication schemes when they become available.

Access control lists can be associated with any file, directory, or servlet. If a file or directory is not explicitly protected by an ACL, it inherits the protection of its parent directory.

If there is no ACL for the entire directory structure, access is granted. If a servlet is not explicitly protected by an ACL, a default is used. If it doesn't exist, access is granted. Servlets can also use their own access-control list, using the security classes available in Jeeves.

Jeeves also makes use of security realms. Realms are used to set broad security policies. When users, groups, or access-control lists are added to the Web server, they are assigned to a realm.

People who have common security needs can be put into a Single realm, such as the adminRealm. When you want to protect a resource, you associate it with an access-control list in a realm. Jeeves comes with two built-in realms, adminRealm and defaultRealm.

Servlet Security

The four basic types of servlets are core servlets, local servlets, signed network servlets, and unsigned network servlets. These servlets are treated differently with respect to security.

The core servlets and local servlets are thought to be trusted and are granted full access to the server's resources. Signed network servlets are granted a limited subset of privileges, as determined by the site administrator. Unsigned servlets are not trusted and are only executed in a restrictive environment, called the *server sandbox*.

Protecting Web Resources

Using the Resource Protection section of the administration Web page (see Figure 24.6), you can assign schemes and realms to Web resources. These resources include documents and servlets.

Adding Users to Security Realms

You can add users to different realms. The easiest way to add users is through the Users screen of the administration Web page (see Figure 24.7). Simply select the realm, and enter the user's name and password.

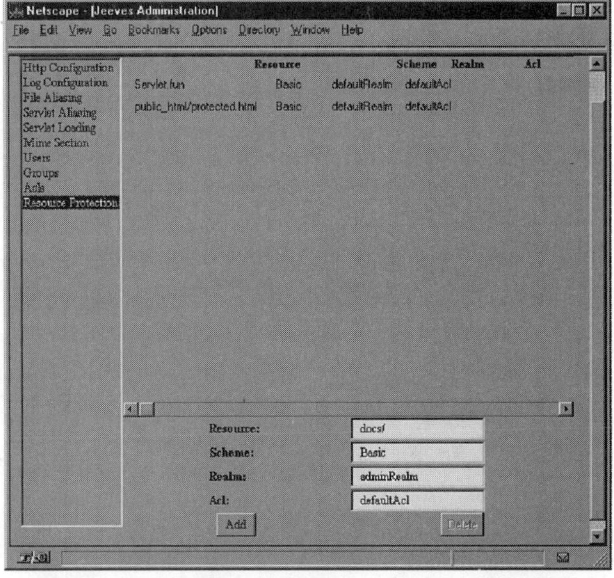

Fig. 24.6
Protecting resources with the administration Web page.

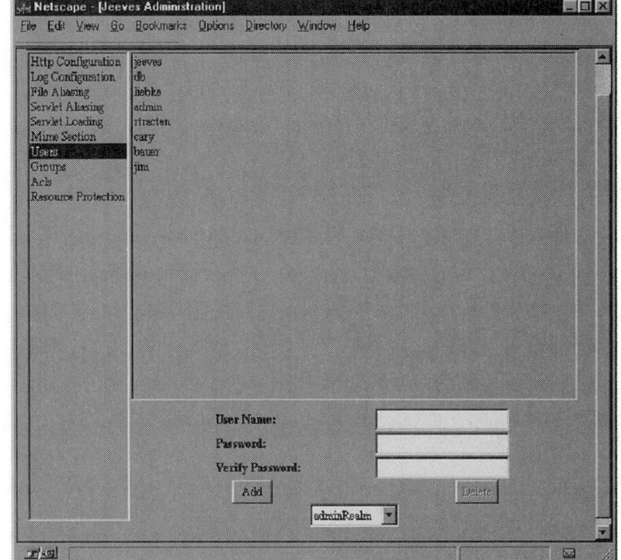

Fig. 24.7
Adding a user to a realm with the Admin applet.

24

Creating Groups of Users

You can group together users who should share the same privileges using the Groups section of the administration Web page (see Figure 24.8). Select the realm and group you want to change and enter the user you want to add. You can also create new groups by entering the new group name in the field above the user name.

Fig. 24.8
Adding a user to a group with the Admin applet.

Creating and Modifying ACLs

You can create new ACLs in a realm or add entries to an existing realm from the ACL screen on the administration Web page (see Figure 24.9). To add an entry to an existing ACL, select it from the center window and click the Add ACL Entry button.

A new window appears. On the far left is a select box with a plus sign and a minus sign. Choose the plus sign to grant privileges or choose the minus sign to restrict them.

The next select box lets you choose whether you are modifying the privileges of a group or of an individual user. There is a text field to enter the group or user name. Finally, select the privileges you want (such as GET, POST, or PUT) for that user or group.

To add a new ACL, choose the Create ACL button. A box appears prompting you for the ACL name. To delete an ACL, select it from the list and choose the Delete ACL button.

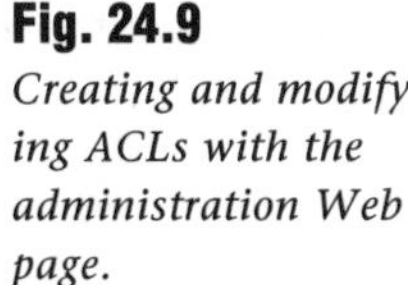

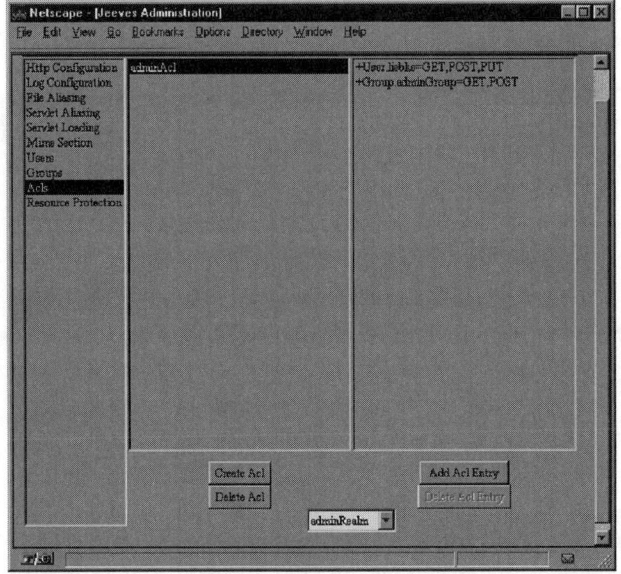

Fig. 24.9 *Creating and modifying ACLs with the administration Web page.*

Extending Jeeves' Functionality with Servlets

Now that you have a basic understanding of the HTTP server architecture and are familiar with the administrative design, you can move on to extending the server's function with servlets.

Creating servlets is like creating applets. Servlets are basically applets without graphical front ends. Both servlets and applets can be loaded dynamically from across a network.

Both applets and servlets are small programs that extend the function of a browser or server, respectively. Both can run on any platform that supports Java and the applet or servlet APIs, respectively.

In this part of the chapter, you are introduced to the Servlet API, and you'll write some generic servlets. You then learn about the additional classes provided by the Jeeves server development toolkit that make extending Web server functions even simpler.

Next, you build a servlet that accesses any database that supports the Java Database Connectivity (JDBC) interface, letting users insert data and search for data from a Web page.

Finally, you use servlets to build a simple example of an autonomous agent system. You'll write a couple of simple agency servlets that provide an environment for roaming autonomous agents.

You'll create an agent that is transported to a remote agency where it gathers some information from a JDBC database. The agency asks the agent where it lives and sends it home.

The agent's home agency stores the agent in a file for later processing. Finally, you'll restore the agent and extract the information it has gathered.

Employing the Servlet API

The Servlet API is Sun's proposed standard for extending Web server function with Java. Other servers that have Java APIs include Netscape, Oracle, and the World Wide Web Consortium's Jigsaw server, which, like Jeeves, is written entirely in Java.

Each of the above servers uses a different API. This reduces Java's inherent platform independence by requiring developers to write different Java programs for each of these servers.

A single Java Web server API will greatly simplify development of Web services. It is not yet clear whether servlets will become the standard that applets have become. But servlets have a lot going for them, not the least of which is the support of Sun, the developer of Java.

The classes associated with the servlet API are in a single package, `java.servlet`. This package includes four Java interfaces: `ServletContext`, `ServletRequest`, `ServletResponse`, and `ServletStub`; and three classes: `Servlet`, `ServletInputStream`, and `ServletOutputStream`.

The server developer must use the four interfaces to make the server comply with the servlet API. You then use the server's implementations of these interfaces along with the `Servlet`, `ServletInputStream`, and `ServletOutputStream` classes to write servlets.

In this section, you learn the basics behind the classes and interfaces that make up the servlet package.

Extending the *Servlet* Class

The `Servlet` class provides the basic function necessary to create servlets. This class includes the methods shown in Table 24.2.

Table 24.2 Methods in the *Servlet* Class

Method Name	Description
`service(ServletRequest, ServletResponse)`	Services a single request from a client.

Method Name	Description
init()	Called by system when servlet is first loaded.
GetInitParameter(String)	Gets the named initialization parameter.
GetServletContext()	Returns the servlet context object.
log(String)	Logs a message to the servlet log.
GetServletInfo()	Returns a string containing information about the servlet.
destroy()	Destroys servlet and cleans up after it.
SetStub(ServletStub)	Sets servlet stub; this is done by the system.

The first step in writing Servlets is extending the `Servlet` class and overriding the `service` method. The following servlet prints "Hello World" to the client browser.

The first step is to get the `OutputStream` from the `ServletResponse` object and create a `PrintStream` with it. Next, you set the response status to `OK` using the static variable `SC_OK` from the `ServletResponse` class.

Then, you set the content type of the response to text/plain and write out the headers. Finally, print the Hello World string to the `PrintStream`.

```
import java.servlet.*;

public class SimpleServlet extends Servlet {
     public void service( ServletRequest req, ServletResponse res ) {
     PrintStream ps = new PrintStream(res.getOutputStream());
     res.setStatus(ServletResponse.SC_OK);
     res.setContentType("text/plain");
     res.writeHeaders();
     ps.println("Hello World");
     ps.flush();
     }
}
```


After you compile the class, load it into the HTTP server using either the servlet.properties file or the servlet loading screen of the administration Web page, as was discussed in the first part of this chapter. You can access the servlet with the following URL:

http://<server>/servlet/<servlet_name>

where `<servlet_name>` is the name you assigned to your servlet when you loaded it into the HTTP server.

Sending Information with the *ServletResponse* Interface

The ServletResponse interface allows you to send information to the client's browser. It includes methods for getting an output stream directed at the client, setting the header information, sending errors to the client, and setting the status of the response. Table 24.3 shows more of ServletResponse's methods.

ServletResponse also includes a list of static integer variables used in setting the response status. The previous example used the SC_OK variable. Other responses include SC_CREATED, SC_NO_CONTENT, SC_MOVED_PERMANENTLY, SC_MOVED_TEMPORARILY, SC_BAD_REQUEST, SC_UNATHORIZED, SC_FORBIDDEN, SC_NOT_FOUND. For a complete list of methods and variables, see the servlet API documentation.

Table 24.3 *ServletResponse* Methods

Method	Description
getOuputStream()	Returns the output stream for writing responses.
SendError(int, String)	Sends an error message to the client.
sendRedirect(String)	Sends a redirect response to the client using a specified redirect URL.
SetContentLength(int)	Sets the content length for this response.
SetContentType(String)	Sets the content type for this response.
SetDateHeader(String, long)	Sets the date header field.
SetHeader(String, String)	Sets the value of a header field.
setIntHeader(String, int)	Sets the value of an integer header field.
WriteHeaders()	Writes the status line and message headers for this response to the output stream.
SetStatus(int)	Sets the status code and a default message for this response.

Receiving Information with the *ServletRequest* Interface

In addition to the `ServletResponse` object, Servlets get a `ServletRequest` object as an argument. This object lets the servlet get information directly from the client making the request, as well as from the server that called the servlet.

`ServletRequest` includes methods for getting an input stream from the client, gathering header information, and extracting path and query information from the requested URL.

Table 24.4 shows the `ServletRequest` methods. For complete information, see the servlet API documentation.

Table 24.4 *ServletRequest* Methods

Method Name	Description
`getAuthType()`	Returns the authentication scheme of the request or null if none.
`GetContentLength()`	Returns the size of the request entity data or -1 if not known.
`getContentType()`	Returns the MIME type of the request entity data.
`GetDateHeader`(String, long)	Returns the value of a date header field.
`getHeader`(String)	Returns the value of a header field.
`getHeader`(int)	Returns the nth header field.
`GetHeaderName`(int)	Returns the name of the nth header field.
`GetInputStream()`	Returns an input stream for reading request data.
`GetIntHeader`(String, int)	Returns the value of an integer header field.
`getMethod()`	Returns the method with which the request was made.
`GetPathInfo()`	Returns optional extra path information following the servlet path and preceding the query. string.
`GetPathTranslated()`	Returns extra path information translated to a real path.
`GetProtocol()`	Returns the protocol and version of the request.

continues

Table 24.4 Continued

Method Name	Description
`GetQueryParameter(String)`	Returns the value of the specified query string parameter.
`GetQueryParameters()`	Returns a hash table of query string parameter values.
`GetQueryString()`	Returns the query string part of the servlet URL.
`GetRemoteAddr()`	Returns the IP address of the agent that sent the request.
`GetRemoteHost()`	Returns name of the host making the request.
`GetRemoteUser()`	Returns the name of the user making the request or null if not known.
`GetRequestPath()`	Returns the part of the request URI that corresponds to the servlet path, plus optional path information.
`GetRequestURI()`	Returns the request URI.
`GetServerName()`	Returns the host name of the server.
`GetServerPort()`	Returns the port number on which this request was received.
`GetServletPath()`	Returns the part of the request URI that refers to the servlet being invoked.

Getting Information with the *ServletContext* Interface

The `getServletContext` method from the `Servlet` class returns a `ServletContext`. This object lets you find out information about the environment in which the servlet is running.

The `getServerInfo` method returns the name and version of the server running. The `getServlet` method returns a servlet with its name, and the `getServlets` method returns an enumeration of all the available servlets in this context.

Using the Jeeves Development Toolkit

In addition to the servlet API, Jeeves includes additional classes that simplify the development of Web services. For example, there are several prebuilt servlets that extend the function of the generic `Servlet` class. These include a form servlet that processes HTML form input and a filter interface that lets you embed servlets in HTML pages using server-side includes.

Sun also includes several sample servlets to get you started. Other classes in the toolkit let you generate HTML, set servlet security, and do other useful tasks.

Processing Form Input with the *FormServlet*

The `FormServlet` greatly simplifies the processing of HTML form input. To process data from a form, extend the `FormServlet` class and override the `sendResponse` method.

The `sendResponse` method doesn't take a `ServletRequest` object as an argument. Instead, it gets a hash table containing the values from the HTML form. The following example shows how to get the value from the form field called `field_name`.

```
Public class SimpleFormServlet extends FormServlet {
    public void sendResponse(ServletResponse res, Hashtable table) {
    String field_value = table.get("field_name");
    ...
    }
}
```

Using the Filter Interface to Embed Servlets in HTML Pages

Using the Jeeves Filter interface, you can create servlets that can be embedded in HTML pages using a server-side include statement. The following server-side include statement calls `myServlet` and passes the `name1` and `name2` parameters to it in the form of a hash table:

```
<SERVLET CODE="myServlet" name1="value1" name2="value2">
```

The following servlet inserts the date into the Web page it is embedded in:

```
import java.servlet.*;
import java.io.*;
import java.util.*;

public class SSIServlet extends Servlet implements Filter {
     public void service(InputStream is, OutputStream os, Hashtable params)
     throws java.io.IOException
     {
     Date now = new Date();
     PrintStream ps = new PrintStream(os);
     ps.println(today);
     ps.flush();
     }
}
```

24

Notice that the `service` method accepts different arguments from normal. Instead of `ServletRequest` and `ServletResponse`, the arguments to service are an `InputStream`, `OutputStream`, and `Hashtable`. The hash table is used to store the parameters passed to the servlet by the server-side include statement.

Generating HTML with the Jeeves HTML Classes

Sun provides a package of classes that generate HTML. The package includes the `HtmlContainer` and `HtmlElement` interfaces, as well as the `HtmlContainerImpl`, `HtmlPage`, `HtmlTag`, `HtmlTagPair`, and `HtmlText` classes.

Start by creating a new `HtmlPage` object. Then, using the `addTag`, `addTagPair`, and `addText` methods, insert the necessary HTML. The following example shows a simple use of these classes:

```
import java.servlet.*;
import sun.server.html
import java.io.*;

public class HtmlServlet extends Servlet {
     pubic service(ServletRequest req, ServletResponse res)
     throws Exception {
     res.setContentType("text/html");
     res.setStatus(ServletResponse.SC_OK);
     OutputStream os = res.getOutputStream();

     HtmlPage page = new HtmlPage("A Simple HTML page");
     page.addTagPair("H1", "This is a Simple HTML Page");
     page.addTag("p");
     page.addText("This page was generated by the sun.server.html package");

     page.write(os);
     os.flush();
     }
}
```

Building a Database Servlet

In this section, you build a Servlet that processes an HTML form and either searches for or inserts data into a JDBC database. This servlet could be used by a site to register new users, process orders, survey users, or enable users to search one of your publicly accessible databases.

Getting the Information from the Users

The first step is to process the form data with a `FormServlet`. This is a generic registration form that asks the user's name, title, company, and address. The following is a `sendResponse` method that returns the information supplied by the user in an HTML table:

```
public void sendResponse(ServletResponse res, Hashtable table)
throws IOException
{
```

```
        PrintStream ps = new PrintStream(res.getOutputStream());
        log("MyServlet running");
        res.setStatus(ServletResponse.SC_OK);
        res.setContentType("text/html");
        res.writeHeaders();

        String name = (String) table.get("name");
        String title = (String) table.get("title");
        String company = (String) table.get("company");
        String address = (String) table.get("address");

        ps.println("<HTML><HEAD>");
        ps.println("<TITLE>Registration Information</TITLE>");
        ps.println("</HEAD><BODY>");
        ps.println("<H2>This is the information you submitted</H2>");
        ps.println("<TABLE Border>");
        ps.println("<CAPTION>Your Registration Information</CAPTION>");
        ps.println("<TR><TD><B>Name</B></TD><TD>" +name +"</TD></TR>");
        ps.println("<TR><TD><B>Title</B></TD><TD>" +title +"</TD></TR>");
        ps.println("<TR><TD><B>Company</B></TD><TD>" +company +"</TD></TR>");
        ps.println("<TR><TD><B>Address</B></TD><TD>" +address +"</TD></TR>");
        ps.println("</TABLE>");
        ps.println("</BODY></HTML>");
        ps.flush();
    }
```

Connecting Your Servlet to a JDBC Database

The next step is to connect to a SQL database. The Java Database Connectivity package makes this possible. The servlet also uses a very simple SQL generator.

The `generator` class takes an object of the `DBRecord` class as an argument and returns a string containing SQL commands. `DBRecord` is a container class that holds the table's name, its primary key, and the names and values of the fields to be changed.

To increase the performance of the database queries, the servlet connects to the database in its `init()` method. This makes the servlet connect to the database as soon as it is loaded.

By telling Jeeves to load the servlet when the server starts up, you can reduce the overhead associated with reestablishing the connection for each request. See the previous section on loading servlets to learn how to make Jeeves load the servlet at startup.

```
Public class JDBCServlet extends FormServlet {
    Connection con;
    Statement stmt;

    public void init() {
    try {
```

```
        Class.forName("imaginary.sql.iMsqlDriver");
        String url = "jdbc:msql://pandora.scripps.edu:1112/userreg";
        connection = DriverManager.getConnection(url, "guest", "");
        } catch (Exception e) {
        System.out.println(e.getMessage());
        e.printStackTrace();
        }
        }
        public void destroy() throws Exception {
        ocn.close();
        }

}
```

The JDBCServlet's `init()` method made the connection to an `msql` database with the `imaginary.sql.iMsqlDriver`. The connection could have been made to any database with a JDBC driver. Even databases that use only ODBC could be used with an ODBC-JDBC bridge.

Note
The Weblogic Company has both pure Java JDBC drivers for most of the major RDBMSs and ODBC-JDBC bridges. To find out more, check out **http://www.weblogic.com/**.

Inserting Data in the Database

The next step is to override the `sendResponse` method. You put the information submitted with the form into a `DBRecord` object, and then you generate a string containing SQL commands with the `SQLgen` object.

Use that string in the `executeQuery` method of the JDBC `Statement` class. The Query returns a `ResultSet` object containing the response to your query, in the case of a search.

Listing 24.1 shows how data is inserted in a JDBC database. When the data is inserted in the database, the user gets an acknowledgment.

Caution
Since the Jeeves Web server is multithreaded, a servlet may be called by several handler threads simultaneously. You must make your servlets thread-safe by using synchronized methods and blocking when necessary.

Listing 24.1 JDBCSERVLET.JAVA—The *sendResponse* Method of the JDBCServlet

```
Public void sendResponse(Servlet res, Hashtable table)
throws Exception
{
     Statement stmt;
     SQLgen dbaction;
     ResultSet rs;

     // Create a new DBRecord object and fill its fields with
     // the values obtained from the HTML form.
     DBRecord rec = new DBRecord();
     rec.setTable("userreg");
     String name = (String) table.get("name");
     if (name.length() > 0) {
     rec.setField(new DBField("name", name);
     }
     String title = (String) table.get("title");
     if (title.length() > 0) {
     rec.setField(new DBField("title", title);
     }
     String company = (String) table.get("company");
     if (company.length() > 0) {
     rec.setField(new DBField("company", company);
     }
     String address = (String) table.get("address");
     if (address.length() > 0) {
     rec.setField(new DBField("address", address);
     }
     String action = (String) table.get("action");
     if (action.equals("Insert")) {
     rec.setActionInsert();
     }

     // Create a generator object with the completed DBRecord object.
     dbaction = new SQLgen(rec);
     // Create a JDBC Statement object.
     stmt = con.createStatement();
     // Execute the SQL query generated by the SQLgen object
     rs = stmt.executeQuery(dbaction.getSQL());
     stmt.close();

     // Create a new PrintStream to output an acknowledgment of the users
     // registration
     PrintStream ps = new PrintStream(res.getOutputStream());
     log("JDBCServlet running");
     res.setStatus(ServletResponse.SC_OK);
     res.setContentType("text/html");
     res.writeHeaders();
     ps.println("<HTML><HEAD>");
     ps.println("<TITLE>Registration Complete</TITLE>");
     ps.println("</HEAD><BODY>");
     ps.println("<H2>Thank you for registering</H2>");
     ps.println("</BODY></HTML>");
     ps.flush();
}
```

Searching the Database

You can make your servlet search the database and insert data into it by adding the following code fragments to the above `sendResponse` method. The first piece checks to see if the form's action was set to search.

If it is, the `action` field of the `DBRecord` object is also set to search. The second piece returns the search results in the form of an HTML table.

```
 if (action.equals("Search")) {
     rec.setActionInsert();
}

...

if (action.equals("Search")) {
     ps.println("<TABLE Border>");
ps.println("<TR><TD><B>Name</TD><TD>Title</TD><TD>Company</TD><TD>Address</TD></TR>");
     while(rs.next()) {
     String name = rs.getString(1);
     String title = rs.getString(2);
     String company = rs.getString(3);
     String address = rs.getString(4);

     ps.println("<TR><TD>" +name +"</TD><TD>" +title +"</TD><TD>" );
     ps.println(company +"</TD><TD>" + address +"</TD></TR>")
     }
     ps.println("</TABLE>");
 }
```

Following is the complete code listing for the JDBC Serlvet. This simple example shows the power of using Java on the server-side. Combining servlets with the JDBC makes a strong argument for server-side Java.

Listing 24.2 shows a simple autonomous agent system that takes advantage of another of Java's powerful features, object serialization.

Listing 24.2 JDBCSERVLET.JAVA—Complete Code for the JDBC Servlet

```
import java.sql.*;
import java.io.*;
import java.util.*;
import sun.server.http.*;
import java.servlet.*;
import db.*;

public class JDBCServlet extends FormServlet {
     Connection con;
     Statement stmt;

     public void init() {
     try {
     Class.forName("imaginary.sql.iMsqlDriver");
```

```
String url = "jdbc:msql://pandora.scripps.edu:1112/userreg";
con = DriverManager.getConnection(url, "guest", "");
} catch (Exception e) {
System.out.println(e.getMessage());
e.printStackTrace();
}
}
public void destroy(){
try {
          con.close();
} catch (Exception e) {
System.out.println(e.getMessage());
e.printStackTrace();
}

}

public void sendResponse(ServletResponse res, Hashtable table)
throws Exception
{
Statement stmt;
SQLgen dbaction;
ResultSet rs;

// Create a new DBRecord object and fill its fields with
// the values obtained from the HTML form.
     DBRecord rec = new DBRecord();
rec.setTable("userreg");
String name = (String) table.get("name");
if (name.length() > 0) {
rec.setField(new DBField("name", name));
}
String title = (String) table.get("title");
if (title.length() > 0) {
rec.setField(new DBField("title", title));
}
String company = (String) table.get("company");
if (company.length() > 0) {
rec.setField(new DBField("company", company));
}
String address = (String) table.get("address");
if (address.length() > 0) {
rec.setField(new DBField("address", address));
}
String action = (String) table.get("action");
if (action.equals("Insert")) {
rec.setActionInsert();
}
     if (action.equals("Search")) {
rec.setActionInsert();
}


// Create a generator object with the completed DBRecord object.
     dbaction = new SQLgen(rec);
     try {
```

24

continues

Listing 24.2 Continued

```
        // Create a JDBC Statement object.
    stmt = con.createStatement();
    // Execute the SQL query generated by the SQLgen object
    rs = stmt.executeQuery(dbaction.getSQL());
    stmt.close();

    // Create a new PrintStream to output an acknowledgment of the users
    // registration
        PrintStream ps = new PrintStream(res.getOutputStream());
        log("JDBCServlet running");
    res.setStatus(ServletResponse.SC_OK);
    res.setContentType("text/html");
    res.writeHeaders();
    ps.println("<HTML><HEAD>");
    ps.println("<TITLE>Registration Complete</TITLE>");
    ps.println("</HEAD><BODY>");
        ps.println("<H2>Thank you for registering</H2>");
        if (action.equals("Search")) {
    ps.println("<TABLE Border>");
    ps.println("<TR><TD><B>Name</TD><TD>Title</TD>");
            ps.println("<TD>Company</TD><TD>Address</TD></TR>");
            while(rs.next()) {
    name = rs.getString(1);
    title = rs.getString(2);
    company = rs.getString(3);
    address = rs.getString(4);

    ps.println("<TR><TD>" +name +"</TD><TD>" +title +"</TD><TD>" );
              ps.println(company +"</TD><TD>" + address
           +"</TD></TR>");

    }
    ps.println("</TABLE>");
    }
           if (action.equals("Insert")) {
        ps.println("<H2>This is the information you submitted</H2>");
    ps.println("<TABLE Border>");
    ps.println("<CAPTION>Your Registration Information</CAPTION>");
    ps.println("<TR><TD><B>Name</B></TD><TD>" +name +"</TD></TR>");
    ps.println("<TR><TD><B>Title</B></TD><TD>" +title +"</TD></TR>");
    ps.println("<TR><TD><B>Company</B></TD><TD>" +company +"</TD></TR>");
    ps.println("<TR><TD><B>Address</B></TD><TD>" +address +"</TD></TR>");
    ps.println("</TABLE>");
    }

    ps.println("</BODY></HTML>");
    ps.flush();

    } catch (Exception e) {
    System.out.println(e.getMessage());
    e.printStackTrace();
    }

}
}
```

Building a Simple Autonomous Agent System with Jeeves

This example shows how servlets can be used to create an environment in which small, self-contained Java programs can roam the Internet, gathering and processing information before returning home for debriefing. This example has five components: the agent, the remote agency servlet, the home agency servlet, the agent launcher, and the agent debriefing program.

The agent launcher instructs the agent of the information it is to retrieve from a particular JDBC database and then transports it to the destination. The remote agency servlet provides an environment where the agent can execute its `run` method, which then queries the specified database.

After that, the remote agency asks the agent where it lives and then sends it on its way. The home agency servlet then accepts the agent and stores it in a file for later debriefing. Finally, the agent debriefing program restores the agent and requests the information it was sent to retrieve.

This is a simple system designed only for illustration. A real system needs to use strict security measures, which Jeeves does provide through a servlet-specific, access-control list.

A real system also needs a way of advertising services that are accessible to agents. This way, agents can find new services themselves.

Using Object Serialization to Transport Agents Across the Internet

Java's object serialization provides transportation for your agent. Object serialization is the process of turning any Java object or graph of objects (an object and all the objects it is made up of) into a stream of information. This stream can be transported using any `OutputStream` or `InputStream` and restored to its original state when it reaches the other side.

Object serialization can be used to give persistence to an object by serializing an object into a file for later retrieval. This is done to the `JDBCAgent` in the following example.

Serializing an object is as easy as creating an `ObjectOutputStream` and calling its `writeObject` method with the object to be serialized as the argument.

```
ObjectOutputStream oos = ObjectOutputStream(socket.getOutputStream());
oos.writeObject(myobject);
```

Deserializing an object is just as straightforward. First, create an `ObjectInputStream` and call its `readObject` method with the object to be deserialized as the argument.

```
ObjectInputStream ois = ObjectInputStream(socket.getInputStream());
ois.readObject(myobject);
```

Note

The object serialization classes are not included with the JDK as of release 1.0.2. They can be downloaded with the Remote Method Invocation package from the Javasoft Web site.

Note

For more information on object serialization, see Sun's white paper: Java Object Serialization Specification, available at the Javasoft Web site (**http://www.javasoft.com/**).

Building the Remote Agency

Start by building the remote agency. The `RemoteAgencyServlet` class extends the `Servlet` class. Its sole purpose in Listing 24.3 is to deserialize the agent, execute the agent's `run` method, ask the agent where it lives, and send it on its way. Again, in a real system, you need to use careful security procedures.

Caution

This agency accepts any Java object that conforms to a simple interface and executes its `run` method. The servlet also bypasses all of Jeeves' built-in security procedures used to protect the server from remote servlets.

This is extremely dangerous in the real world. You should use strict access control on this servlet. At the same time, this example shows the power of servlets and Java.

Note

Jeeves provides an elaborate access-control mechanism that can be used to protect the server from dangerous agents. You can also create servlet-specific authentication procedures with the security classes.

Listing 24.3 REMOTEAGENCYSERVLET.JAVA—*The RemoteAgencyServlet* Class

```
import java.io.*;
import java.servlet.*;
import java.net.*;

public class RemoteAgencyServlet extends Servlet
{
     public String getServletInfo() {
          return "Remote Agent Servlet";
     }
     public void service(ServletRequest req, ServletResponse res)
     throws Exception
     {
     // Load the agent from the client's agent launcher
     ObjectInputStream ois = new ObjectInputStream(req.getInputStream());
     // Cast the incoming object to AgentInterface, which is a simple that
     // all agents must implement.
     AgentInterface agent = (AgentInterface) ois.readObject();
     // Call the agents run method.
     agent.run();

     // Now that the agent has completed its task, find out where it lives.
     URL agenthome = agent.getAgentHome();
     int port = agenthome.getPort();
     String host = agenthome.getHost();
     String file = agenthome.getFile();
     // Now that you know where the agent lives send it on its way.
     // Open up a connection to the agents home, which is a servlet compliant
     // web server.
     Socket socket = new Socket(host, port);
     PrintStream ps = new PrintStream(socket.getOutputStream());
     // Request to HomeAgentServlet from the web server
     ps.println("POST" +file);
     ps.flush();
     // Create an ObjectOutputStream
     ObjectOutputStream oos = new
     ObjectOutputStream(socket.getOutputStream());
     oos.writeObject(agent);
     oos.flush();
     }
}
```

24

Creating a Generic Agent Interface

Using agents from the `AgentInterface` interface allows new agents to be created to run on any servlet that knows the interface. This agent interface is simple, but other methods could be added.

The current interface has only three methods. The `run` method causes the agent to carry out the mission for which it was sent. The `getAgentHome` method is used by the remote agency to determine where to send the agent.

Finally, the `getAuthentication` method is used by the server to authenticate the agent. In this example, `getAuthentication` returns null.

```
import java.net.URL;
public interface AgentInterface {
     public void run();
     public URL getAgentHome();
     public String getAuthentication();
}
```

Implementing a Database Search Agent

The `JDBCAgent` uses the `AgentInterface`. This agent, shown in Listing 24.4, queries a JDBC database using much of the same code as the earlier database example. It has methods for specifying the remote host, database, JDBC driver, and the agent's home.

Listing 24.4 JDBCAGENT.JAVA—The *JDBCAgent* Class

```
import java.sql.*;
import java.io.*;
import java.util.*;
import java.net.URL;
import db.*;

public class JDBCAgent implements AgentInterface
{
     Connection con;
     Statement stmt;
     DBRecord rec;
     JDBCInfo jdbcinfo;
     Vector v;
     URL agenthome;

     public void run() {
     try {
     String url = jdbcinfo.getURL();
     String driver = jdbcinfo.getDriver();
     String user = jdbcinfo.getUser();
     String password = jdbcinfo.getPassword();
```

```
        Class.forName(driver);
        con = DriverManager.getConnection(url, user, password);
        stmt = con.createStatement();
        SQLgen dbaction = new SQLgen(rec);
        ResultSet rs = stmt.executeQuery(dbaction.getSQL());

        while(rs.next()) {
        Hashtable hashtable = new Hashtable();
        hashtable.put("name", rs.getString(1));
        hashtable.put("id", rs.getString(2));
        hashtable.put("company", rs.getString(3));
        hashtable.put("location", rs.getString(4));
        v.addElement(hashtable);
        }
        stmt.close();
        } catch (Exception e) {
        System.out.println(e.getMessage());
        e.printStackTrace();
        }
        }

        public Vector getResultVector() {
        return v;
        }
        public void setQuery(DBRecord rec) {
        this.rec = rec;
        }
        public void setJDBCInfo(JDBCInfo jdbcinfo) {
        this.jdbcinfo = jdbcinfo;
        }
        public void setAgentHome(URL agenthome) {
        this.agenthome = agenthome;
        }
        public URL getAgentHome() {
        return agenthome;
        }
        public String getAuthentication() {
        return null;
        }
}
```


Building the Home Agency

The `HomeAgencyServlet` stores returning agents until the user is ready to debrief them. This servlet deserializes an incoming agent and then stores it in a file (see Listing 24.5).

Listing 24.5 HOMEAGENCYSERVLET.JAVA—The *HomeAgency* Class

```
import java.io.*;
import java.servlet.*;
import java.net.*;
```

continues

Listing 24.5 Continued

```
public class HomeAgencyServlet extends Servlet
{
     public String getServletInfo()
     {
     return "Agent Home Servlet";
     }

     public void service(ServletRequest req, ServletResponse res)
     throws Exception
     {
     // create ObjectInputStream from the InputStream originating a the
RemoteAgencyServlet.
          ObjectInputStream ois = new
          ObjectInputStream(req.getInputStream());
          // Read in the Agent object from the stream.
     AgentInterface agent = (AgentInterface) ois.readObject();
     // open a file to store the agent in until debriefing
     FileOutputStream fos = new
FileOutputStream("/agents/storage/agent99");
     // Create an ObjectOutputStream pointing to the file
     ObjectOutputStream oos = new ObjectOutputStream(fos);
     // Write the agent to the file.
     oos.writeObject(agent);
     oos.flush();
     fos.close();
     }
}
```

Launching the Agent

The `AgentLauncher` sets the agent's mission and then transports it to the `RemoteAgencyServlet`. It uses a class called `JDBCInfo` to set the specific database information.

`JDBCInfo` is a container class that holds information on which database driver to use, the URL, and the user name and password for the database. The `AgentLauncher` then places the query in a `DBRecord` object.

Finally, it contacts the agency servlet on a remote HTTP server and uses object serialization to transport the agent to the remote agency (see Listing 24.6).

Listing 24.6 AGENTLAUNCHER.JAVA—The *AgentLauncher* Class

```
import java.io.*;
import java.util.*;
import java.net.*;
import db.*;

public class AgentLauncher {
     public static void main(String[] argv) throws Exception {
     JDBCAgent jdbcagent = new JDBCAgent();
```

```
        JDBCInfo jdbcinfo = new JDBCInfo();
        jdbcinfo.setDriver("imaginary.sql.iMsqlDriver");
        jdbcinfo.setURL("jdbc:msql://agency.agentworld.com:1112/agentdb");
        jdbcinfo.setUser("agent99");
        jdbcinfo.setPassword("");
        jdbcagent.setJDBCInfo(jdbcinfo);

        DBRecord rec = new DBRecord();
        rec.setTable("agents");
        rec.setPrimaryKey("recordnumber");
        rec.setField(new DBField("location", "North America"));
        rec.setActionSelect();
        jdbcagent.setQuery(rec);

        URL homeurl = new
URL("http://pandora.scripps.edu/servlet/homeagency");
        jdbcagent.setAgentHome(homeurl);

        Socket socket = new Socket("buddha", 8888);
        PrintStream ps = new PrintStream(socket.getOutputStream());
        ps.println("POST /servlet/RemoteAgency");
        ps.flush();
        ObjectOutputStream oos = new ObjectOutputStream(ps);
        oos.writeObject(jdbcagent);
        oos.flush();
        }
}
```

Debriefing the Agent

The `AgentDebriefing` class, shown in Listing 24.7, restores the agent from the file that it is stored in and requests the information it was sent to gather. This program is run by the user when the agent has returned. The `HomeAgency` could have been designed to send mail, letting the user know when an agent returns.

Listing 24.7 AGENTDEBRIEFING.JAVA—The *AgentDebriefing* class 24

```
import java.io.*;
import java.util.*;
import java.net.Socket;
import db.*;

public class AgentDebriefing {
        public static void main(String[] argv) throws Exception {
        JDBCAgent jdbcagent = new JDBCAgent();
        FileInputStream fis = new FileInputStream("/agents/storage/agent99");
        ObjectInputStream ois = new ObjectInputStream(fis);
        JDBCAgent agent = (JDBCAgent) ois.readObject();

        Vector v = agent.getResultVector();
        for (Enumeration e=v.elements(); e.hasMoreElements();) {
```

continues

Listing 24.7 Continued

```
        Hashtable hash = (Hashtable) (e.nextElement());
        System.out.println("Name: " +hash.get("name"));
        System.out.println("id: " +hash.get("id"));
        System.out.println("Company: " +hash.get("company"));
        System.out.println("location: " +hash.get("location"));
        }
        }
}
```

chapter 25

Writing Web Services for Jigsaw

by David P. Boswell

In this chapter

- **Review the architecture of the Jigsaw HTTP server.**
  Begin your tour of the Jigsaw server by going over the modules that make up the server and how they fit together.
- **Review the most important Jigsaw classes.**
  This section will review some of the important Java classes that make up the Jigsaw server. Emphasis will be placed on the many attributes defined in these classes that you can use to extend and control the behavior of Jigsaw.
- **Installation of the Jigsaw HTTP server.**
  You will go through the steps involved in installing the Jigsaw server under the UNIX or Microsoft Windows environment and cover basic server configuration tips and techniques. Your server will be ready to follow along with the examples in the rest of this chapter.
- **Add content to the Jigsaw HTTP server.**
  Adding content to the Jigsaw server involves more than simply placing the files to be exported in the correct location. You will install some existing text files in HTML format and some GIF files in your file system. Next, you will export the resource by indexing it into the Jigsaw server's name space. You will also go through the steps necessary to index an existing Java class into a server resource.
- **Extend the Jigsaw server by adding a Java resource.**
  Experience the real power of the Jigsaw server by writing a Java resource and making it available through your server's name space.
- **Create a filter in Java and add it to the server.**
  Another exciting design feature of the Jigsaw server allows you to add hooks into the request processing loop both before and after the resource has been retrieved. You will write a Java class to implement an access counter using this server feature.
- **Create a Java class to handle the HTTP *POST* method.**
  You will create a Java class to handle the HTTP POST *method, and be ready to replace existing CGI-based form processing using the power of Java. You will also be ready to implement exciting new interactive content on your Web site.*

Jigsaw is the first Web server written entirely in Java that is freely available and uses HyperText Transport Protocol (HTTP). Two of its major design goals are portability and extensibility. The Jigsaw server runs on most machines for which a Java environment is available. The author has tested the server in a number of these environments. Some examples are Microsoft Windows 95/NT, SunMicrosystems Solaris, and Linux. This chapter was developed using Jigsaw running on Linux 2.0 and a port of the Sun JDK. It was also tested with the Kaffe Java interpreter. The Jigsaw server can be extended by writing new resource objects in Java. One possible extension would be a replacement for CGI scripts. Using this extension does not preclude the use of normal CGI scripts. The support of regular CGI scripts allows you to migrate existing CGI applications into Jigsaw. Portability adds tremendous value to the Jigsaw server when you select a hardware and software base for your Web applications. This chapter focuses on the extensibility of the server.

Architectural Overview

Jigsaw is an object-oriented Web server. Each resource exported by the server is mapped to a Java object. Each resource can be configured independently and maintains its own state through a persistency mechanism provided by the Jigsaw runtime.

The major components of the Jigsaw server are the daemon module and the resource module.

Handling the HTTP Protocol with the Daemon Module

The daemon module deals with HTTP. It handles incoming connections creates new client objects, decodes requests, and sends replies.

The most important part of the daemon module is the HTTPD object. This object runs the main processing loop of the server handling incoming connections and managing other objects in the server process, such as:

- The authentication realm manager, which handles authentication of selected server resources.
- The client pool, which handles accepted connections.
- The logger, which logs server activity.
- The root resource of the server, which links the protocol module to the resource modules.
- The resource store manager, which is responsible for wrapping each file or directory into a Resource instance. This module also keeps track of all the loaded resources and unloads them when they do not appear to be needed.

Managing the Server Information Space with the Resource Module

The resource module is responsible for managing the information space of the server. Each exported resource is mapped to an instance of an `HTTPResource`. Each instance is created at configuration time, either manually or by the resource factory.

The resource factory creates `HTTPResource` instances out of existing data. Jigsaw can handle files and directories provided by the underlying file system. Like the rest of Jigsaw, you can extend the resource factory to handle more objects.

The resource module uses two databases, accessible via a forms-based interface. The extension database /Admin/Extensions and the directory template database are accessible at /Admin/DirectoryTemplates.

Maintaining Server State via Object Persistence

Jigsaw resources are persistent objects. They maintain their state across server invocations. A resource that wraps an existing object is created only once during the lifetime of the server. Changing the configuration after a resource has been indexed has no effect on resources that have already been created.

This design feature speeds up the server because indexing an existing object into a resource is a costly process involving the querying of multiple databases, such as the extensions and directory templates database.

If you want to change the configuration of a resource and reindex a selected part of your information space, the `DirectoryResourceEditor` object accessible via **http://your-host.your-domain:9999/Admin** allows you to reindex resources as needed.

If you want the whole site to be reindexed, stop the server, delete all .jigidx files, and restart it. This causes the server to reindex the whole site when it is restarted.

Tip

To do this quickly under UNIX, change to the root of your Jigsaw tree.

Then issue the following command:

```
find . -name .jigidx -exec rm {} \;
```

Under Windows: Start the Windows Explorer and select your Jigsaw directory. Select Tools, Find Files or Folders. Type **.jigidx** in the Names dialog box (note the leading "dot"). Choose Edit Select All and File Delete.

25

Pre and Post Request Processing with Resource Filters

The final important concept of Jigsaw is resource filters. A resource filter is a Java resource that contains a set of attributes and one or more methods. Like all other Jigsaw resources, its attributes are persistent. This provides some powerful possibilities, as you will see later in the filter example

Each HTTP request is processed by a target resource instance. Most resource classes provided by Jigsaw inherit from the `FilteredResource` class. All instances of this class inherit a set of filters that are subclasses of `ResourceFilter`.

This provides a callback to the filter twice during resource processing. Once during lookup, before the target has been selected, the `ingoingFilter` method is called with the request as a parameter. After the request has been processed by the target resource, the `outgoingFilter` method is called with both the request and reply as parameters.

Jigsaw Interface

Jigsaw provides many classes and attributes, listed in Table 25.1, that you can use to extend and control the behavior of the server. For the sake of space, you will only look at classes central to the Jigsaw server design, or those needed by the examples.

The *HTTPResource* Class

`HTTPResource` is the base class of all resources accessible through HTTP. It does not provide any implementation of the HTTP methods.

Table 25.1 Attributes Defined by *HTTPResource*

Attribute	Description
`parent`	The `parent` of a resource is the resource that is responsible for its loading in memory. All resources should have a `parent`, except for the server's root resource, whose parent is `null`. type: This attribute is a computed `ObjectAttribute`. default value: This attribute defaults to that of the resource that loaded it into memory.

Attribute	Description
`url`	This is the location of this resource within the servers exported name-space. It is a string that is parseable into a Java URL. type: This attribute is a computed `StringAttribute`. default value: This attribute defaults to the concatenation of the resource's parent URL attribute with its own name or identifier.
`server`	This is the name of the server that makes this resource accessible through HTTP. type: This attribute is a computed `ObjectAttribute`. default value: This attribute defaults to its parent's server attribute value.
`quality`	This is a rating of the quality of this resource's content. The rating is a number between 0.0 and 1.0. It is used by the `NegotiatedResource` to select among its set of variants. type: This attribute is a editable `DoubleAttribute`. default value: This attribute defaults to 1.0.
`title`	This is the title of this resource. This attribute can be computed from the resource content if the content is an HTML file that has some `<META>` tag, or if it is provided for informational purposes even if the resource's content type is not text/html. type: This attribute is a computed and/or editable `StringAttribute`. default value: This attribute is undefined.
`content-language`	This is the language of the resource. It is used by the `NegotiatedResource` to select among its set of variant resources. The value of this attribute can be extracted from the resource content if it is an HTML file that includes some appropriate `<META>` tag. Otherwise, it is provided for informational purposes. type: This attribute is a computed and/or editable `LanguageAttribute`. default value: This attribute is undefined.
`content-encoding`	This is the encoding method. This can only be a single token as described in the HTTP/1.0 protocol specification. type: This attribute is a computed and/or editable `EncodingAttribute`. default value: This attribute is undefined.
`content-type`	This is the `MIME` type of the resource. type: This attribute is a computed and/or editable `MIMETypeAttribute`. default value: This attribute is undefined.

continues

Table 25.1 Continued

Attribute	Description
`content-length`	This is the length of the resource's content. type: This attribute is a computed `IntegerAttribute`. default value: This attribute is undefined. It is up to subclasses of this resource to either generate it dynamically or cache it from the `FileResource`. The `FileResource` gets this information from calls to the file system.
`last-modified`	This is the date of the last modification to this resource. type: This attribute is a computed and/or editable `DateAttribute`. default value: This attribute is undefined. See the default value of content-length above for additional information.
`expires`	This is the date on which this resource expires. type: This attribute is a computed and/or editable `DateAttribute`. default value: This attribute is undefined. See the default value of content-length above for additional information.
`icon`	This is any icon to be associated with this resource. type: This attribute is an editable `StringAttribute`. default value: This attribute is undefined.
`maxage`	This attribute defines the allowed drift between the real content of a resource and the one that is sent as request replies. The bigger this value, the more efficient the server can be, since it can reuse cached request replies for a longer time. This attribute takes affect only if it is defined and if the resource provides a meaningful last-modified attribute value. type: This attribute is an editable `IntegerAttribute`. default value: This attribute is undefined.

The *FilteredResource* Class

A filtered resource is the resource that supports filters. By itself, a filtered resource does not define any new attributes. However, each of the filters attached to the resource maintain a shadow copy of the target resource attribute values.

So a filtered resource attribute value is looked up this way: First, all its filters are queried to locate the attribute needed. If one of them defines the attribute, then this value is returned.

This allows filters to shadow attribute values based on the processing they do on the resource reply. Otherwise, the appropriate filtered resource attribute value is returned. The `FilteredResource` class inherits from `HTTPResource`.

The *DirectoryResource* Class

The directory resource is the basic resource to export file-system directories. It keeps track of all its children resources, creates them dynamically if needed, and is also able to create negotiated resources on-the-fly. The `DirectoryResource` class inherits `HTTPResource` and `FilteredResource` (see Table 25.2).

Table 25.2 Attributes of *DirectoryResource*

Attribute	Description
`directory`	This is the physical directory that this resource exports. type: This attribute is a computed `FileAttribute` and is not saved. default value: This attribute is computed by concatenating, in the appropriate file-system-dependent way, the parent's resource directory value with this directory identifier.
`storeid`	This is the name of the file to be used as the resource store database in this directory. type: This attribute is an editable `FilenameAttribute` and is mandatory. default value: This attribute is computed by concatenating, in the appropriate file-system-dependent way, the parent's resource directory value with this directory identifier.
`relocate`	Should the directory produce a relocation reply when accessed through an invalid URL? A common way of handling invalid directory access is to produce a relocation reply so that the browser gets access to the directory through a valid URL. The URL **http://www.w3.org/pub** is invalid because pub is a directory. The correct URL is **http://www.w3.org/pub/**. When this flag is set to `true`, the directory resource produces the appropriate relocation reply. type: This attribute is an editable `BooleanAttribute` and is not saved. default value: This attribute value defaults to `true`.

25

continues

Table 25.2 Continued

Attribute	Description
`extensible`	Should this directory automatically stay in sync with the underlying physical directory? The directory resource maintains a cache of its list of children, which may be outdated if you change the directory through direct file system access. When this flag is `true`, the directory resource makes its best effort to stay in sync with the file system by adopting the following lookup algorithm. First, look up children in the cache list. If this fails, check to see if an appropriate file exists. If such a file exists, hand it to the `ResourceIndexer` and install the resulting resource, if any, as a new child of the directory resource. type: This attribute is an editable `BooleanAttribute`. default value: This attribute defaults to `true`.
`index`	This attribute should name an existing child resource that will be used as the index resource of the directory. All accesses to the directory will be delegated this resource. type: This attribute is an editable `StringAttribute`. default value: This attribute is computed by concatenating, in the appropriate file-system-dependent way, the parent's resource directory value with this directory identifier.
`icondir`	This is the name of a directory that holds the icons for this directory. Each `HTTPResource` has an optional icon attribute. When a directory resource needs to produce a listing it dereferences each icon relative to its icon directory. type: This attribute is an editable `StringAttribute`, specifying the path tothe icon directory. default value: This attribute defaults to /icons.
`dirstamp`	This is the date on which the directory resource last checked its consistency against the underlying physical directory. type: This attribute is a computed `DateAttribute` that is noneditable. default value: This attribute defaults to `-1` (undefined).

Attribute	Description
`negotiable`	Should the directory resource automatically create a `NegotiatedResource`? If this flag is true, the directory resource automatically creates negotiable resources on top of normal resources. Each time a new resource is added to the directory, the resource looks for a resource having the new child name with possibly different extensions. If it succeeds, either the resource found is already a negotiated resource, in which case the new child is added as one of its variant resources, or the negotiated resource must not already exist. The directory resource then creates it with only one variant, the new child resource. type: This attribute is an editable `BooleanAttribute`. default value: This attribute defaults to `false`.

The *FileResource* Class

This is the basic resource to process files. It allows you to export files and can be configured to handle the HTTP `PUT` method. The `FileResource` class inherits from `HTTPResource` and `FilteredResource`. The `FileResource` defines three attributes `filename`, `putable`, and `filestamp`, as shown in Table 25.3.

Table 25.3 Attributes of *FileResource*

Attribute	Description
`filename`	This is the optional name of the file to be served by the file resource. By default, the file resource serves the file having the same name as the resource. You can define this attribute to modify the URL to file mapping. For example, you can serve the file foo.html through the name oof.html by setting the foo.html filename attribute to oof.html. type: This attribute is an editable `FilenameAttribute`. default value: This attribute is undefined.
`putable`	Should the file resource support `PUT` requests? If this flag is true, the file resource object handles the HTTP `PUT` method by overwriting the resource's file with the new content. The old content is saved using the emacs backup convention (a ~ is appended to the original file name). Take care when enabling

25

continues

Table 25.3 Continued

Attribute	Description
	this feature. You'll probably want to use an authentication filter to ensure that only authorized users are allowed to change files on the server. type: This attribute is an editable `BooleanAttribute`. default value: This attribute defaults to `false`.
`filestamp`	This is the date on which the file resource last checked its consistency against the underlying physical file. type: This attribute is a computed `DateAttribute` which is noneditable. default value: This attribute defaults to `-1` (undefined).

Installation and Setup of the Jigsaw HTTP Server

Jigsaw is an easy server to install and set up. If you don't already have the Jigsaw server running, the following information will help you get a server installed and running as painlessly as possible.

Start your favorite browser and go to URL

http://www.w3.org/pub/WWW/Jigsaw/#Getting.

Select jigsaw.zip for Microsoft Windows 95/NT or jigsaw.tar.gz for UNIX.

When the file has finished downloading, unzip or gunzip and un-tar, as needed. Both archives unpack into a directory structure starting at Jigsaw. The archive has long filenames so make sure you have an unzip that can handle this situation correctly.

In the following discussion, the term *Windows* refers to Microsoft Windows 95/NT. Similarly, *UNIX* refers to the UNIX operating system.

In this sample setup, unpack the Windows archive to D:\ and /usr/www in UNIX. Call this BASEDIR for short. Make sure to replace BASEDIR as appropriate for your setup. In this example, use D:\ or /usr/www instead of BASEDIR.

Now let the Java interpreter know where to find the Jigsaw classes.

On Windows, type the command:

SET CLASSPATH=BASEDIR\Jigsaw\classes\jigsaw.zip

And on UNIX, choose one of the following, depending on your shell:

SH: CLASSPATH=BASEDIR/Jigsaw/classes/jigsaw.zip ; export CLASSPATH

or

CSH: setenv CLASSPATH BASEDIR/Jigsaw/classes/jigsaw.zip.

You are now ready to run the server for the first time. On Windows, type the following command:

java w3c.jigsaw.http.httpd -host your-host.your-domain -root BASEDIR\Jigsaw\Jigsaw.

If you are running UNIX, type:

java w3c.jigsaw.http.httpd -host your-host.your-domain -root BASEDIR/Jigsaw/Jigsaw.

Replace your-host.your-domain with the host name and domain of your machine.

Jigsaw starts executing, and you should see one of the following:

In Windows:

loading properties from: d:\Jigsaw\Jigsaw\config\httpd.props

[httpd]: listening at:http://your-host.your-domain:9999

In UNIX:

loading properties from: /usr/WWW/Jigsaw/Jigsaw/config/httpd.props

[httpd]: listening at:http://your-host.your-domain:9999

Now start your favorite browser and go to URL

http://your-host.your-domain:9999.

Finally, read the configuration tutorial and other documentation that comes with the server. No configuration changes are needed to follow along with the examples in this chapter.

Note

If your server will be accessible by others, you'll want to use the section on protecting the Admin resource in the Jigsaw documentation.

(http://your-host.your-domain:9999/User/Tutorials/configuration.html#authentication)

Caution

There is a security problem in the current version of Jigsaw. Make sure you understand the implications, especially if you are running UNIX.

As of version 1.0, Jigsaw does not give up its root privileges, so you may want to use another port such as 8080 or the default 9999, and run the server as a normal user. There are plans to add system calls to switch to a nonprivileged user in the next Jigsaw release.

Tip

Using the telnet program, you can verify that your server is working without having to access a browser. On UNIX, type **telnet your-host.your-domain 9999** when you see:

```
Connected to your-host.your-domain
Escape character is "^]".
```

type **HEAD / HTTP/1.0** and press Enter twice.

The server should return:

```
HTTP/1.0 200 OK
Content-Length: 701
Content-Type: text/html
Last-Modified: 25 May 1996 15:05:56 GMT
Server: Jigsaw/1.0a
Date: 22 Aug 1996 23:00:33 GMT
```

You can also start the Windows telnet program and select Connect Remote System. Enter the Host Name and replace the telnet Port with **9999** in the dialog box. Then type the line: **HEAD / HTTP/1.0** and press Enter twice.

Adding Content to the Jigsaw Server

Now that you have the server running, you can add some content. By default, additional content is added to Jigsaw in the BASEDIR/Jigsaw/Jigsaw/WWW directory tree. Be sure you change your directory to the one listed above before continuing.

Obtain either example.zip or example.tar. Unzip or untar the archives as appropriate. This extracts a small collection of html and gif files under the que directory.

Now start your browser and go to **HTTP://your-host.your-domain/que/**. This brings up a directory-style listing of the files just extracted, as seen in Figure 25.1—not quite what you wanted, so now open the URL **HTTP://your-host.your-domain/Admin/Editor/que**.

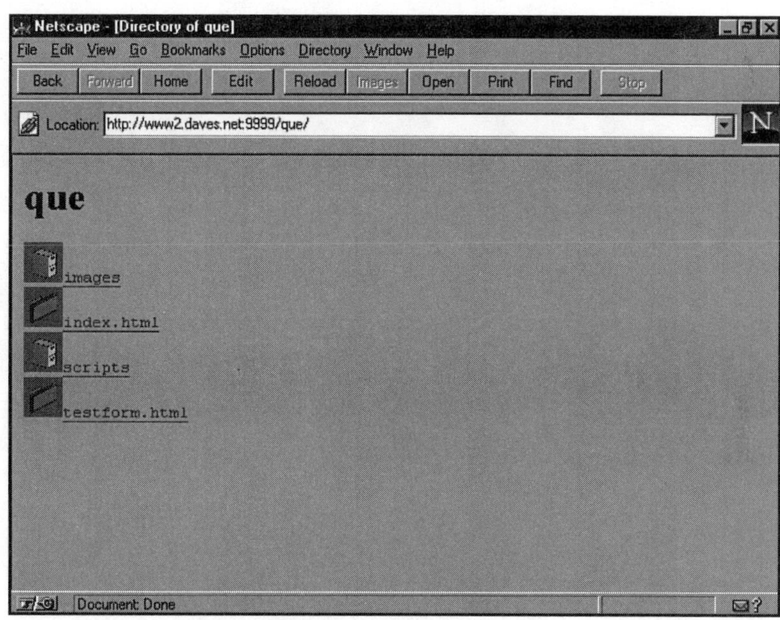

Fig. 25.1
Results of opening ***http://your-host.your-domain:9999/que/***.

Move on to the form now displayed and change the entry index: to index.html. Then click the OK button at the bottom of the page as shown in Figure 25.2. Reopen the URL **HTTP://your-host.your-domain/que/**. This time you see the content of index.html shown in Figure 25.3 instead of the directory listing.

Note

You may need to clear your browser's cache so the URL is displayed correctly.

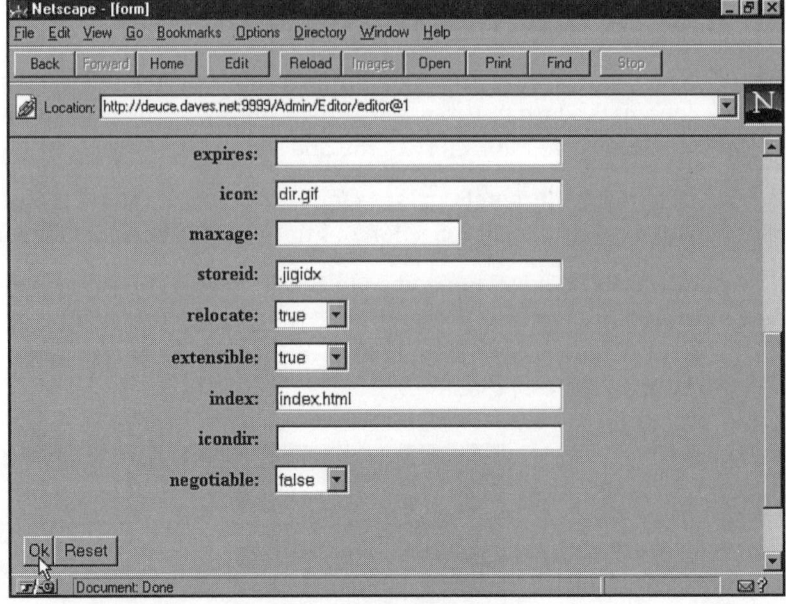

Fig. 25.2
Form to add index.html as the index for the que resource.

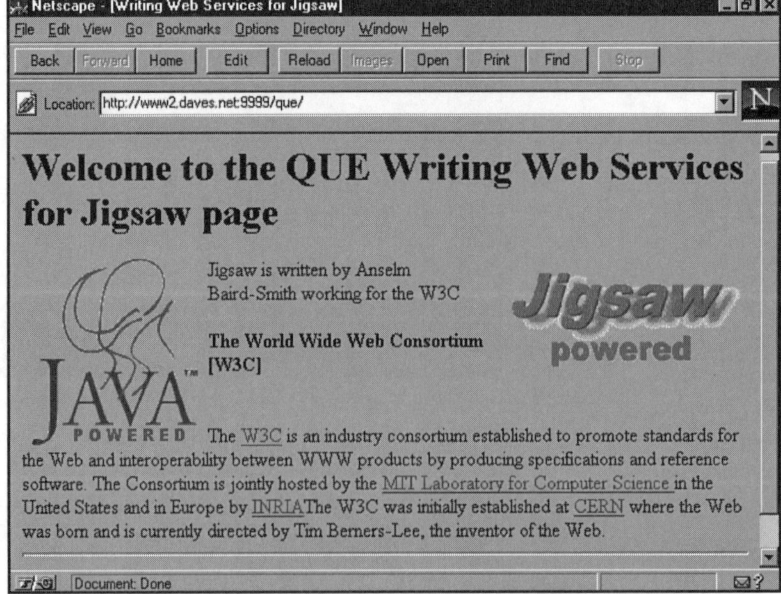

Fig. 25.3
Browser rendered contents of que/index.html.

Finally, add an existing Java class to your que resource.

Open URL **HTTP://your-host.your-domain/Admin/Editor/que** and select the AddingResources link at the bottom of the page. Enter **Memory** in the `name:` field. Enter **w3c.jigsaw.status.GcStat** in the `class:` field and press the OK button as seen in Figure 25.4.

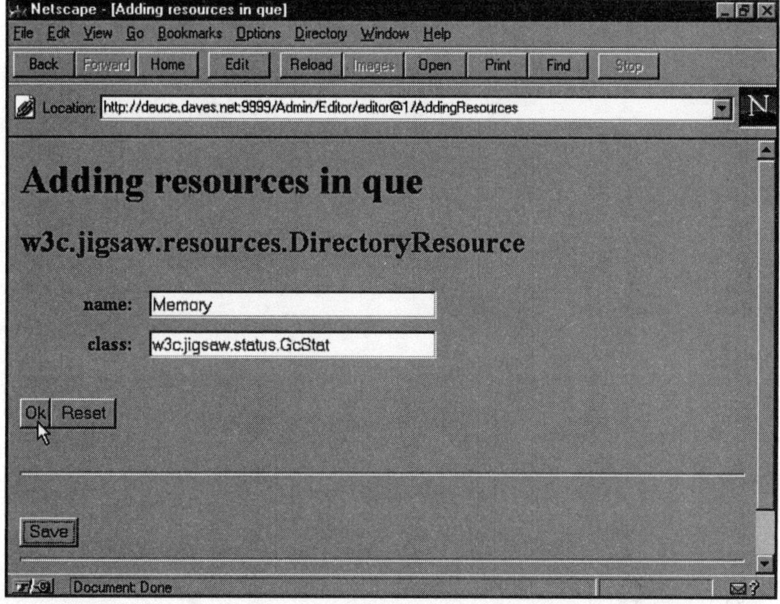

Fig. 25.4
Form to add a Java resource to the server namespace.

Opening the URL **HTTP://your-host.your-domain/que/Memory** should now show the memory status for your server, as seen in Figure 25.5.

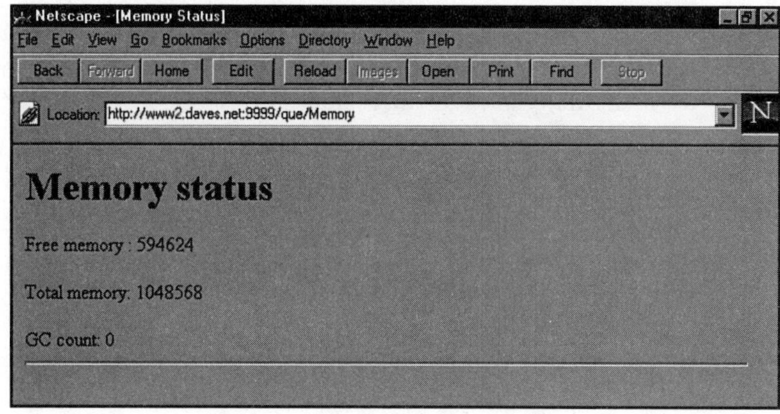

Fig. 25.5
Results of accessing the Java resource added as ***que/Memory****.*

As you can see, it is easy to add existing document trees to the server and specify a start page for the tree.

Extending the Server with Java

You can now get down to writing your own Java classes to extend your server. Start off with something simple.

The first step in writing your resource is choosing a super class, as follows:

- If you are adding a dynamic resource like the `GcStat` class, as described in the previous section, create a subclass of `HTTPResource`.
- If the intent is to serve files, create a subclass of `FileResource`.
- If your resource is being designed to handle forms, create a subclass of `PostableResource`.
- If your new resource will have child resources, create a subclass of `DirectoryResource`.

For this example, use `HTTPResource`. The only other initial decision you need to make is the package name for your new resource. Jigsaw does not impose any restrictions on the name you assign your package as long as the Java interpreter can find it via the `CLASSPATH` environment variable.

Caution
Security Note: Keep in mind the possibility of someone adding code to your server via `CLASSPATH` if it points to a world/group writable directory.

Unzip or untar the classes.zip or classes.tar file to BASEDIR/Jigsaw. This creates files under BASEDIR/Jigsaw/que/que/examples.

You now know enough to create the BASEDIR/Jigsaw/que/que/examples/HelloJigsaw.java (refer to Listing 25.1) source file, as follows:

```
package que.examples

import w3c.jigsaw.http.*;

import w3c.jigsaw.resources.*;
```

```
import w3c.jigsaw.html.*;

public class HelloJigsaw extends HTTPResource {
```

Now you need to decide on the attributes for your new resource. To keep things simple, only deal with the message text returned by your resource.

```
// message attribute index
protected static int ATTR_MESSAGE = -1 ;

static {
   Attribute attrib  = null ;
   Class   HelloClass = null ;

   try {
       HelloClass = Class.forName("que.examples.HelloJigsaw");
   } catch (Exception ex) {
       ex.printStackTrace() ;
       System.exit(1) ;
   }
```

After declaring your attributes, register them with the `AttributeRegistery`. The registry keeps track of all the attributes of all resource classes. For each class the registry knows about, it maintains an ordered list of the attributes declared by the class.

The attribute registry returns an index for each attribute that is registered. You can use the index as a parameter to the `setValue` and `getValue` methods of the `AttributeHolder` class to obtain the attribute value.

```
         // register our message attribute:
         attrib = new StringAttribute("message", "Hello Jigsaw World!",
➥Attribute.EDITABLE);
         ATTR_MESSAGE = AttributeRegistery.registerAttribute
➥(HelloClass, attrib) ;
     }
```

Now, implement the behavior of your resource. The only HTTP method this resource allows is the `GET` method. Generate a reply at each invocation of this resource using the `HtmlGenerator` class provided by Jigsaw.

```
      // Print our message in response to the HTTP GET request

   public Reply get(Request request)
    throws HTTPException {
   // create HTML generator and fill in titles:
       HtmlGenerator gen = new HtmlGenerator("HelloJigsaw");
       gen.append("<h1>Our first Jigsaw extension demo</h1>");
       // print our message:
       gen.append("<p>"+getValue(ATTR_MESSAGE, null));

       // finish off the reply
```

25

```
      Reply rep = request.makeReply(HTTP.OK) ;
      rep.setStream(gen) ;
      return rep ;
   }
}
```

Listing 25.1 *HelloJigsaw.java*—A Class to Respond to the HTTP *GET* Method

```
package que.examples ;

import w3c.jigsaw.http.*;
import w3c.jigsaw.resources.*;
import w3c.jigsaw.html.*;

public class HelloJigsaw extends HTTPResource {
 // message attribute index
 protected static int ATTR_MESSAGE = -1;

 static {
  Attribute attrib  = null;
  Class   HelloClass = null;

  try {
   HelloClass = Class.forName("que.examples.HelloJigsaw");
  } catch (Exception ex) {
   ex.printStackTrace();
   System.exit(1);
  }
  // register our message attribute:
  attrib = new StringAttribute("message", "Hello Jigsaw World!", Attribute.EDITABLE);
  ATTR_MESSAGE = AttributeRegistery.registerAttribute(HelloClass, attrib);
 }

 // Print our message in response to the HTTP GET request

 public Reply get(Request request)
  throws HTTPException {
   // create HTML generator and fill in titles:
   HtmlGenerator gen = new HtmlGenerator("HelloJigsaw");
   gen.append("<h1>Our first Jigsaw extension demo</h1>");
   // print our message:
   gen.append("<p>"+getValue(ATTR_MESSAGE, null));


   // finish off the reply
   Reply rep = request.makeReply(HTTP.OK) ;
   rep.setStream(gen);
   return rep;
 }

}
```

Now add your new resource to the server. First, stop the server and update the `CLASSPATH` environment variable so the server can find your new class.

Under Windows:

```
SET CLASSPATH=BASEDIR\Jigsaw\classes\jigsaw.zip;BASEDIR\Jigsaw\que
```

And on UNIX:

```
SH: CLASSPATH=BASEDIR/Jigsaw/classes/jigsaw.zip:BASEDIR/Jigsaw/que ;
➥export CLASSPATH
```

or

```
CSH: setenv CLASSPATH BASEDIR/Jigsaw/classes/jigsaw.zip:BASEDIR/Jigsaw/que.
```

Restart the server.

Open the URL **http://your-host.your-domain:9999/Admin/Editor/que**.

Select the `AddingResources` link at the bottom of the page.

Type **Hello** in the name: field.

Type **que.examples.HelloJigsaw** in the `class:` field and click OK as shown in Figure 25.6.

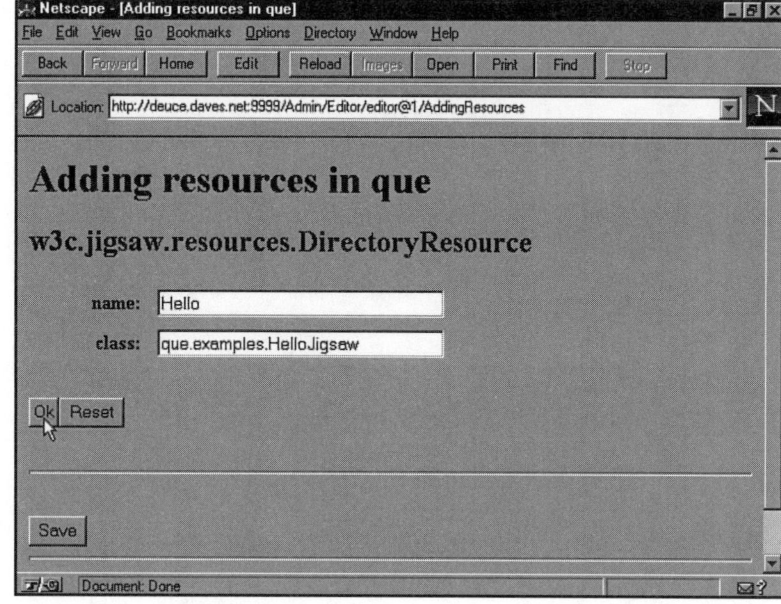

Fig. 25.6
Form to add your `Hello Java` *resource to the server's namespace.*

25

If Jigsaw returns the error message "The field class has an incorrect value," verify that the class name was entered correctly. If the class value is correct, check the CLASSPATH variable in your environment.

You are returned to the Admin/Editor/que screen if the change was successful. Opening URL **http://your-host.your-domain:9999/que/Hello** will execute the new class returning the text "Hello Jigsaw World!"

Writing Resource Filters in Java

As most resource classes provided by Jigsaw descend from FilteredResource, they inherit a set of filters that are sub-classes of ResourceFilter, providing a callback twice during resource processing. Now create a class to use this function (see Listing 25.2).

```
package que.examples.filter;

import w3c.jigsaw.http.*;
import w3c.jigsaw.resources.*;

public class CountingFilter extends ResourceFilter {
   // counter attribute index.
  protected static int ATTR_COUNTER = -1 ;

  static {
    Attribute counterattrib  = null ;
    Class   CountingClass = null ;

    try {
      CountingClass = Class.forName("que.examples.filter.CountingFilter") ;
    } catch (Exception ex) {
      ex.printStackTrace() ;
      System.exit(1) ;
    }
```

Now create an attribute for your class, an integer. This attribute is persistent so this is all you need to do to keep a filtered count for the lifetime of your server.

```
    counterattrib = new IntegerAttribute("counter"
                , new Integer(0)
                , Attribute.EDITABLE) ;
    ATTR_COUNTER = AttributeRegistery.registerAttribute(CountingClass, counterattrib);
  }
```

This method is called during resource lookup with the HTTP request as the parameter.

```
  public synchronized int ingoingFilter(Request request) {
     // get our counter attribute
    int i = getInt (ATTR_COUNTER, 0) ;
    // put it back plus one
    setInt(ATTR_COUNTER, i+1) ;
```

Returning DontCallOutgoing informs the target filtered resource that you have done your work and your outgoingFilter method does not need to be called after resource processing. Also, you do not need to declare an `outgoingFilter` method because your superclass provides an empty method.

```
        return DontCallOutgoing ;
      }
    }
```

Listing 25.2 shows the `CountingFilter` class.

Listing 25.2 *CountingFilter.java*—Count Number of "Hits" on Filtered Resource

```
package que.examples.filter;

import w3c.jigsaw.http.*;
import w3c.jigsaw.resources.*;

public class CountingFilter extends ResourceFilter {
 // counter attribute index.
 protected static int ATTR_COUNTER = -1 ;

 static {
  Attribute counterattrib  = null ;
  Class   CountingClass = null ;

  try {
   CountingClass = Class.forName("que.examples.filter.CountingFilter") ;
  } catch (Exception ex) {
   ex.printStackTrace() ;
   System.exit(1) ;
  }

  counterattrib = new IntegerAttribute("counter"
      , new Integer(0)
      , Attribute.EDITABLE) ;
  ATTR_COUNTER = AttributeRegistery.registerAttribute(CountingClass, counterattrib) ;
 }

 public synchronized int ingoingFilter(Request request) {
  // get our counter attribute
  int i = getInt (ATTR_COUNTER, 0) ;
  // put it back plus one
  setInt(ATTR_COUNTER, i+1) ;
  return DontCallOutgoing ;
 }
}
```

Now plug your filter into the server. If you followed along with the previous section, your server does not need any changes. If not, go back and update your `CLASSPATH` environment variable and restart the server as detailed in the previous section.

Open URL **http://your-host.your-domain:9999/Admin/Editor/que** to edit the properties of the que directory resource. Follow the `AddFilter` link at the bottom of the page.

Enter **que.examples.filter.CountingFilter** in the Filter's `class`: field and click OK, as shown in Figure 25.7. This creates two additional links at the bottom of the `que.examples.filter.CountingFilter` page.

These new links access the properties of the filter. Here you see a single attribute counter that is initially set to 0. You do not need to enter anything in the `identifier`: field on this page.

A link to `ShadowByque.examples.filter.CountingFilter` is also added to the page. This takes you to attributes shadowed by `que.examples.filter.CountingFilter`. Nothing needs to be changed there.

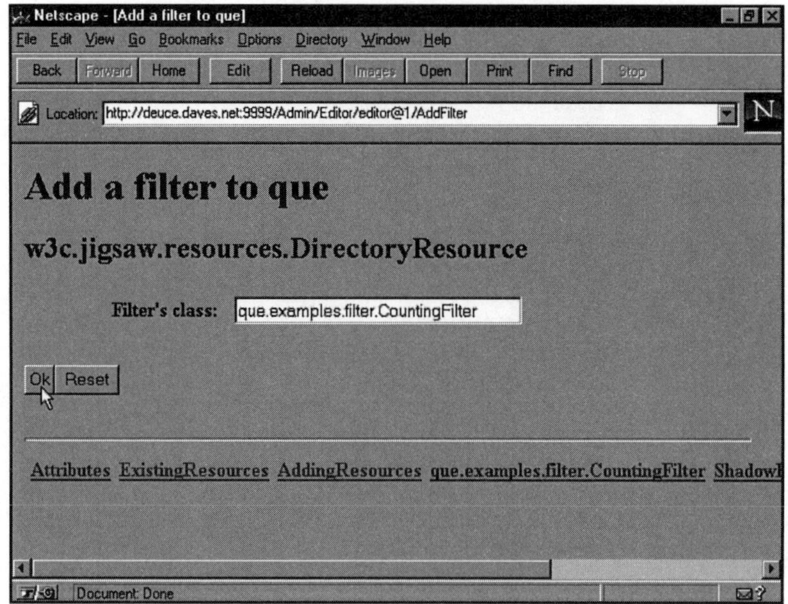

Fig. 25.7
Form to add your Java filter to the server's namespace.

Now when the resource `que` is requested from your server, the `ingoingFilter` method of `CountingFilter` will be called incrementing the integer attribute counter. You can reload the filters attribute page to view the counter as shown in Figure 25.8.

Note

Due to a bug in version 1.0 of Jigsaw, this field display is not updated. You need to restart the server via /Admin/PropertiesEditor for the updates to be viewable.

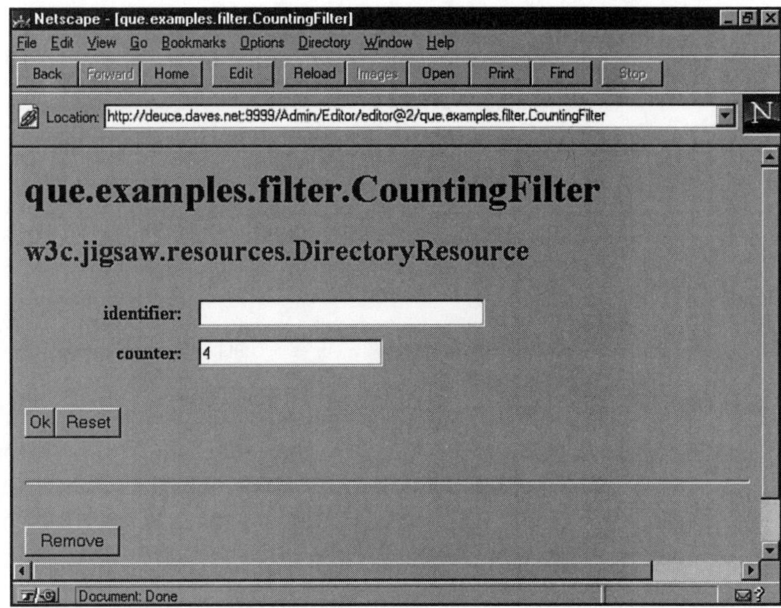

Fig. 25.8
Viewing the value of your counter filter attribute.

Handling Forms and the *POST* Method in Java

Complete your look inside the Jigsaw server by using a class to handle the HTTP POST method (refer to Listing 25.3).

```
package que.examples.postable;

import w3c.jigsaw.forms.*;
import w3c.jigsaw.html.*;
import w3c.jigsaw.http.*;
import w3c.jigsaw.resources.*;

import java.util.*;


public class JigsawPost extends PostableResource
{

 protected static int ATTR_NAME   = -1 ;

 protected final static String NAME   = "Name:";
```

Here you could place any number of form elements as attributes. This code is like the other extension examples you covered in the previous two sections.

```
static {
 Attribute attrib   = null ;
 Class   JPostClass = null ;
```

25

```
try
 {
   JPostClass = Class.forName("que.examples.postable.JigsawPost") ;
  } catch (Exception ex) {
   ex.printStackTrace() ;
   System.exit(1) ;
  }
  // register our attribute(s)
  attrib  = new StringAttribute(NAME , "", Attribute.EDITABLE) ;
  ATTR_NAME = AttributeRegistery.registerAttribute(JPostClass, attrib) ;
}


// method to handle data from POST request
public Reply handle (Request request, URLDecoder data)
 throws HTTPException
{
```

Here you do the work of handling the data resulting from the POST method. Now you could pick up form data, validate it, and perhaps place it in a database or send the data using a Java interface to sendmail. For this example, print out the posted data. This gives you a nice debugging resource.

```
  // print out the variables we received
  // a handy object to have around when testing postable forms
  Enumeration  en = data.keys() ;
  HtmlGenerator gen = new HtmlGenerator ("POST method decoded values") ;
  gen.append ("<p>List of variables and corresponding values:</p><ul>") ;
  while ( en.hasMoreElements () ) {
   String name = (String) en.nextElement() ;
   gen.append ("<li><em>"
        + name+"</em> = <b>"
        + data.getValue(name)
        + "</b></li>");
  }

  gen.append ("</ul>") ;
  Reply reply = request.makeReply(HTTP.OK) ;
  reply.setStream (gen) ;
  return reply ;
 }


}
```

Adding this postable object to the server is like the examples in the previous sections. Open URL **http://your-host.your-domain/Admin/Editor/que**. Select the Adding-Resources link. Enter **PostTest** for the name: field and **que.examples.postable. JigsawPost** for the class: field. Press OK to add the resource as shown in Figure 25.9.

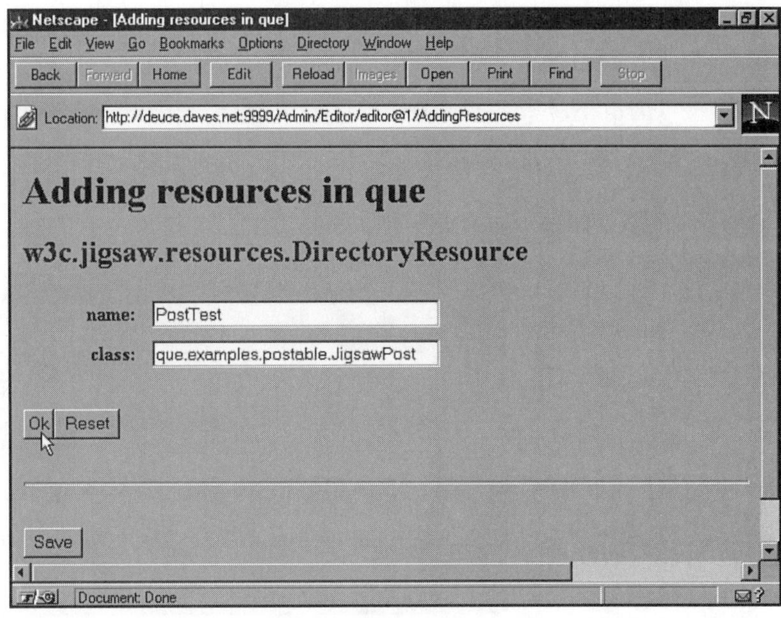

Fig. 25.9
Form adding your PostTest Java resource to the server's namespace.

If you open the URL **http://your-host.your-domain:9999/que/PostTest**, Jigsaw returns the error message "Document not found. The document /que/PostTest is indexed but not available." To test the object, use the following URL:

http://your-host.your-domain:9999/que/PostTest?name=dave;

which returns the output shown in Figure 25.10.

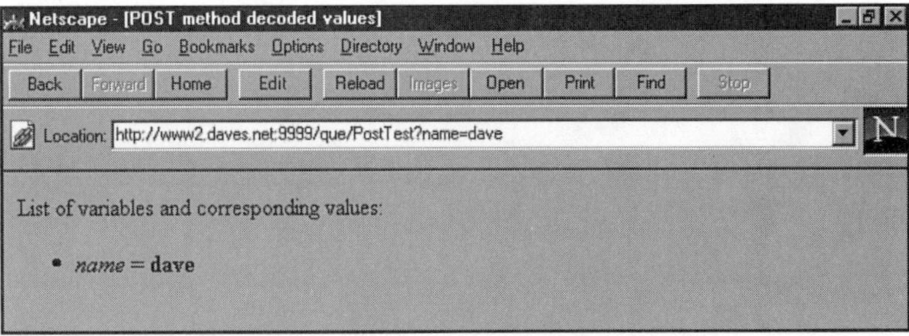

Fig. 25.10
Result of accessing the `PostTest` *resource.*

Normally, to use a resource like this you would use HTML code such as:

```
<FORM METHOD="POST" ACTION="/que/PostTest">Name:
<INPUT TYPE="text" NAME="name" MAXLENGTH=32><br>
<INPUT TYPE="reset" VALUE="Reset">
<INPUT TYPE="submit" VALUE="Ok">
```

An sample form can be viewed with the URL **http://your-host.your-domain:9999/que/testform.html** seen in Figure 25.11.

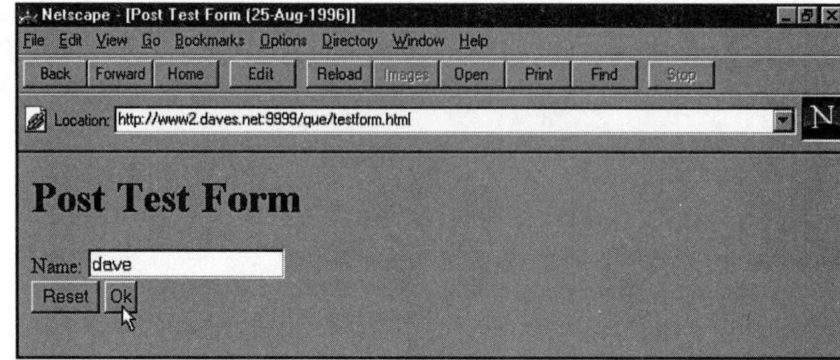

Fig. 25.11
Example of the Post Test HTML form.

Listing 25.3 shows the `JigsawPost` class.

Listing 25.3 *JigsawPost.java*—Class to Implement HTTP *POST* Method

```
package que.examples.postable;

import w3c.jigsaw.forms.*;
import w3c.jigsaw.html.*;
import w3c.jigsaw.http.*;
import w3c.jigsaw.resources.*;

import java.util.*;


public class JigsawPost extends PostableResource
{

 protected static int ATTR_NAME   = -1 ;

 protected final static String NAME   = "Name:";

 static {
  Attribute attrib   = null ;
  Class   JPostClass = null ;
```

```
    try
     {
       JPostClass = Class.forName("que.examples.postable.JigsawPost") ;
     } catch (Exception ex) {
       ex.printStackTrace() ;
       System.exit(1) ;
     }
     // register our attribute(s)
     attrib  = new StringAttribute(NAME , "", Attribute.EDITABLE) ;
     ATTR_NAME = AttributeRegistery.registerAttribute(JPostClass, attrib) ;
   }


   // method to handle data from POST request
   public Reply handle (Request request, URLDecoder data)
    throws HTTPException
   {

    // print out the variables we received
    // a handy object to have around when testing postable forms
    Enumeration  en = data.keys() ;
    HtmlGenerator gen = new HtmlGenerator ("POST method decoded values") ;
    gen.append ("<p>List of variables and corresponding values:</p><ul>") ;
    while ( en.hasMoreElements () ) {
     String name = (String) en.nextElement() ;
     gen.append ("<li><em>"
          + name+"</em> = <b>"
          + data.getValue(name)
          + "</b></li>");
    }

    gen.append ("</ul>") ;
    Reply reply = request.makeReply(HTTP.OK) ;
    reply.setStream (gen) ;
    return reply ;
   }


  }
```

You should now know enough about Jigsaw to add exciting new content to the World Wide Web. Drop me a note and tell me about your projects. My e-mail address is **dave@daves.net**.

PART VI

Java Security

chapter 26

Securing Applets with Digital Signatures

26

by Mark Wutka

In this chapter

- **What are digital signatures?**
  Digital signatures have become an important part of secure transactions. Many people still don't understand what digital signatures are, what they do, and how they work.
- **Securing applets with digital signatures**
  A recent approach to applet security has been to allow applets more access when they have been digitally signed. This allows a trusted software company to create applets that perform more functions than a typical applet.
- **Verifying signatures**
  Digital signatures aren't any good unless you can verify their authenticity. There are several ways you can verify a signature.
- **Potential security problems with digital signatures**
  While digital signatures themselves are very secure, if you are careless in using them, you can open yourself up to security breaches.

One of the biggest hindrances to some Java developers has been the security restrictions placed on applets. Many applet developers want to be able to connect to other sites on the network or to access files on the local hard disk.

You could argue that the restriction on file access is a good thing, since you may soon be writing applets for computers that have no local storage. The network restrictions, however, are another matter.

The reason for the harsh restrictions on network connections is that many users sit safely behind their company's firewall. A firewall protects the company network from outside intruders who might want to steal data or tamper with the systems.

Generally, a firewall allows access out to the Internet but does not allow sites on the Internet to access hosts on the other side of the firewall.

A Java applet with no security restrictions thwarts the firewall because it can access all the hosts on the local network. Anyone who wants to snoop around for data or damage your systems could write an applet that connects to various machines on your network, test the machines for any security holes, and then exploit those holes.

This could all happen without you knowing it. The applet might be a simple scrolling-text applet sending you nice happy messages while it merrily ravages your network.

This security problem comes about because you can download a Java applet and run it without even knowing it. Normally, this is an advantage.

You don't *want* to know that you are downloading applets and you don't want to do anything special to download them. But in the case of security, this is another matter.

When you download a software package, you have a certain amount of trust toward the vendor of the software. If it's a shareware program off some big archive, you might be cautious enough to run a virus checker on the program before you run it. Of course, you should do that all the time, but many people don't learn until they get bitten by a virus.

You are willing, however, to let this program have complete access to your local system. For all you know, it could snoop around your network just as well as an unrestricted applet could.

Many companies get upset at you for loading "unapproved" software for just this reason. You could expose your entire company's network to an outside attack.

You don't usually worry about this sort of thing from a well-known company like Netscape, Sun, or Microsoft. You have some degree of trust in them, partially because you know that they would be out of business if they got a reputation for distributing malicious software.

It would be nice if Java were able to establish some level of trust for each applet it loads. If you were able to verify that an applet came from Sun, you might be willing to give it a lot more access than from pHrEakR's hAvEN. Digital signatures allow you to do precisely that.

What Are Digital Signatures?

A digital signature is an offshoot of data encryption. When you encrypt data, you use a piece of information called a *key* to scramble your data.

The person you send the data to then uses the same key or another key to descramble the data. The several forms of encryption are discussed in Chapter 27, "Encrypting Data."

The encryption used with digital signatures is called *public key encryption.* The idea behind public key encryption is simple. When you want to receive data via public key encryption, you create a public key and a corresponding private key, and then publish the public key for all to see.

Whenever someone wants to send you an encrypted message, they use your public key to encode the data. When you receive it, you use your private key to decode the data.

The trick here is that you can't decode the data with the public key; you can only encrypt it. And it is usually computationally impossible to determine the private key from the public key.

The idea behind a digital signature is that you use a special form of encryption to create a much smaller version of your data. This smaller version of the data is the *signature* of the data.

The encrypted information in a digital signature is not a complete representation of the data—that is, you couldn't decode it and get the original information back. In other words, a digital signature is something of a one-way encoding. You can't get the original information back, but given the original information, you can verify that it was signed with a particular key. Since the signature is generated using all of the original information, if you changed even a tiny part of the original information, the digital signature would be completely different. Furthermore, you can't predict what the new digital signature will be when you change a portion of the original information. This keeps others from tampering with digitally signed information.

When someone sends you digitally signed information, they must send you both the original information and the signature generated for that information. You then use their public key to verify that the signature was generated by them. Unlike normal encryption, where the intent is to hide information, a digital signature is intended to verify the origin and contents of the information.

As shown in Figure 26.1, Bob's Software digitally signs an applet using Bob's private key.

Next, Bob's Software sends you both the applet and the applet's digital signature, as shown in Figure 26.2.

Now, as shown in Figure 26.3, you verify the signature against the applet using Bob's well-known public key. The signature algorithm tells you whether the signature was generated by the private key corresponding to Bob's public key.

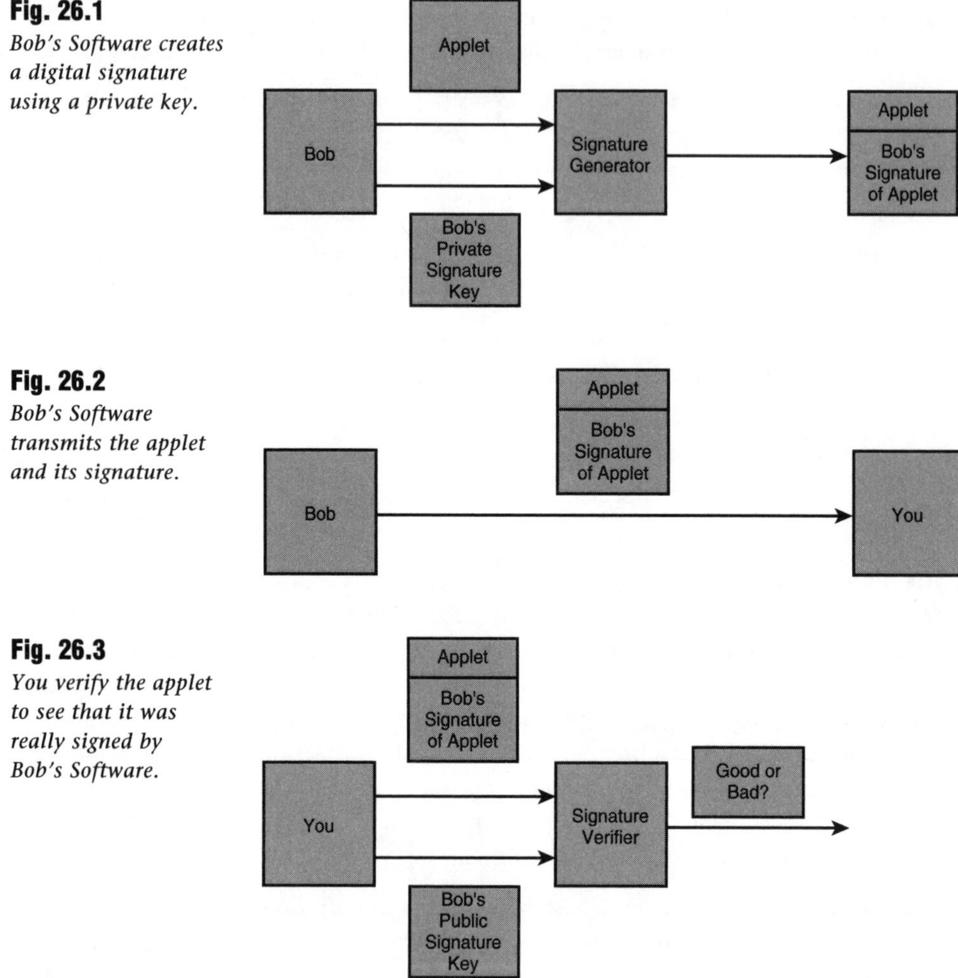

Fig. 26.1
Bob's Software creates a digital signature using a private key.

Fig. 26.2
Bob's Software transmits the applet and its signature.

Fig. 26.3
You verify the applet to see that it was really signed by Bob's Software.

Now, suppose a malicious person who has a bit of ingenuity can intercept the applet transmission from Bob's software and substitute a phony applet. In addition to the phony applet, the malicious person either forwards Bob's original signature or creates a valid digital signature for the applet, but using a different private key.

Figure 26.4 shows a possible scenario for this.

When you receive the phony applet, you check the applet and its signature against Bob's public key, as shown in Figure 26.5. You find that the applet was not sent by Bob's Software.

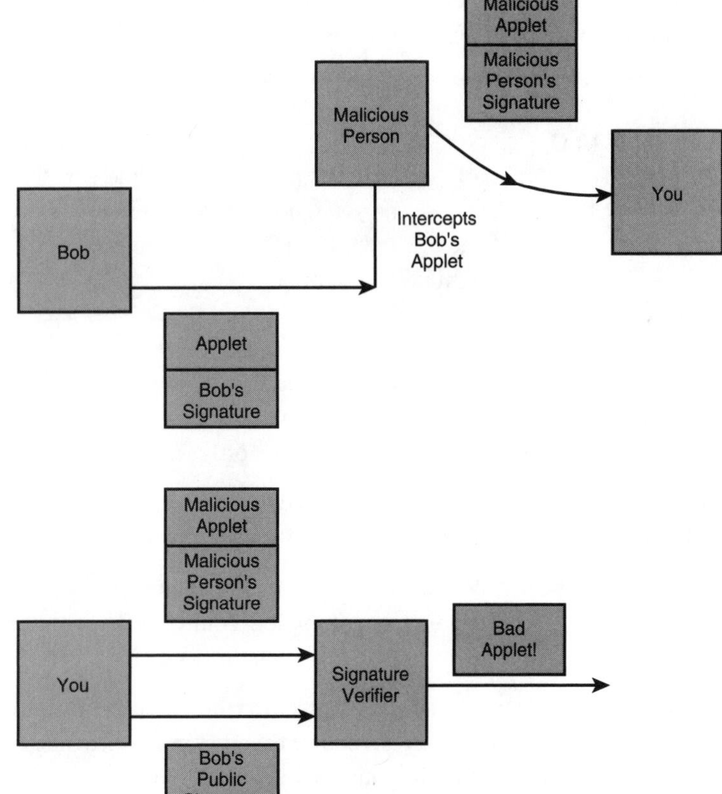

Fig. 26.4
A malicious person intercepts the applet from Bob's Software and substitutes a phony one.

Fig. 26.5
You check the malicious applet and its signature against Bob's public key and find that they don't match.

If the malicious person had sent you the original signature generated by Bob, it would not match the applet since the applet is not the same one Bob's Software generated the signature on.

If the malicious person generates a new signature for the file, it still does not match because it was not generated using Bob's private key. You can discard the applet and call Bob's Software on the phone to ask what's going on.

Allowing More Access for Signed Applets

The whole reason for incorporating digital signatures into Java is to be able to verify that an applet really comes from a certain place. Once you can do this, you can create a set of restrictions or permissions for any applet signed by a certain site.

In other words, you decide how much you trust a particular organization and then decide what you will permit that organization's applets to do on your system.

Note

The Security API from Sun was not available at the time this book was written. It is expected that by the time you read this, the API will be available, as will a preliminary implementation. The information given here is based on Sun's statements about how the security will work.

Digitally signed applets can be restricted to access only certain areas of the network or certain local file systems. For instance, you might create a directory called /usr/local/bob and allow Bob's Software applets to access only that directory.

If Bob's Software decides they want to damage your system, the worst they could do is fill up their own directory until it takes up all your hard disk space.

Suppose you have a Web browser that accepts digital signatures and you download Bob's Software's new hard drive manager applet. Your browser would first verify the signature of the applet and determine that the applet indeed came from Bob's Software.

Next, the browser would consult its security information to see what kind of access Bob's Software is allowed. Presumably, this information would be relayed to the Java SecurityManager running in your browser.

If you download a hard drive manager, you probably have to tell the security system to allow Bob's Software full access to the hard drive. The point is, you must tell the security system what kind of access you want to allow.

Note

The Jeeves server accepts digital signatures on servlets, allowing you to use servlets from other sites and determine how much you are willing to trust the servlets.

Microsoft supports digital signatures for verification of all downloaded code in version 3 of the Internet Explorer. Under the Microsoft scheme, a digitally signed applet is allowed more access to the local machine. Under Sun's security framework, you can control access based on who signs the applet. Under Microsoft's framework, all digitally signed applets have the same amount of access.

Using a Third Party for Applet Signatures

It won't take long for you to tire of setting up security information for every different company you get applets from. There will be a market for trusted third-party verification companies who evaluate the security of applets and their companies, and provide a digital signature for the applet.

Bob's Software would send off a copy of their latest and greatest hard drive manager program to a third-party company like TrustMe, Inc., as illustrated in Figure 26.6.

Fig. 26.6
Bob's Software sends their software to a trusted third party for verification.

TrustMe analyzes the applet and determines if it is doing anything unusual. Or it just verifies the applet, depending on the company. The point is, TrustMe is responsible for ensuring that the applet didn't do anything malicious to your system.

When you download an applet from Bob's Software, you also get the signature generated by TrustMe. As shown in Figure 26.7, your browser sees that the applet is signed by TrustMe and determines the amount of access allowed, based on the restrictions you set up for any applet signed by TrustMe.

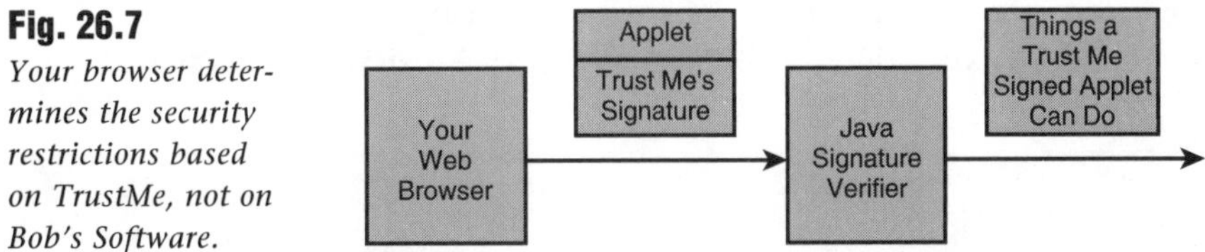

Fig. 26.7
Your browser determines the security restrictions based on TrustMe, not on Bob's Software.

The advantage here is that TrustMe can verify for many different companies. Rather than you having to enter a security policy for each different company, you can enter a policy for a small number of trusted verification companies.

Potential Security Problems with Digital Signatures

For the most part, digital signatures are pretty secure. If used properly, digital signatures are very secure, but carelessness and lack of understanding can compromise that security.

In addition, digital signatures by themselves do not solve all potential security problems. Most of the problems come from putting too much trust in the digital signatures or by assuming that they protect you from something they don't.

Using Phony Signatures

Any time you have a public key system, you need a way to verify that the public key you have is the correct key. Otherwise, someone who wants to slip you a malicious applet could make you think that the public key for Bob's Software is something other than the real key value.

For example, they might send you a fake e-mail saying "To All Bob's Software Customers, Our private key was recently compromised, forcing us to use a new private/public key pair. Please visit our Web site at ...." Of course, the malicious person could give you an incorrect Web site address or, through a process called "spoofing," impersonate Bob's Web site.

This potential security problem is usually handled by using a certification authority (CA). This CA is a trusted signing authority. When you create your own private/public key pair, you send the public key to a CA along with information verifying who you are. The CA then verifies your information and digitally signs your public key with the CA's digital signature.

When you download digitally signed code, you also receive a certificate containing the server's digital signature, signed by the CA. You then use this certificate to verify the signature on the code. In other words, the server is saying to you "Here is some code that I have signed, and here is a copy of my signature that has been notarized by a CA." While the term "certificate" sounds good, it is really just a digitally signed public key.

Caution
It is extremely important that your browser have some built-in knowledge of a CA's key. Everything that comes from the network has the potential of being fake. The browser needs some piece of information that does not come from the network before it can make any assumptions about the validity of network information. In this case, the browser needs the CA's public key so that it can verify that the CA really did sign a particular certificate.

Most certificate authorities have very stringent security procedures to keep people from sabotaging the certification process. A significant risk for a certificate authority is having its private key compromised. Once someone gets the private key for a CA, they can create false certificates. For instance, if you had the private key for a CA, you could create a certificate for Bob's Software and sign it with the CA's key, allowing you to pretend that you are Bob's Software. A good CA uses a system that hides the key from everyone, even the employees at the CA. In these cases, the CA's signature is produced by a machine that cannot reveal the private key. Some of these machines will even destroy the private key if they are tampered with. Overall, the likelihood of someone getting the private key for a CA is very remote.

As technology has improved in the area of security, humans are almost always the weak link in the security chain. You may not be able to get the private key for a CA, but you can bribe someone at a CA to sign a false certificate for you. In other words, you create a certificate that says that you are Bob's Software and get someone at the CA to sign it. Most CA's have fairly stringent security procedures, making even this kind of security breach unlikely. Unfortunately, there is no way to render it completely impossible.

Another potential weakness in the area of phony signatures is that someone might be able to successfully impersonate Bob's Software and obtain a signed certificate from a CA without bribing anyone at the CA. You can always forge credentials, perform spoofing over the network, and tap or reroute phone lines. Of course, this is not an aspect of digital signatures. This situation can occur in everyday business and occasionally does. If you are creating an electronic commerce system, you should be careful which CA's you accept certificates from. A certificate authority that does not take adequate precautions in verifying the identify of a person or corporation makes fraud a lot easier. You don't want to trust certificates from a CA that issues certificates to anyone that mails them a request.

The Pretty Good Privacy (PGP) encryption package uses an interesting alternative to a certification authority. Rather than using a CA, PGP users pass keys around to each other.

The idea is that you generate your own private/public key pair and then give your public key to some friends, who digitally sign your key. In other words, instead of going to a central certificate authority, your friends act as CAs for you (see Figure 26.8).

These people are now your *introducers*. They vouch for you. When a stranger gives you their public key, they also give you a list of signatures from their introducers (see Figure 26.9). This is like giving an employer a list of references.

If you know one of the introducers, you have some idea that you can trust the key. If you don't know any of the introducers, you can't be sure that the key you get is really valid.

This scheme works pretty well for personal use, but it has some drawbacks for business use. For one thing, it is a lot easier for someone untrustworthy to sneak in and get their key verified by normally trustworthy people.

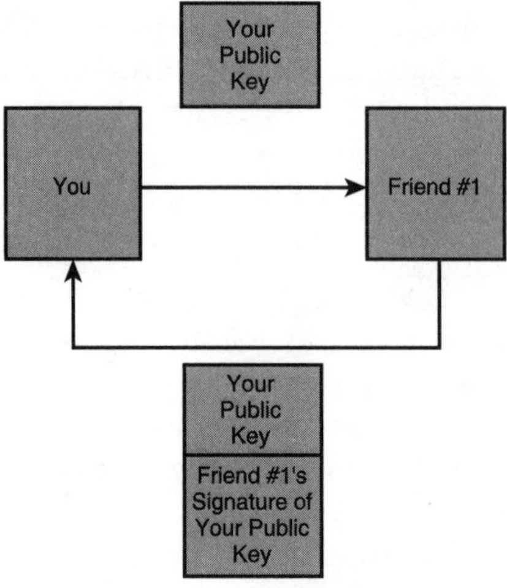

Fig. 26.8
You get your public key signed by people who trust you.

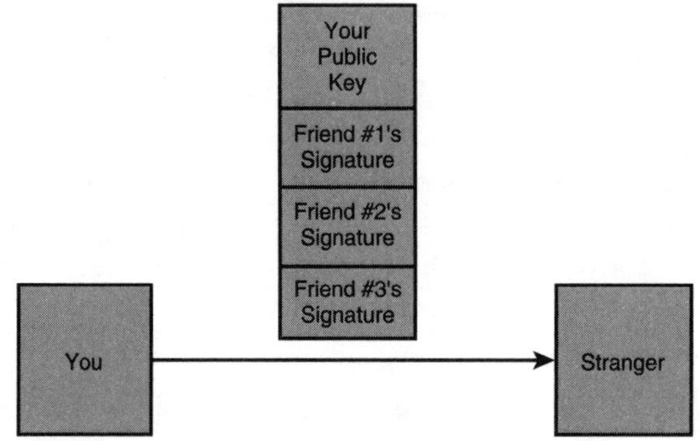

Fig. 26.9
When giving your public key to a stranger, you also give them a list of introducers.

After all, the introducers are usually friends of yours or people you know over the Net. It would be easy for someone to become your "friend" just to get you to introduce them.

Another problem with key passing is that if someone's private key is compromised (stolen), there's no easy way to propagate that information. In other words, you may know Fred and trust people introduced by Fred.

Suppose Fred's private key has been stolen and someone begins creating keys that were supposedly signed by Fred. You may not have heard from Fred in a while and you may not know that his key was stolen. You may end up trusting a malicious person who was supposedly introduced by Fred.

You can also run into this problem using a CA. Because you don't verify certificates with the CA at runtime, which would be a huge performance bottleneck, you don't know immediately if a certificate is no longer valid. To address this problem, there are lists of invalid certificates called Certificate Revocation Lists (CRL). When your browser receives a certificate, it checks it against a CRL to see if the certificate has been revoked.

You may wonder what happens in a few years when the number of revoked certificates has grown tremendously. Wouldn't a CRL be very large and unwieldy? A certificate does not stay on a CRL forever because certificates also have an expiration date. As soon as a certificate expires, it is removed from the list because any browser trying to verify the certificate would reject it for being expired.

Receiving Old Software

Digital signatures verify that a piece of software came from a particular person but they cannot verify that you have the most recent version of software. Someone with a knowledge of the security holes in an old piece of software could feed you that software and then exploit the holes.

For example, suppose Bob's Software Hard Disk Manager Applet version 1.0 has a serious flaw that allows anyone on the Web to access your local file system while the applet is running. Even though Bob's finds the error and corrects it shortly thereafter, a malicious person could save a copy of the applet, along with its valid signature, from Bob's Software.

When you go to load the applet from Bob's, the malicious person could give you the old version of the program and then immediately start accessing your local file system. Figure 26.10 illustrates this problem.

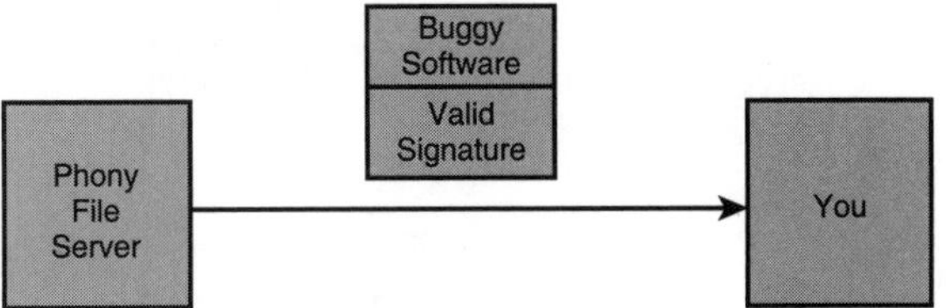

Fig. 26.10
Someone can pass you an old piece of signed software.

As a client, you cannot solve this problem. The software vendor who is supplying you with the applet must do this.

Whenever Bob's Software releases a new version of the software, they should get a new key pair for signing the software. The new pair is registered with the CA, and the *old one must be invalidated.* In other words, you should revoke the signature for the old version of software.

This way, when someone tries to give you the old copy of the applet, you check the revocation list and learn that the signature key for the old copy has been revoked, so you should discard the old version.

Mistaken Trust in Signed Applets

Digital signatures are done behind the scenes in Java. This means that when you load an applet, you don't really know whether it's been signed or not.

You can take comfort in the fact that an unsigned applet or an improperly signed applet is not allowed to wreak havoc on your system. But *you should not assume that an applet came from where you think it did.*

This is not a problem with the digital signature mechanism itself. The problem is in the HTTP protocol (and other networking protocols).

Suppose you have been dealing with Fred's Catering for a while and you have digitally signed applets from Fred's Web page. You know that Fred's is a trustworthy company.

When you order from Fred's, you enter your credit card number in Fred's ordering applet. You cannot assume that the applet really came from Fred's just because you have Fred's public key.

A malicious person who wants to get your credit card number could impersonate Fred's Web page. The applet you run might look exactly like the applet for Fred's (see Figure 26.11). But when you enter your credit card number, it gets shipped off to someone else's list of now-stolen credit card numbers.

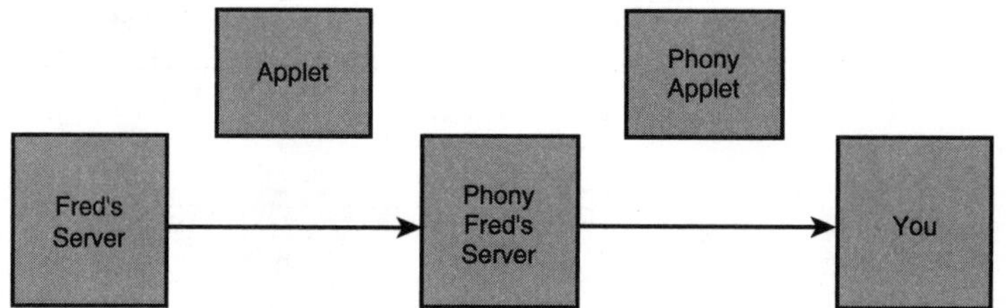

Fig. 26.11
Someone impersonating Fred can pass you a phony applet.

The really clever thieves not only impersonate Fred's. They turn around and impersonate you to Fred's and place your order (see Figure 26.12). That way, you never suspect that someone actually saw your credit card number.

There are other ways of handling this. Just keep in mind that digital signatures do not solve this problem. One way of addressing this problem is to use a secure Web protocol like SSL. This technique is discussed in Chapter 30, "Performing Secure Transactions."

Running a Phony Web Browser

This particular form of attack is pretty far-fetched but certainly feasible for someone who really wants to infiltrate your company. Most Web browsers today are delivered over the Internet, with no encryption and no digital signatures. If someone wants to breach your company's security, they could impersonate the Web browser vendor and feed you a hacked version of the browser.

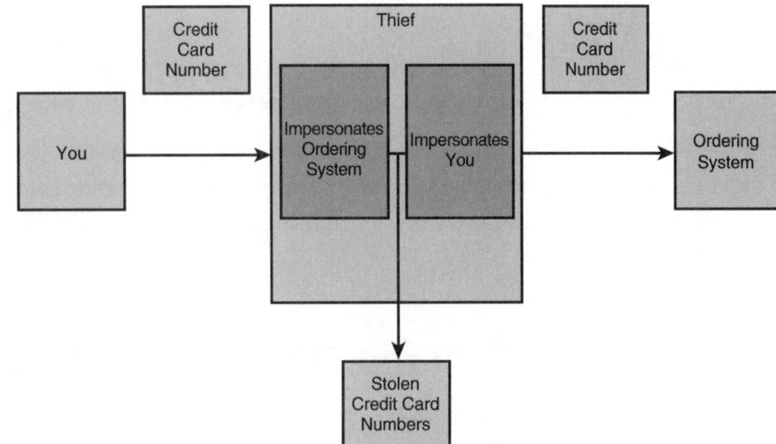

Fig. 26.12
A clever credit card thief looks at your number and then passes the order on to the real company.

Suppose, for instance, that your favorite browser, the Surf-O-Matic, has just been updated and put out for download on the Net. If someone wants to infiltrate your network, they could make you think that their file server was really the Surf-O-Matic file server. You happily download the new browser, unaware that it contains a version of Java that doesn't use certain security restrictions. Figure 26.13 illustrates this problem.

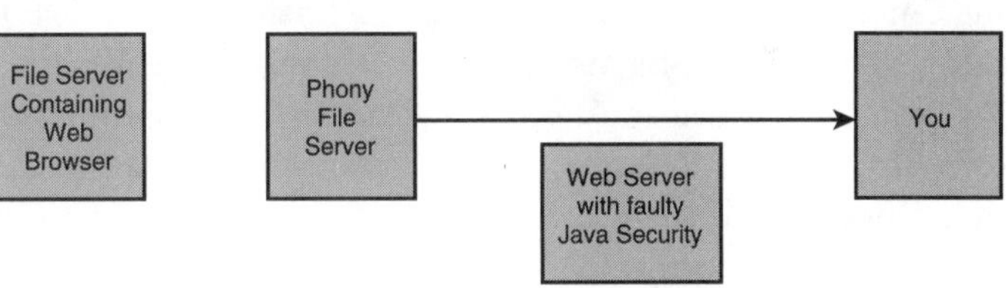

Fig. 26.13
By impersonating a file server, a malicious person can feed you a phony Java environment.

Some time later, you find out that someone has been sneaking into your network and stealing confidential information, and you never suspect your browser because Surf-O-Matic is a trustworthy company.

This is not really a Java problem and it's not one you can solve yourself. It must be solved by Surf-O-Matic and other browser vendors.

You must be able to download a browser and verify it by a digital signature to be sure that it really came from the right vendor. Otherwise, all the nice security within Java is useless.

Unfortunately, this is something of a chicken and egg situation. How do you get the verification software? If you download it off the Net, how do you know it isn't also a phony?

This is one of the more maddening aspects of security. The only thing that keeps this from being a huge problem is that it is not a simple task to impersonate a file server. Even then, you can usually fool only one company at a time, unless you can impersonate the file server to the whole Internet.

Most companies don't have to go to this degree of worry. But if you have highly classified information on your network that people would love to get their hands on, you probably have a big headache right now.

One solution to the fakery problem is to talk to your vendor about getting an encrypted version of the software. Another solution is to send someone over to the company headquarters and get a copy directly from them.

Obtaining a Digital Signature Certificate

For you to digitally sign information, you need a certificate. Unfortunately, certificates are not free. You must buy a certificate from a known CA like Verisign. Many secure Web servers provide registration information for ordering a certificate.

Typically, you must first generate a public/private key pair. This only makes sense because the certificate is just a digitally signed verification of a public key. Next, you send your public key, along with a lot of information about yourself or your company, to the certificate authority. Next, the certificate authority verifies your identity. Depending on the CA, this may be a lengthy process, especially if the CA has a reputation of being very thorough when investigating identities. Companies requesting a certificate from Verisign, for instance, must provide a letter from an authorized representative of the company along with certain official documents like the company's articles of incorporation. Once the CA has verified your identity, it digitally signs your public key and sends you a completed certificate.

For more information, try the Verisign home page at **http://www.verisign.com**.

Other Uses for Digital Signatures

In general, digital signatures are useful in cases where a handwritten signature would normally suffice. For instance, you could use a digital signature to sign e-mail messages so that recipients could be sure that you really sent the mail. This is especially important given the ease at which e-mail may be faked.

Digital signatures may also be used to sign receipts when purchasing goods and services online. It is extremely important to use a secure certification process when setting up an electronic commerce system. You want to ensure that the person who digitally signs the receipt is really the person you think it is. Likewise, when you obtain a digital certificate for performing electronic commerce, it is important that no one be able to forge your certificate. It is extremely important that no one be able to access your private key. Once someone has the private key for your signature, they may forge your signature on any digital receipt. Many digital signature systems store your signature in an encrypted form where you must enter a password any time you go to digitally sign a document. If the signature is not encrypted, any piece of software that can read your local hard disk may be able to find your signature.

If you haven't had much experience with digital signatures yet, that will change. You may soon find that you can't do business without one.

chapter 27

Encrypting Data

27

by Mark Wutka

In this chapter

- **Different types of encryption**
  There are several different types of encryption, each with its own strengths and weaknesses. You have to choose which kind of encryption to use, based on security requirements, performance, and the type of data you are sending.
- **Different kinds of security attacks**
  There are many different ways to break a system's security. You need to know the major ways your system can be attacked in order to properly use an encryption system. Just because you're using encryption doesn't mean your system is safe.
- **Getting and using encryption software**
  There are several encryption libraries available for Java. They each have different purposes and different restrictions.

Data encryption is a touchy subject. Many cryptography algorithms and their implementations are restricted to use within the United States by the National Security Agency (NSA).

It is illegal to export certain kinds of encryption software outside the U.S. There has recently been a push to lift some of these export restrictions, however, because of the greater need for security on the Internet. Many American companies can't sell their software overseas because of the encryption software embedded in their code.

The increase in commerce over the Internet has made encryption a need for some businesses. When you type your credit card number on an order form, you want to be sure that no one can see the information as it passes through the Internet. Since you can't prevent people from snooping on your data, your only hope of safely keeping your credit card number away from prying eyes is to encrypt the data before you send it.

The purpose of encryption is to turn ordinary data into completely random-looking bits. The notion of "completely random-looking" is a real science.

You may think you have some clever little way of encrypting your data but unless you really know cryptography, your scheme can probably be broken easily. Unless you really know what you're doing, stick to the known encryption algorithms and you'll be pretty safe.

Data is encrypted with a key that can be a random string of bits, or some word or phrase that you pick. The key is like a password. It needs the same degree of secrecy and the same care in creating a word or phrase that can't be guessed. The key is used by the encryption algorithm to scramble your data and to unscramble it on the other side.

A data encryption algorithm is called a *cipher*. The data you are encrypting is called *plaintext*, whereas the encrypted version of the data is called *ciphertext*. The process of converting ciphertext back to plaintext is called *decryption*.

Figure 27.1 illustrates a simple use of encryption to pass a coded message.

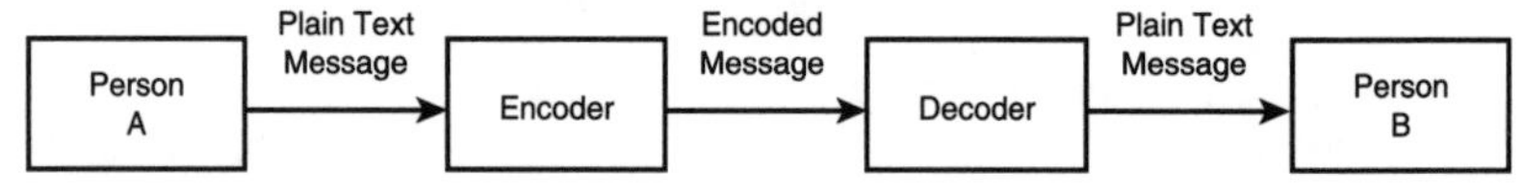

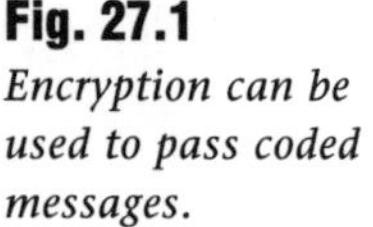

Fig. 27.1
Encryption can be used to pass coded messages.

Data encryption ciphers are grouped into two categories: block ciphers and stream ciphers. The stream cipher is a simple single-character-in, single-character-out cipher. That is, it does the encryption one character at a time.

Each time a stream cipher reads a character, it uses the key and accumulated data from the other characters it has processed to figure out how to scramble the next byte of data. Unlike some of the simple ciphers you may be familiar with, a good stream cipher does not just map one character to another.

If you feed two A's in a row to a stream cipher, chances are you will not get two identical characters in a row in the encrypted text. Figure 27.2 illustrates a stream cipher in action.

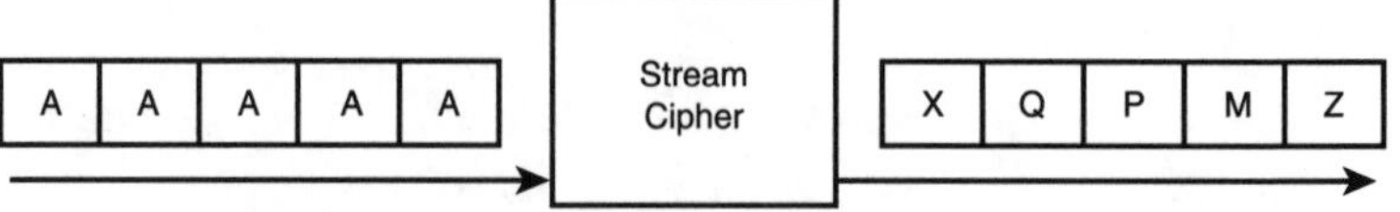

Fig. 27.2
A stream cipher encodes a single character at a time.

A block cipher, on the other hand, encrypts whole blocks of data at a time. Unlike a stream cipher, the block cipher can scramble all the bits in a block so that the bits for the first byte of the block can be scrambled and placed in strange places.

Of course, the key and the actual values of the bits determine what the encoded block looks like. The first bit in a block may end up in one position using a certain key and in a different position using a different key. Figure 27.3 illustrates a block cipher in action.

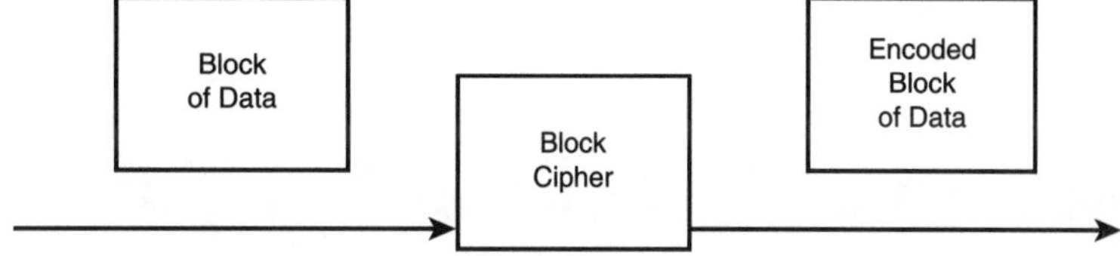

Fig. 27.3
A block cipher scrambles whole blocks of data at one time.

There is another way to classify encryption algorithms, based on the kind of key used. Some algorithms use a private key, also called a *symmetric key*, whereas others use a public/private key pair, called an *asymmetric pair*.

Private key encryption is probably the one you are most familiar with. Two parties agree on a secret key. The sender encrypts the data with the secret key, and the receiver decrypts the data with the same key.

If anyone else finds out the secret key, he or she can spy on the data being exchanged. Figure 27.4 illustrates a data exchange using a private key.

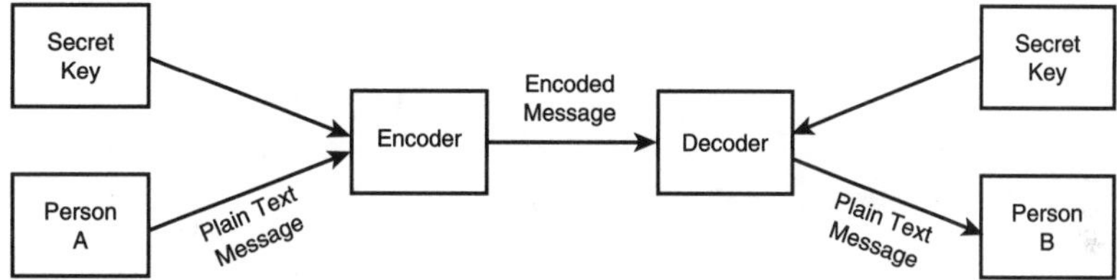

Fig. 27.4
Both parties agree on a private key and use that key for encryption and decryption.

One of the problems with private keys is that you have to find some way of agreeing on the key ahead of time. How do two people exchange encrypted communications if they have no way to exchange keys to begin with? Public key encryption provides a neat solution to this problem.

With public key encryption, everyone who wants to get encrypted data creates a private decryption key and a public encryption key. This is called an *asymmetric key cipher* because the encryption key and the decryption key are different. The important part of this scheme is that although you can determine the public key based on the private key, you cannot figure out the private key from the public key.

Anyone wanting to send you encrypted data would look up your public key, which can be published in a number of ways, and use it to encrypt a message to you. You would receive this message and decrypt it with your private key. Figure 27.5 illustrates a data exchange using a public key.

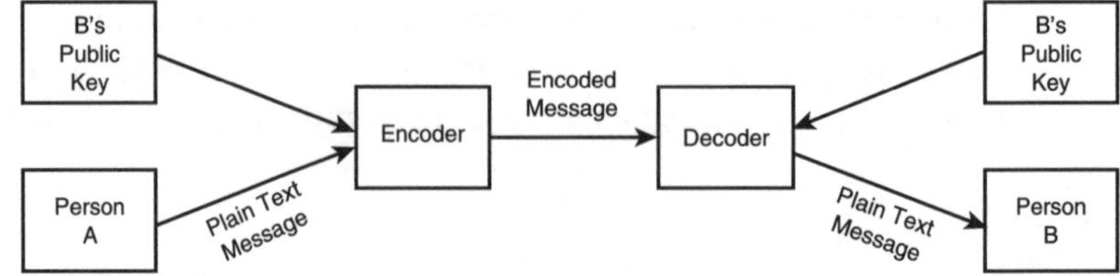

Fig. 27.5
The data is encrypted with the public key and decrypted with the private key.

Choosing the Right Kind of Encryption

Given that a stream cipher handles one byte or even one bit at a time, you might think that a stream cipher is better for encrypting computer login sessions, which are more byte-oriented. As it turns out, block ciphers aren't really too bad for login sessions, since the blocks are often only 64 bits (8 bytes) in size. Essentially, your choice of cipher shouldn't depend on whether it is a block or stream cipher.

Some of the factors that will influence your choice of encryption are:

- **The amount of security needed**

  Some encryption algorithms can be broken in a matter of hours; some would take many years. Others would take several times the anticipated lifetime of the universe to break given machines many times more powerful than the ones in use today.

  Of course, the price you pay for more security is the encryption time, among other things. If the data will be useless in an hour, you don't need an algorithm to protect it for your lifetime.

- **The speed of the algorithm**

  Some algorithms are prohibitively slow for common use. If you need a Cray mainframe to encrypt and decrypt the data in a reasonable time, it probably is not a good choice for an applet.

- **Licensing fees**

  The number of patents for encryption algorithms is amazing compared to the rest of the computing field. Many algorithms, though publicly available, are still patented and subject to licensing fees for commercial use.

- **Availability for Java**

  At the outset, Java and encryption algorithms didn't get along too well. This was because Java is a byte-code-interpreted language, and encryption algorithms need a lot of computations. As Just-in-Time (JIT) compilers have emerged, Java has gotten better at meeting the high demands of these algorithms.

- **Native versus 100 percent Java implementations**

  Several vendors have taken a shortcut to encryption for Java by using some of the more compute-intensive parts of the algorithms as native methods. When you start relying on native methods, you lose the cross-platform advantages of Java.

- **Export restrictions**

  The U.S. has stringent restrictions on the export of encryption software. If your applet uses a restricted algorithm, you could be violating U.S. law if your applet is run by someone outside the U.S. Of course, if you're already outside the U.S., you don't have this problem. Sometimes an entire algorithm is not restricted, only the use of keys above a certain size.

Guarding Against Malicious Attacks

Your choice of private keys versus private/public key pairs depends on what kind of communications you are doing and what are the possible ways someone might attack your communications.

Presumably, the reason you are encrypting your data is to hide something in the data from prying eyes. This hidden information might be a credit card number, it might be the password to another system somewhere, or it might just be personal information.

When you create secure applications, you need to have some idea of the ways someone can attack your application. In general, the two kinds of attack are a simple eavesdropping and an impersonation.

An eavesdropping attack is a passive attack that can be made by monitoring network traffic. You should assume that anyone who might want to listen in on a conversation will have access to such a monitor. Because so many computers can act as network monitors with only a small amount of programming, this is a safe assumption.

An impersonation attack is very insidious: Someone has the ability of impersonating another person or computer. The person sending confidential information sends the information to the impostor rather than to the real recipient. This is typically the hardest attack to defend against and also the hardest attack to use.

You can see how encryption solves various attacks by starting first with a conversation that doesn't involve encryption. Then, as encryption is added to solve various problems, you can see how the attackers respond. Once you are able to see how devious an attacker can be, you can design your applications appropriately.

Figure 27.6 shows a simple conversation between two people with an eavesdropper watching the conversation.

Fig. 27.6
Unencrypted conversations are easy prey for an eavesdropper.

Plain Text Message
Person A
Network Monitor
Person B
Plain Text Message
Eaves-dropper

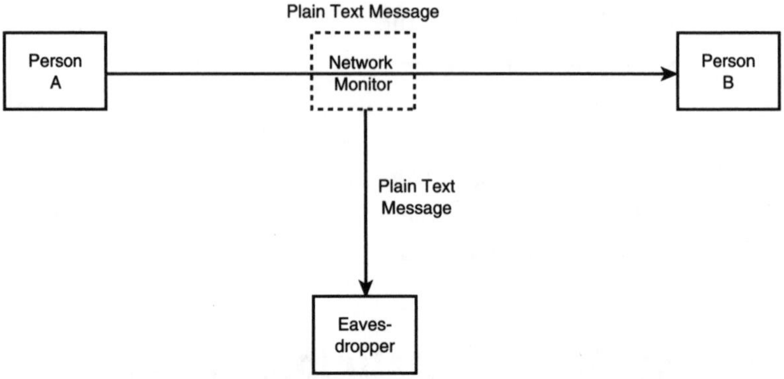

To solve the simple eavesdropping problem, the participants in the conversation agree on a secret key and encrypt their conversation. Now, the eavesdropper doesn't know what they're saying.

In certain cases, the eavesdropper may not need to know what they're saying to make an attack. Suppose, for instance, that the participants in the conversation are an automatic teller machine and a bank.

As shown in Figure 27.7, the eavesdropper records the conversation between the teller machine and the bank as someone at the automatic teller makes a withdrawal.

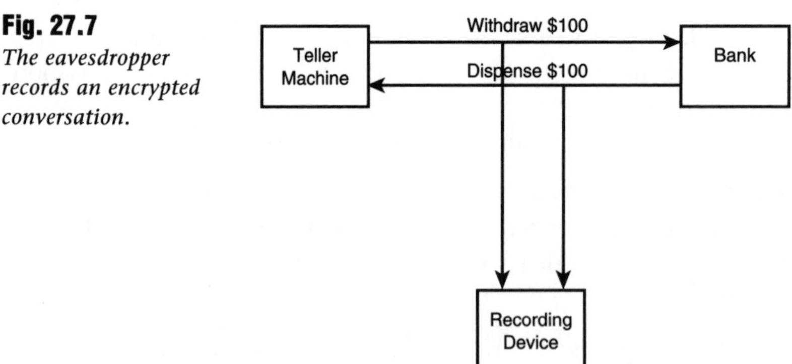

Fig. 27.7
The eavesdropper records an encrypted conversation.

Withdraw $100
Teller Machine
Bank
Dispense $100
Recording Device

Some time later, the eavesdropper taps back into the connection between the bank and the teller machine, and replays the encrypted conversation. This causes the bank to make another cash withdrawal from the customer's account and the teller machine to spit out the cash, as shown in Figure 27.8.

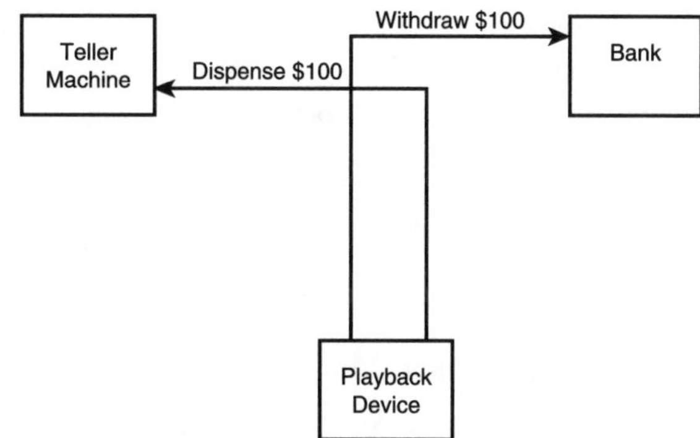

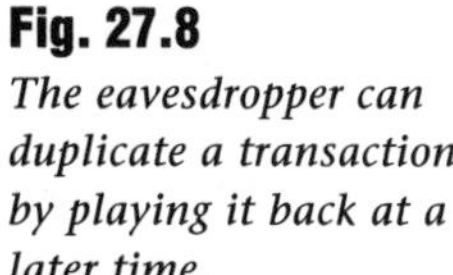
Fig. 27.8
The eavesdropper can duplicate a transaction by playing it back at a later time.

Resisting a Playback Attack

This sort of attack is often useful when encryption is used to set up a login connection or similar session, but the rest of the session is unencrypted. An eavesdropper could play back the login sequence and make a login connection some time after the original login, without ever knowing the secret key.

You can counter the playback attack in the case of a login like this but you should encrypt the entire login session anyway. If someone wants to infiltrate your system, they could interfere with your unencrypted session and send bogus commands, intercepting the responses so you never know they are there.

A simple trick for thwarting the playback attack is to ensure that the messages change slightly from one session to the next—not just that they change, but that they have to change.

A simple solution for this problem is:

1. The receiver generates a random number and sends it to the sender.
2. The sender must use the randomly generated number inside the message it sends to the receiver.
3. The receiver ignores any messages with an invalid number.

Now the eavesdropper cannot play back the messages later because it is highly unlikely that the receiver would generate the same random number the next time. In the worst case, the eavesdropper could get the sender to send a message by replaying a previous number sent by the receiver, but the receiver would ignore the message because it has the wrong number.

The eavesdropper could still wreak havoc by replaying previous messages during the current session. In other words, the eavesdropper waits for the session to begin and starts recording the conversation. At some point, the eavesdropper interferes and plays back an earlier part of the conversation, possibly causing some kind of security breach.

If each message has a sequence number associated with it, however, even that playback attack does not work. Each time a message is sent, it is given a sequence number that is greater than the previous sequence number.

Any out-of-sequence message is ignored. If the eavesdropper plays back a message from earlier in the session, it has a sequence number that is out of order and the message is ignored.

Don't Store Keys in Your Applets

Java makes simple, symmetric communication almost impossible for applets. The problem here is that someone could get your applet, find the secret key, and decrypt a conversation—or impersonate either or both of the participants. You probably still want to use symmetric keys for communication, but the sender needs a way to generate a random session key and send it to the receiver.

Using Public Key Encryption to Exchange Session Keys

One of the reasons you don't see public keys used for encrypting communication channels is that the asymmetric encryption algorithms tend to take a lot longer than symmetric key encryption. Still, public keys are quite useful for passing a random session key to a potential receiver.

The sequence for this is simple:

1. The sender generates a random session key and encrypts it with the receiver's public key.
2. The receiver decrypts the session key using the private key and the two are ready to talk.

Unfortunately, you can't just store the public key in your applet, either. If you do, you open yourself up to an impersonation, or "man-in-the-middle" attack. Java is particularly vulnerable to this kind of attack because the code itself is downloaded over the network.

An impersonator impersonates the receiver to the sender and the sender to the receiver, as shown in Figure 27.9.

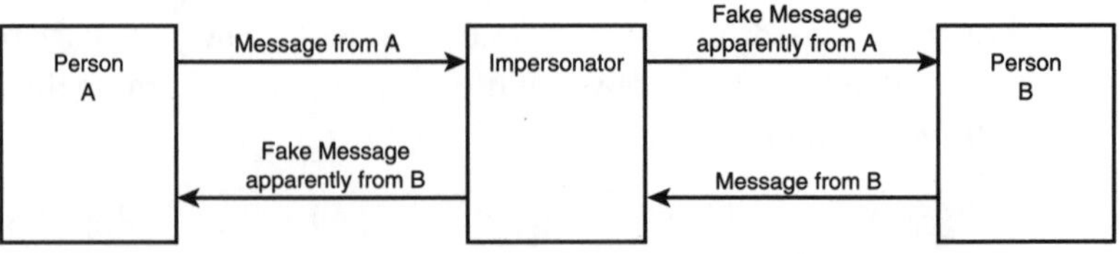

Fig. 27.9
An impersonator sits between two communicating parties and impersonates them both.

Normally, this kind of attack doesn't work with public key encryption unless you can somehow make the sender think the public key is something other than it is. In Java, this turns out to be a simpler task, although digital signatures throw an extra wrench into the works.

If an impersonator wants to set up shop, it first impersonates the receiver. When the server downloads an applet from the receiver, it really downloads the applet from the impersonator. As shown in Figure 27.10, the impersonator has cleverly substituted its own public key in place of the receiver's public key in the applet.

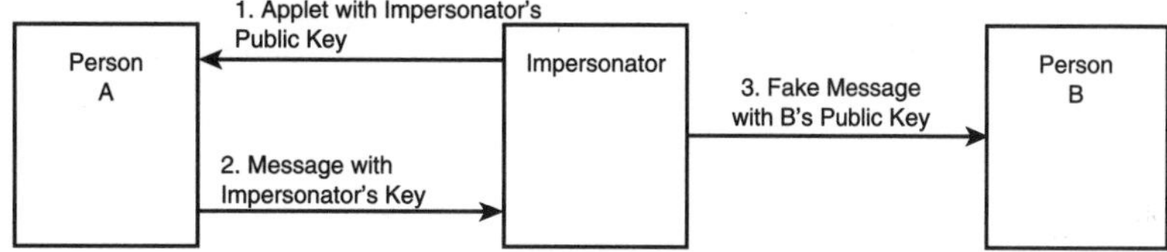

Fig. 27.10
The impersonator gives a phony applet to the sender.

When the sender generates a random session key, it encrypts it with what is now the impersonator's public key and sends the encrypted session key to the impersonator. The impersonator, wanting to spy but not be found out, impersonates the sender by generating a random session key, encrypting it with the receiver's public key, and sending it to the receiver.

As shown in Figure 27.11, the sender now thinks it is talking to the receiver, while the receiver thinks it is talking to the sender. The impersonator, however, is in the middle, watching all the data go by.

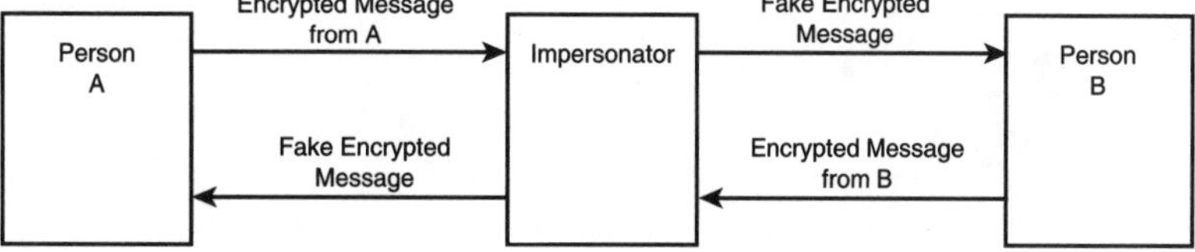

Fig. 27.11
The impersonator is now playing the part of the sender and the receiver.

Anytime the sender sends information to the receiver, the impersonator intercepts it and then passes it on to the real receiver—but not before saving any interesting parts for later use.

As discussed in Chapter 26, "Securing Applets with Digital Signatures," digital signatures can put a damper on this kind of activity but they cannot prevent all attacks. In particular, if the impersonator is able to sign the phony applet with some other valid signature, the sender thinks the applet is okay.

Using Secure HTTP to Thwart Impersonations

The problem with thwarting an impersonation attack is that it needs some piece of secret data on the sender side that the impersonator cannot change. If the server is running an applet that is downloaded from another site, every part of the applet is subject to impersonation.

Secure HTTP pages are not subject to impersonation because the browser uses a certification authority to verify the Web page, much the same way that the digital signature mechanism verifies an applet. The nice thing is that not only is the Web page downloaded securely, everything on the page is downloaded with the same secure mechanism, including applets.

Thus, you can assure your customers that if they connect to your Web page using Secure HTTP, you can guarantee the safety of any information they give to your applets. That is, assuming you are wise enough to encrypt the data before you send it to your server!

Getting Encryption Software

Sun's Security API will eventually provide a number of different encryption schemes, as well as a general interface for encrypting and decrypting information. If you can't wait for Sun, however, you still have a few options.

Caution
The U.S. has some severe export restrictions on encryption software. If you are a U.S. resident, take special note of the warnings on any encryption software you get about whether or not it is restricted. If you don't know whether something is restricted, assume it is and it's probably a safe bet.

Getting SSLava, the Secure Sockets Library

Phaos Technologies (**http://www.phaos.com**) has created an implementation of the secure sockets layer (SSL) protocol. SSL is like the regular network socket implementation you are familiar with but it adds a nice degree of security.

When a client makes an SSL connection with a server, the server provides the client with a digitally signed certificate verifying that it is the intended server. Through a series of checks, the client can determine whether it is the real server or an impostor.

The specification for SSL is publicly available from Netscape Communications. The SSL Version 2 document is located at **http://home.netscape.com/newsref/std/SSL.html**. The proposal for the new SSL Version 3 standard is at **http://home.netscape.com/eng/ssl3/index.html**.

The SSLava library is available for free for noncommercial use, but commercial users must buy a license. SSLava is written entirely in Java, allowing you to use it on any Java-enabled platform. Unfortunately, according to the non-commercial license for SSLava, you cannot redistribute the binary copy of their libraries along with your applet. In other words, if you want someone to run your SSLava applet, they must download SSLava themselves. You do not have these restrictions if you purchase a commercial license.

Caution
If you use SSLava within an applet, make sure that the applet itself is downloaded with a secure protocol. Otherwise, an impostor could replace the real SSLava classes with phony ones and breach your security.

The SSL protocol does solve a number of encryption headaches and it will probably be more widely available in the future. The SSLava product gives you a good way to get your feet wet with SSL.

Note
The SSL protocol is a part of Java 1.1, giving you encryption capabilities on any Java 1.1 platform. While you are waiting for Java 1.1 to be available everywhere, you can use the SSLava libraries.

Getting the Cryptix Library

Systemics, Ltd. (**http://www.systemics.com**) has created an excellent library of encryption classes for Java. Unlike SSLava, some of the Systemics code is used as a native library, making it hard to write applets that use the code.

It does, however, provide a variety of encryption algorithms and is available free for commercial and noncommercial use. Since Systemics is not in the U.S., their software is not subject to the U.S. export restrictions. Still, there may be some patent problems since some of the algorithms used in the library are patented in the U.S.

Systemics recommends that you seek professional legal advice about whether or not you can legally use their software in your country.

Cryptix is handy when you need to do large amounts of encryption. Since it is implemented as a native library, it is very fast. While Cryptix may not be as desirable for applets, it works very well for stand-alone applications.

All of the block ciphers in the Cryptix library are subclasses of the `BlockCipher` class, which has methods to encrypt and decrypt blocks of data. One of the things that appears to be lacking from the library is a way to automatically encrypt or decrypt a multi-block buffer.

This is, in part, because it is hard to handle partial blocks. When the data doesn't fill a complete block, you usually pad the block with zeroes. Unfortunately, you have to figure out where the padding starts when you decrypt the data, which requires that you embed the information in the encryption. If you are willing to accept the padding at the end of an encrypted buffer, it is simple just to break up a buffer into multiple blocks and encrypt each block.

Listing 27.1 shows an input stream filter that decrypts data using the Cryptix library. When you create the stream, you pass it the cipher you want to use.

Listing 27.1 Source Code for *BlockCipherInputStream*

```
import java.io.*;

// This class wraps an input stream filter around the decrypt
// method from the Cryptix java.crypt.BlockCipher
// class. It allows you to decrypt an input stream. You
// can use it to read in an encrypted file as if it were
// unencrypted.

public class BlockCipherInputStream extends FilterInputStream
{
// cipher is the cipher we use to decrypt
     protected java.crypt.BlockCipher cipher;

// currentBlock is the most recent block of data we decrypted. The
// block cipher must work on blocks of data. We build up blocks from
// the input, decrypt them, and let them out byte by byte

     byte[] currentBlock;

// currentChar is the position in currentBlock of the next
// character we return in the read method.

     int currentChar;

// Create a cipher input stream on InputStream in, using the BlockCipher
// cipher.
```

```
     public BlockCipherInputStream(InputStream in,
          java.crypt.BlockCipher cipher)
     {
          super(in);

// save the cipher
          this.cipher = cipher;

// Create a block that is the cipher's block size
          currentBlock = new byte[cipher.blockLength()];

// Flag that we have no characters in the block right now
          currentChar = -1;
     }

// read gets a character from the block we've decrypted,
// If we've exhausted the current block, go read another block.

     public int read()
     throws IOException
     {

// If we've used up all the chars in the block, get another block
          if (currentChar < 0) {
               readNextBlock();
          }

// If we got another block and we're still out of chars, there's
// no chars left to get.

          if (currentChar < 0) return -1;

// Fetch the next char in the block

          int ch = currentBlock[currentChar++];

// If that was the last char in the block, set currentChar to -1
// to show we need to read a new block next time.

          if (currentChar >= currentBlock.length) {
               currentChar = -1;
          }

          return ch;
     }

// readNextBlock reads in another block from input, decrypts it, and
// resets the index for the current character.

     protected void readNextBlock()
     throws IOException
     {

// Read the next character from input.

          for (int i=0; i < currentBlock.length; i++) {
               int ch = in.read();
```

27

continues

Listing 27.1 Continued

```
// If we hit EOF and we only have a partial block, flag it as an error.

                if (ch < 0) {

// If we hit EOF and the current block is empty, we don't need to
// decrypt. Just mark the current character as end-of-block and return.

                    if (i == 0) {
                        currentChar = -1;
                        return;
                    }

// If we get here, it means that we hit EOF in the middle of a block.
// This shouldn't happen because we only encrypt whole blocks.

                    throw new IOException("Incomplete block.");
                }
                currentBlock[i] = (byte)ch;
            }

// Reset the index of the current character
            currentChar = 0;

// Decrypt the current block

            cipher.decrypt(currentBlock);
            return;
        }
}
```

All the `BlockCipherInputStream` does is read whole blocks of encrypted data, decrypt them, and then dole the unencrypted data out one byte at a time through the `read` method. This class is quite handy because you can now use encryption on any data stream, including a network socket.

The companion to this class is the `BlockCipherOutputStream`, which takes one byte at a time, stores the byte in a block, and encrypts each block as it fills up. It then writes out the block onto the output stream it is filtering.

Listing 27.2 shows the `BlockCipherOutputStream`.

Listing 27.2 Source Code for *BlockCipherOutputStream*

```
import java.io.*;

// This class implements an output stream filter that encrypts
// data using an BlockCipher from the Cryptix java.crypt libraries.

public class BlockCipherOutputStream extends FilterOutputStream
{
```

```
// The actual cipher we're using
     protected java.crypt.BlockCipher cipher;

// The current block of data we're writing
     byte[] currentBlock;

// The index of the current character we're writing.
     int currentChar;

// Create an output stream filte rfor a particular cipher
     public BlockCipherOutputStream(OutputStream out,
          java.crypt.BlockCipher cipher)
     {
          super(out);

          this.cipher = cipher;

          currentBlock = new byte[cipher.blockLength()];

          currentChar = 0;
     }

// write adds a character to the output block, and when the buffer
// is full, it encrypts the block and sends it up the filter
     public void write(int ch)
     throws IOException
     {

// Add the character to the block
          currentBlock[currentChar++] = (byte) ch;

// If we've filled the block, encrypt the block and write it out
          if (currentChar >= currentBlock.length) {
               cipher.encrypt(currentBlock);

               out.write(currentBlock);

               currentChar = 0;
          }
     }

// Flush fills out the remainder of the current block with 0's, then
// encrypts the block and writes it out.

     public void flush()
     throws IOException
     {

// If there's a partial block, fill it out with 0's
          if (currentChar > 0) {
               while (currentChar < currentBlock.length) {
                    currentBlock[currentChar++] = 0;
               }

// Encrypt the block and write it out
               cipher.encrypt(currentBlock);

               out.write(currentBlock, 0, currentBlock.length);
```

27

continues

Listing 27.2 Continued

```
                currentChar = 0;
            }

// Do whatever else we have to do to flush the stream
            super.flush();
        }


        public void close()
        throws IOException
        {
// Before closing the stream, flush it.
            flush();

            super.close();
        }
}
```

These classes are fairly small. All they really do is arrange data into a form more suitable for the encryption and decryption routines, which do the hard work.

Listing 27.3 shows a program that tests out both the encryption and decryption streams using a pipe. It uses the IDEA cipher for encryption, which is a patented cipher and must be licensed for commercial use. It can be used noncommercially for free.

Tip

The technique used in the IdeaCrypt program of testing input and output stream filters by using a pipe is a handy technique. You can also use it to test out networking protocols if you are writing both sides of the protocol. The pipe takes only two lines of code to create, compared to the amount of time it takes to set up socket connections.

Listing 27.3 Source Code for *IdeaCrypt.java*

```
import java.io.*;

//
// This program encrypts a block of data using the IDEA
// cipher, then unencrypts it.

public class IdeaCrypt
{
        public static void main(String[] args)
        {
```

```
// encodeMe is the string we want to encode
        String encodeMe = "This is a string to be encoded!!!";

// The IDEA cipher implemented in the Cryptix library uses a 16-byte
// key - that's 128 bits!
        String key = "<Sixteen>ByteKey";

        try {

// The Cryptix library likes the keys and the data to be in byte
// arrays, not strings. We allocate an array for the key and
// copy the key into the array.

            byte[] keyBytes = new byte[key.length()];

// Copy the key string to a byte array.
            key.getBytes(0, key.length(), keyBytes, 0);

// Create an IDEA cipher for our key.
            java.crypt.IDEA cipher = new java.crypt.IDEA(keyBytes);

// In order to demonstrate the encryption and decryption filters, we
// just set up a pipe, so we can write to the pipe and read from it,
// testing the encryption and decryption in one simple program.

            PipedInputStream pipeIn = new PipedInputStream();
            PipedOutputStream pipeOut = new PipedOutputStream(pipeIn);

// Create a decryption filter in the input side of the pipe. It will
// decrypt the data we wrote to the pipe.

            BlockCipherInputStream decrypter =
                new BlockCipherInputStream(pipeIn, cipher);

// Create an encryption filter on the output side of the pipe. This will
// encrypt the data we write to the pipe.

            BlockCipherOutputStream encrypter =
                new BlockCipherOutputStream(pipeOut, cipher);

// Now create a print stream on top of the encryption stream so we can
// write stuff to the pipe using println.

            PrintStream encryptPrint = new PrintStream(encrypter);

// Write out the string to be encrypted
            encryptPrint.println(encodeMe);

            System.out.println("Wrote encrypted string: "+encodeMe);

// Go ahead and flush the print stream and close it.
            encryptPrint.flush();
            encryptPrint.close();

// Create a DataInputStream on the decryption stream. This allows us to
// use readLine to read the data back in.
            DataInputStream decryptIn = new DataInputStream(decrypter);
```

27

continues

Listing 27.3 Continued

```
// Read the unencrypted string
                String unencrypted = decryptIn.readLine();

                System.out.println("Read unencrypted string: "+unencrypted);

            } catch (Exception e) {
                e.printStackTrace();
            }

        }
}
```

Getting the Acme Crypto Package

Jef Poskanzer has written a number of useful Java classes, including an encryption package. You can find his excellent Java software at **http://www.acme.com/java**. The beauty of the Acme package is that it is written entirely in Java. This means that your applets can use encryption and not need the installation of native libraries on the local host.

The Acme Crypto package makes a good complement to the SSLava package. You can use SSLava for a normal encrypted data exchange, and then use Crypto for various areas where the SSL protocol doesn't make sense or is too cumbersome. For instance, you might use the Crypto package to create encrypted data files. The Crypto package is also advantageous if you don't want to buy a commercial license for SSLava but don't want to require that your users download the encryption library themselves.

Caution
The unfortunate aspect of downloadable encryption code is that you may violate the U.S. export restrictions if your site is based in the U.S. and the encryption method you use is restricted. If you are in the U.S. and plan to make your applet available internationally, you should seek professional legal advice about the steps you need to take.

The Crypto package includes several block ciphers, such as DES, DES3, and IDEA. The data encryption standard (DES) algorithm has been around for a number of years and is used heavily around the U.S.

Because of the relatively small key length of DES, information is sometimes encrypted three times with DES, using two different keys. This is called *DES3*.

The IDEA cipher is a relatively new block encryption scheme that is still undergoing some analysis of its security. The IDEA cipher is patented, and you have to get a license if you want to use it commercially.

The owners of the patent, Ascom Systec AG, are based in Switzerland and can be reached over the Net at **idea@ascom.ch**.

In addition to block ciphers, the Crypto package has two stream ciphers. One cipher, the rot13, is a simple substitution cipher that is completely insecure. Rot13 is an alphabetic shift in which A is replaced with M, B is replaced with N, and so on.

It is popular on the UseNet for hiding "spoilers" to games and movies, or for hiding potentially offensive material. Most newsreaders can decrypt rot13 so you can view the hidden information if you choose to. Don't even think of using rot13 as a security tool. It is mainly used for testing.

The RC4 stream cipher is a secure cipher that is both restricted for export and patented. The patent is owned by RSA Data Security Inc., who originally kept the design of RC4 a secret.

Unfortunately for RSA, someone anonymously posted the algorithm to the UseNet in 1994, exposing it to the world. RSA still owns the patent on the algorithm, however, so if you plan to use it in a commercial product, you should contact RSA for licensing information.

The Crypto package also includes `EncryptedInputStream` and `EncryptedOutputStream` filters. You can filter any input or output stream with these filters, using any stream or block cipher in the Crypto package. You can also create new ciphers by subclassing the `BlockCipher` and `StreamCipher` classes.

The Crypto package is used in a remote system-access application in Chapter 28, "Accessing Remote Systems Securely."

chapter 28

Accessing Remote Systems Securely

by Mark Wutka

In this chapter

- **Getting a secure Web server**
  In order to create secure applets, you need a Web server that supports a secure download protocol like the Secure Socket Layer (SSL). There are several servers available on the Internet that provide this capability.

- **Preventing impersonations**
  When users run your applet, they need to feel confident that they are really running your applet. You don't want someone to be able to substitute a phony applet for yours that might corrupt user data or steal important information.

- **Accessing remote data**
  Whenever you are performing secure operations and you need data from a server, you must use a secure protocol to load that data. Otherwise, someone could substitute phony data in place of the real stuff.

- **Passing keys to clients**
  In order to perform secure communications, both parties must have encryption and decryption keys (which may be the same). If you don't have a secure key exchange protocol, someone else could eavesdrop on the conversation.

- **Implementing a secure server**
  You have a few options when creating a server that performs secure communications with its clients. You can create servers that handle only one client (you run multiple servers), or a single server that handles all the clients.

The huge explosion of Internet access is both a blessing and a curse to businesses on the Net. Because Internet data passes over insecure networks, a company must be extremely careful when passing sensitive data over the Internet. In the past, it was difficult for companies to communicate with their employees out in the field, because networking technology was fairly primitive, and laptop computers were not very portable, or too powerful. This was especially a problem for sales force automation. A salesman may be on the road for weeks or months at a time, unable to communicate with the home base. Figure 28.1 illustrates the old design of a sales force automation network.

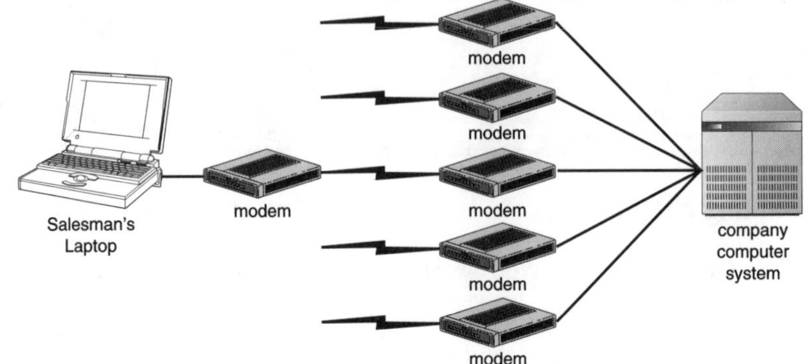

Fig. 28.1
In the past, companies had to create their own sales force automation networks.

Now, laptop computers are extremely powerful with a wide range of networking options, and Internet access is available all over the world. Figure 28.2 shows how the Internet has changed the environment for sales force automation.

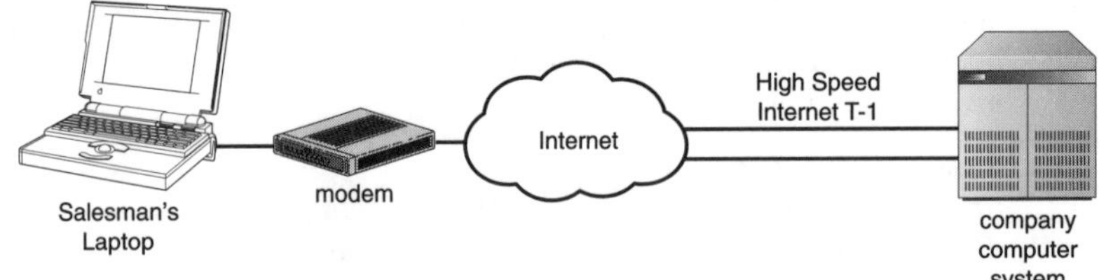

Fig. 28.2
The widespread availability of the Internet eliminates the need for custom networks.

It seems like things should be easier for people on the road, and it is for people at some companies. For others, things haven't gotten any better.

The irony here is that it is still just as difficult to access secure data over the Net. The widespread infiltration of the Internet, which makes it easier for employees to communicate back to their home system, also increases the likelihood that the data can be intercepted. A devious spy from another company could snoop on private data transmissions over the Internet.

In addition, many companies have custom software that must be adapted to work over the Net. Whenever the software is updated, it is very difficult to distribute the new versions to the people in the field. The company must either ship new diskettes, ship out a new laptop, wait until the salesperson is back in the office, or download software over the network. The latter is a very difficult endeavor, most often meeting with failure.

Java can help solve the distribution problem. With Java, you can either write the custom software as applets, which can be cached on the local hard drive (as shown in Figure 28.3), or create a software distribution applet that downloads new versions of the local applications, as shown in Figure 28.4. A digitally signed applet can download updates to the local software, as well as update any information stored on the local hard disk.

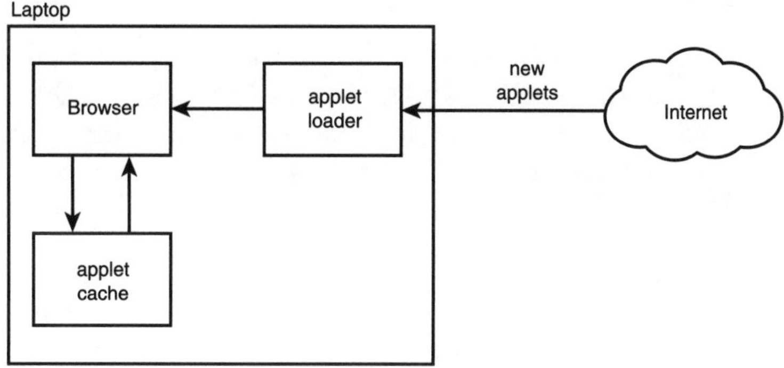

Fig. 28.3
Because applets are downloaded at runtime, you can eliminate some installation headaches.

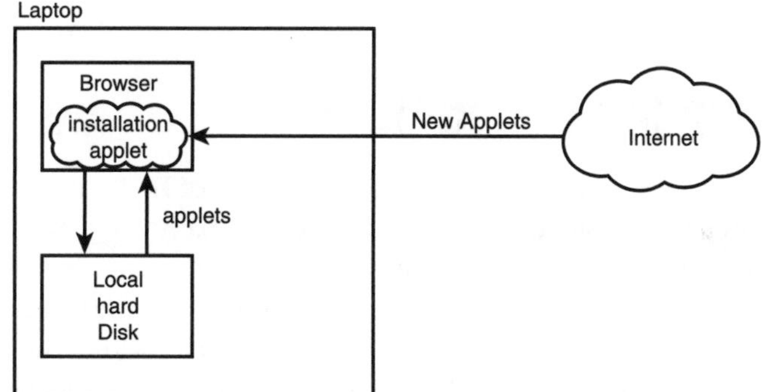

Fig 28.4
A custom software installation applet can also assist in software installation.

You still have the problem of downloading important information without someone intercepting the information. The Secure Socket Layer (SSL) protocol enables you to access Web pages securely. SSL uses a combination of a digitally signed certificate and an encrypted network session.

Getting a Secure Web Server

If you want to use SSL to download your applets, you must get a Web server that supports the SSL protocol. Netscape Communications (**http://home.netscape.com**) has a whole line of Web servers, all of which support the SSL protocol. The secure Web server from Open Market Systems (**http://www.openmarket.com**) also supports SSL.

There is also a version of the Apache Web server that supports SSL. If you are within the United States, you can download the Apache-SSL Web server from Community Connexion, Inc. (**http://www.c2.org**). Apache-SSL is free for non-commercial use. If you want to use it for commercial purposes, you must buy a license from C2.

Caution
Don't forget that it is illegal to export many cryptography programs outside the U.S. If you are outside the U.S., you may not be able to download these programs legally. If you are inside the U.S., you should take extra care to ensure that no one from outside the U.S. can download any secure Web server you might have.

Once you get a secure Web server, you must also get a digitally signed certificate in order to use SSL. There are several certificate authorities around, one of which is Verisign (**http://www.verisign.com**). One of the nice things about the Apache-SSL server is that it will generate a local certificate that you can use for testing. You must still obtain a signed certificate if you want someone else to access your Web server securely.

Preventing Impersonations

The Secure Socket Layer, or another secure form of HTTP, is vital in downloading applets securely. When you download one of your company's applets, you must to be sure that it really came from your company. The digital signature mechanism warns you if you download an unsigned applet, which prevents all but the most devious impersonation attacks. If someone is able to digitally sign an applet with a signature you think is valid, you will not know anything is wrong. Of course, if this happens, it means that you have trusted someone you shouldn't have. Chapter 26, "Securing Applets with Digital Signatures," contains more information about digital signatures and their relationship to applets.

If you use SSL to download your applet, it cannot be impersonated, because SSL ensures that you are talking to the correct Web server.

Accessing Remote Data

You can use SSL to send and receive encrypted data without using any encryption software yourself. The URL class enables you to open up URLs with an https protocol type, which uses SSL for communications. Because of the way the applet security manager works, you cannot intermix http and https URL accesses in a single applet. If your applet was loaded using the http protocol type, you can open URLs only with a protocol type of http. If your applet was downloaded via https, you can open URLs only with a protocol type of https.

What the restriction means is that if you need to download information securely, you must also download the applet securely. It is one of the simple ways that Java protects you from yourself. If you were allowed to download applets insecurely and then download information securely, you would be vulnerable to an impersonation attack.

Since the SSL support is built into the URL class (actually, into the browser itself), you can use the methods discussed in Chapter 6, "Communicating with a Web Server," to store and retrieve files using the URL class. You cannot use any of the socket mechanisms to do this, however.

Passing Keys to Clients

One of the difficulties in performing encrypted communications is agreeing on an encryption key. You have to have a secure way to even agree on a key; otherwise, someone could just eavesdrop on your key exchange and see what key you're using.

Don't Reuse Symmetric Keys

You might be tempted to generate a nice key for symmetric key encryption and let all your applets use that key. Unless you have a foolproof method of ensuring that only trustworthy people can get your applet (which is easier said than done), you run the risk of a malicious person downloading your applet and examining it to find the key you're using.

It should be obvious that just using SSL doesn't prevent someone from stealing your key. SSL only prevents someone from impersonating your server, and from watching your applet being downloaded (since the download is encrypted). The amount of risk involved in reusing a symmetric key isn't worth the trouble.

Using Public Key Encryption to Get a Private Key

Public key encryption is generally very costly. You would not want to carry on an interactive session using public key encryption. Public keys are very handy for exchanging a private key, however.

Suppose you had a client and a server connected together using an insecure TCP/IP socket, as shown in Figure 28.5.

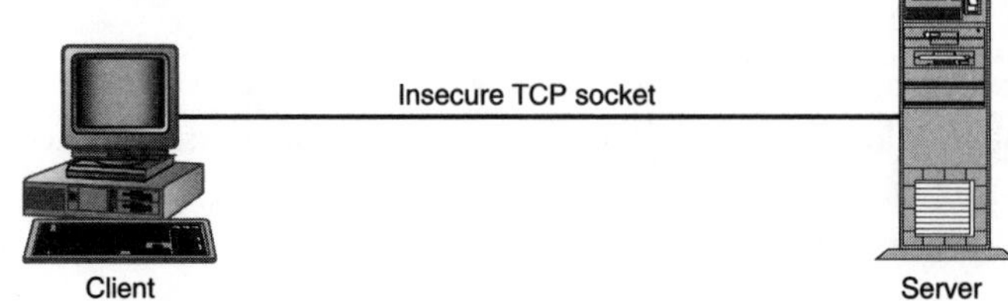

Fig. 28.5
A client connects to a server using an insecure socket.

Next, the client generates a random private encryption key. The client then encrypts the private key using the server's public encryption key and passes the encrypted key to the server, as shown in Figure 28.6.

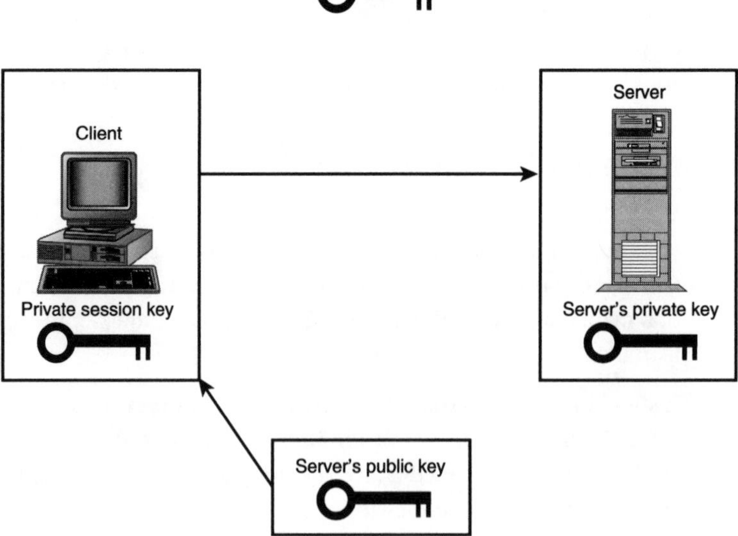

Fig. 28.6
The client encrypts a private key using the server's public key.

Now, the server can decrypt the private session key and the two can use the private key to exchange data. It is safe for you to embed the server's public key in the client applet, because even if someone looked at it, they wouldn't learn anything that isn't already public knowledge. Because each session key is randomly generated, no one else can figure out your session key just by downloading the applet. Anyone who did so would just generate a different key.

Passing a Private Key as an Applet Parameter

Because you are using secure sockets to download your applet, you can take advantage of the fact that the applet and its parent Web page are transmitted in encrypted form. Instead of the client generating the session key and using public key encryption to pass the session key to the server, the server can pass the key to the client applet using the `<PARAM>` tag.

This mechanism has some peculiar drawbacks to it, stemming from the fact that you must use CGI (or its equivalent) to pass the key information back. If you are lucky enough to have a Java Web server that also does SSL, you don't have to worry about this. Unfortunately, since many, if not all, of the current Java Web servers do not support SSL, you have to come up with some unique ways of passing keys around.

Note

Because Java 1.1 includes the SSL protocol, all Java Web servers should soon support SSL.

The problem here is that a CGI program is supposed to generate content in response to a `GET` or a `POST` and then exit. Figure 28.7 illustrates the typical life of a CGI program.

Unfortunately, since the response isn't sent back to the client until the CGI program terminates, by the time the client receives the random private session key, the program that generated the key is gone.

There are a number of ways you can solve this problem. One way is to have your CGI program start up another program that also knows the session key. Once the client knows the session key, it connects to the program started by the CGI program. Figure 28.8 illustrates this sequence.

Fig. 28.7
In response to an http GET *or* POST, *a CGI program starts up, generates a response, and exits.*

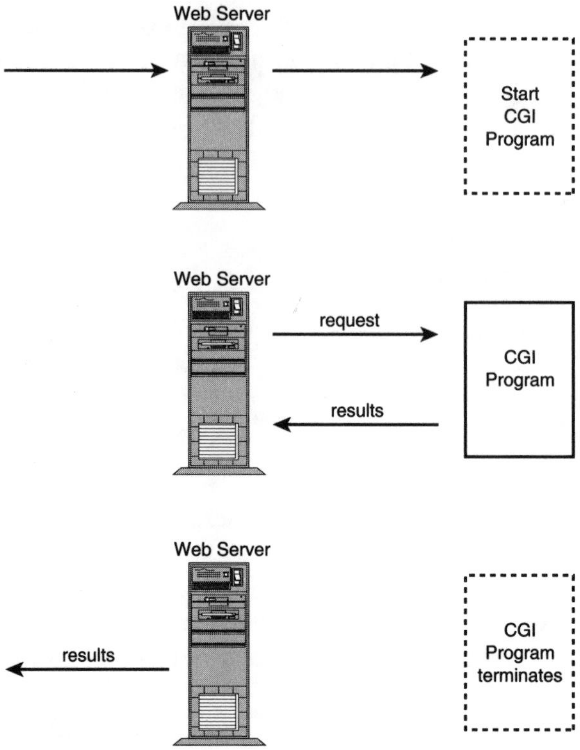

Web Server

Start
CGI
Program

Web Server

request

CGI
Program

results

Web Server

results

CGI
Program
terminates

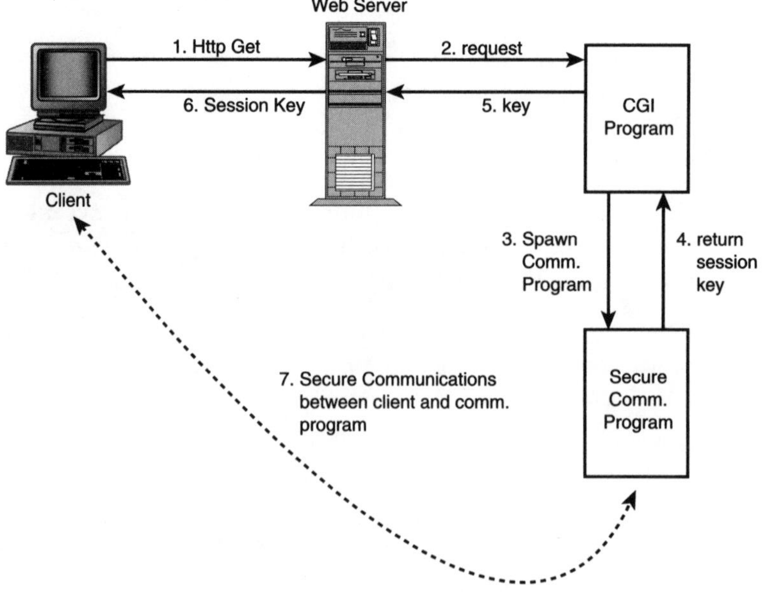

Fig. 28.8
A CGI program can spawn another program that communicates securely with the client.

This solution may be fine for some situations, but it has a number of drawbacks:

- If the spawned program takes a long time to start up, you may bog down your system if you are starting up too many copies of the program at one time. Plus, the client may not be patient enough to wait for the server program to start. The client has to be smart enough to retry if it can't get a connection the first time.
- If the server program needs to use a limited resource, you don't want many simultaneous copies of the program running. For instance, if it accesses a database, you don't want 50 copies of the program all opening database connections. It's even worse if the server needs a resource that can be accessed by only one program at a time.
- Because the client has to connect to the server, the server needs some kind of timer in case the client fails for some reason. You don't want hundreds of old copies just sitting around waiting for a client that will never call. This isn't a big deal, just something you have to take care of.
- It may be expensive on your system to have many copies of the Java virtual machine running at the same time.
- It is tricky for the server program to create a socket and pass that socket number back to the CGI program so it can tell the client where to connect.

Another solution is a bit less taxing on the system resources, but is harder to implement. In this solution, the server is a program that is already running, in the same way that the Web server is always running. When a CGI program starts up, it requests a new session key from the server and then passes the key to the client. The server then listens for an incoming connection. Figure 28.9 illustrates this relationship.

This architecture has some advantages over the previous one:

- With only one copy of the server running, limited resources are not consumed so quickly.
- If the server has a long startup time, you take that hit only once, and probably not while there is a client waiting, because the server is probably started at system boot time.
- You need only one copy of the Java VM to run the server.

This solution also has its drawbacks:

- The server has to handle multiple simultaneous requests. This is usually harder to implement than a single-threaded, single-client server.
- The CGI program has to communicate with the server somehow, either through RMI, CORBA, or a simple socket connection. This takes some startup time.

- You still have the problem of setting up a timer to decide when a client has had a problem and won't be calling.

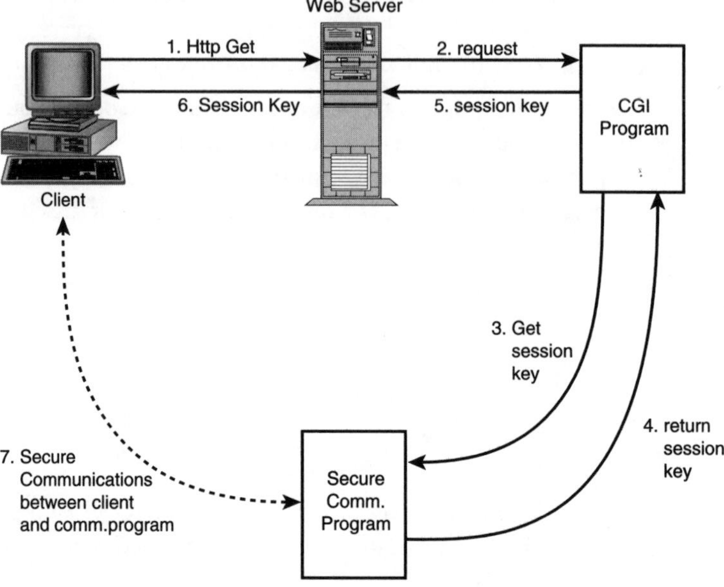

Fig. 28.9
The CGI program gets a key from the server, which was already running.

Implementing a Single-Client Secure Server

If you need something more than a simple http `GET` or `POST` interface and you need encryption, you'll probably have to settle on a socket connection. If you can find a CORBA or RMI implementation that supports encryption, that would be much better.

For a single-client secure server, you need a CGI program that invokes your server program. Since most server programs have a number of similar features, it makes sense to create an abstract class that handles many of the common features. The `SingleSecureServer` class, shown in Listing 28.1, implements a number of useful methods for creating a single-client secure server. The server expects to be started by a CGI program, and passes the port number it is listening on and the secure session key back to the CGI program as output.

Listing 28.1 Source Code for *SingleSecureServer.java*

```
import java.io.*;
import java.net.*;
```

```
// This class implements a single-client secure server. It is implemented
// as an abstract class, leaving your specific server to fill in
// the handleNewClient and makeSessionKey methods.

public abstract class SingleSecureServer extends Object
     implements TimerCallback, Runnable
{
     protected int clientTimeoutPeriod = 300000;     // 5 minute timeout
     protected byte[] sessionKey;

     protected int tickCount;

     protected PrintStream responseStream;

     protected ServerSocket serverSock;

     protected Thread thread;

     public SingleSecureServer(OutputStream responseStream)
     {
          try {
               this.responseStream = new PrintStream(
                    responseStream);
          } catch (Exception e) {
          }
     }

// Called to create the listen socket. Override this if you want a
// specific port number

     public ServerSocket createSocket()
     throws IOException
     {
          return new ServerSocket(0);
     }

// waitForClient waits for a client to connect to the server. It also
// sets up a timer that goes off after a certain amount of time, this
// allows us to quit if the client never connects.

     public void waitForClient()
     {
// Start the timer
          Timer timer = new Timer(this, clientTimeoutPeriod);
          tickCount = 0;
          timer.start();

          while (true) {
               try {
// Accept a new client
                    Socket sock = serverSock.accept();

                    serverSock.close();
// Turn off the timer now
                    timer.stop();

// Do whatever has to be done for the new client
                    handleNewClient(sock);
```

continues

Listing 28.1 Continued

```
                    return;

                } catch (Exception e) {
                }
            }
        }

// This class interfaces with the CGI program in a kludgy way - it
// writes information to the output stream. The CGI program then
// gets an input stream to our output stream and reads the information.
// This method writes out the port number

        public void sendPortNumber(int port)
        {
            responseStream.println(port);
        }

// This method writes out the session key for the CGI program to read
        public void sendSessionKey()
        {
            responseStream.println(keyString(sessionKey));
        }

// This function is provided in the Integer class in JDK 1.0.2
// My poor Linux version is only 1.0.1, so I had to hack one up.

        public static String toHexString(int i)
        {
            char hexBytes[] = new char[2];

            hexBytes[0] = "0123456789abcdef".charAt((i >> 4)&0xf);
            hexBytes[1] = "0123456789abcdef".charAt(i&0xf);

            return new String(hexBytes);
        }

// This method converts a binary session key into a string of hex digits
        public static String keyString(byte[] key)
        {
            String returnVal = "";

            for (int i=0; i < key.length; i++) {
                returnVal += toHexString(key[i]&0xff);
            }

            return returnVal;
        }

// tick is called by the timer when it goes off. The timer is built to
// fire immediately, and then wait for a specific interval before
// going off again. We use the tick count to figure out if this is the
// immediate time, or if the time has elapsed.

        public void tick()
        {
// if tickCount is 1 after we increment it, this is just the first tick
```

```
// so don't do anything
        if (++tickCount == 1) return;

// otherwise, assume the client isn't connecting
        stop();
    }

// start does everything we need - it creates the socket, writes out
// the port number, creates the session key, writes it out, and then
// waits for an incoming client

    public void run()
    {
        serverSock = null;

// Create the socket we're going to listen on
        try {
            serverSock = createSocket();
        } catch (Exception e) {
            return;
        }

// tell the CGI program what the port number is
        sendPortNumber(serverSock.getLocalPort());

// create the session key
        makeSessionKey();

// tell the CGI program what the session key is
        sendSessionKey();

// make sure the CGI program gets all the information
        responseStream.flush();

// wait for a client to connect
        waitForClient();
    }

    public void start()
    {
        thread = new Thread(this);
        thread.start();
    }

    public void stop()
    {
        try {
            serverSock.close();
        } catch (Exception e) {
        }
        thread.stop();
        thread = null;
    }

// handleNewClient does something with the incoming socket, it's
// up to you to decide what
    public abstract void handleNewClient(Socket sock);
```

continues

Listing 28.1 Continued

```
// makeSessionKey generates a session key.
     public abstract void makeSessionKey();
}
```

All your CGI program needs to do is start the server program, read two lines, and generate an HTML page that tells the requesting browser where to get the applet. While you could write the CGI program in any language you choose, Java seems like the ideal choice for this book. Listing 28.2 shows a CGI program that starts up a secure telnet server. This server uses an excellent Java Telnet applet written by Bret Dahlgren. The source code to the applet can be found on the World Wide Web at **http://w3.gwis.com/~thorn/telnet/**. In order to support secure telnet sessions, the Telnet application had to be modified slightly. It now supports a `sessionKey` parameter which, if present, tells it to use encryption for the session. The encryption used is DES3, provided by the Acme cryptography library.

Listing 28.2 Source Code for *SecureLoginStartup.java*

```
import java.net.*;
import java.io.*;

// This is a CGI program that starts up a secure Telnet session
// using a subclass of the SingleSecureServer class. It generates
// an HTML response that refers to a Telnet applet and passes the
// port number and session key to the telnet applet.
// It reads the port number and session key from the SingleSecureServer
// (actually the SecureLoginServer).

public class SecureLoginStartup extends Object
{

// Send an error response to the web browser - something went wrong
     public static void sendErrorResponse(String error)
     {
          System.out.println("Content-type: text/html");

// Gen the HTML on-the-fly. We put it in a string so we can
// compute the content length and be real polite

          String response = "<HTML><HEAD>\n";
          response += "<TITLE> Secure Login Error </TITLE>\n";
          response += "<BODY>\n";
          response += "<H1>Error establishing login.</H1>\n";
          response += "<P>"+error+"\n";
          response += "</BODY></HTML>";

          System.out.println("Content-length: "+response.length());
          System.out.println();
          System.out.println(response);
     }
```

```
// sendNormalResponse sends a web page that loads up the telnet
// applet for a specific port and session key

     public static void sendNormalResponse(int port, String key)
     {
          System.out.println("Content-type: text/html");

// Gen the HTML on-the-fly. We put it in a string so we can
// compute the content length and be real polite

          String response = "<HTML><HEAD>\n";
          response += "<TITLE> Secure Login Session </TITLE>\n";
          response += "<BODY>\n";
          response += "<H1>Secure Login</H1>\n";
          response += "<APPLET codebase=\"/classes\" ";
          response += "code=\"Telnet.class\" ";
          response += "width=600 height=400>\n";
          response += "<PARAM name=\"fields\" value=\"off\">\n";
                response += "<PARAM name=\"host\" value=\"";
                try {
               response += InetAddress.getLocalHost().getHostName();
          } catch (Exception e) {
               response += "localhost";
          }
          response += "\">\n";
          response += "<PARAM name=\"port\" value=\""+port+"\">\n";
          response += "<PARAM name=\"sessionKey\" value=\""+key+"\">\n";
          response += "You need Java for secure logins.\n";
          response += "</APPLET>\n";
          response += "</BODY></HTML>";

          System.out.println("Content-length: "+response.length());
          System.out.println();
          System.out.println(response);
     }

     public static void main(String[] args)
     {
          try {
// Start up the secure server program. You'll probably have to change
// this for your system.
               Process externProcess = Runtime.getRuntime().exec(
                    "/usr/local/java/bin/java SecureLoginServer");

// create an input stream for reading the parameters back from the server
               DataInputStream in = new DataInputStream(
                    externProcess.getInputStream());

// Read the port
               String portLine = in.readLine();
               int port = Integer.parseInt(portLine);

// Read the session key
               String sessionKey = in.readLine();

// Send the web page to the browser
               sendNormalResponse(port, sessionKey);
```

continues

Listing 28.2 Continued

```
            } catch (Exception e) {
                sendErrorResponse(e.toString());
                return;
            }
        }
    }
```

Listing 28.3 shows the HTML information generated by this CGI program:

Listing 28.3 Output from *SecureLoginStartup*

```
Content-type: text/html
Content-length: 378

<HTML><HEAD>
<TITLE> Secure Login Session </TITLE>
<BODY>
<H1>Secure Login</H1>
<APPLET codebase="/classes" code="Telnet.class" width=600 height=400>
<PARAM name="fields" value="off">
<PARAM name="host" value="flamingo">
<PARAM name="port" value="1126">
<PARAM name="sessionKey" value="8b4243347b3a69b8aa12594153c15c8c">
You need Java for secure logins.
</APPLET>
</BODY></HTML>
```

The CGI program is started by a small shell script that sets the Java `CLASSPATH` variable before running:

```
#!/bin/sh
export CLASSPATH=/usr/local/etc/httpd/htdocs/classes:/usr/local/java/lib/classes.zip
/usr/local/java/bin/java SecureLoginStartup
```

The startup sequence for the secure Telnet applet is as follows:

1. The Web browser opens up the URL for the CGI program (actually, the startup script for the CGI program).
2. The CGI program creates an instance of a `SingleSecureServer` and initializes the server.
3. The server opens up a `ServerSocket` to listen for incoming connections and creates a random session key. It returns both the port number and the session key to the CGI program via `System.out`.

4. The CGI program generates an HTML page containing an <APPLET> tag for the Telnet applet and all the important parameters, including the session key.
5. The Telnet applet starts up, connects to the server, and, using the session key for encryption, engages in an encrypted telnet session.

The class that actually creates the telnet connection and passes the information back and forth to the encryption routines is shown in Listing 28.4. It is fairly short. Essentially, it creates the telnet connection, and then uses a simple bridging class to link two streams together.

Listing 28.4 Source Code for *SecureLoginClient.java*

```
import java.io.*;
import java.net.*;
import Acme.Crypto.*;

// This class sets up an encrypted telnet session. It uses the StreamBridge
// class to transfer data between the telnet streams and the encrypted
// streams.

public class SecureLoginClient extends Object implements BridgeCloseCallback
{
     Socket socket;
     StreamBridge bridge1;
     StreamBridge bridge2;
     byte[] sessionKey;

     public SecureLoginClient(Socket socket, byte[] sessionKey)
     {
          this.socket = socket;
          this.sessionKey = sessionKey;
          start();
     }

     public void start()
     {
          try {

// Connect to the telnet port on the local host
               Socket telnetSock = new Socket(
                    InetAddress.getLocalHost(), 23);

// It is vital that you create the encryption streams in the reverse
// order from the other end. In other words, if you create the encrypted
//  output stream first here, you must create the encrypted input stream
// first at the other end. This is because the block cipher streams
// require some initial data over the stream. If you create the input
// streams first, both sides will be waiting for input.

// Connect the output from the telnet stream to the encrypted output
// stream
```

Listing 28.4 Continued

```
                bridge2 = new StreamBridge(
                     telnetSock.getInputStream(),
                     new EncryptedOutputStream(
                          new Des3Cipher(sessionKey),
                          socket.getOutputStream()), this, true);

// Connect the output from the encrypted stream to the telnet stream

                bridge1 = new StreamBridge(
                     new EncryptedInputStream(
                          new Des3Cipher(sessionKey),
                          socket.getInputStream()),
                     telnetSock.getOutputStream(), this, false);

                bridge1.start();
                bridge2.start();

           } catch (Exception e) {
                try {
                     socket.close();
                } catch (Exception ignore) {
                }
                return;
           }
      }

// bridgeClosed is called by the StreamBridge class whenever a
// stream closes. We just close off the socket to make sure
// everything will shut down properly

      public synchronized void bridgeClosed()
      {
           try {
                socket.close();
           } catch (Exception e) {
           }
      }
}
```

The `SecureLoginServer` class, which is a subclass of `SingleSecureServer`, does little more than create a session key and create the `SecureLoginClient` to handle the client connection. Most subclasses of `SingleSecureServer` will probably be this simple. Listing 28.5 shows the `SecureLoginServer` class.

Note

When you generate a random session key, make sure you use a cryptographically secure random number generator. Most of the random number generators you find in programming languages are not good for cryptography because they are too predictable. For instance, if your random number generator has a period of 2^32, it repeats its pattern after 2^32 (about 4 billion) numbers. This may seem like a lot to you, but in terms of breaking codes, it's very small. Even if you generate 128-bit keys, there are only 2^32 possible 128-bit patterns that the random number generator could create, meaning your key is logically only 32 bits. In other words, if someone wanted to try every possible key, he or she would have to try only 2^32 combinations instead of the 2^128 combinations you would expect with a 128-bit key. In addition, most random number generators have some predictability, where a truly secure generator has the appearance of being completely random.

Listing 28.5 Source Code for *SecureLoginServer.java*

```
import java.net.*;
import java.io.*;

// This class is responsible for creating a random session
// key and for creating the class to handle a new client.

public class SecureLoginServer extends SingleSecureServer
{
     public SecureLoginServer(OutputStream out)
     {
          super(out);
     }

// Create a SecureLoginClient to handle the client connection

     public void handleNewClient(Socket sock)
     {
          SecureLoginClient client = new SecureLoginClient(sock,
               sessionKey);
     }

// Generate a random session key
     public void makeSessionKey()
     {
          sessionKey = new byte[16];

          Acme.Crypto.CryptoUtils.randomBlock(sessionKey);
     }

// Start the server with the responses going to System.out, these
// will be picked up by the CGI program.

     public static void main(String[] args)
     {
```

continues

Listing 28.5 Continued

```
        SecureLoginServer server = new SecureLoginServer(
            System.out);

        server.start();
    }
}
```

Finally, the bridging mechanism to link two streams together is very simple. The `StreamBridge` class, shown in Listing 28.6, sets up a thread and constantly reads data from one stream and writes it to another. It can operate in either block mode or single character mode. The single character mode is necessary for the encryption streams, because if you do a block mode read on the encryption stream, it won't return until it fills the entire block. You don't necessarily want it that way.

Tip

The `StreamBridge` class is like a connector for streams. It connects the input of one stream to the output of another stream, and is a little like a pipe in that it results in two streams being connected together, but is unlike a pipe in that you don't have to do any work to send the data over the connected streams.

Listing 28.6 Source Code for *StreamBridge.java*

```
import java.io.*;

// This is a generic class for connecting one stream to another.
// It has a callback to notify you when a stream closes, and
// will operate in either single-character or block-read mode

public class StreamBridge extends Object implements Runnable
{
    InputStream in;
    OutputStream out;
    BridgeCloseCallback callback;
    Thread bridgeThread;
    boolean blockRead;

    public StreamBridge(InputStream in, OutputStream out,
        BridgeCloseCallback callback, boolean blockRead)
    {
        this.in = in;
        this.out = out;
        this.callback = callback;
        this.blockRead = blockRead;
    }
```

```
        public void run()
        {
            int ch;

            try {

// If we support block read, create a block and read as much as
// we can into it each time

                if (blockRead) {
                    byte[] block = new byte[1024];
                    int len = 0;

// Keep reading blocks. We flush the output just in case.
                    while ((len = in.read(block)) > 0) {
                        out.write(block, 0, len);
                        out.flush();
                    }
                } else {

// If we aren't in block-read mode, read a character, write a character
// and flush the stream after writing each char.

                    while ((ch = in.read()) >= 0) {
                        out.write((char)ch);
                        out.flush();
                    }
                }
            } catch (Exception error) {
            }

            callback.bridgeClosed();

            stop();
        }

        public void start()
        {
            bridgeThread = new Thread(this);
            bridgeThread.start();
        }

        public void stop()
        {
            bridgeThread.stop();
            bridgeThread = null;
        }
}
```

You can use this same framework to implement other secure protocols. For example, you could use the POP3 and SMTP classes from Chapter 11, "Sending E-Mail from an Applet," and create a secure mail system. This framework is essentially the "Poor Man's SSL." It uses SSL to get the initial setup information back and forth, and then uses other encryption for the rest of the session.

Implementing a Multiclient Secure Server

If you want to implement a secure server that handles multiple simultaneous sessions, you have to do a little more work. As it turns out, however, if you are careful in the design of your single-client server, you can reuse large amounts of it.

The difference between the single-client and multiclient approach is that the multiclient server is always running, whereas the single-client server is spawned by the CGI program.

The interesting thing here is that the CGI program has to communicate with both servers in a similar way. It needs to know the port number and session key regardless of the type of server implementation. Similarities like this are usually an indication that there may be some code reuse brewing somewhere.

For a multiclient server, your CGI program can use a socket connection to get the port number and session key. Since the `SingleSecureServer` is already set up to run as a thread, it is ridiculously simple to make a multiclient server that just spawns new instances of a `SingleSecureServer` every time a CGI program connects to it.

It's ridiculously simple *now*, but it wasn't in the first design of the `SingleSecureServer`. Originally, the `SingleSecureServer` didn't run as a thread. Its `run` method was called something else, and it didn't implement `Runnable`. When it came time to create a multiclient server, I realized that it took only a few changes to adapt the single-client server so it could run either way. This is what I call "reuse by re-engineering."

Sometimes, you go to design a new system and discover that there is another class that almost works for you, but not quite. With a little change, the class could do what you need and still perform its previous functions. You run the risk of introducing bugs back into the original system, but it surely beats having to keep two copies of almost identical code.

As you make these small design changes, try to make a note of what you had to change. Not necessarily a detailed description, but a general one. You will start to see common themes—design strategies that you have taken in the past that inhibit code reuse. The next time you design a class, keep those previous problems in mind, and maybe your class will not need to be changed. This accumulated knowledge is what really makes a good object-oriented designer.

To support multiple simultaneous clients using the `SingleSecureServer` framework, you need a server that listens for socket connections from the CGI program and then spawns new `SingleSecureServer` threads. Listing 28.7 shows the `MultiLoginServer` class that does this.

Listing 28.7 Source Code for *MultiLoginServer.java*

```
import java.net.*;
import java.io.*;

// This class is responsible for creating a random session
// key and for creating the class to handle a new client.

public class MultiLoginServer extends Object implements Runnable
{
     protected Thread thread;
     protected ServerSocket serverSock;

     public MultiLoginServer(int listenPort)
     throws IOException
     {
// Create the socket that CGI program will connect to
          serverSock = new ServerSocket(listenPort);
     }

     public void run()
     {
          while (true) {
               Socket sock = null;

// Accept a new client connection
               try {
                    sock = serverSock.accept();
               } catch (Exception ignore) {
                    continue;
               }

// Spawn a server to handle the new connection
               try {
                    SecureLoginServer server =
                         new SecureLoginServer(
                              sock.getOutputStream());
                    server.start();

// If there was an error, close down the socket
               } catch (Exception oops) {
                    try {
                         sock.close();
                    } catch (Exception ignore) {
                    }
               }
          }
     }

     public void start()
     {
          Thread thread = new Thread(this);
          thread.start();
     }

     public void stop()
     {
```

continues

Listing 28.7 Continued

```
          thread.stop();
          thread = null;
     }

     public static void main(String[] args)
     {
          int port = 1234;

// Allow the port address to be set as a property

          String portStr = System.getProperty("port");

// Parse the port address
          try {
               port = Integer.parseInt(portStr);
          } catch (Exception ignore) {
          }

// Start the server
          try {
               MultiLoginServer server = new MultiLoginServer(port);
               server.start();
          } catch (Exception e) {
               e.printStackTrace();
               System.exit(1);
          }
     }
}
```

Finally, the CGI program that connects to the multiclient server is similar to the single-client CGI program. The only difference between the two programs is in their `main` methods. This being the case, it makes sense to just create a subclass of the single-client CGI program and create a new `main`. Listing 28.8 shows the multiclient CGI program.

Listing 28.8 Source Code for *MultiLoginStartup.java*

```
import java.net.*;
import java.io.*;

// This is a CGI program that starts up a secure Telnet session
// using a multi-client server that should already be running.
// It connects to the server to get the port number and session
// key which it passes back to the client.

public class MultiLoginStartup extends SecureLoginStartup
{
     public static void main(String[] args)
     {
          try {

               int port = 1234;
```

```
// Allow the port to be set as a system property
               String portStr = System.getProperty("port");

// Parse the port value
               try {
                    port = Integer.parseInt(portStr);
               } catch (Exception e) {
               }

// Connect to the login server
               Socket sock = new Socket(InetAddress.getLocalHost(),
                    port);

// create an input stream for reading the parameters back from the server
               DataInputStream in = new DataInputStream(
                    sock.getInputStream());

// Read the client port
               String portLine = in.readLine();
               int clientPort = Integer.parseInt(portLine);

// Read the session key
               String sessionKey = in.readLine();

// Send the web page to the browser
               sendNormalResponse(clientPort, sessionKey);

          } catch (Exception e) {
               sendErrorResponse(e.toString());
               return;
          }
     }
}
```

Creating Other Secure Remote Access Programs

You can use the `SingleSecureServer` class as a framework for implementing other secure remote access programs. Frankly, this solution is not the optimal one, because you have to work on the socket level. With RMI and CORBA available in Java, you shouldn't have to open up raw sockets for simple communications. They are still useful when you need to grab a large chunk of raw data, but for passing messages back and forth, sockets are a step backwards.

Be on the lookout for an ORB product that supports secure communications. If there isn't one now, there should be soon. Security is a growing issue on the Internet.

PART VII

Doing Business over the Web with Java

chapter 29

Creating a Java Shopping Cart

by Mark Wutka

In this chapter

- **Starting with a basic design**
  When you design a system, you frequently start with the core object model and then build the user interface on top of it. There are a few things you can do to make this an easier task.
- **Creating a parts catalog**
  Before you put items into your shopping cart, you need some way to find out what's available. You need some kind of catalog interface to present the information in a reasonable form.
- **Creating the shopping cart**
  Once you have the basic design of the system done and you have a catalog of available items, it is fairly simple to make a shopping cart for storing the items. The shopping cart is also responsible for sending orders to the Web server.

One of the popular mechanisms in electronic commerce is the electronic shopping cart. When you are shopping over the Web, you can select numerous items that go into your virtual shopping cart. The shopping cart keeps a continuous list of what you want to buy and how much it costs. When you have finished selecting items, you simply push a button and place your order.

One of the problems with many CGI shopping carts is that all the shopping cart information resides on the Web server. Every time you add an item to your cart, you have to communicate with the Web server. If you have a slow connection, it may take you quite a while to select the items. A Java applet is an ideal place for a shopping cart. It can manage the items locally rather than saving them on the Web server. When you decide that it's time to place your order, the Java applet sends your order to the Web server.

Designing a Basic Shopping Cart

One of the themes you have been hearing over and over again in this book is that you should separate the application from the user interface. In the case of the shopping cart, this guideline still holds true. You create a simple framework for a shopping cart and then attach a user interface to it. The first thing you need to do is figure out how the shopping cart will work. The cart itself is nothing fancy; it is just a container of items.

Before you start writing the shopping cart, you should spend a little time on the items that go in the cart. You probably need some sort of name for the item, a price, and maybe a quantity. The quantity value is handy if you don't want to have multiple instances of the same item in your cart. For instance, if you are ordering tires, you can either have four separate instances of a tire item, or have one tire item with a quantity of four. Listing 29.1 shows a simple implementation of a shopping cart item. It contains a name, a price, a quantity, and also an URL that refers to a description of the item.

Listing 29.1 Source Code for *ShoppingCartItem.java*

```
// This class contains data for an individual item in a
// shopping cart.

import java.net.URL;

public class ShoppingCartItem implements Cloneable
{
      public String itemName;
      public int itemCost;
      public int quantity;
      public URL descriptionURL;

      public ShoppingCartItem()
      {
      }

      public ShoppingCartItem(String itemName, int itemCost,
            int quantity, URL descriptionURL)
      {
            this.itemName = itemName;
            this.itemCost = itemCost;
            this.quantity = quantity;
            this.descriptionURL = descriptionURL;
      }

// The add method is a quick method for combining two similar
// items. It doesn't perform any checks to insure that they are
// similar, however. You use this method when adding items to a
// cart, rather than storing two instances of the same item, you
// add the quantities together.
```

```
        public void add(ShoppingCartItem otherItem)
        {
                this.quantity = this.quantity + otherItem.quantity;
        }

// The subtract method is similar to the add method, but it
// removes a certain quantity of items.

        public void subtract(ShoppingCartItem otherItem)
        {
                this.quantity = this.quantity - otherItem.quantity;
        }

// You can store items in a hash table if you implement hashCode. It's
// always a good idea to do this.

        public int hashCode()
        {
                return itemName.hashCode() + itemCost;
        }

// The equals method does something a little dirty here, it only
// compares the item names and item costs. Technically, this is
// not the way that equals was intended to work.

        public boolean equals(Object other)
        {
            if (this == other) return true;

            if (!(other instanceof ShoppingCartItem))
                 return false;

            ShoppingCartItem otherItem =
                 (ShoppingCartItem) other;

            return (itemName.equals(otherItem.itemName)) &&
                 (itemCost == otherItem.itemCost);
        }

// Create a copy of this object

        public ShoppingCartItem copy()
        {
            return new ShoppingCartItem(itemName, itemCost,
                 quantity, descriptionURL);
        }

// Create a printable version of this object

        public String toString()
        {
            return itemName+" cost: "+itemCost+" qty: "+quantity+" desc: "+
                 descriptionURL;
        }
}
```

Note

One interesting thing about the `ShoppingCartItem` class is that it cheats when it comes to object equality. It treats any two objects with the same name and cost as being equal. If they have different quantities, they are still considered equal. This is usually not a good idea, since it can lead to confusion, but in this particular instance, it works nicely. If you have an item with some quantity value, you can search through the cart for the same object (ignoring the quantities) and if you find a matching object, you can just add their quantities together.

The next item on the agenda is the shopping cart itself. Since this is a very simple model of a cart, independent of the user interface, the cart should be observable. In other words, other objects should be able to watch the shopping cart to see when it changes. This allows you to write a user interface that updates itself whenever the cart is changed, yet you keep the user interface code out of the cart. The `Observer/Observable` mechanism is very handy for this sort of thing. The shopping cart is a subclass of the `Observable` class. Whenever the cart changes, it sends a notification to its observers. When you implement an observable object, you frequently need to notify the observers of different types of changes. For instance, in the shopping cart, you can add an item, remove an item, or change the quantity of an item. Since there is only one way to notify the observers that a change has taken place, you need to cram all that information into a single method call. You can accomplish this by creating an object that holds the information about the change. Listing 29.2 shows the `ShoppingCartEvent` class that holds the change information.

Listing 29.2 Source Code for *ShoppingCartEvent.java*

```
public class ShoppingCartEvent
{
// Define the kinds of changes that can take place
      public static final int ADDED_ITEM = 1;
      public static final int REMOVED_ITEM = 2;
      public static final int CHANGED_ITEM = 3;

// item is the item that is affected
      public ShoppingCartItem item;

// eventType is the kind of change that has taken
// place (add/remove/change)
      public int eventType;

      public ShoppingCartEvent()
      {
      }
```

```
        public ShoppingCartEvent(ShoppingCartItem item,
             int eventType)
        {
             this.item = item;
             this.eventType = eventType;
        }
}
```

Now you can create the shopping cart itself. All you really need is a vector object for storing the cart items and a variable for the total cost so far. You must also be sure that you always notify your observers whenever the cart changes. Another object may be keeping a duplicate record of all the items in the cart. If you add or remove an item from the cart without sending a notification, the other object will no longer have an accurate representation of the shopping cart. Listing 29.3 shows the `ShoppingCart` object.

Listing 29.3 Source Code for *ShoppingCart.java*

```
import java.applet.*;
import java.awt.*;
import java.net.*;
import java.util.*;

// This class is a simple container of shopping cart items.
// It is observable, which means that it notifies any interested
// classes whenever it changes.

public class ShoppingCart extends Observable
{
      protected Vector items;    // the items in the cart
      protected int total;       // the total item cost so far

      public ShoppingCart()
      {
           items = new Vector();
           total = 0;
      }

// Add a new item and update the total

      public void addItem(ShoppingCartItem newItem)
      {

// See if there's already an item like this in the cart
          int currIndex = items.indexOf(newItem);

          ShoppingCartEvent event = new ShoppingCartEvent();

          if (currIndex == -1) {
// If the item is new, add it to the cart
               items.addElement(newItem);
               event.item = newItem;
               event.eventType = ShoppingCartEvent.ADDED_ITEM;
```

continues

Listing 29.3 Continued

```
                } else {

// If there is a similar item, just add the quantities
                ShoppingCartItem currItem =
                     (ShoppingCartItem)
                     items.elementAt(currIndex);

                currItem.add(newItem);
                event.item = currItem;
                event.eventType = ShoppingCartEvent.CHANGED_ITEM;
           }

           total += newItem.itemCost * newItem.quantity;

// Tell the observers what just happened
           setChanged();
           notifyObservers(event);
      }

// Remove item removes an item from the cart. Since it removes
// n items from the cart at a time, if there are more than n items
// in the cart, it just subtracts n from the quantity.

      public void removeItem(ShoppingCartItem oldItem)
      {
// Find this object in the cart
           int currIndex = items.indexOf(oldItem);
           ShoppingCartEvent event = new ShoppingCartEvent();

           if (currIndex == -1) {
// If it wasn't there, just return, assume everything's okay
                return;
           } else {
                ShoppingCartItem currItem =
                        (ShoppingCartItem)
                        items.elementAt(currIndex);

// If you are trying to subtract more items than are in the cart,
// adjust the amount you want to subtract so it is equal to the
// number of items in the cart.

                if (oldItem.quantity > currItem.quantity) {
                     oldItem.quantity = currItem.quantity;
                }

// Adjust the total
                total -= oldItem.itemCost * oldItem.quantity;

                currItem.subtract(oldItem);

                event.item = currItem;
                event.eventType = ShoppingCartEvent.CHANGED_ITEM;

// If the quantity drops to 0, remove the item entirely
```

```
                if (currItem.quantity == 0) {
                     items.removeElementAt(currIndex);
                     event.eventType =
                        ShoppingCartEvent.REMOVED_ITEM;
                }

                }

// Tell everyone what happened

          setChanged();
          notifyObservers(event);
     }

// getItems returns a copy of all the items in the cart

     public ShoppingCartItem[] getItems()
     {
          ShoppingCartItem[] itemArray =
               new ShoppingCartItem[items.size()];

          items.copyInto(itemArray);

          return itemArray;
     }
}
```

Now that you have the basic framework for a shopping cart, you can work on a user interface for it.

Creating a Shopping Cart User Interface

The user interface for an electronic shopping cart is rarely a simple thing. Many shopping cart interfaces are incredibly complex, but also extremely easy to use. You can keep the interface pretty simple and still create a useful shopping cart, however.

If you think about the structure of a shopping cart application, you'll see that it really has two parts to it—the shopping cart and the catalog. When you are buying items, you look through the catalog of available items and select the ones you want. The catalog then sends these items to the shopping cart.

At some point, you go over to the shopping cart and review what you have selected. You may decide to put some of the items back, in which case the shopping cart must remove them from its list and possibly return them to the catalog. There are a number of ways to design a system like this. One of the more interesting ways is to create two separate applets—a catalog applet and a shopping cart applet.

Tip

It is frequently useful to split the user interface into separate applets. Many times, you can reuse one of the applets in another project without going through the pain of separating out the other parts of the user interface.

In order to implement this system with multiple applets, you need a way for the applets to locate each other. While applets can use the `AppletContext` class to find each other, your best bet is the `AppletRegistry` class, which was introduced in Chapter 10, "Inter-Applet Communication." The `AppletRegistry` class is an observable class, which means that an applet can be notified whenever new applets are loaded. If you don't use the registry, you must be prepared to occasionally poll for the other applets in case your applet starts up first.

For a simple user interface, you may decide to present a scrollable list of items both in the catalog and in the shopping cart. Unfortunately, the AWT `List` class leaves much to be desired when it comes to scrollable lists. The biggest problem with the `List` class is that is only stores strings. Since the strings you store in the scrollable lists are the strings the user sees, you can't really hide any information in them. For instance, if you look at the information stored in the `ShoppingCartItem` class, you realize that you don't want the URL for the item's description clogging up space in the list.

Listing 29.4 shows an `ObjectList` class that allows you to associate an object with each entry in a scrollable list.

Listing 29.4 Source Code for *ObjectList.java*

```
import java.awt.*;
import java.util.*;

// This class is a special version of a scrollable list that
// associates an object with each element in the list.

public class ObjectList extends List
{
     Vector objects;   // the objects that correspond to list entries

     public ObjectList()
     {
          objects = new Vector();
     }

     public ObjectList(int items, boolean multiSelect)
     {
          super(items, multiSelect);
          objects = new Vector();
```

```
    }

    public synchronized void addObject(Object ob)
    {
// add a string version of the object to the list
        super.addItem(ob.toString());

// add the object itself to the object vector
        objects.addElement(ob);
    }

    public synchronized void addObject(Object ob, int position)
    {
// add a string version of the object to the list
        super.addItem(ob.toString(), position);

// add the object itself to the object vector
        if (position >= objects.size()) {
            objects.addElement(ob);
        } else {
            objects.insertElementAt(ob.toString(),
                position);
        }
    }

    public synchronized void addObject(String label, Object ob)
    {
// Allow the object to be assigned a label independently of the object
        super.addItem(label);
        objects.addElement(ob);
    }

    public synchronized void addObject(String label, Object ob,
        int position)
    {
// Allow the object to be assigned a label independently of the object
        super.addItem(label, position);
        if (position >= objects.size()) {
                objects.addElement(ob);
        } else {
                objects.insertElementAt(ob.toString(),
                        position);
        }
    }

    public synchronized void delObject(Object ob)
    {
// See if the object is in the vector
        int index = objects.indexOf(ob);

// If not, just return
        if (index < 0) return;

// Remove the object from the vector
        objects.removeElementAt(index);
```

continues

Listing 29.4 Continued

```
// Remove the list entry
            super.delItem(index);
        }

        public synchronized Object getSelectedObject()
        {
// Get the index of the current selection
            int i = getSelectedIndex();

            if (i == -1) return null;

// Return the object currently selected
            return objects.elementAt(i);
        }

        public synchronized Object[] getSelectedObjects()
        {
// Get the indices of all the selected objects
            int[] selectedItems = getSelectedIndexes();

// Create an array of all the selected objects
            Object[] whichObjects = new Object[
                selectedItems.length];

            for (int i=0; i < selectedItems.length; i++) {
                whichObjects[i] = objects.elementAt(i);
            }

            return whichObjects;
        }

        public int indexOf(Object ob)
        {
// Locate a particular object
            return objects.indexOf(ob);
        }

        public Object objectAt(int index)
        {
// Return the object at a particular index
            return objects.elementAt(index);
        }

        public void replaceObject(Object ob, int index)
        {
// Change a specific entry in the vector
            replaceItem(ob.toString(), index);

// Change a specific entry in the list
            objects.setElementAt(ob, index);
        }

        public void replaceObject(String label, Object ob, int index)
        {
// Change a specific entry in the vector
```

```
            replaceItem(label, index);

// Change a specific entry in the list
            objects.setElementAt(ob, index);
        }
}
```

Note

You should use the `ObjectList` class in place of the `List` class in many, if not all, situations. It is important to be able to associate objects with the entries in a list, and even more important to keep the content of the list strings down to the bare minimum needed by the user.

Creating a Catalog Applet

The catalog interface should allow a user to browse through the items that are for sale. You should at least provide some sort of description. If you are selling software or online services, it would be even better to offer a small sample. This would also be true for music or video recordings. While Java doesn't have the ability to display many of these kinds of media yet, that capability is coming. For now, you can take advantage of the wonderful infrastructure of the Web and use simple URLs to describe the product. That way, you can include audio and video clips as you see fit.

Since the catalog and the shopping cart are different applets, they need some way to communicate back and forth. The `ShoppingCart` class is the perfect mechanism for this. Whenever someone selects an item from the catalog, the catalog applet adds the item to the `ShoppingCart` class. The shopping cart applet is an observer of the `ShoppingCart` class and sees the new item immediately.

Tip

If you recall the Model-View-Controller paradigm, which was discussed in Chapter 9, "Creating Reusable Graphics Components," the `ShoppingCart` class represents the model of the data. The catalog represents the controller, since it takes user input and translates it into changes in the model. The shopping cart applet is the view of the model, since it displays the items stored in the actual cart. The shopping cart applet also acts as a controller since it also takes input.

When the catalog applet starts up, it looks for the shopping cart applet via the applet registry. When it finds the other applet, it calls `getShoppingCart` to locate the instance of the `ShoppingCart` class that the two applets will share. Listing 29.5 shows the `ItemPickerApplet` class, which implements the user interface for the catalog portion of the shopping cart system.

Listing 29.5 Source Code for *ItemPickerApplet.java*

```
import java.awt.*;
import java.applet.*;
import java.net.*;
import java.util.*;
import java.io.*;

// This class represents the catalog portion of a shopping cart.
// You can select items and then either view a description of
// the item or add the item to the shopping cart.

public class ItemPickerApplet extends Applet implements Observer
{
      ObjectList items;
      ShoppingCart cart;
      AppletRegistry registry;

      public void init()
      {
// Watch the applet registry to see when the Shopping Cart applet
// becomes active
            registry = AppletRegistry.instance();
            registry.addObserver(this);

            items = new ObjectList();

// Get the URL of the list of items that are for sale
            String itemURL = getParameter("itemList");
            if (itemURL != null) fetchItems(itemURL);

// Put the items in the center of the screen
            setLayout(new BorderLayout());
            add("Center", items);

            checkForShoppingCart();

// Add this applet to the registry
            registry.addApplet("Item Picker", this);
      }

      public void checkForShoppingCart()
      {
// See if the shopping cart has been loaded yet
            Applet applet = registry.findApplet("Shopping Cart");
            if (applet == null) return;

            ShoppingCartApplet cartApplet = (ShoppingCartApplet)
```

```
                applet;

// Get the shopping cart used by the shopping cart applet
            cart = cartApplet.getShoppingCart();

// Create the panel for adding items
            Panel southPanel = new Panel();

// Set up some command buttons for adding and describing items
            southPanel.add(new CommandButton("Describe Item",
                new ItemPickerDescribe(this)));
            southPanel.add(new CommandButton("Add Item",
                new ItemPickerAdd(this)));

            add("South", southPanel);
        }

        public void update(Observable obs, Object ob)
        {
            if (cart != null) return;

            checkForShoppingCart();
        }

// When someone presses the "Add Item" button, the doAdd method
// is called.
        public void doAdd()
        {
// Find out what object was selected
            Object ob = items.getSelectedObject();

            if (ob == null) return;

// Add the item to the cart
            cart.addItem(((ShoppingCartItem)ob).copy());
        }

// When someone presses "Describe Item", the doDescribe method
// is called.

        public void doDescribe()
        {

// Find out which object was selected
            Object ob = items.getSelectedObject();

            if (ob == null) return;

            ShoppingCartItem item = (ShoppingCartItem) ob;

// If it has a description URL, open it up in another frame
            if (item.descriptionURL != null) {
                getAppletContext().showDocument(
                    item.descriptionURL, "descframe");
            }
        }
```

continues

Listing 29.5 Continued

```
// parseItem extracts an item name, cost, and URL from a string. The
// items should be separated by ¦'s.
     public void parseItem(String str)
     {
          StringTokenizer tokenizer = new StringTokenizer(str, "¦");

          if (tokenizer.countTokens() < 3) return;

          String name = tokenizer.nextToken();

          int cost = 0;
          try {
               cost = Integer.parseInt(tokenizer.nextToken());
          } catch (Exception ignore) {
          }

          URL descURL = null;

          try {
               descURL = new URL(tokenizer.nextToken());
          } catch (Exception ignore) {
          }

          items.addObject(name,
               new ShoppingCartItem(name, cost, 1, descURL));

     }

// fetchItems gets a list of available items from the web server and
// uses parseItem to parse the individual items. If a line begins with
// the # character, it is ignored (# is typically a comment character).

     public void fetchItems(String urlName)
     {
          try {
               URL url = new URL(urlName);

               DataInputStream inStream =
                    new DataInputStream(
                         url.openStream());

               String line;

               while ((line = inStream.readLine()) != null) {
                    if (line.charAt(0) == '#') continue;
                    parseItem(line);
               }
          } catch (Exception e) {
          }
     }
}
```

Notice that the ItemPickerApplet uses the CommandButton class that was also introduced in Chapter 10, "Inter-Applet Communication." The CommandButton class did not have to be

changed at all in order to be used with this application. The only necessary items are a few command classes that provide the glue between the command buttons and the catalog applet. Listing 29.6 shows the `ItemPickerDescribe` command class. The other command classes are almost identical to the `ItemPickerDescribe` class.

Listing 29.6 Source Code for *ItemPickerDescribe.java*

```
public class ItemPickerDescribe extends Object implements Command
{
     ItemPickerApplet cart;

     public ItemPickerDescribe(ItemPickerApplet cart)
     {
          this.cart = cart;
     }

     public void doCommand()
     {
          cart.doDescribe();
     }
}
```

Creating the Shopping Cart Applet

Now that most of the hard work has been done, the shopping cart interface itself is fairly easy. Basically, the shopping cart applet must be an observer of the shopping cart. Whenever the applet receives an update notification telling it that the shopping cart has changed, the applet simply changes its local list of items, which is a scrollable list (actually, it's an `ObjectList`). The shopping cart applet is also responsible for sending the order to the Web server. For posting data to the Web server, you can adapt the `PostSockURL` or `URLPost` classes from Chapter 6, "Communicating with a Web Server." Listing 29.7 shows the `ShoppingCartApplet` class.

Listing 29.7 Source Code for *ShoppingCartApplet.java*

```
import java.applet.*;
import java.awt.*;
import java.util.*;
import java.net.*;
import java.io.*;

// This class provides a user interface for the ShoppingCart class

public class ShoppingCartApplet extends Applet
     implements Observer
{
```

continues

Listing 29.7 Continued

```
    protected ShoppingCart cart;
    protected ObjectList itemList;
    protected TextField customerName;
    protected TextField totalField;

    public ShoppingCartApplet()
    {
// Make this class an observer of the shopping cart
        cart = new ShoppingCart();
        cart.addObserver(this);

// Create the list of objects in the cart
        itemList = new ObjectList();

// Create the field for the total cost so far
        totalField = new TextField(10);
        totalField.setEditable(false);
        totalField.setText("Total: "+cart.total);

        setLayout(new BorderLayout());

// Create a field for the customer name
        customerName = new TextField(20);

// Combine the label and the name field on a single panel
        Panel namePanel = new Panel();
        namePanel.add(new Label("Customer Name: "));
        namePanel.add(customerName);

// Put the name field up at the top and the item list in the center
        add("North", namePanel);
        add("Center", itemList);

// Create buttons for removing items and placing an order and put
// them along the bottom.

        Panel southPanel = new Panel();
        southPanel.add(new CommandButton(
             "Remove Item",
             new ShoppingCartRemove(this)));
        southPanel.add(new CommandButton(
             "Place Order",
             new ShoppingCartOrder(this)));
        southPanel.add(totalField);

        add("South", southPanel);

// Tell the applet registry about this applet
        AppletRegistry.instance().addApplet("Shopping Cart", this);
    }

    public String makeItemString(ShoppingCartItem item)
    {
        return item.itemName+"   Qty: "+item.quantity+
```

29

```
                "  Cost: "+item.itemCost;
        }

        public void update(Observable whichCart, Object ob)
        {
            ShoppingCartEvent event = (ShoppingCartEvent) ob;

            if (event.eventType == ShoppingCartEvent.ADDED_ITEM) {
// If there is a new item in the cart, add it to the scrollable list
                itemList.addObject(makeItemString(event.item),
                    event.item);
                totalField.setText("Total: "+cart.total);
                itemList.validate();
            } else if (event.eventType ==
// If an item has been removed from the cart, remove it from the list
                ShoppingCartEvent.REMOVED_ITEM) {
                itemList.delObject(event.item);
                totalField.setText("Total: "+cart.total);
                itemList.validate();
            } else if (event.eventType ==
                ShoppingCartEvent.CHANGED_ITEM) {
// If an item has changed, update the list
                int index = itemList.indexOf(event.item);
                itemList.replaceObject(makeItemString(
                    event.item), event.item, index);
                totalField.setText("Total: "+cart.total);
                itemList.validate();
            }
        }

// If the user clicks on "Remove Item," remove it from he list
        public void doRemove()
        {
            Object ob = itemList.getSelectedObject();
            if (ob == null) return;

            ShoppingCartItem item = ((ShoppingCartItem)ob).copy();
            item.quantity = 1;
            cart.removeItem(item);
        }

// doPlaceOrder uses PostSockURL to post the order to a web
// server. You will need to customize this method to fit your needs.

        public void doPlaceOrder()
        {
            try {
                URL postURL = new URL(
                    getDocumentBase().getProtocol(),
                    getDocumentBase().getHost(),
                    getDocumentBase().getPort(),
                    "/shopping");

                ByteArrayOutputStream byteOut =
                    new ByteArrayOutputStream();
                PrintStream outStream =
                    new PrintStream(byteOut);
```

continues

Listing 29.7 Continued

```
                outStream.println("Custname: "+
                     customerName.getText());
                ShoppingCartItem[] items = cart.getItems();
                for (int i=0; i < items.length; i++) {
                     outStream.println(
                          items[i].itemName+"|"+
                          items[i].quantity);
                }

                String response = PostSockURL.post(postURL,
                     byteOut.toString());
                System.out.println(response);
           } catch (Exception e) {
                e.printStackTrace();
           }

      }

      public ShoppingCart getShoppingCart()
      {
           return cart;
      }
}
```

Figure 29.1 shows the shopping cart applet in action.

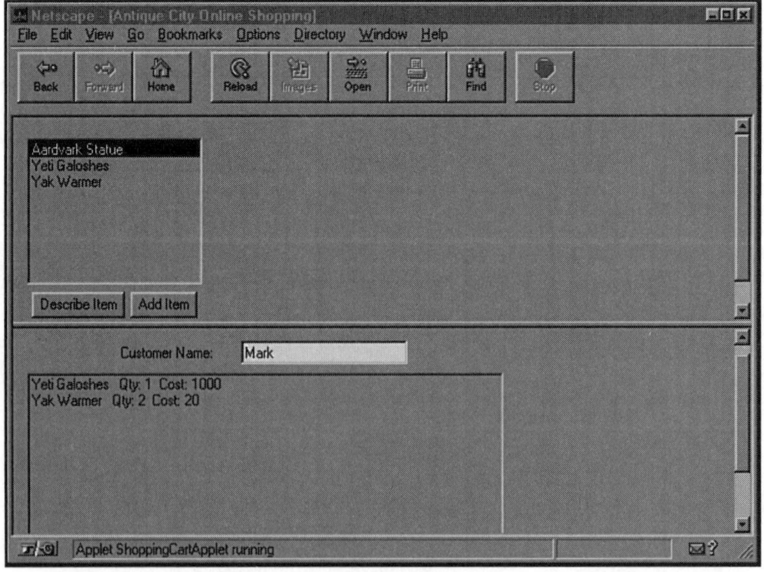

Fig. 29.1
The shopping cart applet works in conjunction with a catalog applet.

When you request a description of an item, the catalog applet opens another browser window for viewing descriptions. Since the descriptions are simple URLs, you can include any data that you could normally place on a Web page. Figure 29.2 shows the description window for the shopping cart applet.

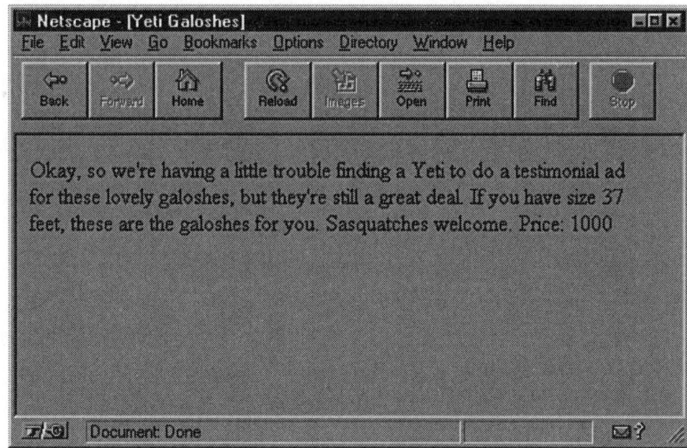

Fig. 29.2
An item description can be described by simple HTML pages.

In addition to providing an introduction to electronic shopping carts, this chapter reuses several key components from previous chapters. This makes the programs in this chapter easier to write, and it shows that the components that were presented as being reusable really *are* reusable.

One of the upcoming additions to Java, the Java Electronic Commerce Framework (JECF), will help you when developing shopping cart applications. Your shopping cart will be allowed to conduct financial transactions with the user's Java Wallet, which provides payment via credit card access, electronic cash, and other forms of electronic transactions. Chapter 31, "Java Electronic Commerce Framework (JECF)," provides an overview of the services provided by the JECF.

Finally, remember to use secure communications when performing any transactions that involve personal information such as credit card numbers or social security numbers. It is a good idea to provide secure access at all times, because some customers will want all aspects of a transaction to be hidden from prying eyes.

chapter 30

Performing Secure Transactions

by Mark Wutka

In this chapter

- **Digitally signing orders**
  Digital signatures enable you and your customer to verify each other's identity. A digital signature can also be used to sign orders and receipts just like a handwritten signature.
- **Encrypting communications**
  To ensure your customer's privacy and security, you should encrypt all communications between the customer and your server.
- **Using Netscape servers for secure transactions**
  Netscape's Web servers support the Secure Socket Layer (SSL) protocol, enabling you to create Web services that are safely encrypted.
- **Creating a secure ordering system**
  Using a combination of a Netscape Web server and the SSL protocol, you can create an ordering system that is secure and tamper-proof.

When you do business on the Web, you need to assure your customers that their personal information is safe. Obviously, you need to keep the credit card numbers secure, but sometimes you need to protect more than that. Sometimes the contents of an order need to be kept quiet. You may be selling items or services of a personal nature, for instance. Sometimes competitors can learn about a company's plans just by analyzing their recent orders.

Obviously, you need to provide Web services that support encryption to keep the contents of the services private. For you to really do this securely, you need a signed digital certificate, registered with some trusted certificate authority. To protect your customers, you should also allow customers to verify themselves with signed certificates, as well.

As digital commerce becomes more mainstream, digital signatures will continue to grow in importance. Your digital signature may one day be as important, or even more important, than your handwritten signature. Unfortunately, digital signatures are still rather expensive to maintain. The average user isn't going to pay a fee to a certificate authority just to keep their signature on file.

At some point, however, there should be a cheaper way to keep digital signatures on file. It may be a service offered by credit card companies, who have a vested interest in preventing fraud. It is also possible that other signature mechanisms will be available soon.

Letting Customers Digitally Sign Orders

Security is making its way onto the Web slowly, but its pace is increasing. With the increasing need to secure browsers and servers, more companies are able to offer secure services. There are enough companies doing business without security, however, so that the ability to do a secure transaction is a competitive advantage.

One of the next new features will be personal digital signatures. Each customer will have their own signature, or set of signatures. By letting a customer digitally sign an order, you protect yourself and your customer.

From the customer's standpoint, being able to digitally sign orders means that other people can't place phony orders using the customer's name and credit card number. This gives the customer extra security, knowing that even if someone had their credit card number, they couldn't place an order on your system.

This mechanism also protects you from the same kind of fraud. You don't want someone else placing phony orders using the names of your good customers. When you receive a digitally signed order, you know that it came from the person who signed the order.

Your customer places an order, digitally signing it to verify that it is their order. The customer then sends both the order and the digital signature to you, as shown in Figure 30.1.

At this point, you can confirm the customer's identity by verifying it with a certificate authority. If someone were trying to create a fake order, they would not know the customer's digital signature key, so they would not be able to sign the order.

In the future, credit card companies might require digital signatures on all electronic transactions. This could cut down on fraud, as long as people keep their private signature keys away from prying eyes. There are a number of signature exchange protocols that may be required for credit card transactions. The credit card company would need your signature on a receipt, as well as the customer's.

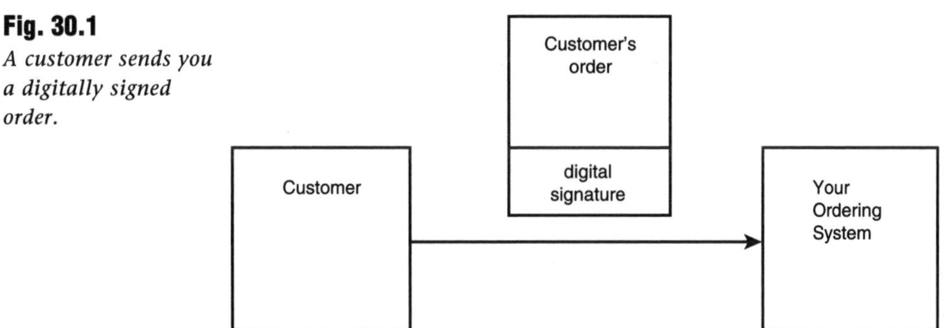

Fig. 30.1
A customer sends you a digitally signed order.

After a customer sends you a digitally signed order, you create an electronic credit card receipt and digitally sign it, then pass it to the customer, as shown in Figure 30.2.

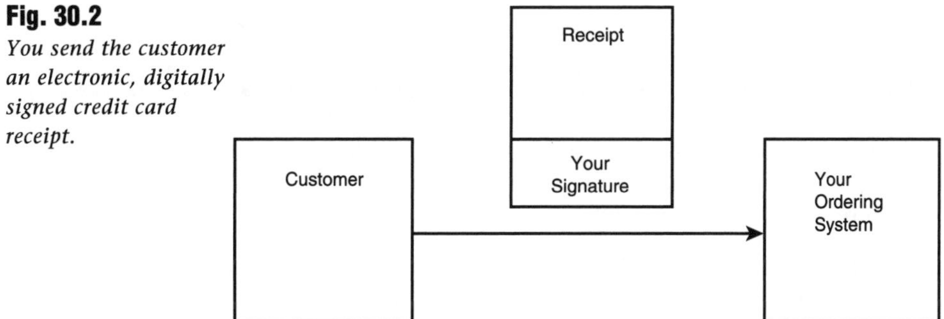

Fig. 30.2
You send the customer an electronic, digitally signed credit card receipt.

Figure 30.3 illustrates the next step in the sequence. The customer verifies your signature on the receipt, then digitally signs the receipt and sends it back.

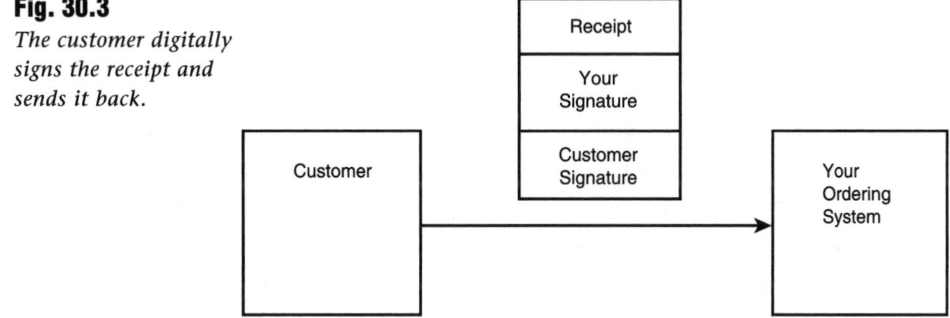

Fig. 30.3
The customer digitally signs the receipt and sends it back.

Now, you have a signed receipt to send to the credit card company which shows that the customer agrees to the transaction. The credit card company can verify the customer's signature.

You can also use digital signatures to prevent the transmission of credit card numbers over the Internet. In this case, you need some way to get the customer's credit card number up front, as well as the public key for their digital signature. You keep their credit card number in a secure database, along with their signature key and the customer account number.

Now, when a customer places an order, they give you only their customer number, which you use to look up their credit card number. Since you also require that the order is digitally signed, someone else couldn't use that customer's account number.

It is conceivable that you could perform unencrypted transactions this way, however, you still need to use a secure download method to download the Java applets that will perform the transaction. Otherwise, you have the potential for someone to create a phony applet, as discussed in Chapter 27, "Encrypting Data."

Using Encryption in All Network Communications

At the moment, the only encryption mechanism that is readily accessible to Java applets is through the SSL protocol built into the Web browsers. Unfortunately, not all Java-enabled browsers support SSL.

Future releases of Java will include a security library with many encryption routines. This will eventually allow remote-object systems, like RMI and CORBA, to support encrypted sessions. This is extremely important. You don't want to be tied to the restrictions of http communications, as you are when using https URLs (SSL-enabled URLs).

Creating Java Services for Netscape Servers

While it would be nice to write secure Web services using a Java Web server like Jeeves or Jigsaw, these servers do not yet support secure protocols such as SSL. If you were really desperate to use one of these, you could write a CGI script on a secure server to forward requests to the non-secure Java Web server and then relay the results back. This is not a very pretty solution, however.

Netscape's Web servers support server-side Java programs, which Netscape calls "server-side applets." In addition, Netscape's Web servers support the SSL protocol, allowing you to create secure transactions. You used the SSL protocol in Chapter 28 to download an applet securely. For secure transactions, you also use it to transmit data.

Netscape took a more traditional CGI-like approach to server-side Java. Every time the server gets a request that is serviced by a server applet, the server creates a new instance of the server applet and invokes that applet's `run` command. When the applet has serviced the request and sent a result, the applet terminates.

If you look at the `HttpApplet` class, and its parent class, `ServerApplet`, you'll notice that they are similar to CGI. Instead of environment variables for the various HTTP header values, there are methods to retrieve the interesting header values. You can retrieve any value from the header using the `getHeader` method, like:

```
String contentType = getHeader("Content-type");
```

The `ServerApplet` class also provides methods to get an input stream and an output stream for the client connection. In CGI, these are mapped to the standard input and standard output streams. The `getInputStream` and `getOutputStream` methods are defined as follows:

```
public InputStream getInputStream() throws IOException
public OutputStream getOutputStream() throws IOException
```

When your `HttpApplet` is ready to return a response to the client, it calls the `returnNormalResponse` method:

```
public boolean returnNormalResponse(String contentType) throws IOException
```

The `returnNormalResponse` method returns true if you need to send a response. The reason for this is that there is an HTTP request type called "HEAD" that doesn't expect a response. The `returnNormalResponse` method returns false if the incoming request was a HEAD request. If you are returning an HTML form, you should use "text/html" for the `contentType` parameter. If you are returning non-HTML text, you should use a `contentType` of "text/plain."

Creating a Server-Side "Hello World"

You now have enough information to write the ubiquitous "Hello World" program for a Netscape Web server. Listing 30.1 shows the `ServerHello class`, which generates a "Hello World" page in HTML.

Listing 30.1 Source Code for *ServerHello.java*

```
import netscape.server.applet.*;
import java.io.PrintStream;

public class ServerHello extends HttpApplet {
```

continues

Listing 30.1 Continued

```
        ServerHello() {}

        public void run() throws Exception {

            if (returnNormalResponse("text/html")) {
                  PrintStream out = getOutputStream();

               out.println("<HTML><HEAD>");
               out.println("<TITLE>Hello World!</TITLE>");
               out.println("</HEAD>");

               out.println("<BODY>");
               out.println("<H1>Hello World!</H1>");
               out.println("</BODY></HTML>");
                }
        }
}
```

Figure 30.4 shows the very simple output from this applet on a Web browser.

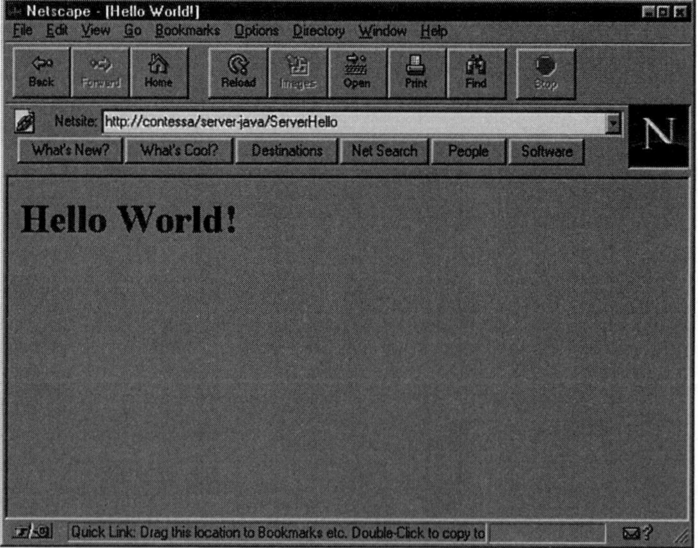

Fig. 30.4
Server-side Java applets may generate HTML output.

Installing a New Server-Side Java Applet

The Netscape Web servers store all the Java applets in a single directory. From the root directory of the server, the applets are installed in `plugins/java/applets`. When you install a new applet, you just copy the .class file into that directory, and restart the server.

Tip

While it seems to go against the "on-demand" loading concept taken by many Java environments, Netscape Web servers load all the Java applets at startup, taking the speed hit up front, instead of when the applet is requested.

Once you install a server-side Java applet, you can run it using an URL of this form:

```
http://host_name/server-java/applet_name
```

For example, if you were running the ServerHello applet on a host called `pandora.contessa.com`, you would use the following URL:

```
http://pandora.contessa.com/server-java/ServerHello
```

Handling Forms from Server-Side Applets

It is very simple to handle forms in a server-side applet. The `HttpApplet` class takes the same approach as the servlet API by returning the form parameters in a hash table. You simply call the `getFormData` method, like this:

```
Hashtable formItems = getFormData();
```

Listing 30.2 shows a server-side applet that displays a form, and then receives the submitted form. It is able to do both of these things because the form results are sent using an HTTP `POST`, while the initial input form is retrieved via `GET`. The applet simply checks to see what HTTP method was used to invoke it.

Listing 30.2 Source Code for *FormDemo.java*

```
import netscape.server.applet.*;
import java.io.PrintStream;
import java.util.Hashtable;
import java.util.Enumeration;

// This is a Netscape server-side applet that generates a
// form which posts information back to this same applet.

public class FormDemo extends HttpApplet {

        FormDemo() {}

        public void run() throws Exception {

          if (returnNormalResponse("text/html")) {
```

continues

Listing 30.2 Continued

```
// If this applet was retrieved with a GET, send the input form
               if (getMethod().equals("GET")) {
                    sendInputForm();
               } else {
// Otherwise, this must have been a post, so retrieve the posted data
                    processForm();
               }
          }
     }

     protected void sendInputForm()
     throws Exception
     {
               PrintStream out = getOutputStream();

// Send the header
          out.println("<HTML><HEAD>");
          out.println("<TITLE>Java-Five Needs Input!</TITLE>");
          out.println("</HEAD>");

          out.println("<BODY>");
          out.println("<H1>Give Me Some Input!</H1>");

// Send the input form
          out.println("<FORM action=\"/server-java/FormDemo\" "+
               "method=POST>");

// Input field titled "First Name"
          out.println("First Name: ");
          out.println("<INPUT type=\"text\" name=\"First Name\">");
          out.println("<P>");

// Input field titled "Last Name"
          out.println("Last Name: ");
          out.println("<INPUT type=\"text\" name=\"Last Name\">");
          out.println("<P>");

// Button to submit the form
          out.println("<INPUT type=submit><P>");
          out.println("</FORM>");
          out.println("</BODY></HTML>");
        }

     protected void processForm()
     throws Exception
     {
               PrintStream out = getOutputStream();

// Send the initial part of the response

          out.println("<HTML><HEAD>");
          out.println("<TITLE>OOOOH!!  Input!! MMM!!</TITLE>");
          out.println("</HEAD>");

          out.println("<BODY>");
```

```
            out.println("<H1>Thanks for the input!</H1>");
            out.println("Just for the record, here's what you sent:<P>");

    // Get the fields from the form
            Hashtable formData = getFormData();

    // For each field on the form, print the value
            Enumeration keys = formData.keys();
            while (keys.hasMoreElements()) {
                 String key = (String) keys.nextElement();

                 out.println(key+": "+formData.get(key)+"<P>");
            }
            out.println("</BODY></HTML>");
        }
    }
```


Figure 30.5 shows the initial input form from this applet, while Figure 30.6 shows the results from the submission of the form.

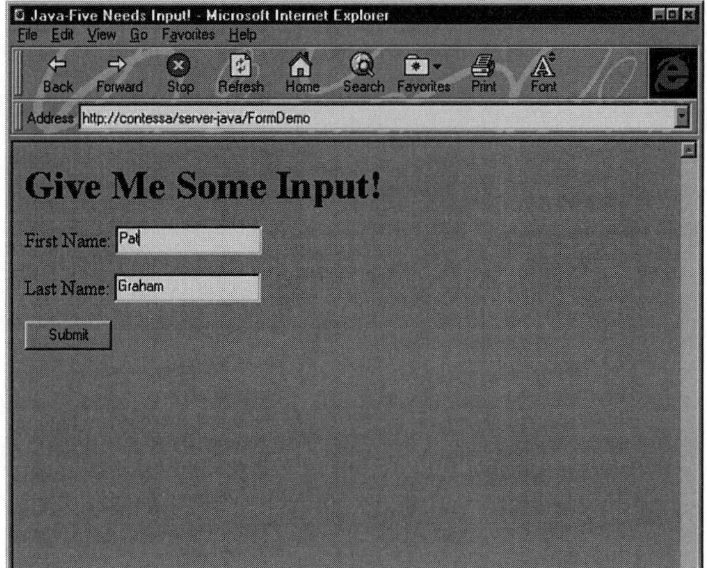

Fig. 30.5
The FormDemo *applet displays a simple input form.*

Sending Files as a Response

Instead of generating HTML or other content straight from Java, you can create server-side applets that return other files. For example, you might be creating an on-demand audio or video library controlled by a server-side applet. The applet verifies the client's access, handles any billing information, and then tells the server to return the requested file. The `returnFile` method lets you tell the server which file to return. The method is defined like this:

```
public void returnFile(String contentType, File file)
throws IOException
```

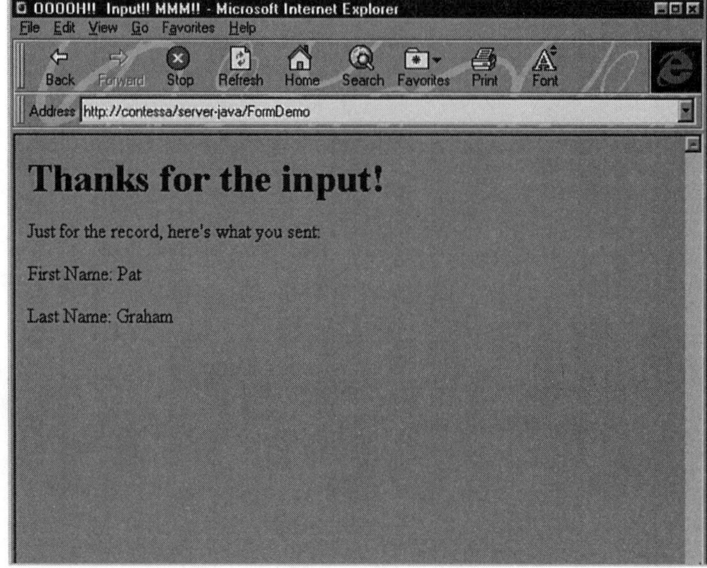

Fig. 30.6
The `FormDemo` *applet processes its own input form.*

The file is an absolute pathname; it is not relative to the root directory of the Web server. This means that a server-side applet can return any file on the system, as long as it has sufficient permissions.

If the server can figure out the type of the file based on its suffix (like `.gif` or `.mov`), you don't have to specify the content type when you return a file. In these cases, you can use the alternate version of `returnFile`:

```
public void returnFile(File file) throws IOException
```

Listing 30.3 shows a minimal server-side applet that returns an image file. Since the filename ends with ".jpg," the applet doesn't have to specify the content type.

Listing 30.3 Source Code for *ShowPicture.java*

```
import netscape.server.applet.*;
import java.io.File;

public class ShowPicture extends HttpApplet {
```

```
        ShowPicture() {}

        public void run() throws Exception {
          returnFile(new File("\\pictures\\kaitlynn.jpg"));
        }
}
```

Figure 30.7 shows the picture returned by this applet. Notice that there is no surrounding text, only an image.

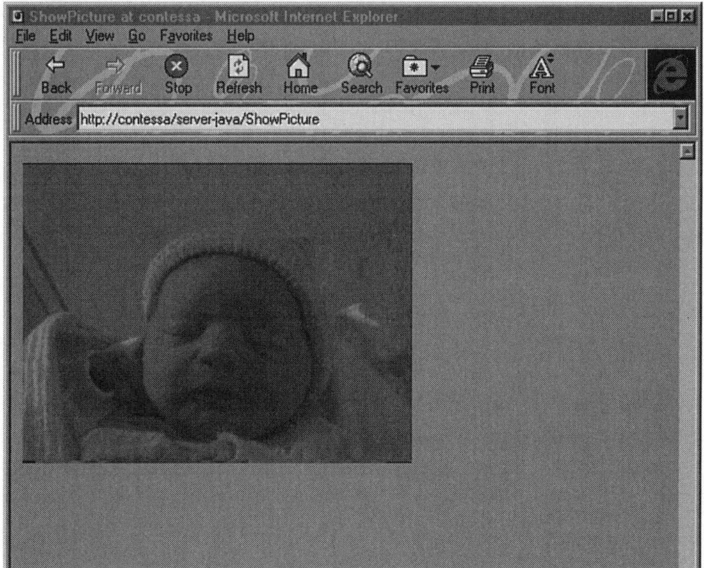

Fig. 30.7
A server-side applet can return images, movies, and audio files.

Returning Multi-Part Responses

Multi-part responses are a neat little hack to HTTP that allow you to perform primitive kinds of animation. The idea is that, instead of sending a single response to the client, you send multiple responses. This allows you to send a series of images as an animation, or display a page of information that occasionally updates itself. The `returnMultipartResponse` method in the `HttpApplet` class allows your server-side Java programs to return multi-part responses:

```
public boolean returnMultipartResponse(String subtype)
     throws IOException
```

The `subtype` value should either be "mixed" or "x-mixed-replace." Once you send the multi-part response header, you send responses normally, using the `returnNormalResponse` method.

When you generate a multi-part response, you keep the connection to the client open until you tell the client that you are through sending responses. In a server-side applet, you tell the client you are through sending responses by calling the `endMultipartResponse` method:

```
public void endMultipartResponse() throws IOException
```

Listing 30.4 shows a server-side applet that displays the current time using a multi-part response. It updates the time every five seconds.

Listing 30.4 Source Code for *Multipart.java*

```
import netscape.server.applet.*;
import java.io.PrintStream;
import java.util.Date;

// This applet sends a multi-part response that displays the
// current time every 5 seconds.

public class Multipart extends HttpApplet {

        Multipart() {}

        public void run() throws Exception {

// Tell the server we are sending a multi-part response

          if (returnMultipartResponse("x-mixed-replace")) {

                PrintStream out = getOutputStream();

                while (true) {

// Send the next part of the response
                     returnNormalResponse("text/html");

                     out.println("<HTML><HEAD>");
                     out.println("<TITLE>Web Clock</TITLE>");
                     out.println("</HEAD>");

                     out.println("<BODY>");
                     out.println("<H1>Current Time</H1>");
                     out.println(new Date());
                     out.println("<P>");
                     out.println("</BODY></HTML>");

// Wait a little while before sending another
                     Thread.sleep(5000);
                }
                 }
        }
}
```

Maintaining Information Between Applet Invocations

One of the advantages to the Servlet API is that there is only one instance of a particular servlet and it stays around after a request completes. The Netscape server-side applets don't work that way. There are multiple instances of a particular applet, and the instances go away after completing their assigned task.

This is not a difficult problem to get around, however. All you need to do is set up another class that is implemented as a singleton. In other words, there is only one instance of the class. Listing 30.5 shows an example singleton class.

Listing 30.5 Source Code for *PersistentInfo.java*

```
import java.util.Vector;

// This is a singleton class that maintains a vector of
// strings. Since the constructor is protected, the only
// way you can get an instance of this class is by calling
// the instance method, which returns the single shared
// copy of the class.

public class PersistentInfo
{
// singleInstance is the lone instance of this class
     protected static PersistentInfo singleInstance;

// info is the vector of strings
     protected Vector info;

// instance returns the lone instance of this class, and creates one
// if there isn't one already.

     public synchronized static PersistentInfo instance()
     {
          if (singleInstance == null) {
               singleInstance = new PersistentInfo();
          }
          return singleInstance;
     }

     protected PersistentInfo()
     {
          info = new Vector();
     }

// getInfo returns an array of the strings stored in the info vector

     public synchronized String[] getInfo()
     {
          String[] strings = new String[info.size()];

          info.copyInto(strings);
```

continues

Listing 30.5 Continued

```
          return strings;
     }

// addInfo adds another string to the info list

     public synchronized void addInfo(String newInfo)
     {
          info.addElement(newInfo);
     }
}
```

The `PersistentInfo` class stays active while the Java VM is running. This means that any instances of `HttpApplet` can access the info in `PersistentInfo` at any time. You can use this method to keep database connections open, or keep open a session with a host that may take a long time to set up.

Tip

If you use singleton classes with your applets, be especially careful about using synchronization. While you may not be explicitly creating threads, each `HttpApplet` object runs in its own thread.

Listing 30.6 shows a server-side applet that uses the `PersistentInfo` object. The applet generates a form with a single text field. Any information in the text field is added to the `PersistentInfo` object.

Listing 30.6 Source Code for *PersistDemo.java*

```
import netscape.server.applet.*;
import java.io.PrintStream;
import java.util.Hashtable;
import java.util.Enumeration;

// This is a Netscape server-side applet that generates a
// form which posts information back to this same applet.
// It uses a second class called PersistentInfo.
// The PersistentInfo class sticks around, so information
// is preserved for future instances of this class.

public class PersistDemo extends HttpApplet {

        PersistDemo() {}

        public void run() throws Exception {
```

```
            if (returnNormalResponse("text/html")) {

// If this applet was retrieved with a GET, send the input form
                  if (getMethod().equals("GET")) {
                        sendInputForm();
                  } else {
// Otherwise, this must have been a post, so retrieve the posted data
                        processForm();
                  }
            }
      }

      protected void sendInputForm()
      throws Exception
      {
                  PrintStream out = getOutputStream();

// Send the header
            out.println("<HTML><HEAD>");
            out.println("<TITLE>Persistent Information Demo</TITLE>");
            out.println("</HEAD>");

            out.println("<BODY>");

            out.println("<H1>Current information:</H1>");

// Print out the strings currently stored in the PersistenceInfo class

            String strings[] = PersistentInfo.instance().getInfo();

            for (int i=0; i < strings.length; i++) {
                  out.println(strings[i]+"<P>");
            }

            out.println("<H1>Please enter some new information</H1>");

// Send the input form
            out.println("<FORM action=\"/server-java/PersistDemo\" "+
                  "method=POST>");

// Input field titled "First Name"
            out.println("Information: ");
            out.println("<INPUT type=\"text\" name=\"Information\">");
            out.println("<P>");

// Button to submit the form
            out.println("<INPUT type=submit><P>");
            out.println("</FORM>");
            out.println("</BODY></HTML>");
          }

      protected void processForm()
      throws Exception
      {
// Get the fields from the form
            Hashtable formData = getFormData();
```

continues

Listing 30.6 Continued

```
// If there's any information, add it to the PersistentInfo class
          String newInfo = (String) formData.get("Information");
          if (newInfo != null) {
               PersistentInfo.instance().addInfo(newInfo);
          }

// Put up another form so we can get more input
          sendInputForm();
     }
}
```

Figure 30.8 shows the output from this server-side applet.

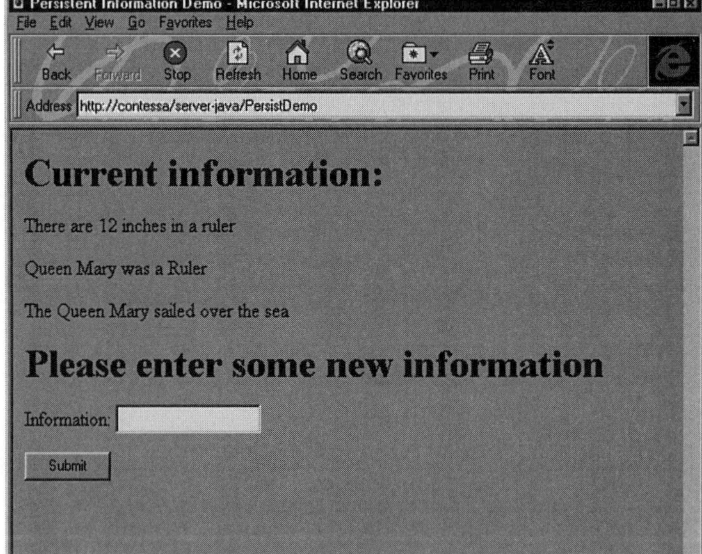

Fig. 30.8
A singleton object can preserve information for multiple `HttpApplet` *instances.*

Making Server-Side Applets Work on Different Web Servers

If you need to create secure server-side Java objects, whether they are applets or servlets, you want to do the tough work only once. In fact, you want to write the application only one time.

After that, you may have to do a little work hooking your application into the local Web server. This goes back to one of the basic design principles, where you design the application without considering the user interface. When you run an application on a Java Web server, the applet or servlet represents the user interface.

Try to create the application without regard to the user interface. Don't return HTML forms from the application itself, and don't let it parse HTML. Instead, dedicate your servlet, or server-side applet, to handling HTML and invoking methods on a separate application object.

This method will allow you to provide multiple forms of access to your application. You might have a Web interface and a CORBA interface to the same application simultaneously.

Performing Secure Transactions

The only mechanism currently available for performing a secure transaction with Java is through https URLs. Furthermore, the only Web servers that currently support Java on the server side, and https, are the Netscape Web servers.

Caution
If the URL for your service starts with http and not https, your transactions are *not* encrypted.

This will certainly not be the case forever, though. As security becomes integrated into the Java environment, more Web servers, and other systems, will support encryption and digital signatures. The trick, as always, is to design and build your applications so you can run them now, but keep them flexible enough to embrace other technologies as they become available.

Listing 30.7 shows a framework for a simple ordering system. Notice that the system doesn't have any knowledge of applets or servlets—just ordering.

Listing 30.7 Source Code for *TheStore.java*

```
// A dummy storefront that has some items for sale.
// The store doesn't record its transactions, however.

public class TheStore
{
// Make sure there's only one instance of the store
```

continues

Listing 30.7 Continued

```
     protected static TheStore singleInstance;

     protected StoreItem items[];

     public static TheStore instance()
     {
          if (singleInstance == null) {
               singleInstance = new TheStore();
          }
          return singleInstance;
     }

// Create a store with some items
     protected TheStore()
     {
          items = new StoreItem[3];

          items[0] = new StoreItem("Dongle", 199);
          items[1] = new StoreItem("Widget", 599);
          items[2] = new StoreItem("Tweaker", 799);
     }

// Return a list of available items

     public StoreItem[] getItems()
     throws StoreException
     {
          try {
               return (StoreItem[]) items.clone();
          } catch (Exception e) {
               return null;
          }
     }

// A dummy routine for purchasing products

     public void purchase(String customerId, String itemList[])
     throws StoreException
     {
// Normally you would do something here to record the purchase
     }
}
```

This class also uses some auxiliary classes, which are shown in Listings 30.8 and 30.9.

Listing 30.8 Source Code for *StoreException.java*

```
public class StoreException extends Exception
{
     public StoreException(String why)
     {
          super(why);
```

```
     }
}
```

Listing 30.9 Source Code for *StoreItem.java*

```
public class StoreItem
{
     public String itemName;
     public int price;

     public StoreItem(String itemName, int price)
     {
          this.itemName = itemName;
          this.price = price;
     }
}
```

Now that the first step has been taken, and there is an application defined, you can start creating different interfaces into the application. Since you already have some examples of server-side applets that present HTML forms and parse them, it is fairly simple to create a similar applet that places orders with this application. Listing 30.10 shows an HTML front end for this application.

Listing 30.10 Source Code for *HTMLStoreFront.java*

```
import netscape.server.applet.*;
import java.io.PrintStream;
import java.util.Hashtable;
import java.util.Vector;
import java.util.Enumeration;

// This class implements an HTML interface for the TheStore class.

public class HTMLStoreFront extends HttpApplet {

        HTMLStoreFront() {}

        public void run() throws Exception {

          if (returnNormalResponse("text/html")) {

// If this applet was retrieved with a GET, send the input form
                if (getMethod().equals("GET")) {
                     sendInputForm();
                } else {
// Otherwise, this must have been a post, so retrieve the posted data
                     processForm();
                }
          }
```

continues

Listing 30.10 Continued

```
    }

    protected void sendInputForm()
    throws Exception
    {
              PrintStream out = getOutputStream();

// Send the header
          out.println("<HTML><HEAD>");
          out.println("<TITLE>The Store</TITLE>");
          out.println("</HEAD>");

          out.println("<BODY>");
          out.println("<H1>What would you like to order?</H1>");

// Send the input form
          out.println("<FORM action=\"/server-java/HTMLStoreFront\" "+
               "method=POST>");

          out.println("<P>Customer ID #: ");
          out.println("<INPUT type=text name=\"customerID\">");
          out.println("<P>");
// List the items on sale from the store, and their prices
          StoreItem[] items = TheStore.instance().getItems();

          for (int i=0; i < items.length; i++) {
               out.println("<INPUT type=checkbox name=\""+
                    items[i].itemName+"\" value=off>");
               out.println(items[i].itemName+"     "+
                    items[i].price+"<P>");
          }

// Button to submit the form
          out.println("<INPUT type=submit><P>");
          out.println("</FORM>");
          out.println("</BODY></HTML>");
       }

    protected void processForm()
    throws Exception
    {
              PrintStream out = getOutputStream();

// Get the fields from the form
          Hashtable formData = getFormData();

          Vector partOrder = new Vector();
          String customerID = null;

// For each field on the form, see if the checkbox is on

          Enumeration keys = formData.keys();
          while (keys.hasMoreElements()) {
               String key = (String) keys.nextElement();
```

```
// If we got the customerID field, save it and go on

                if (key.equals("customerID")) {
                     customerID = (String) formData.get(key);
                     continue;
                }

// If the checkbox was on for this part, add it to the parts vector

                partOrder.addElement(key);
           }

           String[] orderItems = new String[partOrder.size()];

           partOrder.copyInto(orderItems);

           try {
                TheStore.instance().purchase(customerID, orderItems);

// Send a success response
                out.println("<HTML><HEAD>");
                out.println("<TITLE>The Store - Order Completed");
                out.println("</TITLE>");
                out.println("</HEAD>");

                out.println("<BODY>");
                out.println("<H1>Order Complete. ");
                out.println("Thanks for the business!</H1>");

                out.println("<P>Items on your order:<P>");
                for (int i=0; i < orderItems.length; i++) {
                     out.println(orderItems[i]+"<P>");
                }

           } catch (Exception e) {

// If we got an error ordering, print the reason
                out.println("<HTML><HEAD>");
                out.println("<TITLE>The Store - Order Aborted!");
                out.println("</TITLE>");
                out.println("</HEAD>");

                out.println("<BODY>");
                out.println("<H1>Order Aborted!</H1>");
                out.println("Here's why:<P>");
                out.println(e+"<P>");
           }
           out.println("</BODY></HTML>");
      }
}
```

Plain old HTML forms are pretty boring. You really want to liven up your ordering system by running a Java applet on the client side, right? You can do this, and still keep everything secure!

You can use the technique outlined in Chapter 6, "Communicating with a Web Server," for posting to a URL. This will allow you to send secure data to a server-side applet, which can then interpret the posted data and send a response.

Rather than making your applet parse the form returned by the `HTMLStoreFront` class, you can create a similar class that is friendly to applets. Instead of sending HTML data, it sends plain text in a format that the applet can easily read. Listing 30.11 shows such a class.

Listing 30.11 Source Code for *AppletStoreFront.java*

```
import netscape.server.applet.*;
import java.io.PrintStream;
import java.util.Hashtable;
import java.util.Vector;
import java.util.Enumeration;

// This class implements a secure interface for the TheStore class.
// This interface is used by client-side applets to store and
// retrieve data securely.

public class AppletStoreFront extends HttpApplet {

        AppletStoreFront() {}

        public void run() throws Exception {

          if (returnNormalResponse("text/plain")) {

// If this applet was retrieved with a GET, send the input form
                if (getMethod().equals("GET")) {
                     sendItemList();
                } else {
// Otherwise, this must have been a post, so retrieve the posted data
                     processOrder();
                }
          }
     }

     protected void sendItemList()
     throws Exception
     {
                PrintStream out = getOutputStream();

          StoreItem[] items = TheStore.instance().getItems();

          for (int i=0; i < items.length; i++) {
               out.println(items[i].itemName);
               out.println(items[i].price);
          }
        }

     protected void processOrder()
     throws Exception
```

```
      {
                PrintStream out = getOutputStream();

  // Get the fields from the form
            Hashtable formData = getFormData();

            Vector partOrder = new Vector();
            String customerID = null;

  // For each field on the form, see if the checkbox is on

            Enumeration keys = formData.keys();
            while (keys.hasMoreElements()) {
                 String key = (String) keys.nextElement();

  // If we got the customerID field, save it and go on

                 if (key.equals("customerID")) {
                      customerID = (String) formData.get(key);
                      continue;
                 }

  // add the part to the parts vector

                 partOrder.addElement(key);
            }

            String[] orderItems = new String[partOrder.size()];

            partOrder.copyInto(orderItems);

            try {
                 out.println("OK");
            } catch (Exception e) {
                 out.println("ERROR: "+e);
            }
      }
  }
```

Once again, you haven't had to change a single line of code in the original application class. All you do is add new user interfaces for it. You could follow this same track and create an RMI interface and a CORBA interface to this application. Of course, if you can't get a secure version of RMI or CORBA yet, you can't do secure transactions.

chapter 31

Java Electronic Commerce Framework (JECF)

31

by Eric Ries

In this chapter

- **Performing online transactions**
  The JECF is a framework that enables you to create many kinds of online services. You may be creating an online credit card system, or you may be creating an online game network that makes charges against an online credit card system.
- **Securing the Java wallet**
  The Java Wallet is a powerful and dangerous concept. You have a wallet that is made up of live programs, not dead pieces of plastic like your real-life wallet. The JECF contains many security measures to keep these live programs from doing things they shouldn't.
- **Creating wallet services**
  Wallet services, also known as cassettes, are extremely flexible. One cassette may be an electronic version of your normal credit card, while another may implement digital cash. A cassette can also perform financial services like income tax computation or budgeting.

The Internet has provided a tremendous opportunity for business. Many millions have already been made by businesses related to the Internet and companies that have taken advantage of the Internet's unique features. Like any financial medium, the Internet has sparked concerns about the safety and reliability of doing business online. Part of this hesitation stems from the fact that there is no real standard for conducting secure, safe, and simple transactions online. Although several methods do exist for Internet commerce, they are all built upon proprietary protocols and existing, static payment methods. Although most of these systems now have secure encryption-based security, none provides a comprehensive solution for developers and entrepreneurs seeking to conduct business over the Internet.

This is where the JECF comes into play. As an open, cross-platform, extensible API, it has all the advantages of Java without the drawbacks of proprietary protocols. In short, it is the first all-inclusive solution for online commerce.

Note

Although the JECF is still only in the specification phase, it is important to understand the concepts behind it. You may not be able to create an application using the JECF today, but you can start planning for it today. You can design your current applications so they can take advantage of the JECF when it becomes available. A good system designer always looks to the horizon to see what's coming and designs with future extensions in mind.

The Difficulties of Electronic Commerce

The problems associated with online commerce are many. Understanding why the JECF is so well-suited to the task of conducting business online requires a full understanding of the difficulties involved.

Theft of Information

The first main difficulty in electronic commerce is, ironically, both the easiest to solve and the source of the most consternation: the theft of important information. People who are wary of electronic commerce fear that their credit card number, or other personal information, will be stolen by "hackers" or other miscreants and used for illicit purposes. Luckily, with the advent of public-key encryption, and its implementation in the Java Security API and Netscape's Secure Sockets Layer (SSL) 3.0, intercepting encrypted information across the Internet is nearly impossible.

Fraudulent Programs

Good encryption does not necessarily equal good security, however. Especially with a comprehensive commerce system, there are many points at which a hostile applet or application could gain access to sensitive system information. These problems can potentially increase in an object-oriented environment such as Java. For instance, an applet posing as a legitimate service provider could make illegitimate charges on a user's credit card, unless sufficient preventative measures are taken.

Proprietary Solutions

Other barriers to electronic commerce include proprietary protocols and solutions. Every time a developer tries to write an application for conducting online commerce, he or she must overcome the same set of problems (encryption, security, and so on) from scratch. This is redundant and makes commercial Internet development expensive and time-consuming. In addition, developers who use existing protocols are often locked in to a specific commerce system. For instance, many credit card companies have their own centralized network for conducting electronic transactions. However, in order to access this network, developers must use the protocols established by that specific company—which may or may not be compatible with other companies. An application that supports many protocols can become bulky and hard to manage.

Static Solutions

Further, existing commerce solutions are based on existing forms of commerce—mainly credit cards and checks. A comprehensive solution must account for many other forms of transactions, and most importantly, must be able to adapt to future forms, like game tokens, cash cards, "smart" cards, and so on. A dynamic extensible architecture such as this is essentially absent from the field of Internet commerce.

Platform-Dependence

Even commerce systems that overcome these problems often run into the barrier of single-platform support. Because the Internet is made up of numerous types of computers running many different operating systems, a commerce system needs to support this wide range.

Creating Online Services with the JECF

Every aspect of the JECF was designed to combat one of these potential problems in an online transaction. One offshoot of this is that many parts of the API are complex, often taking two or three steps to accomplish—securely—what might have been accomplished in one insecure step. Also keep in mind that, as of August, 1996, the full JECF API has not been published; it is still under development by JavaSoft and its corporate partners. All JavaSoft has done thus far is to publish a theoretical framework (the JECF White Paper) that details what the goals and structure of the finished API will be. Do not be surprised if this changes somewhat in the months to come.

The JECF, like all other Java APIs, is made up of several key classes. They are divided into several packages based on their function. These separate pieces interact to provide the full functionality of the JECF. Each component acts independently in order to increase the security of the whole system. They are all contained in something called the Java Wallet, which manages all transactions relating to the user.

The JECF is centered around the Java Wallet. Each user has his or her own wallet which contains a number of cassettes. Cassettes are to a wallet what an applet is to a browser. Cassettes provide some form of financial service to a wallet. In a way, cassettes are like credit cards. When you are shopping and go to pay for something, you open your wallet and select an appropriate credit card (or that old-fashioned cash stuff). When you perform an online transaction, you may select a payment cassette from your wallet. The online service then interacts with your cassette, which may, in turn, interact with your credit card company or an electronic cash server.

Storing Information in the Wallet Database

One of the most important parts of the Java Wallet is the Wallet database. This stores all kinds of information about the Wallet's owner, including a record of all previous transactions conducted using the Wallet. Because of the sensitive but useful nature of this information, the Wallet must be simultaneously secure yet robust and accessible—never an easy compromise! Each cassette is allowed to keep its own data in the Wallet database. When you write a cassette, you can count on the Wallet database being available so you can store any data that you may need the next time the cassette is used.

Keeping Data Safe

The Wallet database provides only limited access to its information. Access to the database is managed by a system of `Permit` objects that designate certain roles to various components. Components wishing to gain access to the database can have one of three roles: `DatabaseOwner` (the Wallet, the Wallet's owner, and any classes designated by the user), `DatabaseUser` (any applet, cassette, or component seeking to use some information stored in the database), and `DatabaseMaintainer` (applets and objects that perform maintenance or non-financial functions on the database). These roles are delegated by the database based upon a user-configurable understanding of which objects are to be trusted with the various roles. When an object applies for a `Permit` from the database, it must be authenticated and digitally signed by a trusted agency. The user has final control over which objects get access to what information.

The Wallet database can also give access to specific `Table` or `Row` objects. These classes comprise the internal structure of the Wallet database, and each class operates independently to ensure the security of its contents. Permits can be registered at this level, so that outside objects can be given access to only a small part of the database rather than the entire thing. Table and Row permits and roles are the same as those used in the `database` class, only they apply to a smaller region of the database.

Performing Transactions

The Wallet database has classes for conducting all kinds of transactions. These include record-keeping transactions, as well as user interactions and exchanges of money, goods, or services. Each type of transaction has its own class type that determines its parameters and functionality. Transactions can also be extended to include more interesting exchanges, such as barter agreements or contracts. Further, the JECF can create tallies, which are essentially electronic receipts for products purchased. All of this provides a robust framework for conducting commerce.

Database Transactions and User Transactions

These are the two most common forms of transactions in the database. Database transactions include the storage of transaction information and are discussed in detail in the "Backing out Pending Transactions" section of this chapter. User transactions are those in which the Wallet's owner makes a purchase using a payment cassette, and are discussed throughout this chapter, most notably in the shopping cart and cassette sections.

Making Electronic Purchases

An exchange transaction is an extension of the standard user transaction in which money is exchanged for goods. In an exchange transaction, any kind of value can be traded, including money, but also including trades for stock, goods, services, time, and so on. In fact, this opens up the possibility of having online contracts, which could be legally as legitimate and binding as paper contracts. This requires that digital signing be extended from applets and cassettes to create *signable documents*, which requires a whole other set of protocols and classes for authenticating user signatures and enforcing contracts signed online. These issues, however, are still a long way off — signable applets will probably not become a reality until 1997, and signable documents will probably take another year.

Performing Multi-Party Transactions

Complex transactions are just like regular exchange transactions, except that they can include more than two parties. This is ideal for multiple-party sales, or loans involving a third party. This could also make it possible for groups of people to form contracts with companies—perhaps an online mutual fund could contract with all of its members at once. This type of transaction has the advantage of being fully adaptable to a variety of circumstances—it is not locked into traditional two-party contracts, but can be used for just about anything. This helps maintain the dynamic nature of the JECF.

Implementing Digital Cash with Microtransactions

Microtransactions are used by companies to issue cash substitutes such as cash cards or tokens. These transactions allow small, predefined charges to be made against a preauthorized account. This would allow gaming companies to issue online tokens redeemable for games, with the money charges being made against a special company account. Or, a company could issue coupons or vouchers that could be used to purchase certain products from a third party, which would be paid out of the issuing company's account. Microtransactions are important because they allow companies to engage in non-cash sales and promotions. Because many people are wary about spending their own money online, this gives Internet vendors the opportunity to let users "win" tokens or coupons and then redeem those for prizes. Services such as Riddler (**http://www.riddler.com**) allow users to play games and earn "CAPS," which can be redeemed for certain prizes that the company buys. While this is effective, the JECF allows such companies to issue same-as-cash tokens that can be redeemed at other vendor locations, thus freeing them to provide a much wider variety of services.

Implementing a *Shopping Cart* Applet with the JECF

The process of purchasing products is handled by a `Shopping Cart` applet. This is the basic unit of user interaction. When a user chooses to make a purchase, it is this applet which must load the necessary JECF components and ensure that the transaction completes successfully. It is also responsible for authenticating the user and establishing a secure link. Rather than completing a sale in one step, as many online commerce programs do today, the `Shopping Cart` uses a three-step process.

First, the user selects the goods to be purchased from the vendor. Next, the applet shows a tally of the items selected and allows the user to select a payment method. Before the final transaction is conducted, the applet constructs a page displaying the total prices registered by the Java Wallet. This is different from the previous tally page, because this one is constructed locally—displaying the *actual* charges incurred rather than the ones displayed by the vendor. If these two sets of prices do not match, the user can abort the transaction. This is the vendor's only chance to charge money to the user's account (or credit card, and so on.); they cannot charge more or less than is registered with the Wallet. Further, no financial information about the user is transmitted to the vendor; all transactions are handled by the Wallet on a separate secure link.

Offering Services with Cassettes

The actual work of transacting money is done by small portable objects called *Cassettes*. Each Cassette implements a specific *payment* or *service* protocol. Cassettes are provided by vendors, who may or may not charge a fee for their use. Cassettes are a convenient method for software distribution, because any Java object (applet, servlet, and so on) can become a cassette by simply conforming to the JECF `Cassette` Interface. This means that currently existing Java products will have an easy transition to the JECF.

Registering Payments with Payment Cassettes

Payment cassettes are provided by money management companies such as banks and credit card providers. These cassettes contain the necessary instructions to access a user's account with one of these companies. From the user's perspective, this provides a convenient way to add new payment instruments; they simply request a cassette corresponding to a particular credit card or bank account. From the standpoint of companies, this provides an easy way to give their customers online access to their accounts in a secure, standard, cross-platform way.

Creating Other Wallet Services

The other kind of cassette is called a *service cassette*. These cassettes are modules that provide non-payment kinds of services, such as accounting or budget management. Service cassettes are used mainly to access and maintain the user's financial database. For instance, a tax cassette might automatically fill out online tax forms for a user based upon his or her online purchases. This provides developers with an ideal way to create lightweight, portable financial applications without requiring the user to enter in redundant data; all records are kept securely by the Java Wallet. Only cassettes that are designated as safe by the user have access to the Java Database.

Ensuring Cassette Security

The JECF takes many measures to ensure the security of the user's data, and to prevent access to it by a malicious applet or cassette. One of the most important security measures implemented in the JECF is *digital signing*. This is a process whereby one or more trusted entities certify that a particular piece of Java code is safe and reliable. If the code is tampered with in any way, the digital signature is invalidated, thus ensuring that Java applets or packages remain unchanged since their last digital signature.

Digitally Signing Cassettes

JECF cassettes require a digital signature in order to gain access to the Java Wallet database. Based on a cassette's signature, the User can assign to the cassette a level of "trust." This trust is used by the Wallet to grant various *roles* to the cassette. A role determines what parts of the JECF system a cassette or applet can access. As an example, Sun describes a service Cassette that provides backup and restore services for the Java Wallet database. This Cassette needs to be granted a "maintenance" role in order to gain read and write privileges for the database.

Controlling Cassette Access

Two important classes to maintaining Cassette and Wallet security are the `PassPhrase` and Access Control List (ACL) classes. These two classes are used to determine which roles are assigned to which cassettes. Although only loosely defined in the prerelease API, the `PassPhrase` class will provide user authentication services for each wallet, thus preventing unauthorized access by any user other than the owner of the wallet. Each wallet must have a `PassPhrase` associated with each user. The ACL provides a similar service for cassettes loaded into the wallet. Just like each wallet must have a `PassPhrase`, each wallet component or cassette must have an ACL that determines what other components or cassettes can gain access to it. This requires signing and other authentication routines in each and every Wallet component. Although this is cumbersome, having each object operate separately makes the whole system much more secure.

Creating Unique Cassette Identities

The identity of a Cassette is provided by the entity that signed it. Every Cassette must have a special `Identity` object that is used to give the user (and the JECF system) accurate information about the behaviors of the cassette. This `Identity` is digitally signed to prevent tampering. Further, to prevent another cassette from "borrowing" its signed status, the cassette makes use of a `Ticket` object. `Tickets` are an indirect method of accessing the `Identity` object. Because of security considerations, the `Identity` object cannot be directly accessed; this might allow a malicious applet to steal its `Identity`. Instead, a Cassette generates a `Ticket` object based upon its `Identity`. Although a `Ticket` can be created from an `Identity`, the reverse is not true. When queries are made of the `Ticket`, it fetches the required information from the Cassette `Identity`, but does not contain this information itself. The process is very much like the pointers used by Java to represent data in memory; the `Ticket` (pointer) allows the data (`Identity`) to be accessed, but does not actually contain the data itself. This, combined with the digital signature and shopping cart security measures, makes it virtually impossible for anyone to gain access to a user's personal financial information by posing as a legitimate vendor.

Dealing with System Failures

Another important aspect of the Java Wallet is the way in which it ensures reliable transactions. Even more so than in the "real" world, Internet transactions are prone to both human and computer error. The Internet itself is chaotic and fluctuating, and a huge number of problems could easily arise during the simplest of transactions. Servers going down, power outages, software or hardware bugs, viruses, and incompetent operators can all interrupt a transaction at any stage. In order for an electronic commerce system to be fully robust, it must be able to handle such problems with style and grace. It should also give users and vendors a way of resolving any disputes that arise from botched transactions. The JECF provides methods for both canceling a transaction that has encountered errors and also for resolving transaction disputes between users and vendors.

Backing out Pending Transactions

A transaction is never permanently written to the Wallet database until it is completely finished. During the various stages of the transaction, information is posted to the Pending Transactions list. If, for any reason, the transaction is interrupted before it is complete, the information contained in the Pending Transactions list can be used to undo any monetary exchange that has taken place. This protects the user from any damages that might result from accidental computer failure. It also helps prevent a malicious applet from making unauthorized charges by faking a failure of some kind.

Creating a Problem-Reporting System

Despite all of the measures the Java Wallet takes to prevent a dispute from arising from an erroneous transaction, these are still possible. For instance, if a transaction is interrupted en route to the vendor, but is still transmitted by the payment Cassette to a credit card company, a user might wind up paying for a product they never received. Although this scenario is unlikely, the JECF still provides a method to resolve disputes among any combination of the buyer, seller, and cassette vendor. This functionality is implemented in the `Problem` class, which allows for convenient correspondence between any of the three parties. This eliminates the need for tedious phone calls, conference calls, and hard copies of correspondence. Instead, parties use the Problem Resolution System to send Problem reports back and forth. These can be easily responded to, and allow problem troubleshooters to keep track of each problem separately. All transactions are sent and received via e-mail, so problems can be answered immediately.

JECF Availability

The JECF API is expected to be released as an "alpha" test product in the last quarter of 1996. Currently, only a brief White Paper and code outline are available, although JavaSoft says it is reviewing the API with major commerce vendors. Many companies have also endorsed the JECF concept, but only time will tell which products will support it. In any event, the JECF will definitely not be ready for full-fledged application development until sometime in 1997, possibly even as late as 1998. Until that time, developers and users will have to make do with existing inferior, yet viable, solutions.

Getting More Information About the JECF

More information is available on the Internet at any of the following locations:

- **http://java.sun.com/products/commerce/** JavaSoft's JECF pages
- **commerce@java.sun.com** JavaSoft's e-mail address for queries regarding the JECF
- **http://www.yahoo.com/Business and Economy/Companies/Computers/Software/Financial/Electronic Commerce/** Yahoo!'s Electronic Commerce listing
- **http://java.sun.com/javaone/abstracts.html** Session abstracts from the JavaOne conference. Includes several talks about the JECF, as well as slides in Adobe's PDF format
- **http://www.gamelan.com** Repository of all Java things
- **http://www.teamjava.com** Site devoted to Java developers and companies
- **http://www.javaworld.com** Online magazine, good site for the latest Java news and information
- **http://www.visa.com/** Visa's home page, good site for information about online commerce solutions

Although still a long way off, the JECF is one of the most exciting new additions to the Java API. If adopted by the Internet, business, and legal communities (it already has a long list of sponsors), the JECF could one day replace, or at least enhance, the current process of selling products and completing contracts. This is one of the truly revolutionary ramifications of Java's development and it promises abundant benefits. As long as it is implemented cautiously and thoroughly, the Java Electronic Commerce Framework could become the most significant and secure form of commerce yet devised.

PART VIII

Java and Legacy Systems

chapter 32

Encapsulating Legacy Systems

by Mark Wutka

In this chapter

- **Designing for the future, not the past**
  When you write programs to access older systems, you should focus on what the system does and not the exact formats it uses. Otherwise, you could be left with unwieldy formats long after the legacy system has been unplugged.
- **Linking the old and the new**
  When you replace an older system with a new one, you may have to hook the older system into the newer one. Sometimes, you need to hook new workstations to the older system; sometimes, you need the old terminals to access the new system.
- **Creating open interfaces with CORBA**
  Although your old system may never run CORBA, you can create a CORBA interface that accesses the old system. This gives the old system the appearance of a CORBA interface, allowing other clients to access it.
- **Using the interface you prefer**
  When you create an interface into an older system, you don't have to use the same interface as the old system. You can change function names, parameters, data types, even the sequence of commands. Decide how you want the interface to look and then worry about accessing the older system.
- **Encapsulating several systems**
  You can use encapsulation to make multiple systems have the appearance of a single system. There are some dangers involved with this, however.
- **Real-world examples**
  Encapsulation is used every day in companies all over the world. It often helps to see how other companies deal with older systems.

Keeping up with technology is one of the constant problems that most businesses face. You buy a top-of-the-line database system and a year later, after you've spent considerable time converting your organization over to the new database, the database is obsolete. If you try to keep your systems on the leading edge all the time, you'll probably spend more time and money changing systems than you do using them. More likely, you'll keep the old system for a long, long time. Most of these older systems are referred to as "legacy" systems, and while they may not be on the forefront of technology, they are still the lifeblood of many businesses.

By the time you decide to switch systems, all your applications are so heavily tied to the legacy system that you have to rewrite all your applications, making it even more expensive to switch. You have to factor these costs into your decision to switch. You don't switch just to use new technology. You switch because a new system will save you money. If you are more heavily tied to the legacy system, you are more willing to keep using it, because the cost of switching is more than the cost of maintaining the existing system. It is obvious that you could reduce the cost of upgrading and changing systems if you could design your applications so they weren't as dependent on specific products.

As you design new applications, you don't want your design to be constrained by the limits of the current system. Obviously, the implementation will have these constraints, but you want to leave room to grow. Rather than attacking this problem on a per-application basis, take a step back and look at the systems you have today, and try to put a prettier face on them.

You can use a technique called encapsulation to make a legacy system look like a newer system. There is no magic here, since you can't really make the old system work just like a newer one. It won't run any faster, or magically perform some new functions. What encapsulation does is break your dependence on the exact interfaces of the legacy system. For example, suppose you have an MVS system from IBM, and if you are at a large corporation, you probably do. While MVS is expanding its accessibility, you still have some limitations. Suppose, for instance, that you don't have an MVS TCP/IP gateway available and you must use IBM's proprietary SNA protocol to access MVS. How are you going to write an applet to access MVS data? You aren't going to find a copy of the Netscape Navigator that comes with SNA built in. What you can do, however, is write a program that sits in between MVS and the applet and does the necessary translation. Figure 32.1 illustrates an example configuration.

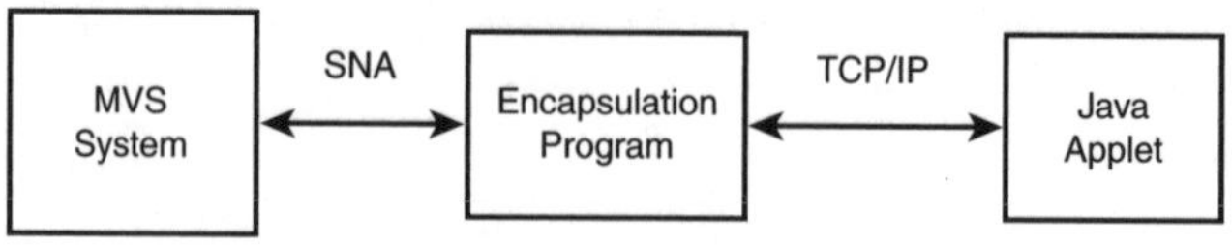

Fig. 32.1
An encapsulation program puts a more friendly face on a legacy system.

Focusing on Function, not Form

One of the biggest traps you run into when writing an application is focusing only on the exact form of the data you can get or the exact commands that you can give to the legacy system. What you want to do instead is concentrate on what the legacy system actually does.

For example, suppose you have an ordering system and you want to create a Java applet that can place orders. Assume that you have the following commands on your ordering system:

- `START TRANSACTION <customer ID>` Begins the ordering process for a particular customer.
- `LIST PARTS` Gets a list of available parts.
- `ORDER <part number> <quantity>` Adds a part to the list of parts being ordered.
- `REMOVE <part number>` Removes a part number from the current list.
- `END TRANSACTION` Completes the order.
- `ABORT TRANSACTION` Cancels the order.

As you can see by this set of commands, the ordering system requires a high degree of interaction. This set of commands is the "form" of the legacy system. Its function is that it creates orders of parts for your customers. That may seem like a subtle point, but it is very important. One of the reasons we spend so much money re-engineering old applications is that they were too heavily tied to the form of the legacy system.

If you got a new ordering system, the likelihood of the commands being different is fairly high. Most systems use their own set of commands. The function should still be the same for a new system, however. You'll still be using a system to create orders. If you focus on the function of the system and don't worry as much about the actual commands, your applications will adapt to new systems more readily.

Of course, there is a trade-off here. You have to do a little extra work to translate from the legacy system to the application. That's where the encapsulation comes in.

You could, for example, create an encapsulation that placed an entire order at once. It would have methods to list the available parts and place an order. The encapsulation program would translate the order placement into the series of commands expected by the legacy system. Figure 32.2 illustrates how this might take place.

This form of encapsulation is actually a design pattern known as a "facade."

Fig. 32.2
An encapsulation can present an interface different from the legacy system.

Providing Access to New Systems

One of the reasons you encapsulate legacy systems is that you want to move to a more modern computing platform. Sometimes the move is on the server side, and sometimes the move is on the client side. For instance, you may want to keep your old mainframe, but upgrade some or all of your workstations to inexpensive Web terminals. Sometimes you want to upgrade the central server or mainframe, but you can't afford to upgrade all your terminals out in the field.

You can often use encapsulation to facilitate a system upgrade. For instance, an airline has a large network of very old terminals, the kind you see every day at the airport. These terminals are connected via a network to a group of mainframes. Now, you realize that it is much more cost effective to develop applications on a UNIX or NT system. In fact, many of your users already have workstations that support a nice graphical interface. Unfortunately, you still have to support the users out in the field, with their old-fashioned terminals. Do you develop your new application on the old mainframe, or do you aim for the new technology? Figure 32.3 illustrates this dilemma.

Ideally, the answer to this problem is that you aim for the new technology. Wherever you have to use your legacy technology, encapsulate it and put a pretty face on it.

The practice of separating the application from the user interface is really going to shine for you when you have to deal with legacy systems. If you design your application as you would like it to be, rather than constrain it by the way things are, you can make the existing system fit.

Tip

While "vision" is an overused term these days, you need vision when you design applications. You need to be able to look beyond what you have right now and see where you want to be, then work toward that goal. You'll never escape the legacy system if you keep designing it into your new applications.

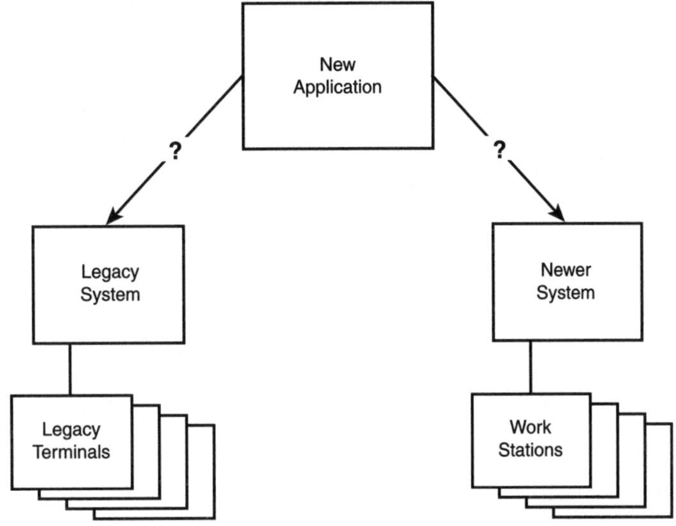

Fig. 32.3
It is difficult to decide whether to extend the legacy system, or put an application on a new system.

You design your application the way you want, then adapt the legacy systems to fit your application, not vice versa. For example, suppose you design a new e-mail system using Java for both the client and server. Figure 32.4 illustrates a possible configuration.

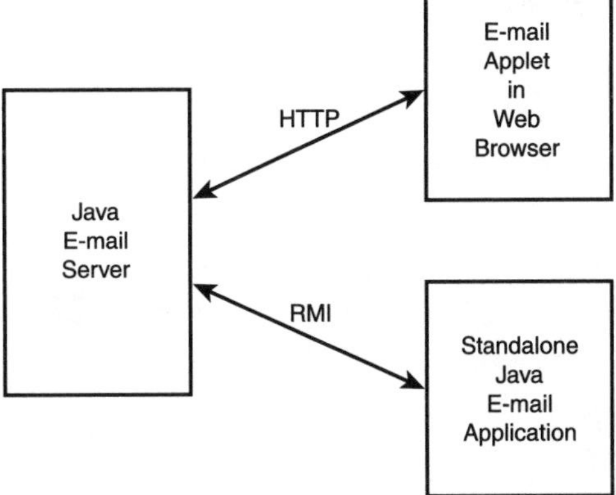

Fig. 32.4
A Java e-mail system.

Now that you have your application designed, you concentrate on encapsulating the legacy system to fit into the new application structure. In the case of the e-mail system, you may want to allow the old legacy terminals to access the system. You create an object or a server that looks like a legacy host to the terminals, but looks like a client to the e-mail system. This object would translate the new-user interface into something the legacy terminals understand. Figure 32.5 shows an example of this.

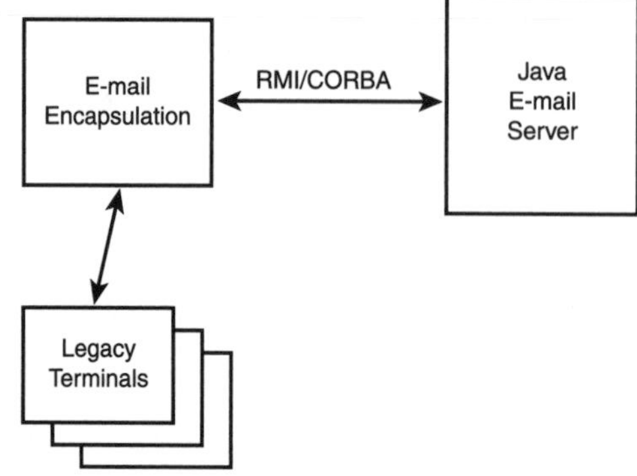

Fig. 32.5
You can translate a new-user interface into something a legacy terminal understands.

You could take a different approach with the new application. Suppose you want to use the existing e-mail application on the legacy system. Maybe it is too expensive or difficult to get the legacy terminals to access the new e-mail application. You could create an object that translates the old e-mail interface into something that looks like the new application, as far as the clients are concerned. Figure 32.6 illustrates this configuration.

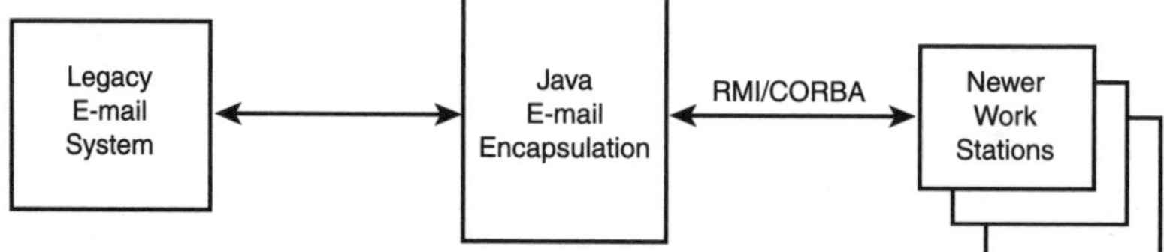

Fig. 32.6
You can translate a legacy interface into something newer clients can deal with.

Note

In both of the previous examples, the encapsulation was based on the clear separation between the application and user interface. Once you separate them, you can translate different application interfaces and user interfaces into something that fits your design.

Using CORBA to Open Up a Closed System

Once you come up with a way to get data out of your legacy system, you should make it available to other applications using a mechanism that is likely to be supported by many systems. CORBA is a reasonable choice for this, since it is a well-known standard that has been growing in popularity for the last few years. Even if Java's popularity suddenly wanes in favor of something else, you still have a CORBA interface that you could access from other languages.

Figure 32.7 shows some of the ways you can access a legacy system if the encapsulation provides a CORBA interface.

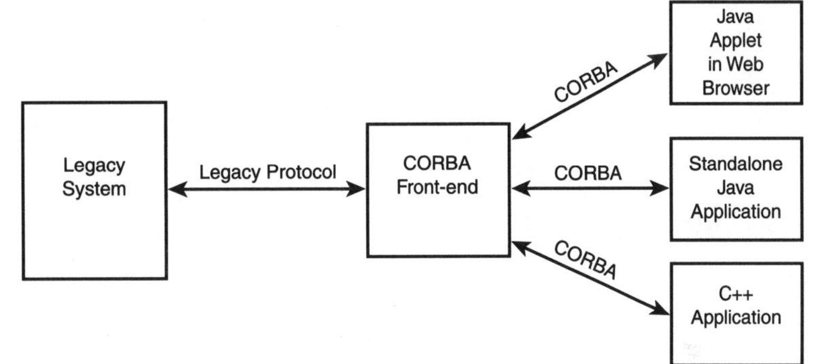

Fig. 32.7
CORBA expands the accessibility of an encapsulated system.

Encapsulating a TCP/IP System

If your legacy system can be accessed over the network via TCP/IP, it will be easy for you to access the legacy system. This doesn't mean that it will be easy to write the encapsulation. You may wonder why you even need extra code to encapsulate the system when an applet could make a TCP/IP connection straight to the legacy system (assuming the security restrictions didn't get in the way). Remember that you aren't just encapsulating the access to the system, you are encapsulating the functions it provides.

You don't want to tie your applet to the specific interface provided by the legacy system. This way, if you upgrade the legacy system, you change only the encapsulation, but the applets that talk to the encapsulation don't need to change.

Encapsulating with Native Method Calls

Even if your legacy system can run Java, you may still need to create an encapsulation layer. Java may not be able to access the applications running on the legacy system. You can create native methods to handle these situations.

You also may need native methods if you have a special interface card or special interface software to access your legacy system. For example, many IBM systems can only be accessed using the SNA networking protocol. You occasionally need a special interface card to talk to these systems, but many times you just need special networking drivers. Either way, you need a native method to access the special card or drivers.

Figure 32.8 illustrates a typical native method encapsulation.

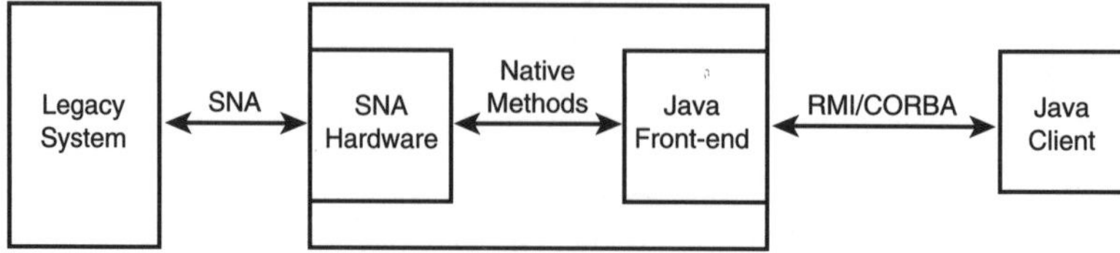

Fig. 32.8
You often need native methods to access a legacy system.

Wrapping Java Around a Native Interface

Suppose your ordering system came with a C library that let you perform all the functions you needed. You could start and end transactions, get a parts list, and add and remove parts from an order. You could create a Java class to access the C library via native method calls.

Listing 32.1 shows a Java interface to the ordering system, with native method calls to the C library.

Listing 32.1 Source Code for *Ordering.java*

```
package ordering;

// this class provides an interface to an ordering system. It makes
// calls to native C methods which take care of accessing the real
// system.

public class Ordering extends Object
{
// transactionID is the transaction id returned by the C interface
// to the ordering system. Each call to the ordering system must
// be accompanied by the transaction ID.

     int transactionID;

// Create an instance of an Ordering object, which begins an ordering
// transaction.

     public Ordering(String customerId)
     throws OrderingException
     {
          transactionID = startTransaction(customerId);
     }
```

```
// Add a part to the current order

     public void orderPart(String partNumber, int quantity)
     throws OrderingException
     {
          orderPart(transactionID, partNumber, quantity);
     }

// remove a part from the current order

     public void removePart(String partNumber)
     throws OrderingException
     {
          removePart(transactionID, partNumber);
     }

// finish the order

     public void endTransaction()
     throws OrderingException
     {
          endTransaction(transactionID);
     }

// abort the order

     public void abortTransaction()
     throws OrderingException
     {
          abortTransaction(transactionID);
     }

// These methods are implemented in a local DLL

     protected native int startTransaction(String customerId)
          throws OrderingException;

     public native static String[] listParts();

     protected native void orderPart(int txnID, String partNumber,
          int quantity) throws OrderingException;

     protected native void removePart(int txnID, String partNumber)
          throws OrderingException;

     protected native void endTransaction(int txnID)
          throws OrderingException;

     protected native void abortTransaction(int txnID)
          throws OrderingException;
}
```

Note

The methods in the `Ordering` class are not quite a straight pass-through to the real ordering system. Rather, it provides a slightly higher level of abstraction. It considers an `Ordering` object to be a transaction, and hides the transaction ID from the users of the Java class. You will find that many C libraries return information that you must use for future function calls. You don't actually use the information. Instead, since the library has no way of grouping method calls and data together, like an object does, the library makes you handle the data and forces you to pass it to whatever functions need it. When you design a Java interface to a native library, keep information like this hidden within the Java class. Don't let the public methods pass back anything that isn't useful.

Writing Native Methods in C

Once you have defined a Java class with native methods, you must write the native methods yourself. You can't simply call any arbitrary C function from Java, you almost always have to create a C function that calls the real function you want.

The reason you can't call any arbitrary C function is that native Java methods must conform to a strict naming scheme that combines the method name, the Java class name, and the package name. For example, the declaration for the native C `endTransaction` method would look like this:

```
void ordering_Ordering_endTransaction(
      struct HOrdering_Ordering *thisPtr, long txnID)
```

Java always passes a "this" pointer to its native methods, which precludes the use of calling any old C function as a native method. Typically, your native methods will turn around and call other C functions, however.

For instance, your `ordering_Ordering_endTransaction` function would probably call the `endTransaction` function in the C library that came with your ordering system.

When you create a Java class with native methods, you have to generate a special header file that contains declarations for the C implementation. You create the header using the `javah` command. Once the `Ordering` class has been compiled in Java, you issue the following command:

```
javah ordering.Ordering
```

This will generate a header file called `ordering_Ordering.h`. Next, you must generate a set of stubs, which Java uses to invoke your native methods. You also use the `javah` command for this, but you must include the `-stubs` option:

```
javah -stubs ordering.Ordering
```

This will create a C file called `ordering_Ordering.c`. You must compile and link this file into a shared library, along with your native methods. Listing 32.2 shows a skeletal implementation of the native methods for the Ordering class.

32

Listing 32.2 Source Code for *orderingImpl.c*

```
#include "ordering_Ordering.h"

/* This is an absolutely skeletal implementation of the
   native methods for the Ordering class. The only method
   that does anything is the listParts method, which returns
   an array of strings. The rest of the methods are dummies.
*/

int nextId = 1;          /* For returning different transaction ID's */

/* parts is a list of values that will be returned in listParts */

char *parts[] = {
     "12345 Widget",
     "23456 Deluxe Widget",
     "55534 Thing",
     "30038 Zippy"
};

struct Hjava_lang_String;
long ordering_Ordering_startTransaction(struct Hordering_Ordering *thisPtr,
     struct Hjava_lang_String *customerId)
{
     return nextId++;
}

HArrayOfString *ordering_Ordering_listParts(struct Hordering_Ordering *thisPtr)
{
     HArrayOfString *retval;
     ClassArrayOfString *strs;
     int i;

/* Create an array of strings that will contain 4 strings */
     retval = (HArrayOfString *) ArrayAlloc(T_CLASS, 4);

/* If we couldn't allocate the memory, throw a Java exception */
     if (retval == NULL) {
         SignalError(EE(), "java/lang/OutOfMemoryException", NULL);
         return NULL;
     }
```

continues

Listing 32.2 Continued

```
/* ArrayAlloc allocated an array of objects, this call makes it an
   array of strings */

    unhand(retval)->body[4] = (HString *)
        FindClass(EE(), "java/lang/String", TRUE);

/* Get a pointer to the array of strings */
     strs = unhand(retval);

/* Fill the array of strings with Java strings */

     for (i=0; i < 4; i++) {
          strs->body[i] = makeJavaString(parts[i], strlen(parts[i]));
     }

     return retval;
}

void ordering_Ordering_orderPart(struct Hordering_Ordering *thisPtr,
     long txnID, struct Hjava_lang_String *part, long quantity)
{
}

void ordering_Ordering_removePart(struct Hordering_Ordering *thisPtr,
     long txnID, struct Hjava_lang_String *part)
{
}

void ordering_Ordering_endTransaction(struct Hordering_Ordering *thisPtr,
     long txnID)
{
}

void ordering_Ordering_abortTransaction(struct Hordering_Ordering *thisPtr,
     long txnID)
{
}
```

The skeletal implementation in Listing 32.2 doesn't interface with a real ordering system. Chances are, a real system wouldn't have exactly these methods. For one thing, there are too many things left out. However, for the purposes of illustration, assume that there really is a system that uses the above methods. Once you can access a legacy system, you can change the way it is accessed, as you will see later in this chapter in the section titled "Presenting a Different Interface."

Encapsulating by Emulating a User

Sometimes, the only way you can access a legacy system is by interacting with it as if you were a user. This method is more commonly known as "screen-scraping." You basically parse the individual output screens of the legacy application, and generate input to it as if you were a user.

This type of encapsulation is often combined with other methods. For instance, your legacy system may support TCP/IP, but you have to do screen-scraping to get the information from the system, as illustrated in Figure 32.9.

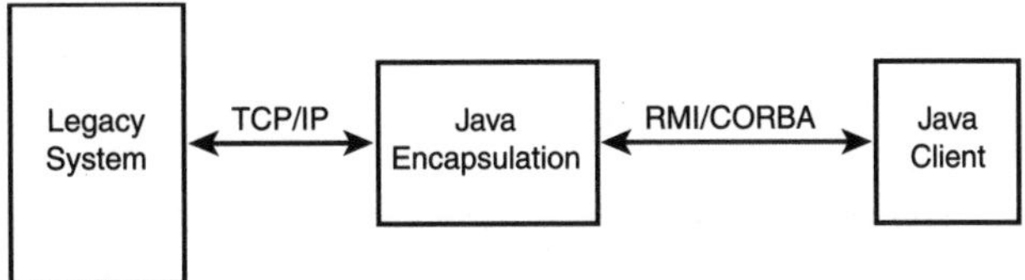

Fig. 32.9
Even when a legacy system has TCP/IP, you may have to resort to screen-scraping.

Sometimes, the only access you can get with a native method is as a terminal to the application, and not directly into the application itself.

You may have to sink so low as to connect up via a modem or a serial cable to do asynchronous communications. You would almost certainly need native methods to do this, although under UNIX, you may be able to get away with doing file I/O. Figure 32.10 illustrates this kind of configuration.

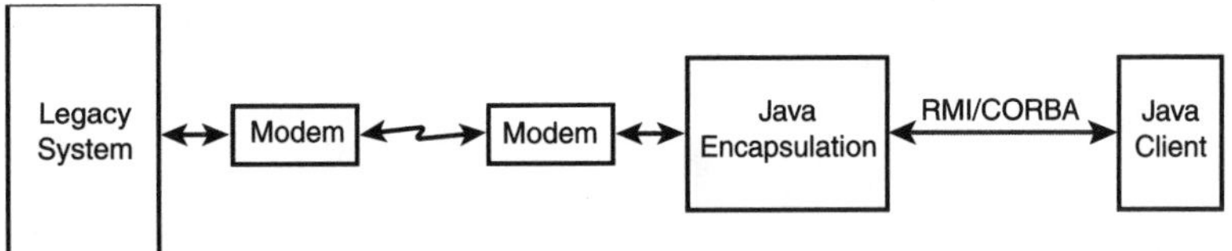

Fig. 32.10
Sometimes, the only way to get data from a legacy system is via a modem or serial connection.

Getting Assistance from the Legacy System

There's no rule that says that the legacy system can't have an active role in the encapsulation. Many times, you can add code to the legacy system in a few strategic places and open up the system to encapsulation. You can often create simple messaging protocols to pass data to and from the legacy system without having to resort to scraping screens.

Presenting a Different Interface

The remnants of a legacy system can stay around long after the system itself is gone. Many times, applications that originally interfaced with the legacy system still do things the way the legacy system did, even though there is no reason for it.

Note

This situation occurs outside the computer industry as well. A woman was preparing a ham for a family dinner when her daughter asked her why she cut the end off the ham. The woman replied that her mother always did it. The woman then asked *her* mother why she always cut the end off the ham. Her mother replied, "So it would fit in the pan."

If you are encapsulating a legacy system, you have the ability to change the interface into the system to some degree. If the legacy system does something in a strange way, use the encapsulation to hide it.

Take the ordering system shown previously, for example. When you create an order, you have to begin a transaction, add parts, then either end or abort the transaction. Maybe you don't want to work that way anymore. You might be better off building an order at the client side, then have the client send the entire order, which is then fed into the system.

This would be more in line with the way Web services work. You try to do everything in one message, since there is no concept of a session on a Web server. Of course, designing your system to work *only* as a session-less system may also be a bad thing. Do what makes sense for your application.

Tip

You can use this technique when writing an application to use an interface that has not yet been completely specified or is changing. You decide on the interface your application will use, and write your application. When the real interface is completed, write an object that translates from one interface to the other.

The ordering system is a good candidate for a different interface. You can easily create an object that lets you place orders in a single, session-less method call, rather than the group of calls in the current interface.

Listing 32.3 shows a simple class with a static method that places an order using the `Ordering` class.

Listing 32.3 Source Code for *Orders.java*

```
package ordering;

public class Orders extends Object
{
     public static void placeOrder(String customerID,
          PartOrder[] parts) throws OrderingException
     {
          Ordering ordering = new Ordering(customerID);

          for (int i=0; i < parts.length; i++) {
               ordering.orderPart(parts[i].part,
                    parts[i].quantity);
          }

          ordering.endTransaction();
     }
}
```


Listing 32.4 shows the `PartOrder` class, which encapsulates the information for a single entry in the ordering system.

Listing 32.4 Source Code for *PartOrder.java*

```
package ordering;

public class PartOrder extends Object
{
     public String part;
     public int quantity;

     public PartOrder()
     {
     }

     public PartOrder(String part, int quantity)
     {
          this.part = part;
          this.quantity = quantity;
     }
}
```

As you can see, the `placeOrders` method is much easier to use than the regular `Ordering` object. In a typical ordering system, this simplified interface may be a disadvantage. If this were an airline reservations system, you would have to book all your seats at once and hope that no one got a seat you wanted before you did. When you have a session-based system, you reserve the seats (or the parts) as your transaction progresses. If you abort the transaction, the things you have reserved get freed up for someone else. You will have to decide if you are willing to give up this functionality. It may or may not be worth the cost of a simplified interface.

Combining Multiple Systems

One of the more interesting aspects of encapsulation is combining various pieces to present a single, uniform system. It is a task that is both interesting and challenging. A simple example of this might be adding additional customer information to a customer database. For example, suppose your customer database stored the customer's account number, name, shipping address, phone number, and fax number. Now, suppose you have created a new shipping system that allowed customers to get software from you via ftp. You want to add information to the customer database to support this.

If would be nice if you could just add all this information to your legacy system, but maybe that wouldn't be the best thing. Maybe it is so difficult to get data out of the legacy system quickly that your ftp server couldn't service all the requests in a reasonable time.

You can create a separate database containing the information for the ftp server. Your encapsulation would then store information in both the ftp database and the legacy database. Whenever you retrieve information, the encapsulation queries both systems for the information you need.

Tip

Some systems have the ability to maintain information across multiple databases. You should see if your legacy system supports this kind of thing on its own before you attempt to write it yourself. That's a good idea in any situation. A good transaction processing (TP) monitor will also handle this kind of situation.

Figure 32.11 shows an encapsulation that stores data in two places.

There can be some serious drawbacks to this approach, so you need to be very careful if you decide to try it.

Handling Deletions Originating in the Legacy System

If the encapsulation provides the only access to the legacy system, you can control things a lot more easily. If the legacy system is still accessed through some other means, like legacy terminals, you can get into some serious synchronization problems. If someone removes a customer from the legacy database, the other databases don't know about it. If you require all the databases to be in absolute synchronization at all times, this can be a major pain.

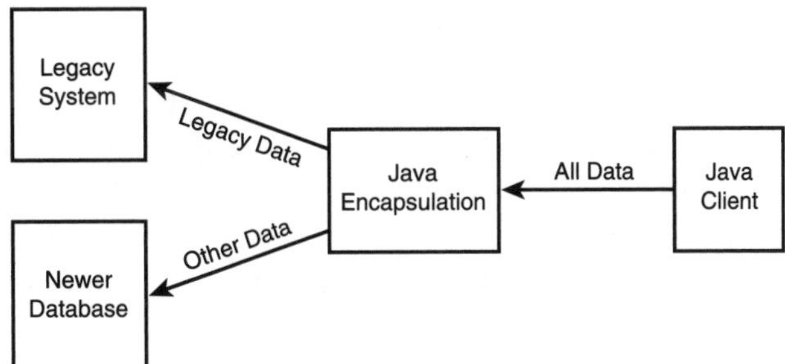

Fig. 32.11
An encapsulation can make multiple databases look like one.

You can alleviate this problem by always checking with the legacy database to make sure a record exists. For instance, suppose you removed a customer from the legacy database for some reason, and then that customer tried to access the ftp server. Even though all the information necessary for the ftp is stored in the other database, the encapsulation still checks with the legacy system and learns that the customer account is no longer there.

The problem with this kind of approach is that it is slow. The other database may be a lot quicker than the legacy system, but because you must check with the legacy system each time, you don't realize the speed benefit.

If you are willing to accept a small possibility of discrepancies, you can remove the speed blockage caused by the legacy system. You could run a synchronization program that verified that a particular customer was in both databases, and removed any customers from the other database when they disappear from the legacy database. For a large database, this may be unfeasible.

Some legacy systems keep a transaction log, so you could run a synchronization program that looked for deletions in the transaction log and perform the deletion on the other database. This is a very reasonable solution. You don't have to perform a large number of queries to synchronize the database.

If you are only accessing the databases through the encapsulation, this problem doesn't occur, because the encapsulation knows whenever data is deleted. You may still have some problems if one database is down. You may need a two-phase commit protocol.

Using a Two-Phase Commit Protocol

A two-phase commit protocol allows you to make sure an operation can be performed, and then perform it. The idea is that when you have an operation that spans multiple databases, you tell each database, "This is what I want to do, are you ready to do it?" Each database gets ready to perform the operation, or replies that it can't. This is the first phase.

The second phase occurs when all of the databases have responded that they can perform the operation (most of them have actually performed the operation, but not committed it as permanent). You now tell the databases to commit the operation. If one of them fails at this point, you assume that it will be taken care of by the database. In other words, it is the database's responsibility to complete the transaction once it has said that it can.

If, during the first phase, any database refuses to perform the operation, you tell all the databases to back out of the operation. Again, it is the responsibility of the databases to undo whatever changes have been made.

If you have a system that supports the two-phase commit protocol, chances are you can also find a good TP monitor that will supervise the two-phase commit, freeing you from having to write it. If you use a TP monitor, you can always use the native method mechanism to create a Java interface to the TP monitor.

Implementing a Two-Phase Commit

When your system doesn't support a two-phase commit, you can either perform a single-phase transaction and log any errors that come up, or you can implement your own two-phase commit. Unless you're anticipating a large number of failures, you may be better off just logging any problems.

Caution
Writing your own two-phase commit protocol is decidedly non-trivial. You should have a firm grasp of database techniques before you attempt this.

When a database system performs a two-phase commit, it writes the transaction to a log, then performs the transaction without committing it. If the transaction is aborted, it undoes the changes. The log is used in case the database fails during the transaction. Once the database has responded in the first phase, it must be able to either commit or abort the transaction.

Generally, you implement a two-phase commit by saving enough information to be able to restore things to the way they were before the transaction, then performing the transaction. If the transaction is aborted, you put things back the way they were.

If you have a locking mechanism on the legacy system, you should use it while waiting for a commit or abort in the second phase. If you have performed a change in the first phase and another transaction is able to come in and use the changed version of the data, you may not be able to back out of the change. If you are able to lock the data against changes, this can't happen.

Some Real-World Examples

If you've never been through a legacy system migration before, you are probably overwhelmed by the number of options and the lack of certainty with which they have been presented. Legacy system migration is often a difficult struggle. The best thing you can do is to approach it with a set of strategies and an open mind, and see what comes up.

An Example Legacy System

Suppose you are working with an airline, with a cluster of mainframes, a wide-area network, and thousands of old terminals spread all over the world. The terminals are connected to the mainframe via the wide-area network. Figure 32.12 illustrates this configuration.

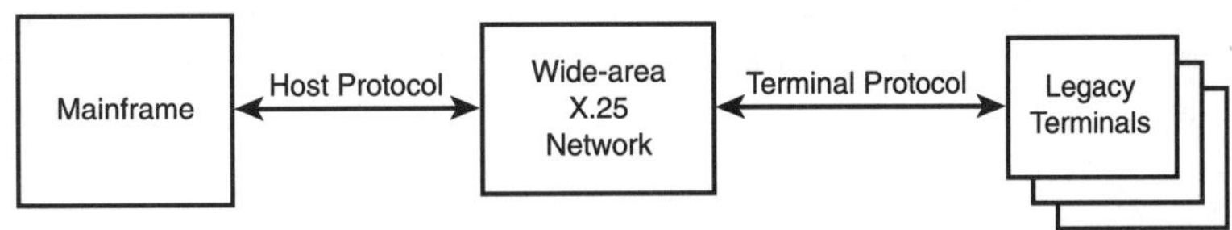

Fig. 32.12
Many legacy systems have a network, one or more mainframes, and a group of terminals.

Note

The following examples are adapted from actual running systems. Your systems may be radically different, but the steps you take are roughly the same.

Since you are probably not familiar with the kind of system normally found at an airline, here are thumbnail sketches of the mainframe, the WAN, and the terminals.

- The mainframes run an operating system from IBM called Transaction Processing Facility (TPF). It is commonly used by large airlines and financial institutions. For this particular site, the only connectivity to the mainframes is via thick cables called "channel cables." The channel is like an overgrown two-way parallel port. The applications running on the mainframe are very tightly intertwined, and generally difficult to maintain.
- The terminals are very old, rugged terminals that run a proprietary airline data protocol that is completely incompatible with modern data terminals. These legacy terminals can display only uppercase letters, digits, and a small set of other characters. In addition, they operate in block mode, as opposed to single-character mode. That is, when someone enters data at the terminal, nothing is sent until the person presses the "enter" or "send" key. The idea of "press any key to continue" is unheard of on these terminals. Some users in the corporate offices have modern PCs, using special gateways to talk to the legacy mainframe.
- The wide-area network is a fairly robust packet-switched network that speaks the IBM channel protocol and the proprietary terminal protocol. In addition, it supports a number of other protocols, including the X.25 standard. This network is very modular and programmable.

Creating a New Application for the Existing Terminal Base

Suppose you want to create a company-wide e-mail system. You are faced with a number of choices:

- You could write the e-mail system on the existing mainframes. This would entail great cost and would not provide any neat GUI features for the more modern terminals.
- You could buy an off-the-shelf e-mail system and put PCs out in the field to run it. This is probably the first thing many people think of. Unfortunately, it may be even more costly than implementing the e-mail system in the mainframe. After all, you not only have to buy millions of dollars worth of PCs, you also have to put in a distributed LAN infrastructure, and possibly a new wide-area network to support it.
- You could write a custom e-mail system on a modern server, UNIX or NT, for example, provide full GUI access to the modern terminals, and provide an encapsulation for the legacy terminals so they can send and receive mail, too.

Assume that you want to save the company millions of dollars and create a modern e-mail system while encapsulating the legacy terminals.

In keeping with the philosophy of not letting the legacy system drag down your design, you design an e-mail system that allows you to send full ASCII text messages, as well as attach binary files to the messages.

Note

Hopefully, you considered buying such a product off-the-shelf. There is far too much custom software that needs to be written for you to spend your time writing things that have already been done a million times.

Armed with your new design, you try to determine how to fit the legacy terminals into the plan. Normally, you have only the mainframe and the terminals to deal with. In this case, however, you have a third element—the network. You could place an encapsulation in two different places. Figure 32.13 shows a scheme where you encapsulate the mail system by making it look like the wide-area network to the terminals. The terminals send information to your encapsulation thinking it is the wide-area network.

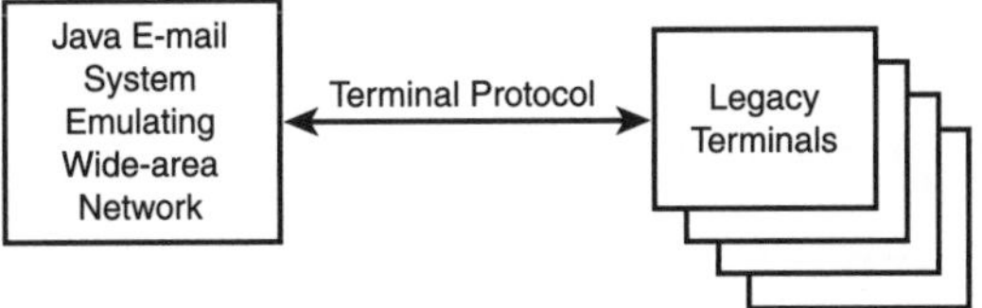

Fig. 32.13
You can encapsulate the mail system by emulating the network.

Your other option is to make your mail application hook into the network and behave like the mainframe. Figure 32.14 illustrates this configuration.

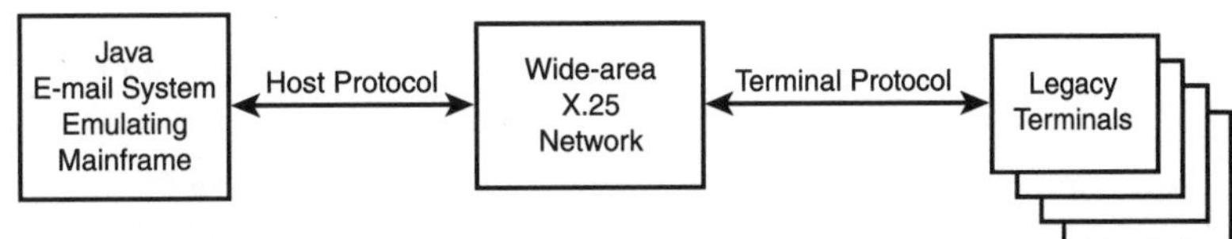

Fig. 32.14
You can also encapsulate the mail system by emulating a mainframe.

Note

There is a third option, which is using the mainframe as the front-end for the application, and passing data from the mainframe to the application. In this particular solution, however, you want to avoid writing code on the mainframe.

Each choice brings its own problems. If you try to emulate the wide-area network, you will probably experience some headaches because you'll have to install code wherever the network connects to the terminals. In general, you want to hook in at as few places as possible, preferably one.

If you try to emulate the mainframe, you want to avoid having to set up your own IBM channel and performing the channel protocol. If you get desperate, you can operate that way. In this case, however, there is a better option.

Recall that the network is highly programmable and supports X.25. Also remember that you may often reap huge benefits by adding a little code to the legacy system to open it up to your encapsulation. By adding some code to the network, you can use X.25 to emulate a mainframe rather than using the channel protocol.

Note

The notion of emulating a legacy host is like a reverse screen-scraping. Rather than pulling data off screens generated by a legacy system, you're generating the screens.

Figure 32.15 illustrates this configuration.

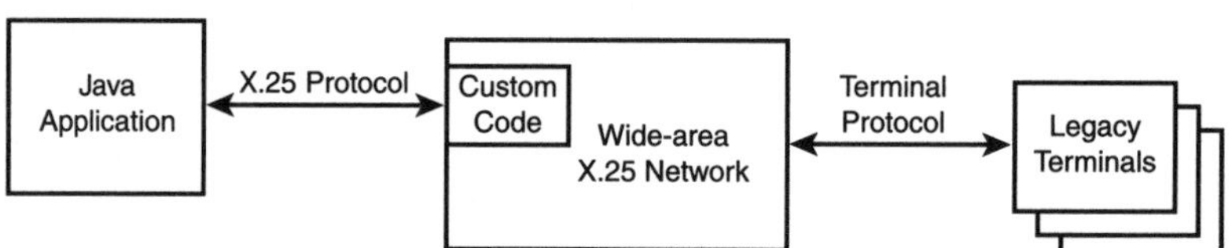

Fig. 32.15
A little interface code in the network makes for a simple encapsulation.

Now that you have a way to emulate a host via X.25, you must decide how you will use the X.25 protocol. You will need to use a native method call of some sort, or, as an alternative, you can create a program in C or C++ that accesses the X.25 line and communicates with users of the X.25 line via TCP/IP. In other words, you create an X.25 server.

Figure 32.16 shows how a Java program could access an X.25 network via this X.25 server.

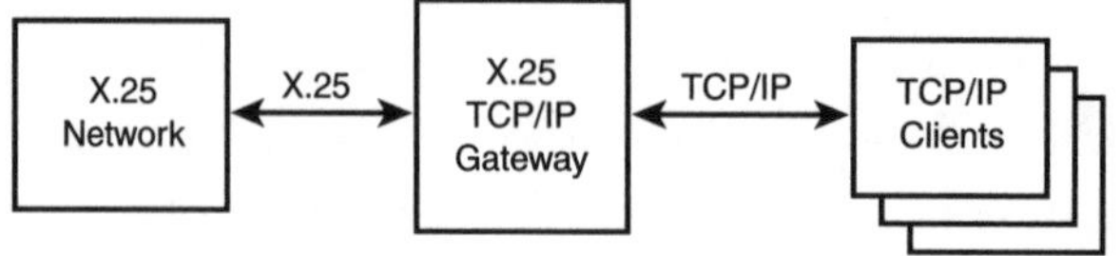

Fig. 32.16
A Java program uses a TCP/IP server to access the X.25 network.

Tip

This technique of creating small servers to handle specific interfaces or devices is a reasonable choice for data streams. This is much more efficient than CORBA, since you are just passing large blocks of data without interpreting it. CORBA is much better for message-based communications and remote method invocations.

At this point, you have the connectivity problem solved. You can communicate with the network from your Java program, and you will be able to exchange whatever information you need in order to emulate a mainframe.

Now, you actually implement the encapsulation. The job of the encapsulation is to take a command from a legacy terminal and turn it into a method invocation in the e-mail system, then gather the results and display them in a form that the terminal will understand.

The encapsulation acts like a client to the e-mail system and like a server to the legacy terminal population. Figure 32.17 shows the e-mail system with PC-based clients and legacy terminal clients.

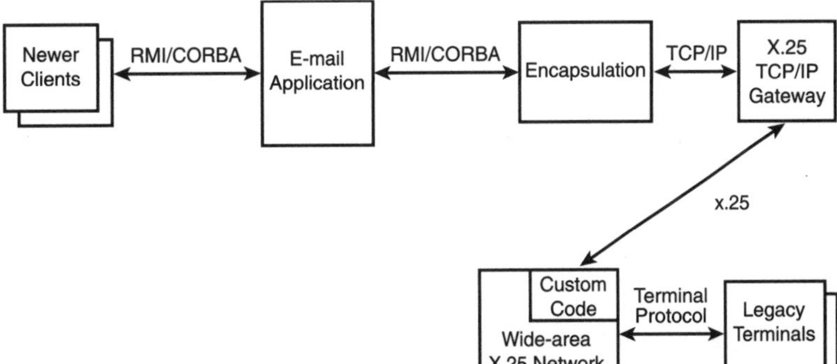

Fig. 32.17
The e-mail system interacts with both legacy terminals and PC-based terminals.

As you can see, the e-mail system is not limited by the constraints of the legacy terminal population, but it is still able to service those terminals. Your e-mail system is able to work in the world of distributed clients, where its users may be reading their mail from hand-held terminals and other devices.

Creating a New Interface for an Existing Application

Suppose you wanted to create a new interface for a legacy application. In this case, assume that you are trying to put a pretty front-end on an airline reservation system.

Your first task, before you even think about connectivity, is designing your reservation system.

Remember, your system doesn't have to work exactly the same way that the existing system does. You'll probably want to simplify the interface and require as little typing as possible.

This is especially important if your goal is to allow agents at the airport to walk around with small hand-held terminals and provide assistance to passengers from outside the confines of a desk. This allows for more personalized service, and this is where you are really going to realize the benefits of Java.

Again, for the sake of simplicity, assume that you have come up with a good, user-friendly design. You aren't ready to move the airline's reservation off the mainframe, however. So, if anyone is going to use your new application, you're going to have to encapsulate the existing reservations system and make it look like your new application.

Now it's time to look at connectivity. Again, you have the mainframe, the network, and the legacy terminals. Start with a simple screen-scraping and proceed from there. In other words, the encapsulation is going to emulate a terminal. You again have choices for where you put your encapsulation:

- You can create an encapsulation that looks like the wide-area network, making the mainframe think it is talking to the network when it is really talking to your encapsulation. This would let your encapsulation emulate whole groups of terminals at once.
- You can hook your encapsulation into the network as a terminal, or cluster of terminals, using the network's X.25 interface.
- You can write software to emulate an actual legacy terminal, which would be both a huge hassle and a huge waste of time.

The X.25 interface looks like the best candidate here because it's cheap and non-proprietary. Plus, you could use the same X.25 server from the e-mail system to access X.25 from Java.

Figure 32.18 shows the relationship between the encapsulation, the X.25 server, and the mainframe.

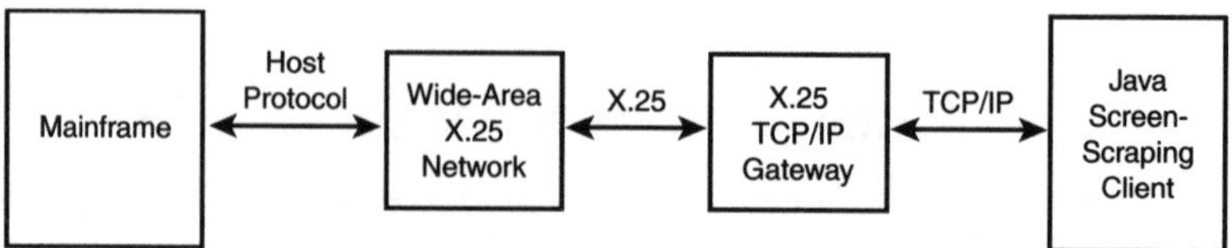

Fig. 32.18
The network's X.25 interface permits easy emulation of a legacy terminal.

In a screen-scraping setup, your encapsulation logs on to the host system with the same commands that a user would normally type. If you are screen-scraping an IBM 3270 application, there's good news and bad news. The bad news is that 3270 screens are no fun to emulate. The good news is that there are some libraries to help you. In the airline example, however, there are no libraries to assist you. After all, it's not like there would be a big customer base for such a library.

You must figure out what commands you would have to enter on the legacy system to perform each task that your new application needs to perform. This may involve single commands to the legacy system, or it may involve a whole series of commands.

Tip

If at all possible, try to minimize the number of extra commands your library has to perform each time. For instance, you don't want it to go through a complete login sequence every time it needs to do commands. Do the minimum number of commands that will ensure that your terminal is set up the way you expect.

Once you have your screen-scraping code written, the other side of your encapsulation acts like the server for your new application. In other words, to the regular clients, it looks like the new system. To the legacy system, it looks like a terminal or a group of terminals. Figure 32.19 shows this screen-scraping encapsulation.

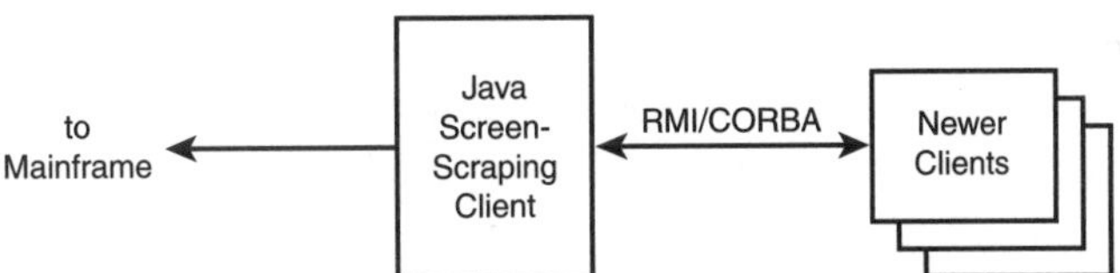

Fig. 32.19

A screen-scraping encapsulation is sometimes your only choice.

The screen-scraping method of encapsulation is often useful when adding new code to the legacy system is impossible, or cost-prohibitive. Screen-scraping is well-suited for rapid prototyping, however. You can throw a functioning model together fairly quickly, without having to add code to the legacy system.

As a mechanism for a production system, however, screen-scraping has some serious drawbacks:

- If the output for a particular command changes, it could throw the screen-scraping code off and give you incorrect results.
- If the screen-scraper gets out of sync with the host, you can get very strange results.
- Screen-scraping can be very slow, and often performs more commands than it needs to.

The nice thing here, however, is that once you have a functioning system, you can work on improving it. If you can get raw data out of the legacy system, you will be much happier. The trick with some systems, like the airline reservation system, is that it wasn't built to give out data in a raw form, so you must add custom code.

When you want to receive raw data from the legacy system, you must decide how the legacy system should deliver the data. The channel interface is a very fast interface, but it takes more work. If you are in a hurry, you may be better off finding an easier solution.

Note

This reluctance to directly hook up to an IBM channel is specific to the airline reservation system. If you are connecting to a regular SNA host, this is a very viable solution, and there are many software/hardware packages available that do this.

You also have the option of making some kind of binary data stream to a terminal, which would most likely require a lot of cooperation from both the legacy system and the network.

The network makes a nice option here. With a little code on the reservation system and on the network, you can get data over the X.25 interface. The legacy system passes data to the network over the channel, and the network hands it to you via the X.25 interface.

Yet again, you have the X.25 server program to keep your Java encapsulation from needing any native methods to access X.25. Unlike screen-scraping, you don't have to perform a series of commands. You can work out a set of messages to be passed between the reservation system and your encapsulation. You won't have to go through the pain of extracting information from text output stream. Instead, the information you need will be laid out in specific places in the messages sent from the reservation system.

Figure 32.20 shows how a Java encapsulation program can use X.25 to exchange binary data with the legacy host.

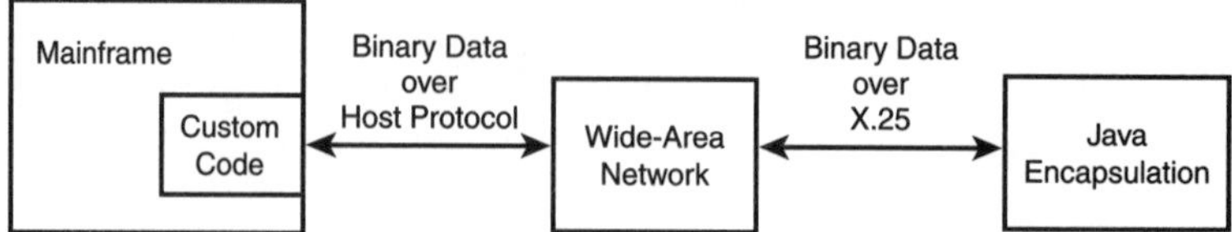

Fig. 32.20
Your encapsulation can exchange binary data with the legacy system.

Assuming you have the time and the resources, a direct channel connection to the mainframe is the best option in terms of bandwidth. When you need such an interface, you may be better off finding a firm that specializes in channel communications and getting them to write the channel interface code.

Assuming you have a way to speak your system's channel code, you should create something similar to the X.25 server. It should speak channel protocol on one side and TCP/IP on the other. Again, this means that you can connect a Java application to the channel gateway with a simple socket instead of creating non-portable native methods.

As with the X.25 solution, when passing information over the channel, you need to figure out what data your encapsulation needs to send and receive, and then add code on the legacy system to handle the requests. Figure 32.21 shows a channel-based encapsulation configuration.

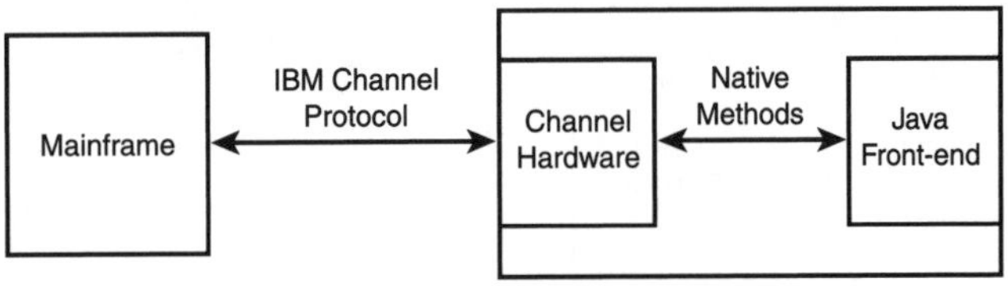

Fig. 32.21
A direct channel connection to a mainframe gives you high-speed access to data.

Clearing a Path for Migration off the Legacy System

When you encapsulate part of a system in order to use newer technology, you gain more than just the use of the newer technology. You gain a path for migrating off the legacy system.

This whole use of encapsulation boils down to one thing—changing a system in pieces rather than tackling the whole thing at once.

Encapsulation helps insulate you from "flash cuts" where everyone suddenly switches over to a new system. While there are cases when these cuts work, many times you end up switching back and forth while all the bugs are worked out. You'll still have these situations where you go back and forth, but you don't have to switch everything at once.

A typical migration path for upgrading both the legacy system and the legacy terminals usually requires at least one encapsulation. The kind of encapsulation you use depends on which part you want to change first.

Tip

No matter which part of your system you want to change first, the first step in migrating away from the legacy system is always the same. You have to figure out what the new system is going to look like. Until you do that, you can't change a thing.

When you decide to migrate your terminal population first, you must create an encapsulation for the legacy system. You encapsulate the part you aren't changing. As shown in Figure 32.22, you first encapsulate the legacy system, creating what looks like a server for your new application design.

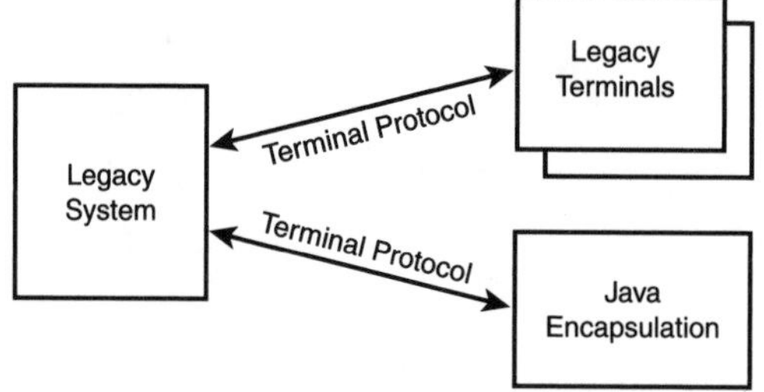

Fig. 32.22
When migrating legacy terminals, you first encapsulate the legacy system.

Next, you begin to migrate your terminal population over to the new application design. Since the old terminals and the new terminals are still accessing the same legacy system, you don't run into any coordination problems. Figure 32.23 shows how your terminal population might look halfway through the migration.

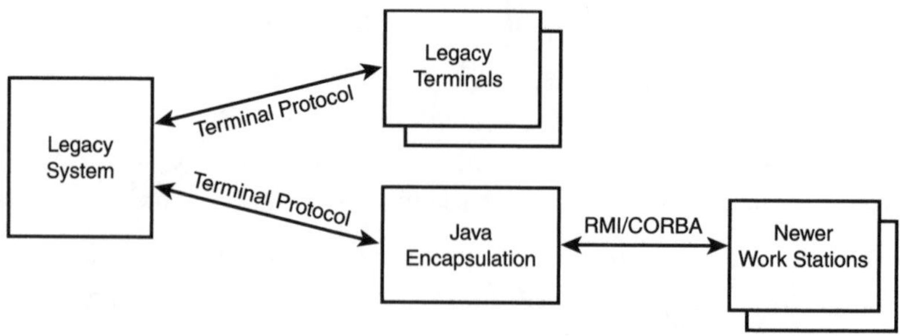

Fig. 32.23
New workstations use the encapsulation to access the legacy system.

Finally, when all the terminals have been migrated over to the new application design, you can create a new server to replace the legacy system, as shown in Figure 32.24.

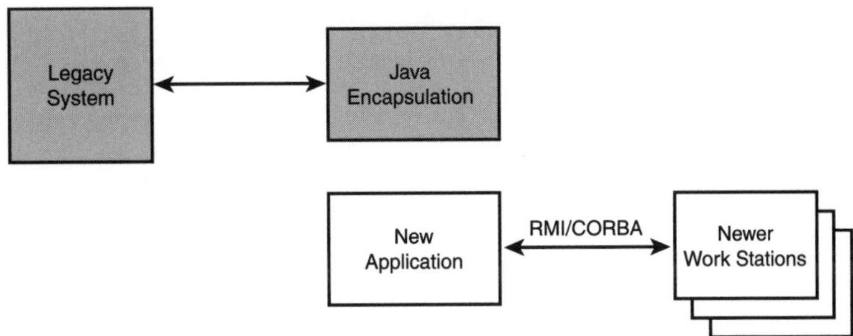

Fig. 32.24
Once the legacy terminals are gone, you can replace the legacy system.

32

When you migrate the legacy system first, you encapsulate the terminal population first. In other words, you create an encapsulation that translates commands from the legacy terminals into commands understood by the new application design. Figure 32.25 illustrates this encapsulation.

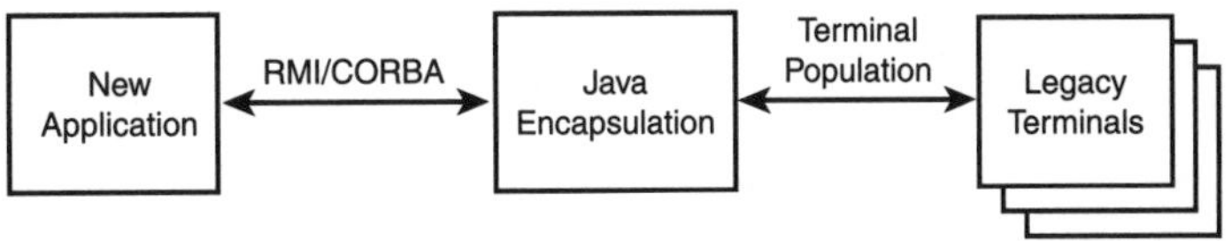

Fig. 32.25
A terminal encapsulation allows legacy terminals to access the new system.

Once the new system is in place, you can migrate your terminals over to the newer terminals. Again, since the new terminals access the same system as the old system, you don't have any coordination problems—there is only one system running. Figure 32.26 illustrates this migration in the process of changing the terminals over.

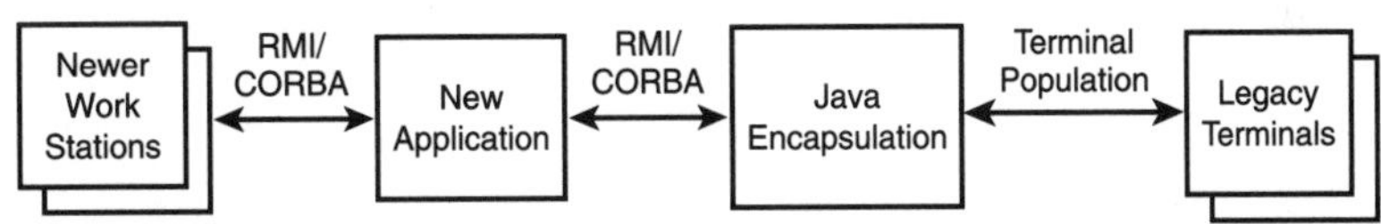

Fig. 32.26
Legacy terminals and new workstations access the new system.

Finally, when you have migrated the last terminal over to the new application design, you are done.

Legacy system is a lot harder than it sounds. The techniques presented in this chapter represent your battle strategy. You use them to attack each new legacy system in a different way. Even though you have a good strategy, you still have to fight the battle—or write the code, in this case. That's where the real fun begins. Each system has its own challenges. You may not enjoy it while you're doing it, but sometime down the road, you'll enjoy recounting all the peculiarities of each system you worked with. They all have their own personalities, brought about by years of tweaks and changes.

Legacy system migration is crucial to bringing more companies onto the Internet and really advancing into the information age. Very few companies want to create a new system from scratch just so they can be on the Net.

chapter 33

Web-Enabling Legacy Systems

33

by Mark Wutka

In this chapter

- **Accessing legacy data**
  Because your legacy system is probably not Web-aware, and your Web server probably can't access the legacy system directly, you need to create an encapsulation to access the legacy data.
- **Creating servlets for legacy data**
  Once you've created a legacy system encapsulation in Java, you can use it in a Java Web server, like Jeeves, to provide Web access to legacy data.

Many companies get their feet wet on the Web by creating a static display-only page. This may be nice from a marketing perspective, but Web surfers find little use for these pages. The real power of the Web is that you can provide a way for customers to interact with your business.

When customers can do business with your company over the Web, they can conduct business at any time of day, from anywhere in the world. They don't have to wait for a salesman, they aren't stuck on hold waiting for an operator—you can give them all the information they need and the power to place orders right at their fingertips.

One of the reasons more companies aren't operating this way is that so many companies have older systems that aren't very Web-friendly. IBM has begun to address this problem for many of their customers, providing Web server software for the AS/400 line, and gateway software to access CICS systems. Chapter 34, "Interfacing with CICS Systems," shows you ways to access a CICS system.

If your company has a legacy system that needs to be accessed from the Web, you can use the encapsulation techniques from Chapter 32, "Encapsulating Legacy Systems," to help you.

Using Encapsulations to Access Legacy Data

When you want to connect a legacy system to the Web, you will probably want the Web server to act as a client to the legacy system. You must first figure out what kind of things you want to do on the Web, then design an interface to the legacy system that supports the functions you want.

Using the encapsulation techniques you learned in Chapter 32, you create an object that both interacts with the legacy system and presents a nice Java front-end to it.

Aiming for Session-Less Transactions

Typical Web accesses are session-less. In other words, each time you access a document on the Web server, or post data to it, you set up a new connection to the server. From the Web server's point of view, this means that it never knows when a particular user is going to send another message.

In a session-oriented system, there is a distinct session initiation, an exchange of messages, and a session shutdown. The nice thing about session-oriented transactions is that you don't have to do everything at once. For instance, if you are booking a number of flights on an airline, you can try to book the first flight. If that succeeds, you book the second flight. If the first flight is full, you can try an alternate. Once you have selected the flights you want, you finish the transaction and everything is saved. You could also abort the transaction, canceling all your reservations automatically.

You can't do this kind of thing with session-less transactions. You have to do everything you want at one time. For instance, you would try to book your whole flight itinerary. If it failed for some reason, you'd make adjustments and try the whole thing again. This is generally less convenient for you but more convenient for the server.

If your legacy system already supports a session-less transaction system, you don't really have to do anything. If not, you can use encapsulation to fake it. When your Web server receives a request and invokes a method in your encapsulation, the encapsulation performs all the steps required to complete the transaction. In other words, it establishes a session, exchanges information with the legacy system, then finishes the transaction.

Storing Session Information in the Web Page

Sometimes, you want to keep the session-oriented transaction protocol, either because it is convenient or because you have no choice. In these situations, your Web server needs to be able to take an incoming request and determine which session it belongs to.

The easiest way to do this is to store a session identifier on the Web page in a hidden variable. Whenever you process a request, you look for this hidden variable. If it isn't there, you can assume that it's a new session. You associate this session identifier with whatever data you need to keep for your session with the legacy system. Typically, you would store the session identifier in a hash table.

Note
In order to keep a session going like this, you cannot use CGI. A CGI program would terminate after each request, taking down the session with the legacy system. The Java Servlet API is very well-suited for this kind of task, however.

From the time a client first initiates a session, the sequence would go like this:

1. The client accesses the URL for the Web service.
2. The Web service creates a session with the legacy system, then creates a unique session identifier and stores the session information in a hash table using the session identifier as a key.
3. The Web service returns an HTML page to the client that contains fields for entering data for the session, along with a hidden field containing the session identifier.
4. The client enters some data for the session and clicks the submit button.
5. The Web service reads in the fields from the client's page, including the session identifier. It uses this identifier to locate the session with the legacy system.
6. The Web service updates the current transaction with whatever information was sent by the client, and returns another HTML page containing the same session identifier.
7. When the client signals that it wants to finish the transaction, the server uses the session identifier again to locate the session with the legacy system. It then asks the legacy system to finish the transaction and close down the session.
8. The server removes the session information from the hash table, because the session has been completed.

Listing 33.1 shows a servlet that uses a simple sequence number for a session ID. It uses a text field to build up a string of text. Anytime text is entered in the field, it appends the text to the current session text. It also provides a checkbox to signal that the transaction is complete.

Listing 33.1 Source Code for *SessionServlet.java*

```
import java.io.*;
import java.util.*;
import java.servlet.*;
import sun.server.html.*;

// This servlet uses hidden variables to keep track of
// a session. When it starts a new session, it sets a
// hidden sessionId variable in the web page. Whenever
// the 'submit' button is clicked, the hidden sessionId
// is transmitted to the servlet.

public class SessionServlet extends Servlet
{

// The sessions table maps session id's to session information. For
// this example, the session information is just a string containing
// the text added during the session.

     protected Hashtable sessions;

// Just for demonstration purposes, we use a simple integer
// variable for generating session id's.

     protected int nextSessionNumber;

     public void init()
     {
          nextSessionNumber = 0;
          sessions = new Hashtable();
     }

// Start new session is called when a request comes in that
// does not contain a session id. This routine should generate
// a new session id and perform the necessary session setup.

     protected String startNewSession()
     {
// Generate a new session id
          String sessionId = ""+nextSessionNumber++;

// Set up the session information in the session table (start
// with an empty string).
          setSessionInfo(sessionId, "");

          return sessionId;
     }

// getSessionInfo returns the information associated with
```

```
// a session - in this case, the information string.

     protected String getSessionInfo(String sessionId)
     {
          return (String) sessions.get(sessionId);
     }

// setSessionInfo stores session-related information in the
// sessions table.

     protected void setSessionInfo(String sessionId, String info)
     {
          sessions.put(sessionId, info);
     }

// finishSession is called to complete a transaction and close
// down the session.

     protected void finishSession(String sessionId)
     {
          sessions.remove(sessionId);
     }

     public void service(ServletRequest req, ServletResponse resp)
     {

          boolean isNewSession = false;
          boolean isExpired = false;
          boolean isFinished = false;

// get a table of variables from the web page
          Hashtable params = req.getQueryParameters();

// get the session id from the page
          String sessionId = (String) params.get("sessionId");

// if there was no session id, start up a new session
          if (sessionId == null) {
               sessionId = startNewSession();
               isNewSession = true;
          }

// get the session info for this session
          String sessionInfo = getSessionInfo(sessionId);

// if there was no session info, it must be an old/invalid session id
          if (sessionInfo == null) {
               isExpired = true;
          }

// get the text item to be added to the session information
          String newStuff = (String) params.get("item");

// if there is text in the "item" field and the session id
// isn't expired, add the item to the session info and save it.

          if (!isExpired && (newStuff != null)) {
```

continues

Listing 33.1 Continued

```
                sessionInfo += newStuff + "\n";
                setSessionInfo(sessionId, sessionInfo);
            }

// See if the "finished" flag was checked
            String finishedFlag = (String) params.get("finished");

            isFinished = (finishedFlag != null) &&
                finishedFlag.equals("on");

// Start generating the response

            resp.setContentType("text/html");
            try {
                resp.writeHeaders();
            } catch (IOException e) {
                e.printStackTrace();
                return;
            }

// Create a response page

            HtmlPage page = new HtmlPage("Session-Oriented Service");

// We always respond with a form of some kind, the action
            page.addText("<FORM action=\"/servlet/SessionServlet\">");

// If the transaction isn't finished, and the session id hasn't
// expired, generate a form for entering text, including the
// hidden session id, and a checkbox for signalling the last
// entry in the transaction.

            if (!isFinished && !isExpired) {

// Add the hidden sessionId field
                page.addText("<INPUT type=\"hidden\""+
                    " name=\"sessionId\""+
                    " value=\""+sessionId+"\">");

// Print out the current session info
                page.addText("<P>Current transaction text:<P>");
                page.addText(sessionInfo+"<P>");

// Create the field for adding new text
                page.addText("<P>New text to add: ");
                page.addText("<INPUT type=\"text\" name=\"item\">");

// Create the checkbox for signalling the end of the transaction
                page.addText("<P>Check here when finished: ");
                page.addText("<INPUT type=\"checkbox\""+
                    " name=\"finished\">");

// Create the submit buttin
                page.addText("<P>");
                page.addText("<INPUT type=\"submit\">");
```

```
// If this is a new session, let the user know
               if (isNewSession) {
                    page.addText("<P>Congratulations, you've started a "+
                         "new session!<P>");
               }

// If the "finished" box was checked, finish the session and
// create a simple form to start another transaction
          } else if (isFinished) {

// Close down the session
               finishSession(sessionId);

               page.addText("<P>Your transaction is completed.<P>");
               page.addText("<P>Press 'Submit' to start another.<P>");
               page.addText("<INPUT type=\"submit\">");

// If the session id had expired, print a message about it and create
// a button to start another transaction.

          } else if (isExpired) {
               page.addText("<P>Uh oh! Your session has expired!");
               page.addText("<P>Press 'Submit' to start another.<P>");
               page.addText("<INPUT type=\"submit\">");
          }

// Finish off the form
          page.addText("</FORM>");

// Write the HTML page to the response output stream
          try {
               page.write(resp.getOutputStream());
          } catch (IOException e) {
               e.printStackTrace();
          }
     }
}
```

Figure 33.1 shows the output from the `SessionServlet` servlet.

Using HTTP Cookies to Preserve Session Information

One of the ugly parts of hidden variables is that they show up as part of the URL. If your browser shows the current location, you can see the session ID embedded within the URL. Aside from a security risk, which will be discussed shortly, the hidden variable causes unnecessary clutter in the URL.

The cookie protocol provides a nice alternative to hidden variables. Actually, cookies are intended more for permanent information. In other words, cookies were intended to be saved by the browser and used every time you run the browser. If you don't give a cookie an expiration date, however, the browser doesn't save it to disk. The cookie disappears when you exit the browser.

33

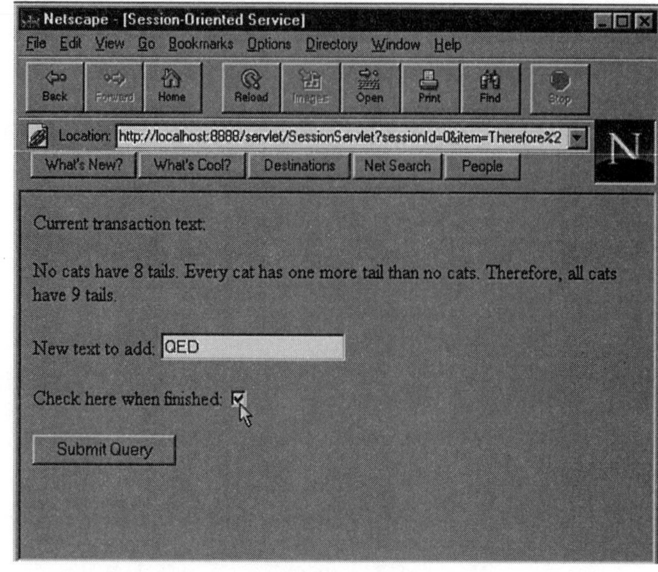

Fig. 33.1
You can maintain a session ID using a hidden variable.

The only sticky point is that there is not a clean way to erase a cookie. In the case of a session, you want to erase the session cookie when the session is terminated. You can kludge around the lack of an erase mechanism by setting the session ID to some phony value like "erased." Whenever the session ID cookie has a value of "erased," treat it as though it were null.

Jeeves has a built-in cookie class, making it very easy to parse cookies and generate them. All you have to do, in order to use cookies instead of hidden variables, is change the way you read and write the information.

For instance, in the previous example, you read the session ID by saying:

```
Hashtable params = req.getQueryParameters();
String sessionId = (String) params.get("sessionId");
```

To use a cookie instead, you have to use a few more lines. You must first get the cookie string from the header:

```
// get the cookie value(s)
String cookieStr = req.getHeader("Cookie");
```

Then, if there were a cookie string, you must extract the `sessionId` cookie:

```
Cookie cookie = null;

String sessionId = null;

// If there was a cookie string, convert it to a cookie object
// and then fetch the sessionId value
```

```
if (cookieStr != null) {
      cookie = new Cookie(cookieStr);

      sessionId = cookie.getValues("sessionId");

// Netscape doesn't seem to like to erase a cookie while it's still
// running, so we hack around it by creating a session id of "erased"
      if ((sessionId != null) &&
            sessionId.equals("erased")) {
            sessionId = null;
      }
}
```

Unlike the hidden variable example, you still have to write out cookie information when the session ID has expired or you have finished the transaction. As you now know, you can't simply erase a cookie, so we have a special kludge to handle erasing the cookie:

```
// If we need to write out a session id, create a cookie and
// write it out.

if (!isFinished && !isExpired) {
      cookie = new Cookie("sessionId", sessionId);
      cookie.setPath("/servlet/SessionCookie");
      resp.setHeader("Set-Cookie", cookie.toString());
} else {

// If expired or finished, set the sessionId to "erased"

      cookie = new Cookie("sessionId", "erased");
      cookie.setPath("/servlet/SessionCookie");
      resp.setHeader("Set-Cookie", cookie.toString());
}
```


Choosing a Good Session Identifier

If you are concerned about security (and you should be), you need to be very careful when creating a session identifier. The technique used in the preceding example, where you just use a sequential numbering system, is completely unacceptable.

The reason you need to be careful with the session identifier is that someone could come along and take over someone else's session if they could guess the session identifier. Even though there are 4 billion possible identifiers in a 32-bit number, you can figure out where the current count is by setting up your own session and seeing what session ID you have been assigned. Then you could guess in the neighborhood of that session ID number.

Don't think that cookies prevent this, either. Just because you can't see the cookie from the browser doesn't mean that someone couldn't write a program that establishes a session and prints out the cookie value it was given. You could use the cookie code in Chapter 6, "Communicating with a Web Server," to do that.

As you've heard so many times, you have to start with secure communications. You have to ensure that no one can spy on another user and figure out their session ID. Once someone gets the session ID, it's all over. They can take over someone else's session. Next, you need to generate a reasonable session ID. Actually, a random session key that you might generate for secure private key communications would work in this situation. When you generate the session ID, you need to check your session ID table to make sure that you haven't chosen an ID that is already in use.

Clearing Out Old Sessions

One of the difficulties in trying to maintain a session in a session-less world is that the server never knows when a client has decided it doesn't want to talk anymore. Obviously, a client is going to tell you whether it wants to abort a transaction, or end one. But what do you do if the client completely forgets about you?

For instance, the client browser could crash and lose the session key. You probably don't have a good way to recover the key, especially since any such mechanism would make you vulnerable to impersonations. At some point, your service must decide that a client session is never going to complete.

The simplest way to age out old sessions is to store the last access time somewhere in your session information. Then, at periodic intervals, a background thread goes through the entire table of sessions and removes every session that has not been accessed within a certain time period.

The only thing you have to do in this case is figure out what a reasonable time period is. It might be 15 minutes, it might be an hour, it might be a week. The timeout period depends on the kind of interaction people do with your server. Generally, give your users more than a reasonable amount of time to perform their transactions. If a normal transaction is five minutes, maybe you should give them an hour or more. If it takes an hour, give them a day.

Accessing Legacy Data from Servlets

Hopefully, you have been creating your legacy system encapsulations in Java, or at least designed them to be Java-friendly. If this is the case, you can use Java servlets to quickly put your legacy system out on the Web.

Conceptually, you have a servlet running in a Java Web server that communicates with your legacy system encapsulation, which, in turn, talks to your legacy system. Figure 33.2 illustrates this relationship.

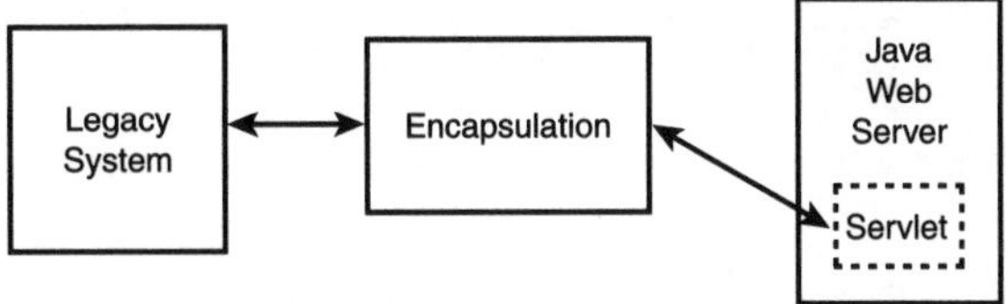

Fig. 33.2
Web access to legacy system involves a servlet and an encapsulation.

One of the things that makes system design so interesting is the number of ways you can implement a system. The trick, of course, is choosing the best way, or at least striking a good balance, between the different factors that affect performance and maintainability.

The most basic way to access legacy data from a servlet is to have the servlet and the legacy encapsulation code running in the same Java environment. Figure 33.3 illustrates this configuration.

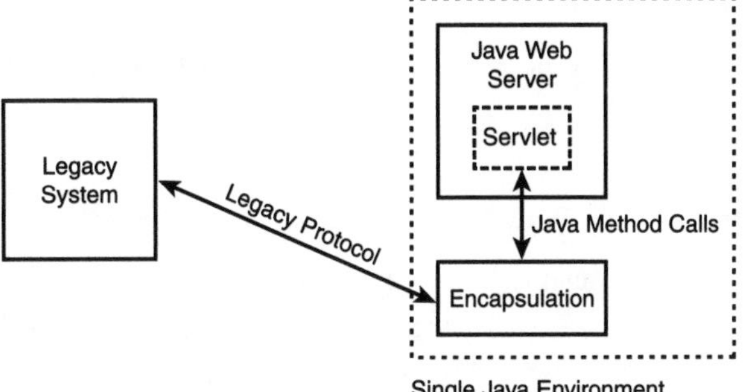

Fig. 33.3
In the most basic configuration, the servlet and encapsulation reside in the same place.

This configuration can support all the different types of encapsulations from Chapter 32. For example, you can invoke methods on an encapsulation that uses native methods. Listing 33.2 shows an extremely basic servlet that invokes the `listParts` native method in the `Ordering` class from Chapter 32.

Listing 33.2 Source Code for *NativeServlet.java*

```
import java.io.*;
import java.util.*;
import java.servlet.*;
import sun.server.html.*;

// This servlet displays a list of parts from the ordering
// system. It shows that a servlet can invoke native methods.

public class NativeServlet extends Servlet
{

     public void init()
     {
```

continues

Listing 33.2 Continued

```
// Load the native library
        System.load("ORDERING.dll");
    }

    public void service(ServletRequest req, ServletResponse resp)
    {

// Start generating the response

        resp.setContentType("text/html");
        try {
            resp.writeHeaders();
        } catch (IOException e) {
            e.printStackTrace();
            return;
        }

// Create a response page

        HtmlPage page = new HtmlPage("Native Encapsulation Service");


        try {

// Get the list of parts from the "legacy system"

            String[] parts = ordering.Ordering.listParts();

// Display the parts list
            for (int i=0; i < parts.length; i++) {
                page.addText(parts[i]+"<P>");
            }
        } catch (Exception e) {
            page.addText(e.toString());
        }

// Write the HTML page to the response output stream
        try {
            page.write(resp.getOutputStream());
        } catch (IOException e) {
            e.printStackTrace();
        }
    }
}
```

You don't have to restrict the servlet from running in the same Java environment as the legacy system encapsulation, however. You can use CORBA, RMI, or even TCP/IP to link the servlet to the encapsulation. Figure 33.4 shows an example configuration using RMI.

Listing 33.3 shows a banking servlet that retrieves an account balance from the banking service in Chapter 16, "Creating 3-Tier Distributed Applications with RMI."

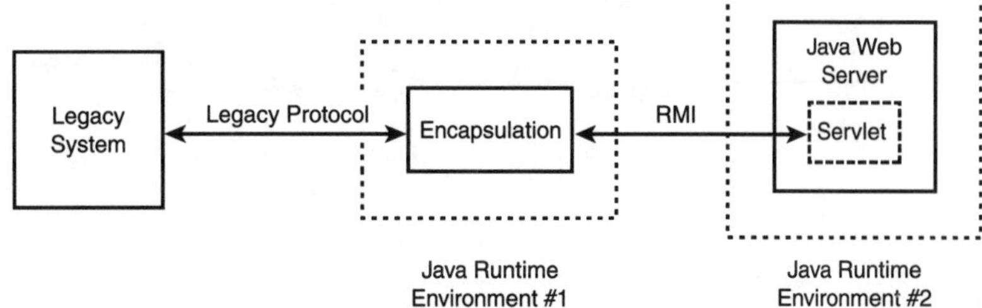

Fig. 33.4
A servlet can use RMI to access a legacy system encapsulation.

33

Listing 33.3 Source Code for *BankBalance.java*

```
import java.io.*;
import java.util.*;
import java.servlet.*;
import sun.server.html.*;

import java.rmi.server.StubSecurityManager;
import java.rmi.Naming;

import banking.*;

// This servlet displays a bank balance using RMI to invoke methods
// on the banking service.

public class BankBalance extends Servlet
{

     public void init()
     {
// Set the security manager for RMI
          System.setSecurityManager(new StubSecurityManager());
     }

     public void service(ServletRequest req, ServletResponse resp)
     {

// Start generating the response

          resp.setContentType("text/html");
          try {
               resp.writeHeaders();
          } catch (IOException e) {
               e.printStackTrace();
               return;
          }

          HtmlPage page = new HtmlPage("Banking Service");

          Account myAccount = new Account(
               "AA1234", "1017", Account.CHECKING);

          try {
```

continues

Listing 33.3 Continued

```
// Get a stub for the BankingImpl object (the stub implements the
// Banking interface).

               Banking bank = (Banking)Naming.lookup("NetBank");

// Check the initial balance
               page.addText("<P>My balance is: "+
                    bank.getBalance(myAccount)+"<P>");

          } catch (Exception e) {
               page.addText(e.toString());
          }
// Create a response page


// Write the HTML page to the response output stream
          try {
               page.write(resp.getOutputStream());
          } catch (IOException e) {
               e.printStackTrace();
          }
     }
}
```

Servlets are a big advantage over CGI when you need to do session-oriented transactions with a legacy system. Servlets stick around between requests, so the sessions with the legacy system are preserved for the next time. You already have a framework for tracking these sessions; all you need to do is put it together with your legacy system encapsulation and you're ready to hit the Web.

chapter 34

Interfacing with CICS Systems

34

by Mark Wutka

In this chapter

- **Accessing CICS from Java**
  The Java-CICS gateway from IBM allows a Java program to run CICS programs and retrieve the results. Although there are some limitations on how you invoke CICS programs, you should be able to do almost anything you need to.
- **Accessing a CICS System from the Web**
  Once you are able to access CICS data, you can provide a Web interface to the CICS system. Because you can access CICS from Java, it makes sense to use a Java Web server to access the data.
- **Accessing CICS with CORBA**
  CORBA gives you more flexibility than normal HTTP Web access. You can use the Java-CICS gateway and one of the Java CORBA products to create a CORBA interface to a CICS system. This allows any CORBA client to access the CICS system.

IBM's Customer Information Control System (CICS) is an extremely popular transaction processing system. Sites all over the world use CICS for ordering, inventory, accounting, and almost any other business application you can think of. While CICS itself is still a very active operating system, it can be considered a "legacy" system with respect to the Internet.

IBM, realizing the potential of the Internet, has taken huge strides in opening up their products to the Internet. They have created gateways for the AS/400 line of computers and have been pushing them as Web servers. There is also a TCP/IP gateway available for MVS systems, which has been a boon to many MVS shops.

In the area of CICS, IBM has created a CICS Web gateway that allows you to create CGI scripts that make calls into CICS. Rather than just stick with that, however, IBM took a major step forward and created the Java-CICS gateway. The Java-CICS gateway allows a Java applet or application to send requests to a CICS system and receive responses. This gateway sits between the CICS system and your Java programs and translates TCP/IP requests from the Java side into SNA or TCP/IP requests on the CICS side. Figure 34.1 shows the relationship between the Java-CICS gateway, a CICS system, and your Java program.

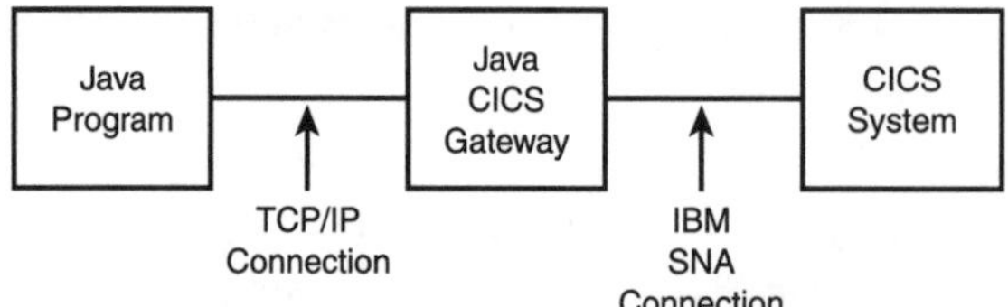

Fig. 34.1
The Java-CICS gateway connects Java programs to CICS systems.

Tip
The Java-CICS gateway is an excellent example of a non-Java encapsulation program that is Java-friendly.

A Thumbnail Sketch of CICS

CICS is a transaction-processing system that performs a number of very handy functions. First and foremost, it manages multiple simultaneous transactions, some of which may be distributed across multiple machines.

The main focus of CICS is processing transactions. You group operations in a transaction into Logical Units of Work (LUW). You can have multiple LUWs in a single transaction. For instance, booking a seat on an airplane would be considered an LUW. Your entire reservation is a transaction, made up of one or more LUWs (after all, you are probably booking seats on multiple flights).

Like other transaction systems, CICS has the ability to abort or "roll back" a transaction. For instance, when you book a seat on an airplane, you want that booking to be visible immediately. If you get the last seat on a plane, you don't want someone else booking that same seat. If you suddenly decide that you don't want to fly at all, the friendly airline agent helping you build the reservation would then abort the transaction. The CICS system would undo all your seat bookings. This kind of feature is usually associated only with database systems, but CICS is not a database system. You still need a database system to use CICS—either IBM's DB2 database or a variety of popular relational databases.

CICS started out back before personal computers hit the scene, so it is well-versed in communicating with older "legacy" terminals like the IBM 3270 series. IBM has done a good job in keeping CICS up-to-date with clients, and today it supports clients on a large number of platforms, including Windows NT, OS/2, and various flavors of UNIX. CICS didn't remain stuck in the "character mode" frame of mind, either. You can buy automated tools for building Graphical User Interfaces for CICS.

CICS also has the ability to communicate with a variety of clients, and even other CICS servers. It supports the popular TCP/IP protocol, as well as IBM's proprietary SNA protocol and even NetBIOS.

For more information about CICS, visit the CICS home page on the Web at **http://www.hursley.ibm.com/cics/**.

The CICS External Call Interface

The External Call Interface (ECI) is a mechanism used by CICS to allow non-CICS clients to invoke programs under CICS. CICS has a remote procedure call mechanism called DPL (Distributed Program Link) which allows a CICS program to start up a CICS program on another CICS host. ECI works exactly the same way as DPL, except that the program that originates the call is not running under CICS.

CICS applications are built as a series of programs, where one program runs another program, which is why you can do almost anything you need with ECI.

To run a CICS program using ECI, you must supply CICS with a user name and password, as well as the name of the program you want to run. You pass data to the program via a block of data called the `COMMAREA` block. The contents of the block vary from program to program. There is no fixed format to the block. Typically, however, you pass text information in the block. If you have to pass a numeric value, you pass numbers as a text string.

You must also pass information about the LUW for your transaction. A unit of work can span multiple ECI calls, if it needs to. An LUW is similar to a transaction in a relational database. As you make changes over the course of an LUW, the changes are not visible to the rest of the system until you commit the LUW, that is, until you save it. If there is a failure of some kind, CICS will undo the changes made so far in the current LUW, but not the previous LUWs.

When you make an ECI call, you pass an LUW token, which is like a session ID for the LUW. When you start a new LUW, you pass a token called ECU_LUW_NEW. CICS will then generate an LUW token value for subsequent ECI calls for this LUW. You must also pass an extend mode parameter for the LUW. You pass either a value of ECI_EXTENDED or ECI_NO_EXTEND. It's very easy to determine when to use ECI_EXTENDED and when to use ECI_NO_EXTEND. You use ECI_NO_EXTEND on the last ECI call in an LUW, and ECI_EXTENDED for all others. If you have only one call in the LUW, it's both the first and last call, so it is sent with the ECI_NO_EXTEND parameter.

Sometimes, you realize you want to back out the LUW (undo the changes) or commit it without actually calling another program. You can use an extend mode of ECI_COMMIT to commit the current LUW, or ECI_BACKOUT to back out the changes in the current LUW.

In addition to the preceding parameters, which are part of the regular ECI interface, you must pass an additional parameter to the Java-CICS gateway. You must supply the name of the CICS server you want to talk to, because the gateway can talk to many different servers.

The Java-CICS Gateway API

While the ECI may seem fairly complicated to you so far, the Java API is actually very simple. In fact, the API consists of only two classes—the JGateConnection class and the ECIRequest class.

The JGateConnection class represents a connection to a Java-CICS gateway server. You can create multiple connections to a single server, or to different servers. You can perform only one ECI call at a time over a single connection. You can perform as many ECI calls as you like over one connection, just one at a time.

The constructor for the JGateConnection class takes two parameters—the name and port number of the gateway server you are connecting to. For example:

```
JGateConnection cicsGateway = new JGateConnection(
"gateway.myplace.com", 4321);
```

Once you have created the connection, you use the flow method to send ECI requests to the gateway. The flow method takes an ECIRequest object as its only parameter. Any information returned from the ECI call is stored in the Commarea array in the ECIRequest.

You create an ECIRequest by passing its constructor the name of the CICS server, the user name, password, Commarea, extend mode, and LUW token.

Suppose you had a CICS program called "BOOKSEAT" that booked a seat on an airline flight. Furthermore, assume that the name of the CICS server is "RES," and that the user name and password are **airjava** and **whee**, respectively. Also, assume that you must store a 4-digit flight number, a 5-digit date in the form DDMMM, and a 3-letter seat number in the Commarea. The following code segment would create the ECIRequest to book seat 35B on flight 5050 on January 12. Also, this is a one-shot LUW, so use an extend mode of ECI_NO_EXTEND, and an LUW token of ECI_LUW_NEW.

```
byte[] commarea = new byte [12];
// A quickie to copy a string into a byte array
"505012JAN35B".getBytes(0, 12, commarea, 0);
ECIRequest request = new ECIRequest("RES", "airjava", "whee",
     "BOOKSEAT", commarea, ECI_NO_EXTEND, ECI_LUW_NEW);
```

To send this request to CICS, you use the flow method in the JGateConnection object, like this:

```
cicsGateway.flow(request);    // send the ECI request
```

Once you send the request, you can check the CICS return code, which is stored in the Cics_Rc variable in the ECIRequest object. If the request completed successfully, the Cics_Rc value should be 0.

Creating Multiple-Call LUWs

The one-shot, or single-call, LUW is very simple to make, and will probably cover most situations for you. When you do a multiple-call LUW, there are a few extra things you have to deal with:

- On the first ECI call, you must sent an LUW token of ECI_LUW_NEW, and the extend mode must be ECI_EXTENDED.
- After the first ECI call completes, you must save the LUW token returned by the CICS system, which is stored in the Luw_Token variable in the ECIRequest object. You must pass this Luw_Token variable as the LUW token for subsequent ECI requests for this LUW.
- On the last ECI call, you must set the extend mode to ECI_NO_EXTEND.
- If you want to commit or back out the current LUW, you set the extend mode to ECI_COMMIT or ECI_BACKOUT.

Tip

If you reuse the same ECIRequest object for each ECI call in an LUW, the Luw_Token variable will already contain the correct LUW token value. You need to change only the token value when you start a new LUW.

Suppose you want to book a round-trip flight using the BOOKSEAT program illustrated previously. Because you want this to be a single LUW, that is, you want to book both seats as a single transaction, you call BOOKSEAT twice as part of a single LUW. The following code books seat 35B on flight 5050 on January 12 and seat 12A on flight 1313 on January 13 as a single LUW:

```
byte[] commarea = new byte [12];
// A quickie to copy a string into a byte array
"505012JAN35B".getBytes(0, 12, commarea, 0);
// Book the first flight leg
ECIRequest request = new ECIRequest("RES", "airjava", "whee",
     "BOOKSEAT", commarea, ECI_EXTENDED, ECI_LUW_NEW);
cicsGateway.flow(request);     // send the ECI request
// Now copy in the return flight leg
"131313JAN12A".getBytes(0, 12, commarea);
// Change the extend mode on the ECI request to ECI_NO_EXTEND
request.Extend_Mode = ECI_NO_EXTEND;
// Book the second flight leg
cicsGateway.flow(request);     // send the ECI request
```

Caution
Be careful when creating multiple-call LUWs. If there is a significant amount of time between calls, you could keep system resources locked unnecessarily. Remember that CICS keeps certain locks on data while an LUW is in progress.

Creating Web Interfaces to CICS

Even before IBM came out with the Java-CICS gateway, you were able to provide Web access into CICS systems. Using a CICS TCP/IP gateway, you could write CGI scripts that used ECI to run programs on the CICS system. Figure 34.2 illustrates this configuration.

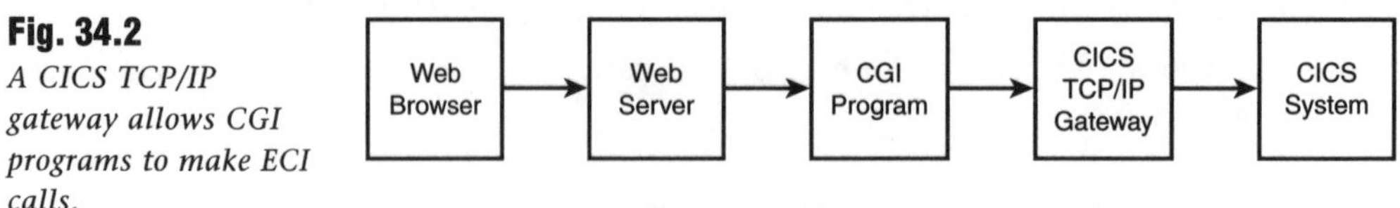

Fig. 34.2
A CICS TCP/IP gateway allows CGI programs to make ECI calls.

As usual, this solution suffered from the usual problems of CGI—the CGI program exited after each request, and you had fairly high session-startup costs.

As you might guess, a Java Web server is an excellent alternative to CGI when accessing CICS. You could, if you wanted, create a servlet that talked to a CICS TCP/IP gateway, but there's no need to do this when IBM has already created the Java-CICS gateway.

You can create Java servlets that execute CICS programs. The advantage to the servlets is that they can use existing connections to the CICS gateway, eliminating the session startup overhead you get with CGI. Figure 34.3 illustrates the relationship between the servlet, the Java-CICS gateway, and the CICS system.

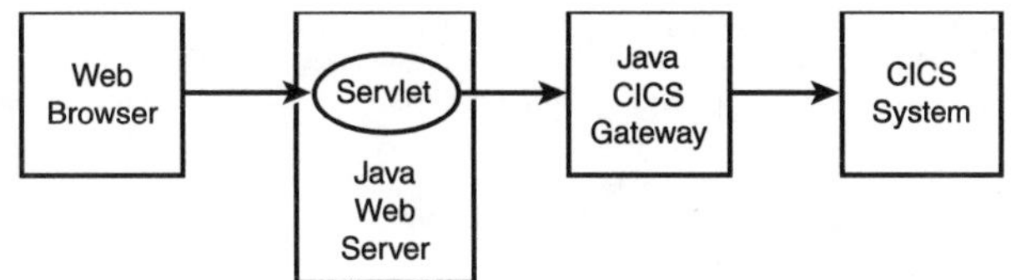

Fig. 34.3
The Java servlet relating to the Java-CICS gateway and the CICS system.

You can use the techniques outlined in Chapter 33, "Web-Enabling Legacy Systems," to preserve session information, so you can perform multiple-call LUWs via Web requests.

Recall that in Chapter 33, you created a session ID variable that was used as a lookup value for the session-related information. In the CICS case, the session components you are concerned with are the `JGateConnection` and the `Luw_Target` for the LUW. Using these two values, you can create an ECI request for an existing LUW. The following class saves the information for the session:

```
public class LUWSession
     public JGateConnection connection;
     public int LUWTarget;
     public LUWSession(JGateConnection connection,
          int LUWTarget)
     {
          this.connection = connection;
          this.LUWTarget = LUWTarget;
```

Providing a CORBA Interface to CICS

It would be really nice if there were a standard CORBA interface into CICS, but in the meantime, you can provide your own CORBA access to CICS in a variety of ways.

Creating a CORBA-CICS Gateway

You may want to use the Java-CICS gateway from a number of CORBA clients, maybe even non-Java clients. One way you can do this is to define an IDL interface that mimics the ECI interface. The following IDL definition creates one such interface:

```
module CICS {
// Define the different values for the extend mode
     enum ExtendType {
          ECI_NO_EXTEND,
          ECI_EXTENDED,
          ECI_BACKOUT,
          ECI_COMMIT
     };
// Define the constant for a new LUW token
     const long ECI_LUW_NEW = 0;
// Set up a data type for the commarea
     typedef sequence<octet> byteArray;
     interface ECI {
// Define the flow method that will send calls to CICS
          void flow(in string serverName, in string programName,
               in string userName, in string password,
               inout byteArray commarea,
               in long extendMode, inout long luwToken);
     };
};
```

The preceding interface should look very familiar because it is the same as the Java-CICS gateway API. It simply wraps a CORBA framework around the old API. You still have to do the work of implementing the CORBA server, but all it would do is create an ECI request, pass it to a `JGateConnection` object, and update the `luwToken` value. This is not necessarily the best way to create a CORBA interface to CICS, however. Figure 34.4 illustrates how this CORBA-CICS gateway fits in with the client, the Java-CICS gateway, and the CICS system.

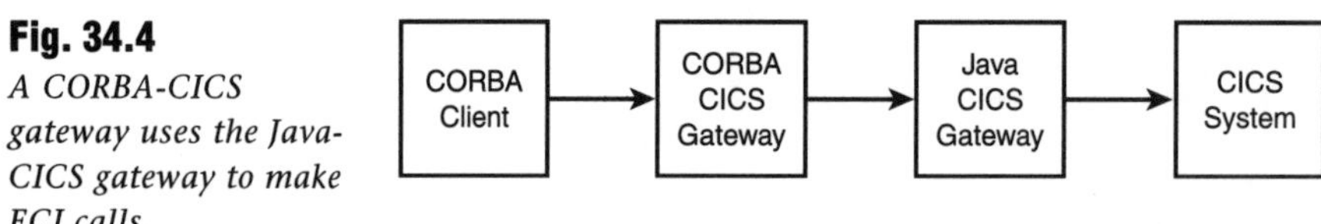

Fig. 34.4
A CORBA-CICS gateway uses the Java-CICS gateway to make ECI calls.

The reason you probably want to avoid setting things up this way is that you don't want to carry the CICS-specific features into your future versions. In other words, an interface like this is one of those cases where the remnants of a legacy system can stay embedded in your application long after the legacy system has departed. For example, suppose you write all your applications to use this ECI interface over CORBA. You're now passing all sorts of different requests using the same method call. The only difference between the requests is the program name and the contents of the `Commarea`.

Now, suppose you replace your CICS system with a newer one. If you don't want to replace all your existing applications, you have to create an encapsulation that maps the program name and `Commarea` information to whatever the new system needs. Someone looking at an application cannot determine what a particular ECI call does without knowing what the CICS program did.

Creating CORBA Interfaces to CICS Programs

Following the encapsulation principles from Chapter 32, look at the CICS system as an application or group of applications to see what it actually does. For example, the BOOKSEAT program from earlier in this chapter can be represented by the following IDL interface:

```
module Reservations {
     struct Date {
          short year;
          short month;
          short day;
     };
     interface Booking {
          void bookSeat(in short flightNumber,
               in Date date, in string seat);
     };
};
```

Your CORBA server for this interface would invoke the BOOKSEAT program in the CICS system. Unlike the previous CORBA interface, this one is not tied to the CICS system. Remember that the dates in the CICS reservations system were specified in DDMMM format, like 04JUL or 25DEC. Because other systems may not use a notation like that, the CORBA Reservations module defines a generic date class that the CORBA server can then convert into whatever format it needs to.

HotJava

chapter 35

35

Adding Additional Protocols to HotJava

by David Baker

In this chapter

- **How protocol handlers can help you**
  Protocol handlers empower you to implement new application protocols.
- **Extending HotJava**
  HotJava, Sun's browser and toolkit for network computing, supports protocol handlers. Using HotJava, you can access new types of Internet servers.
- **Using protocol handlers in your own applications**
  Protocol handlers can also be utilized by your own network applications.

An essential feature that Java attempts to impart to computing is extensibility. Over time, newer and better means of communicating will be created. Application protocols will evolve and programs must be able to adapt. Support for new protocols can be added to Java and the HotJava browser through *protocol handlers*.

Protocol handlers are a key tool for maintaining an adaptable environment with Java. They extend support to new URL schemes, which can access new application protocols, or present existing ones in new ways.

Writing a Protocol Handler

Protocol handlers enable you to accomplish two tasks: first, you can implement a client for a defined network application protocol, as demonstrated in the previous chapters; second, you can associate this implementation with a new URL scheme. Thus, you can create the code necessary to assign meaning to a new URL scheme.

Note

All URLs are classified into schemes. The scheme is the label prior to the first colon. Common schemes are http, ftp, and gopher.

A scheme generally identifies an application protocol, and thus Java references often describe the scheme as being the protocol portion of the URL. However, a scheme need not identify a particular protocol.

The distinction is important when you implement more complex protocol handlers that implement new URL schemes built upon existing protocols. For instance, a useful protocol handler would be one that created a search scheme, which connected to various Web search engines and returned a unified hit list.

HotJava can make use of new protocol handlers; this is part of the vision guiding HotJava's ongoing development. The intention is that programs like HotJava should have very little core intelligence, providing only a framework for extensibility. When new protocols are invented, HotJava will transparently download a new handler and the user can then access the resource.

You can also utilize protocol handlers in your own applications. By installing a new protocol handler and using a registration facility termed a *factory*, URL objects can use these handlers just as the standard protocols are used.

Protocol handlers are not a factor new to your Java programming. In fact, any time an URL object was used to obtain a resource in the previous chapters, a handler inherent in the JDK was used. With the steps that follow, you can create your own handlers to build on this existing set.

The examples within this chapter implement the NICNAME/WHOIS protocol, defined in RFC 954. WHOIS is used by Internic, the domain name registration and directory project, to enable individuals to query their database. WHOIS can be used at **rs.internic.net**, but other sites utilize this service. By opening a TCP socket to the standard port 43, a query can be entered and the response read.

Tip

More information on this protocol is available at

http://www.cis.ohio-state.edu/htbin/rfc/rfc954.html

Caution
Java is case-sensitive. Even if your system doesn't treat upper and lower case characters within directory names differently, use the case of the letters as shown within these instructions.

Step One: Decide Upon a Package Name

A protocol handler must be placed into a clearly-defined package. This package must end in `protocol.scheme` where *scheme* is the new URL scheme. Generally, new packages also include the domain name and author identifier of the distributor. Thus, in this example the following package will be used:

```
ORG.netspace.dwb.protocol.whois
```

Step Two: Create the Directories

The necessary code for the protocol handler must be placed into a directory named in correlation to the package name identified. This directory should reside within a directory into which your own Java code is placed, usually called `classes` within your home directory.

35

Listing 35.1 shows an example for creating these directories under Windows NT and Windows 95.

Lising 35.1 Creating the Directories Under Windows NT and Windows 95

```
%HOMEDRIVE%
cd %HOMEPATH%
mkdir classes
mkdir classes\ORG
mkdir classes\ORG\netspace
mkdir classes\ORG\netspace\dwb
mkdir classes\ORG\netspace\dwb\protocol
mkdir classes\ORG\netspace\dwb\protocol\whois
```

The process is similar under the UNIX operating system, as shown in Listing 35.2.

Listing 35.2 Creating the Directories Under UNIX

```
cd ~
mkdir classes
mkdir classes/ORG
```

continues

Listing 35.2 Continued

```
mkdir classes/ORG/netspace
mkdir classes/ORG/netspace/dwb
mkdir classes/ORG/netspace/dwb/protocol
mkdir classes/ORG/netspace/dwb/protocol/whois
```

Step Three: Set Your *CLASSPATH*

The CLASSPATH environment variable tells the Java compiler and interpreter where to find Java classes, enabling the dynamic linking feature of the Java execution environment. When installing the JDK, HotJava, or a Java-aware browser, you may have set the CLASSPATH environment variable. If this is so, it is critical that you avoid overwriting that data. First, you must find out what your CLASSPATH current setting is. Under Windows NT/95, just type the following command:

```
SET
```

Look for the CLASSPATH value. Under UNIX systems, you can display the CLASSPATH value with this command:

```
ECHO $CLASSPATH
```

Now you need to reset your CLASSPATH, including the previous data, if any. Under Windows 95, if your CLASSPATH was `.;C:\JAVA\LIB\CLASSES.ZIP`, you can add the following line to your AUTOEXEC.BAT and reboot:

```
SET CLASSPATH=.;%HOMEDRIVE%%HOMEPATH%\CLASSES;C:\JAVA\LIB\CLASSES.ZIP
```

Under Windows NT, presuming that the CLASSPATH value was the same as under the Windows 95 example, use the System Control Panel to add a CLASSPATH environment variable with the value `.; %HOMEDRIVE%%HOMEPATH%\CLASSES;C:\JAVA\LIB\CLASSES.ZIP`.

Under UNIX, assume that your old CLASSPATH was `.:/usr/java/lib`. If you are using the C shell, place the following into your .cshrc file:

```
setenv CLASSPATH .:${HOME}:/usr/java/lib
```

If you are on a UNIX system using the Korn or a POSIX-compliant shell, add the following line to whatever file your ENV environment variable points. If ENV is unset, then you could add the line to your `~/.profile` file:

```
CLASSPATH=.:${HOME}:/usr/java/lib
export CLASSPATH
```

Step Four: Implement the Protocol

Within the directory created in Step Two, create a class that extends `URLConnection`. This class should have a constructor that takes an URL object as an argument and calls its superclass with that object. In addition, most protocol handlers should extend the following methods:

```
public void connect() throws IOException;
```

This method should connect to the remote resource and perform the network transaction, as appropriate.

```
public String getContentType();
```

This method should indicate the MIME content type of the data returned by the object.

```
public synchronized InputStream getInputStream()
   throws IOException;
```

This returns an `InputStream` containing the data from the remote system.

Listing 35.3 shows the class used to implement the WHOIS protocol. This class supports the URL formats shown in Table 35.1.

Table 35.1 WHOIS URL Syntax

URL	Meaning
`whois:`*`query`*	Connect to `rs.internic.net` and submit `query`.
`whois:/`*`query`*	Identical to "`whois:query.`"
`whois://`*`host/query`*	Instead of connecting to `rs.internic.net`, connect to WHOIS service on `host` and submit `query`.
`whois://`*`host:port/query`*	Instead of using port 43, connect to `host` at the specified `port` and submit `query`.

35

Listing 35.3 *whoisURLConnection.java*

```
// This is the package identified for this protocol handler.
package ORG.netspace.dwb.protocol.whois;

import java.io.*;    // Import the package names used.
import java.net.*;

/**
 * This class implements a connection to the new "whois"
 * URL scheme.
 * @author David W. Baker
 * @version 1.0
 */
class whoisURLConnection extends URLConnection {
   // Some defaults for the WHOIS protocol implementation:
   //    site defaults to rs.internic.net
```

continues

Listing 35.3 Continued

```
//    port defaults to 43
//    query defaults to QUIT
private static final String DEF_SITE = "rs.internic.net";
private static final int DEF_PORT = 43;
private static final String DEF_QUERY = "QUIT";
private static final String CONT_TYPE = "text/html";
static final int URL_BASE = 16;
InputStream fromHandler;   // Input from the handler
Socket whoisSocket;        // Socket for communication
boolean gotQuery = false;  // Did we get the data?

/**
 * Given a URL will instantiate a whoisURLConnection
 * object.
 * @param getURL The URL to contact.
 */
whoisURLConnection(URL getURL) {
   super(getURL); // Call superclass with the URL.
}

/**
 * Connect to the WHOIS server, obtain, and format the
 * data.
 * @exception java.io.IOException Indicates a problem
 *    connecting to URL.
 */
public void connect() throws IOException {
   String whoisSite;
   int whoisPort;
   String whoisQuery;
   PrintStream toApp;   // Send data to app using handler.
   DataInputStream fromWhois = null;
   PrintStream toWhois = null;
   String dataLine;

   // Set up piped streams for communication between
   // this handler and the application using it.
   PipedOutputStream pipe = new PipedOutputStream();
   toApp = new PrintStream(pipe);
   fromHandler = new PipedInputStream(pipe);

   // Get host from the URL, using default if omitted.
   if (url.getHost().length() == 0) {
      whoisSite = DEF_SITE;
   } else {
      whoisSite = url.getHost();
   }
   // Get port from the URL, using default if omitted.
   if (url.getPort() < 1) {
      whoisPort = DEF_PORT;
   } else {
      whoisPort = url.getPort();
   }
   // Get file from the URL, using default is "/"
   if (url.getFile().equals("/")) {
      whoisQuery = DEF_QUERY;
```

```
      } else {
         whoisQuery = url.getFile().substring(1);
      }
      // Decode the query from the URL.
      whoisQuery = decodeURL(whoisQuery);
      // Open a socket to the whois server.
      whoisSocket = new Socket(whoisSite,whoisPort);
      // Open streams to communicate with the whois server.
      fromWhois =
         new DataInputStream(whoisSocket.getInputStream());
      toWhois =
         new PrintStream(whoisSocket.getOutputStream());
      // Send the query to the server.
      toWhois.println(whoisQuery);
      // Print out some HTML.
      toApp.println("<!DOCTYPE HTML PUBLIC \"-//IETF//DTD "
                    + "HTML//EN\">");
      toApp.println("<HTML>");
      toApp.println("<HEAD>");
      toApp.println("<TITLE>Whois Query for: " + url
                    + "</TITLE>");
      toApp.println("</HEAD>");
      toApp.println("<BODY>");
      toApp.println("<H1>Whois Query for : " + url
                    + "</H1>");
      toApp.println("<PRE>");
      // Loop through the data from the whois server,
      // printing it all out within the preformatted
      // text section.
      while ((dataLine = fromWhois.readLine()) != null) {
         toApp.println(dataLine);
      }
      // Some last HTML.
      toApp.println("</PRE>");
      toApp.println("</BODY>");
      toApp.println("</HTML>");
      toApp.flush();       // Flush the pipe.
      toWhois.close();     // Close the streams.
      fromWhois.close();
      whoisSocket.close(); // Close the socket.
      toApp.close();       // Close one end of the pipe.
      gotQuery = true;     // Data has been obtained.
   }

   /**
    * Determine the content type of the data returned.
    * @return The content type.
    */
   public String getContentType() {
      return CONT_TYPE;
   }

   /**
    * Obtain a stream to get data from this protocol handler.
    * @return The stream to read data.
    */
   public synchronized InputStream getInputStream()
      throws IOException {
```

35

continues

Listing 35.3 Continued

```
        // If where has not been obtained, connect()
        if (!gotQuery) {
           connect();
        }
        // Return the stream.
        return fromHandler;
     }

     /**
      * This method decodes the URL encoded format.
      * i.e. %XX -> char and + to space
      * @param decode The String to decode.
      * @return The decoded String.
      */
     protected String decodeURL(String decode) {
        StringBuffer decoded = new StringBuffer();
        char nextChar;
        String encString;
        Integer encInteger;

        // Go through the String character by character.
        for(int index=0; index < decode.length(); index++) {
           // Get the next character in the String.
           nextChar = decode.charAt(index);
           // If the character is +, then convert it to
           // a space.
           if (nextChar == '+') {
              decoded.append(" ");
           }
           // If the character is a %, then the next two
           // characters store the value of the encoded
           // character.
           else if (nextChar == '%') {
              // Create an Integer object containing the
              // integer value of the next two characters
              // in the string, assuming a base 16 notation.
              encInteger = Integer.valueOf(
                 decode.substring(index+1,index+3),URL_BASE);
              // Increment our counter by 2 - we just read
              // two characters.
              index += 2;
              // Return the int value within the Integer
              // and then cast that into a char type.
              nextChar = (char)encInteger.intValue();
              // Add the coded character.
              decoded.append(nextChar);
           }
           // Otherwise, just add the character.
           else {
              decoded.append(nextChar);
           }
        }
        // Return the decoded string.
        return decoded.toString();
     }
  }
```

The whoisURLConnection constructor merely makes the appropriate call to the URLConnection superclass, passing it the URL object. The connect() method is where all of the work is done. First, it creates a number of streams for reading in data and passing it back to your Java application. Next, it uses various URL class methods to parse the URL, supporting the formats identified in Table 35.1. The default values of the host (for example, "rs.internic.net") and port (i.e., "35") are stored within static final variables. Then, the connect() method opens a TCP socket connection to the remote system, sends the query, and prepares to read the response. It reads in the query response, embedding it within HTML. Finally, connect() closes the streams and TCP socket.

The getContentType() method is used to indicate that the returned data is an HTML document. getInputStream() returns the PipedOutputStream, into which this protocol handler has pushed the formatted data. The Java application uses this stream to access the data obtained by the new protocol handler.

The whoisURLConnection has an additional protected method called decodeURL(). Certain characters, such as spaces and other special characters, cannot be represented literally within URLs, and these characters are encoded with a special format. For example, a space is encoded as %20. Since your WHOIS query may need to use such characters, the WHOIS protocol handler must have a method to decode this data. decodeURL() is called from the connect() method, and examines a string byte-by-byte. When it encounters a percent-sign, it uses the next two characters as the Unicode value to the encoded character.

Step Five: Create the *Handler* Class

Within the same directory, you must create a file called Handler.java. The Handler class must extend the URLStreamHandler class and return an instance of the class created in Step Four. Listing 35.4 shows the Handler class for the WHOIS protocol.

Listing 35.4 *Handler.java*

```
// This is the package identified for this protocol handler.
package ORG.netspace.dwb.protocol.whois;

import java.net.*;   // Import the package names used.

/**
 * This class is a subclass of URLStreamHandler and provides
 * an implementation of the abstract openConnection() method
 * to support the "whois" scheme.
 * @author David W. Baker
 * @version 1.0
 */
```

continues

Listing 35.4 Continued

```
public class Handler extends URLStreamHandler {
  /**
   * Given a URL return an appropriate URLConnection.
   * @param requestedURL The URL instance to contact.
   * @return The connection to the resource.
   */
   public synchronized URLConnection
      openConnection(URL requestedURL) {
      return new whoisURLConnection(requestedURL);
   }
}
```

Step Six: Compile the Sources

Use `javac` to compile the sources created in Steps Four and Five, leaving the compiled class files in the originating directory.

Using Protocol Handlers with HotJava

Eventually, as part of HotJava's vision, protocol handlers will be dynamically downloaded and utilized. At the time of this writing, this feature is not yet supported by HotJava. Protocol handlers must be manually installed, as previously described, in order for HotJava to utilize them.

Note

The Netscape Navigator supports a different mechanism for extending the browser. A Netscape *plug-in* can implement a new application protocol using a special API. No specific plans seem to have been stated by Netscape regarding the support of protocol handlers such as HotJava. More information on Netscape Plug-ins is available from:

http://home.netscape.com/eng/mozilla/3.0/handbook/plugins/

The Microsoft Explorer also supports add-ins and ActiveX, OLE Controls. ActiveX can accomplish many of the same tasks as Netscape Plug-ins and Java can. As with Netscape, no stated plans are apparent with respect to protocol handlers and the Explorer. More information on ActiveX is available from:

http://www.microsoft.com/intdev/controls/controls-f.htm

Once a protocol handler has been installed, the following additional steps are necessary to use it within your HotJava browser.

Note

JavaSoft makes the HotJava browser and instructions for its installation available at <URL:**http://www.javasoft.com/java.sun.com/HotJava/CurrentRelease/installation.html**>.

Step One: Update the *properties* File

You must instruct HotJava to load additional protocol handlers. This is done by updating the `properties` file, which is located within the `.hotjava` directory in your home directory.

Within this file, you must set the `java.protocol.handler.pkgs` property to include the new protocol package. The value to add should be everything from the `protocol` token leftward. Thus, you want to add the following line for your WHOIS protocol handler:

```
java.protocol.handler.pkgs=ORG.netspace.dwb.protocol
```


If you already have this property set within your HotJava properties file, append a pipe character (i.e., |) to the end of the line and then add `ORG.netspace.dwb.protocol`. This syntax enables you to install several new protocol handlers, like the following:

```
java.protocol.handler.pkgs=COM.company.protocol|ORG.netspace.dwb.protocol
```

Step Two: Run HotJava

Start up HotJava and test out the new protocol handler. Go under the File menu, select Open Page, and type the following text into the URL field:

```
whois:internic.net
```

Figure 35.1 shows what should be displayed within the HotJava window.

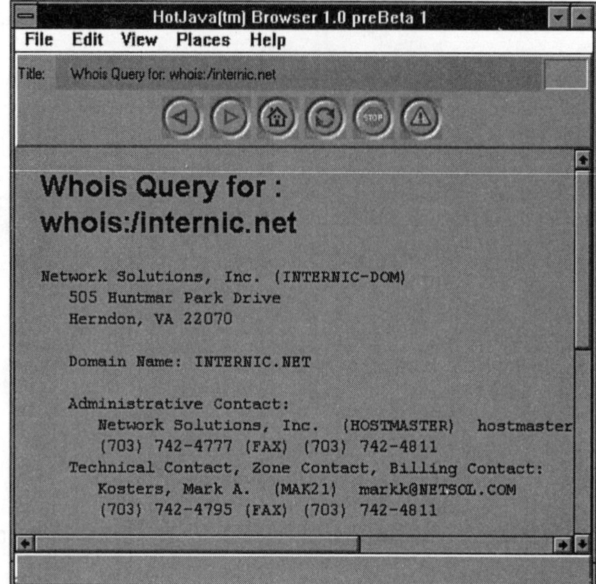

Fig. 35.1
HotJava using the WHOIS protocol handler.

Using Protocol Handlers with Your Own Applications

The usefulness of new protocol handlers extends beyond the HotJava browser. They can also be utilized within your own applications; the key step being a method to register the new protocol handler using a concept known as a factory.

As an example, a simple application will be developed to make use of the WHOIS protocol handler. FetchWhois will take its arguments and send them as a query to the WHOIS service at `rs.internic.net`. The source of this example is shown in Listing 35.5.

Listing 35.5 *FetchWhois.java*

```
import java.net.*;   // Import the package names used.
import java.io.*;

/**
 * This is an application which uses our new whois
 * protocol handler to obtain information.
 * @author David W. Baker
 * @version 1.1
 */
public class FetchWhois {

   /**
    * The method launches the application.
```

```
     * @param args Arguments which are the query string.
     */
    public static void main (String args[]) {
       if (args.length < 1) {
          System.err.println(
             "usage: java FetchWhois query string");
          System.exit(1);
       }
       FetchWhois app = new FetchWhois(args);
    }

    /**
     * This constructor does all of the work of obtaining
     * the data from the server.
     * @param args The tokens of the query string.
     */
    public FetchWhois(String args[]) {
       String encodedString;   // Hold the URL encoded query.
       String nextLine;        // Line from the handler.
       URL whoisURL;           // URL to whois resource
       URLConnection whoisAgent;  // Connection to whois.
       DataInputStream input;     // Stream from whois.

       // Create a buffer to place in all of the query
       // string tokens.
       StringBuffer buffer = new StringBuffer();
       // Append all of the tokens to the buffer.
       for(int index = 0; index < args.length; index++) {
          buffer.append(args[index]);
          if (index < args.length-1) {
             buffer.append(" ");
          }
       }
       // URL encode the query buffer.
       encodedString = URLEncoder.encode(buffer.toString());
       // Set the factory to register the whois handler.
       URL.setURLStreamHandlerFactory(new whoisUSHFactory());
       try {
          // Create the whois URL object.
          whoisURL = new URL("whois:" + encodedString);
          // Open the connection.
          whoisAgent = whoisURL.openConnection();
          // Get an input stream from the whois server.
          input =
             new DataInputStream(whoisAgent.getInputStream());
          // Print out the data line-by-line.
          while((nextLine = input.readLine()) != null) {
             System.out.println(nextLine);
          }
          input.close(); // Close the stream.
       } catch(MalformedURLException excpt) {
          System.err.println("Mailformed URL: " + excpt);
       } catch(IOException excpt) {
          System.err.println("Failed I/O: " + excpt);
       }
    }
}
```

35

continues

Listing 35.5 Continued

```
/**
 * This class implements the URLStreamHandlerFactory
 * interface to register the whois protocol handler.
 * @see java.net.URLStreamHandlerFactory
 */
class whoisUSHFactory implements URLStreamHandlerFactory {
   /**
    * This method returns the protocol handler to the
    * calling object.
    * @param scheme The URL scheme to be obtained.
    * @return The protocol handler.
    * @see java.net.URLStreamHandlerFactory#createURLStreamHandler
    */
   public URLStreamHandler
      createURLStreamHandler(String scheme) {
      // Make sure that this is for a whois URL
      if (scheme.equalsIgnoreCase("whois")) {
         // If so, create the handler and return it.
         return
            new ORG.netspace.dwb.protocol.whois.Handler();
      // Otherwise print an error message and return null.
      } else {
         System.err.println("Unknown protocol: " + scheme);
         return null;
      }
   }
}
```

The *main()* Method: Starting *FetchWhois*

The simple `main()` method checks to see that the program was invoked properly. It then creates a `FetchWhois` object, passing it the array of command line arguments.

The *FetchWhois* Constructor: Where the Work Gets Done

The constructor is where the connection to `rs.internic.net` is opened through the use of your new protocol handler. The key line is where it uses the `setURLSreamHandlerFactory()` static method from the URL class. This is where `FetchWhois` directs new URL instances to the new WHOIS protocol handler, using the `whoisUSHFactory` described later.

The constructor uses a `StringBuffer` to consolidate the array of command line arguments into a single `String`, and then uses the static `encode()` method of `URLEncoder` to properly format the data. Then, it creates an URL object with the new whois URL scheme. Finally, it opens a connection to the URL and receives the WHOIS data.

The *whoisUSHFactory* Class: Registering the Protocol Handler

The URL class uses a `URLStreamHandlerFactory` implementation to choose an appropriate protocol handler. In order to use the WHOIS protocol handler, you must implement the `URLStreamHandlerFactory` interface. The constructor should take a `String` that contains the scheme of the URL object being instantiated. `whoisUSHFactory` checks to ensure that the scheme is `whois`, and if so, returns an instance of the WHOIS `Handler`. Otherwise, it returns `null`.

Running *FetchWhois*

Compile `FetchWhois` with `javac` and then try running it by using the following command. The program should print an HTML document that contains the same data as when you used the `whois` URL within HotJava.

```
java FetchWhois internic.net
```

HotJava will soon support dynamically downloaded protocol handlers, enabling a much more flexible use of this feature. Manually installing these extensions will continue to be a useful alternative.

More on *URLStreamHandlerFactory*

The `URLStreamHandlerFactory` class is a means of passing out specific protocol handlers for each supported protocol handler. In Listing 35.5, you used a custom factory called `whoisUSHFactory`. This factory supported only one scheme, `whois`. However, factories can be much more general, and can support both custom protocol handlers and those provided within the JDK.

Listing 35.6 shows another application, `ParseURL`, which uses its own `URLStreamHandlerFactory` implementation. This application will take a series of URLs, including new URL schemes, as command line arguments and then print out how the URL class parses them. This demonstrates how the URL class deals with different forms of URLs.

Listing 35.6 *ParseURL.java*

```
import java.net.*;

/*
 * This simple application demonstrates how a custom
 * URLStreamHandlerFactory can be used to provide custom-
```

continues

Listing 35.6 Continued

```
 * written protocol handlers as well as those within the
 * JDK. This program uses a dummy protocol handler so that
 * it can construct a URL object to unknown protocols and
 * parse out that URL.
 * @author David W. Baker
 * @version 1.0
 */
public class ParseURL {

  /**
   * This method allows ParseURL to be executed as a
   * stand-alone application. It takes a series of URLs
   * as arguments and then prints out the various portions
   * of those URLs.
   * @param args The command-line arguments.
   */
  public static void main(String[] args) {
    URL urlToParse;    // We use this to parse each URL.

    // First, we must use the custom URLStreamHandlerFactory
    // which is included below.
    URL.setURLStreamHandlerFactory(new ParseURLFactory());
    // Go through each command-line argument.
    for(int index = 0; index < args.length; index++) {
      try {
        // Create the URL object.
        urlToParse = new URL(args[index]);
        // Print the URL to be parsed.
        System.out.println("Parsing URL: " + args[index]);
        // Print out the various portions of the URL.
        System.out.println("\tScheme:\t" +
                           urlToParse.getProtocol());
        System.out.println("\tHost:\t" +
                           urlToParse.getHost());
        System.out.println("\tPort:\t" +
                           urlToParse.getPort());
        System.out.println("\tFile:\t" +
                           urlToParse.getFile());
        System.out.println("\tRef:\t" + urlToParse.getRef());
        System.out.println("==============================");
      } catch(MalformedURLException excpt) {
        // We should catch this exception, but our custom
        // URLStreamHandlerFactory will ensure such is
        // never thrown.
        System.err.println("Malformed URL: " + args[index]);
        System.err.println(excpt);
      }
    }
  }
}

/**
 * This custom URLStreamHandlerFactory allows us to create
 * URL objects that will use the JDK protocol handlers for
 * known schemes. If the scheme is not one of those within
```

```
 * the JDK, we create an instance of our DummyHandler and
 * return that. If this factory returned null instead,
 * a MalformedURLException would be thrown for unknown
 * schemes.
 */
class ParseURLFactory implements URLStreamHandlerFactory {
  public URLStreamHandler createURLStreamHandler(String
                                                  scheme) {
    // First, go through the JDK's protocol handlers for
    // known URL schemes. All of these protocol handlers
    // reside within sun.net.www.protocol.<scheme>.
    if (scheme.equalsIgnoreCase("http")) {
      return new sun.net.www.protocol.http.Handler();
    }
    if (scheme.equalsIgnoreCase("ftp")) {
      return new sun.net.www.protocol.ftp.Handler();
    }
    if (scheme.equalsIgnoreCase("gopher")) {
      return new sun.net.www.protocol.gopher.Handler();
    }
    if (scheme.equalsIgnoreCase("file")) {
      return new sun.net.www.protocol.file.Handler();
    }
    if (scheme.equalsIgnoreCase("mailto")) {
      return new sun.net.www.protocol.mailto.Handler();
    }
    // If it is none of the above, create an instance of our
    // dummy URLStreamHandler.
    return new DummyHandler();
  }
}

/**
 * This is a dummy protocol handler. This handler will allow
 * us to create a URL object for this scheme, but we won't
 * be able to retrieve any data through it.
 */
class DummyHandler extends URLStreamHandler {
  /**
   * This method will only return null. Data cannot be
   * obtained from this handler.
   * @param u The URL to obtain data from.
   * @return A null URLConnection.
   */
  public URLConnection openConnection(URL u) {
    return null;
  }
}
```

`ParseURL` also elucidates how the `MalformedURLException` is created for unknown schemes. If the factory being used with your application doesn't return a protocol handler for a scheme, any attempt to create an URL instance with such a scheme will throw a `MalformedURLException`. In `ParseURL`, however, you prevent this from occurring so that you can see how new URLs are parsed.

`ParseURL` has three classes, `ParseURL`, `ParseURLFactory`, and `DummyHandler`. The first is the only public class and is used to invoke the application. The `main()` method within the `ParseURL` class sets the `URLStreamHandlerFactory` to your custom one, `ParseURLFactory`. It then iterates through the command line arguments, creating URL instances for each and then printing out the portions of each URL.

The `ParseURLFactory` is your custom factory. It inspects the scheme of the URL instance to be created. If the scheme happens to be one of the standard schemes supported within the JDK, it returns the corresponding protocol handler. All of these protocol handlers within the JDK are contained within the package `sun.net.www.protocol.`*`scheme`*. If the `scheme` is not one of the standard ones, `ParseURLFactory` returns an instance of `DummyHandler`, rather than `null`. If `null` were returned, a `MalformedURLException` would be thrown if you attempted to create any URLs with non-standard schemes.

The `DummyHandler` class does very little, as its name suggests. This class allows you to create URL instances for non-standard schemes. You can then parse such URLs with methods like `getHost()` and `getFile()` without having to create a protocol handler for each new scheme. However, `DummyHandler` does not implement any connection mechanism. Thus, you will not be able to obtain any data through non-standard URL instances that use the `DummyHandler`.

To test your `ParseURL` application, first compile it with the Java compiler. Then execute it with the Java interpreter with one or more URLs as arguments. For instance, invoking it with:

```
java ParseURL http://www.yahoo.com/ newscheme:newstuff
```

returns the following information:

```
Parsing URL: http://www.yahoo.com/
        Scheme: http
        Host:    www.yahoo.com
        Port:    -1
        File:    /
        Ref:     null
==============================
Parsing URL: newscheme:newstuff
        Scheme: newscheme
        Host:
        Port:    -1
        File:    /newstuff
        Ref:     null
==============================
```

chapter 36

Adding New MIME Types to HotJava

36

by David Baker

In this chapter

- **What content handlers can do**
  With content handlers, you can capitalize upon the flexibility of Java.
- **Using new content handlers with HotJava**
  You can plug in content handlers to view different data formats through HotJava.
- **Using content handlers**
  Your own Java applications can also utilize the power of content handlers.

Files on the Internet come in various formats, each of which is used to convey specific information. There are different image file formats, sound clips, video information, and HTML pages. When these documents are transmitted on the Web with the HTTP protocol, a particular MIME content type is used in order to identify how that file should be interpreted.

New document formats are constantly being introduced to the World Wide Web. However, before you can use these new formats, your browser or other applications must understand how to interpret them. Extensibility is part of the nature of the Java execution environment and the HotJava browser. To manage new MIME types, Java and HotJava can be extended through content handlers.

Content handlers are Java's way of dealing with various data formats, such as text files, images, and sounds. By creating new content handlers, additional data types can be processed and rendered. They empower you to add new functionality to your Web browser and quickly develop applications to utilize new file formats.

Writing Content Handlers

Documents on the Web are transmitted with a MIME content type identifier indicating to the receiving agent how the data is formatted. The client must understand how to decode and render that data. A content handler is a Java class that is called by either an URL or `URLConnection` object. The content handler obtains an input stream from the calling object and then receives data from that stream. It then processes the data and returns an object that contains that data.

Java and HotJava provide a core set of content handlers to manage commonly used types. You can write your own handlers to deal with new content types. This empowers you to extend your Java applications or your HotJava browser to understand new document formats.

The process of creating new content handlers is quite similar to creating protocol handlers. If you have read the previous chapter, some of these instructions will seem quite familiar. As an example, this chapter demonstrates a content handler that processes plain text documents, overriding the existing handling.

Note

The example in this chapter provides the somewhat frivolous task of making incoming text files appear as though spoken by a famous bald cartoon character inclined towards hunting rabbits.

The process of creating protocol handlers is very similar to that of content handlers, and is described in the section "Writing a Procotol Handler," in Chapter 35, "Adding Additional Protocols to HotJava."

Step One: Decide upon a Package Name

Like protocol handlers, content handlers must reside within a specific package. This package must end with *`content.type`* where `type` is the MIME type of the data. For instance, the type of `text/plain` documents is text, while for `image/gif`, it is `image`. As with the previous chapter, I append `ORG.netspace.dwb` to indicate the distribution source and author to obtain the following:

```
ORG.netspace.dwb.content.text
```

See "Step One: Decide on a Package Name" in Chapter 35, "Adding Additional Protocols to HotJava," to see the corresponding process for protocol handlers.

Step Two: Create the Directories

Caution
Java is case-sensitive. Even if your system doesn't treat upper- and lowercase characters within directory names differently, use the case of the letters as shown within these instructions.

The content handler class must be placed into a directory that corresponds to the package name. Such directories usually reside within a directory called classes in your home directory. For Windows NT and Windows 95 users, the following sequence of commands accomplishes this at the command prompt:

Note
If you have previously installed other content handlers, protocol handlers, or personal Java classes, you may have already created some of the following directories.

```
%HOMEDRIVE%
cd %HOMEPATH%
mkdir classes
mkdir classes\ORG
mkdir classes\ORG\netspace
mkdir classes\ORG\netspace\dwb
mkdir classes\ORG\netspace\dwb\content
mkdir classes\ORG\netspace\dwb\content\text
```


For UNIX users, the analogous commands are:

```
cd~
mkdir classes
mkdir classes/ORG
mkdir classes/ORG/netspace
mkdir classes/ORG/netspace/dwb
mkdir classes/ORG/netspace/dwb/content
mkdir classes/ORG/netspace/dwb/content/text
```

Step Three: Set Your *CLASSPATH*

The CLASSPATH environment variable tells the Java compiler and interpreter where to find Java classes, enabling the dynamic linking feature of the Java execution environment. When installing the JDK, HotJava, or a Java-aware browser, you might have set the CLASSPATH environment variable. If so, it is critical that you avoid overwriting that data.

Follow these steps:

1. Find out what your CLASSPATH current setting is. Under Windows NT/95, just type the following command from the command prompt:

```
SET
```

Note

The CLASSPATH can indicate as many Java libraries as you have installed. The base directory of each library should be contained within the CLASSPATH, each separated by a ':' under UNIX systems or a ';' under Windows 95 and Windows NT systems. The part of the CLASSPATH which is only a period indicates that the current working directory should be searched for appropriate class files, making developing new Java classes more convenient.

2. Look for the CLASSPATH value. Under UNIX systems, you can display the CLASSPATH value with this command:

```
ECHO $CLASSPATH
```

3. Reset your CLASSPATH, including the previous data, if any. Under Windows 95, if your CLASSPATH was

```
.;C:\JAVA\LIB\CLASSES.ZIP
```

4. you can add the following line to your AUTOEXEC.BAT and reboot

```
SET CLASSPATH=.;%HOMEDRIVE%%HOMEPATH%\CLASSES ;C:\JAVA\LIB\CLASSES.ZIP
```

5. Under Windows NT, presuming that the CLASSPATH value was the same as under the Windows 95 example, you would use the System Control Panel to add a CLASSPATH environment variable with the value:

```
.;%HOMEDRIVE%%HOMEPATH%C:\JAVA\LIB\CLASSES.ZIP
```

6. Under UNIX, assume that your old CLASSPATH was `.:/usr/java/lib`. If you are using the C shell, place the following into your CSHRC file:

```
setenv CLASSPATH .:/home/myid/classes:/usr/java/lib
```

7. If you are on a UNIX system using the Korn or a POSIX-compliant shell, add this line to whatever file your ENV environment variable points. If ENV is unset, then you could add the following line to your ~/.PROFILE file:

```
CLASSPATH=.:/home/myid/classes:/usr/java/lib
```

Step Four: Write the Content Handler

The content handler must be a class that extends `java.net.ContentHandler`. It must also have the same name as the subtype of the MIME content-type it processes. That is, for `image/gif`, the class should be called `gif`, while my example that overrides the normal `plain/text` handler should be named `text`.

The class must have a `getContent()` method that takes a `URLConnection` as an argument and returns a generic `Object`. For now, HotJava supports the following returned `Object` instances:

- A `String` object that appears as plain text within the HotJava window
- An instance of `sun.awt.image.InputStreamImageSource`, allowing HotJava to load the image
- An `InputStream` object that opens the Save to Disk dialog box
- A `Thread` instance that launches an external helper application

The code for the example used in this chapter is shown in listing 36.1. This content handler has only one method—`getContent()`. It obtains an `InputStream` from the `URLConnection` object and then enters an infinite loop. Within the loop, it reads the incoming characters and makes a number of substitutions, altering the text to appear as though spoken by our cartoon friend.

The filtered characters are placed into a `StringBuffer()` object. Once the last character is read, the `read()` method returns `-1`, and the content handler breaks from the loop. It closes the `InputStream` and then returns a `String` object.

Note
If there is an exception, the method returns a `String` providing information about the problem.

Listing 36.1 ***plain.java***

```
// This is the package identified for this content handler.
package ORG.netspace.dwb.content.text;

import java.lang.*;  // Import the package names used.
import java.net.*;
import java.io.*;
```

continues

Listing 36.1 Continued

```
/**
 * This is a text/plain content handler which "fuddifies"
 * the text it receives.
 * @author David W. Baker
 * @version 1.1
 * @see sun.net.ContentHandler
 */
public class plain extends ContentHandler {
     // Stream to receive text/plain file from.
     private InputStream input;
     // Some standard replacement strings.
     private static final String QUIET = "(be vewy quiet, ";
     private static final String HEH = ", eheheheh.";
     private static final String SCREWY = "? Awe you scwewy?";
     private static final String RASCAL = ", you wascal!";
     private static final String MISCREANT =
                                                                ", you miscweant:";
     /**
     * This method returns an Object containing the
     * processed content from the given URLConnection.
     * @param contentConn Connection used to obtain the content.
     * @return The content.
     * @see sun.net.ContentHandler#getContent
     */
     public Object getContent(URLConnection contentConn) {
          // Create a buffer to store the filtered data.
          StringBuffer fuddBuff = new StringBuffer();
          int intChar;      // A int representation of a char.
          char nextChar; // A char.

          try {
               // Get the input.
               input  = contentConn.getInputStream();
               // Loop infinitely.
               filter: while(true) {
                    // Read in next character.
                    intChar = input.read();
                    // Make sure we aren't at the end.
                    if (intChar == -1) {
                         break filter;  // Break if end.
                    }
                    // Convert it to a char.
                    nextChar = (char)intChar;
                    // Substitute "(" for QUIET
                    if (nextChar == '(') fuddBuff.append(QUIET);
                    // Substitute "W" for "L"
                    else if (nextChar == 'L') fuddBuff.append('W');
                    // Substitute "w" for "l"
                    else if (nextChar == 'l') fuddBuff.append('w');
                    // Substitute "R" for "W"
                    else if (nextChar == 'R') fuddBuff.append('W');
                    // Substitute "r" for "w"
                    else if (nextChar == 'r') fuddBuff.append('w');
                    // For periods at the end of the file or periods
                    // followed by whitespace, substitute HEH.
                    else if (nextChar == '.') {
```

```
                        intChar = input.read();
                        if (intChar == -1) {
                            fuddBuff.append(HEH);
                            break filter;  // Break if end.
                        }
                        nextChar = (char)intChar;
                        if (nextChar == ' ')
                            fuddBuff.append(HEH + " ");
                        else fuddBuff.append("." + nextChar);
                    }
                    // For ? the end of the file or ?
                    // followed by whitespace, substitute SCREWY.
                    else if (nextChar == '?') {
                        intChar = input.read();
                        if (intChar == -1) {
                            fuddBuff.append(SCREWY);
                            break filter;  // Break if end.
                        }
                        nextChar = (char)intChar;
                        if (nextChar == ' ')
                            fuddBuff.append(SCREWY + " ");
                        else fuddBuff.append("?" + nextChar);
                    }
                    // For ! at the end of the file or !
                    // followed by whitespace, substitute RASCAL.
                    else if (nextChar == '!') {
                        intChar = input.read();
                        if (intChar == -1) {
                            fuddBuff.append(RASCAL);
                            break filter;  // Break if end.
                        }
                        nextChar = (char)intChar;
                        if (nextChar == ' ')
                            fuddBuff.append(RASCAL + " ");
                        else fuddBuff.append("!" + nextChar);
                    }
                    // For : at the end of the file or :
                    // followed by whitespace, substitute MISCREANT.
                    else if (nextChar == ':') {
                        intChar = input.read();
                        if (intChar == -1) {
                            fuddBuff.append(MISCREANT);
                            break filter;  // Break if end.
                        }
                        nextChar = (char)intChar;
                        if (nextChar == ' ')
                            fuddBuff.append(MISCREANT + " ");
                        else fuddBuff.append(":" + nextChar);
                    }
                    else fuddBuff.append(nextChar);
                }
                input.close();
            } catch(IOException excpt) {
                return "Unable to load document: "
                                + contentConn.getURL();
            }
            return fuddBuff.toString();
        }
    }
```

Step Five: Compile the Source

Use `javac` to compile the content handler, and leave the compiled class within the directory created in Step Two (i.e., "`classes\ORG\netspace\dwb\content\text`" for NT/95 or "`classes/ORG/netspace/dwb/content/text`" for UNIX). Thus, if you created the `plain.java` program within that directory, you would merely issue change to that directory and then issue this command:

```
javac plain.java
```

Be sure to leave the `.class` file within the bottom "`text`" directory.

Tip

If you choose to create the plain.java file somewhere else, you use the `-d` option to the Java compiler in order to automatically place the .class file into the proper place. For example:

```
javac -d classes/ORG/netspace/dwb/content/text plain.java
```

Using Content Handlers with HotJava

As with protocol handlers, HotJava's goal is to eventually support dynamically downloaded content handlers. For now, only manually installed handlers are supported, created as described in the earlier section "Writing Content Handlers." In addition, at the time of this writing, HotJava supports only content handlers that extend existing MIME types. That is, the example can override the handling of `text/plain`, but HotJava does not support one that handles a new content-type like `text/fuddify`.

HotJava also needs to deal with the conflict between MIME type names and Java class names. MIME content-types can, and under certain circumstances should, contain hyphens. However, hyphens are not allowed in Java class identifiers. Because the class of the content handler must be the same as the MIME content subtype, this presents an obvious problem.

The following steps illustrate how to use the new content handler, as created in the previous section, with the HotJava browser.

Note

JavaSoft makes the HotJava browser and instructions for its installation available at <URL:**http://www.javasoft.com/java.sun.com/HotJava/CurrentRelease/installation.html**>.

Step One: Disable Special MIME Handling

On certain systems, a file called `mailcap` may have been created to indicate that a special helper application should be used for an incoming MIME type, regardless of which browser is loading the data. If such a file exists, ensure that any line indicating special processing is removed for the content-type you want your handler to process. Thus, remove any entry for `text/plain` for this example.

Step Two: Update the PROPERTIES File

HotJava stores per-user customizations in a file called PROPERTIES. This file is located within a directory named ".hotjava" that resides within your home directory. Edit this file to set the `java.content.handler.pkgs` property. You want to add everything up to the `content` token in the content handler's package. When HotJava is searching for a content handler appropriate to a specific MIME type, it will append the MIME type to this value and look for a Java package of that name; then, it looks for a Java class within that package that has the same name as the MIME subtype. If this property has not been set, add the following line to use the example handler:


```
java.content.handler.pkgs=ORG.netspace.dwb.content
```

If that property has already been set, append a pipe character (|) and `ORG.netspace.dwb.content`. For example:

```
java.content.handler.pkgs=COM.company.content¦ORG.netspace.dwb.content
```

Note

When editing the HotJava properties file, be sure to use a text editor or, if you are using a word processor, save the file as text.

Step Three: Run HotJava

Execute HotJava and load up a text file to see the "fuddified" information. Figure 36.1 demonstrates this effect upon the HTML RFC. To view this page yourself, go under the File menu, select Open Page, and then enter the following:

```
ftp://ds.internic.net/rfc/rfc1866.txt
```

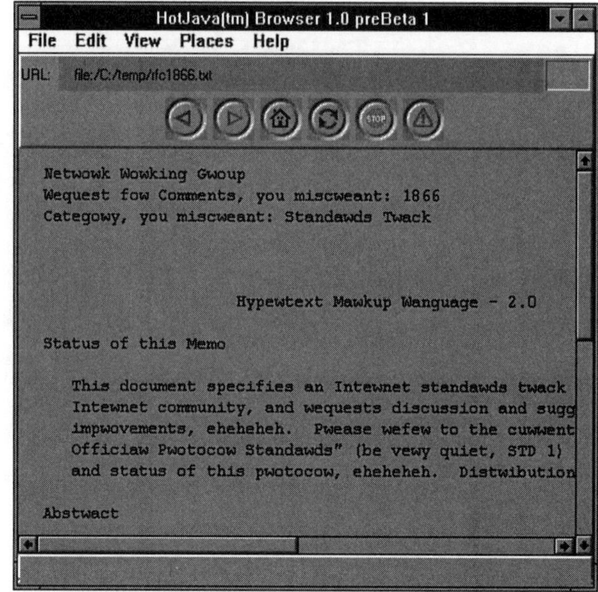

Fig. 36.1
When HotJava uses the Fuddify content handler, the HTML spec looks slightly more interesting.

Using Content Handlers with Your Own Applications

Content handlers can be used by your own applications, in addition to their usefulness with HotJava. Content handlers use a concept similar to protocol handlers for registering a new handler, that of a *factory*. The `FetchFuddify` application, shown in Listing 36.2, demonstrates this functionality.

Listing 36.2 *FetchFuddify.java*

```
import java.net.*;      // Import package names used.
import java.io.*;

/**
 * This is an application which utilizes the new
 * text/plain content handler which "fuddifies"
 * the text.
 * @author David W. Baker
```

```
 * @version 1.1
 */
public class FetchFuddify {
     /**
      * This method starts the application.
      * @param args The program arguments - should be URL.
      */
     public static void main (String args[]) {
          // Check the arguments.
          if (args.length != 1) {
               System.err.println("usage: " +
                    "java FetchFuddify <url of Fudd document>");
               System.exit(1);
          }
          // Create an instance of FetchFuddify to do its stuff.
          FetchFuddify app = new FetchFuddify(args[0]);
     }

     /**
      * This constructor does all of the work of obtaining
      * the data with the appropriate content handler and
      * sending it to standard output.
      * @param url The URL to obtain.
      */
     public FetchFuddify(String url) {
          URL fuddURL;                    // URL object to resource.
          URLConnection fuddConn; // Connection to resource.
          Object fuddObject;          // Object returned.

          // Register the content handler with our ow
          // factory.
          URLConnection.setContentHandlerFactory(
               new fuddifyCHFactory());
          try {
               // Create the URL object with the command line
               // argument used.
               fuddURL = new URL(url);
               // Open the connection.
               fuddConn = fuddURL.openConnection();
               // Get the content.
               fuddObject = fuddConn.getContent();
               // Convert the content to a String and print it.
               System.out.println(fuddObject.toString());
          } catch(MalformedURLException excpt) {
               System.err.println("Mailformed URL: " + excpt);
          } catch(IOException excpt) {
               System.err.println("Failed I/O: " + excpt);
          }
     }
}

/**
 * This class implements the ContentHandlerFactory
 * interface to register our own content handler.
 * @see java.net.ContentHandlerFactory
 */
```

36

continues

Listing 36.2 Continued

```
class fuddifyCHFactory implements ContentHandlerFactory {
     /**
      * This method returns our own customer content
      * handler when given a "text/plain" content type.
      * @param contenttype MIME type - should be "text/plain".
      * @return The content handler to use.
      * @see java.net.ContentHandlerFactory#createContentHandler
      */
     public ContentHandler
          createContentHandler(String contenttype) {
          // Ensure the content type is "text/plain".
          if (contenttype.equalsIgnoreCase("text/plain")) {
               // Create an instance of our content handler.
               return new ORG.netspace.dwb.content.text.plain();
          }
          // Otherwise, print an error message and return null.
          System.err.println("Unknown data type: "
               + contenttype);
          return null;
     }
}
```

Start *FetchFuddify*

The `main()` method checks to see that the program was invoked with a single argument, which corresponds to the URL of a text file to filter. Then it creates a `FetchFuddify` object, passing it the `String` command line argument.

The constructor performs the essential task in using a new content handler: invoking the `static` method of the `URLConnection` class, `setContentHandlerFactory()`. Factories should be a familiar concept, this time allowing the `URLConnection` class to choose an appropriate content handler. The `setContentHandlerFactory` takes an object that implements the `java.net.ContentHandlerFactory` interface. This example's implementation, `fuddifyCHFactory`, is described next in "The `ContentHandlerFactory` Implementation."

The constructor then creates an `URL` object and opens a connection to the resource. It calls the `getContent()` method of the `URLConnection` class, which causes the code of the content handler to be invoked. `getContent()` returns an `Object`, which the constructor converts to a `String` with the `toString()` method and prints to standard output.

The *ContentHandlerFactory* Implementation

This interface enables you to register new content handlers with the `URLConnection` class. A class that implements this interface must have a `createContentHandler()` method. This method takes a `String` instance containing the value of the MIME content-type of the resource being accessed. This method returns a `ContentHandler` object.

The example first checks to see that the `contenttype` argument is `text/plain`. It then creates an instance of the content handler and returns it. If the method is called with a `contenttype` other than `text/plain`, it returns `null`.

Running the Application

First, make sure you've already installed the appropriate content handler, as described in "Writing Content Handlers." Compile the FetchFuddify application and then invoke it with the URL of a text file available somewhere on the Web. For instance, the following will "fuddify" a release notes document from JavaSoft:

```
java FetchFuddify http://chatsubo.javasoft.com/current/doc/rmi/release-notes.txt
```

Which will generate:

```
Wemote Method Invocation (be vewy quiet, WMI) notes fow wewease Awpha2.

- WMI is suppowted fow Java appwications and in the AppwetViewew.

- WMI wequiwes wocaw instawwation of the wmi package appwopwiate fow
  Sowawis ow Win95/NT.

- Any appwication that expowts wemote objects must be awwowed
  by the SecuwityManagew to use SewvewSockets to wisten fow and accept
  incoming socket connections, eheheheh.

- Appwets may not expowt wemote objects since theSecuwityManagew
  pwevents using SewvewSocket, eheheheh.  This wiww be suppowted in a futuwe
  update.
```


It is promised that with the 1.0 release version of HotJava, dynamically downloaded content handlers will be supported. Once realized, this will allow HotJava to be extended on demand with little effort from the enduser. When you encounter a new document type, HotJava will automatically download and install the new content handler necessary to render the data.

chapter 37

Creating Multi-User Programs in Java

37

by Mark Wutka

In this chapter

- **Designing multi-user applications**
  There are a few special details you must deal with when designing a multi-user application. Many of the problems are typical of client/server applications. One of the most helpful things you can do is to design the application to be protocol-independent.
- **Adding socket-based access to multi-user applications**
  Once you have designed your application, you can add a socket interface to it. Because sockets provide a low-level interface to the network, you need to create a way to exchange messages between the server and its clients.
- **Adding RMI access to multi-user applications**
  You can wrap an RMI interface around your application, allowing clients to access your server with RMI while others are using sockets. Since RMI is a high-level interface, you don't have to create your own custom messaging system.

One thing that attracts thousands of people to the Internet is its interactive nature. The popularity of multi-user chat programs like IRC and various multi-user games like MUDs (Multi-User Domain/Dungeon/Dimension) illustrates that fact very clearly.

In the beginning, multi-user programs were all text-based. There are many early multi-user programs that predate the Internet. Many multi-user programs are still text-based, but they are beginning to get graphical front ends (another form of encapsulation!).

Other programs have grown out of single-user versions. Game manufacturers, for instance, have begun to support Internet connections. This allows game users to play against each other over the Internet.

Java adds something that these off-the-shelf games don't really have. You can download a Java game and play it on any Java-enabled platform immediately. You can even create a game server that manages the connections between players. Whenever you add new games to the server, the players download new Java applets that present the user interface for the new games.

The multi-user paradigm isn't restricted to games, of course. You can set up various kinds of collaborative applications, so people can solve problems and complete tasks from separate parts of the world.

Designing Multi-User Applications

A multi-user application is a slight variation on the typical client/server application. The only difference is that information passes from one client through the server to other clients. On a typical client/server application, information flows only from the client to the server and back. Figure 37.1 illustrates this difference.

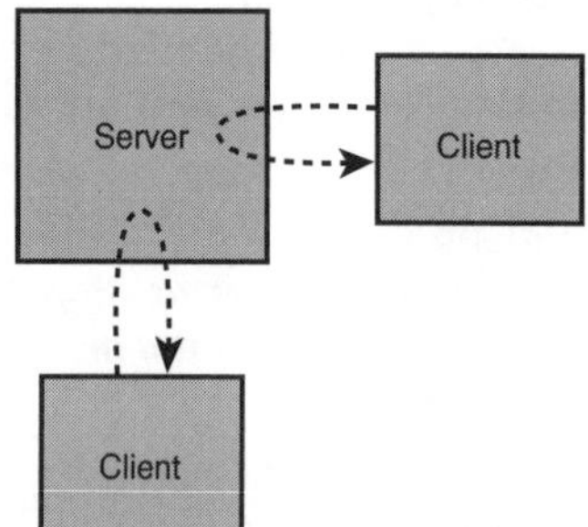

Fig. 37.1 *Information flows between users in a multi-user application.*

When you design a multi-user application, you should try to ignore the network if possible. You can't fully discount the network, of course. You have to remember that there is a high amount of overhead between the client and the server. You want to minimize the number of interactions between the client and server.

Tip

If your server needs to invoke methods in the client, define the client as an interface. This allows you to implement the client side in different ways, while not tying the server to a particular set of client implementations.

When you create your application, you first create the server, and a client interface if needed. Next, you create encapsulations for the various network protocols and remote object systems you want to support. Figure 37.2 shows an example configuration, where the server can be accessed through TCP sockets and RMI.

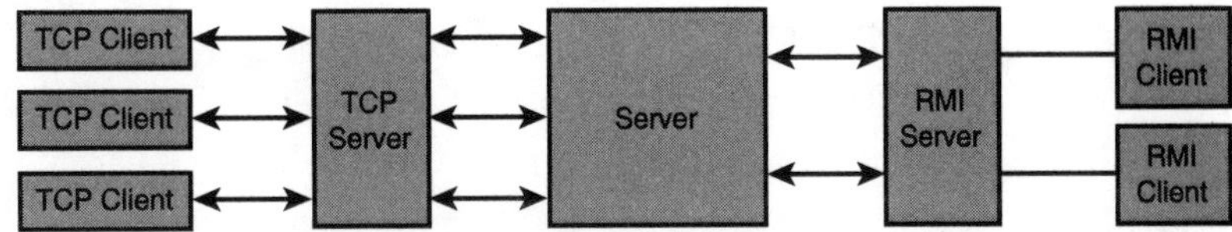

Fig. 37.2
Through encapsulation, your application can support multiple protocols.

Tip

As far as the server is concerned, the networking protocol is the user interface for the server. You are really just following the principle of separating the application from the user interface.

Listing 37.1 shows a server for a simple chat system. The server relays chat messages to the other users, and notifies the users whenever a new client enters the system or an existing client leaves.

Listing 37.1 Source Code for *ChatServer.java*

```
package chat.server;

import java.util.Vector;
import java.util.Hashtable;
import java.util.Enumeration;

// This is a simple chat application. It allows clients to enroll
// under a particular name, and send messages to each other.
// Messages are sent to the client via the ChatClient interface.

public class ChatServer
{
// clients is a table that maps a client name to a ChatClient
// interface
     protected Hashtable clients;

     public ChatServer()
     {
          clients = new Hashtable();
     }

// Add client adds a new client to the system and tells the other
// clients about the new client.

     public synchronized void addClient(String name,
ChatClient client)
```

continues

Listing 37.1 Continued

```
     {

// If the client picks a name that is already here,
// disconnect the new client, let the old one keep its name.

          if (clients.get(name) != null) {
               client.disconnect();
               return;
          }

// Add the new client to the table
          clients.put(name, client);

// Tell the other clients about this new client
          sendEnterMessage(name);
     }

     public synchronized void removeClient(String name)
     {
          ChatClient client = (ChatClient) clients.get(name);
          if (client != null) {
               clients.remove(name);
               sendLeaveMessage(name);
          }
     }

// removeClient removes a client from the chat system and tells
// the other clients about it.

     public synchronized void removeClient(ChatClient client)
     {

// We remove by ChatClient, not by name. We have to enumerate through
// all the clients to find out the name of this client.

          Enumeration e = clients.keys();

          while (e.hasMoreElements()) {
               String key = (String) e.nextElement();

// If we found the right name for this client, remove them and
// tell everyone about it.
               if (clients.get(key) == client) {
                    clients.remove(key);
                    sendLeaveMessage(key);
               }
          }
     }

// sendChat is called by a client to send a message to the
// other clients

     public synchronized void sendChat(String name, String message)
     {
          Enumeration e = clients.elements();
```

```
// Enumerate through all the clients and send them the chat message
// Note that this will send a message back to the original
// sender, too.

          while (e.hasMoreElements()) {
               ChatClient client = (ChatClient) e.nextElement();

               client.incomingChat(name, message);
          }
     }

// sendEnterMessage tells all the clients when a new client
// has arrived

     public synchronized void sendEnterMessage(String name)
     {
          Enumeration e = clients.elements();

// Enumerate through all the clients and tell them about
// the new client

          while (e.hasMoreElements()) {
               ChatClient client = (ChatClient) e.nextElement();

               client.userHasEntered(name);
          }
     }

// sendLeaveMessage tells all the clients that a client has left

     public synchronized void sendLeaveMessage(String name)
     {
          Enumeration e = clients.elements();

// Enumerate through all the clients and tell them who left

          while (e.hasMoreElements()) {
               ChatClient client = (ChatClient) e.nextElement();

               client.userHasLeft(name);
          }
     }

// getUserList returns a list of all the users on the system

     public synchronized String[] getUserList()
     {
          Enumeration e = clients.keys();

// Create an array to hold the user names
          String[] nameList = new String[clients.size()];

// Copy the user names into the nameList array
          int i = 0;
          while (e.hasMoreElements()) {
              nameList[i++] = (String) e.nextElement();
          }
```

37

continues

Listing 37.1 Continued

```
// Return the name list
            return nameList;
        }
}
```

Since this server needs to invoke methods on the client, it defines a `ChatClient` interface that all clients to this system must implement. Listing 37.2 shows this `ChatClient` interface.

Listing 37.2 Source Code for *ChatClient.java*

```
package chat.server;

public interface ChatClient
{
     public void incomingChat(String who, String chat);
     public void userHasEntered(String who);
     public void userHasLeft(String who);

     public void disconnect();
}
```

Again, it is important to note that there is no mention of a specific networking protocol. These two classes represent the core application. If you design all your applications this way, you will have no trouble adding other ways to access your application.

Adding Socket-Based Access to Multi-User Applications

Once you have created an application, you can put a socket-based front end on it, allowing clients to access it over the network. Sockets are a low-level means of communication, and are simple to set up. Sockets are good for sending streams of bytes over the network. For sending messages, however, you have to do a bit more work.

It is very easy to create a socket-based server. First, you create a `ServerSocket` object that listens for incoming connections. Next, you use the `accept` method to wait for incoming connections. The `accept` method returns an instance of a `Socket` class, which represents the connection to the new client. After that, you can use `getInputStream` and `getOutputStream` to get streams to reading from and writing to the new client.

Creating a Socket-Based Server

The socket-based server is a separate class from the original application class. The socket server is just a setup-man. It accepts new socket connections and then creates objects that interact with the real application and pass the results back to the socket-based client. The socket-based server itself never interacts with the application server.

Figure 37.3 illustrates a socket-based client connecting to the socket server.

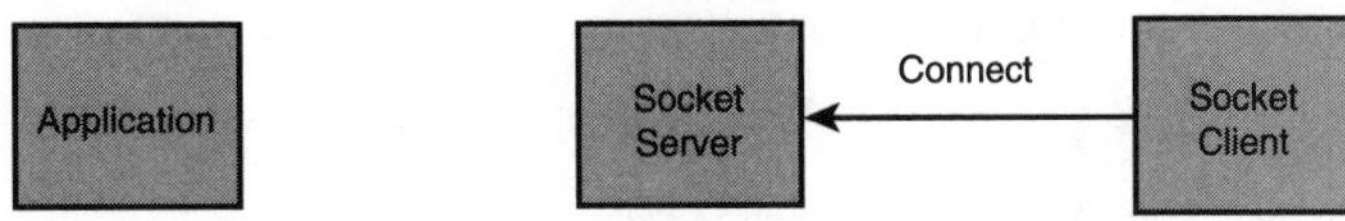

Fig. 37.3
A socket-based client connects to the socket server.

Next, the server creates a socket-based client object, which implements the application's client interface. The socket server also tells the new client object where to find the application object. Figure 37.4 illustrates this step.

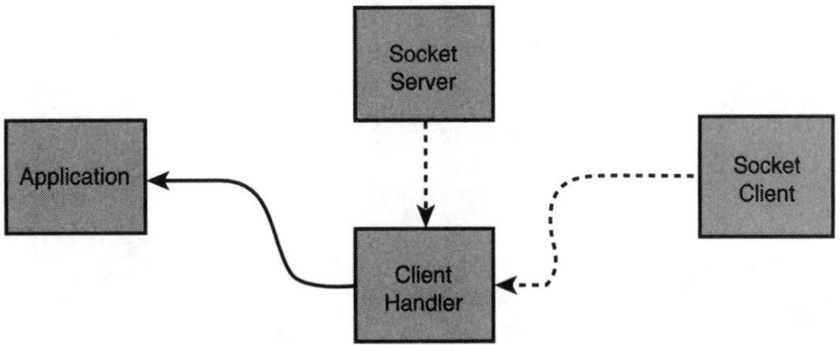

Fig. 37.4
The socket server creates a socket-based client object to handle the connection.

Finally, the socket-based client object interacts with the application, passing information over the socket connection to the user on the other end. Figure 37.5 shows this interaction. 37

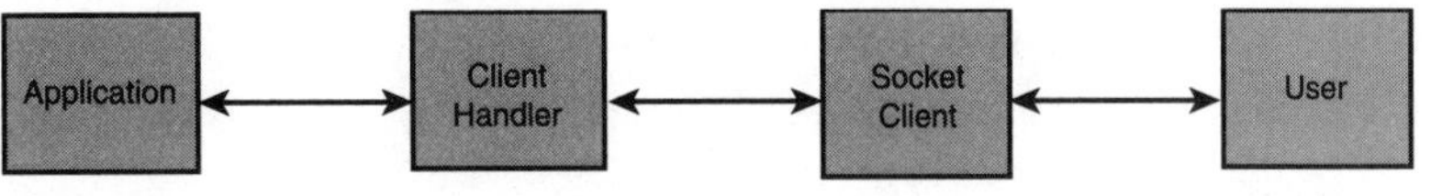

Fig. 37.5
The socket-based client communicates directly with the application.

Listing 37.3 shows a very basic TCP socket server that creates client objects to do the real dirty work.

Listing 37.3 Source Code for *TCPChatServer.java*

```
package chat.tcp.server;

import java.net.*;
import java.io.*;

import chat.server.*;

// This class implements a simple TCP server that listens
// for incoming connections. It creates a TCPChatClient object
// to handle the actual connection.

public class TCPChatServer extends Object implements Runnable
{
// serverSocket is the socket we are listening on
     protected ServerSocket serverSocket;

// server is a reference to the application object, which we
// pass to the TCPChatClients

     protected ChatServer server;
     protected Thread myThread;

     public TCPChatServer(ChatServer server, int port)
     throws IOException
     {
          serverSocket = new ServerSocket(port);

          this.server = server;
     }

     public void run()
     {
          while (true) {
               try {
// Accept a new connection
                    Socket newConn = serverSocket.accept();

// Create a client to handle the connection
                    TCPChatClient newClient = new TCPChatClient(
                         server, newConn);

// Start the client (it's runnable)
                    newClient.start();

               } catch (Exception e) {
               }
          }
     }

     public void start()
     {
          myThread = new Thread(this);
          myThread.start();
     }
```

```
        public void stop()
        {
            myThread.stop();
            myThread = null;
        }
    }
```

Sending Messages over Sockets

The client handler is where the real work is done. Sending messages over a TCP socket is a tricky matter. There are no message boundaries in TCP; it's just a stream of bytes. This means that if you write 50 bytes to the stream, the program on the other end might read it as two groups of 25 bytes, or 50 single bytes.

There are two ways to approach this problem. One way is to have the client and server know what kind of data is being sent at any time and have them read that correct number of bytes. Typically, you would send a message type followed by the message bytes. The program reading the information would determine the length and content of the data based on the message type.

The other solution is to put a message length in front of any message you send over the socket. For example, if you want to send 223 bytes, you write out 223 as a 4-byte integer value, followed by the 223 bytes of data. The program on the other end reads the 4-byte length and then sees that the length is 223 bytes.

There are advantages and disadvantages to each approach. When you send messages as arrays of bytes, you have to take the extra step of putting the data into the array, rather than writing it directly to the socket. If you determine the length of the data based on context, you have to ensure that both ends of the connection are using the exact same format. In other words, if one side sends a message containing an integer and a string, the other side had better be expecting an integer and a string. If you send a message type that the other side doesn't understand, it can never recover. It has no idea how many bytes there are in the message data.

The `TCPChatClient` shown in Listing 37.4 combines both of these methods. It sends a 4-byte message type, followed by the data length, and then the data. It uses `DataInputStream` and `DataOutputStream` filters on top of the socket connections so it can write different data types easily. The `TCPChatClient` class implements the `ChatClient` interface that the `ChatServer` class uses to send a message to a particular client. For each different protocol you support in a chat server, you will have a different class that implements the `ChatClient` interface.

Listing 37.4 Source Code for *TCPChatClient.java*

```
package chat.tcp.server;

import java.io.*;
import java.net.*;

import chat.server.*;
import chat.tcp.common.TCPChatMessageTypes;

// This class acts like a client of the ChatServer application. It
// translates messages from a TCP socket into requests for the chat
// server, and translates method invocations from the server into
// TCP messages.

public class TCPChatClient extends Object
implements ChatClient, Runnable
{
// server is the ChatServer application we are a client of
     protected ChatServer server;

// clientSock is the socket connection to the user
     protected Socket clientSock;

// inStream and outStream are Data streams for the socket. This allows
// us to send information in forms other than an array of bytes

     protected DataInputStream inStream;
     protected DataOutputStream outStream;

// clientName is the name the user wants to be known by
     protected String clientName;

     protected Thread myThread;

     public TCPChatClient(ChatServer server, Socket clientSock)
     throws IOException
     {
          this.server = server;
          this.clientSock = clientSock;

// get data streams to the socket

          inStream = new DataInputStream(
               clientSock.getInputStream());

          outStream = new DataOutputStream(
               clientSock.getOutputStream());

// The first thing that the user sends us is
// the name they want to use
          clientName = inStream.readUTF();

// Add ourself to the server application
          server.addClient(clientName, this);
     }
```

```
// The next few methods implement a really simple messaging protocol:
// 4 byte Integer message type
// 4 byte message length
// <message length> bytes of data

// userHasEntered is called by the server whenever there's a new user
// the data part of the message is just the name of the user who has
// entered.

     public void userHasEntered(String who)
     {
          try {
// Write the message type
               outStream.writeInt(TCPChatMessageTypes.ENTER);
// Write the message length
               outStream.writeInt(who.length());
// Write the user's name
               outStream.writeBytes(who);
          } catch (Exception e) {
               server.removeClient(this);
          }
     }

// userHasLeft is called by the server whenever there's a new user
// the data part of the message is just the name of the user who has
// left.
     public void userHasLeft(String who)
     {
          try {
               outStream.writeInt(TCPChatMessageTypes.LEAVE);
               outStream.writeInt(who.length());
               outStream.writeBytes(who);
          } catch (Exception e) {
               server.removeClient(this);
          }
     }

// incomingChat is called by the server whenever someone sends a message.
// The data part of the message has three parts:
// the length of the name of the person sending the message (the
// length value itself is a 4-byte integer)
// the name of the person sending the message
// the chat message

     public void incomingChat(String who, String chat)
     {
          try {
               outStream.writeInt(TCPChatMessageTypes.CHAT);
               outStream.writeInt(who.length() + chat.length() + 4);
               outStream.writeInt(who.length());
               outStream.writeBytes(who);
               outStream.writeBytes(chat);
          } catch (Exception e) {
               server.removeClient(this);
          }
     }
```


continues

Listing 37.4 Continued

```
// disconnect is called by the server when the client has
// been disconnected from the server. We just close down the
// socket and stop this thread.

     public void disconnect()
     {
          try {
               clientSock.close();
          } catch (Exception e) {
          }
          stop();
     }
```

The rest of the `TCPChatClient` class deals with messages coming in from the client. The `run` method reads in an integer message type as the first part of the message. It then calls an appropriate method to handle the rest of the message. The `handleChatMessage` method reads an incoming chat message and passes it on to the server to be distributed to the rest of the clients. Because this protocol is extremely simple, there are no other message types defined.

Because you may want to add protocol types at some point, the server should be able to receive messages it does not understand without completely dying. In this case, because the length of the message is always sent after the message type, the `skipMessage` method can read in and then ignore any message that the server doesn't understand. You should always provide some sort of safety mechanism like this. Someone may take this server and really expand it and then write a nice client for it. If that client then accesses an original version of the server, it should still be able to safely use the original version without the server dying.

If you decide to change the contents of a particular message, you should assign that message a new message type and continue to support the old type. If you added a date field to the incoming chat message, you can't expect all the clients to suddenly support the new field. You should be able to handle incoming chat messages with or without the date field. One of the best ways to handle this is by adding a second message type.

Version numbers are another common device used for handling multiple formats for a particular message. When the client connects to the server, it tells the server which version of the messaging protocol it uses. If it uses version 2, for instance, it will be sending a date field in every chat message, while version 1 clients don't send the date field (see Listing 37.5).

Listing 37.5 Source Code for *TCPChatClient.java* (continued)

```
// handleChatMessage reads an incoming chat message from the user and
// sends it to the server. The data part of the message is just the
// chat message itself.

     public void handleChatMessage()
     throws IOException
     {
// Get the message length
          int length = inStream.readInt();
          byte[] chatChars = new byte[length];

// Read the chat message
          inStream.readFully(chatChars);

          String message = new String(chatChars, 0);

// Send the chat message to the server
          server.sendChat(clientName, message);
     }

// If we get a message we don't understand, skip over it. That's
// why we have the message length as part of the protocol.

     public void skipMessage()
     throws IOException
     {
          int length = inStream.readInt();
          inStream.skipBytes(length);
     }

     public void run()
     {
          while (true) {
               try {

// Read the type of the next message
                    int messageType = inStream.readInt();

                    switch (messageType) {

// If it's a chat message, read it
                         case TCPChatMessageTypes.CHAT:
                              handleChatMessage();
                              break;

// For any messages whose type we don't understand, skip the message
                         default:
                              skipMessage();
                              return;
                    }
               } catch (Exception e) {
                    server.removeClient(clientName);
                    return;
               }
```

37

continues

Listing 37.5 Continued

```
            }
        }
        public void start()
        {
            myThread = new Thread(this);
            myThread.start();
        }

        public void stop()
        {
            myThread.stop();
            myThread = null;
        }
    }
```

The `TCPChatClient` class uses message types defined in an interface called `TCPChatMessageTypes`, which is shown in Listing 37.6.

Listing 37.6 Source Code for *TCPChatMessageTypes.java*

```
package chat.tcp.common;

public interface TCPChatMessageTypes
{
     public static final int CHAT = 1;
     public static final int ENTER = 2;
     public static final int LEAVE = 3;
}
```

The user-side client program is pretty simple to write. It needs to connect to the `TCPChatClient` and pass chat messages to it. It must also read any messages sent by the server. Since the user-side client is reading from two different places, it needs at least two threads. The `RunTCPClient` class, shown in Listing 37.7, uses a second class called `TCPChatReader` to read messages coming from the `TCPChatServer`. The `TCPChatReader` class calls methods in `RunTCPClient` to actually display the results of a message from the server. In this simple example, the `RunTCPClient` class just prints the messages to `System.out`. If you were making a chat applet, however, you would display incoming messages differently. You could still use the `TCPChatReader` with a chat applet.

Listing 37.7 Source Code for *RunTCPClient.java*

```
import java.net.*;
import java.io.*;

import chat.server.*;
```

```
import chat.tcp.common.TCPChatMessageTypes;
import chat.tcp.client.*;

// Class is a client for the TCPChatServer object. It reads chat
// messages from System.in and relays them to the chat server.
// It displays any information coming back from the chat server.

public class RunTCPClient extends Object implements ChatClient
{
     public RunTCPClient()
     {
     }

// Display a message when there's a new user
     public void userHasEntered(String who)
     {
          System.out.println("--- "+who+" has just entered ---");
     }

// Display a message when someone exits
     public void userHasLeft(String who)
     {
          System.out.println("--- "+who+" has just left ---");
     }

// Display a chat message
     public void incomingChat(String who, String chat)
     {
          System.out.println("<"+who+"> "+chat);
     }

     public void disconnect()
     {
          System.out.println("Chat server connection closed.");
          System.exit(0);
     }

     public static void main(String args[])
     {
          int port = 4321;

// Allow the port to be set from the command line (-Dport=4567)

          String portStr = System.getProperty("port");
          if (portStr != null) {
               try {
                    port = Integer.parseInt(portStr);
               } catch (Exception ignore) {
               }
          }

// Allow the server's host name to be specified on the command
// line (-Dhost=myhost.com)

          String hostName = System.getProperty("host");
          if (hostName == null) hostName = "localhost";
```

37

continues

Listing 37.7 Continued

```
          try {


// Connect to the TCPChatServer program

               Socket clientSocket = new Socket(hostName, port);

               DataOutputStream chatOutputStream =
                    new DataOutputStream(
                         clientSocket.getOutputStream());

               DataInputStream chatInputStream =
                    new DataInputStream(
                         clientSocket.getInputStream());

               DataInputStream userInputStream =
                    new DataInputStream(System.in);

               System.out.println("Connected to chat server!");
// Prompt the user for a name
               System.out.print("What name do you want to use? ");
               System.out.flush();

               String myName = userInputStream.readLine();

// Send the name to the server
               chatOutputStream.writeUTF(myName);

               RunTCPClient thisClient = new RunTCPClient();

// Start up a reader thread that reads messages from the server
               TCPChatReader reader = new TCPChatReader(
                    thisClient, chatInputStream);

               reader.start();

// Read input from System.in

               while (true) {

                    String chatLine = userInputStream.readLine();

                    sendChat(chatOutputStream, chatLine);

               }

          } catch (Exception e) {
               System.out.println("Got exception:");
               e.printStackTrace();
               System.exit(1);
          }
     }

// sendChat sends a chat message to the TCPChatServer program

     public static void sendChat(DataOutputStream outStream,
```

```
String line)
     throws IOException
     {
          outStream.writeInt(TCPChatMessageTypes.CHAT);
          outStream.writeInt(line.length());
          outStream.writeBytes(line);
     }
}
```

The `TCPChatReader` class reads messages from the chat server. Rather than display the messages itself, it invokes methods in another object. This enables you to customize the display of information without changing the `TCPChatReader` class. Listing 37.8 shows the `TCPChatReader` class.

Listing 37.8 Source Code for *TCPChatReader.java*

```
package chat.tcp.client;

import java.io.*;

import chat.server.*;
import chat.tcp.common.TCPChatMessageTypes;

// This class sets up a thread that reads messages from the
// TCPChatServer and then invokes methods in an object
// implementing the ChatClient interface.

public class TCPChatReader extends Object implements Runnable
{
     protected ChatClient client;
     protected DataInputStream inStream;
     protected Thread myThread;

     public TCPChatReader(ChatClient client,
DataInputStream inStream)
     {
          this.client = client;
          this.inStream = inStream;
     }

     public void run()
     {
          while (true) {
              try {
                    int messageType = inStream.readInt();

// Look at the message type and call the appropriate method to
// read the message.

                    switch (messageType) {
                         case TCPChatMessageTypes.CHAT:
                             readChat();
                              break;
```

continues

37

Listing 37.8 Continued

```
                    case TCPChatMessageTypes.ENTER:
                         readEnter();
                         break;

                    case TCPChatMessageTypes.LEAVE:
                         readLeave();
                         break;

                    default:
                         skipMessage();
                         break;
               }
          } catch (Exception e) {
               client.disconnect();
          }
     }
}

public void start()
{
     myThread = new Thread(this);
     myThread.start();
}

public void stop()
{
     myThread.stop();
     myThread = null;
}

// readChat has the toughest job in reading the message, and it's not
// really that tough. The message length is the total length of the
// bytes sent. It is followed by the length of the name of the person
// sending the chat, and then the name itself. This method has to
// compute the length of the chat string by subtracting the length of
// the name, and 4 bytes for the name length.

     public void readChat()
     throws IOException
     {
// Get the total message length
          int length = inStream.readInt();

// Get the length of the name of the person sending the chat
          int whoLength = inStream.readInt();

// Compute the length of the chat, subtract the length of the name,
// and 4 bytes for the length that was sent.

          int chatLength = length - whoLength - 4;

// Read in the name of the person sending the chat
          byte[] whoBytes = new byte[whoLength];
          inStream.readFully(whoBytes);
          String whoString = new String(whoBytes, 0);
```

```
// Read in the chat
            byte[] chatBytes = new byte[chatLength];
            inStream.readFully(chatBytes);
            String chatString = new String(chatBytes, 0);

// Pass the chat to the object that will display it

            client.incomingChat(whoString, chatString);
     }

     public void readEnter()
     throws IOException
     {
            int length = inStream.readInt();
            byte[] whoBytes = new byte[length];
            inStream.readFully(whoBytes);

            String whoString = new String(whoBytes, 0);

            client.userHasEntered(whoString);
     }

     public void readLeave()
     throws IOException
     {
            int length = inStream.readInt();
            byte[] whoBytes = new byte[length];
            inStream.readFully(whoBytes);

            String whoString = new String(whoBytes, 0);

            client.userHasLeft(whoString);
     }

     public void skipMessage()
     throws IOException
     {
            int length = inStream.readInt();
            inStream.skipBytes(length);
     }
}
```


Other Issues When Dealing with Sockets

When you write socket-based servers, you have to take care of all the problems that RMI and CORBA normally take care of. For instance, if a client has a very slow network link, you may have threads that start blocking when trying to write to the client. This can cause the server to appear hung for some users.

Just as you created a thread to read from a client, you can create a thread to write to a client. You can then create a pipe stream for sending data to the write thread. The write thread would read data from the pipe and write it to the client's socket connection.

You also have the problem of deciding when a user's connection is hung. Usually when a client disappears, the socket connection closes. Sometimes, however, the network never receives a message to close down the connection. You may be queuing up data for a client that will never read it.

One way to solve this problem is to keep track of how long a write thread has been trying to write data to a client. The write thread sets a flag indicating that it is trying to write and stores the current time before calling the `write` method. You then create a thread that runs in the background checking all the write threads. If it finds a thread that is trying to write and it has been trying to write for a certain time period (maybe 10-15 minutes), it closes down the connection to the client.

Adding RMI Access to Multi-User Applications

You don't have to implement too many complex client/server applications using sockets before you wish for something better. It is a huge hassle to send messages over a socket manually. You must either write some libraries to help you, or better yet, use a system that takes care of messaging for you. RMI and CORBA fit this bill perfectly.

When you create server encapsulations with RMI and CORBA, you have to set things up a little differently. The TCP server created client objects that actually handled the connection. In this design, the TCP server is acting like a factory; it produces the objects that handle the connections. The factory model for a TCP server is somewhat automatic, because the `ServerSocket` class behaves like a factory of `Socket` objects.

When you establish a connection using RMI or CORBA, you connect directly to an object. There is no new object created on the server side. This makes it a little more difficult to create multiple-client objects. You can solve this pretty easily by creating an object that creates connection handling objects. A client would enroll to this factor object, as illustrated in Figure 37.6.

The factory object then creates a new connection handling object and passes the enrolled client a reference to the new connection handler. The client and the connection handler now communicate directly; the factory object is no longer involved. Figure 37.7 illustrates this relationship.

Listing 37.9 shows an RMI interface definition for a simple factory object.

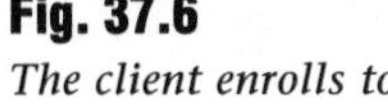

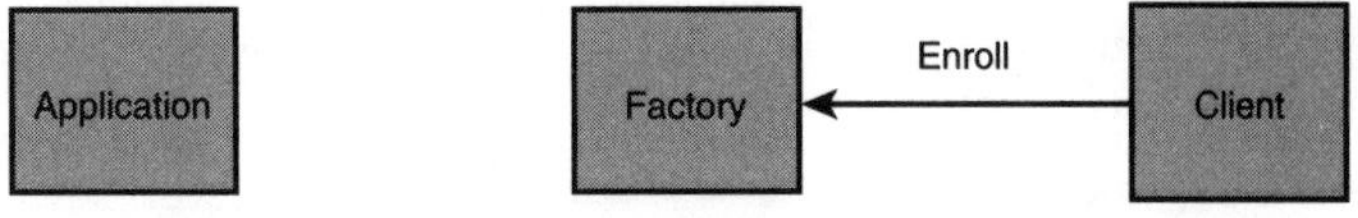

Fig. 37.6
The client enrolls to the factory object.

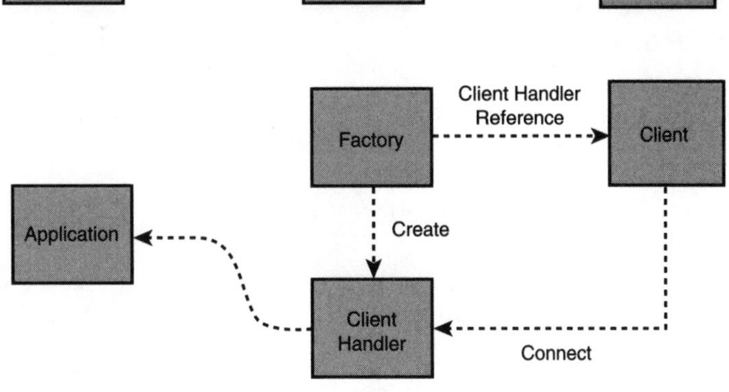

Fig. 37.7
The factory creates a connection handler object that communicates with the client.

Listing 37.9 Source Code for *RMIChatEnrol.java*

```
package chat.rmi;

public interface RMIChatEnrol extends java.rmi.Remote
{
     public RMIChatServer enrol(String name, RMIChatClient client)
          throws java.rmi.RemoteException;
}
```

Listing 37.10 shows the RMI implementation for this factory. It simply identifies itself to the RMI registry (the RMI naming service) and then creates new `RMIChatServerImpl` objects in response to an enroll request from a client.

Listing 37.10 Source Code for *RMIChatEnrolImpl.java*

```
package chat.rmi;

import java.rmi.server.UnicastRemoteServer;
import java.rmi.server.StubSecurityManager;

import chat.server.*;

// This class is a factory for RMIChatServerImpl objects. Whenever
// a client enrolls, it creates a new RMIChatServerImpl and returns
// it to the client.

public class RMIChatEnrolImpl extends UnicastRemoteServer
     implements RMIChatEnrol
{
     ChatServer server;
```

continues

Listing 37.10 Continued

```
     public RMIChatEnrolImpl(ChatServer server)
     throws Exception
     {
          this.server = server;

// Find out what name this object should use in the RMI registry
          String name = System.getProperty("rmiName", "chat");

// Identify this object to the registry
          java.rmi.Naming.rebind("chat", this);
     }

     public RMIChatServer enrol(String name, RMIChatClient client)
     throws java.rmi.RemoteException
     {
// Create a new RMIChatServerImpl and return it to the client
          return new RMIChatServerImpl(server, name, client);
     }
}
```

Once the connection handler is created, it needs to be able to communicate with the client, and the client needs to communicate back. Under RMI, this requires two more interfaces. Listing 37.11 shows the `RMIChatClient` interface, which is implemented by the client. The connection handler calls methods in `RMIChatClient` in response to method calls from the chat application.

Listing 37.11 Source Code for *RMIChatClient.java*

```
package chat.rmi;

public interface RMIChatClient extends java.rmi.Remote
{
     public void incomingChat(String who, String chat)
          throws java.rmi.RemoteException;

     public void userHasEntered(String who)
          throws java.rmi.RemoteException;

     public void userHasLeft(String who)
          throws java.rmi.RemoteException;

     public void disconnect()
          throws java.rmi.RemoteException;
}
```

The `RMIChatServer` interface is implemented by the connection handler. The client invokes the `sendChat` method in this interface to send a chat message to the chat application. Listing 37.12 shows the `RMIChatServer` interface.

Listing 37.12 Source Code for *RMIChatServer.java*

```
package chat.rmi;

public interface RMIChatServer extends java.rmi.Remote
{
     public void sendChat(String chat)
throws java.rmi.RemoteException;
     public void disconnect() throws java.rmi.RemoteException;
}
```

Unlike the complex `TCPChatClient` class, the `RMIChatServerImpl` class is extremely straightforward. It doesn't have to cram messages down a socket, and it doesn't have to interpret any data. All it does is invoke methods on the remote client or on the chat application. Listing 37.13 shows the `RMIChatServerImpl` class.

Listing 37.13 Source Code for *RMIChatServerImpl.java*

```
package chat.rmi;

import java.rmi.server.UnicastRemoteServer;
import java.rmi.server.StubSecurityManager;

import chat.server.*;

// This class is actually an RMI encapsulation for the
// ChatClient interface. It implements the methods in the
// ChatClient interface and invokes the corresponding method
// in the RMIChatClient interface.

// It also handles messages coming from the client. When the
// sendChat method is invoked via RMI, it turns around and
// invokes sendChat in the chat application.

public class RMIChatServerImpl extends UnicastRemoteServer
     implements RMIChatServer, ChatClient
{
     protected ChatServer server;
     protected String name;
     protected RMIChatClient client;

     public RMIChatServerImpl(ChatServer server, String name,
          RMIChatClient client)
     throws java.rmi.RemoteException
     {
          this.server = server;
          this.name = name;
          this.client = client;

          server.addClient(name, this);
     }
```

continues

37

Listing 37.13 Continued

```
public void incomingChat(String who, String chat)
{
     try {
          client.incomingChat(who, chat);
     } catch (Exception e) {
          try {
               client.disconnect();
          } catch (Exception ignore) {
          }
          server.removeClient(name);
          client = null;
     }
}

public void userHasEntered(String who)
{
     try {
          client.userHasEntered(who);
     } catch (Exception e) {
          try {
               client.disconnect();
          } catch (Exception ignore) {
          }
          server.removeClient(name);
          client = null;
     }
}

public void userHasLeft(String who)
{
     try {
          client.userHasLeft(who);
     } catch (Exception e) {
          try {
               client.disconnect();
          } catch (Exception ignore) {
          }
          server.removeClient(name);
          client = null;
     }
}

public void disconnect()
{
     try {
          client.disconnect();
     } catch (Exception ignore) {
     }
     server.removeClient(name);
     client = null;
}

public void sendChat(String chat)
     throws java.rmi.RemoteException
{
     server.sendChat(name, chat);
```

```
        }
    }
```

The actual client program that you run is very simple, too. Unlike the TCP program, it doesn't need to spawn a separate thread, since RMI is running as a separate thread. The program can concentrate on reading input from the user. Listing 37.14 shows the `RMIChatClientImpl` object, which is the actual application that a user would run.

Listing 37.14 Source Code for *RMIChatClientImpl.java*

```
import java.net.*;
import java.io.*;

import java.rmi.server.UnicastRemoteServer;
import java.rmi.server.StubSecurityManager;

import chat.server.*;
import chat.rmi.*;

// This class is an RMI client for the chat application

public class RMIChatClientImpl extends UnicastRemoteServer
implements RMIChatClient
{
     public RMIChatClientImpl()
     throws java.rmi.RemoteException
     {
     }

// The following 4 methods are callbacks from the
// RMIChatServerImpl class.

     public void userHasEntered(String who)
     throws java.rmi.RemoteException
     {
          System.out.println("--- "+who+" has just entered ---");
     }

     public void userHasLeft(String who)
     throws java.rmi.RemoteException
     {
          System.out.println("--- "+who+" has just left ---");
     }

     public void incomingChat(String who, String chat)
     throws java.rmi.RemoteException
     {
          System.out.println("<"+who+"> "+chat);
     }

     public void disconnect()
     throws java.rmi.RemoteException
```

37

continues

Listing 37.14 Continued

```
     {
          System.out.println("Chat server connection closed.");
          System.exit(0);
     }

     public static void main(String args[])
     {
// Get the name of the enroll factory

          String chatName = System.getProperty("rmiName", "chat");

// Must have a stub security manager!
          System.setSecurityManager(new StubSecurityManager());

          try {

// Get the name the user wants to use
               System.out.print("What name do you want to use? ");

               System.out.flush();

               DataInputStream userInputStream =
                    new DataInputStream(System.in);

               String myName = userInputStream.readLine();

// Create an instance of this object to receive callbacks
               RMIChatClient thisClient = new RMIChatClientImpl();

// Locate the RMIChatEnrol object
               RMIChatEnrol enrol = (RMIChatEnrol)
                    java.rmi.Naming.lookup(chatName);

// Enrol to the chat system
               RMIChatServer server = enrol.enrol(myName, thisClient);

// Free up the enrol object, we don't need it any more
               enrol = null;

// Read lines from the user and pass them to the server

               while (true) {

                    String chatLine = userInputStream.readLine();

                    server.sendChat(chatLine);

               }

          } catch (Exception e) {
               System.out.println("Got exception:");
               e.printStackTrace();
               System.exit(1);
          }
     }
}
```

All you need now is a class to start up the chat application and set up the TCP and RMI front ends for the application. Because the application implementation is separate from the networking protocols, you can run both TCP and RMI interfaces to a single chat application. This means that RMI users and TCP users can talk together. Listing 37.15 shows the `RunServer` class that starts up everything.

Listing 37.15 Source Code for *RunServer.java*

```
import chat.tcp.server.TCPChatServer;
import chat.server.ChatServer;
import chat.rmi.*;

import java.rmi.server.StubSecurityManager;

// This class starts up the chat application and the TCP and RMI
// front ends.

public class RunServer
{
     public static void main(String[] args)
     {
          try {

// Start the chat application
               ChatServer server = new ChatServer();

               int port = 4321;

               String portStr = System.getProperty("port");
               if (portStr != null) {
                    try {
                         port = Integer.parseInt(portStr);
                    } catch (Exception ignore) {
                    }
               }

               System.setSecurityManager(new StubSecurityManager());

// Start the RMI server
               RMIChatEnrol rmiEnrol = new RMIChatEnrolImpl(
                    server);

// Start the TCP server
               TCPChatServer tcpServer = new TCPChatServer(
                    server, port);

               tcpServer.start();
          } catch (Exception e) {
               System.out.println("Got exception starting up:");
               e.printStackTrace();
          }
     }
}
```

37

You should be able to use these classes as a starting point for any multi-user application you want to write. Always remember, however, to keep the application separated from the network protocols.

PART X

Java and Multimedia

chapter 38

Creating On-Demand Multimedia Services

by George Menyhert

In this chapter

- **Learn what makes Java so useful for on-demand applications**
  Java is compact, portable, and has many multimedia features built in.
- **Use an on-demand audio applet**
  Take a look at a simple applet used to play streaming audio.
- **See how audio is added to an applet**
  This section very quickly shows you how to add audio to an applet.
- **Take a detailed look at code samples from the applet**
  This is a line-by-line review of the code that adds audio capability to the applet.
- **Discover some of Java's shortcomings**
  Java is relatively new and the current version presents some drawbacks.
- **Look ahead to new Java features**
  Java development is exploding; a new set of features is on the way.

The World Wide Web has served as an agent of change for many industries. Even old, stable technologies like telephone service are swaying to the rhythm of the Net. Very shortly, the content we now call multimedia will be available as an on-demand stream, first to your desktop, then to your set top, and finally to your palmtop. The promise is that you will receive the content of the exact type you want, as much as you want, anywhere you want.

Java will probably play an important role in this media explosion. If ever there was a right programming language in the right place at the right time, this surely looks like it. Pay-Per-View and Content On-Demand are terms that you are probably already familiar with. Java holds the promise of creating high quality products for these new application areas.

Java's Suitability for On-Demand Applications

Why is Java particularly suited for on-demand access of multimedia over the network? Take a look at the process of doing an on-demand multimedia application using C++.

The following shows your list of concerns if developing a multimedia application using C++:

- Develop a client and server that can communicate over the Internet.

On the server Side:

- Server listens for a connection on a given port.
- Once a connection is made, handshaking occurs.
- Client makes its request.
- Server interprets the request and processes it.
- Server needs to understand the digital media file format. (If the format is unknown, you have problems.)
- Server reads file and sends it over the network.
- Communications are monitored for loss of connectivity, interrupts, and socket transfer rates.
- When the transaction completes, the communication line is terminated.

On the client Side:

- Client initializes itself and presents a UI to the user and waits for input.
- User selects clip; client contacts the server and establishes a connection.
- Client requests the clip and waits for data.
- Data is read from the socket and is sent to the output device.
- Data stream is complete; communication socket is closed and the output device is closed.

The server application can be fairly platform-independent; however, it has platform-specific modules controlling the file system and other operating system-specific aspects. It also needs basic knowledge of the underlying media if it is to transfer the data efficiently (can the headers be left out, what data packing is most appropriate?).

The client software is very platform-specific. At best, the user interface uses a standard library that can be linked on different platforms. More likely, sections of it need to be rewritten for the various platforms. The client also needs to control the output device and understand the translation, if any, between the file data format and the required hardware data format. The client needs intimate knowledge of network communications. Finally, the client needs to be distributed to customers; this is a major marketing problem. The customer wants the audio or video "on-demand" (read *now*). Can you imagine an on-demand system where users need to have the foresight to order an application a couple of days before they have the desire to watch and listen?

There are some libraries available for C++ that help alleviate some of the problems—a commercial implementation of CORBA for the communications issues, various UI libraries for the user interface—but none deal comprehensively with the problem areas of network multimedia.

Java addresses many of these problems. The underlying steps remain, but the Java execution environment removes many of the implementation details from the developer. For example, instead of developing a server from scratch (or even modifying and reusing an existing server), the product can be developed as an applet. The communication issues are completely removed from the process. There is no need to develop a server at all. Any off-the-shelf Web server works.

Any application (or applet) developed with Java is platform-independent. Therefore, creating graphical elements, displaying images, playing audio, and processing events are not only done with the same source code, but the same compiled binary code.

The Java built-in media API removes many file format- and output hardware-dependent issues. For example, audio clips can be streamed over the network and played on any system without regard to the various output devices or streamed data formats.

Because the majority of the underlying functionality is supplied by the Web server/ browser system, the distributed Java executable is very small. The example developed for this chapter is approximately 9K. Due to its extremely compact size, it can be downloaded over the Web in less time than most images. This solves the problem of distribution and provides instant access.

To review, Java is suitable for multimedia because:

- It is portable.
- It is compact.
- It can handle streaming data.
- It is distributed in a client/server topology.
- It has built-in multimedia classes.

Using the On-Demand Audio Applet

This applet is not intended to be a commercial On-Demand audio server. It is a simple example of how audio can be added to an applet.

Logging In

To login to the On-Demand Audio Applet:

1. Start your favorite Java-capable browser.
2. Open the file OnDemand.html with your browser.

   The text string Applet OnDemand running is displayed on your browser's status line when the applet is fully loaded. The login dialog appears as in Figure 38.1.

Fig. 38.1
*Enter **anonymous** in the Username text field.*

3. Click in the Username text field.
4. Enter the text string **anonymous** in lowercase letters.
5. Click the Login button.

Playing Audio Clips

To play audio clips:

1. Double-click the name of the Artist.

   A list of the artist's songs appears in the Songs list.

2. Double-click the name of the song that you want to play.

   Wait for a few moments. It takes a while for the audio clips to load. Copyright and other facts appear in the Information list when the song is loaded (see Figure 38.2).

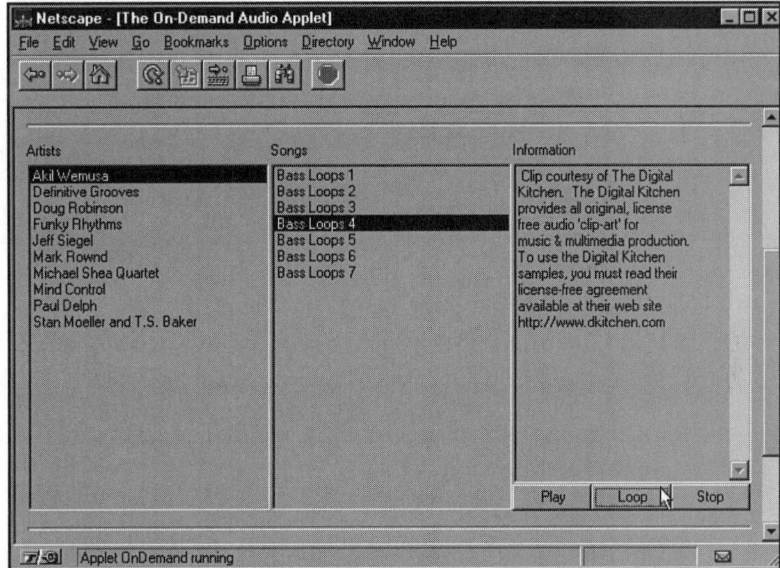

Fig. 38.2
The OnDemand applet is ready to play an audio stream.

3. Use the audio controls Play, Loop, and Stop to control the audio stream.

Adding Sound to Applets

Adding sound to a Java applet is *extremely* simple. There are only two steps: Identify the audio source, and play the clip. In general, the audio functionality is only available via the applet class. Although it is possible to run an applet as an application, there are many limitations to applets executed in this mode (including media streaming). However, there are some available work-arounds. See Chapter 13, "Running Applets as Applications," for details about the techniques and limitations of running applets as applications and ways of overcoming these limitations.

To specify the source of the sound clip, use the applet method `getAudioClip`. It requires one or two arguments—either a base URL and a relative file path packed as a String, or a complete URL. For example, to attach an `AudioClip` object to an audio file stored in a folder in your applet's HTML location, try the following:

```
AudioClip rockinTune = this.getAudioClip(getDocumentBase(),
"rocking.au");
```

Tip

Getting the audio clip this way is usually very slow the first time it is done in an applet. This is due to dynamic class loading.

When you are running these applets over the Internet, *each* instantiation of an `AudioClip` is extremely slow. This is because the `AudioClip` object does not truly stream the audio data. It downloads and buffers the data at the time of instantiation.

You need to give users some feedback so they don't cancel the operation. Try a call to `showStatus` that states something like, "Initializing audio. Please wait...". Changing the cursor to a wait state would be ideal, but is not possible in applets.

`getAudioClip` returns a reference to an `AudioClip` object. You can then use this object to play the audio clip when you are ready. To do this, simply call the `AudioClip.play` method

```
rockinTune.play();
```

You can also stop the playback using `AudioClip.stop` method and play back continuously using the `AudioClip.loop` method.

Caution

The supported list of audio file formats is limited. Currently, you can use only 8-bit, 8000Hz, single-channel (mono) Next/Sun AU files with G711 µ-law compression. Note that files with a higher sample rate may produce hissing on playback.

On-Demand Music Applet Code Review

Playing audio in an applet over the network involves only two method calls. It is simple to expand on this to create a fully functional online, on-demand music applet (see the previous section, "Using the On-Demand Audio Applet"). There are four basic elements to this on-demand music applet:

- Registration screen where a user signs in (later used for billing).
- Browse the system for songs of interest.
- Play a song.
- Register the transaction on the server (for billing).

The first three elements are addressed here. The fourth element involves writing to files on the server and is addressed in Chapter 8, "Reading and Writing Files from an Applet." The sample code does have comments showing where to implement the transaction registration.

Applet Architecture

To keep the system as flexible as possible, all of the applet options are controlled by configuration files and parameters in the applet HTML. There are four parameters. Each parameter is the name of a configuration file. They are:

- `userfile`—contains a list of accepted users.
- `imagefile`—the start-up image.
- `artistfile`—the configuration file containing a list of artists.
- `transactionfile`—the name of the file to record the transactions to (this final parameter is not used).

Specifying the file names as parameters and designing the applet to be based on configuration files allows a single, simple applet to be used by a wide variety of users without any code modification by the programmer. All flexible values are specified in the files—the image file, the acceptable user names, the list of artists, the names of the files containing the songs for each artist, the names of the audio files associated with each song, and the detailed information for each song. These can be easily modified and don't even require the user to reload the applet.

Due to the simplicity of this applet, there is no need to generate a host of new classes. The sample includes a total of two new classes: one subclass of `applet`, and a utility class that aids in file input and string parsing (`FileParser`). If the applet were expanded, separate classes would probably be desirable for each element listed earlier.

Initialization and Registration

First, the applet performs initialization, and the registration interface is prepared. During initialization, the applet reads the required filenames from the parameter list. Also, an `Image` object is created using one of the parameters as a filename. Finally, the rest of the user interface is created and organized (see Listing 38.1). The applet then waits for events. See the `OnDemand.init` method in the OnDemand.java source file on the CD.

Here, the initialization parameters are specified in the HTML.

Listing 38.1 Initialization Parameters in the HTML

```
<APPLET code="OnDemand.class" width=600 height=300>
<PARAM name="userfile" value="user.txt">
<PARAM name="imagefile" value="image.gif">
<PARAM name="artistsfile" value="art.txt">
<PARAM name="transactionfile" value="tran.txt">
</APPLET>
...
```

First, the initialization parameters are set, then an image is read, as shown in Listing 38.2.

Listing 38.2 Reading the Initialization Parameters and Creating the Image Object in the Java Applet

```
// get the input parameters
userFileName = getParameter("userfile");
imageFileName = getParameter("imagefile");
artistFileName = getParameter("artistsfile");
transactionFileName = getParameter("transactionfile");
...

// get the startup image
startUpImage = getImage(getDocumentBase(),imageFileName);

...
```

When the Login button is pressed, the method `OnDemand.confirmLogin` is called. It retrieves the requested user name from the text field, reads the contents of the user file (specified in the parameter list), and compares the selected name to the retrieved list (see Listing 38.3). If the name matches, the interface is cleared and `OnDemand.startUI` is called to begin the main program. If the name does not match one of the names in the configuration file, the text field is cleared and the login form remains on the screen.

Tip

To improve performance, user configuration files could be read asynchronously at startup.

Note

This applet is not intended as a commercial application; a more sophisticated applet uses encryption or digital signatures to secure its communications (see

Chapters 26-28 in Part VI, "Java Security," for more details). It also provides a dialog box if the login fails, and a password is then required. To implement a `password` text field, see `TextField.setEchoCharacter`.

Listing 38.3 Confirming the Username

```
// get the specified UID
userName = userNameField.getText();
...
// read the file contents and pack the lines of text into a
// vector of strings
userFileContents = FileParser.parseFile(getDocumentBase(),
                          userFileName);

...
// loop over the acceptable usernames and compare the specified UID
int i;
int total = userFileContents.size();
for(i=0; i<total; i++) {

 try {
 String tempString = (String)userFileContents.elementAt(i);

 // compare the strings
 if( userName.compareTo(tempString)
 == 0) {

 // the strings are the same, let them log in
 startUI();

 return;
 }

 }
 catch (ArrayIndexOutOfBoundsException e) {
 // do nothing since we are sure not to be out of the bounds
 }
}

...
```

Song Selection

Once the user is logged in, two text lists are displayed. The first is a list of artists; the second is a list of songs by that artist. The first list is read from the artist file (one of the initialization parameters). When an artist is selected, `OnDemand.selectArtist` is called and the artist's line from the configuration file is parsed and the song list filename is retrieved. Then, the song list is read (see Listing 38.4).

Listing 38.4 Reading the Song List in Response to an Artist Being Selected

```
...

//
// get the selected artist
//
int index = artistList.getSelectedIndex();

...

// get the selected artist configuration line
String temp = (String)artistFileContents.elementAt(index);

//
// read the contents of the artist's song file. the name of the
// song file is the second argument in the artists file.
//
songFileContents = FileParser.parseFile(getDocumentBase(),
                            FileParser.parseField(temp,2));
...
```

When a song is selected, `OnDemand.selectSong` is called, the song's configuration line is parsed, and the song filename and informational message is retrieved. Then, the song information is displayed using the song filename retrieved from the configuration files; the `AudioClip` object is created (see Listing 38.5).

Listing 38.5 Parsing the Song Configuration Line

```
//
// get the selected song from the list
//
int index = songList.getSelectedIndex();

// notify the user of wait condition
showStatus("Initializing audio. Please wait...");
...

// get the song info string the song's configuration line
String line = (String)songFileContents.elementAt(index);

//
// create the audio clip
//
sound = getAudioClip(getDocumentBase(),
            FileParser.parseField(line,2));

//
// populate the text area
//
FileParser.populateTextArea(songInfo,
                FileParser.parseField(line,3),
                songInfo.getColumns()-10);
...
```

Caution

Double-clicking is used in this example to select items from the list. This can be confusing since one click highlights a new item. If the user is not paying attention, there may be confusion between which clip is selected and which is highlighted. To alleviate this problem, subclass `List` and override the `handleEvent` operation. Look for the event IDs of `Event.LIST_SELECT` and `Event.LIST_DESELECT` with the target a list region. See the Java API documentation for details.

Playing the Songs

Once a song is selected, there is little remaining to do. If the user presses any of the audio control buttons (play, stop, loop), the appropriate `AudioClip` command is executed. If the action is play or loop, `OnDemand.logTransaction` is called to log the information of the transaction. In the example, `logTransaction` is a stub with comments in it to aid in later implementation.

Java Shortcomings

Although Java is a very powerful language, there are a number of things that can be improved:

- Media streaming is available only via applets that are executed in the environment of a robust Web browser (see Chapter 13, "Running Applets as Applications," for details and work-arounds). It is not possible to use the appletviewer to run or debug these applets. The current debug method is a slow process of loading your applet into a Web browser, checking it out, and then editing your Java source. This in itself is not so bad, but some browsers buffer your classes (even if you try to force a reload). You must relaunch your browser each time you want to test another feature. Also, it is difficult to get any debug feedback via `System.out` because some Web browsers do not supply a standard out.
- Currently the `AudioClip` is limited to a very specific file format and even a specific range of parameters within that format (Sun/Next audio file with one channel, μ-law compression, and 8KHz sample rate). This limitation should be removed.
- Java needs to include video streaming.
- True data streaming should be implemented to reduce initialization delay times in the instantiation of objects. Currently, the AudioClip objects download and buffer the audio data upon initialization. There may be some room for compromise using built-in asynchronous transfers.

- Ultimately, the streams need to have more user feedback control. For example, the user should be able to pause and scrub through an audio clip.
- Visual media types (images, and in the future, video) should be subclasses of components or have containers that can accept them as components.
- The current Javasoft API documentation is fairly weak when it comes to educating a new developer. Although it is excellent for reference, a Programmer's Guide with detailed information on difficult topics like the Layout Managers would be beneficial.

New Features

Java is evolving; look for the following changes that will affect the development of multimedia applications:

- Video implementation

  Improvements will include both latency-sensitive and -insensitive video and will accommodate both streaming and stored video sources.
- Enhanced Audio

  Enhancements will include support for sampled and synthesized audio as well as 3-D spatial audio sources. Streaming and stored audio sources will be supported.
- MIDI support

  Support will include timed-event streams, loadable synthesizers, and effects.
- High performance 2-D object animation

  2-D support will include sprites with transparency, programmed sprite behaviors, scrolling background images, aggregation and hierarchical compositing, and image-transformation effects.
- Improvements to 2-D graphics and imaging

  2-D graphics support will include affine transformations (translate, rotate, skew, and so on) on points and paths; compositing, which will allow overlays, blending, and transparency; image filters, including features such as table lookup, convolve, and sharpen; and paint enhancements, including gradients, and patterns.

chapter 39

Implementing a Multimedia Encyclopedia

39

by George Menyhert

In this chapter

- **Learn why Java is a good choice for multimedia encyclopedias**
  Java is compact, portable, can run on Personal Digital Assistants (PDA), and is already based on a client/server architecture.
- **Use a multimedia encyclopedia written in Java**
  This is a very simple applet that shows how quickly an applet can be developed and still provide a useful feature set.
- **See how sound and images are added to an applet**
  This reviews the key objects and methods necessary to add audio and video to an applet.
- **Take a look at code samples**
  This is a relatively detailed look at the code that shows how the applet was constructed and how it works.
- **Look at specific Java shortcomings**
  It surely would be nice to play a video stream (you probably will not have to wait long).
- **Find out about a series of features that will improve Java**
  A video API will make Java considerably more useful for multimedia.

Knowledge is dynamic. Science and industry march on heedless of the headaches that this evolving picture of the universe gives publishers and authors around the world. Even information that we think of as static does not rest peacefully. Discoveries are made every day that change the way that we look upon historical events. The Dead Sea Scrolls are unearthed; a meteorite from Mars with tantalizing clues of life is discovered; the Titanic is raised from the ocean's floor. Not only is knowledge dynamic but so is language, teaching methodology, and culture. There are methods of displaying information today that were not possible several years ago.

Now, look at our feeble attempts to deal with dynamic information. Reprinted books? CD-ROMs? Something is wrong. How do you update the copy of Encarta that you've had on your machine for three years? The *possibility* of solutions is only now starting to emerge with increased use of the Internet, graphical browsers, and portable, small, powerful software applets written in Java.

Java's Suitability for Multimedia Applications

Java is useful for multimedia applications because it is portable, is compact, can handle streaming data, and can provide encryption. In addition, it is already based on the client/server model and will support PDAs easily. Please see Chapter 38, "Creating On-Demand Multimedia Services," for a more detailed discussion of each of these topics.

Java Is Portable

Java already runs on every popular computing platform. The same code runs on PCs, Macintoshes, and UNIX workstations.

Java Is Compact

The Multimedia Encyclopedia applet in this chapter is only 9K in size. This is critically important when dealing with the small bandwidth of phone lines (or an even smaller bandwidth for some mobile applications).

Java Can Handle Streaming Data

Encyclopedias are huge and will only get bigger. Can you imagine downloading a new version every day? Rather than downloading, storing and then playing data, Java lets you *stream* data. That is, the data flows through the device. You don't worry about your radio storing enough sound to play continuously. Why should your computer, or other digital devices, be any different?

Java Is Based on the Client/Server Model

Ideally, you want your multimedia encyclopedia to be updated constantly. This is not possible without adopting a client/server model. Fortunately, that is the model used by Java. The distribution of data is a nightmare using traditional media. If the distribution of data is difficult, so is the distribution of more powerful indexing or playback technologies. Using Java, the executable part of the product can be updated as frequently as the data. I'm sure that when folks look at Encarta's interface, they think it's kind of clunky and wonder why it doesn't look more like Internet Explorer. With Java, IUs are as easy to modify and distribute as the data.

Java Supports PDAs Easily

Today, Java can run on PDAs; all you need is a *mini-browser*. As an example, assume that you need to develop a Multimedia Tour Book for an art museum that runs on a PDA. The application lets visitors arrange a detailed personal tour and spend time at the exhibits that are of particular interest to them. In this case, you do not need a full commercial browser like Netscape; rather, you need a browser that can handle text, hypertext, and multimedia. This browser can be optimized for your specific requirements, reducing code size and increasing performance. Because this application is written in Java, tourists can take this same tour at home on their PCs, either before or after their visit, simply by accessing the museum's Web site.

Using the Multimedia Encyclopedia

This applet is designed as a public domain multimedia encyclopedia; it provides all the features of a Multimedia Encyclopedia short of video streaming. It is a good example of an application that can be written in a few hours and still be very useful and easy to improve in the future. Remember, the next time a user accesses the encyclopedia, he or she could see a greatly improved user interface, as well as better content.

To use the Multimedia Encyclopedia:

1. Start your favorite Java-capable browser.
2. Open the file Chapter48/Encyc.html with your browser.

   The text string, Applet Encyc running, displays on your browser's status line when the applet is fully loaded (see Figure 39.1).
3. Double-click the name of the topic that you want to see.

   An image of the topic appears (see Figure 39.2).
4. Click the Listen button to hear the associated audio clip.
5. Click the Index button to go back to the topics list.

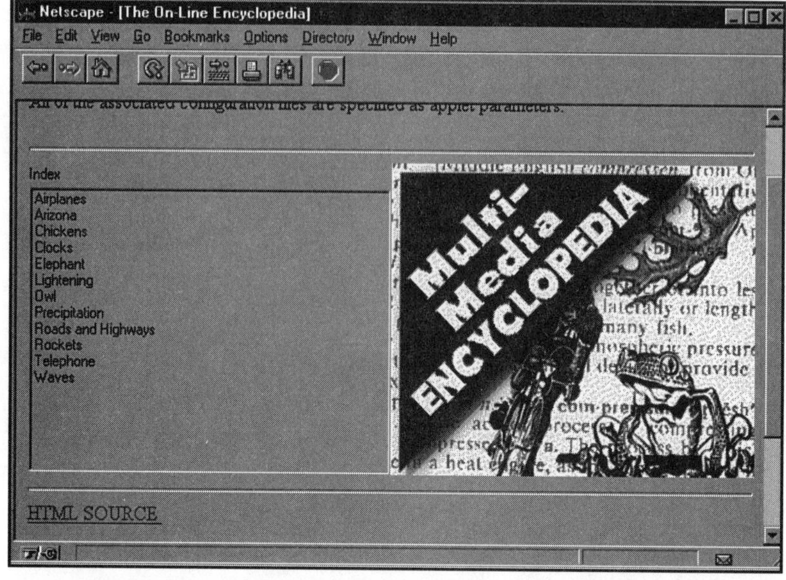

Fig. 39.1
The Multimedia's welcome screen and topics list are loaded.

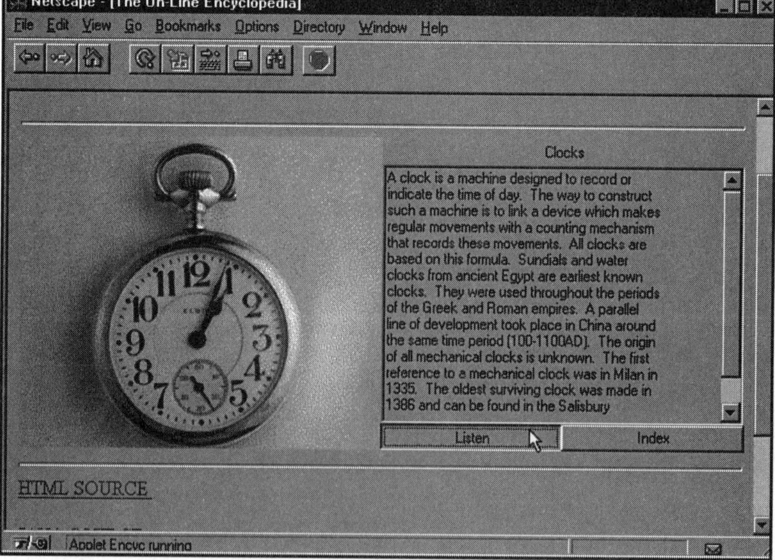

Fig. 39.2
An image of the topic along with the applet's controls can be seen here.

Adding Images and Sound to Applets

Adding sound and pictures to Java applets is very simple. This is also discussed in Chapter 4, "Displaying Images," and Chapter 38, "Creating On-Demand Multimedia Services." Both media types are handled in similar ways. Simply obtain a reference to an object of the correct media type; then display the media. The media functionality is available only via the applet class. Although it is possible to run an applet as an application, there are many limitations to applets executed in this mode (including media streaming). However, there are some available work-arounds. See Chapter 13, "Running Applets as Applications," for details on the techniques and limitations of running applets as applications and ways of overcoming these limitations.

To select the source of a sound clip, call the method `Applet.getAudioClip`. This method is overloaded and has two invocations. A sound file can be referenced either by a base URL and a relative file path, or by its absolute URL. To include audio in your applet, add the following line:

```
AudioClip sound =
myApplet.getAudioClip(getDocumentBase(), "sound.au");
```

Tip

Getting the audio clip this way is usually very slow the first time it is done in an applet. This is due to dynamic class loading.

When you are running these applets over the Internet, *each* instantiation of an `AudioClip` is extremely slow. This is because the `AudioClip` object does not truly stream the audio data. It downloads and buffers the data at the time of instantiation.

You need to give users some feedback so they don't cancel the operation. Try a call to `showStatus` that states something like, "Initializing audio. Please wait...". Changing the cursor to a wait state would be ideal, but is not possible in applets.

This sample creates an object that references the sound file, sound.au, in the same location as the applet's URL. To play the sound clip, simply invoke the `AudioClip.play` method. You can also stop and loop (continually play back) the audio clip. The following line shows how to play a sound:

```
sound.play();
```

Tip

Using the loop functionality can be very helpful for background sounds. Instead of downloading long sound files, you can loop short sound files. Looping a sound file will play it over and over without pause. This will shorten download time without sacrificing quality.

Caution

The supported list of audio file formats is extremely limited. Currently, you can use only 8-bit, 8000Hz, single-channel (mono) NEXT/Sun AU files with G711 μ-law compression. Note that files with a higher sample rate may produce hissing on playback.

Adding images to your applet is very similar to adding audio. The primary difference is that the image does not have a `draw` method to display itself, whereas the audio clip contains its own play method. To attach to a particular image, call the `Applet.getImage` method. The URL (or a base URL and relative path) can be specified just like the `AudioClip`, as follows:

```
Image thePicture = myApplet.getImage(getDocumentBase(), "image.gif");
```

An image object can reference either JPEG (JFIF) or GIF images. To display the image, add a call to `Graphics.drawImage`. This is usually done in the applet's (or component's) overridden `paint` method. The following example explains how to display an image object. Note that the call to `myApplet.getGraphics` is made because only a `Graphics` object can display an `Image`:

```
Graphics g = myApplet.getGraphics();
g.drawImage(thePicture, 20, 40, myApplet);
```

The method `Graphics.drawImage` is overloaded and has four implementations. They vary based on whether or not a default background or output resolution is specified. If an output resolution is specified, the image is scaled as it is rendered to the screen.

Images can also be created or altered by your applet, and they can be rendered on or off screen. For more information, see Chapter 4, "Displaying Images." Also, refer to the `ImageProducer` class and the `java.awt.image` package.

Tip

Unfortunately, images are not components in the Java libraries. This means that they cannot be added directly to a layout. If you want to add images to a display that contains components, you probably need to subclass `Canvas`. Your subclass must at least override the `Component.paint` method. Add the `Graphics.drawImage` method to the paint method. This is illustrated in the sample code `ImageCanvas.java`. To develop a more robust `ImageCanvas`, you should also override the `Component.preferredSize`, `Component.minimumSize`, and `Component.size` methods to return the actual image dimensions. This makes the resulting component the correct dimensions.

The On-Line Multimedia Encyclopedia In-Depth

We have discussed how to add sound and pictures to your applet; an on-line multimedia encyclopedia is a simple extension of these tools. The only thing to add is some descriptive text, an index, and a few control buttons.

Applet Architecture

To make the applet as flexible as possible, all of the display options are specified as either applet parameters or in configuration files. The encyclopedia cover page (image file name) and the index file are specified in the applet parameter list. The topic configuration filename is a field in the index file (associated with the index listing), which references a file that contains fields specifying an image filename, a sound filename, and a textual description of the topic. Thus, the encyclopedia can be easily modified without changing the underlying Java source code.

Due to the simplicity of this example, there is no need to create a large set of new classes. However, due to their nature, *some* new classes are straightforward, obvious, and well-behaved. These classes are `ImageCanvas` and `FileParser`. The `FileParser` class was not actually created for this sample. It was originally developed for the sample in Chapter 38, "Creating On-Demand Multimedia Services." Follow good object practice here and reuse it.

39

`FileParser` aids in configuration file input, file and field parsing, and text region population (loading the fields from the file into specified text regions). `ImageCanvas` is a component that displays an image within its body. The `ImageCanvas` is required in order to include an image in a display that also contains buttons and other widgets. The `Canvas` allows an image to be displayed as part of a component. If the image is not a component, no space is reserved for it by the Layout Managers. Listing 39.1 is an example of a basic `ImageCanvas`.

Listing 39.1 Implementing a Basic *ImageCanvas*

```
public class ImageCanvas extends Canvas {

 private Image theImage;

 // image canvas constructor
 public ImageCanvas(Image that) {
 theImage = that;
 }

 // draw the canvas
 public void paint(Graphics g) {
 // draw the image
 g.drawImage(theImage, 0, 0, this);
 }

}
```

Index Window

The encyclopedia consists of two screens. The first is the index screen; it contains a list of indexes and the encyclopedia cover page (image). Double-clicking a list topic takes you to the topic screen. Listing 39.2 shows the major steps required to display an image in a `Canvas` on the interface.

Listing 39.2 Creating the Cover Page Image Object and Placing It in an *ImageCanvas*

```
...

// get the startup image
Image startUpImage = getImage(getDocumentBase(),imageFileName);

// create the intro image canvas component
introImage = new ImageCanvas(startUpImage);

//
// Create the GUI. Notice that the image canvas is a component and
// can be handled by the Layout Managers like any other component.
//
```

```
setLayout(new GridLayout(1,2));
add(indexPanel);
add(introImage);

...
```

Note

There is no need to explicitly draw the image, because its parent component `ImageCanvas` draws the image in its paint method.

Topic Window

The topic window displays the topic's image, a text region containing the topic information, a *Listen* button to play the sound clip associated with the image, and an *Index* button that takes you back to the original index screen.

Again, the `ImageCanvas` is employed to place and display the image component. The `AudioClip` object is created and tied to the Listen button. Listing 39.3 shows the major steps required to create `Image` and `Audio` objects. Listing 39.4 is an example of binding sound playback to a button action.

Listing 39.3 Creating Media Objects and Adding Them to the Applet

```
...

//
// Create the image, image canvas, and audioclip objects.
// Sometimes the audio initialization takes some time, so post a
// message to the user.
//
showStatus("Initializing the audio. Please wait...");
sound = getAudioClip(getDocumentBase(), audioName);
Image theImage = getImage(getDocumentBase(), imageName);
ImageCanvas theCanvas = new ImageCanvas(theImage);
showStatus("");

// add the items to the applet
setLayout(new GridLayout(1,2));
add(theCanvas);
add(textPanel);

...
```

Listing 39.4 Play the Sound in Reaction to the Listen Button

```
//
// watch for button events
//
public boolean action(Event event, Object arg) {

 // the listen button was pressed
 if(event.target == listenButton)
 sound.play();

 // didn't find anything of interest. see if my parent wants it.
 else
 return super.action(event,arg);

 return true;
}
```

Shortcomings

Following are some shortcomings of Java for developing this multimedia encyclopedia:

- Visual media types (images and video) should be subclasses of components or should have containers that can accept them as components.

Tip

Until this happens, try subclassing `Canvas` and overriding the `paint` method. Also, override the `minimumSize`, `preferredSize`, and `size` method to make the panel conform to the image size.

- Currently, the `AudioClip` is limited to a very specific file format and even a specific range of parameters within that format (Sun/NEXT audio file with one channel, μ-law compression, and 8KHz sample rate). This limitation should be removed.
- Media streaming is available only via applets that are executed in the environment of a robust Web browser (see Chapter 13, "Running Applets as Applications," for details and work-arounds). It is not possible to use the appletviewer to run or debug these applets. The current debug method is a slow process of loading your applet into a Web browser, checking it out, and then editing your Java source. This in itself is not so bad, but some browsers buffer your classes (even if you try to force a reload). You must relaunch your browser each time you want to test another feature. Also, it is difficult to get any debug feedback via `System.out`, because some Web browsers do not supply a standard out.

- Java needs to include video streaming.
- Java should include 3-D world streaming for support of these potentially important types for a multimedia encyclopedia.
- Ultimately, the streams need to have more user feedback control. For example, the user should be able to pause and scrub video and audio clips.
- True data streaming should be implemented to reduce initialization delay times in the instantiation of objects. There may be some room for compromise using built-in asynchronous transfers.
- There is no way to synchronize graphical events with audio playback. There should be a time-based synchronization method. This will need to be easily integrated with video streaming.

New Features

Java is evolving; look for the following changes that will affect the development of multimedia applications:

- Video implementation

  Improvements will include both latency-sensitive and insensitive video and will accommodate both streaming and stored video sources.
- Enhanced audio

  Enhancements will include support for sampled and synthesized audio, as well as 3-D-spatial audio sources. Streaming and stored audio sources will be supported.
- MIDI support

  Support will include timed event streams, loadable synthesizers, and effects.
- High-performance 2-D object animation

  2-D support will include sprites with transparency, programmed sprite behaviors, scrolling background images, aggregation and hierarchical compositing, and image transformation effects.
- Improvements to 2-D graphics and imaging

  2-D graphics support will include affine transformations (translate, rotate, skew, and so on) on points and paths; compositing, which will allow overlays, blending, and transparency; image filters including features such as table lookup, convolve, and sharpen; paint enhancements, including gradients and patterns.

- Addition of 3-D geometry and behavior

  3-D geometry features will include immediate, retained, and compiled-retained 3-D graphics; high-level specification of behavior and control of 3-D objects; a generalized morphing engine; and high-resolution coordinate anchors.

- A new Java object—the servlet

  Servlets are Java objects that can be downloaded from the server at runtime. These servlets provide increased capabilities for communicating with the server. In a simple case, they can be used to replace the rather awkward CGI scripts that are currently being used.

PART XI

Java and Embedded Systems

chapter 40

Implementing Java Interfaces for Non-Traditional Devices

by Mark Wutka

In this chapter

- **The challenges of hand-held devices**
  Java was originally designed to run on a small, hand-held device. These types of devices are different from the traditional desktop platform because they lack many of the features you often expect, such as disks or a keyboard.
- **The new computing model**
  As more intelligent devices become available, the model of computing you use at home and at work will change. You will no longer be able to point to a single device and say, "That's my computer."
- **Supporting non-traditional devices**
  Your applications may be run on a hand-held device in the near future. If you design your application well, it won't matter where the application runs. There are a few simple design principles you can employ to make your application friendly to non-traditional devices.
- **Adapting user interfaces to non-traditional devices**
  You can't always rely on a nice, big screen when designing an application. You can't even rely on a keyboard. There are steps you can take to support non-traditional devices in your user interface while still taking advantage of a traditional workstation.
- **Creating reusable components for small devices**
  You can create components that support small devices while still presenting a traditional interface. These components should work without a keyboard or mouse. If you design these components carefully, you can reuse them in many applications without changing them.

One of the most interesting aspects of Java is that it was originally designed to work on a small hand-held device, making it very friendly toward these devices. Java is also a self-contained environment; that is, it is more than just a programming language. You can run Java programs wherever you can implement the Java runtime environment.

Java promises to allow you to run programs in places you never expected. For example, you can have a mobile terminal mounted in your car, maybe as an extension to your cellular phone. Within the next year, you may see television sets that can also access the Internet and run Java programs. You will soon see Java showing up in cellular phones and Personal Digital Assistants (PDAs).

These devices come with their own set of advantages and limitations. If you get your systems ready for these devices, you can get a jump on your competition.

Characteristics of Non-Traditional Devices

One of the most common characteristics you find in these new computing devices is that they have little or no local disk storage. While this may change in the future, you can design around it fairly easily. In fact, you have probably already tackled this problem thanks to the current applet security restrictions.

Many of these new devices have small display screens. This stretches your user interface design skills quite a bit, because you need to come up with creative ways to display information without requiring reading glasses.

You will also have an interesting time getting input from these devices. For example, a cellular phone typically has about 16 to 20 buttons, 12 of which are the standard telephone buttons of 0 through 9, #, and *. Many PDAs have a full keyboard, while others, like the Newton, have only a pen. You may also be dealing with touch-screen interfaces, which are often approached like pen-based systems.

One of the things you should be able to count on for most of these devices is network connectivity. After all, with no local storage, they either have to have all their code built-in, or they must be able to download code from the network.

The New Computing Model

Right now, you probably have a number of different information sources in your home. You have one or more phone lines, maybe even a digital ISDN line, probably cable TV or a satellite dish, and, of course, you have television and radio waves drifting through the air. For each of these information sources, you have different receivers that relay the information to you. Figure 40.1 shows the typical information sources coming into a home and their receivers.

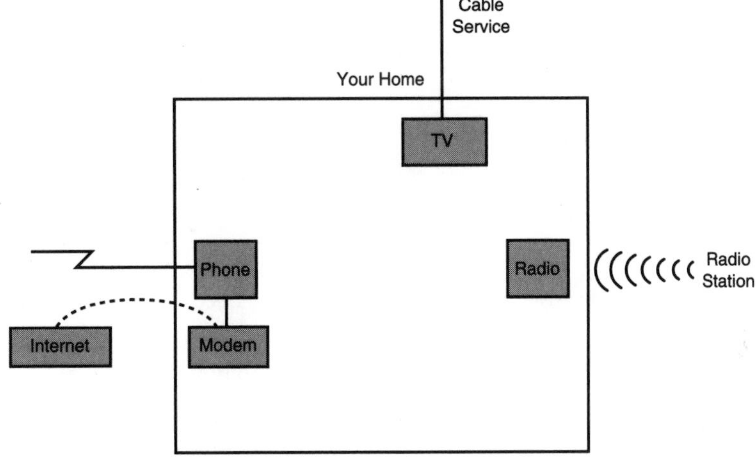

Fig. 40.1
Your home has many different information sources.

You also have a number of information sources that you bring into your house manually—that is, not electronically. For instance, you may receive a newspaper. You also buy books, videotapes, and CDs.

These information sources are beginning to blend together, however, thanks to improvements in technology. Newspapers are now available on the Web, as are recent news reports. There are online books and magazines, and audio and video clips are becoming very popular.

Cable TV companies are beginning to offer cable modems that allow you to access the Web with a direct digital connection, similar to ISDN. Within the next few years, you may start seeing phone, cable TV, and Internet access combined into a single service, available over a single connection to your house. Figure 40.2 illustrates how this changes your sources of information.

This combination of information sources is only half the picture. You soon will have many more devices in your house that want to communicate with you and other devices. Right now, you use your personal computer for surfing the Web, but when you get a Web-enabled TV, you may want both of them to share your Internet access. You may already have a PDA or a laptop computer, and have probably experienced the fun of trying to share data between the PDA or laptop and your desktop system.

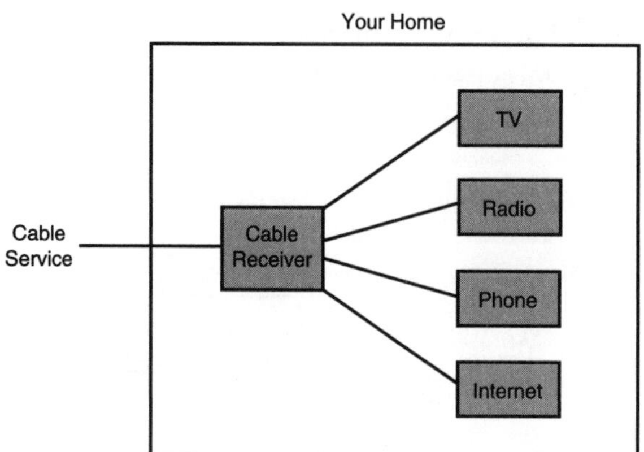

Fig. 40.2
You may soon get several kinds of information from a single source.

As more and more of your household devices become Java-enabled, more of them will require network access. You will soon have a need for your own home network. Figure 40.3 illustrates a typical home network configuration.

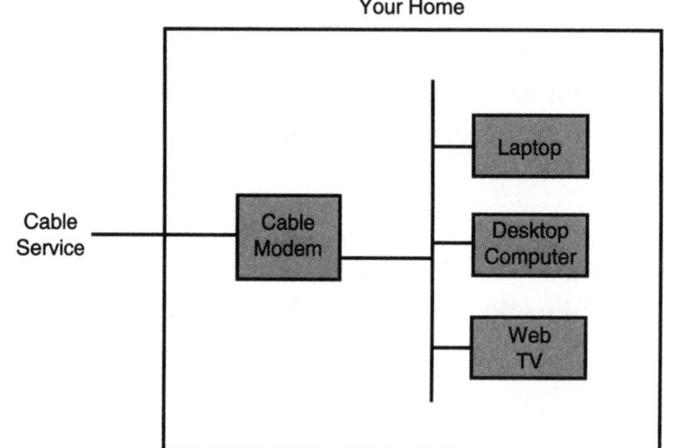

Fig. 40.3
With so many network-aware devices at home, you will need your own home network.

As more and more of the applications you use every day become Java-enabled, you will be able to run them in the different devices on your home network. For instance, you may have an address book program that you might need to access from your phone, your TV, or your desktop computer (if you still have one). Applications for these new devices will consist of one or more applets implementing the user interface and communicating with a server application, as shown in Figure 40.4.

It is entirely possible that your desktop computer, as you know it, will change. Right now, you probably have a keyboard, a monitor, a CPU, a modem, and a printer. Figure 40.5 illustrates the typical home computer of today.

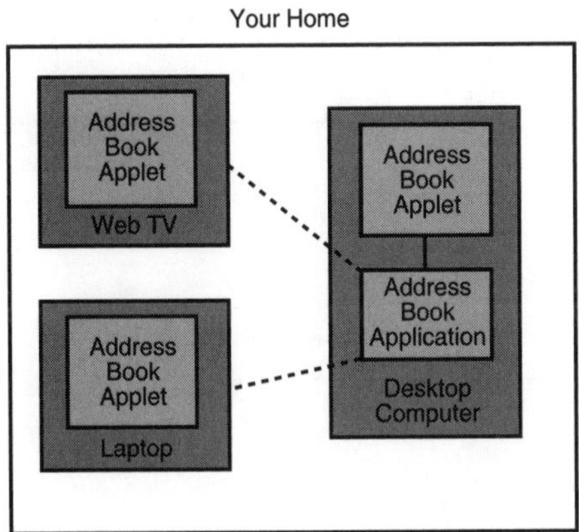

Fig. 40.4
The Java-enabled devices in your home will often just implement a user interface for an application.

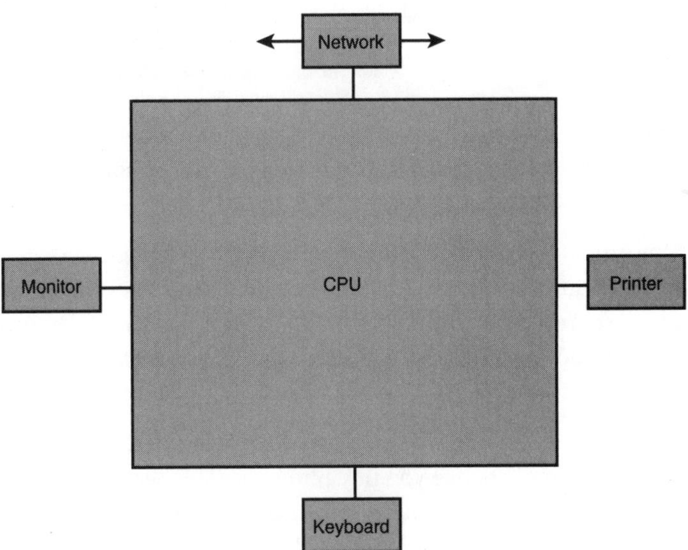

Fig. 40.5
A typical home computer configuration.

In your future home network, you still need these devices, of course, but some of these components need to be shared with other devices in your house. Your CPU becomes the computing server for your house. All your applications run on it. Your printer either is connected to your CPU or plugs directly into the network. Your monitor and keyboard are replaced by a network computer or a Web TV. You probably can buy a cheap box that turns your current monitor and keyboard into a network computer. Your modem is either attached to the network or replaced by whatever device gives you connectivity to the outside world—maybe a cable or an ISDN terminal adaptor. Figure 40.6 shows how the components of your home computer fit into a home network.

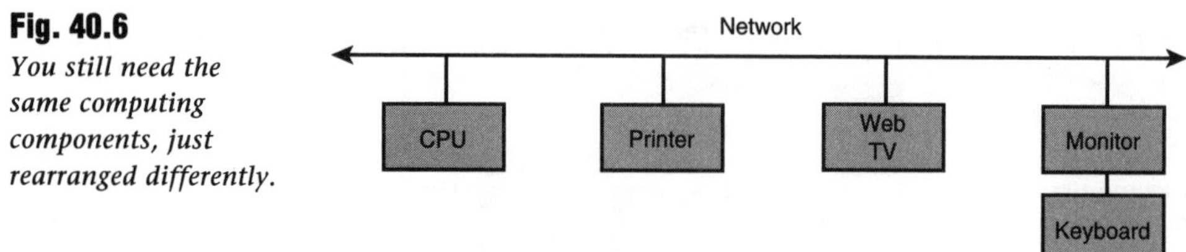

Fig. 40.6
You still need the same computing components, just rearranged differently.

You may eventually be able to control your lights and thermostat from a home network. After you have a network running throughout your home, the possibilities for new devices are endless. Figure 40.7 illustrates some of the possible devices that can be on your home network.

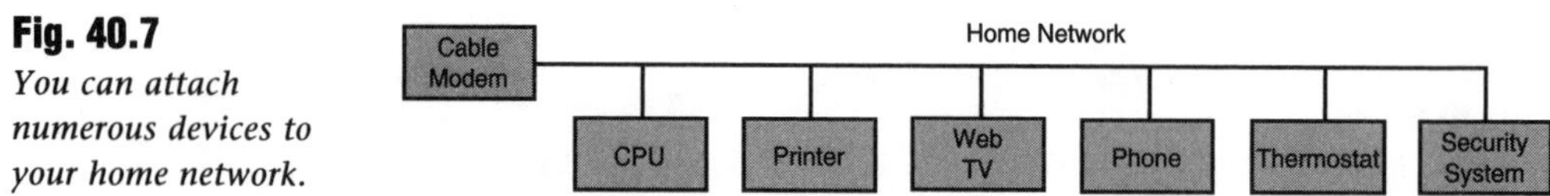

Fig. 40.7
You can attach numerous devices to your home network.

This brings up a sticky situation, however. The more things that are accessible on your home network, the more critical it is to prevent people from accessing your home network from the outside.

Unfortunately, you can't simply block out any incoming requests, because you may want to access information on your home server from your car, which may also have its own network. You need a home firewall system that prevents malicious network attacks, and enables you to control who can access information in your home and what information they can access.

It is possible that, some day, you will no longer need your CPU. You will be able to buy computing services like you buy phone or cable services. Your computing services provider supplies the applications you use over the Internet. This provider also maintains the applications, making sure that the most recent versions are available. In addition, the provider would perform the often-ignored task of backing up your data.

There are advantages and disadvantages to giving up the administration of your computing server. On the positive side, you no longer have to keep up with the current versions of software. You don't have to go out and install new packages; your provider should have whole application suites ready for immediate use. You don't have to make backups, either. In the simplest case, you can subscribe to such a service, then go out and buy a Java-enabled TV and a network printer, plug them into the wall, and go.

Designing Applications to Support Non-Traditional Devices

In case you haven't noticed, this book has been pushing you toward an application model that is friendly to small, non-traditional devices. The specific design principles for this application model are as follows:

- Separate the user interface from the application logic This allows you to create various interfaces for the same application.
- Avoid large, monolithic applications Try to break up the functionality into smaller classes that can be downloaded on demand.
- Use standard libraries whenever possible Smaller devices will probably have enough local code to communicate on the network, hopefully using RMI or CORBA. Some, if not all, will include JDBC, because it is one of the core Java libraries. The less you have to download to the device, the better off you are.
- Avoid complex, prolonged transactions Most of the time, remote devices need to get small pieces of information quickly. Obviously there are exceptions, but something like an address book should be small and quick.

Separating the User Interface from the Application

Many times, the separation of the application from the user interface is a difficult task. After you have done it a few times, however, it gets easier. When an application's goal is the rendering of an image, the line between application and user interface becomes a little fuzzier.

For example, suppose you are writing an application that displays weather radar images. The application needs to retrieve the weather images, but the user interface is responsible for displaying them. How do you separate them?

Actually, there's not always a clear-cut answer to this. Sometimes the distinction can be gray. If your weather application allows you to zoom in on an image or overlay other information on top of the image, do you do that in the application or the user interface?

Tip

If your application needs to know the characteristics of the display area, that is a good indication that you haven't clearly separated the user interface from the application.

There's a tradeoff involved here. It is extremely costly for your server to generate images for every client whenever the client needs to zoom the image. You would be much better off if the client were doing that processing. You must balance that against the fact that you have to put the zooming code onto the client, which may be a burden to the client.

Tip

Design involves a series of tradeoffs that result in different decisions for different applications.

It is often very easy to let pieces of the user interface leak into the application. For instance, suppose you create an ordering system that presents the user with a list of parts. The user can select any number of parts on the list, and press the Order button to order the parts. You might be tempted to have the application keep track of which parts the user has selected. In other words, the interface between the application and the user interface might include methods to select and deselect parts, and then place the order, like this:

```
public void selectPart(String partName);
public void deselectPart(String partName);
public void placeOrder();
```

This is not a good separation, however. The user interface has leaked over into the application. This often happens because you have taken too granular a view of what is going on. The application is responsible for ordering parts. It is not responsible for identifying which parts should be ordered.

Tip

If the interface between an application and a user interface closely reflects the various components of the user interface, you may not have separated them very well.

When you look at the `selectPart-deselectPart-placeOrder` interface, you can almost see what the designer was thinking—a multiple-selection scrolling list of parts and an Order button. The interface should really just contain a method to place an order, like this:

```
public void placeOrder(String[] partNames);
```

Now the application doesn't have any notion of the interaction between the user and the user interface, as it did when it had methods for selecting and deselecting parts.

Avoiding Large, Monolithic Applications

When you design an application, you may think in terms of the whole application, treating all the little things it does as a part of the whole. This results in huge applications that take a long time to download.

Take a word processor, for instance. You have a spelling checker, a thesaurus, a mailing list handler, an outline generator, and all sorts of other features. However, you don't necessarily want to load all of these features when the program starts up.

Note

A word processor not only serves as a good example of a typically monolithic application, it also illustrates one of the compromises you have to make when separating the user interface from the application. Conceptually, the document you are editing belongs to the application side. If you were to send every little editing command over to the application, you may never get anything done, unless you happen to have a very fast network. You have to create a balance, where you bring over portions of the text for editing, and occasionally mirror the text back to the application.

Different features of your application have their own special interfaces. Rather than downloading these to the client at startup time, you can use Java's dynamic loading mechanism to postpone the loading of these special interfaces.

You can also cut down on the interdependence between various interface components if you create each interface component as an AWT panel, or better yet, as an applet. That's really where the term *applet* comes from. They aren't whole applications, they are pieces of applications.

Because the special interfaces are panels or applets (which are panels themselves), you can create a special section of your display for the special interfaces, or use a card layout manager to switch between different panels. The other parts of your user interface don't have to know anything else about the interface.

The Java component interface, known as Beans, promises to provide additional support for this, allowing your special interfaces to plug themselves into the current application in a seamless way.

Sticking to Standard Libraries

One of the toughest things to balance when developing for small devices is the use of third-party libraries. There are many excellent third-party libraries available that allow you to do some really fancy things, but these libraries have to be downloaded to the client, which means extra startup time.

Tip

Third-party libraries don't always mean extra download time. If a library provides functionality that you would have to write anyway and it is smaller than anything you could write in a reasonable amount of time, go ahead and use it.

The important thing here is that you don't write anything that is already available in the standard Java libraries. If you have your own special remote method invocation system, consider replacing it with RMI, at least for Java client-server communications. You save a tremendous amount of time, because the RMI code is part of the standard Java libraries (as of Java 1.1).

Tip

Keep in mind that non-Java components, such as ActiveX, are probably not going to be available on these smaller clients. You should be very wary of these components when designing user interfaces that may run on small clients.

Avoiding Long, Complex Transactions

If you are performing a long, complex task, there is a good chance you won't be able to get around a long, complex transaction from the user interface. Many times, however, the task itself is simple, but the way you access the data is complex. Just because you have a complex database doesn't mean you have to punish the user by presenting them with a complex user interface. In other words, don't make something complicated out of a simple task.

For example, if you have an address book program, provide a way to simply look up someone by name, like this:

```
public String getAddress(String name);
```

If you can define an operation as a single method call, do it. Don't open up a session, create a logon, or require multiple method calls if you can avoid it.

Designing User Interfaces for Small Devices

For someone coming from a background of designing user interfaces for desktop systems, the world of small hand-held devices is a rude awakening. Instead of focusing on pretty interfaces, you must focus on simple, self-documenting interfaces.

When designing user interfaces for small hand-held devices, there is a set of design principles that you should follow:

- The interface should be obvious and self-documenting   You should be able to figure out how to use the interface just by looking at it or by playing around with it for a minute or two. You can't rely on online help.
- No extraneous pictures or information   Screen space is precious, as is download time. Don't put anything on the screen that isn't used to perform a task.
- Keep everything readable   Don't just shrink down an interface from the desktop and expect someone to use it. If you are searching for smaller fonts so you can fit more text on the screen, you're doing something wrong.
- Support multiple sources of input   If your user interface must run on a cellular phone, you had better be able to use it with only a phone keypad.

Creating Obvious, Self-Documenting Interfaces

Is there a help key on an automatic teller machine? That's a tough question to answer, because you've probably never needed one. When you create user interfaces for hand-held devices, you want the interface to be so obvious that no one ever needs a help key or a manual.

Note

You can get a better understanding of what makes a good interface and what makes a bad one by studying different devices. An automatic teller is one such example. Your VCR is another. How many VCRs have you seen that are actually simple to program? Even with on-screen programming? Why are they more difficult? Consider how you might make a better one.

Avoiding Extraneous Pictures or Information

40

There are two main reasons for avoiding extraneous pictures in your interface: time and space. You shouldn't waste time downloading images that aren't necessary, and you shouldn't waste precious screen space.

Note

Screen space doesn't just refer to the number of pixels on the screen when it comes to small devices. The screens are typically only a few inches wide. It doesn't matter if they are 50 pixels wide or 1,000 pixels wide. There is a limit to the amount of readable information you can show.

This doesn't mean that you should avoid pictures altogether. You may find that a few simple icons describe the use of the device just as well as text. The advantage to the icons is that they are not language-dependent. Anyone can use an icon-based user interface no matter what language they speak.

When you create icons for your interface, however, keep them simple. If you need arrows pointing in certain directions, don't download some ray-traced image of a marble arrow. Either download a simple arrow image, or use the `Graphics` class to paint the arrow yourself.

Keeping Everything Readable

Any user interface that requires generous amounts of squinting or high-powered reading glasses is a bad interface. If you have to cram that much information onto the screen, you should break it up into multiple screens that you can scroll through back and forth. Imagine if you made a hard-to-read interface that was used in a car. You don't want people wrecking because they had to lean over and put their faces an inch from the screen to read it.

Because many small devices have poor resolution, the larger you make your letters, the more readable they are. Obviously, bigger letters are more readable. The point here is that letters on a small device are generally less readable than letters of the same size on a desktop computer.

Supporting Multiple Sources of Input

Input sources present almost as big a portability problem as varying processors or operating systems. If you want to create a single user interface that runs on any device, you will face a huge challenge.

Some of the different types of input sources you might find on a hand-held device are as follows:

- Small keyboard with arrows and most ASCII characters, but no function keys
- Numeric telephone keypad with a few extra keys
- A pen that functions like a mouse
- A touch-screen, which is like a pen, but with a big, fat pointer device called a finger
- A voice-recognition system

The fact that some devices may not even have separate input sources poses a huge problem. If you have to support a pen or touch-screen interface, you have to leave room on the screen for the items the user can select.

Because you can't always count on letters being present when you have a keypad, you have to support the limited set of buttons on a telephone keypad.

These are serious issues that may be addressed by the manufacturers of these devices as they become more prevalent. Unfortunately, this technology is too new for anyone to have considered the problem. In the past, you had to write custom programs for each hand-held device, so you could make safe assumptions about what kind of input source might have been present.

With the advent of Java, you can no longer make that assumption, so you must adjust. The following are some strategies you can take when approaching this problem:

- Create a loader applet that figures out what kind of input source is present and then loads an applet specialized for that kind of input source.
- Provide multiple means of performing an operation. For instance, allow the 2 key on a phone keypad to work like the up arrow on a regular keyboard.
- Provide small touchable icons. If someone has a touch screen or a pen, this may be the only way to enter input. You may also create a special icon that brings up a small touchable keyboard or keypad.
- Force your users to run different applets depending on what kind of input source they have. This is not a very good solution, but sometimes you don't have much choice.

Creating Reusable Components for Small Devices

As you begin to build applets for small devices, you will need a toolkit of components to help you build interfaces quickly, without having to add a lot of custom code to adapt to different input sources. If anything has to adapt, it should be the components and not the applets.

Using the *CardLayout* Layout Manager as a Stack

On a small device, you don't have the luxury of multiple window frames. Because you usually need all the space you can get, you can use a card layout to achieve something similar to a dialog box. The idea is that when you would normally open a dialog box, you create a new panel and use the card layout to display the new panel.

You are really using the card layout like a stack. Whenever you add a new panel, you are pushing it on top of what you are doing now. When you are through, you want to go back to the previous card. For a scheme like this, you need a panel that knows how to push itself onto the card stack and pop itself back off.

For convenience, define a `StackLayout` class that is really just a `CardLayout`. This helps cut down on the confusion if you happen to use the `CardLayout` class in several places. Listing 40.1 shows the `StackLayout` class.

Listing 40.1 Source Code for *StackLayout.java*

```
import java.awt.CardLayout;
// This class is used as a layout manager for use with the PushablePanel
// class. It works exactly like the CardLayout, but the PushablePanel
// looks for a StackLayout explicitly, so you can safely use CardLayouts
// in your panels without pushing a PushablePanel on top of them.
public class StackLayout extends CardLayout
{
     public StackLayout()
     {
     }
     public StackLayout(int hgap, int vgap)
     {
          super(hgap, vgap);
     }
}
```

Now, when a panel pushes itself onto a stack layout, it adds itself to the end of the stack and tells the stack layout to display the last element. You may want to make custom user interface components that can pop up panels at any time. This presents a small difficulty, because you always add the panels to the container that uses a stack layout. This means that each user interface component would have to have a reference to that container. If a component is nested several containers deep, this is unacceptable.

However, you can make a pushable panel that searches for the correct container. Whenever a component pops up one of these panels, the panel searches for the container that uses a stack layout for a layout manager. It does this by using the `getParent` method in the current component and continuing to search parents. Listing 40.2 shows the `PushablePanel` class that works with the `StackLayout` layout manager.

Listing 40.2 Source Code for *PushablePanel.java*

```
import java.awt.*;
// This class implements a panel that can push itself onto a StackLayout
// and pop itself off again.
public class PushablePanel extends Panel
{
     protected Container parentContainer;
     protected StackLayout stackLayout;
     public PushablePanel()
     {
          parentContainer = null;
          stackLayout = null;
     }
// Push this panel onto the current stack layout. Given a component, find
// a container whose layout manager is a stack layout, and push this panel
// on top of it. By doing this, any object can push a new panel without
// having a reference to the layout manager.
     public void push(Component comp)
     {
          while (comp != null) {
// If the current component is a Container, see if it uses a StackLayout
               if (comp instanceof Container) {
                    Container cont = (Container) comp;
                    LayoutManager layout = cont.getLayout();
// If the current container uses a StackLayout, we've found our container
                    if (layout instanceof StackLayout) {
                         parentContainer = cont;
                         stackLayout = (StackLayout)layout;
                         break;
                    }
               }
// Try the next component up the line
               comp = comp.getParent();
          }
// If we found a container with a StackLayout, add this component to
// the container.
          if (parentContainer != null) {
               parentContainer.add(this);
               stackLayout.last(parentContainer);
          }
     }
     public void pop()
     {
// To pop this panel off the stack, move the stack layout to the previous
// panel (the StackLayout is really a CardLayout) and then remove this
// panel from the stack.
          if (parentContainer != null) {
               stackLayout.previous(parentContainer);
               parentContainer.remove(this);
          }
     }
}
```

Creating a Keyboard/Keypad Input Filter

One of the difficulties in creating a user interface that works for different hand-held devices is that you can't always count on certain input devices being present. If you are running an applet on a cellular phone, you may not be able to count on a mouse-like pointing device. This is a problem for creating buttons. You have to come up with a way to make hot keys for each button on the panel. This requires the cooperation of the button and the panel itself. The panel has to examine each keystroke and figure out whether the keystroke is a hot key for a button. Remember, you can't count on a mouse to change the input focus, so when you hit a key, the key press event may first go to another component and then filter up to the panel.

Listing 40.3 shows a `SmallDevicePanel` that runs all keystrokes through a filter class that relays them to other components. The panel is also a pushable panel.

Listing 40.3 Source Code for *SmallDevicePanel.java*

```
import java.awt.*;
// This class implements a PushablePanel that can filter keystrokes
// to implement hot keys for various user interface components.
public class SmallDevicePanel extends PushablePanel
{
// InputFilter maps key codes to components and passes keystroke events
// to those components.
     protected InputFilter filter;
// The empty constructor creates an input filter by default
     public SmallDevicePanel()
     {
          filter = new InputFilter();
     }
// This constructor allows you to create an unfiltered panel, which
// makes this object nothing more than a PushablePanel.
     public SmallDevicePanel(boolean filtered)
     {
          if (filtered) {
               filter = new InputFilter();
          } else {
               filter = null;
          }
     }
// Add a component and if it can have an input filter, set its filter
     public Component add(Component comp)
     {
          if ((filter != null) &&
               (comp instanceof FilteredComponent)) {
               ((FilteredComponent)comp).setFilter(filter);
          }
          return super.add(comp);
     }
// Add a component and if it can have an input filter, set its filter
     public Component add(String name, Component comp)
     {
```

```
          if ((filter != null) &&
               (comp instanceof FilteredComponent)) {
               ((FilteredComponent)comp).setFilter(filter);
          }
          return super.add(name, comp);
     }
// Add a component and if it can have an input filter, set its filter
     public Component add(Component comp, int position)
     {
          if ((filter != null) &&
               (comp instanceof FilteredComponent)) {
               ((FilteredComponent)comp).setFilter(filter);
          }
          return super.add(comp, position);
     }
// Filter any keypresses and pass them to the input filter class
     public boolean handleEvent(Event evt)
     {
          if (filter == null) return super.handleEvent(evt);
          if (evt.id == Event.KEY_PRESS) {
               return filter.filter(evt);
          }
          return super.handleEvent(evt);
     }
}
```

The `SmallDevicePanel` class requires a helper class called `InputFilter` that actually maps the keystrokes to a component. The components register the keystrokes they want with the input filter. Listing 40.4 shows the `InputFilter` class.

Listing 40.4 Source Code for *InputFilter.java*

```
import java.awt.*;
import java.util.*;
// This class implements a keystroke filter that allows you to
// create hot keys for various components. It uses a hash table
// to look up the keystrokes.
public class InputFilter extends Object
{
     protected Hashtable filterTable;
     protected boolean filtering;
     public InputFilter()
     {
          filterTable = new Hashtable();
          filtering = false;
     }
// Map a single key value to a component
     public void add(int ch, Component receiver)
     {
          filterTable.put(new Integer(ch), receiver);
     }
// Map a range of key values to a component
     public void add(int from, int to, Component receiver)
     {
```


continues

Listing 40.4 Continued

```
          for (int i=from; i <= to; i++) {
               filterTable.put(new Integer(i), receiver);
          }
     }
// Unmap a key, but only if it belongs to this receiver.
     public void remove(int ch, Component receiver)
     {
          Integer key = new Integer(ch);
          if (filterTable.get(key) == receiver) {
               filterTable.remove(key);
          }
     }
// Unmap a range of keys, but only if they belong to this receiver
     public void remove(int from, int to, Component receiver)
     {
          for (int i=from; i <= to; i++) {
               Integer key = new Integer(i);
               if (filterTable.get(key) == receiver) {
                    filterTable.remove(key);
               }
          }
     }
// This method actually performs the filtering. It uses a flag to
// see if it is already filtering an event. This way, if it passes
// the event to a component and the event gets all the way back up to
// the panel that has the filter, we don't filter it again. Otherwise, we'd
// have an infinite recursion, and that is a bad thing.
     public synchronized boolean filter(Event evt)
     {
// If we're already filtering an event, go away
          if (filtering) return false;
// Now we definitely are filtering an event
          filtering = true;
// See if there's a component that wants this keystroke
          Component comp = (Component) filterTable.get(
               new Integer(evt.key));
// If nobody wanted this keystroke, unset the filtering flag and return
          if (comp == null) {
               filtering = false;
               return false;
          }
// Send this event to the component that wants it
          boolean retval = comp.postEvent(evt);
// We're through filtering
          filtering = false;
// Return the result that came from postEvent
          return retval;
     }
}
```

An interesting feature of the `SmallDevicePanel` and the `InputFilter` is that they allow the components themselves to specify what keystrokes they want to receive. The `SmallDevicePanel` class checks each component to see whether it implements the `FilteredComponent` interface, shown in Listing 40.5.

Listing 40.5 Source Code for *FilteredComponent.java*

```
// This interface is implemented by any component that wants
// hot keys controlled by the InputFilter class.
public interface FilteredComponent
{
     public void setFilter(InputFilter filter);
}
```

If a component implements the `FilteredComponent` interface, the `SmallDevicePanel` class calls the `setFilter` method in the component. At that time, the component tells the filter what keystrokes it is interested in. You can safely use regular components with the `SmallDevicePanel` class, because it explicitly checks for the `FilteredComponent` interface first. It doesn't do anything if a component doesn't implement the interface.

Listing 40.6 shows the `ShortcutButton` class, which allows you to specify a character as a shortcut for the button.

Listing 40.6 Source Code for *ShortcutButton.java*

```
import java.awt.*;
// This class implements a button that has a shortcut character.
// It works in conjunction with the SmallDevicePanel and InputFilter classes.
public class ShortcutButton extends Button implements FilteredComponent
{
     protected int shortcut;
     protected InputFilter filter;
// Create a button with a specific label and shortcut character
     public ShortcutButton(String label, int shortcut)
     {
          super(label);
          filter = null;
          this.shortcut = shortcut;
     }
// Whenever this button becomes enabled, re-register the shortcut key
// with the input filter.
     public synchronized void enable()
     {
          if (filter != null) {
               filter.add(shortcut, this);
          }
          super.enable();
     }
// Whenever this button becomes disabled, unregister the shortcut key
     public synchronized void disable()
     {
          if (filter != null) {
               filter.remove(shortcut, this);
          }
          super.disable();
     }
```

40

continues

Listing 40.6 Continued

```
// If we get a keypress event and the key pressed is the shortcut key,
// generate an ACTION_EVENT event for this button.
     public boolean handleEvent(Event evt)
     {
          if ((evt.id == Event.KEY_PRESS) &&
               (evt.key == shortcut)) {
               return postEvent(new Event(this,
                    Event.ACTION_EVENT, getLabel()));
          }
          return super.handleEvent(evt);
     }
// setFilter is called by the SmallDevicePanel class when this button
// is added to the panel. The button then registers the shortcut key
// with the input filter.
     public void setFilter(InputFilter filter)
     {
          this.filter = filter;
          if ((filter != null) && isEnabled()) {
               filter.add(shortcut, this);
          }
     }
}
```

Creating a Pop-Up Keypad for Pen and Touch-Screen Users

One of the ways you can address the problem of multiple input sources is by creating special entry pads for those users with only a pen or touch-screen interface. For example, if you have a field where you are entering numbers, allow the pen-based users to click the field and pop up a numeric input pad with buttons for the various digits.

Listing 40.7 shows a `NumericInputField` that is geared toward small devices. It supports the `FilteredComponent` interface, so it gets keystrokes via the `InputFilter` class, if necessary. Furthermore, if you click the field itself, it creates a `NumberPad` class, which is a `SmallDevicePanel`, and pushes the pad onto the current display.

Listing 40.7 Source Code for *NumericInputField.java*

```
import java.awt.*;
// This class implements a text field for entering integers.
// Because of some of the peculiarities of text fields, it sets
// the field to be non-editable and handles the keystroke events
// manually. It allows * to be used as a delete key to key out
// potential cell-phone users.
public class NumericInputField extends TextField implements FilteredComponent
{
     protected int numDigits;
     protected InputFilter filter;
// When you create the field, you give a limit to the number of digits
```

```
    public NumericInputField(int numDigits)
    {
        super(numDigits);
        this.numDigits = numDigits;
        setEditable(false);
    }
    public boolean handleEvent(Event evt)
    {
// If we get a keypress, check to see if the key is a number
        if (evt.id == Event.KEY_PRESS) {
            if ((evt.key >= '0') && (evt.key <= '9')) {
// We got a number, see if there's room to add another digit
                if (getText().length() >= numDigits) {
                    return true;
                }
// To add a digit, we create an array of 1 character, turn it into a
// string, and then add that to the current digit string
                char ch[] = new char[1];
                ch[0] = (char)evt.key;
                setText(getText()+new String(ch));
                return true;
// If we get a '*', remove the last character in the digit string
            } else if (evt.key == '*') {
                String currText = getText();
                int len = currText.length();
                if (len > 0) {
                    setText(currText.substring(0, len-1));
                }
                return true;
            }
            return false;
// If we get a mouse down event, pop up a keypad for entering a number
        } else if (evt.id == Event.MOUSE_DOWN) {
            if (getParent() instanceof NumberPad) return true;
            doPad();
            return true;
// If we get an action event, see if it is an action from the number pad.
// When you click "OK" on the number pad, it generates an ACTION_EVENT
// and will send it to you if you ask. In this case, when we get that
// event, we pop the pad back off the stack layout.
        } else if (evt.id == Event.ACTION_EVENT) {
            if (evt.target instanceof NumberPad) {
                NumberPad pad = (NumberPad)evt.target;
                setText(""+pad.getValue());
                pad.pop();
                return true;
            } else {
                return false;
            }
        } else {
            return super.handleEvent(evt);
        }
    }
// doPad creates a number pad and pushes it onto the stack layout
    public void doPad()
    {
```


continues

Listing 40.7 Continued

```
            NumberPad pad = new NumberPad(numDigits, this);
            pad.push(this);
        }
// getValue returns the numeric value of the digit string
        public int getValue()
        {
            try {
                return Integer.parseInt(getText());
            } catch (Exception e) {
                return 0;
            }
        }
// setFilter tells the input filter what characters we are interested in
        public void setFilter(InputFilter filter)
        {
            this.filter = filter;
            if (isEnabled()) {
                filter.add('0', '9', this);
                filter.add('*', this);
            }
        }
// If this component becomes enabled, re-register the keystrokes
// with the input filter
        public void enable()
        {
            if (filter != null) {
                filter.add('0', '9', this);
                filter.add('*', this);
            }
        }
// If this component becomes disabled, unregister the keystrokes
// with the input filter
        public void disable()
        {
            if (filter != null) {
                filter.remove('0', '9', this);
                filter.remove('*', this);
            }
        }
}
```

The `NumberPad` class used by the `NumericInputField` class is a very simple panel of 12 buttons (0 through 9, *, and #). It passes the digits and the * key on to the `NumericInputField` class, and uses the # as an OK button, causing the pad to pop off the screen, sending you back to the previous screen. Listing 40.8 shows the `NumberPad` class.

Listing 40.8 Source Code for *NumberPad.java*

```
import java.awt.*;
// NumberPad creates a pushable panel of buttons
// that resembles a telephone keypad. It has the
```

```
// digits 0-9 and also * and #. It uses the * key
// as delete and # as OK.
public class NumberPad extends SmallDevicePanel
{
     protected NumericInputField inputField;
     protected int numDigits;
     protected Component notifyMe;
// Creates a number pad which will generate an ACTION_EVENT to
// itself when OK is pressed.
     public NumberPad(int numDigits)
     {
          this.numDigits = numDigits;
          notifyMe = this;
          createPad();
     }
// Creates a number pad that sends the ACTION_EVENT to another
// component when OK is pressed. This allows the NumericInputField
// class to pop up a number pad and receive an action event when
// OK is pressed.
     public NumberPad(int numDigits, Component notifyMe)
     {
          this.numDigits = numDigits;
          this.notifyMe = notifyMe;
          createPad();
     }
// Create the buttons for the pad
     protected void createPad()
     {
          inputField = new NumericInputField(numDigits);
          setLayout(new BorderLayout());
          add("North", inputField);
          Panel buttonPanel = new Panel();
          buttonPanel.setLayout(new GridLayout(4, 0));
          buttonPanel.add(new Button("1"));
          buttonPanel.add(new Button("2"));
          buttonPanel.add(new Button("3"));
          buttonPanel.add(new Button("4"));
          buttonPanel.add(new Button("5"));
          buttonPanel.add(new Button("6"));
          buttonPanel.add(new Button("7"));
          buttonPanel.add(new Button("8"));
          buttonPanel.add(new Button("9"));
          buttonPanel.add(new Button("* DEL"));
          buttonPanel.add(new Button("0"));
          buttonPanel.add(new Button("# OK"));
          add("Center", buttonPanel);
     }
// Return the integer value in the number pad
     public int getValue()
     {
          return inputField.getValue();
     }
// This method handles all the button presses for the keypad. The
// digit that each button represents is conveniently stored as
// the first digit in the label.
     public boolean action(Event evt, Object whichAction)
     {
```


continues

Listing 40.8 Continued

```
// If this event isn't for a button, we don't handle it
          if (!(evt.target instanceof Button)) {
               return false;
          }
          char ch = ((String)whichAction).charAt(0);
// If we get any of the characters that the numeric input field might
// be interested in, pass them along to it.
          if (((ch >= '0') && (ch <= '9')) ||
               (ch == '*')) {
               inputField.postEvent(
                    new Event(evt.target, evt.when,
                         Event.KEY_PRESS,
                         evt.x, evt.y, ch, 0));
               return true;
// If we get a '#', post an action event
          } else if (ch == '#') {
               return notifyMe.postEvent(new Event(this,
                    Event.ACTION_EVENT, new Boolean(false)));
          }
          return super.handleEvent(evt);
     }
}
```

Listing 40.9 shows a very simple test program that demonstrates the various components presented in this chapter. It creates a numeric input field and a button with a shortcut key of #. The idea is that it can be used by a client who has only a telephone keypad, or by someone who has only a pointing device. If you have only a pointing device, you can click the numeric input field to bring up a keypad to enter a number.

Listing 40.9 Source Code for *TestField.java*

```
import java.awt.*;
import java.applet.*;
// This is a simple test applet for the SmallDevicePanel and
// the NumericInputField classes. It creates a numeric field and
// a shortcut button.
public class TestField extends Applet
{
     NumericInputField inField;
     Button okButton;
     public void init()
     {
          setLayout(new StackLayout());
          SmallDevicePanel startPanel = new SmallDevicePanel();
          startPanel.setLayout(new BorderLayout());
          inField = new NumericInputField(8);
          startPanel.add("North", inField);
          okButton = new ShortcutButton("# OK", '#');
          startPanel.add("South", okButton);
          add(startPanel);
     }
```

```
        public boolean action(Event evt, Object whichAction)
        {
            if (evt.target instanceof Button) {
                System.out.println("Your number is "+
                    inField.getValue());
            }
            return false;
        }
    }
```

Figure 40.8 shows the test applet in operation. The applet itself violates one of the design principles in that it is not self-documenting. Its purpose is just to demonstrate the numeric input field.

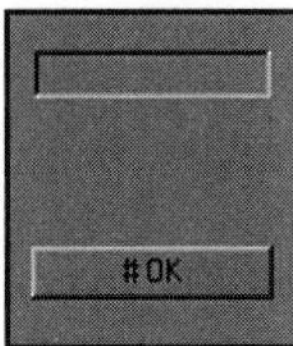

Fig. 40.8
Your interfaces should support different input sources.

Figure 40.9 shows the number pad that pops up by the numeric input field. You could use this same approach to create a small pop-up keyboard.

Fig. 40.9
Create auxiliary panels to help users with limited input sources.

Whereas these classes may help you get going when designing interfaces for small devices, you really need a full development library geared toward these devices. Hopefully, one will be available by the time Java-enabled hand-held devices become prevalent. Otherwise, you'll have to create many components from scratch.

Index

Symbols

A

B

C

D

E

F

J - K

M

N

O

Q - R

S

X - Y - Z

Complete and Return this Card for a *FREE* Computer Book Catalog

Thank you for purchasing this book! You have purchased a superior computer book written expressly for your needs. To continue to provide the kind of up-to-date, pertinent coverage you've come to expect from us, we need to hear from you. Please take a minute to complete and return this self-addressed, postage-paid form. In return, we'll send you a free catalog of all our computer books on topics ranging from word processing to programming and the internet.

r. ☐ Mrs. ☐ Ms. ☐ Dr. ☐

ame (first) ☐☐☐☐☐☐☐☐☐☐☐ (M.I.) ☐ (last) ☐☐☐☐☐☐☐☐☐☐☐☐☐☐☐

ldress ☐☐☐☐☐☐☐☐☐☐☐☐☐☐☐☐☐☐☐☐☐☐☐☐☐☐☐☐☐☐☐☐☐☐☐

ty ☐☐☐☐☐☐☐☐☐☐☐☐☐☐☐ State ☐☐ Zip ☐☐☐☐☐ ☐☐☐☐

one ☐☐☐ ☐☐☐ ☐☐☐☐ Fax ☐☐☐ ☐☐☐ ☐☐☐☐

ompany Name ☐☐☐☐☐☐☐☐☐☐☐☐☐☐☐☐☐☐☐☐☐☐☐☐☐☐☐☐☐☐☐☐☐

mail address ☐☐☐☐☐☐☐☐☐☐☐☐☐☐☐☐☐☐☐☐☐☐☐☐☐☐☐☐☐☐☐☐☐

Please check at least (3) influencing factors for purchasing this book.

- ont or back cover information on book ☐
- ecial approach to the content ☐
- ompleteness of content ☐
- uthor's reputation ☐
- iblisher's reputation ☐
- ook cover design or layout ☐
- dex or table of contents of book ☐
- ice of book ☐
- ecial effects, graphics, illustrations ☐
- ther (Please specify): ______________ ☐

. How did you first learn about this book?

- aw in Macmillan Computer Publishing catalog ☐
- ecommended by store personnel ☐
- aw the book on bookshelf at store ☐
- ecommended by a friend ☐
- eceived advertisement in the mail ☐
- aw an advertisement in: ______________ ☐
- ead book review in: ______________ ☐
- ther (Please specify): ______________ ☐

. How many computer books have you purchased in the last six months?

- his book only ☐
- books ☐
- 3 to 5 books ☐
- More than 5 ☐

4. Where did you purchase this book?

- Bookstore ☐
- Computer Store ☐
- Consumer Electronics Store ☐
- Department Store ☐
- Office Club ☐
- Warehouse Club ☐
- Mail Order ☐
- Direct from Publisher ☐
- Internet site ☐
- Other (Please specify): ______________ ☐

5. How long have you been using a computer?

- ☐ Less than 6 months
- ☐ 6 months to a year
- ☐ 1 to 3 years
- ☐ More than 3 years

6. What is your level of experience with personal computers and with the subject of this book?

	With PCs	With subject of book
New	☐	☐
Casual	☐	☐
Accomplished	☐	☐
Expert	☐	☐

Source Code ISBN: 0-7897-0935-x

7. Which of the following best describes your job title?

- Administrative Assistant ☐
- Coordinator ☐
- Manager/Supervisor ☐
- Director ☐
- Vice President ☐
- President/CEO/COO ☐
- Lawyer/Doctor/Medical Professional ☐
- Teacher/Educator/Trainer ☐
- Engineer/Technician ☐
- Consultant ☐
- Not employed/Student/Retired ☐
- Other (Please specify): ________ ☐

8. Which of the following best describes the area of the company your job title falls under?

- Accounting ☐
- Engineering ☐
- Manufacturing ☐
- Operations ☐
- Marketing ☐
- Sales ☐
- Other (Please specify): ________ ☐

9. What is your age?

- Under 20 ☐
- 21-29 ☐
- 30-39 ☐
- 40-49 ☐
- 50-59 ☐
- 60-over ☐

10. Are you:

- Male ☐
- Female ☐

11. Which computer publications do you read regularly? (Please list)

____

Comments: ________

Fold here and scotch-tape to mail

NO POSTAGE NECESSARY IF MAILED IN THE UNITED STATES

BUSINESS REPLY MAIL

FIRST-CLASS MAIL PERMIT NO. 9918 INDIANAPOLIS IN

POSTAGE WILL BE PAID BY THE ADDRESSEE

ATTN MARKETING
MACMILLAN COMPUTER PUBLISHING
MACMILLAN PUBLISHING USA
201 W 103RD ST
INDIANAPOLIS IN 46290-9042

Before using any of the software on this disc, you need to install the software you plan to use. If you have problems with this CD-ROM, please contact Macmillan Technical Support at (317) 581-3833. We can be reached by e-mail at **support@mcp.com** or by CompuServe at **GO QUEBOOKS**.

Read This Before Opening Software